T0304233

Foundations of Statistics
for Data Scientists

CHAPMAN & HALL/CRC
Texts in Statistical Science Series
Joseph K. Blitzstein, *Harvard University, USA*
Julian J. Faraway, *University of Bath, UK*
Martin Tanner, *Northwestern University, USA*
Jim Zidek, *University of British Columbia, Canada*

Recently Published Titles

Randomization, Bootstrap and Monte Carlo Methods in Biology
Fourth Edition
Bryan F. J. Manly, Jorje A. Navarro Alberto

Principles of Uncertainty, Second Edition
Joseph B. Kadane

Beyond Multiple Linear Regression
Applied Generalized Linear Models and Multilevel Models in R
Paul Roback, Julie Legler

Bayesian Thinking in Biostatistics
Gary L. Rosner, Purushottam W. Laud, and Wesley O. Johnson

Linear Models with Python
Julian J. Faraway

Modern Data Science with R, Second Edition
Benjamin S. Baumer, Daniel T. Kaplan, and Nicholas J. Horton

Probability and Statistical Inference
From Basic Principles to Advanced Models
Miltiadis Mavrakakis and Jeremy Penzer

Bayesian Networks
With Examples in R, Second Edition
Marco Scutari and Jean-Baptiste Denis

Time Series
Modeling, Computation, and Inference, Second Edition
Raquel Prado, Marco A. R. Ferreira and Mike West

A First Course in Linear Model Theory
Second Edition
Nalini Ravishanker, Zhiyi Chi, Dipak K. Dey

Foundations of Statistics for Data Scientists
With R and Python
Alan Agresti and Maria Kateri

For more information about this series, please visit: https://www.crcpress.com/Chapman--Hall/CRC-Texts-in-Statistical-Science/book-series/CHTEXSTASCI

Foundations of Statistics for Data Scientists

With R and Python

Alan Agresti and Maria Kateri

CRC Press
Taylor & Francis Group
Boca Raton London New York

CRC Press is an imprint of the
Taylor & Francis Group, an **informa** business

A CHAPMAN & HALL BOOK

First edition published 2022
by CRC Press
6000 Broken Sound Parkway NW, Suite 300, Boca Raton, FL 33487-2742

and by CRC Press
2 Park Square, Milton Park, Abingdon, Oxon, OX14 4RN

ISBN: 978-0-367-74845-6 (hbk)
ISBN: 978-1-003-15983-4 (ebk)

DOI: 10.1201/9781003159834

Typeset in LM Roman
by KnowledgeWorks Global Ltd.

Contents

Preface

This book presents an overview of the *foundations*—the key concepts and results—of statistical science. The primary intended audience is undergraduate students who are training to become data scientists. This is not a book, however, about how to become a data scientist or about the newest methods being used by data scientists or about how to analyze "big data" and the wide variety of types of data with which data scientists deal. It is a book that has the purpose of teaching potential data scientists the foundations of one of the core tenets of data science—statistical science.

Statistical science is by now a large subject, having many distinct specialties. This book highlights the topics with which we believe that any data scientist should be familiar: descriptive statistical methods, probability distributions, the inferential statistical methods of confidence intervals and significance testing, and linear and generalized linear modeling. When combined with courses that a student majoring in Data Science would take in computer science and mathematics, this book provides the background needed to follow this introduction to statistical science by studying specialized areas of it.[1]

This book assumes that students have knowledge of calculus, so we can focus on *why a statistical analysis works* as well as *how to do it*. University statistical science courses that require a calculus background often have the name *Mathematical Statistics*. We avoid this term in the title of our book, as we do not want students to think that statistical science is a subfield of mathematics or that complex mathematics is necessary to be proficient in understanding and applying statistical science. In fact, we mainly use only basic calculus tools of differentiation and integration, and then only for some topics. Compared to the content of traditional mathematical statistics textbooks, our book has less emphasis on probability theory, derivations of probability distributions of transformations of random variables, decision theory, and statement and formal proof of theorems. It introduces some modern topics that do not normally appear in such texts but are especially relevant for data scientists, such as generalized linear models for non-normal responses, Bayesian and regularized model-fitting, and classification and clustering. The greatest difference from a traditional mathematical statistics book, however, is that this book shows how to implement statistical methods with modern software and illustrates statistical concepts and theory using simulations.

To use and properly interpret methods of modern statistical science, computational skills are as important as mathematical skills. Besides using mathematics to show "why it works," we use computational simulations and Internet apps to help provide intuition about foundational results such as behavior of sampling distributions and error rates for statistical inferences. Throughout the book, examples with real data show how to use the free statistical software R to implement statistical methods. The book also contains software appendices that present greater detail about R as well as introducing Python for statistical analyses. The Python appendix shows analyses for the examples analyzed in the chapters with R, so an instructor can easily use the text in a course that has Python as its primary software. Since

---

[1]Such as multivariate analysis, nonparametrics, categorical data analysis, design and sample survey methods, time series, longitudinal data analysis, survival analysis, decision theory, Bayesian statistics, stochastic modeling, computational methods of statistics, and smoothing and nonlinear modeling

the book focuses on the foundations of statistical science, it has less emphasis on some practical issues of data analysis, such as preparing and cleaning data files. However, the software appendices also introduce additional analyses that supplement the examples presented in the chapters. A regularly-updated website `http://stat4ds.rwth-aachen.de` for the book has all data files analyzed and longer versions of the software appendices as well as an appendix about the use of `Matlab` for statistical analyses. The data files are also available at `www.stat.ufl.edu/~aa/ds` and at the GitHub site `https://github.com/stat4DS/data`.

Use of this book as a course textbook

Chapters 1–6 of this book are designed as a textbook for an introductory course on statistical science for undergraduate students majoring in Data Science or Statistics or Mathematics. Some instructors may prefer to skip some of the less central or more technical material, such as Sections 3.4, 4.9, 5.7, 5.8, and 6.7. (These and other such sections and subsections have an * next to their titles.) With all nine chapters and the extra material presented in the R and `Python` appendices, it is also appropriate for a two-term sequence of courses. The book also can serve programs that have a heavy focus on statistical science, such as econometrics and operations research. It also should be useful to graduate students in the social, biological, and environmental sciences who choose Statistics as their minor area of concentration, so they can learn about the foundations that underlie statistical methods that they use. An instructor can use either R or `Python` as the main software for the course, as the examples in the main part of the text use R but the same examples are shown with `Python` in its appendix.

Each chapter contains many exercises for students to practice and extend the theory and methods. The exercises are grouped into two parts: Exercises in *Data Analysis and Applications* request that students perform data analyses similar to the ones presented in that chapter. Exercises in *Methods and Concepts* relate directly to the foundations aspect of the book. They ask questions about properties of statistical methods, conceptual questions about their bases, as well as extend that chapter's results. An appendix contains outlines of solutions for the odd-numbered exercises.

This book is by no means a complete overview of statistical science. The field is large and grows more every year, with areas being developed now that did not even exist in the twentieth century. However, we do believe it provides a solid introduction to the core material with which we believe any data scientist should be familiar.

In preparing this book together, Agresti (`agresti@ufl.edu`) has taken main responsibility for the chapter material and Kateri (`maria.kateri@rwth-aachen.de`) has taken main responsibility for the appendices about R and `Python` statistical software and the expanded appendices about R, `Python`, and `Matlab` at the book's website. We welcome any comments or suggestions that you care to send either of us that we can take into account in future editions of this book.

Acknowledgments

Thanks to several friends and colleagues who provided comments on various versions of this manuscript or who provided data sets or other help, including Alessandra Brazzale, Jane Brockmann, Brian Caffo, Sir David Cox, Bianca De Stavola, Cristina Cuesta, Travis Gerke, Sabrina Giordano, Anna Gottard, Ralitza Gueorguieva, Bernhard Klingenberg, Bhramar Mukherjee, Ranjini Natarajan, Madan Oli, Euijung Ryu, Alessandra Salvan, Nicola Sartori, Elena Stanghellini, Stephen Stigler, Gerhard Tutz, Roberta Varriale, Larry Winner, and Daniela Witten. Thanks to Hassan Satvat for help in setting up the book's website and to Bernhard Klingenberg for developing the excellent apps at `www.artofstat.com` that are often cited in the book. Many thanks to Joyce Robbins, Mintaek Lee, Jason M. Graham, Christopher Gaffney, Tumulesh Solanky, and Steve Chung for providing helpful reviews to

CRC Press of our manuscript. Finally, special thanks to John Kimmel, Executive Editor of Statistics for Chapman & Hall/CRC Press, for his encouragement and support in this book project.

ALAN AGRESTI and MARIA KATERI
Gainesville Florida and Brookline Massachusetts, USA;
Aachen, Germany

April 2021

1

Introduction to Statistical Science

Compared to mathematics and the physical and natural sciences, statistical science is quite young. The statistical methods that you'll learn about in this book were mainly developed within the past century. Modern computing power is causing a revolution in the sorts of data analyses that are possible, so new methods are continually being developed. In recent years, new statistical methods have resulted from challenges in analyzing data in diverse fields, such as medicine (e.g., genetic data relating to disease presence, data for personalized medical decisions) and business (e.g., data on consumer buying behavior, data from experiments comparing advertising strategies). This book presents the foundations underlying the methods of statistical science, explaining when and why these methods work, and shows how to use statistical software to apply them.

Statistical software also has become increasingly powerful and easily available. This has had benefits in the data analyses that are now possible, but a danger is that prospective data scientists might think that statistical science is merely a computational toolbox consisting of a variety of algorithms. A goal of this book, by contrast, is to show that *the methods of statistical science result from a unified theory*, although that theory itself has slight variations in the way it is implemented or interpreted. Another danger of the ubiquity of statistical software is that prospective data scientists might expect that software can automatically perform good data analyses without input from the user. We'll see, however, that careful thought is needed to decide which statistical methods are appropriate for any particular situation, as they all make certain assumptions, and some methods work poorly when the assumptions are violated. Moreover, a data scientist needs to be able to interpret and explain the results that software yields.

In this chapter, we introduce statistical science as a field that deals with describing data and using them to make inferences. We define types of *variables* that represent how measured characteristics can vary from observation to observation. We also introduce *graphical and numerical methods* for describing the data. When a study can use *randomization* in collecting the data or conducting an experiment, data analysts can exploit the random variation to make reliable estimations and predictions.

1.1   Statistical Science: Description and Inference

You already have a sense of what the word ***statistics*** means. You regularly hear statistics quoted about sports events, the economy, medical research, and opinions, beliefs, and behaviors of people. In this sense, a statistic is merely a number calculated from ***data*** —the observations that provide information about the subject matter. But the field of ***statistical science*** has a much broader sense—as a field that gives us a way of gathering and analyzing the data in an objective manner.

DOI: 10.1201/9781003159834-1

Statistical science

Statistical science is the science of developing and applying methods for collecting, analyzing, and interpreting data.

Many methods of statistical science incorporate reasoning using tools of *probability*. The methods enable us to deal with uncertainty and variability in virtually all scientific fields. With statistical methods, we learn from the data while measuring, controlling, and communicating uncertainty.

1.1.1   Design, Descriptive Statistics, and Inferential Statistics

Statistical science has three aspects:

1. **Design**: Planning how to gather relevant data for the subject matter of interest.

2. **Description**: Summarizing the data.

3. **Inference**: Making evaluations, such as estimations and predictions, based on the data.

Design refers to planning a study so that it yields useful data. For example, for a poll taken to determine public opinion on some issue, the design specifies how to select the people to interview and constructs the questionnaire for interviews. For a research study to compare an experimental diet with a standard diet to address obesity, the design specifies how to obtain people for the study, how to determine which people use each diet, and specifies the characteristics to measure to compare the diets.

Description refers to summarizing the data, to mine the information that the data provide. For any study, the raw data are a complete listing of observations that can be overwhelming for comprehension. To present the results, we reduce the data to simpler and more understandable form without distorting or losing much information. Graphs, tables, and numerical summaries such as averages and percentages are called **descriptive statistics**.

Inference refers to using the data to make estimations and other sorts of evaluations, such as predictions. These evaluations take into account random variability that occurs with the characteristics measured and the resulting uncertainty in decision-making. For instance, suppose that in the study comparing two diets, the people on the experimental diet had an average weight loss of 7.0 kilograms. What can we say about the average weight change if hypothetically *all* obese people used this diet? An inferential statistical method provides an interval of numbers within which we can predict that the average weight change would fall. The analysis might enable us to conclude, with small probability of being wrong, that the average weight change for all obese people would fall between 5.6 and 8.4 kilograms. Another inferential statistical method would enable us to decide whether that average weight change is greater than would be obtained with a standard diet or no special diet. Other inferential statistical methods evaluate whether weight change is associated with characteristics other than the diet, such as a person's gender, race, age, attained education, and amount of weekly exercise. Data-based evaluations such as estimations and predictions are called **statistical inferences**.

Descriptive statistics and *inferential statistics* are the two main types of methods for analyzing data. Researchers use them to answer questions such as, "Does the experimental diet have a beneficial effect in reducing obesity, and is it more effective than a standard diet?" "How does the sales of a product compare if we place an advertisement for it at websites, or in mailings, or in newspapers, or on TV programs?" "Do states in the U.S.

that have stronger gun control laws tend to have lower murder rates, taking into account socioeconomic factors?" "Is student performance in Canada associated with the amount of money spent per student, the size of the classes, or the teachers' salaries?" "Do a majority of all New Zealanders favor legalization of marijuana?"

1.1.2 Populations and Samples

The entities on which a study makes observations are called the sample *subjects*. Usually the subjects are individual people, such as in a survey, but they need not be. For example, an agricultural experiment might have cows as subjects if its goal is to compare milk yields for different diets. An ecological survey might have different forest areas as subjects in a study of species diversity. Subjects in social surveys might be people, families, schools, or counties.

Although we obtain data for the sample subjects, our ultimate interest is on the *population* from which the sample is taken.

Population and sample

The *population* is the total set of subjects of interest. A *sample* is the set of subjects from the population for which data are available.

The goal of most data analyses is to learn about populations. But it is almost always necessary, and more practical, to observe only samples from those populations. For example, polling organizations such as the Gallup poll (`www.gallup.com`) and the Pew Research Center (`www.pewresearch.org`) usually sample about 1000–2000 Americans to gather information about opinions and beliefs of the population of *all* adult Americans.

Inferential statistics provide evaluations about a population, based on data from a sample. For example, a survey taken in the U.S. in 2018 asked, "Do you believe in heaven?" The population of interest was all adults in the United States. Of the 1141 sampled subjects, 81% answered *yes*. We would be interested, however, not only in those 1141 people but in the *population* of more than 250 million adults in the U.S. An inferential method presented in Chapter 4 estimates that the population percentage believing in heaven almost certainly falls between 78% and 84%. That is, the sample value of 81% has a "margin of error" of 3%. Inferential statistical analyses can predict characteristics of entire populations quite well by selecting samples that are very small relative to the population size. In this book, we'll learn why this works.

1.1.3 Parameters: Numerical Summaries of the Population

To distinguish between a descriptive statistic calculated for a sample and the corresponding characteristic of the population, we use the term *parameter* for the population characteristic.

Parameter

A *parameter* is a numerical summary of a population.

In practice, our primary interest is in the values of parameters rather than sample descriptive statistics. For example, in viewing the results of a poll before an election, we would be more interested in the *population* percentages favoring the various candidates than in the *sample* percentages for the people interviewed. However, parameter values are almost always unknown. The sample and statistics describing it help us to make inferences about the unknown parameter values.

A key aspect of statistical inference involves reporting the *precision* of the sample statistic that estimates the population parameter. For the example on belief in heaven, the reported margin of error of 3% predicted how close the *sample* value of 81% was to the unknown *population* percentage. The other key aspect relates to the *probability* with which we obtain that precision. For instance, a statistical inference might state that we can be 95% sure that the sample value of 81% differs from the population value by no more than 3%.

1.1.4   Defining Populations: Actual and Conceptual

Usually the population to which inferences apply is an actual set of subjects, such as all adult residents of a nation. Sometimes, though, the inferences refer to a *conceptual* population—one that does not actually exist but is hypothetical.

For example, suppose a medical research team investigates a newly proposed drug for treating a virus by conducting a study at several medical centers. Such a medical study is called a *clinical trial*. The study would compare virus patients who are given the new drug to other virus patients who instead receive a standard treatment or a placebo, using descriptive statistics such as the percentages who respond positively. In applying inferential statistical methods, the researchers would like their inferences to apply to the conceptual population of *all* people suffering from the virus now or at some time in the future.

1.2   Types of Data and Variables

The observations gathered on the characteristics of interest are the *data*. For example, a survey of 1000 people to analyze opinions about the legalization of same-sex marriage might also observe characteristics such as political party affiliation, frequency of attending religious services, number of years of education, annual income, marital status, race, and gender. The data for a particular subject would consist of observations such as (opinion = do not favor legalization, political party = Republican, religiosity = attend services once a week, education = 12 years, annual income in the interval 40–60 thousand dollars, marital status = married, race = White, gender = male).

1.2.1   Data Files

Statistical software analyzes data organized in the spreadsheet form of a ***data file***:

- Any one row of a data file contains the observations for a particular subject (e.g., person) in the sample.

- Any one column of a data file contains the observations for a particular characteristic (e.g., opinion about legalized same-sex marriage).

The *number* of subjects in the data file, called the ***sample size***, is denoted by n. If we observe 10 characteristics for a sample of $n = 2000$ people, then the data file has 2000 rows and 10 columns.

Throughout this book, we use the statistical software R to illustrate statistical analyses. This software package is available to download for free at www.r-project.org. In R, we save a data file as a *data frame*,[1] which is the fundamental data structure required by many R functions. Figure 1.1 shows the use of R to read a data file called `Survey.dat` (containing data from a student survey mentioned in Exercise 1.2) from a directory on a computer, save it as a data frame called *Opinions*, and display it.

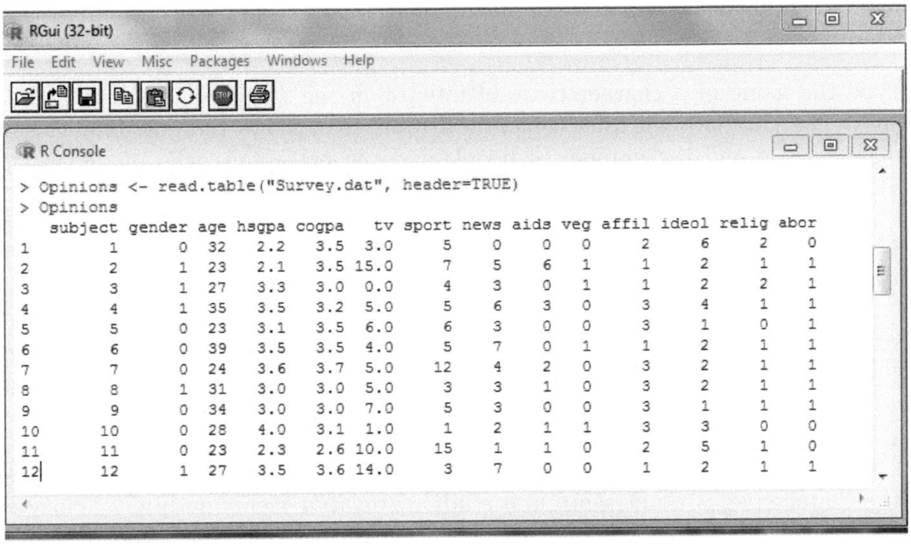

```
> Opinions <- read.table("Survey.dat", header=TRUE)
> Opinions
   subject gender age hsgpa cogpa   tv sport news aids veg affil ideol relig abor
1        1      0  32   2.2   3.5  3.0     5    0    0   0     2     6     2    0
2        2      1  23   2.1   3.5 15.0     7    5    6   1     1     2     1    1
3        3      1  27   3.3   3.0  0.0     4    3    0   1     1     2     2    1
4        4      1  35   3.5   3.2  5.0     5    6    3   0     3     4     1    1
5        5      0  23   3.1   3.5  6.0     6    3    0   0     3     1     0    1
6        6      0  39   3.5   3.5  4.0     5    7    0   1     1     2     1    1
7        7      0  24   3.6   3.7  5.0    12    4    2   0     3     2     1    1
8        8      1  31   3.0   3.0  5.0     3    3    1   0     3     2     1    1
9        9      0  34   3.0   3.0  7.0     5    3    0   0     3     1     1    1
10      10      0  28   4.0   3.1  1.0     1    2    1   1     3     3     0    0
11      11      0  23   2.3   2.6 10.0    15    1    1   0     2     5     1    0
12      12      1  27   3.5   3.6 14.0     3    7    0   0     1     2     1    1
```

FIGURE 1.1 Part of a R session for loading and displaying a data file.

Existing archived collections of data are called ***databases***. Many databases result from a survey or study of some type, but some are existing records of data that result from other purposes. An example is a database of patients' electronic medical records. With the increasing variety of data that can be recorded electronically, not all data files have the format of a traditional data file with entries that are numbers or characters. For example, in medical records, some observations for some subjects may be images, such as a mammogram, a chest x-ray, or a brain scan,[2] or a continuous streaming of data over time, such as monitoring of heart-rate, respiratory-rate, blood pressure, and temperature.

1.2.2 Example: The General Social Survey (GSS)

Some databases are freely available on the Internet. An important database in the U.S. contains results since 1972 of the *General Social Survey* (GSS), conducted every other year by the National Opinion Research Center at the University of Chicago. It gathers information using personal interviews of a sample of about $n = 2000$ subjects from the U.S. adult population to provide a snapshot of opinions and behaviors. Researchers use it to investigate how adult Americans answer a wide diversity of questions, such as, "Do you believe in life after death?" and "Would you be willing to pay higher prices in order to protect the environment?" Similar social surveys occur in other countries, such as the General Social Survey administered by Statistics Canada, the British Social Attitudes Survey, and the Eurobarometer survey and European Social Survey for nations in the European Union.

It is easy to get summaries of data from the GSS database:

---

[1] For details, see Section A.0.3 of the R Appendix.
[2] See `https://aimi.stanford.edu/research/public-datasets` for examples of data files of this type.

- Go to the website `https://sda.berkeley.edu/archive.htm` at the Survey Documentation and Analysis site at the University of California, Berkeley.

- Click on the most recently available *General Social Survey (GSS) Cumulative Datafile*. You will then see a "variable selection" listing in the left margin of characteristics measured over the years, and a menu on the right for selecting particular characteristics of interest.

- Type the name of a characteristic of interest in the *Row* box, and click on *Run the table*. The GSS site will then generate a table that shows the possible values for the characteristic and the number of people and the percentage who made each possible response.

For example, in one survey the GSS asked "About how many good friends do you have?" The GSS name for this characteristic is NUMFREND. The table that the GSS provides shows that the responses of 1, 2, 3, 4, 5, and 6 good friends had the percentages 6.1, 16.2, 15.7. 14.2, 11.3, and 8.8, respectively, with the remaining 27.7% spread around the other possible responses.

1.2.3 Variables

For the characteristics we measure in a study, *variability* occurs naturally among subjects in a sample or population. For instance, variation occurs from student to student in their college grade point average (GPA). A study to investigate the factors mainly responsible for that variability might also observe other characteristics that vary among students, such as high school GPA, college board score, time per day spent studying, time per day watching TV or browsing the Internet, and whether at least one parent attended college. Any characteristic that we can measure for the subjects is called a **variable**. The term reflects that values of the characteristic *vary* among subjects.

> ## Variable
> A **variable** is a characteristic that can vary in value among subjects in a sample or population.

The values the variable can take form a *measurement scale*. The valid statistical methods for a variable depend on its measurement scale. We treat a numerical-valued variable such as number of good friends differently than a variable measured with categories, such as (*yes, no*) for whether employed. We next present two ways to classify variables. The first type refers to whether the measurement scale consists of numbers or categories. The second type refers to the fineness of measurement—the number of values in the measurement scale.

1.2.4 Quantitative Variables and Categorical Variables

A variable is called **quantitative** when the measurement scale has numerical values that represent different magnitudes of the variable. Examples of quantitative variables are number of good friends, annual income, college GPA, age, and weight.

A variable is called **categorical** when the measurement scale is a set of categories. Examples of categorical variables are marital status (with categories such as *single, married, divorced, widowed*), primary mode of transportation to work (*automobile, bicycle, bus, subway, walk*), preferred destination for clothes shopping (*downtown, Internet, mall, other*), and favorite type of music (*classical, country, folk, jazz, rap/hip-hop, rock*). Categorical variables having only two categories, such as whether employed (*yes, no*), are called **binary**.

For categorical variables, distinct categories differ in quality, not in numerical magnitude. Categorical variables are often called **qualitative**.

Categorical variables have two types of measurement scales. For some categorical variables, such as the ones just mentioned, the categories are unordered. The scale does not have a "high" or "low" end. The categories are then said to form a **nominal scale**. By contrast, some categorical scales have a natural *ordering* of values. The categories form an **ordinal scale**. Examples are perceived happiness (*not too happy, pretty happy, very happy*), headache pain (*none, slight, moderate, severe*), and political philosophy (*very liberal, slightly liberal, moderate, slightly conservative, very conservative*).

1.2.5 Discrete Variables and Continuous Variables

Another classification refers to the *number* of values in the measurement scale.

> ## Discrete and continuous variables
>
> A quantitative variable is **discrete** if it can take a set of distinct, separate values, such as the nonnegative integers (0, 1, 2, 3, …). It is **continuous** if it can take an infinite continuum of possible real number values.

Examples of discrete variables are one's number of good friends, number of computers in household, and number of days playing a sport in the past week. Any variable phrased as "the number of …" is discrete, because we can list its possible values (*0, 1, 2, 3, …*). Examples of continuous variables are height, weight, age, distance a person walks in a day, winning time in a marathon race, and how long a cell phone works before it needs recharging. It is impossible to write down all the distinct potential values, because they form an interval of infinitely many real-number values. A person's age, for example, could take the value 20.6294473 … years.

In practice, we round continuous variables when measuring them, so the actual measurement is discrete. We say that an individual is 20 years old whenever that person's age is somewhere between 20 and 21. On the other hand, some variables, although discrete, have a very large number of possible values. In measuring annual income in dollars, the potential values are 0, 1, 2, 3, …, up to some very large value in many millions. Statistical methods for continuous variables are used for quantitative variables that can take a very large number of values, regardless of whether they are theoretically continuous or discrete.

1.2.6 Associations: Response Variables and Explanatory Variables

Most studies have more than one variable. With multivariable analyses, we say that an **association** occurs between two variables if certain values of one variable tend to go with certain values of the other. For example, consider religious affiliation, with categories (*Catholic, Protestant, Muslim, Jewish, Other*), and ethnic group, with categories (*African-American, Anglo-American, Hispanic, Other*). In the United States, Anglo-Americans are more likely to be Protestant than are Hispanics, who are overwhelmingly Catholic. African-Americans are even more likely to be Protestant. An association exists between religious affiliation and ethnic group, because the percentage of people having a particular religious affiliation changes as ethnic group changes.

When we study the association between two variables, usually one is an outcome variable on which comparisons are made at levels of the other variable. The outcome variable is called the **response variable**. The variable that defines the groups is called the **explanatory variable**. The analysis studies how the outcome on the response variable *depends on* or is *explained by* the value of the explanatory variable. For example, when we describe how religious affiliation depends on ethnic group, religious affiliation is the response variable. In a comparison of men and women on annual income, annual income is the response variable and gender is the explanatory variable.

Most studies have one response variable and multiple explanatory variables. Sometimes the response variable is called the **dependent variable** and the explanatory variables are called the **independent variables**. We prefer not to use these terms, because the terms *independent* and *dependent* are used in statistical science for many other things, and the terminology suggests causal interpretations that are usually inappropriate.

1.3 Data Collection and Randomization

When we apply inferential methods of statistical science to parameters for some population, the quality of the inferences depends on how well the *sample* represents the *population*.

1.3.1 Randomization

Randomization is a mechanism for achieving good sample representation of a population in a survey or an experiment.

> ### Simple random sample
>
> A **simple random sample** of n subjects from a population is one in which each possible sample of size n has the same probability (chance) of being selected.

With simple random sampling, everyone has the same chance of inclusion in the sample, so it is fair. It tends to yield a sample that resembles the population. This reduces the chance that the sample is seriously biased in some way, leading to inaccurate inferences about the population.

Suppose that a researcher in a medical center plans to compare two drugs for some adverse condition. She has four patients with this condition, and she wants to randomly select two to use each drug. Denote the four patients by P_1, P_2, P_3, and P_4. In selecting $n = 2$ subjects to use the first drug, the six possible samples are

$$(P_1, P_2), (P_1, P_3), (P_1, P_4), (P_2, P_3), (P_2, P_4), (P_3, P_4).$$

More generally, let N denote the population size. The population has $\binom{N}{n}$ possible samples of size n. For example, a population of size $N = 4$ has $\binom{4}{2} = 4!/[2!(4-2)!] = 6$ possible samples of size $n = 2$. You could select the simple random sample by placing the four people's names on four identical ballots and selecting two blindly from a hat. This is unwieldy with the larger values for N and n usual in practice, and these days software can easily select the sample from a list of the population members using a *random number generator*.

We illustrate for random selection of $n = 5$ students out of a class of size $N = 60$. We assign the numbers $01, 02, \ldots, 60$ to the class members and generate five random numbers between 01 and 60. With the statistical software R, the `sample` function performs simple random sampling from a numbered population list:[3]

---

[3]We suggest that you read the Basics and Chapter 1 sections in this book's R Appendix to learn more about R and its use for descriptive statistical analysis.

```
> sample(1:60, 5)    # Comments about R commands follow the # symbol
[1] 11 55 48 59 29   # output line [1] shows the five integers randomly generated
```

The sample of size 5 selects the students numbered 11, 55, 48, 59, 29.

The *simple* adjective in "simple random sample" distinguishes this type of sampling from more complex sampling schemes that also have elements of randomization. For instance, *stratified random sampling* schemes divide the population into separate groups ("strata") and then select a simple random sample from each stratum. This is useful for comparing groups on some variable when a particular group is relatively small and may not be adequately represented in a simple random sample. *Cluster random sampling* schemes divide the population into a large number of clusters, such as city blocks, and select a simple random sample of the clusters. This is useful when a complete listing of the population is not available.

1.3.2   Collecting Data with a Sample Survey

Some studies sample people from a population and interview them to collect data. This method of data collection is called a **sample survey**. The interview could be a personal interview, telephone interview, or self-administered questionnaire. Implementing a sample survey requires finding or constructing a valid *population list* for selecting the sample. A major challenge with collecting data with sample surveys is *nonresponse*—a significant percentage of those sampled refuse to be interviewed or don't respond on some items.

The *General Social Survey*, introduced in Section 1.2.2, is a sample survey. The GSS uses a random sampling design that is more complex than simple random sampling, incorporating multiple stages and clustering to make the survey easier to implement, but it ensures adequate coverage by giving each family the same chance of inclusion.

1.3.3   Collecting Data with an Experiment

Some studies use a planned **experiment** to generate data. An experiment compares subjects on a response variable under different conditions. Those conditions, which are levels of an explanatory variable, are called *treatments*. For instance, the treatments might be different drugs for treating some illness, compared in a clinical trial. The researcher specifies a plan for how to assign subjects to the treatments, called the *experimental design*. Good experimental designs use randomization to determine which treatment a subject receives. This reduces bias and allows us to use statistical inference.

For example, the Physicians' Health Study Research Group at Harvard Medical School designed an experiment to analyze whether regular intake of aspirin reduces mortality from heart disease. Of about 22,000 physicians, half were randomly chosen to take an aspirin every other day. The remaining half took a placebo, which had no active agent. After five years, rates of heart attack were compared. By using randomization to determine who received which treatment, the researchers knew the groups would roughly balance on all variables that could affect heart attack rates, such as age and quality of health. If the physicians could decide on their own which treatment to take, the groups might have been out of balance on some important factor. For instance, if younger physicians were more likely to select aspirin, then a lower heart attack rate among the aspirin group could occur merely because younger subjects are less likely to suffer heart attacks.

In medical research, *randomized clinical trials* are experiments using randomization that have been the gold standard for many years. But experiments are now used to address questions in an increasing variety of areas. For instance, the economists at Harvard and Massachusetts Institute of Technology (MIT) who won the Nobel Prize in 2019 pioneered the use of experiments to determine the policies that best improve the lives of the poor.[4] They randomly selected participants for anti-poverty programs, such as to evaluate if access to textbooks or access to remedial instruction improves education results. Randomized experiments have addressed diverse topics such as how to improve child nutrition, protect forests, and reduce gender discrimination.

1.3.4   Collecting Data with an Observational Study

In many application areas, it is not possible to conduct experiments to answer the questions of interest. We cannot randomly assign subjects to the groups we want to compare, such as levels of gender or race or educational level or annual income or usage of guns. Many studies merely *observe* the outcomes for available subjects on the variables of interest, without any experimental control of the subjects. Such studies are called **observational studies**. Sample surveys are examples of observational studies.

Sometimes we can envision an experiment that would help us answer some question, but the experiment would be *unethical* to conduct, so observational studies are used instead. For example, in the mid-20th century some researchers decided to investigate whether an association exists between lung cancer and smoking. The researchers could have answered the question by taking a group of youngsters, randomly splitting them into two groups, and instructing one group to smoke a pack of cigarettes each day and the other group not to smoke at all. Then, after 50 years, the study would have compared the percentages of smokers and non-smokers who got lung cancer. Such an experiment would not have been ethical or feasible to conduct, and the answer was needed at that time itself and not 50 years later, so it was necessary to use observational studies to address this issue. One useful approach sampled hospital patients, matching each adult suffering from lung cancer to an adult control of similar age who did not have it,[5] and compared the lung-cancer group with the control group in terms of how much they had smoked in the past.

1.3.5   Establishing Cause and Effect: Observational versus Experimental Studies

With observational studies, making causal conclusions based on comparing groups on a response variable is dangerous because the groups may be imbalanced on other variables that affect the response outcome. This is true even with random sampling. For instance, suppose we plan to compare performance on some standardized exam for Black, Hispanic, and White students. If White students have a higher average score, a variety of variables might account for that difference. Perhaps, on the average, White students have higher parents' attained education or higher parents' income or better quality of school attended. Those or other key variables may not even have been measured in the study.

Establishing *cause and effect* definitively is not possible with an observational study.[6] Unmeasured variables, referred to as *lurking variables*, could be responsible for associations observed in the data. By contrast, with an experiment that randomly assigns subjects to treatments, those treatments should balance on any unmeasured variables, at least approximately. For example, in the Harvard Medical School study of the association between heart attack prevalence and taking aspirin or placebo, those taking aspirin would not tend to be

---

[4]See www.nytimes.com/2019/11/29/business/economics-nobel.html

[5]Such a study is called a *matched case–control study*. It is a *retrospective* type of observational study, which compares groups, such as those with and without some medical condition, by "looking into the past" to measure relevant variables.

[6]Section 6.2.4 discusses this issue in more detail.

younger or of better health than those taking placebo. Because a randomized experiment balances the groups being compared on lurking variables, one can better establish cause and effect with it than with an observational study.

1.4 Descriptive Statistics: Summarizing Data

Descriptive statistics summarize the information that the data contain. Before calculating and analyzing descriptive statistics, you need to be cautious about complications such as missing data or improperly recorded data that can cause software to fail to work or to give invalid output.[7] Furthermore, the data readily accessible to us may be unstructured and messy. The process of organizing and cleaning the data and bringing them into an appropriate form of a data file for further statistical analysis is called *data wrangling*. This is an important preliminary stage of any statistical analysis and may take substantial time.

This section presents descriptive statistics for quantitative variables in clean data files. Tables and graphs describe the data by showing the number of times various outcomes occurred. The two key features to describe numerically are the *center* of the data and the *variability* of the data around the center.

1.4.1 Example: Carbon Dioxide Emissions in European Nations

Environmental scientists study how the increasing levels of carbon dioxide (CO_2) emissions around the world over time are associated with climate change reflected by the rising temperatures of "global warming." To illustrate methods of this section, we analyze recent UN data on carbon dioxide emissions per capita, in metric tons, for 31 nations in Europe. The emissions range between 2.0 for Albania and 9.9 for the Netherlands. We do not consider trends over time here, but it has been estimated that CO_2 emissions in the U.S. have doubled since the 1950s and are about 150 times higher than in 1850.

We can use R to read and view the `Carbon` data file from the book's website:

```
> Carbon <- read.table("http://stat4ds.rwth-aachen.de/data/Carbon.dat", header=TRUE)
                        # header=TRUE if variable names are at top of data file
> head(Carbon, 3)       # head(Carbon, n) shows n observations at top of data file
    Nation  CO2         # tail(Carbon, n) shows n observations at end of data file
1  Albania   2.0
2  Austria   6.9
3  Belgium   8.3
```

1.4.2 Frequency Distribution and Histogram Graphic

A *frequency distribution* is a listing of the possible values for a variable, together with the number, proportion, or percentage of observations at each value. For a discrete variable with relatively few values, the distribution lists each possible value. For a continuous variable or a discrete variable with many possible values, those values are divided into intervals.

The next output uses R to construct a frequency distribution for the CO_2 values in the `Carbon` data file, using intervals of width 1.0 metric ton. The most common interval was 5.0 up to but not including 6.0, with a percentage occurrence of 25.8%.

---

[7] Section A.1.4 in the R Appendix shows the use of R software for identifying missing data and conducting descriptive statistical analyses without them.

```
> breaks <- seq(2.0, 10.0, by=1.0) # frequency dist. intervals of width 1 between 2 and 10
> freq <- table(cut(Carbon$CO2, breaks, right=FALSE))
> freq                 # with right=FALSE, right-most value not included in interval
  [2,3)   [3,4)   [4,5)   [5,6)   [6,7)   [7,8)   [8,9)  [9,10)
      1       3       7       8       5       1       3       3
> cbind(freq, freq/nrow(Carbon)) # Frequency distribution of CO2 values, showing
            freq                  # intervals of CO2 values, followed by frequency
  [2,3)        1  0.03225806      # (freq) and proportion, which divides freq by
  [3,4)        3  0.09677419      # nrow(Carbon) = number of rows in data frame = 31
  [4,5)        7  0.22580645
  [5,6)        8  0.25806452
  [6,7)        5  0.16129032
  [7,8)        1  0.03225806
  [8,9)        3  0.09677419
  [9,10)       3  0.09677419
> hist(Carbon$CO2, xlab="CO2", ylab="Proportion", freq=FALSE) # histogram
> plot(density(Carbon$CO2))       # smooth-curve approximation of histogram (not shown)
```

A graph of the frequency distribution of a continuous variable or a discrete variable with intervals of values is called a ***histogram***.[8] Each interval of possible values has a bar over it, with height representing its number, proportion or percentage of observations. For the data on European CO_2 values, Figure 1.2 shows the histogram constructed using the `hist` function in R. For highly discrete variables, such as categorical variables, a graph that has a separate bar over each distinct value is called a ***bar graph***.

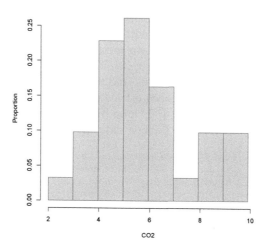

FIGURE 1.2 Histogram for frequency distribution of European CO2 values.

The *shape* of a histogram is informative. For a continuous variable, if we could increase n indefinitely with the number of intervals simultaneously increasing, so their width narrows, the shape would gradually approach a smooth curve.[9] For a smooth-curve approximation for any n, a bell-shaped appearance indicates that most subjects tend to fall near a central value. See Figure 1.3. The parts of the curve for the lowest values and the highest values are called the *tails* of the distribution. Often, one tail is much longer than the other. A distribution is then said to be ***skewed***: *skewed to the right* or *skewed to the left* according to which tail is longer.

---

[8]Section A.1.2 of the R Appendix presents options for constructing histograms.

[9]This curve can be approximated with the `density` function in R. See the code above (plot not shown) and Exercise 1.18.

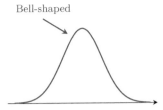
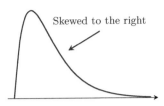

FIGURE 1.3 Smooth curve versions of bell-shaped and skewed frequency distributions: The longer tail indicates the direction of skew.

The `Carbon_West` data file at the book's website adds four non-European Western nations to the `Carbon` data file for Europe, with CO2 values of 15.4 for Australia, 15.1 for Canada, 7.7 for New Zealand, and 16.5 for the U.S. As an exercise, load that data file and form the histogram of CO2 values. The relatively large values for 3 of the 35 nations yields an extended right-tail reflecting skewness to the right.

1.4.3 Describing the Center of the Data: Mean and Median

For a sample, we use subscripts to identify particular observations in a data file. For example, we express the first three observations of a variable denoted by y as y_1, y_2, y_3.

How can we describe a typical observation for a quantitative variable, for example, describing the *center* of the data? A commonly used measure is the ***mean***.

Mean

The ***mean*** is the sum of the observations divided by the number of them. For a variable y with n observations y_1, y_2, ..., y_n in a sample from some population, the mean $\bar{y}$ is

$$\bar{y} = \frac{y_1 + y_2 + \cdots + y_n}{n} = \frac{\sum_{i=1}^{n} y_i}{n}.$$

The next section explains how the mean is the *center of gravity* of the data. Because of this, with small n, the mean can be highly influenced by an observation that falls well above or well below the rest of the data. Such an observation is called an ***outlier***. Here is an example: The owner of Leonardo's Pizza Joint reports that the mean annual income of his seven employees is $56,600. In fact, the annual incomes are $15,400, $15,600, $15,900, $16,400, $16,400, $16,600, and $299,900. The $299,900 income, which is the owner's income, is an outlier. The mean computed for the other six observations alone equals $16,050, quite different from the overall mean of $56,600.

The other commonly used measure of center for a quantitative variable is the ***median***. It is the middle value,[10] being larger than 50% of the other observations and smaller than 50%. For highly skewed distributions, this is a more representative summary of the center than is the mean. To illustrate, for the ordered income observations for the seven employees of Leonardo's Pizza, the median is $16,400. In particular, the median is *resistant* to outliers. When the highest observation of $299,900 is increased to $1,000,000, the median is still $16,400.

A measure sometimes reported with discrete data (quantitative or categorical) is the ***mode***, which is the most common outcome. For the GSS data on number of good friends,

---

[10] When n is even, the median is the midpoint between the two middle observations.

the most common response was 2, which is the mode. A frequency distribution that has two distinct peaks is called *bimodal*.

1.4.4 Describing Data Variability: Standard Deviation and Variance

To describe quantitative data more fully, we describe not only the center but also the *variability* about that center. The difference between the largest and smallest observations, called the **range**, is a simple way to do this. The range incorporates only the two most extreme observations, however, so it is sensitive to outliers and does not reflect how far observations other than those two fall from the center.

More useful measures of variability use the distances of *all* the observations from the center. For observation i, the **deviation** of y_i from the mean $\bar{y}$ is $(y_i - \bar{y})$. The deviation is *positive* when y_i falls *above* the mean and *negative* when y_i falls *below* the mean. Calling the mean the *center of gravity* of the data reflects that the sum of the positive deviations equals the negative of the sum of negative deviations. That is, the sum of all the deviations,

$$\sum_{i=1}^{n}(y_i - \bar{y}) = \sum_{i=1}^{n} y_i - n\bar{y} = n\bar{y} - n\bar{y} = 0.$$

Because of this, measures of variability use the squares or the absolute values of the deviations.

Standard deviation and variance

For a variable y with n observations $y_1, y_2, ..., y_n$ in a sample from some population, the **standard deviation** s is

$$s = \sqrt{\frac{\sum_{i=1}^{n}(y_i - \bar{y})^2}{n-1}} = \sqrt{\frac{(y_1 - \bar{y})^2 + (y_2 - \bar{y})^2 + \cdots + (y_n - \bar{y})^2}{n-1}}.$$

The standard deviation is the positive square root of the **variance** s^2,

$$s^2 = \frac{\sum_{i=1}^{n}(y_i - \bar{y})^2}{n-1}.$$

The variance is approximately an average of the squared deviations. The units of measurement are the squares of those for the original data, so the standard deviation is simpler to interpret: s is a sort of *typical distance* of an observation from the mean. Also, *the larger the standard deviation, the greater the spread of the data.* The value of s is nonnegative, with $s = 0$ only when all observations have the same value. The denominator of s^2 uses $(n-1)$, rather than n, because this version of the measure naturally arises in inferential statistical methods.[11]

The magnitude of s partly reflects the shape of the frequency distribution. If the distribution is approximately bell-shaped, then:[12]

1. About 68% of the observations fall between $\bar{y} - s$ and $\bar{y} + s$.

2. About 95% of the observations fall between $\bar{y} - 2s$ and $\bar{y} + 2s$.

---

[11]With data for an entire population, we replace $(n-1)$ by n; the variance is then precisely the mean squared deviation. In using a sample to *estimate* variability around the population mean, whose value is unknown, Section 4.4.6 shows that the bias due to the numerator of s^2 having the *sample* mean instead of the *population* mean is eliminated when we use $(n-1)$ rather than n in the denominator.

[12]Section 2.5.1 will show where these percentages come from.

3. All or nearly all observations fall between $\bar{y} - 3s$ and $\bar{y} + 3s$.

Figure 1.4 is a graphical portrayal. To illustrate, suppose that grades on an exam are bell-shaped around $\bar{y} = 70$, with $s = 10$. Then, about 68% of the exam scores fall between 60 and 80, about 95% fall between 50 and 90, and all or nearly all fall between 40 and 100.

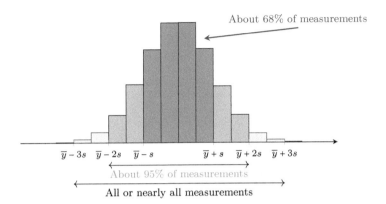

FIGURE 1.4 The standard deviation and mean determine approximate percentages in certain ranges for bell-shaped distributions.

Regardless of the shape of a frequency distribution, it is rare for observations to fall many standard deviations from the mean. The Russian mathematician Pafnuty Chebyshev proved in 1867 that *for any $k \geq 1$, the proportion of observations that fall at least k standard deviations from the mean can be no greater than $1/k^2$*. The result is called **Chebyshev's inequality**.[13] For example, no more than 4% of the observations can fall at least five standard deviations from the mean. Percentages for most data sets, however, are much closer to the bell-shaped percentages than to the Chebyshev upper bounds.

1.4.5 Describing Position: Percentiles, Quartiles, and Box Plots

Besides center and variability, another way to describe a distribution is with a measure of *position*. The **pth percentile** is the point such that $p\%$ of the observations fall below or at that point and $(100 - p)\%$ fall above it.[14] For example, for $p = 95$, the 95th percentile falls above 95% of the observations and below 5% of them. The 50th percentile is the *median*. *Quantiles* are percentiles expressed in proportion form. For example, the 95th percentile is also called the 0.95 quantile.

Two especially useful percentiles are the the 25th percentile, called the **lower quartile**, and the 75th percentile, called the **upper quartile**. The quartiles together with the median split the distribution into four parts, each containing one-fourth of the observations. The middle half of the data falls between the lower and upper quartiles. The **interquartile range**, denoted by IQR, is the difference between the upper quartile and the lower quartile. Unlike the ordinary range, the IQR is not affected by outliers and takes into account variability by observations other than the most extreme ones.

---

[13]Sometimes it is referred to as the *Bienaymé–Chebyshev inequality*, since essentially the same result was shown by the French mathematician I. J. Bienaymé in 1853.

[14]This definition is imprecise, because no value or an infinite number of real numbers may have *exactly* $p\%$ falling below or at it. Software uses more elaborate definitions that make adjustments to yield precise values. The adjustments are tiny for large n.

The median, the upper and lower quartiles, and the maximum and minimum values provide a ***five-number summary*** of positions. Software can easily find these values as well as other percentiles and summary measures. For instance, with R, here is the five-number summary and the mean and standard deviation for the variable labeled as CO2 in the `Carbon` data file:

```
> summary(Carbon$CO2)            # 1st Qu = lower quartile, 3rd Qu = upper quartile
   Min.   1st Qu.   Median    Mean   3rd Qu.    Max.
  2.000    4.350    5.400   5.819    6.700    9.900
> c(mean(Carbon$CO2), sd(Carbon$CO2), quantile(Carbon$CO2, 0.90))
                90%
5.819355 1.964929 8.900000 # mean, standard deviation, 0.90 quantile
> boxplot(Carbon$CO2, xlab="CO2 values", horizontal=TRUE)
```

The five-number summary is the basis of a graphical display called the ***box plot***. The *box* contains the central 50% of the data, from the lower quartile to the upper quartile. The median is marked by a line drawn within the box. The dashed lines extending from the box, called *whiskers*, contain the outer 50% of the data except for outliers, which are marked separately.[15] For example, Figure 1.5 shows the box plot for the European CO2 values. The shape indicates that the right-tail of the distribution, which corresponds to the relatively large values, is slightly longer than the left tail. The plot reflects the slight skewness to the right of the observations.

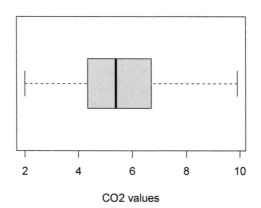

FIGURE 1.5 Box plot of CO2 values for European nations.

Many studies compare different groups on some variable. Side-by-side box plots are useful for making comparisons. To illustrate, Figure 1.6 shows side-by-side box plots of the number of murders per 100,000 population in 2018 for the 50 states and the District of Columbia (D.C.) in the U.S. and for the 10 provinces of Canada. The figure shows that the murder rates in the U.S. tended to be much larger, have much greater variability, and have an extremely large outlier (the murder rate of 24.2 in D.C.). Here is R code to construct this plot and organize summary statistics by group:[16]

```
> Crime <- read.table("http://stat4ds.rwth-aachen.de/data/Murder2.dat", header=TRUE)
> boxplot(Crime$murder ~ Crime$nation, xlab="Murder rate", horizontal=TRUE)
```

[15]An observation is identified as an *outlier* if it falls more than 1.5(IQR) below the lower quartile or above the upper quartile and as an *extreme outlier* if more than 3(IQR) away. The box plot is one of many methods of ***exploratory data analysis*** proposed in a landmark book by John Tukey (1977).

[16]Section A.1.3 shows other ways to present statistics by the level of a second variable.

```
> tapply(Crime$murder, Crime$nation, summary)   # applies summary to murder, by nation
$Canada
   Min. 1st Qu.  Median    Mean 3rd Qu.     Max.
  0.000   1.030   1.735   1.673   1.875    4.070
$US
   Min. 1st Qu.  Median    Mean 3rd Qu.     Max.
  1.000   2.650   5.000   5.253   6.450   24.200
```

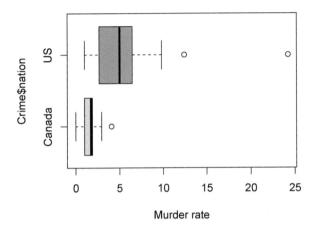

FIGURE 1.6 Side-by-side box plots for U.S. and Canadian murder rates.

1.5   Descriptive Statistics: Summarizing Multivariate Data

For statistical analyses with two or more variables, descriptive methods investigate *associations* between the response variable and the explanatory variables. For a quantitative response variable and categorical explanatory variable, we can compare means or medians on the quantitative variable for the groups that are formed by the categories of the explanatory variable and display results in a side-by-side box plot, such as the R output above and Figure 1.6 show for murder rate and nation. We next present descriptive methods for pairs of quantitative variables and for pairs of categorical variables.

1.5.1   Bivariate Quantitative Data: The Scatterplot, Correlation, and Regression

For a pair of quantitative variables, we can plot values for the explanatory variable on the horizontal (x) axis and for the response variable on the vertical (y) axis. The values of the two variables for any particular observation form a point relative to these axes. A *scatterplot* portrays the n observations as n points.

For example, Figure 1.7 plots the relation in the U.S. for the 50 states and D.C. between x = percent of people in state who own guns and y = suicide rate, measured as the annual number of suicides per 100,000 people in the state. The scatterplot for the 51 observations shows that relatively high values of x tend to occur with relatively high values of y, partly reflecting that guns are used in slightly more than half of all suicides in the U.S.

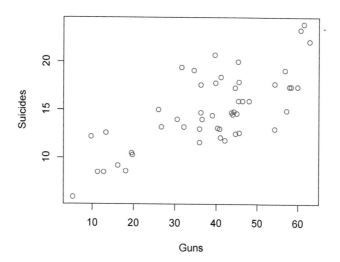

FIGURE 1.7 Scatterplot relating state-level data in the U.S. on percent gun ownership and suicide rate.

Chapter 6 presents two ways to describe such a trend. The **correlation** describes the strength of the association, in terms of how closely the data follow a *straight line trend.* For Figure 1.7, the correlation is 0.74. The positive value means that the suicide rate tends to go *up* as gun ownership goes *up*. The correlation takes values between −1 and +1. The larger it is in absolute value, the stronger the association. A **regression analysis** provides a straight-line formula for predicting the response variable from the explanatory variable. For the data in Figure 1.7, this equation is

$$\text{Predicted suicide rate} = 7.390 + 0.1936(\text{gun ownership}).$$

For a state with $x = 5.2$ (the lowest value in this sample, which is for D.C.), the predicted suicide rate is $7.390 + 0.1936(5.2) = 8.40$. For a state with $x = 62.8$ (the highest value, which is for Wyoming), the predicted suicide rate is $7.390 + 0.1936(62.8) = 19.55$.

Chapter 6 derives formulas for the correlation and the regression line. It is simple to implement them with software, as shown next with R.

```
> GS <- read.table("http://stat4ds.rwth-aachen.de/data/Guns_Suicide.dat", header=TRUE)
> Guns <- GS$guns; Suicides <- GS$suicide
> plot(Guns, Suicides)           # scatterplot with arguments x, y
> cor(Guns, Suicides)            # correlation
[1] 0.7386667
> summary(lm(Suicides ~ Guns))   # lm(y ~ x) is "linear model" for
Coefficients:                    # response variable y and explanatory variable x
             Estimate
(Intercept)  7.39008             # intercept of line fitted to data points
Guns         0.19356             # slope of line
```

1.5.2   Bivariate Categorical Data: Contingency Tables

For two categorical variables, a **contingency table** is a rectangular table that cross-classifies the variables. The *cells* show the combinations of categories and their counts. For instance,

TABLE 1.1 Contingency table cross-classifying political party identification (ID) and race.

	Political Party ID		
Race	Democrat	Independent	Republican
Black	281	66	30
Other	124	77	52
White	633	272	704

Table 1.1 is a contingency table for political party identification (ID = Democrat, Independent, or Republican) and race, using data from the 2018 General Subject Survey.

Treating political party ID as the response variable, we can summarize by finding percentages in each ID category, by race. For instance, 44% of Whites and 8% of Blacks identified as Republicans. The following code uses R with the **PartyID** data file at the book's website to construct the contingency table and find the ID proportions separately for each category of race:

```
> PID <- read.table("http://stat4ds.rwth-aachen.de/data/PartyID.dat", header=TRUE)
> PID
        race         id
1      white    Democrat
...
2238   other  Republican       # 2238 subjects in data file
> table(PID$race, PID$id)       # forms contingency table (not shown here; see Table 1.1)
> options(digits=2)
> prop.table(table(PID$race, PID$id), margin=1)  # For margin=1, proportions
        Democrat Independent Republican           # sum to 1.0 within rows
  black     0.75        0.17       0.08
  other     0.49        0.30       0.21
  white     0.39        0.17       0.44
> mosaicplot(table(PartyID$race, PartyID$id))     # graphical portrayal of cell sizes
```

As an exercise, check what the **mosaicplot** function portrays. Contingency tables extend to multi-dimensional tables to handle several variables at once.

1.5.3 Descriptive Statistics for Samples and for Populations

This chapter has introduced commonly-used graphical and numerical descriptive statistics. We introduce others in later chapters and in the book and website appendices. Of descriptive statistics, the mean $\bar{y}$ and the standard deviation s are the most commonly reported measures of center and variability. The correlation and the regression slope are commonly reported measures of association. Since the values of these statistics depend on the sample selected, they vary in value from sample to sample. In this sense, they are also variables.

For example, for a population, Stanford–Binet IQ scores have a bell shape and are scaled to have a mean of 100 and standard deviation of 16. The following R code randomly samples 30 people from a bell-shaped population with this center and spread and finds $\bar{y}$ and s and constructs a histogram. Then it repeats with another sample of size 30, to show that $\bar{y}$ and s and the histogram shape vary from sample to sample.

```
> y1 <- rnorm(30, 100, 16)      # randomly sample normal distribution (Sec. 2.5.1)
> mean(y1); sd(y1); hist(y1)    # histogram (not shown)
[1] 102.7339                    # mean
[1] 11.64643                    # standard deviation
> y2 <- rnorm(30, 100, 16)      # another random sample of size n=30
> mean(y2); sd(y2); hist(y2)
[1] 99.17068   # mean and standard deviation change for each sample of size n=30
[1] 16.52736
```

Do this several times to investigate how $\bar{y}$ and s vary from sample to sample around the population values. You will observe that the histogram may portray the population poorly, sometimes even showing multiple modes. Now do this several times with $n = 1000$ instead of 30. The statistics will vary less from sample to sample, and the histogram will better portray the population. Chapter 3 shows that, for a particular value of n, we can predict how much $\bar{y}$ varies among samples.

Inferential statistical methods use sample descriptive statistics to make predictions about corresponding parameters for the population. In this text, *lower-case Greek letters denote population parameters and Roman letters denote sample statistics.* For example, $\bar{y}$ and s denote a sample mean and standard deviation, and μ and σ denote the population mean and standard deviation. For the IQ sampling just shown, $\mu = 100$ and $\sigma = 16$, whereas $\bar{y} = 102.73$ and $s = 11.65$ for the first sample of 30 observations and $\bar{y} = 99.17$ and $s = 16.53$ for the second sample. We use π for a population proportion.

Before learning about inferential statistical methods, however, you need some basic tools of *probability*, which serves as the language for expressing uncertainty about inferences. Probability is the subject of Chapter 2.

1.6   Chapter Summary

The field of statistical science includes methods for

- designing research studies,

- summarizing the data (*descriptive statistics*),

- making estimations and predictions using the data (*inferential statistics*).

Statistical methods apply to observations in a *sample* taken from a *population*. With randomization, samples are likely to be representative of the population. For a *simple random sample*, every possible sample has the same chance of selection. *Statistics* summarize sample data, while *parameters* summarize entire populations. Inferential statistics use sample data to make predictions about population parameters.

A *data file* has a separate row of data for each subject and a separate column for each characteristic. Statistical methods analyze data on *variables*, which are characteristics that vary among subjects.

- Numerically measured variables, such as family income and number of children in a family, are *quantitative.*

- Variables taking values in a set of categories, such as race and gender, are *categorical.*

- Variables are also classified as *discrete*, such as categorical variables and quantitative variables that take values in a set of separate numbers (e.g., 0, 1, 2, ...), or *continuous*, having a continuous, infinite set of possible values.

Descriptive statistics summarize key characteristics of the data. A *frequency distribution* lists numbers of observations for possible values or intervals of values of a variable. For a quantitative variable, a *histogram* uses bars over possible values or intervals of values to portray a frequency distribution. It shows whether the distribution is approximately bell-shaped or skewed to the right (longer tail pointing to the right) or to the left. A *box plot* portrays the quartiles (25th and 75th percentiles), the extreme values, and any outliers. Table 1.2 summarizes the most important numerical measures that describe the *center* of n observations and their *variability* (spread).

TABLE 1.2 Summary of descriptive statistical measures of center and variability.

Measure	Definition	Interpretation
Center		
Mean	$\bar{y} = (\sum_i y_i)/n$	Center of gravity
Median	Middle observation of ordered sample	50th percentile, splits sample into two equal parts
Variability		
Standard deviation	$s = \sqrt{\sum(y_i - \bar{y})^2/(n-1)}$	If bell-shaped, 68%, 95%, nearly all within $s, 2s, 3s$ of $\bar{y}$

Bivariate statistics summarize the **association** between two variables and how the outcome on a **response variable** depends on the value of an **explanatory variable**.

- For quantitative variables, a **scatterplot** graphs the observations as points with axes for the variables. The **correlation** describes the strength of straight-line association and the **regression line** can predict the response variable using the explanatory variable.

- For categorical variables, a **contingency table** shows the number of observations at the combinations of possible category outcomes for the two variables.

Exercises

Data Analysis and Applications

1.1 In the 2018 election for Senate in California, a CNN exit poll of 1882 voters stated that 52.5% voted for the Democratic candidate, Diane Feinstein. Of all 11.1 million voters, 54.2% voted for Feinstein.

    (a) What was the (i) subject, (ii) sample, (iii) population?

    (b) Identify a relevant statistic and corresponding parameter.

1.2 The `Students` data file at http://stat4ds.rwth-aachen.de/data shows responses of a class of 60 social science graduate students at the University of Florida to a questionnaire that asked about *gender* (1 = female, 0 = male), *age*, *hsgpa* = high school GPA (on a four-point scale), *cogpa* = college GPA, *dhome* = distance (in miles) of the campus from your home town, *dres* = distance (in miles) of the classroom from your current residence, *tv* = average number of hours per week that you watch TV, *sport* = average number of hours per week that you participate in sports or have other physical exercise, *news* = number of times a week you read a newspaper, *aids* = number of people you know who have died from AIDS or who are HIV+, *veg* = whether you are a vegetarian (1 = yes, 0 = no), *affil* = political affiliation (1 = Democrat, 2 = Republican, 3 = independent), *ideol* = political ideology (1 = very liberal, 2 = liberal, 3 = slightly liberal, 4 = moderate, 5 = slightly conservative, 6 = conservative, 7 = very conservative), *relig* = how often you attend religious services (0 = never, 1 = occasionally, 2 = most weeks, 3 = every week), *abor* = opinion about whether abortion should be legal in the first three months of pregnancy (1 = yes, 0 = no), *affirm* = support affirmative action (1 = yes, 0 = no), and *life* = belief in life after death (1 = yes, 2 = no, 3 = undecided). You will use this data file for some exercises in this book.

    (a) Practice accessing a data file for statistical analysis with your software by going to the book's website and copying and then displaying this data file.

    (b) Using responses on *abor*, state a question that could be addressed with (i) descriptive statistics, (ii) inferential statistics.

1.3 Identify each of the following variables as categorical or quantitative: **(a)** Number of smartphones that you own; **(b)** County of residence; **(c)** Choice of diet (vegetarian, nonvegetarian); **(d)** Distance, in kilometers, commute to work

1.4 Give an example of a variable that is **(a)** categorical; **(b)** quantitative; **(c)** discrete; **(d)** continuous.

1.5 In analyzing data about patients who developed Covid-19 from coronavirus, many research studies used the scale (1. Death; 2. Hospitalized with invasive ventilation; 3. Hospitalized with non-invasive ventilation; 4. Hospitalized with supplemental oxygen; 5. Hospitalized, not requiring supplemental oxygen but requiring ongoing medical care; 6. Hospitalized, not requiring ongoing medical care (quarantine or awaiting rehab); 7. Not hospitalized, limitation on activities; 8. Not hospitalized, no limitations on activities). Is this categorical scale *nominal* or *ordinal*? Why?

1.6 Give an example of a variable that is **(a)** technically discrete but essentially continuous for purposes of data analysis; **(b)** potentially continuous but highly discrete in the way it is measured in practice.

1.7 The student directory for a large university has 400 pages with 130 names per page, a total of 52,000 names. Using software, show how to select a simple random sample of 10 names.

1.8 Explain whether an experiment or an observational study would be more appropriate to investigate the following:

    (a) Whether cities with higher unemployment rates tend to have higher crime rates.

    (b) Whether a Honda Accord hybrid or a Toyota Prius gets better gas mileage.

    (c) Whether higher college grade point averages tend to occur for students who had higher scores on college entrance exams.

    (d) Whether design A or design B for an Internet page makes a person more likely to buy the product advertised.

1.9 For the GSS data on number of good friends (search at `https://sda.berkeley.edu/sdaweb/analysis/?dataset=gss18` for variable NUMFREND), the responses (1, 2, 3, 4, 5, 6, 7, 8, 9, ... , 96+) had percentages of (6.1, 16.2, 15.7. 14.2, 11.3, 8.8, 1.2, 2.4, 0.7, ..., 0.8). Report the median and the mode. Would you expect the mean to be smaller, the same, or larger than the median? Why?

1.10 Analyze the `Carbon_West` data file at the book's website by **(a)** constructing a frequency distribution and a histogram, **(b)** finding the mean, median, and standard deviation. Interpret each.

1.11 According to Statistics Canada, for the Canadian population having income in 2019, annual income had a median of $35,000 and mean of $46,700. What would you predict about the shape of the distribution? Why?

1.12 Give an example of a variable that is nonnegative but has the majority of its sample values at 0, so the median is not especially informative despite the skew.

1.13 A report indicates that public school teacher's annual salaries in New York city have an approximate mean of $69,000 and standard deviation of $6,000. If the distribution has approximately a bell shape, report intervals that contain about (a) 68%, (b) 95%, (c) all or nearly all salaries. Would a salary of $100,000 be unusual? Why?

1.14 In 2017, according to the Kaiser Family Foundation (www.kff.org), the five-number summary for the U.S. statewide percentage of people without health insurance had minimum = 3% (Massachusetts), lower quartile = 6%, median = 8%, upper quartile = 9.5%, and maximum = 17% (Texas). Interpret the quartiles and the interquartile range, and sketch a box plot.

1.15 According to www.salary.com, the mean salary (in dollars) of secondary school teachers in the United States in 2019 varied among states with a five-number summary of maximum = 67,600 (California), upper quartile = 64,700, median = 55,500, lower quartile = 53,100, and minimum = 51,600 (South Dakota). Sketch a box plot, and indicate whether the distribution seems to be symmetric, skewed to the right, or skewed to the left.

1.16 Access the most recent General Social Survey at https://sda.berkeley.edu/archive.htm. Entering TVHOURS for the row variable and year(2018) in the selection filter, you obtain data on hours per day of TV watching in the U.S. in 2018.

(a) Construct the frequency distribution for the values 0, 1, 2, 3, 4, 5, 6, 7 or more. How would you describe its shape?

(b) Find the median and the mode.

(c) Check *Summary statistics* in the output options, and report the mean and standard deviation. From these, explain why you would not expect the distribution to be bell-shaped.

1.17 From the Murder data file at the book's website, use the variable *murder*, which is the murder rate (per 100,000 population) for each state in the U.S. in 2017 according to the FBI Uniform Crime Reports. At first, do not use the observation for D.C. (DC). Using software:

(a) Find the mean and standard deviation and interpret their values.

(b) Find the five-number summary, and construct the corresponding box plot. Interpret.

(c) Now include the observation for D.C. What is affected more by this outlier: The mean or the median? The range or the inter-quartile range?

1.18 The Income data file at the book's website reports annual income values in the U.S., in thousands of dollars.

(a) Using software, construct a histogram. Describe its shape.

(b) Find descriptive statistics to summarize the data. Interpret them.

(c) The *kernel density estimation* method finds a smooth-curve approximation for a histogram. At each value, it takes into account how many observations are nearby and their distance, with more weight given those closer. Increasing the *bandwidth* increases the influence of observations further away. Plot a smooth-curve approximation for the histogram of income values, using the `density` function in R. Summarize the impact of increasing and of decreasing the bandwidth (option `bw` in the `density` function) substantially from the default value.[17]

(d) Construct and interpret side-by-side box plots of income by race (B = Black, H = Hispanic, W = White). Compare the incomes using numerical descriptive statistics.

1.19 The `Houses` data file at the book's website lists the selling price (thousands of dollars), size (square feet), tax bill (dollars), number of bathrooms, number of bedrooms, and whether the house is new (1 = yes, 0 = no) for 100 home sales in Gainesville, Florida. Let's analyze the selling prices.

(a) Construct a frequency distribution and a histogram. Describe the shape.

(b) Find the percentage of observations that fall within one standard deviation of the mean. Why is this not close to 68%?

(c) Construct a box plot, and interpret.

(d) Use descriptive statistics to compare selling prices according to whether the house is new.

1.20 Refer to the previous exercise. Let y = selling price and x = size of home.

(a) Construct a scatterplot. Interpret. Identify any observation that seems to fall apart from the others.

(b) Find the correlation. Interpret.

(c) Find the regression line. Interpret the slope, and find the predicted selling price for a home of (i) 1000 square feet, (ii) 4000 square feet.

1.21 For the `Students` data file introduced in Exercise 1.2, summarize the relationship between *hsgpa* and *cogpa* using correlation and regression. Find the predicted college GPA of a student who had a high school GPA of 4.0.

1.22 Using the `Happy` data file, construct the contingency table relating marital status and happiness. Which variable is the natural response variable? Report the proportions in its categories, separately at each category of the explanatory variable, and interpret.

1.23 For the `Students` data file introduced in Exercise 1.2, construct and summarize a contingency table relating religiosity and opinion about legalized abortion.

1.24 The `UN` data file at the book's website has United Nations data for 42 nations on per capita gross domestic product (GDP, in thousands of dollars), a human development index (HDI, which has components referring to life expectancy at birth, educational attainment, and income per capita), a gender inequality index (GII, a composite measure reflecting inequality in achievement between women and men in reproductive health, empowerment, and the labor market), fertility rate (number of births per woman), carbon dioxide emissions per capita (CO2, in metric tons), a homicide rate (number of homicides per 100,000 people), prison population (per 100,000 people), and percent using the Internet.

---

[17]The default is the so-called *Silverman's rule of thumb*, option `bw = "nrd0"`.

(a) Conduct a descriptive statistical analysis of the prison rates. Summarize your conclusions, highlighting any unusual observations.

(b) Using a command like cor(cbind(GDP, HDI, GII, ..., Internet)) in R, construct a *correlation matrix* showing the correlation for each pair of variables. Which pair has the strongest association?

(c) Conduct correlation and regression analyses to study the association between CO2 use and GDP. Show how the predicted CO2 varies as GDP goes from its minimum to its maximum value in this sample.

1.25 The ScotsRaces data file at the book's website shows the record times for men and for women for several hill races in Scotland. Use graphical and numerical descriptive statistics to compare the men's winning times with the women's winning times. Summarize your analyses in a short report, with software output as an appendix.

1.26 Refer to the previous exercise. Explanatory variables listed in the data file are the distance of the race and the climb in elevation. Use graphical and numerical descriptive statistics to summarize the men's winning times and their relationship with the race distance and climb. Summarize your analyses in a one-page report.

1.27 A study of sheep[18] analyzed whether the sheep survived for a year from the original observation time (1 = yes, 0 = no) as a function of their weight (kg) at the original observation. Using Sheep data file at the text website, use graphical and numerical methods of this chapter to compare weights of the sheep that survived to weights of the sheep that did not survive. Summarize the results of your analysis in a few sentences.

Methods and Concepts

1.28 The beginning of Section 1.2 mentioned a potential survey to observe characteristics such as opinion about the legalization of same-sex marriage, political party affiliation, frequency of attending religious services, number of years of education, annual income, marital status, race, and gender. Describe two ways you could select one of these variables as a response variable and the others as explanatory variables, and explain the reasoning for these choices.

1.29 A *systematic random sample* of n subjects from a population of size N selects a subject at random from the first $k = N/n$ in the population list and then selects every kth subject listed after that one. Explain why this is not a simple random sample.

For the following two multiple-choice questions, select the best response.

1.30 A simple random sample of size n is one in which:

(a) Every nth member is selected from the population.

(b) Each possible sample of size n has the same chance of being selected.

(c) There must be exactly the same proportion of women in the sample as is in the population.

(d) You keep sampling until you have a fixed number of people having various characteristics (e.g., males, females).

---

[18]Summarized in article by T. Coulson, *Oikos*, **121**: 1337–1350 (2012); thanks to Prof. M. K. Oli for the data from this study.

    (e) A particular minority group member of the population is less likely to be chosen than a particular majority group member.

    (f) All of the above.

1.31 If we use random numbers to take a simple random sample of 50 students from the 6500 undergraduate students at the University of Rochester:

    (a) We would never get the random number 1111, because it is not a random sequence.

    (b) The draw 1234 is no more or less likely than the draw 1111.

    (c) Since the sample is random, it is *impossible* that it will be non-representative, such as having only females in the sample.

    (d) Since the sample is random, it is impossible to get the sequence of random numbers 0001, 0002, 0003, ..., 0049, 0050.

1.32 With an Internet search, find a study that used an (a) experiment; (b) observational study. In each case, describe how the sample was obtained and summarize results.

1.33 An article[19] in the *New England Journal of Medicine* (October 12, 2012) observed a correlation of 0.79 for 23 countries between per capita annual chocolate consumption and the number of Nobel laureates per 10 million population. Was this study an experiment or an observational study? Can we conclude that increasing chocolate consumption increases the chance of a Nobel prize? Why or why not?

1.34 A research study funded by Wobegon Springs Mineral Water, Inc., discovers that children with dental problems are less common in families that regularly buy bottled water than in families that do not. Explain why this association need not reflect a causal link between drinking bottled water and having fewer dental problems. Identify lurking variables that could be responsible for the result, and explain how.

1.35 Suppose that grade-point averages at your university are bell-shaped with mean 3.0 and standard deviation 0.3. Randomly sample n students several times for $n = 20$ (using a function such as `rnorm` in R), and then repeat several times for $n = 1000$, each time constructing a histogram. What does this suggest about the difficulty of determining the shape of a population distribution when n is small?

1.36 Construct a set of data for which the mean and median are identical.

1.37 Suppose you estimate the mean number of friends that members of Facebook have by randomly sampling 100 members of Facebook and (i) averaging the numbers of friends that they have, (ii) averaging how many friends the friends of those members have. Which estimate do you think would be larger? Why? (*Hint*: See article by J. A. Paulos, *Scientific American*, Feb. 1, 2011.)

1.38 To measure center, why is the (a) median sometimes preferred over the mean? (b) mean sometimes preferred over the median? (*Hint*: A wide variety of highly discrete frequency distributions can have the same median.) To illustrate, in your answers use the variables annual income for (a) and number of times you played a sport in the past week for (b).

1.39 To measure variability, why is the (a) standard deviation s usually preferred over the range? (b) interquartile range often preferred over the range?

---

[19]See `www.nejm.org/doi/full/10.1056/NEJMon1211064`

1.40 The largest value in a sample is moved upwards so that it is an extreme outlier. Explain how, if at all, this affects the mean, median, range, and interquartile range.

1.41 To investigate how $\bar{y}$ can vary from sample to sample of size n, for the simulation from a bell-shaped population shown at the end of Section 1.5.3, take **(a)** 10,000 random samples of size $n = 30$ each; **(b)** 10,000 random samples of size $n = 1000$ each. In each case, form a histogram of the 10,000 $\bar{y}$ values and find their standard deviation. Compare results and explain what this simulation reveals about the impact of sample size on how study results can vary. (Chapter 3 shows that in sampling from a population with standard deviation 16, the theoretical standard deviation of $\bar{y}$ values is $16/\sqrt{n}$.)

1.42 The Internet site www.artofstat.com/web-apps has useful apps [20] for illustrating data analyses and properties of statistical methods.

   (a) Using the *Explore Quantitative Data* app, construct a sample of 20 observations on y = number of hours of physical exercise in the past week having $\bar{y} < s$. What aspect of the distribution causes this to happen?

   (b) Using the *Explore Linear Regression* app with the *Draw Own* option, create 20 data points that are plausible for x = number of hours of exercise last week and y = number of hours of exercise this week. Describe your data by the correlation and by the linear regression line, and interpret them.

1.43 For a sample with mean $\bar{y}$, show that adding a constant c to each observation changes the mean to $\bar{y} + c$, and the standard deviation s is unchanged. Show that multiplying each observation by c changes the mean to $c\bar{y}$ and the standard deviation to $|c|s$.

1.44 Suppose the sample data distribution of $\{y_i\} = \{y_1, \ldots, y_n\}$ is very highly skewed to the right, and we take logs and analyze $\{x_i = \log(y_i)\}$.

   (a) Is $\bar{x} = \log(\bar{y})$? Why or why not?

   (b) Is median$(\{x_i\}) = \log[\text{median}(\{y_i\})]$? Why or why not?

   (c) To summarize $\{y_i\}$, we find $\bar{x}$ and then use $\exp(\bar{x})$. Show that $\exp(\bar{x}) = (\prod_i y_i)^{1/n}$, called the **geometric mean** of $\{y_i\}$.

1.45 Find the Chebyshev inequality upper bound for the proportion of observations falling at least **(a)** 1, **(b)** 2, **(c)** 3 standard deviations from the mean. Compare this to the approximate proportions for a bell-shaped distribution. Why are the differences so large?

1.46 The R output in Section 1.5.2 shows a mosaicplot function. Implement it for the PartyID data. Do an Internet search and look at the R Appendix to this book to learn about *mosaic plots*, and describe what the plot shows you. (The mosaic function in the vcd package constructs more sophisticated mosaic plots.)

1.47 The *least squares* property of the mean states that the data fall closer to $\bar{y}$ than to any other number c, in the sense that

$$\sum_i (y_i - \bar{y})^2 < \sum_i (y_i - c)^2.$$

Prove this property by treating $f(c) = \sum_i (y_i - c)^2$ as a function of c and deriving the value of c that minimizes it.

---

[20] The apps at that website were developed by Dr. Bernhard Klingenberg.

1.48 For a sample $\{y_i\}$ of size n, $\sum_i |y_i - c|$ is minimized at c = median. Explain why this property holds. (Hint: Starting at c = median, what happens to $\sum_i |y_i - c|$ as you move away from it in either direction?)

1.49 The Delphi group at Carnegie-Mellon University has tracked statistics about coronavirus. Figure 1.8 is a scatterplot of U.S. statewide data compiled between x = percentage wearing masks and y = percentage knowing someone with Covid-19 symptoms. Which do you think best describes the scatterplot?

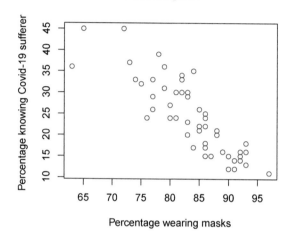

FIGURE 1.8 Scatterplot for data file CovidMasks at book's website, showing U.S. statewide data in October 2020 of percentage of people wearing masks in public all or most of the time and percentage of people knowing someone who has had Covid-19 symptoms

   (a) Correlation = −0.85 and predicted $y = 112.9 - 1.06\ x$
   (b) Correlation = −0.85 and predicted $y = 112.9 + 1.06\ x$
   (c) Correlation = 0.85 and predicted $y = 112.9 - 1.06\ x$
   (d) Correlation = 0.85 and predicted $y = 112.9 + 1.06\ x$

2

Probability Distributions

This chapter introduces *probability*, the language used to describe uncertainty, such as in inferential statistical analyses. We first define probability and give basic rules for calculating probabilities. *Random variables* specify possible values of variables in experiments or observational studies that incorporate randomization. A *probability distribution* summarizes random variation in the values of a random variable by specifying probabilities for all the possible outcomes. Probability distributions are themselves summarized by measures of center and variability, such as the mean and standard deviation. These measures are *expected values*, describing what we expect, on the average, with observations taken at random from a probability distribution.

Like ordinary variables, random variables can be *discrete* or *continuous*. The most important probability distributions for discrete random variables are the *binomial* for binary outcomes and the *Poisson* for count outcomes. The most important probability distributions for continuous random variables are the *normal*, which has a bell shape over the real line, and the *gamma*, which is skewed to the right over positive real number values.

Joint probability distributions describe how two or more random variables co-vary. The *correlation* describes their strength of association, with *independence* being the absence of any association.

2.1   Introduction to Probability

In everyday life, the term *probability* is used in an informal manner to mean the *chance* of an outcome. But this definition is rather vague. For studies that can employ *randomization* for gathering data, a more precise definition relates to how often that outcome occurs.

2.1.1   Probabilities and Long-Run Relative Frequencies

For random phenomena, such as observations in a randomized experiment, the probability of an outcome refers to the proportion of times the outcome would occur in a very long sequence of like observations.

> **Probability**
>
> For an observation of a random phenomenon, the **probability** of a particular outcome is the proportion of times that outcome would occur in an indefinitely long sequence of like observations, under the same conditions.

Probabilities are sometimes expressed as percentages. For this definition, a weather forecast that the probability of rain tomorrow is 0.20, or 20%, means that in a long run of repeated observations of days with atmospheric conditions like those expected tomorrow, rain would occur on 20% of the days. We could simulate the outcome for tomorrow by

DOI: 10.1201/9781003159834-2

generating a random digit from $(0, 1, 2, \ldots, 9)$, where 2 of the 10 possible outcomes (say, 0 and 1) denote *rain* and the other 8 possible outcomes denote *no rain*; for example, using R:

```
> sample(0:9, 1)       # randomly generate 1 integer between 0 and 9
[1] 8
```

The outcome of the simulation was an 8, representing no rain. Let's simulate for a week under the same conditions:

```
> sample(0:9, 7, replace=TRUE)   # with replace=TRUE, numbers replaced,
[1] 5 8 1 9 8 9 5                 # each selection has same choice set
```

In this simulation, it rains on day 3 but not on any of the other six days.

The outcome on a particular day corresponds to flipping an unbalanced coin that has probability 0.20 of a head, where we identify the *head* outcome with *rain*. More generally, we can simulate how often rain occurs in n days by flipping a coin n times, when each flip has probability 0.20 of a head and probability 0.80 of a tail. We can do this using the R function `rbinom`, which provides simulations with binary outcomes for each observation.[1] Here is the result for 1 simulation of $n = 7$ days:

```
> rbinom(1, 7, 0.20) # 1 simulation of 7 coin flips, probability 0.20 of head
[1] 3                 # outcome is 3 heads in 7 flips (i.e., rain on 3 days)
> rbinom(7, 1, 0.20) # Or, 7 simulations of 1 coin flip, probability 0.20 of head
[1] 0 1 0 0 0 0 1     # 1 = head, 0 = tail; simulated outcome is rain on days 2 and 7
```

For the first simulation, it rained on 3 of the 7 days. The proportion $3/7 = 0.43$ is quite far from the stated probability of 0.20. But a probability is a *long-run* relative frequency, in theory letting the number of days $n \to \infty$. Let's see what happens with much larger n for a simulation:

```
> rbinom(1, 100, 0.20)
[1] 18                    # proportion 0.180; 18 heads in 100 coin flips
> rbinom(1, 1000, 0.20)
[1] 204                   # proportion 0.204
> rbinom(1, 10000, 0.20)
[1] 2010                  # proportion 0.2010
> rbinom(1, 100000, 0.20)
[1] 20032                 # proportion 0.2003
> rbinom(1, 1000000, 0.20)
[1] 199859                # proportion 0.1999; 199859 heads in 1000000 coin flips
```

According to this simulation, the proportions of days of rain out of $n = (100, 1000, 10000, 100000, 1000000)$ days are $(0.180, 0.204, 0.201, 0.2003, 0.1999)$. The proportion converges to 0.2000 as n increases indefinitely. Figure 2.1 illustrates how the proportion stabilizes as n increases.

The long-run sequence of like observations for a definition of probability is not always appropriate. For example, it is not meaningful for the probability that intelligent life exists elsewhere in the universe or for the probability that a new business is successful, because no long-run sequence of observations is available. We must then rely on *subjective* beliefs rather than *objective* data. In fact, an alternative definition of probability is subjective:

Subjective definition of probability: The probability of an outcome is the degree of belief that the outcome will occur, based on all the available information.

---

[1]Besides assuming the same probability for each coin flip, this function assumes that observations are "independent events" in a sense to be introduced in Section 2.1.6; for instance, whether it rains one day is not influenced by whether it rained the previous day.

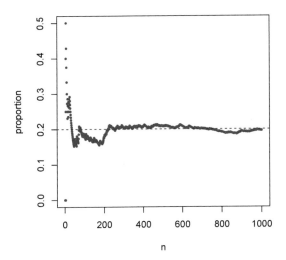

FIGURE 2.1 Simulation of the proportions of times an outcome occurs in n observations, for $n = 1, 2, \ldots, 1000$. The probability of an outcome (here, 0.20) is the value that this proportion converges to as n increases indefinitely.

A branch of inferential statistical science, called *Bayesian statistics*,[2] uses subjective probability as its foundation. In this book, we primarily use the long-run "frequentist" probability definition in presentations of inferential statistics, but we also show how to conduct corresponding Bayesian statistical inference. We'll see that with sufficient data, conclusions derived by the frequentist and the Bayesian approaches are substantively the same.

Yet another approach to probability begins with three mathematical axioms for it and then develops rules that it satisfies. Section 2.1.3 presents the elements of this approach, which is consistent with both the long-run frequentist and subjective definitions of probability.

2.1.2 Sample Spaces and Events

For a random phenomenon, the set of all the possible outcomes is called the ***sample space***, denoted by S. For example, suppose you ask three people whether marijuana use should be legal, with possible responses *yes* and *no*. The sample space of possible responses by (person 1, person 2, person 3) is $S =$ {(yes, yes, yes), (yes, yes, no), (yes, no, yes), (no, yes, yes), (yes, no, no), (no, yes, no), (no, no, yes), (no, no, no)}. An ***event*** is any subset of a sample space. For example, the event A that all three people give the same response is $A =$ {(yes, yes, yes), (no, no, no)}.

The *complement* of an event A, denoted by A^c, consists of all points in the sample space S that are *not* in A. The *intersection* of events A and B, denoted by AB (or $A \cap B$), consists of the points that are in A *and* in B. If $A =$ {(yes, yes, yes), (no, no, no)} and $B =$ {(yes, yes, yes), (yes, yes, no), (yes, no, yes), (yes, no, no)} is the event that the first person supports legalization, then $AB =$ {(yes, yes, yes)}. The *union* of events A and B, denoted by $A \cup B$, consists of the points that are in A *or* in B or in both events. Here, $A \cup B =$ {(yes, yes,

---

[2] Named in honor of Thomas Bayes, who discovered a probability rule presented in Section 2.1.5 on which it is based.

yes), (yes, yes, no), (yes, no, yes), (yes, no, no), (no, no, no)}. The key words are *and* for intersection and *or* for union.

2.1.3 Probability Axioms and Implied Probability Rules

Next, we present some rules that probabilities satisfy, based on three *axioms*[3] that are a mathematical basis for the subject.

> **Probability axioms**
>
> Let $P(A)$ denote the probability of the event A. All probabilities satisfy
>
> 1. **$P(A) \geq 0$.**
>
> 2. **For the sample space S, $P(S) = 1$.**
>
> 3. **If A and B are disjoint, containing no common outcomes, then**
> $$P(A \cup B) = P(A) + P(B).$$

In summary, probabilities are nonnegative, the total probability for all the possible outcomes equals 1, and the probability of a union of events is the sum of the separate probabilities when the events do not overlap.

Here is an illustration of axiom 3: In a survey to estimate the population proportion favoring legalized marijuana, let A represent the event that the estimate based on the sample of people surveyed is much too low, say more than 0.05 *below* the population proportion. Let B represent the event that the estimate is more than 0.05 *above* the population proportion. These are distinct outcomes, so A and B are disjoint. If $P(A) = P(B) = 0.01$, then the total probability that the estimate is in error by more than 0.05 is $P(A \cup B) = P(A) + P(B) = 0.01 + 0.01 = 0.02$.

Other probability rules follow from these axioms, such as the following three basic rules:

- **$P(A^c) = 1 - P(A)$**

  The probability that an event does *not* occur (that is, the *complement* event occurs) is 1 minus the probability that it does occur (see Figure 2.2). We can also express this rule as $P(A) + P(A^c) = 1$, which is the same as $P(A \cup A^c) = P(S)$. The rule follows from the probability axioms because A and A^c are disjoint events that have union S.

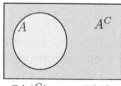

$$P(A^C) = 1 - P(A)$$

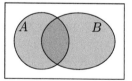

$$P(A \cup B) = P(A) + P(B) - P(AB)$$

FIGURE 2.2 Representation of probabilities $P(A^C)$ and $P(A \cup B)$.

- **$P(A \cup B) = P(A) + P(B) - P(AB)$**

  When we add $P(A)$ to $P(B)$, the intersection AB enters twice, so we make the $-P(AB)$

---

[3]Proposed in 1933 by a Russian mathematician, Andrey Kolmogorov

correction (see Figure 2.2). This rule generalizes the third axiom, in which $P(AB) = 0$ for disjoint events because AB is then the empty set.

A probability of an event A, given than an event B occurred, is called a **conditional probability**. It is denoted by $P(A \mid B)$.

- $P(A \mid B) = \frac{P(AB)}{P(B)}$

Placing $P(B)$ in the denominator corresponds to *conditioning on* (i.e., restricting to) the sample points in B, and it requires $P(B) > 0$. We place $P(AB)$ in the numerator to find the fraction of event B that is also in event A (see Figure 2.3).

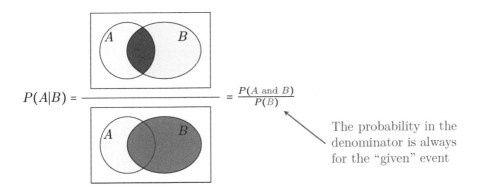

$$P(A|B) = \frac{}{} = \frac{P(A \text{ and } B)}{P(B)}$$

The probability in the denominator is always for the "given" event

FIGURE 2.3 Representation of conditional probability $P(A \mid B) = P(AB)/P(B)$.

2.1.4 Example: Diagnostics for Disease Screening

Medical diagnostic tests help to detect when a person has a certain disease. These include imaging devices such as the mammogram for diagnosing breast cancer. A diagnostic test is said to be *positive* (+) if it states that the disease is present and *negative* (−) if it states that the disease is absent. We denote the true disease status by $D = yes$ and $D^c = no$. The two correct diagnoses are a positive diagnostic outcome when the person has the disease and a negative outcome when a person does not have it. Given that the person has the disease, the conditional probability $P(+ \mid D)$ that the diagnostic test is positive is called the **sensitivity**. Given that the person does not have the disease, the conditional probability $P(- \mid D^c)$ that the diagnostic test is negative is called the **specificity**. Ideally, these are both very high. For mammograms, Table 2.1 shows typically reported values, sensitivity = 0.86 and specificity = 0.88.

The sensitivity $P(+ \mid D)$ is informative, but more relevant to a person who receives a positive diagnosis is the conditional probability $P(D \mid +)$ of truly having the disease, called the *positive predictive value*. How can we find conditional probabilities about *disease, given diagnosis,* when we know conditional probabilities about *diagnosis, given disease*? From the definition of conditional probability,

$$P(D \mid +) = \frac{P(+ \text{ and } D)}{P(+)}.$$

Now, expressing the + event in terms of its two disjoint parts,

$$P(+) = P(+ \text{ and } D) + P(+ \text{ and } D^c).$$

TABLE 2.1 Conditional probabilities of diagnosis given true disease status, for breast cancer mammograms.

Disease Status (Breast Cancer)	Mammogram Diagnosis Positive (+)	Negative (−)	Total
Yes (D)	0.86	0.14	1.0
No (D^c)	0.12	0.88	1.0

Re-expressing the conditional probability formula $P(B \mid A) = P(AB)/P(A)$ as $P(AB) = P(B \mid A)P(A)$ we have

$$P(+ \text{ and } D) = P(+ \mid D)P(D), \quad P(+ \text{ and } D^c) = P(+ \mid D^c)P(D^c).$$

In summary,[4] $P(+) = P(+ \mid D)P(D) + P(+ \mid D^c)P(D^c)$, so the probability of disease given a positive diagnosis is

$$P(D \mid +) = \frac{P(+ \mid D)P(D)}{P(+ \mid D)P(D) + P(+ \mid D^c)P(D^c)}.$$

The sensitivity and specificity reported in Table 2.1 for diagnosing breast cancer are $P(+ \mid D) = 0.86$ and $P(+ \mid D^c) = 0.12$. Suppose that the probability that a woman has the disease is $P(D) = 0.01$. Then,

$$P(D \mid +) = \frac{0.86(0.01)}{0.86(0.01) + 0.12(0.99)} = 0.0675.$$

Of those who receive a positive diagnosis, fewer than 7% actually have the disease. To get intuition about this surprising result, we construct a tree diagram showing predicted outcomes for a typical sample of size 100. We first branch from the root according to whether a woman truly has breast cancer (event D) and then branch according to the test result (see Figure 2.4). Since $P(D) = 0.01$, of the 100 women, we expect about $0.01(100) = 1$ to have the disease and 99 not to have it. For the 1 who has the disease, we expect to observe a positive result, since its probability is 0.86. Of the 99 who do not have the disease, we expect a positive result for about $99(1 - 0.88) \approx 12$ of them. So, we would expect about 13 women to have a positive diagnosis, but only 1 of them to actually have the disease, a proportion of $1/13 = 0.077$.

2.1.5 Bayes' Theorem

The reasoning we have used in the diagnostic test example is an application of a probability result known as **Bayes' theorem**, named after a British Presbyterian minister who discovered it.[5] For events A and B, if we know all the conditional probabilities involving A, given B and given B^c, and we know $P(B)$, then we can find the conditional probability of B given A.

---

[4] This decomposition is a special case of the *rule of total probability*; see Exercise 2.28.

[5] It was published, in 1763, two years after his death. Exercise 2.30 shows a more general version of the theorem.

Bayes' theorem

For any two events A and B in a sample space with $P(A) > 0$,

$$P(B\,|\,A) = \frac{P(A\,|\,B)P(B)}{P(A\,|\,B)P(B) + P(A\,|\,B^c)P(B^c)}.$$

The diagnostic test example applied this result with B as the event D of having the disease and A as the event $+$ of a positive diagnosis.

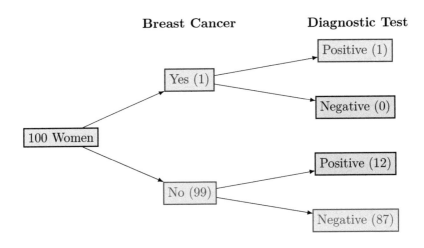

FIGURE 2.4 Tree diagram showing predicted true breast cancer disease status and diagnostic test results for a typical sample of 100 women.

2.1.6 Multiplicative Law of Probability and Independent Events

The diagnostic test example used $P(+\,|\,D)$ and $P(D)$ to find $P(+$ and $D)$, by translating the definition of conditional probability to a corresponding multiplicative relationship, $P(+$ and $D) = P(+\,|\,D)P(D)$. Generally, for two events A and B, the **multiplicative law of probability** states that

$$P(AB) = P(A\,|\,B)P(B) = P(B\,|\,A)P(A).$$

Sometimes A and B are **independent** events, in the sense that $P(A\,|\,B) = P(A)$, that is, whether A occurs does not depend on whether B occurs. In that case, the previous rule simplifies:

When A and B are independent events, $P(AB) = P(A)P(B)$.

For example, suppose that 60% of a population supports a carbon tax to reduce carbon dioxide emissions and consequent global warming. In random sampling of two people, let A denote the event that person 1 supports the carbon tax and let B denote the event that person 2 supports it. Then $P(A) = 0.60$ and $P(B) = 0.60$. With random sampling, successive observations are independent, so the probability that *both* people support a carbon tax is

$$P(A \text{ and } B) = P(A)P(B) = 0.60 \times 0.60 = 0.36.$$

This extends to multiple independent events. For 10 randomly sampled people, the probability that all 10 support a carbon tax is $0.60 \times 0.60 \times \cdots \times 0.60 = (0.60)^{10} = 0.006$.

2.2   Random Variables and Probability Distributions

For a sample space for a random phenomenon, the probabilities of interest usually refer to quantitative summaries of the sample points.

Random variable

For a random phenomenon, a ***random variable*** is a function that assigns a numerical value to each point in the sample space.

For example, in asking three people about whether marijuana use should be legal, the sample space is S = {(yes, yes, yes), (yes, yes, no), (yes, no, yes), (no, yes, yes), (yes, no, no), (no, yes, no), (no, no, yes), (no, no, no)}. The *number* of people who say *yes* is a random variable that assigns the values (3, 2, 2, 2, 1, 1, 1, 0) to the eight sample points. *We use upper-case letters to represent random variables, with lower-case versions for particular possible values.* For instance, if Y = number of people favoring legalization, then y = 2 is a possible value for Y.

Since a random variable refers to a random phenomenon, each possible outcome has a probability that it occurs. The *random variable* terminology reflects that the outcome varies from observation to observation according to random variation that can be summarized by probabilities.

Probability distribution

A ***probability distribution*** lists the possible outcomes for a random variable and their probabilities.

Like quantitative variables, random variables can be discrete or continuous. Each type has its own form for a probability distribution.

2.2.1   Probability Distributions for Discrete Random Variables

For *discrete* random variables, the outcomes are the distinct, separate values that the random variable can assume, usually integers. Let $P(y)$ denote the probability that the discrete random variable Y takes value y. Then,

$$0 \le P(y) \le 1 \quad \text{and} \quad \sum_{\text{all } y} P(y) = 1,$$

where the sum is over all the possible values.

For a simple random sample of n = 3 people, let Y = the number who say *yes* to supporting legalized marijuana. When exactly half the population would respond *yes*, each of the eight sample points {(yes, yes, yes), (yes, yes, no), (yes, no, yes), (no, yes, yes), (yes, no, no), (no, yes, no), (no, no, yes), (no, no, no)} is equally likely. Table 2.2 displays the probability distribution for Y and Figure 2.5 portrays it.

Discrete probability distributions have functions, called ***probability mass functions***, that generate the probabilities for the possible outcomes of a random variable. The function

$$f(y) = \binom{3}{y}\left(\frac{1}{2}\right)^3 = \frac{3!}{y!(3-y)!}\left(\frac{1}{8}\right), \quad y = 0, 1, 2, 3,$$

yields the probabilities in Table 2.2, because $(1/2)^3$ = 1/8 is the probability of each sample point and $[3!/y!(3-y)!]$ is the number of combinations of points in which y of the 3

TABLE 2.2 Probability distribution for Y = number who support legalized marijuana in a random sample of $n = 3$, when half the population support legalization

y	$P(y)$
0	1/8
1	3/8
2	3/8
3	1/8
Total	1.0

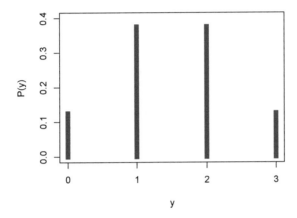

FIGURE 2.5 The probability distribution of Y in Table 2.2.

outcomes are *yes*. For example, 3 sample points have $y = 2$, so the probability that $Y = 2$ is $f(2) = [3!/2!(3-2)!](1/2)^3 = 3(1/2)^3 = 3/8$. What is the probability mass function if the population proportion supporting legalization differs from $1/2$, for arbitrary sample size n? The *binomial distribution*, to be introduced in Section 2.4.1, handles such cases.

2.2.2 Example: Geometric Probability Distribution

When each observation has two possible outcomes, such as (head, tail) for a coin flip or (yes, no) for favoring legalization of marijuana, generically we refer to the two outcomes as *success* and *failure*. Suppose that for each observation the probability[6] of a success is π, the probability of a failure is $1 - \pi$, and the results of the observations are independent events. Let Y = the number of the observation in which we first observe a success, for fixed $0 < \pi \le 1$. Then Y is a random variable with possible values 1, 2, 3. .... What is the probability mass function for Y?

The probability that $Y = 1$ is the probability that a success occurs on the first observation, namely π. To obtain $y = 2$, in two observations we need a failure and then a success. By the probability for an intersection of two independent events, this is the product of the probabilities, or $(1 - \pi)\pi$. Likewise, $y = 3$ occurs with probability $(1 - \pi)(1 - \pi)\pi$, $y = 4$ occurs with probability $(1 - \pi)(1 - \pi)(1 - \pi)\pi$, and so on, so the probability mass function

---

[6]We use π to denote a population proportion or a probability.

for the observation number of the first success is

$$f(y) = (1 - \pi)^{y-1}\pi, \quad y = 1, 2, 3, \ldots. \tag{2.1}$$

This probability distribution is called the **geometric distribution**. For example, if each time you play tennis with a friend, the probability you win the match is $\pi = 0.40$, then the probability that your first win is on the third match is $(0.60)^2(0.40) = 0.144$.

The geometric random variable is discrete but has an infinite number of possible values, namely all the positive integers. It is not continuous, because the possible values are not an interval *continuum*, but rather separate and distinct.[7] The sum of the probabilities for the possible outcomes is

$$\pi + (1 - \pi)\pi + (1 - \pi)^2\pi + (1 - \pi)^3\pi + \cdots = \pi[1 + (1 - \pi) + (1 - \pi)^2 + (1 - \pi)^3 + \cdots]$$
$$= \pi[(1-\pi)^0 + (1-\pi)^1 + (1-\pi)^2 + (1-\pi)^3 + \cdots] = \pi \sum_{k=0}^{\infty}(1-\pi)^k = \pi\left[\frac{1}{1-(1-\pi)}\right] = 1,$$

since the sum in brackets is the sum of the terms in a geometric series.

2.2.3   Probability Distributions for Continuous Random Variables

Continuous random variables have an infinite continuum of possible values. Their probability distributions assign probabilities to *intervals* of real numbers rather than individual values. The probabilities are determined by a **probability density function**. The *area* under the function over an interval of values, which equals its integral over that interval, is the probability that the random variable falls in that interval.

The integral over all possible values equals 1, corresponding to a total probability of 1. Since the area over a single point is 0, the probability of any single point is 0. That is why we instead assign probabilities to intervals.[8]

2.2.4   Example: Uniform Distribution

The *support* of a random variable is the set of points for which the probability density or mass function is positive. Some continuous random variables have support in a finite range, such as all real numbers in the interval [0, 1]. For instance, a dental study might observe for each tooth in a subject's mouth, the proportion covered with plaque. An environmental study might observe for each of several regions, the proportion of the area that is green space. The probability density function

$$f(y) = 1, \ 0 \le y \le 1, \quad f(y) = 0, \ y < 0 \text{ or } y > 1,$$

provides probabilities for the random variable Y that selects a real number at random from the interval [0, 1]. The probability distribution is called the **uniform distribution**. Figure 2.6 portrays the probability density function of a uniform random variable Y over this interval.

For $0 \le a < b \le 1$, the uniform random variable has

$$P(a < Y < b) = \int_a^b f(y)dy = \int_a^b 1dy = y \Big|_{y=a}^{y=b} = (b - a).$$

---

[7] In mathematics, this is the distinction between a *countable* and *uncountable* infinity.

[8] In practice, single points have probabilities > 0 because of imprecise measurement. If Y = weight is measured to the nearest kilogram, we regard, for example, $P(Y = 70)$ as $P(69.5 \le Y \le 70.5)$.

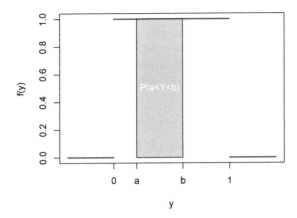

FIGURE 2.6 Probability density function of a uniform random variable over the interval [0, 1], highlighting the probability that it falls between a and b.

This is also $P(a \leq Y \leq b)$, $P(a \leq Y < b)$, and $P(a < Y \leq b)$, since the probability of a single point is 0.

More generally, for a positive number θ, we can define a uniform random variable Y having support over the interval $[0, \theta]$. It has a constant probability density function of $f(y) = 1/\theta$ over that interval and 0 elsewhere, since $\int_{y=0}^{\theta}(1/\theta)dy = 1$. For example, for $\theta = 100$, here's the result of using R to simulate a single uniform random variable over the interval [0, 100], with the result rounded to five decimal places:

```
> runif(1, min=0, max=100) # simulate uniform random variable between 0 and 100
[1] 10.52683
```

More generally yet, for any two real numbers $L < U$ for lower and upper bounds, the uniform random variable Y having support over the interval $[L, U]$ has a constant probability density function of $f(y) = 1/(U - L)$ over that interval and 0 elsewhere.

The uniform distribution over [0, 1] is a special case of the family of *beta distributions*, which have a variety of shapes over that interval.[9] Uniform random variables can also be *discrete*. An example is a random number generator that has equal probability for each integer in a set of integers, such as provided by the `sample` function in R.

2.2.5 Probability Functions (*pdf*, *pmf*) and Cumulative Distribution Function (*cdf*)

For convenience, we abbreviate *probability density function* for continuous random variables by *pdf* and *probability mass function* for discrete random variables by *pmf*. When there is no reason to identify a random variable as continuous or discrete, we shall merely refer to the *probability function*.

For both discrete and continuous random variables, the probability distribution is also specified by the **cumulative distribution function** (*cdf*).

---

[9]The beta distribution is introduced in Exercise 2.70 and Section 4.7.2.

Cumulative distribution function

The probability $P(Y \leq y)$ that a random variable Y takes value $\leq y$ is called a *cumulative probability*. The *cumulative distribution function* is $F(y) = P(Y \leq y)$, for all real numbers y.

By convention, we denote a *pdf* or *pmf* by lower-case f and a *cdf* by upper-case F. For continuous random variables, we obtain the *cdf* F from the *pdf* f by integrating over all values up to y,

$$F(y) = P(Y \leq y) = \int_{-\infty}^{y} f(u)du.$$

For discrete random variables, we obtain the *cdf* from the *pmf* by summing over all values up to y. In either case, the *cdf* increases monotonically from 0 below the lowest possible value for the random variable up to 1 at the highest possible value.

For example, the uniform random variable defined over $[0,1]$ has *pdf* $f(y) = 1$ over that interval and $f(y) = 0$ elsewhere. For any $0 \leq y \leq 1$,

$$F(y) = \int_{-\infty}^{y} f(u)du = \int_{0}^{y} (1)du = y,$$

with $F(y) = 0$ for all $y < 0$ and $F(y) = 1$ for all $y > 1$ (see Figure 2.7). The uniform random variable Y having support over the interval $[0,\theta]$ has *pdf* $f(y) = 1/\theta$ over that interval. Its *cdf* is $F(y) = y/\theta$ over $[0,\theta]$ and $F(y) = 0$ for all $y < 0$ and $F(y) = 1$ for all $y > \theta$.

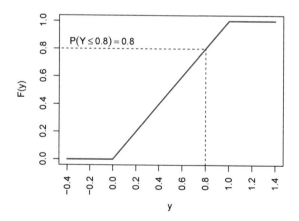

FIGURE 2.7 The cumulative distribution function (*cdf*) for a uniform random variable defined over the interval $[0,1]$, for which $F(y) = y$ over that interval.

Because we obtain the *cdf* for a continuous random variable by integrating the *pdf*, we can obtain the *pdf* from the *cdf* by differentiating it. For example, since $F(y) = y$ for the uniform distribution over $[0,1]$, the *pdf* is $f(y) = \partial F(y)/\partial y = 1$ over $[0,1]$.

2.2.6   Example: Exponential Random Variable

Consider the *pdf* with support over the positive real line,

$$f(y) = e^{-y}, \ y \geq 0, \quad f(y) = 0, \ y < 0, \tag{2.2}$$

shown in Figure 2.8. This is a special case of the ***exponential*** probability distribution, to be introduced in Section 2.5.5. You can verify that this is a legitimate *pdf*, as it is nonnegative and integrates to 1 over the real line.

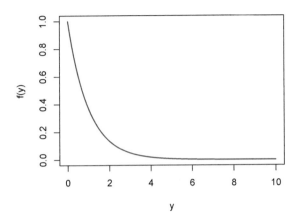

FIGURE 2.8 The *pdf* $f(y) = e^{-y}$ for $y > 0$ is an example of an exponential distribution.

The exponential *cdf* takes value 0 for $y < 0$. For nonnegative y values, the *cdf* is

$$F(y) = \int_0^y e^{-u}\, du = -e^{-u}\Big|_{u=0}^{u=y} = 1 - e^{-y} \text{ for } y \geq 0.$$

The *cdf*, shown later in the chapter in Figure 2.13, increases from $F(y) = 0$ at $y = 0$ to $F(y) = 1$ as y increases indefinitely toward ∞.

2.2.7 Families of Probability Distributions Indexed by Parameters

When a probability function $f(y)$ is indexed by particular values, we add those after a semicolon. For example, for the geometric random variable Y = number of the observation for the first success, with probability π of a success on each observation, a separate *pmf* $f(y; \pi) = (1 - \pi)^{y-1}\pi$ exists over the positive integers for each value of $0 < \pi \leq 1$. For the uniform distribution defined over $[0, \theta]$, a separate *pdf* $f(y; \theta) = 1/\theta$ exists for each positive real number θ. We refer to the index as a *parameter*. This terminology reflects that we often use probability distributions to describe a population of interest, and typically we do not know the parameter values and we use the data to estimate them.

The parameter values determine summary characteristics of the distribution. For example, for Y = number of the observation for the first success, we expect to observe larger values for Y when the probability π of a success on each observation is smaller. For a uniform distribution over $[0, \theta]$, we expect that values of Y tend to be larger when θ is larger. We next show how to summarize characteristics of a probability distribution.

2.3   Expectations of Random Variables

Just as we can summarize frequency distributions of variables by descriptive measures such as means and standard deviations, the same is true of probability distributions of random variables. For example, the mean of a probability distribution is the mean of the values the corresponding random variable would assume in an indefinitely long sequence of independent observations.

2.3.1   Expected Value and Variability of a Discrete Random Variable

Table 2.2 showed that the probability distribution of Y = number supporting legalized marijuana in a random sample of 3 people, when half the population support it, has $P(0) = 1/8$, $P(1) = 3/8$, $P(2) = 3/8$, $P(3) = 1/8$. If we repeatedly randomly sampled 3 people and observed y, then in the long run, we expect $y = 0$ to occur $1/8$ of the time, $y = 1$ to occur $3/8$ of the time, $y = 2$ to occur $3/8$ of the time, and $y = 3$ to occur $1/8$ of the time. In observing y in 1000 random samples of size 3, for instance, we expect about

$$125 \ 0\text{'s}, \ 375 \ 1\text{'s}, \ 375 \ 2\text{'s}, \ \text{and} \ 125 \ 3\text{'s}.$$

We would expect the mean of the 1000 observations to equal approximately

$$\frac{(125)0 + (375)1 + (375)2 + (125)3}{1000} = \frac{1500}{1000} = 1.50.$$

This calculation has the form

$$0\left(\tfrac{1}{8}\right) + 1\left(\tfrac{3}{8}\right) + 2\left(\tfrac{3}{8}\right) + 3\left(\tfrac{1}{8}\right) = \sum_{y=0}^{3} yP(y),$$

the sum of the possible outcomes times their probabilities. For any discrete random variable, the mean of the probability distribution has this form. It is called the *expected value* of Y.

Expected value of a discrete random variable

The ***expected value*** of a discrete random variable Y with *pmf* $f(y)$ is

$$E(Y) = \sum_{y} yf(y),$$

with the sum taken over all possible values y of Y. Because of the interpretation of $E(Y)$ as a long-run mean, such as a population mean, it is also denoted by μ.

The terminology *expected value* reflects that $E(Y)$ is the value we expect for the mean in an indefinitely long series of observations of Y. To illustrate, let's randomly generate ten million values of Y = number of *successes* in $n = 3$ binary "trials," with probability 0.50 of a success on each trial, and then average the ten million observations. In R, the function rbinom(r, n, π) simulates r experiments, in each case finding the number of successes in n binary trials with probability π of a success on each. [10]

```
> y <- rbinom(10000000,3,0.50)  # simulate 10000000 times the no. of successes in 3 trials
> head(y, 10)                   # the first 10 of the 10 million observations generated
[1] 2 2 0 2 3 2 2 2 1 2
```

---

[10]Each simulation is an example of a *binomial experiment*, introduced with the corresponding *binomial distribution* in Section 2.4.1.

```
> mean(y); sd(y)
[1] 1.499741              # mean of the 10 million observations
[1] 0.8662191             # standard deviation of the 10 million observations
```

The mean is very close to $E(Y) = 1.50$ that we found from the definition, $E(Y) = \sum_y y f(y)$.
   We can also describe the *spread* of a probability distribution, which reflects long-run *variability* of observations from that probability distribution.

Standard deviation and variance of a discrete random variable

For a discrete random variable Y with *pmf* $f(y)$ and $E(Y) = \mu$, the *variance* is denoted by σ^2 and defined to be

$$\sigma^2 = E(Y - \mu)^2 = \sum_y (y - \mu)^2 f(y),$$

the average squared deviation of Y from the mean, with the sum taken over all the possible values for y. The *standard deviation*, denoted by σ, is the positive square root of the variance.

As with sample data, the standard deviation is simpler to interpret than the variance, because the units of measurement are the same as the original units. Larger values for σ reflect greater spread of the probability distribution.
   The variance of a discrete (or continuous) random variable has an alternative formula, resulting from the derivation

$$
\begin{aligned}
\sigma^2 &= E(Y - \mu)^2 = \sum_y (y - \mu)^2 f(y) = \sum_y (y^2 - 2y\mu + \mu^2) f(y) \\
&= \sum_y y^2 f(y) - 2\mu \sum_y y f(y) + \mu^2 \sum_y f(y) = E(Y^2) - 2\mu E(Y) + \mu^2 = E(Y^2) - \mu^2.
\end{aligned}
$$

We used (1) $E(cY) = c[E(Y)]$ for any constant c, because we can take c outside the sum, and (2) for any constant c, $E(c) = c$, because $\sum_y cf(y) = c\sum_y f(y) = c(1) = c$. In summary, the alternate formula is

$$\text{var}(Y) = \sigma^2 = E(Y^2) - \mu^2. \tag{2.3}$$

To illustrate, for the probability distribution of Y = number supporting legalized marijuana in a random sample of 3 people, when half the population support it, we found that the *pmf* $f(0) = 1/8$, $f(1) = 3/8$, $f(2) = 3/8$, $f(3) = 1/8$ has $E(Y) = \sum_y y f(y) = 1.50$. Also,

$$E(Y^2) = \sum_y y^2 f(y) = 0^2\left(\frac{1}{8}\right) + 1^2\left(\frac{3}{8}\right) + 2^2\left(\frac{3}{8}\right) + 3^2\left(\frac{1}{8}\right) = 3.00,$$

so $\sigma^2 = E(Y^2) - \mu^2 = 3.00 - (1.50)^2 = 0.750$ and $\sigma = 0.866$. The standard deviation agrees with the value found in the R simulation above of ten million observations.

2.3.2   Expected Values for Continuous Random Variables

Analogous formulas apply for expectations of a continuous random variable, replacing summation signs by integrals.

Expected value and variability of a continuous random variable

For a continuous random variable Y with probability density function $f(y)$,

$$E(Y) = \mu = \int_y yf(y)dy, \quad \text{variance } \sigma^2 = E(Y - \mu)^2 = \int_y (y - \mu)^2 f(y)dy,$$

and the standard deviation σ is the positive square root of the variance.

To find the variance, we can use the alternate formula (2.3), that is, $\sigma^2 = E(Y^2) - \mu^2$. An advantage of it is that after finding μ we need only to evaluate $E(Y^2) = \int_y y^2 f(y)dy$ rather than to integrate the squared deviation around μ.

2.3.3 Example: Mean and Variability for Uniform Random Variable

When Y is a uniform random variable over the interval $[0, \theta]$, such as for $\theta = 1$ with the standard uniform,

$$f(y; \theta) = 1/\theta, \ 0 \le y \le \theta, \quad f(y; \theta) = 0 \text{ elsewhere.} \tag{2.4}$$

The expected value of this uniform random variable is

$$E(Y) = \int_0^\theta yf(y; \theta)dy = \int_0^\theta y\left(\frac{1}{\theta}\right)dy = \left.\frac{y^2}{2\theta}\right|_0^\theta = \frac{\theta^2}{2\theta} = \frac{\theta}{2}.$$

To find the variance and standard deviation, we first find

$$E(Y^2) = \int_0^\theta y^2 f(y; \theta)dy = \int_0^\theta y^2\left(\frac{1}{\theta}\right)dy = \left.\frac{y^3}{3\theta}\right|_0^\theta = \frac{\theta^3}{3\theta} = \frac{\theta^2}{3}.$$

Therefore, using formula (2.3), this uniform random variable has variance

$$\sigma^2 = E(Y^2) - \mu^2 = \frac{\theta^2}{3} - \left(\frac{\theta}{2}\right)^2 = \frac{\theta^2}{12}.$$

The standard deviation is $\sigma = \theta/\sqrt{12}$. The variability is greater when θ is greater, as the *pdf* then spreads over a wider interval.

For $\theta = 100$, a uniform random variable over $[0, 100]$ has mean $\theta/2 = 50.00$ and standard deviation $\theta/\sqrt{12} = 28.87$. Let's use R to randomly generate ten million such uniform random variables and then find their sample mean and standard deviation:

```
> y <- runif(10000000, min=0, max=100)        # runif simulates uniform random variable
> head(y, 5)          # first 5 of ten million generated (to 6 decimal places)
[1] 69.738396 10.630499 45.303774  6.350559 54.988320
> mean(y); sd(y)      # mean and standard deviation of ten million simulated uniform rv's
[1] 50.01878          # close to theoretical values of 50.00 and 28.87
[1] 28.86978
```

The values vary randomly with a mean of 50.0 and standard deviation of 28.9.

2.3.4 Higher Moments: Skewness

The expected values $E(Y)$ and $E(Y^2)$ are examples of **moments** of a random variable and its probability distribution. The expected value $E[(Y - \mu)^2]$ is called a **central moment**.

The third central moment $E(Y - \mu)^3$ describes **skewness**. This measure equals 0 when the probability distribution is symmetric, such as the uniform distribution. It is positive when the distribution is skewed to the right and negative when it is skewed to the left. So that its value does not depend on the units of measurement, skewness is summarized by

$$\text{Skewness coefficient} = \frac{E(Y - \mu)^3}{\sigma^3}.$$

For example, if we multiply Y by 10, the distribution is ten times as spread out, but the shape does not change. For this scale change, $E(Y - \mu)^3$ multiplies by 10^3, but so does σ^3, and the ratio stays constant.

Random variables that must take a positive value are often skewed to the right, with skewness values above 1 indicating substantial skew. An example is the exponential *pdf*, $f(y) = e^{-y}$ for $y > 0$, illustrated in Figure 2.8. For it, you can show that $\mu = 1$, $\sigma = 1$, and $E(Y - \mu)^3 = 2$, so the skewness coefficient $[E(Y - \mu)^3]/\sigma^3 = 2$. The positive skewness reflects the long tail to the right.

2.3.5 Expectations of Linear Functions of Random Variables

For a random variable Y with expected value μ_Y and standard deviation σ_Y, consider the *linear* transformation

$$X = a + bY.$$

If Y is a continuous random variable, then the expected value of X is

$$\begin{aligned}
\mu_X &= E(X) = E(a + bY) = \int (a + by)f(y)dy = a\int f(y)dy + b\int yf(y)dy \\
&= a(1) + bE(Y) = a + b\mu_Y.
\end{aligned}$$

The mean of a linear transformation is identical to the linear transformation of the mean. The variance of X is

$$\begin{aligned}
\sigma_X^2 &= \text{var}(X) = E[X - E(X)]^2 = E[(a + bY) - (a + b\mu)]^2 = E[b(Y - \mu)]^2 \\
&= b^2[E(Y - \mu)^2] = b^2\sigma_Y^2.
\end{aligned}$$

The standard deviation of X is $\sigma_X = |b|\sigma_Y$. As a special case, for any constant c,

$$E(cY) = cE(Y) \text{ and } \text{var}(cY) = c^2\text{var}(Y). \tag{2.5}$$

For example, suppose X is weight in pounds and Y is weight in kilograms. Since 1 kilogram equals 2.2 pounds, $X = 2.2Y$, so $\mu_X = 2.2\mu_Y$ and $\sigma_X = 2.2\sigma_Y$.

Although the mean of a *linear* transformation equals the linear transformation of the mean, this is not the case for *nonlinear* functions. For a nonlinear function g, $E[g(Y)] \neq g[E(Y)]$. For instance, for the square function $g(t) = t^2$, $E(Y^2) \neq [E(Y)]^2$. In fact, from equation (2.3), $\sigma^2 = E(Y^2) - \mu^2 = E(Y^2) - [E(Y)]^2$, and since $\sigma^2 \geq 0$, necessarily $E(Y^2) \geq [E(Y)]^2$. The function $g(t) = t^2$ is an example of a *convex* function, which is bowl-shaped.[11] **Jensen's inequality** states that for convex functions, $E[g(Y)] \geq g[E(Y)]$. For example, for the convex function $g(t) = t^2$, $E[g(Y)] = E(Y^2)$ and $g[E(Y)] = [E(Y)]^2 = \mu^2$, so $E(Y^2) \geq \mu^2$.

---

[11]Technically, a *convex* function is one that has nonnegative second derivative everywhere, so the first derivative is always increasing. *Concave* functions are mound-shaped and have first derivative always decreasing.

2.3.6   Standardizing a Random Variable

A common linear transformation of Y for statistical analysis is

$$Z = \frac{Y - \mu}{\sigma}.$$

This transformation is called **standardizing** Y. The random variable Z represents the *number of standard deviations* that Y falls from its mean. For example, when the observed value of Z is $z = 2$, then y falls 2 standard deviations above μ, whereas when $z = -0.8$, it falls $8/10$ of a standard deviation below μ.

A standardized random variable has mean and variance

$$E(Z) \;=\; E\!\left[\frac{Y-\mu}{\sigma}\right] = \frac{E(Y-\mu)}{\sigma} = \frac{E(Y)-E(\mu)}{\sigma} = \frac{\mu-\mu}{\sigma} = 0,$$

$$\mathrm{var}(Z) \;=\; \mathrm{var}\!\left[\frac{Y-\mu}{\sigma}\right] = \frac{\mathrm{var}(Y-\mu)}{\sigma^2} = \frac{E(Y-\mu)^2}{\sigma^2} = \frac{\sigma^2}{\sigma^2} = 1.$$

Regardless of the scale for the original random variable Y, the values of Z vary around 0 with a standard deviation of 1.

2.4   Discrete Probability Distributions

We next introduce the most important families of probability distributions for statistical analyses. We consider discrete random variables in this section and continuous random variables in the following one.

2.4.1   Binomial Distribution

For many experiments and observational studies, the following conditions hold:

1. Each of n observations has two possible outcomes, which we refer to as *success* and *failure*. Corresponding random variables $Y_1, Y_2, \ldots, Y_n$ take value 1 for success and 0 for failure.

2. The probabilities for the two outcomes are the same for each observation. We denote them by $\pi = P(Y_i = 1)$ and $(1 - \pi) = P(Y_i = 0)$.

3. The outcomes of the observations are independent. That is $\{Y_i\}$ are independent random variables, in the sense that events involving distinct $\{Y_i\}$ are independent.[12]

The process of generating $\{Y_i\}$ under these three conditions is called a **binomial experiment with n trials**. Another name for such binary observations is **Bernoulli trials**. The random variable Y = number of successes in the n trials is called a **binomial random variable**. In terms of the binary random variables $\{Y_i\}$, $Y = \sum_i Y_i$ and takes integer values between 0 and n.

The binomial experiment is a good representation for observing a binary outcome when a sample survey uses simple random sampling. For example, if π is the population proportion who say *yes* in response to a question with possible outcomes (*yes, no*), then the probability

---

[12]We explain *independence of random variables* in a more general sense in Section 2.6.6.

of responding *yes* is π for each person in a simple random sample, and how one person in the sample responds is independent of how another responds.

Consider the sequence of observations $(y_1, y_2, \ldots, y_n) = (1, 1, 0, 0, 0, \ldots, 0)$ in which the first two trials are successes and the other $n - 2$ are failures. With independent trials, the probability of this sequence is the probability of the intersection of n independent events, and therefore has probability

$$P(Y_1 = 1)P(Y_2 = 1)P(Y_3 = 0)P(Y_4 = 0)\cdots P(Y_n = 0) = \pi^2(1 - \pi)^{n-2}.$$

However, the $y = 2$ successes in the n trials could have occurred in any of $\binom{n}{2} = n(n-1)/2$ different locations, not just the first two. Thus, $P(Y = 2) = \binom{n}{2}\pi^2(1-\pi)^{n-2}$. More generally, we can find this when the number of successes y is any integer between 0 and n.

Binomial distribution

The probability mass function for the probability of y successes in n independent binary trials, with probability π of success on each trial for $0 \le \pi \le 1$, is

$$f(y; n, \pi) = \binom{n}{y}\pi^y(1-\pi)^{n-y}, \quad y = 0, 1, 2, \ldots, n. \tag{2.6}$$

This is the ***binomial distribution*** with index n and parameter π, denoted by $\mathrm{binom}(n, \pi)$.

2.4.2 Example: Hispanic Composition of Jury List

A list contains the names of all adults living in a city who may be called for jury duty. Reflecting the city's population, the proportion of Hispanics on the list is 0.20. Twelve people are selected from the list for a trial, supposedly at random. None are Hispanic. Would this be very unusual if the choices truly were made at random?

Of the 12 selected, let Y denote the number of Hispanics. For random sampling, the $\mathrm{binom}(12, 0.20)$ distribution applies. For each y between 0 and 12, the probability of selecting y Hispanics and $12 - y$ non-Hispanics equals

$$f(y; n, \pi) = f(y; 12, 0.20) = \frac{12!}{y!(12-y)!}(0.20)^y(0.80)^{12-y}, \quad y = 0, 1, 2, \ldots, 12.$$

The probability of selecting $y = 0$ Hispanics equals

$$f(0; 12, 0.20) = \frac{12!}{0!12!}(0.20)^0(0.80)^{12} = (0.80)^{12} = 0.069.$$

This would be unusual, but not dramatically so. The probability of selecting one Hispanic equals

$$f(1; 12, 0.20) = \frac{12!}{1!11!}(0.20)^1(0.80)^{11} = 12(0.20)(0.80)^{11} = 0.206.$$

Table 2.3 shows the binomial distribution for all the possible y values. For contrast, it also shows the binomial distribution when $\pi = 0.50$, which is symmetric, and when $\pi = 0.80$.

You can easily find and plot binomial probabilities with software and apps on the Internet.[13] Figure 2.9 shows two of the distributions in Table 2.3. Here is R code for displaying probabilities and plotting them:

---

[13]Such as at `www.artofstat.com/web-apps`

```
> y = seq(0, 12, 1)                    # y values between 0 and 12 with increment of 1
> plot(y, dbinom(y,12,0.2), type="h")  # plots binomial probabilities when n=12, pi=0.2
> dbinom(y, 12, 0.2)                    # displays the binomial probabilities
```

TABLE 2.3 Binomial distributions with $n = 12$ and $\pi = 0.20, 0.50,$ and 0.80. The binomial distribution is symmetric when $\pi = 0.50$.

y	$f(y; 12, 0.20)$	$f(y; 12, 0.50)$	$f(y; 12, 0.80)$
0	0.069	0.000	0.000
1	0.206	0.003	0.000
2	0.283	0.016	0.000
3	0.236	0.054	0.000
4	0.133	0.121	0.001
5	0.053	0.193	0.003
6	0.016	0.226	0.016
7	0.003	0.193	0.053
8	0.001	0.121	0.133
9	0.000	0.054	0.236
10	0.000	0.016	0.283
11	0.000	0.003	0.206
12	0.000	0.000	0.069

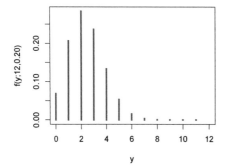 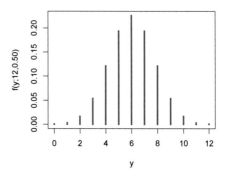

FIGURE 2.9 Binomial distributions with $n = 12$ and $(1)\,\pi = 0.20$, $(2)\,\pi = 0.50$. The binomial is symmetric when $\pi = 0.50$.

2.4.3   Mean, Variability, and Skewness of Binomial Distribution

We find the mean and variance of a binomial random variable by finding the mean and variance for a single binary trial, and then using the result that a binomial random variable is the sum of the results of n independent, identical binary trials. First, for trial i,

$$E(Y_i) = \sum_{y_i=0}^{1} y_i P(y_i) = 0 \times (1 - \pi) + 1 \times \pi = \pi.$$

Using a result to be shown in Section 2.6.5 that expectations are additive, the binomial distribution for $Y = \sum_i Y_i$ has mean

$$E(Y) = E(\sum_{i=1}^{n} Y_i) = \sum_{i=1}^{n} E(Y_i) = n\pi.$$

If we flip a fair coin $n = 100$ times, the expected number of heads is $n\pi = 100(0.50) = 50$.

Next, because Y_i takes only values 0 and 1, $Y_i^2 = Y_i$, and $E(Y_i^2) = E(Y_i) = \pi$. Therefore, using formula (2.3),

$$\text{var}(Y_i) = E(Y_i - \pi)^2 = E(Y_i^2) - [E(Y_i)]^2 = \pi - \pi^2 = \pi(1 - \pi).$$

Because the n trials are independent, the binomial distribution for $Y = \sum_i Y_i$ has variance that also equals the sum of the variances, using a result to be shown in Section 3.2.1. So, a binomial random variable has

$$\sigma^2 = \text{var}(Y) = \text{var}(\sum_{i=1}^{n} Y_i) = \sum_{i=1}^{n} \text{var}(Y_i) = n\pi(1 - \pi).$$

The standard deviation is $\sigma = \sqrt{n\pi(1 - \pi)}$.

One can show that the skewness coefficient for the binomial distribution is

$$\text{Skewness coefficient} = \frac{E(Y - \mu)^3}{\sigma^3} = \frac{(1 - 2\pi)}{\sqrt{n\pi(1 - \pi)}}.$$

The distribution is symmetric (skewness = 0) when $\pi = 0.50$ but becomes increasingly skewed as π moves toward 0 or 1, especially when n is relatively small. The distribution has close to a symmetric, bell shape when the skewness coefficient has absolute value no greater than about 0.30. The distribution in Figure 2.9 with $n = 12$ and $\pi = 0.20$ has skewness coefficient $(1 - 2\pi)/\sqrt{n\pi(1 - \pi)} = [1 - 2(0.20)]/\sqrt{12(0.20)(0.80)} = 0.43$.

2.4.4 Example: Predicting Results of a Sample Survey

Each week the Gallup Poll surveys about 1500 Americans to gauge the popularity of the U.S. President. Newspoll surveys about 1500 Australians each month to gauge the popularity of their prime minister. Similar surveys in other nations, such as YouGov in the UK and NEWS Colmar Brunton in New Zealand, sample anywhere from 1000 to several thousand people to gauge a leader's popularity. When a prime minister enjoys a 60% popularity rating among the entire population, about how many people in a survey of 1500 people would we expect to support her or him?

Let Y denote the number in the survey who express support. If the survey used a simple random sample,[14] then Y has a binom(1500, 0.60) distribution. The distribution is described by

$$\mu = n\pi = 1500(0.60) = 900, \quad \sigma = \sqrt{n\pi(1 - \pi)} = \sqrt{1500(0.60)(0.40)} = 19.$$

The skewness coefficient is

$$\text{Skewness coefficient} = \frac{(1 - 2\pi)}{\sqrt{n\pi(1 - \pi)}} = \frac{1 - 2(0.60)}{\sqrt{1500(0.60)(0.40)}} = -0.011,$$

so this binomial distribution is bell-shaped. From the approximations introduced in Section

---

[14]Polls such as the Gallup Poll are random, but more complex than a simple random sample.

1.4.4, the probability is about 0.95 that Y falls within 2 standard deviations of the mean. This is the interval from 862 to 938. Almost certainly Y falls within 3 standard deviations of the mean, between 843 and 957. Let's use R to find the actual probability falling within 2 and 3 standard deviations of the mean, with the `pbinom` function for cumulative binomial probabilities:

```
> mu <- function(n,pi){n*pi}                    # function: binomial mean
> sigma <- function(n,pi){sqrt(n*pi*1-pi)}   # function: binomial standard deviation
> Psd <- function(n,pi,k){pbinom(mu(n,pi)+k*sigma(n,pi), n, pi)  # function: prob. within
                          - pbinom(mu(n,pi)-k*sigma(n,pi), n, pi)} # k std. dev. of mean
> n=1500; pi=0.60
> Psd(n, pi, 2)
[1] 0.9519324                    # probability within k=2 standard deviations of mean
> Psd(n, pi, 3)
[1] 0.9971083                    # probability within k=3 standard deviations of mean
```

2.4.5 The Sample Proportion as a Scaled Binomial Random Variable

The binomial random variable Y is the *number* of successes in n trials. We denote[15] the *proportion* of successes Y/n by $\hat{\pi}$. For a constant c, since $E(cY) = cE(Y)$ and $\text{var}(cY) = c^2\text{var}(Y)$,

$$E(\hat{\pi}) = E\left(\frac{Y}{n}\right) = \frac{E(Y)}{n} = \frac{n\pi}{n} = \pi,$$

$$\text{var}(\hat{\pi}) = \text{var}\left(\frac{Y}{n}\right) = \left(\frac{1}{n}\right)^2 \text{var}(Y) = \left(\frac{1}{n}\right)^2 n\pi(1-\pi) = \frac{\pi(1-\pi)}{n}.$$

The standard deviation of the probability distribution of $\hat{\pi}$ values is $\sqrt{\pi(1-\pi)/n}$. It decreases as the sample size n increases. The sample proportion tends to be closer to π as n increases.

For a simple random sample of size $n = 1500$ when $\pi = 0.60$, the sample proportion $\hat{\pi}$ has mean 0.60 and standard deviation $\sqrt{(0.60)(0.40)/1500} = 0.01265$. The probability is about 0.95 that $\hat{\pi}$ falls within $0.60 \pm 2(0.01265)$, which is about 0.600 ± 0.025, or $(0.575, 0.625)$.

2.4.6 Poisson Distribution

The binomial distribution applies with n independent binary trials. But sometimes discrete data do not result from a fixed number of trials. For instance, if Y = number of automobile accidents today on motorways in Italy, there is no fixed upper bound n for Y. Since Y must take a nonnegative integer value, its distribution should place its mass on that range.

A simple probability distribution taking all the nonnegative integers as possible value is the **Poisson**.[16] It is used for counts of events that occur randomly over time (or space) when (1) counts of events in disjoint periods are independent, (2) it is essentially impossible to have two or more events simultaneously, and (3) the rate of occurrences is constant. The Poisson distribution has probabilities that depend on a single parameter, $\mu > 0$.

---

[15] In Chapter 4 we'll denote the *estimate* of a parameter by putting a circumflex over the parameter symbol. Here, $\hat{\pi}$ is an estimate of π.

[16] Named after Siméon Denis Poisson, the French mathematician who introduced it in 1837

Poisson distribution

The **Poisson** probability distribution with parameter $\mu > 0$ has probability mass function

$$f(y; \mu) = \frac{e^{-\mu}\mu^y}{y!}, \qquad y = 0, 1, 2, \ldots. \qquad (2.7)$$

These probabilities sum to 1, because

$$\sum_y f(y; \mu) = \sum_{y=0}^{\infty} \frac{e^{-\mu}\mu^y}{y!} = e^{-\mu} \sum_{y=0}^{\infty} \frac{\mu^y}{y!} = e^{-\mu}e^{\mu} = 1.$$

The Poisson distribution has mean

$$\begin{aligned}
E(Y) &= \sum_{y=0}^{\infty} y f(y; \mu) = e^{-\mu} \sum_{y=0}^{\infty} \frac{y\mu^y}{y!} = e^{-\mu}\mu \sum_{y=1}^{\infty} \frac{\mu^{y-1}}{(y-1)!} \\
&= e^{-\mu}\mu \sum_{y=0}^{\infty} \frac{\mu^y}{y!} = e^{-\mu}\mu e^{\mu} = \mu.
\end{aligned}$$

Likewise, you can show that $E(Y^2) = \mu + \mu^2$, so that

$$\mathrm{var}(Y) = E(Y^2) - [E(Y)]^2 = (\mu + \mu^2) - [\mu]^2 = \mu.$$

As the mean increases, so does the variability of the Poisson distribution.

The Poisson distribution is unimodal. Its mode equals the integer part of μ. Its skewness coefficient is $E(Y - \mu)^3/\sigma^3 = 1/\sqrt{\mu}$. It is skewed to the right but becomes more bell-shaped[17] as μ increases, the degree of skew being minor when $\mu > 10$ (i.e., skewness coefficient less than about 0.3).

The Poisson distribution applies as an approximation[18] for the binomial when n is very large and π is very small, with $\mu = n\pi$. For example, suppose Y = number of *deaths* today in auto accidents in Italy (rather than the number of *accidents*). Then, Y has an upper bound. If we can treat each of the 50 million people driving in Italy as independent binary trials with probability 0.0000001 of dying today in an auto accident, then Y is a binomial random variable with $n = 50000000 = 5.0 \times 10^7$ and $\pi = 0.0000001 = 1.0 \times 10^{-7}$. This is approximately Poisson with $\mu = n\pi = 50000000(0.0000001) = 5$. Figure 2.10 shows the close resemblance between the two distributions.

2.4.7 Poisson Variability and Overdispersion

A key feature of the Poisson distribution is that its variance equals its mean. If the mean daily number of Italian motorway automobile accidents is $\mu = 100$, the variability from day to day is much greater than if $\mu = 10$.

A Poisson distribution with $\mu = 100$ has standard deviation $\sqrt{\mu} = 10$. Since it is bell-shaped, nearly the entire distribution falls within $100 \pm 3(10)$, or between 70 and 130. Similarly, the probability is about 0.95 that Y falls in [80, 120]. Here are the exact probabilities, using the ppois function in R for Poisson cumulative probabilities and the dpois function for finding individual probabilities:

```
> ppois(130, 100) - ppois(69, 100) # Poisson cdf at 130 - Poisson cdf at 69
[1] 0.9976323
```

---

[17] The Poisson distribution app at www.artofstat.com/web-apps shows shapes for various μ.
[18] This is how the distribution was derived in 1837 by Poisson.

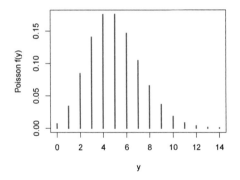 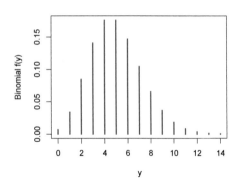

FIGURE 2.10 The Poisson distribution with $\mu = 5$ and the binomial distribution with $n = 50000000$ and $\pi = 0.0000001$.

```
> ppois(120, 100) - ppois(79, 100) # probability within 2 standard deviations of mean
[1] 0.9598793
> y = seq(60, 140, 1)        # y values between 60 and 140 with increment of 1
> plot(y, dpois(y, 100))     # plot of Poisson probabilities when mean=100
```

Here we have used that $P(70 \le Y \le 130) = P(Y \le 130) - P(Y \le 69)$.

The Poisson distribution is simple, having a single parameter that is both the mean and the variance. However, this is also a weakness, because sample count data often show more variability than the Poisson allows. For example, sometimes the mode is 0 but the mean is considerably larger. This could be the case for a random variable such as Y = number of movies seen in a theater last year, where it is not inconceivable that a population would have $\mu = 5.4$ but mode = 0. With $\mu = 5.4$, the Poisson distribution has a mode of 5 (the integer part of the mean).

The Poisson–binomial connection also shows how the Poisson may fail, in violating the assumptions for a binomial experiment. In analyzing Y = number of deaths per day in auto accidents in Italy, the probability π of death in a given day would vary from person to person, depending on driving performance and how much time they spent in autos. The Poisson condition of a constant rate would also be violated, as the rate would vary from day to day according to variables such as the density of traffic and weather conditions. So, the expected number of deaths would also vary from day to day. When we consider a distribution that applies over a long period of time, the overall distribution might average many Poisson distributions, each with their own mean. That overall distribution would exhibit more variability than a single Poisson can. This situation is called ***overdispersion***.

Section 7.5.2 introduces an alternative distribution for count data, the *negative binomial*. It arises from a type of averaging of Poisson distributions with different means. As a consequence, it has a second parameter and permits the variance to be larger than the mean. It also permits the mode to be 0 even when the mean is much larger than 0.

2.5   Continuous Probability Distributions

Sections 2.2.4 and 2.2.6 introduced the *uniform* and the *exponential* as two examples of probability distributions of continuous random variables. We now introduce two distributions for continuous random variables that have greater scope. The *normal distribution* is important partly because members of the normal family have a bell shape that approximates well the distributions of many variables in the real world but mainly because it is a key distribution for methods of statistical inference. The *gamma distribution* is a family of skewed distributions over the positive real line that contains the exponential as a special case as well as another distribution (the *chi-squared*) used in some methods of statistical inference.

2.5.1 The Normal Distribution

Each normal distribution is specified by its mean μ and its standard deviation σ. For any real number μ and any $\sigma > 0$, a normal distribution exists having that mean and standard deviation.

Normal distribution

The **normal distribution** is characterized by the probability density function

$$f(y; \mu, \sigma) = \left(\frac{1}{\sqrt{2\pi}\sigma}\right) e^{-(y-\mu)^2/2\sigma^2}, \quad -\infty < y < \infty, \tag{2.8}$$

where μ and $\sigma > 0$ are parameters and π is the mathematical constant 3.1416... .

We abbreviate by writing that Y has a $N(\mu, \sigma^2)$ distribution, denoted $Y \sim N(\mu, \sigma^2)$.

The *pdf* for the normal distribution has a symmetric, bell-shape that describes well histograms for many variables that are continuous or have a large number of possible values. It is the most important probability distribution for statistical inference. For example, the next chapter shows that many statistics that estimate population parameters vary from sample to sample according to a normal distribution, even when the sample data do *not* come from a normal distribution.

The normal *pdf* has probability within any particular number of standard deviations of μ that is the same for all normal distributions. This probability (rounded) equals 0.68 within 1 standard deviation, 0.95 within 2 standard deviations, and 0.997 within 3 standard deviations, as shown in Figure 2.11. These agree with the proportions stated in Section 1.4.4 as an aid to interpreting standard deviations for bell-shaped distributions. The *pdf* is positive over the entire real line, but nearly the entire distribution falls between $\mu - 3\sigma$ and $\mu + 3\sigma$.

The central normal probabilities of 0.68, 0.95, and 0.997 come from integrating the normal *pdf* over the regions $\mu \pm \sigma$, $\mu \pm 2\sigma$, and $\mu \pm 3\sigma$. The normal *pdf* does not have a closed-form integral, so this is done numerically and can be implemented simply with software, as the next section shows.

2.5.2 The Standard Normal Distribution

The normal distribution having $\mu = 0$ and $\sigma = 1$ is called the **standard normal distribution**. It has *cdf* denoted by Φ and *pdf* denoted by ϕ. The *pdf* has equation

$$\phi(z) = \frac{1}{\sqrt{2\pi}} e^{-z^2/2}, \quad -\infty < z < \infty. \tag{2.9}$$

For the standard normal distribution, the number that falls z standard deviations from the mean is $\mu + z\sigma = 0 + z(1) = z$.

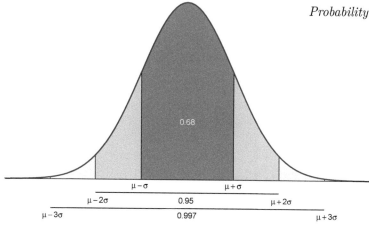

FIGURE 2.11 For every normal distribution, the probability equals (rounded) 0.68 within σ of μ, 0.95 within 2σ of μ, and 0.997 within 3σ of μ.

Because the normal *pdf* does not have a closed form for its integral, we cannot express its *cdf* as an ordinary function. However, the *cdf* is widely available in tables, in software, and in apps.[19] The R function `pnorm` gives cumulative probabilities for the standard normal distribution. We can use it to directly find the central probabilities that fall within 1, 2, and 3 standard deviations of the mean of a normal distribution:

```
> pnorm(1) - pnorm(-1)
[1] 0.6826895           # probability within 1 standard deviation of mean
> pnorm(2) - pnorm(-2)
[1] 0.9544997           # probability within 2 standard deviations of mean
> pnorm(3) - pnorm(-3)
[1] 0.9973002           # probability within 3 standard deviations of mean
```

As Section 2.3.6 explained, to *standardize* a random variable, we subtract the mean and divide by the standard deviation. When Y has a $N(\mu, \sigma^2)$ distribution, the standardized version

$$Z = \frac{Y - \mu}{\sigma}$$

has a standard normal distribution. More generally, *any linear transformation of a normal random variable has a normal distribution.* Chapters 4 and 5 show that some methods of inferential statistics convert values of certain statistics to standardized variables that have approximate standard normal distributions. The value z of Z is then called a *standardized score*, or z-score for short.

2.5.3 Examples: Finding Normal Probabilities and Percentiles

According to a recent *Current Population Reports*, self-employed individuals in the United States work an average of 45 hours per week, with a standard deviation of 15. If this distribution is approximately normal, about what proportion work between 50 and 70 hours? We can answer this directly in R with the general version of the `pnorm` function that has arguments for specified means and standard deviations for a normal *cdf*:

```
> pnorm(70,45,15) - pnorm(50,45,15) # pnorm(70,45,15) = cumulative probability
[1] 0.32165                         # below 70 when mean = 45, standard deviation = 15
```

---

[19]For example, see the normal distribution app at www.artofstat.com.

To the extent that the normal approximation is good, about a third of self-employed individuals in the U.S. work between 50 and 70 hours per week.

Stanford–Binet IQ scores are discrete but have approximately a normal distribution with $\mu = 100$ and $\sigma = 16$ in the U.S. population. What is the approximate 99th percentile (0.99 quantile) of IQ scores, that is, the IQ score that falls above 99% of IQ scores? In R, we can find normal percentiles (quantiles) using the qnorm function for quantiles:

```
> qnorm(0.99,100,16) # 0.99 normal quantile when mean = 100, standard deviation = 16
[1] 137.2216
```

This calculation uses the value of z such that $\mu + z\sigma$ falls above 99% of a normal distribution. From the standard normal,

```
> qnorm(0.99)
[1] 2.326348
```

so the 0.99 quantile is $z = 2.326$ standard deviations above the mean. For the IQ scores, it is $100 + 2.326(16) = 137$.

We can also use percentiles to compare scores from different normal distributions. For instance, suppose that when you applied to college, you took a SAT exam and scored 550, whereas your friend took the ACT exam and scored 30. Which score is relatively better, if the SAT has $\mu = 500$ and $\sigma = 100$ and the ACT has $\mu = 18$ and $\sigma = 6$? An SAT score of $y = 550$ is 0.50 standard deviations above the mean, whereas the ACT score of $y = 30$ is 2.0 standard deviations above the mean. In this relative sense, the ACT score is higher. If the distributions of SAT and ACT are approximately normal, it corresponds to a higher percentile:

```
> pnorm(550, 500, 100); pnorm(30, 18, 6)
[1] 0.6914625    # SAT = 550 is approximate 69th percentile
[1] 0.9772499    # ACT =  30 is approximate 98th percentile
```

2.5.4 The Gamma Distribution

Many continuous random variables can take only positive values. Often, their distribution is skewed to the right, such as when μ is relatively close to 0 but y values can be quite large.

A family of probability densities that has a variety of shapes that are unimodal but skewed to the right has *pdf* with support over the positive real line that is proportional to

$$e^{-\lambda y}y^{k-1}, \quad y \geq 0,$$

for parameters $\lambda > 0$ and $k > 0$. To convert the function $e^{-\lambda y}y^{k-1}$ to a proper *pdf*, we divide it by a constant so that it integrates to 1.0 over the positive real line. That constant is $\int_0^\infty e^{-\lambda y}y^{k-1}dy$. Now, as a function of k, an integral of the form

$$\Gamma(k) = \int_0^\infty e^{-x}x^{k-1}dx$$

is called the *gamma function*. It has the property $\Gamma(k+1) = k\Gamma(k)$. For k a positive integer, $\Gamma(k) = (k-1)! = (k-1)(k-2)\cdots(1)$. Substituting $x = \lambda y$ and $dx = \lambda dy$,

$$\Gamma(k) = \int_0^\infty \lambda^k e^{-\lambda y}y^{k-1}dy$$

Therefore, $\int_0^\infty e^{-\lambda y}y^{k-1}dy = \Gamma(k)/\lambda^k$, and the function of form $e^{-\lambda y}y^{k-1}$ becomes a *pdf* when we divide it by $\Gamma(k)/\lambda^k$.

Gamma distribution

The *gamma distribution* is characterized by the probability density function

$$f(y; k, \lambda) = \frac{\lambda^k}{\Gamma(k)} e^{-\lambda y} y^{k-1}, \ y \geq 0; \quad f(y; \lambda, k) = 0, \ y < 0, \qquad (2.10)$$

for parameters $k > 0$ and $\lambda > 0$; k is a *shape parameter* and $1/\lambda$ is a *scale parameter*.

The gamma distribution has mean and standard deviation

$$\mu = k/\lambda, \quad \sigma = \sqrt{k}/\lambda, \qquad (2.11)$$

so that $\sigma = \mu/\sqrt{k}$. For fixed k, the standard deviation is proportional to the mean, the distribution being more spread out when the mean is greater. The first plot in Figure 2.12 shows [20] the *pdf* for $k = 10$ and three values for μ. The gamma density is skewed to the right, with skewness equal to $2/\sqrt{k}$. The index k is called a *shape parameter*. As k increases, the skewness decreases and the *pdf* has more of a bell shape. The second plot in Figure 2.12 shows the *pdf* with $\mu = 10$ and three values for k. The mode is 0 when $k \leq 1$ and otherwise is $(k-1)/\lambda$. The index $1/\lambda$ is called a *scale parameter* (Exercise 2.48). The mean and standard deviation are proportional to it.

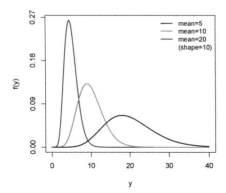 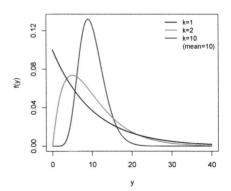

FIGURE 2.12 Gamma distributions with (1) shape parameter $k = 10$ and $\mu = 5, 10, 20$, (2) $\mu = 10$ and shape parameter $k = 1, 2,$ and 10. For fixed shape parameter, the standard deviation increases as the mean (and the scale parameter μ/k) increases. For fixed mean, the distribution is more bell-shaped as the shape parameter increases (and scale parameter μ/k decreases).

We can derive moments of a gamma distribution by direct integration. For example,

$$\begin{aligned}
\mu &= \int_0^\infty y f(y; \lambda, k) dy = \int_0^\infty \frac{\lambda^k}{\Gamma(k)} y e^{-\lambda y} y^{k-1} dy \\
&= \frac{\Gamma(k+1)}{\lambda \Gamma(k)} \int_0^\infty \frac{\lambda^{k+1}}{\Gamma(k+1)} e^{-\lambda y} y^{(k+1)-1}.
\end{aligned}$$

---

[20]The R function for this is `dgamma(y, shape, scale)`. The scale parameter $1/\lambda = \mu/k$ is $= \mu/10$ for the first plot and $10/k$ for the second plot.

In this form, the argument of the integral is a gamma *pdf* having parameters λ and $k^* = k+1$. Thus, the integral equals 1. But then since $\Gamma(k+1) = k\Gamma(k)$, the constant outside the integral is k/λ, so that $\mu = k/\lambda$.

A special case of the gamma distribution is especially important, being a key probability distribution for statistical inference. The ***chi-squared distribution*** is the family of gamma distributions with $\lambda = 1/2$ and with an index called the *degrees of freedom* (*df*) that equals $2k$ and is a positive integer. For it, $\mu = df$ and $\sigma^2 = 2(df)$. Chapters 4–7 give details and show how to use the chi-squared distribution.

2.5.5 The Exponential Distribution and Poisson Processes

Another special case of the gamma distribution is the ***exponential distribution***, sometimes called *negative exponential*. The general form of this distribution is the gamma distribution with shape parameter $k = 1$,

$$f(y; \lambda) = \lambda e^{-\lambda y}, \quad y \geq 0. \tag{2.12}$$

It is skewed to the right with $\mu = \sigma = 1/\lambda$ and median $= 0.693/\lambda$. Section 2.2.6 introduced the special case with $\lambda = 1$, with *pdf* shown in Figure 2.8. The *pdf* with $k = 1$ in Figure 2.12 is the exponential with $\lambda = 0.1$. The exponential *cdf* is

$$F(y; \lambda) = P(Y \leq y) = \int_0^y \lambda e^{-\lambda u} du = 1 - e^{-\lambda y}, \quad y \geq 0.$$

The exponential distribution has a connection with the Poisson distribution. For a random phenomenon occurring over time, let the random variable Y_t equal the number of occurrences by time t. Suppose that Y_t has a Poisson distribution with mean λt; that is, λ is the *rate* of occurrence. Such a random phenomenon is called a ***Poisson process***. Now, let T denote the *waiting time* until we observe the first occurrence of the Poisson process. The event that $T \leq t$ is equivalent to the event $Y_t \geq 1$. So, for any $t \geq 0$, T has *cdf*

$$F(t) = P(T \leq t) = P(Y_t \geq 1) = 1 - P(Y_t = 0).$$

From the Poisson distribution with mean λt, $P(Y_t = 0) = e^{-\lambda t}(\lambda t)^0/0! = e^{-\lambda t}$, so $F(t) = 1 - e^{-\lambda t}$. Therefore, T has the exponential distribution with parameter λ. It can be shown that the waiting time between any two successive occurrences of a Poisson process also has this exponential distribution. If the number of major payments Y_t that an insurance company makes by week t is a Poisson process with rate $\lambda = 0.20$, then the time between any two successive payments has the exponential distribution with mean $1/\lambda = 5$ weeks. Because of this Poisson connection, λ in the exponential distribution or the more general gamma distribution (2.10) is often referred to as a *rate parameter*.[21]

2.5.6 Quantiles of a Probability Distribution

For a continuous random variable, the *p*th quantile (100*p* percentile) is the point q at which $F(q) = p$. For instance, the 0.50 quantile (the median) is the point q at which $F(q) = 0.50$. The point q is determined by $q = F^{-1}(p)$, where F^{-1} is the *inverse function*[22] that maps from the possible p values between 0 and 1 back to the real values that Y can take.

---

[21] Generally, the sum of n independent exponential random variables has the gamma distribution (2.10) with shape parameter $k = n$ and rate parameter λ; here we used $n = 1$.

[22] For F^{-1} to exist, F must be strictly increasing over the range of possible values for Y. This is true for the commonly-used continuous distributions.

For instance, for the exponential distribution, the *cdf* is $F(y; \lambda) = 1 - e^{-\lambda y}$, so the *p*th quantile q satisfies $F(q; \lambda) = 1 - e^{-\lambda q} = p$. Solving, we find $q = -\log(1 - p)/\lambda$. For example, for the exponential distribution with $\lambda = 1.0$, shown in Figure 2.8, the 0.40 quantile (40th percentile) is $q = -\log(1 - 0.40)/1.0 = 0.511$. Likewise, we can verify with R that the 0.05 quantile (5th percentile) is 0.051 and the 0.95 quantile (95th percentile) is 2.996:

```
> qexp(0.05, 1); qexp(0.40, 1); qexp(0.95, 1) # 0.05, 0.40, 0.95 quantiles of exponential
[1] 0.05129329                                 # distribution with parameter lambda = 1.0
[1] 0.510826 # 0.40 quantile is -log(1 - 0.40)/1.0 = 0.511
[1] 2.995732 # 0.95 quantile is -log(1 - 0.95)/1.0 = 2.996
```

Figure 2.13 shows the *cdf* of the exponential distribution with $\lambda = 1$. We use the inverse of this function to get the 0.40 quantile by starting at 0.40 on the vertical axis of *cdf* probability values, going over horizontally to the *cdf*, and then down to the horizontal axis of exponential random variable values at 0.511.

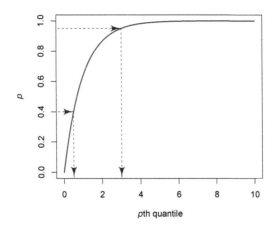

FIGURE 2.13 The *cdf* of an exponential distribution with $\lambda = 1$ and the inverse *cdf* mapping. To find the 0.40 quantile, go from 0.40 on the vertical *cdf* probability scale to 0.511 on the horizontal scale of exponential random variable values. Likewise, the 0.95 quantile is 2.996.

For a discrete random variable, the *cdf* is a step function. For any particular value p, no value q may satisfy $F(q) = p$. The *p*th quantile is then defined as the minimum q such that $F(q) \geq p$. For an example, see Section A.2.2 of the R Appendix.

2.5.7   Using the Uniform to Randomly Generate a Continuous Random Variable

For a continuous random variable Y with *cdf* F, consider the transformed random variable, $X = F(Y)$. Then, X can take values only between 0 and 1. For $0 < x < 1$, its *cdf* G is

$$G(x) = P(X \leq x) = P[F(Y) \leq x] = P[Y \leq F^{-1}(x)] = F[F^{-1}(x)] = x.$$

From Section 2.2.5, $G(x) = x$ is the *cdf* of a uniform random variable over the interval [0, 1]. That is:

▶ For a continuous random variable Y with *cdf* F, $X = F(Y)$ has this uniform distribution.

Because F is the integral of the *pdf* f, the transformation $X = F(Y)$ is called the **probability integral transformation**.

This result is useful for generating random variables. With software that can generate a uniform random variable X, we can generate a random variable Y having cdf F by generating X and then letting $Y = F^{-1}(X)$. For example, if Y has an exponential distribution, then $X = F(Y; \lambda) = 1 - e^{-\lambda Y}$ has a uniform distribution. To randomly generate an exponential, we randomly generate a uniform random variable X over $[0, 1]$ and then find $Y = -\log(1 - X)/\lambda$. The following R code does this a million times, with $\lambda = 0.50$, for which the exponential distribution has mean and standard deviation equal to 2.

```
> X <- runif(1000000)      # 1000000 randomly generated uniforms over [0, 1]
> Y <- -log(1 - X)/(0.50) # Histogram of randomly generated Y values should
> mean(Y); sd(Y); hist(Y) # resemble exponential pdf with lambda = 0.50,
[1] 2.000083
[1] 2.00032                # which has mean = standard deviation = 2.0
```

2.6 Joint and Conditional Distributions and Independence

Table A.1 in the R Appendix in this book lists the probability distributions introduced in the previous two sections and others introduced in later chapters as well as the names used to access them in R. Most statistical analyses, however, deal simultaneously with two or more random variables. Probability distributions can then specify probabilities about joint values of the random variables or about values of one of them conditional on values for the others.

2.6.1 Joint and Marginal Probability Distributions

A **joint probability distribution** specifies probabilities for all the possible combinations of values of the random variables. In this section, we mainly focus on the *bivariate* case, for two random variables X and Y.

For continuous random variables, a joint *pdf* $f(x, y)$ specifies the joint probability distribution. It integrates to 1.0 over the plane of possible (x, y) values. For discrete random variables, most commonly both X and Y are categorical, X with r categories and Y with c categories. The joint *pmf* specifies rc probabilities, with $f(x, y) = P(X = x, Y = y)$ the probability that X is in category x and Y is in category y, satisfying $\sum_{x=1}^{r} \sum_{y=1}^{c} f(x, y) = 1$.

The probability distribution of a single random variable, considered by itself without reference to any other random variable, is called a **marginal distribution**. A joint probability function determines marginal probability functions by integrating or summing over the others. For the discrete case of X having r categories and Y having c categories, for instance, the marginal probability functions are $f_1(x) = \sum_{y=1}^{c} f(x, y)$ for $x = 1, \ldots, r$ and $f_2(y) = \sum_{x=1}^{r} f(x, y)$ for $y = 1, \ldots, c$.

2.6.2 Example: Joint and Marginal Distributions of Happiness and Family Income

We illustrate a discrete joint probability distribution[23] with Table 2.4, which shows results based on a recent General Social Survey when respondents were asked, "Would you say that you are very happy, pretty happy, or not too happy?" and "Compared with American families in general, would you say your family income is below average, average, or above average?" Let X denote the row number for family income and let Y denote the column number for happiness. Table 2.4 shows the proportions of people at the nine combinations of categories, which are called the *cells* of the table.

TABLE 2.4 Sample joint distribution of happiness by family income, with marginal distributions shown by the row and column totals.

Relative Family Income	Happiness			Total
	Not too happy	Pretty happy	Very happy	
Below average	0.080	0.198	0.079	0.357
Average	0.043	0.254	0.143	0.440
Above average	0.017	0.105	0.081	0.203
Total	0.140	0.557	0.303	1.000

In Table 2.4, the marginal distributions are in the margins of the table. The column total probabilities (0.140, 0.557, 0.303) form the marginal distribution of Y = happiness, and the row total probabilities (0.357, 0.440, 0.203) form the marginal distribution of X = relative family income.

2.6.3 Conditional Probability Distributions

A *conditional probability distribution* specifies probabilities for the outcome of one random variable, conditional on the outcome for another random variable. In the discrete case, we can find the conditional distribution by applying the conditional probability rule $P(A \mid B) = P(AB)/P(B)$. In the continuous or discrete cases, when X and Y have joint probability function $f(x,y)$ and marginal probability functions $f_1(x)$ and $f_2(y)$, the conditional probability function for Y given $X = x$ is

$$f(y \mid x) = \frac{f(x,y)}{f_1(x)}.$$

When we distinguish between the random variables as response and explanatory, we form conditional distributions over the response categories. In Table 2.4, treating happiness as the response random variable, conditional on a person reporting average family income, their probabilities for the three categories of happiness are

$$\frac{0.043}{0.440} = 0.10, \quad \frac{0.254}{0.440} = 0.58, \quad \frac{0.143}{0.440} = 0.32.$$

Like ordinary probability distributions, a conditional distribution has moments that describe it. For instance, for a continuous random variable Y, the **conditional expectation**

---

[23]This table is based on a survey of 1943 Americans, so it is a *sample* joint distribution that estimates the joint probability distribution for the *population*.

of Y at a particular value x of X is its mean,

$$E(Y \mid X = x) = \int_y y f(y \mid x) dy.$$

For example, suppose that in a week an insurance company has to make X payments for claims from auto accidents, and X has a Poisson distribution with mean 10. The payment for accident i is Y_i euros, so the total payment in the week is $Y = Y_1 + \cdots + Y_X$ euros. Suppose that each payment Y_i has a $N(9000, 3000^2)$ distribution. Then conditional on $X = x$, Y is the sum of x independent normal random variables each having mean 9000, which we'll see in Section 3.2.6 has a normal distribution with mean $9000x$. Given $X = x$, the conditional expectation is $E(Y \mid X = x) = 9000x$.

In this example, how can we find $E(Y)$ without observing X but knowing only its distribution? A useful result, called the *law of iterated expectation*, says that[24]

$$E(Y) = E[E(Y \mid X)],$$

where the outside expectation is with respect to the distribution of X. Here, based on the number of payments X having a Poisson distribution with mean 10 and $E(Y \mid X) = 9000X$, we have $E(Y) = E[E(Y \mid X)] = E(9000X) = 9000E(X) = 9000(10) = 90,000$, the product of the normal and Poisson means.

2.6.4 Trials with Multiple Categories: The Multinomial Distribution

Section 2.4.1 introduced the binomial distribution for the number of successes in n independent observations of a binary variable. Nominal and ordinal response variables have more than two possible outcomes. Let c denote the fixed number of mutually exclusive outcome categories. We denote their probabilities by $(\pi_1, \pi_2, \ldots, \pi_c)$, where $\sum_j \pi_j = 1$. For n independent trials, we let the random variable Y_j, $j = 1, \ldots, c$, count the number of cases that fall in category j. Each Y_j takes values between 0 and n, but the possible values for the joint probability distribution of $(Y_1, \ldots, Y_c)$ are constrained by $\sum Y_j = n$. In a realization of n independent observations, the number of possible samples for which y_1 fall in category 1, y_2 fall in category 2, $\ldots$, y_c fall in category c, where $\sum_j y_j = n$, equals $[n!/(y_1!y_2!\cdots y_c!)]$, called the *multinomial coefficient*. Each such possible sample has probability $\pi_1^{y_1} \pi_2^{y_2} \cdots \pi_c^{y_c}$, so the total joint probability of the sample counts $(y_1, y_2, \ldots, y_c)$ equals

$$P(Y_1 = y_1, Y_1 = y_2, \ldots, Y_c = y_c) = \left(\frac{n!}{y_1!y_2!\cdots y_c!}\right) \pi_1^{y_1} \pi_2^{y_2} \cdots \pi_c^{y_c}. \tag{2.13}$$

The probability distribution of all such possible samples is called the ***multinomial distribution***.

Multinomial distribution

For n independent trials with c possible outcome categories having probabilities $(\pi_1, \pi_2, \ldots, \pi_c)$ with $\sum_j \pi_j = 1$, the joint probability mass function for the numbers of outcomes $\{y_j\}$ in those categories, where $\sum_j y_j = n$, is

$$f(y_1, y_2, \ldots, y_c; n, \pi_1, \pi_2, \ldots, \pi_c) = \left(\frac{n!}{y_1!y_2!\cdots y_c!}\right) \pi_1^{y_1} \pi_2^{y_2} \cdots \pi_c^{y_c}. \tag{2.14}$$

This is the ***multinomial distribution*** with index n and parameters $(\pi_1, \pi_2, \ldots, \pi_c)$.

---

[24]This result is discussed further in Section 7.5.1.

The binomial distribution is the special case with $c = 2$ categories. The multinomial distribution is actually $(c-1)$-dimensional, because $Y_c = n - (Y_1 + \cdots + Y_{c-1})$ and $\pi_c = 1 - (\pi_1 + \cdots + \pi_{c-1})$. For instance, the binomial special case with $c = 2$ has number of failures determined by the number of successes. It can be expressed merely as $Y_1 \sim \text{binom}(n, \pi_1)$, rather than as $(Y_1, Y_2) \sim \text{multinom}(n, \pi_1, \pi_2)$, with the understanding in the binomial expression that $Y_2 = n - Y_1$ and $\pi_2 = 1 - \pi_1$.

Section 2.4.2 illustrated the binomial distribution with an example about the composition of a jury, for which the list of potential jurors had proportion Hispanic of 0.20. Suppose also that the list had proportion African-American of 0.30 and proportion White of 0.50, and that of 12 people selected for a trial from the list, 0 were Hispanic, 1 was African-American, and 11 were White. For random selections, the probability of such a sample is

$$\left(\frac{12!}{0!1!11!}\right)(0.20)^0(0.30)^1(0.50)^{11} = 12(0.30)(0.50)^{11} = 0.00176.$$

The multinomial coefficient equals 12, representing that the sole African-American chosen could have been the first person selected, or the second, ..., or the twelfth. We can also find this using R:

```
> dmultinom(c(0, 1, 11), prob=c(0.20, 0.30, 0.50))
[1] 0.001757812
```

The probability of selecting *at least 11* White people from the list is

$$\frac{12!}{0!1!11!}(0.20)^0(0.30)^1(0.50)^{11} + \frac{12!}{1!0!11!}(0.20)^1(0.30)^0(0.50)^{11} + \frac{12!}{0!0!12!}(0.20)^0(0.30)^0(0.50)^{12},$$

which is 0.00317, very unlikely.

For the multinomial distribution, the marginal distribution of each Y_j is binomial with n trials and success probability π_j. When the jury-list counts (Y_1, Y_2, Y_3) for (Hispanic, African-American, White) have the multinomial distribution with $n = 12$ and $(\pi_1, \pi_2, \pi_3) = (0.20, 0.30, 0.50)$, then the count Y_3 of Whites selected for the jury has the binom(12, 0.50) distribution. The constraint $\sum_j Y_j = n$ affects the possible values for conditional distributions. For instance, given $Y_3 = 11$ in $n = 12$ selections, the possible values for Y_1 or for Y_2 are only 0 and 1.

2.6.5 Expectations of Sums of Random Variables

A useful property of expectations for jointly distributed random variables is that they have an *additive* property: The expected value of a sum of random variables is the sum of the expected values. For instance, for random variables X and Y that have a joint *pdf* $f(x,y)$ and marginal *pdfs* $f_1(x)$ for X and $f_2(y)$ for Y,

$$\begin{aligned} E(X+Y) &= \int_y \int_x (x+y)f(x,y)dxdy = \int_y \int_x xf(x,y)dxdy + \int_y \int_x yf(x,y)dxdy \\ &= \int_x x\left[\int_y f(x,y)dy\right]dx + \int_y y\left[\int_x f(x,y)dx\right]dy = \int_x xf_1(x)dx + \int_y yf_2(y)dy \\ &= E(X) + E(Y). \end{aligned}$$

More generally, for a set of n random variables, continuous or discrete,

$$E(Y_1 + Y_2 + \cdots + Y_n) = E(Y_1) + E(Y_2) + \cdots + E(Y_n). \tag{2.15}$$

Here is an application of this additive property: Consider a sample survey that obtains observations $\{y_i\} = \{y_1, \ldots, y_n\}$. Before the data are collected, the observations $\{Y_i\}$ are random variables, as is the sample mean $\overline{Y}$. Their values are unknown and vary from sample to sample. With simple random sampling, the $\{Y_i\}$ come from the same distribution, with common mean μ. Then, with sample size n,

$$E\left(\sum_{i=1}^n Y_i\right) = \sum_{i=1}^n E(Y_i) = n\mu,$$

$$E(\overline{Y}) = E\left[\frac{\sum_{i=1}^n Y_i}{n}\right] = \frac{1}{n}\left[E\left(\sum_{i=1}^n Y_i\right)\right] = \frac{1}{n}(n\mu) = \mu.$$

If a study were to take many simple random samples of size n from a population, then in the long run, the mean of the sample means would equal the population mean μ. In practice, of course, a study takes a single sample of size n rather than many samples of size n each. But in Section 3.2 we'll see how this result is relevant to practical applications, after we learn how also to find the standard deviation of the probability distribution of $\overline{Y}$.

2.6.6 Independence of Random Variables

When we study the joint probability distribution of two random variables, certain questions naturally arise: Is there a "correlation," such as with the values of Y tending to increase as values of X increase? Or are X and Y "independent" random variables?

Independent random variables

Two random variables X and Y with marginal probability functions $f_1(x)$ and $f_2(y)$ are ***independent*** when

$$f(x \mid y) = f_1(x) \text{ and } f(y \mid x) = f_2(y)$$

for all possible values x of X and y of Y. Then, their joint probability function $f(x, y)$ satisfies

$$f(x, y) = f_1(x)f_2(y) \text{ for all } x \text{ and } y.$$

When X and Y are independent, the conditional distributions are the same as the marginal distributions, and the joint probability function is the product of the marginal probability functions. In the discrete case, this factorization holds because the events that $X = x$ and that $Y = y$ are independent events in the sense explained in Section 2.1.6. Since $P(Y = y \mid X = x) = P(X = x, Y = y)/P(X = x)$, when $P(Y = y \mid X = x) = P(Y = y)$ for all x and y,

$$P(X = x, Y = y) = P(X = x)P(Y = y).$$

Independence between two random variables extends to *mutual independence* for multiple random variables. The random variables $(Y_1, Y_2, \ldots, Y_n)$ are ***mutually independent*** if their joint probability function f factors as a product of the marginal probability functions, that is,

$$f(y_1, \ldots, y_n) = f_1(y_1) \cdots f_n(y_n) \text{ for all values } (y_1, \ldots, y_n).$$

This implies that they are also *pairwise* independent, for instance $f(y_1, y_2) = f_1(y_1)f_2(y_2)$ for all values (y_1, y_2). However, pairwise independence of each pair of a set of random variables does not imply mutual independence. Exercise 2.58 shows an example.

2.6.7 Markov Chain Dependence and Conditional Independence

When observations occur over time, studies often focus on the dependence of the response Y_t at time t on the previously observed responses $(y_1, y_2, \ldots, y_{t-1})$. A ***Markov chain*** is a sequence[25] for which, for all t, the conditional distribution of Y_t, given $y_1, \ldots, y_{t-1}$, is identical to the conditional distribution of Y_t given y_{t-1} alone. That is, given y_{t-1}, Y_t is independent of $Y_1, \ldots, Y_{t-2}$. Knowing the most recent observation, information about previous observations before it does not help with predicting the next observation.

In a sequence of bets based on coin flips, for each flip suppose you win \$1 with a head and lose \$1 (i.e., win −1 dollar) with a tail. Let Y_t denote the total of your winnings and losings after t bets. With a balanced coin, $P(Y_t = y_{t-1} + 1 \mid y_1, \ldots, y_{t-1}) = P(Y_t = y_{t-1} - 1 \mid y_1, \ldots, y_{t-1}) = 1/2$. Given y_{t-1}, the probability distribution of Y_t does not depend on $(y_1, \ldots, y_{t-2})$, so $\{Y_t, t = 1, 2, \ldots\}$ is a Markov chain. It is an example of a type of Markov chain called a ***random walk***.

Two random variables that are independent, conditional on others, are said to be ***conditionally independent***.[26] In a Markov chain, Y_t and any of $Y_1, Y_2, \ldots, Y_{t-2}$ are conditionally independent, given Y_{t-1}. If we know y_{t-1}, then to predict Y_t, it does not help at all to also know $y_1, \ldots, y_{t-2}$.

2.7 Correlation between Random Variables

When random variables X and Y are not independent, certain values of X tend to go with certain values of Y. An *association* exists between them. When we randomly sample (X, Y) from their joint probability distribution with marginal means (μ_X, μ_Y), a *positive association* exists if, on the average, $(X - \mu_X)(Y - \mu_Y)$ takes a positive value; that is, if when $X > \mu_X$, then typically $Y > \mu_Y$, and when $X < \mu_X$, then typically $Y < \mu_Y$. A *negative association* exists if, on the average, $(X - \mu_X)(Y - \mu_Y)$ takes a negative value.

2.7.1 Covariance and Correlation

The expected value of $(X - \mu_X)(Y - \mu_Y)$ is called the ***covariance***.

Covariance

The ***covariance*** between random variables X and Y having $E(X) = \mu_X$ and $E(Y) = \mu_Y$ is

$$\text{cov}(X, Y) = E[(X - \mu_X)(Y - \mu_Y)].$$

The covariance can take any real-number value. Its size depends on the units of measurement. For example, if X is measured in kilograms and we change units to pounds, then the values of X multiply by 2.2, as does the marginal mean μ_X and standard deviation σ_X and the covariance between X and any other random variable. To make the measure free of the units of measurement, we divide each difference in the covariance definition by the standard deviation. The expected product of the *standardized* variables is called the ***correlation***.

---

[25] Named after the Russian mathematician Andrey Markov, who from 1906 conducted research about sequences of random variables that have this property

[26] More precisely, X and Y are conditionally independent, given Z, if $f(x, y \mid z) = f_1(x \mid z) f_2(y \mid z)$ for all x, y, and z.

Correlation

The ***correlation*** between a random variable X having $E(X) = \mu_X$ and $\text{var}(X) = \sigma_X^2$ and a random variable Y having $E(Y) = \mu_Y$ and $\text{var}(Y) = \sigma_Y^2$ is

$$\text{corr}(X,Y) = E\left[\left(\frac{X - \mu_X}{\sigma_X}\right)\left(\frac{Y - \mu_Y}{\sigma_Y}\right)\right] = \frac{\text{cov}(X,Y)}{\sigma_X \sigma_Y}. \qquad (2.16)$$

The correlation falls between -1 and $+1$, equaling ± 1 when the joint distribution falls perfectly on a straight line, $+1$ when the slope is positive and -1 when the slope is negative (Exercise 2.64). The larger the correlation is in absolute value, the stronger is the association in a linear sense.

By the additivity property of expectation and constants factoring out of expected values, formula (2.3) noted that $\text{var}(Y) = E(Y^2) - [E(Y)]^2$. Likewise, since

$$\begin{aligned} \text{cov}(X,Y) &= E[(X - \mu_X)(Y - \mu_Y)] = E(XY - \mu_X Y - X\mu_Y + \mu_X \mu_Y) \\ &= E(XY) - \mu_X E(Y) - \mu_Y E(X) + \mu_X \mu_Y = E(XY) - \mu_X \mu_Y, \end{aligned}$$

an alternate formula for the covariance that enables simpler calculation is

$$\text{cov}(X,Y) = E(XY) - [E(X)][E(Y)].$$

2.7.2 Example: Correlation between Income and Happiness

To illustrate covariance and correlation, we consider the two hypothetical joint distributions in Table 2.5 for X = family income and Y = happiness. Family income and happiness are both *ordinal* variables, having a natural ordering of the categories (Section 1.2.4). For some analyses, data analysts treat ordinal variables as quantitative by assigning ordered scores to the categories. For simplicity, we assign the row and column numbers, (1, 2, 3), to X and to Y and find the covariance and the correlation.

TABLE 2.5 Joint probability distributions showing (a) positive correlation, (b) zero correlation yet dependence.

(a) Family Income	Happiness 1	2	3	(b) Family Income	Happiness 1	2	3	Total
1	0.2	0.1	0.0	1	0.15	0.0	0.15	0.3
2	0.1	0.2	0.1	2	0.00	0.4	0.00	0.4
3	0.0	0.1	0.2	3	0.15	0.0	0.15	0.3
Total	0.3	0.4	0.3	Total	0.3	0.4	0.3	1.0

For each marginal distribution in Table 2.5, $E(X) = E(Y) = 1(0.3) + 2(0.4) + 3(0.3) = 2.0$. To find the marginal standard deviations, we first find $E(X^2) = E(Y^2) = 1^2(0.3) + 2^2(0.4) + 3^2(0.3) = 4.60$, from which the variances are $E(X^2) - [E(X)]^2 = E(Y^2) - [E(Y)]^2 = 0.60$ and the standard deviations are $\sigma_X = \sigma_Y = \sqrt{0.60}$. To find $E(XY)$, for each cell we multiply the product of the X score and Y score by the probability in that cell, and then add over the nine cells. For case (a) in Table 2.5,

$$E(XY) = (1 \times 1)(0.2) + (1 \times 2)(0.1) + \cdots + (3 \times 3)(0.2) = 4.40,$$

so that $\text{cov}(X,Y) = E(XY) - [E(X)][E(Y)] = 4.40 - (2.0)(2.0) = 0.40$. The correlation is

$$\text{corr}(X,Y) = \frac{\text{cov}(X,Y)}{\sigma_X \sigma_Y} = \frac{0.40}{\sqrt{(0.60)(0.60)}} = 0.667.$$

The two random variables exhibit a moderately strong positive correlation, that is, a tendency for happiness to be higher when family income is higher. Here is how R can do this calculation:

```
> probabilities <- c(0.2, 0.1, 0.0, 0.1, 0.2, 0.1, 0.0, 0.1, 0.2)
> x <- c(1, 1, 1, 2, 2, 2, 3, 3, 3); y <- c(1, 2, 3, 1, 2, 3, 1, 2, 3)   # scores
> library(wCorr)      # after entering install.packages("wCorr")
> weightedCorr(x, y, weights=probabilities)
[1] 0.6666667
```

2.7.3 Independence Implies Zero Correlation, but Not Converse

When two random variables are independent, just as the joint probability function factors into the product of marginal probability functions, so do expectations factor. For example, suppose X and Y have joint *pdf* $f(x,y)$ and marginal *pdf*'s $f_1(x)$ and $f_2(y)$, and $f(x,y) = f_1(x)f_2(y)$. Then,

$$
\begin{aligned}
E(XY) &= \int_y \int_x xy f(x,y)\,dx\,dy = \int_y \int_x xy f_1(x)f_2(y)\,dx\,dy \\
&= \left[\int_x x f_1(x)\,dx\right]\left[\int_y y f_2(y)\,dy\right] = [E(X)][E(Y)].
\end{aligned}
$$

Independence implies that $\text{cov}(X,Y) = E(XY) - [E(X)][E(Y)] = 0$, and therefore $\text{corr}(X,Y) = 0$.

Although independence implies $\text{corr}(X,Y) = 0$, *zero correlation does not imply independence*. For example, consider case (b) in Table 2.5. Given that family income is in category 2, a person necessarily has happiness in category 2. Given that family income is in category 1 or in category 3, happiness is equally likely to be in category 1 or category 3. The conditional distribution on happiness depends on the level of family income, so X and Y are not independent. Yet, you can verify that for the joint distribution in (b), $E(X) = 2$, $E(Y) = 2$, and $E(XY) = 4$, so $\text{cov}(X,Y) = 0$ and $\text{corr}(X,Y) = 0$. The correlation describes strength of a *linear* association, which case (b) does not exhibit.

Although zero correlation need not imply independence, an equivalence exists between the two conditions for some distributions. The most important case is the bivariate normal distribution, presented next. For it, zero correlation *does* imply independence. We will learn more about the correlation in Section 6.1.5.

2.7.4 Bivariate Normal Distribution *

Since the probability function of the conditional distribution relates to that of the joint distribution by $f(y \mid x) = f(x,y)/f_1(x)$, we can specify the joint distribution in terms of conditional and marginal distributions by $f(x,y) = f(y \mid x)f_1(x)$. Thus, we can randomly generate a value from the joint probability distribution of a bivariate random variable (X,Y) by randomly generating X from its marginal distribution and then generating Y from its conditional distribution, given that $X = x$. For example, suppose the 1000 students taking Freshman Calculus at a large state university have score X on the midterm exam that has a $N(70, 10^2)$ distribution. Given that $X = x$, suppose that the score Y on the final exam has

---

*Sections with an asterisk are optional.

a $N[70+0.60(x-70), 6^2]$ distribution. That is, $E(Y \mid x) = 70+0.60(x-70)$, so students who scored higher on the midterm tend to score higher on the final. We now use R to generate 1000 values from these distributions:

```
> x <- rnorm(1000, 70, 10) # simulate n=1000 from normal, mean = 70, standard dev. = 10
> y <- rnorm(1000, 70 + 0.6*(x - 70), 6) # E(Y | x) = 70 + 0.6*(x - 70)
> plot(x, y)
```

Figure 2.14 shows the 1000 values generated from the joint distribution for the midterm and final exam scores. This joint distribution is the *bivariate normal distribution*.

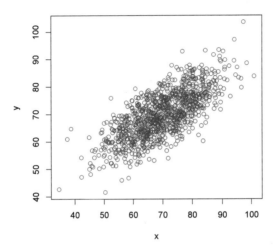

FIGURE 2.14 Simulation of the 1000 observations from a bivariate normal distribution for which a midterm exam score X has a $N(70, 10^2)$ distribution and the conditional distribution of the final exam score Y, given $X = x$, is $N[70 + 0.60(x - 70), 6^2]$.

▶ When a random variable X has a normal distribution and the conditional distribution of Y, given $X = x$, has a normal distribution with mean a linear function of x for a particular variance, then the joint probability distribution of (X,Y) is the *bivariate normal distribution*.

The *pdf* of a bivariate normal distribution has the appearance of a bell-shape in three-dimensional space. The *pdf* of (X,Y) is

$$f(x,y) = \frac{1}{2\pi\sigma_X\sigma_Y\sqrt{1-\rho^2}}e^{-\frac{1}{2(1-\rho^2)}\left[(\frac{x-\mu_X}{\sigma_X})^2-2\rho(\frac{x-\mu_X}{\sigma_X})(\frac{y-\mu_Y}{\sigma_Y})+(\frac{y-\mu_Y}{\sigma_Y})^2\right]}, \quad -\infty < x,y < \infty,$$

where $\rho = \mathrm{corr}(X,Y)$. The *pdf* plots as a surface in 3-dimensional space for which X has a bell shape at each value y of Y, Y has a bell shape at each value x of X, and its tilt reflects the sign and magnitude of the correlation (see Figure 2.15).

Dividing a bivariate normal *pdf* by the $N(\mu_X, \sigma_X^2)$ marginal *pdf* and doing some simplification yields the result that the *pdf* $f(y \mid x) = f(x,y)/f_1(x)$ of the conditional distribution of Y given $X = x$ is also normal. The mean of the normal conditional distribution is

$$E(Y \mid X = x) = \mu_Y + \rho\frac{\sigma_Y}{\sigma_X}(x - \mu_X).$$

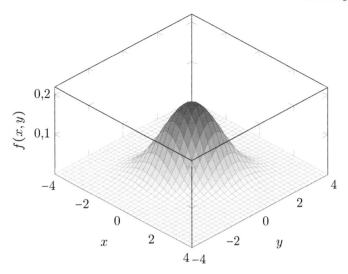

FIGURE 2.15 The *pdf* of a bivariate normal distribution.

Plotted as a function of x, $E(Y \mid X = x)$ is a straight line, with slope $\rho(\sigma_Y/\sigma_X)$ that is proportional to the correlation. When $\sigma_X = \sigma_Y$, the slope is exactly the correlation. At $x = \mu_X$, $E(Y \mid X = x) = \mu_Y$. Chapter 6 shows how to use sample data to estimate the correlation and equations of this type that describe the association between two quantitative variables.

Conditional distributions have higher moments as well as means. The variance of a conditional distribution is the expected squared distance from the conditional mean. The normal conditional distribution of Y given $X = x$ has variance

$$\sigma^2_{Y|X} = E[Y - E(Y \mid X)]^2 = E\{Y - [\mu_Y + \rho\frac{\sigma_Y}{\sigma_X}(X - \mu_X)]\}^2 = E\{(Y - \mu_Y) - [\rho\frac{\sigma_Y}{\sigma_X}(X - \mu_X)]\}^2$$

$$= E(Y - \mu_Y)^2 + \left(\rho\frac{\sigma_Y}{\sigma_X}\right)^2 E(X - \mu_X)^2 - 2\left(\rho\frac{\sigma_Y}{\sigma_X}\right)E(X - \mu_X)(Y - \mu_Y)$$

$$= \sigma^2_Y + \left(\rho\frac{\sigma_Y}{\sigma_X}\right)^2 \sigma^2_X - 2\left(\rho\frac{\sigma_Y}{\sigma_X}\right)\rho\sigma_X\sigma_Y = \sigma^2_Y(1 - \rho^2),$$

using that $E(X - \mu_X)(Y - \mu_Y) = \text{cov}(X, Y) = \rho\sigma_X\sigma_Y$. The variance $\sigma^2_Y(1 - \rho^2)$ of the conditional distribution of Y given X is smaller than the variance σ^2_Y of the marginal distribution of Y. The larger the value of $|\rho|$, the smaller the conditional variance. As $|\rho|$ approaches 1, the conditional variance approaches 0 and the joint bivariate normal distribution falls more tightly along a straight line.

The bivariate normal distribution extends to a ***multivariate normal distribution***. It has a mean and a standard deviation for each component random variable and a correlation for each pair of the random variables that describes their strength of association. Each marginal distribution is normal, the conditional distribution of one component given the others is normal, and any linear combination of the components (such as a difference between two of them) has a normal distribution. Many multivariate statistical methods are based on the assumption that the data come from a multivariate normal distribution.

2.8 Chapter Summary

For an observation in a random sample or a randomized experiment, the **probability** of a particular outcome is the proportion of times that the outcome would occur in a very long sequence of observations. Probabilities of **events** in a **sample space** satisfy rules such as:

- The **complement** probability of A *not* occurring is $P(A^c) = 1 - P(A)$.

- The **conditional probability** that A occurs, given that B occurs, is $P(A \mid B) = P(AB)/P(B)$, where AB is the event that both A and B occur.

- **Independent** events satisfy $P(AB) = P(A)P(B)$.

A **random variable** is a numerical measurement of the outcome of a random phenomenon.

- A **probability distribution** specifies probabilities for the possible values of a random variable by a **probability mass function** (*pmf*) for a *discrete* random variable and a **probability density function** (*pdf*) for a *continuous* random variable.

- A probability distribution has summary measures of the center and variability, called **expected values**. For instance, the mean and variance of a discrete random variable Y with probability mass function $f(y)$ are

$$\mu = E(Y) = \sum_y y f(y) \quad \text{and} \quad \sigma^2 = E(Y - \mu)^2 = \sum_y (y - \mu)^2 f(y).$$

The most important discrete probability distributions are:

- The **binomial distribution** specifies probabilities for the *number of successes* in n independent binary trials, when each trial has probability π of success.

- The **Poisson distribution** specifies probabilities for nonnegative counts of independent events that occur randomly over time or space with a certain rate.

The most important continuous probability distributions are:

- The **normal distribution** has a symmetric bell-shaped *pdf* specified by the mean μ and standard deviation σ. The probability is 0.68 within $\mu \pm \sigma$, 0.95 within $\mu \pm 2\sigma$, and nearly 1.0 within $\mu \pm 3\sigma$. The *standard normal distribution* has $\mu = 0$ and $\sigma = 1$.

- The **gamma distribution** has *pdf* that is skewed to the right over positive values. The **exponential distribution** is a special case for which the *pdf* has mode at 0 and continually decreases as y increases over the positive real line.

- The **uniform distribution** has constant *pdf* over some interval, such as [0, 1].

Table A.1 in the R Appendix lists these and other probability distributions used in this text and shows their parameters and their names in R.

   Joint probability distributions specify probabilities about joint values of two or more random variables. Two random variables are independent if this is completely determined by the **marginal distributions**. The **correlation** falls between −1 and +1 and describes the degree to which the joint distribution falls along a straight line, with independence implying a correlation of 0. A **conditional probability distribution** specifies probabilities about values of one random variable, conditional on values for the others.

Exercises

Data Analysis and Applications

2.1 For the rain simulation example in Section 2.1.1, but with probability of rain 0.30 on any given day, simulate the outcome (**a**) on the next day, (**b**) the next 10 days. (**c**) Simulate the proportion of days of rain for the next (i) 100 days, (ii) 10,000 days, (iii) 1,000,000 days. Use the simulation to explain the long-run relative frequency definition of probability.

2.2 Data analysts often implement statistical inference methods by setting the probability of a correct inference equal to 0.95. Let A denote the event that an inference for the population about men is correct. Let B represent the event of a corresponding inference about women being correct. Suppose that these are independent events.

    (a) Find the probability that (i) *both* inferences are correct, (ii) *neither* inference is correct.

    (b) Construct the probability distribution for Y = number of correct inferences.

    (c) With what probability would each inference need to be correct in order for the probability to be 0.95 that *both* are correct?

2.3 According to recent data at the FBI website, of all Blacks slain in the U.S., 85% are slain by Blacks, and of all Whites slain, 93% are slain by Whites. Let Y = victim's race and X = offender's race

    (a) Which conditional distribution do these probabilities refer to, Y given X, or X given Y?

    (b) Given that a murderer was White, what other probability do you need to estimate the conditional probability that the victim was White? To illustrate, fix a value of 0.60 for that other probability and find the conditional probability.

2.4 A wine connoisseur is asked to match five glasses of red wine with the bottles from which they came, representing five different grape types.

    (a) Set up a sample space for the five guesses.

    (b) With random guessing, find the probability of getting all five correct.

2.5 Suppose that a person is equally likely to be born on any of 365 days of the year.

    (a) For three people selected randomly, explain why the probability that they all have different birthdays is $[(365)(364)(363)]/365^3$.

    (b) Show that if at least 23 people attend a social party, the probability exceeds 0.50 that at least two people have the same birthday. State any further assumptions needed for your solution. (The R function **pbirthday(n)** gives the probability that at least 2 of n people have the same birthday.)

    (c) Use a simulation to show that if 50 people attend the party, the probability is 0.97 of at least one common birthday. (If results seem counterintuitive, notice how the number of *pairs* of attendees increases as the number of attendees n increases.)

2.6 Let Y denote the number of people known personally in one's lifetime who committed suicide. According to a recent General Social Survey, for a randomly chosen person in the U.S., the probability distribution of Y is approximately: $P(0) = 0.48, P(1) = 0.24, P(2) = 0.15, P(3) = 0.07, P(4) = 0.03, P(5) = 0.02, P(6) = 0.01$. Find the mean of the probability distribution. Using equation (2.3), find the standard deviation.

2.7 For the simulation at the end of Section 2.3.1, explain why you could also simulate the mean with a single binomial experiment of 30 million observations and probability 0.50 of a head for each, dividing by 10,000,000. Do this and compare the result to the theoretical expected value.

2.8 Each time a person shops at a grocery store, the event of catching a cold or some other virus from another shopper is independent from visit to visit and has a constant probability over the year, equal to 0.01.

(a) In 100 trips to this store over the course of a year, the probability of catching a virus while shopping there is $100(0.01) = 1.0$. What is wrong with this reasoning?

(b) Find the correct probability in (a).

2.9 A quiz has ten multiple-choice questions, with five possible answers for each. A student who is completely unprepared randomly guesses the answer for each question. Let Y denote the number of correct responses.

(a) Find the probability that the students gets (i) all 10, (ii) none of the questions correct.

(b) Find the mean and standard deviation of the probability distribution of Y.

2.10 A method of statistical inference has probability 0.05 of yielding an incorrect result. How many independent times can the method be used until the probability of all the inferences being correct is less than 0.50?

2.11 Show that for the binomial distribution to have absolute value of the skewness coefficient $< c$ for any particular $c > 0$ requires $n > (1 - 2\pi)^2/c^2\pi(1 - \pi)$. Show that when $\pi = 0.20$, having skewness < 0.3 (and thus close to a symmetric, bell shape) requires $n > 25$.

2.12 A basketball player has probability 0.80 of making any particular free throw (a standardized shot taken 15 feet from the basket).

(a) For a season with 200 free throw attempts, use the mean and standard deviation of a binomial distribution to state an interval within which the player has probability about 0.95 of making (i) that many free throws, (ii) that proportion of free throws. State any assumptions you make.

(b) When the player attempts n free throws, as n increases, would you expect the probability to increase, or to decrease, that the **(i)** *proportion* of successful free throws is between $0.80 - 0.05$ and $0.80 + 0.05$? **(ii)** *number* of successful free throws is between $0.80n - 5$ and $0.80n + 5$? Explain your answers.

2.13 In his autobiography *A Sort of Life*, British author Graham Greene described a period of severe mental depression during which he played Russian roulette—putting a bullet in one of the six chambers of a pistol, spinning the chambers to select one at random, and then firing the pistol once at his head.

(a) Greene states that he did this six times and was lucky that none of them resulted in a bullet firing. Find the probability of this outcome.

(b) Suppose he had kept playing this game until the bullet fired. Let Y denote the number of the game on which it fires. Find the *pmf* for Y. Of which family of probability distributions is this a member?

2.14 To assess the popularity of the prime minister in Italy, each of several sample surveys takes a simple random sample of 1000 people from the population of 40 million adults in Italy.

(a) With 10 surveys, find the probability that none sample a particular person, Vincenzo in the village of Ferrazzano in the region of Molise.

(b) How many surveys need to be taken for Vincenzo to have probability 0.5 of being in at least one of them?

(c) Report the probability distribution of Y = number of first survey that has Vincenzo in the sample.

2.15 Each week an insurance company records Y = number of payments because of a home burning down. State conditions under which we would expect Y to approximately have a Poisson distribution.

2.16 Each day a hospital records the number of people who come to the emergency room for treatment.

(a) In the first week, the observations from Sunday to Saturday are 10, 8, 14, 7, 21, 44, 60. Do you think that the Poisson distribution might describe the random variability of this phenomenon adequately. Why or why not?

(b) Would you expect the Poisson distribution to better describe, or more poorly describe, the number of weekly admissions to the hospital for a rare disease? Why?

2.17 An instructor gives a course grade of B to students who have total score on exams and homeworks between 800 and 900, where the maximum possible is 1000. If the total scores have approximately a normal distribution with mean 830 and standard deviation 50, about what proportion of the students receive a B?

2.18 Normal probabilities and percentiles:

(a) Find the z-value for which the probability that a normal variable exceeds $\mu + z\sigma$ equals (i) 0.01 (ii) 0.025 (iii) 0.05.

(b) Find the z-value such that for a normal distribution the interval from $\mu - z\sigma$ to $\mu + z\sigma$ contains probability (i) 0.90, (ii) 0.95, (iii) 0.99.

(c) Find the z-values such that $\mu + z\sigma$ is the (i) 75th, (ii) 95th, (iii) 99th percentile of a normal distribution.

(d) Show that the upper quartile equals $\mu + 0.6745\sigma$ and the interquartile range is IQR = 1.349σ.

2.19 Lake Wobegon Junior College admits students only if they score above 400 on a standardized achievement test. Applicants from group A have a mean of 500 and a standard deviation of 100 on this test, and applicants from group B have a mean of 450 and a standard deviation of 100. Both distributions are approximately normal, and both groups have the same size.

(a) Find the proportion not admitted for each group.

(b) Of the students who are not admitted, what proportion are from group B?

(c) A state legislator proposes that the college lower the cutoff point for admission to 300, thinking that the proportion of not-admitted students who are from group B would decrease. If this policy is implemented, determine the effect on the answer to (b).

2.20 Create a data file with the income values in the **Income** data file at the text website.

(a) Construct a histogram or a smooth-curve approximation for the *pdf* of income in the corresponding population by plotting results using the **density** function in R (explained in Exercise 1.18).

(b) Of the probability distributions studied in this chapter, which do you think might be most appropriate for these data? Why? Plot the probability function of that distribution having the same mean and standard deviation as the income values. Does it seem to describe the income distribution well?

2.21 Plot the gamma distribution by fixing the shape parameter $k = 3$ and setting the scale parameter = 0.5, 1, 2, 3, 4, 5. What is the effect of increasing the scale parameter? (See also Exercise 2.48.)

2.22 Consider the mammogram diagnostic example in Section 2.1.4.

(a) Show that the joint probability distribution of diagnosis and disease status is as shown in Table 2.6. Given that a diagnostic test result is positive, explain how this joint distribution shows that the 12% of incorrect diagnoses for the 99% of women not having breast cancer swamp the 86% of correct diagnoses for the 1% of women actually having breast cancer.

(b) The first test for detecting HIV-positive status had a sensitivity of 0.999 and specificity of 0.9999. Explain what these mean. If at that time 1 in 10,000 men were truly HIV-positive, find the positive predictive value. Based on this example, explain the potential disadvantage of routine diagnostic screening of a population for a rare disease.

TABLE 2.6 Joint probability distribution for disease status and diagnosis of breast cancer mammogram, based on conditional probabilities in Table 2.1

Disease	Diagnosis from Mammogram		
Status	Positive (+)	Negative (−)	Total
Yes (D)	0.0086	0.0014	0.01
No (D^c)	0.1188	0.8712	0.99

2.23 The `Afterlife` data file at the book's website contains data from the 2018 General Social Survey on postlife = belief in the afterlife (1 = yes, 2 = no) and religion (1 = Protestant, 2 = Catholic, 3 = Jewish, other categories excluded). Using these data, form a contingency table and use it to illustrate sample versions of a joint distribution, marginal distributions, and conditional distribution of postlife given religion.

2.24 Consider the jury list example in Section 2.6.4, but with $(\pi_1, \pi_2, \pi_3) = (0.25, 0.25, 0.50)$ for (Hispanic, African-American, White).

   (a) With $n = 12$, the expected counts are (3, 3, 6). Use the multinomial distribution to find the probability of this result.

   (b) Suppose the 12 chosen for a trial had 10 Whites. With random selection, would this be unlikely? Answer based on the probability that *at least* ten Whites would be chosen.

2.25 For the example in Section 2.7.4 in which a midterm exam score X has a $N(70, 10^2)$ distribution and the conditional distribution of the final exam score Y given $X = x$ is $N(70+0.60(x-70), 6^2)$, use the formula $E(Y) = E[E(Y \mid X)]$ to find $E(Y)$.

2.26 Refer to Table 2.4 cross classifying happiness with family income.

   (a) Find and interpret the correlation using scores (i) (1, 2, 3) for each variable, (ii) (1, 2, 3) for family income and (1, 4, 5) for happiness.

   (b) Construct the joint distribution that has these marginal distributions and exhibits independence of X and Y.

2.27 The distribution of X = heights (*cm*) of women in the U.K. is approximately $N(162, 7^2)$. Conditional on $X = x$, suppose Y = weight (*kg*) has a $N(3.0+0.40x, 8^2)$ distribution. Simulate and plot 1000 observations from this approximate bivariate normal distribution. Approximate the marginal means and standard deviations for X and Y. Approximate and interpret the correlation.

Methods and Concepts

2.28 Show the **rule of total probability**: If a sample space S partitions into disjoint events $B_1, \ldots, B_c$ (the union of which is S), then $P(A) = P(A \mid B_1)P(B_1) + \cdots + P(A \mid B_c)P(B_c)$.

2.29 **De Morgan's law** states, for the case of two events, $(A \cup B)^c = A^c B^c$. Show this with a Venn diagram, and explain how the law generalizes to p events $A_1, \ldots, A_p$.

2.30 For discrete random variables X and Y, derive the following generalization of Bayes' Theorem (Section 2.1.5):

$$P(X = x \mid Y = y) = \frac{P(Y = y \mid X = x)P(X = x)}{\sum_a P(Y = y \mid X = a)P(X = a)},$$

where the denominator sum is over all the possible values a for X. State the corresponding result for $P(B_j \mid A)$ for an event A and a sample space that partitions into disjoint events $\{B_1, \ldots, B_c\}$.

2.31 For continuous random variables, formulate a version of Bayes' Theorem to obtain $f(x \mid y)$ from the functions $f(y \mid x)$ and $f_1(x)$.

2.32 On a multiple-choice exam, with k possible responses for each question, a student knows the answer with probability π and has to guess the answer randomly with probability $(1-\pi)$. Given that a student correctly answers a question, find the probability they truly knew the answer. Evaluate the expression you derive when $k = 5$ and π is (i) 0.90, (ii) 0.10.

2.33 For discrete random variables X and Y, suppose $P(Y = y \mid X = x) = P(Y = y)$ for all possible values x of X and y of Y. Show that $P(X = x \mid Y = y) = P(X = x)$ for all those values.

2.34 If events A and B are independent, then are A and B^c independent, or dependent? Show which is the case.

2.35 Although an observation of a continuous random variable is a particular value, explain why each possible value has probability 0. Justify this in the context of the relative frequency interpretation of probability.

2.36 Let X be a uniform distribution over $[L, U]$ with $L < U$.

  (a) Specify the *pdf* of X and find $E(X)$.

  (b) From Section 2.3.3, a uniform random variable Y over $[0, 1]$ has mean $1/2$ and standard deviation $1/\sqrt{12}$. Express X as a linear function of Y and use this relation and results in Section 2.3.5 about expectations of linear functions of random variables to find μ and σ for the distribution of X.

  (c) Report μ and σ when X = SAT (Scholastic Aptitude Test) score has a uniform distribution between 200 and 800. Check your answer by finding $\bar{x}$ and s for a million randomly generated observations from this distribution.

2.37 For independent observations with probability of success π on each, specify the probability mass function of Y = number of failures until the first success.[27]

2.38 For a geometric random variable with probability function (2.1), show that (**a**) the *cdf* is $F(y) = 1 - (1-\pi)^y$ for $y = 1, 2, \ldots$; (**b**) $E(Y) = 1/\pi$.

2.39 For the Poisson distribution, show that $E[Y(Y-1)] = \mu^2$. Use this to show that $E(Y^2) = \mu + \mu^2$ and thus $\text{var}(Y) = \mu$.

2.40 Let Y be your waiting time in a line at a grocery store. Let Y_1, Y_2, ... be the waiting times of other people. Let N = the number of people that must be in lines at the store until someone has to wait longer than you. If the waiting times are independent and have the same continuous probability distribution, explain why (**a**) $P(N > n) = P(Y > \max(Y_1, \ldots, Y_n)) = 1/(n+1)$, for $n = 1, 2, \ldots$; (**b**) $E(N) = \infty$.

2.41 Use formula (2.8) for the normal *pdf* to show that the *pdf* is symmetric.

2.42 Show that the binomial probability mass function (2.6) converges to the Poisson when you substitute $\pi = \mu/n$ and let $n \to \infty$ with μ fixed.

2.43 Consider the exponential *pdf* $f(y; \lambda) = \lambda e^{-\lambda y}$ and *cdf* $F(y; \lambda) = 1 - e^{-\lambda y}$, for $y \geq 0$.

  (a) Find the median.

  (b) Find the lower quartile and the upper quartile.

  (c) Find μ by showing that it equals $1/\lambda$ times the integral of a gamma *pdf*. Explain why μ is greater than the median.

  (d) Find σ by finding $E(Y^2)$ using a gamma *pdf* and using expression (2.3).

2.44 For the gamma *pdf* (2.10), find $E(Y^2)$ and use it together with $\mu = k/\lambda$ to find $\text{var}(Y)$.

---

[27]This is an alternative formulation of the *geometric distribution*.

2.45 Reparameterizing the gamma distribution by replacing λ by k/μ, show that

$$f(y; k, \mu) = \frac{(k/\mu)^k}{\Gamma(k)} e^{-ky/\mu} y^{k-1}, \ y \ge 0 \tag{2.17}$$

For this parameterization, show that the expressions in (2.11) simplify to $E(Y) = \mu$ and $\sigma = \mu/\sqrt{k}$. So, for fixed k, as the mean grows, so does the standard deviation. This is the case in practice for many positively-valued variables, such as income, in which groups with larger mean also tend to have larger standard deviation.

2.46 Section 2.5.5 showed that the waiting time T for the first occurrence of a Poisson process has the exponential distribution with parameter λ. For this distribution, show that $P(T > u + t \mid T > u) = P(T > t)$. By this *memoryless* property, if an event has not occurred by time u, the additional time needed to observe an occurrence is the same as if we started to observe the process at time 0.

2.47 When a probability function is symmetric and its moments exist, explain why $E(Y - \mu)^3 = 0$, so the skewness coefficient $= 0$.

2.48 A probability distribution has a *scale parameter* θ if, when you multiply θ by a constant c, all values in the distribution multiply by c. It has a *location parameter* θ if, when you increase θ by a constant c, all values in the distribution increase by c.

   (a) For a scale parameter θ, the distribution of Y/θ does not depend on θ. Show that for the gamma distribution (2.10) with $\theta = 1/\lambda$, Y/θ has mean and variance not dependent on θ.

   (b) For a location parameter θ, the *pdf* is a function of $y - \theta$ and the distribution of $Y - \theta$ does not depend on θ. For a normal distribution, show that μ is a location parameter.

2.49 Section 2.4.5 showed that for a binom(n, π) random variable, the sample proportion $\hat{\pi}$ has standard deviation $\sqrt{\pi(1 - \pi)/n}$. Use this to explain why $\hat{\pi}$ tends to be closer to π as n increases. Thus, in the rain simulation in Section 2.1.1, the relative frequency for a particular outcome converges as n increases to a number that we regard as the probability of that outcome.

2.50 The **Markov inequality** states that when $P(Y \ge 0) = 1$, then $P(Y \ge t) \le E(Y)/t$.

   (a) When Y is discrete over the nonnegative integers, prove this by explaining why $E(Y) \ge \sum_{y \ge t} yf(y) \ge \sum_{y \ge t} tf(y) = tP(Y \ge t)$.

   (b) If X is any random variable with mean μ and variance σ^2, apply the Markov inequality with $Y = (X - \mu)^2$ to prove **Chebyshev's inequality** that $P(|X - \mu| \ge k\sigma) \le 1/k^2$.

   (c) Consider $k = 1$ in Chebyshev's inequality. Specify a probability distribution for which $P(|X - \mu| \ge \sigma) = 1$.

2.51 By **Jensen's inequality**, convex functions satisfy $E[g(Y)] \ge g[E(Y)]$. Use this to prove that for concave functions, $E[g(Y)] \le g[E(Y)]$. Apply the appropriate cases to $\log(Y)$ and $1/Y$ for a positively-valued random variable Y.

2.52 The *pdf* f of a $N(\mu, \sigma^2)$ distribution can be derived from the standard normal *pdf* ϕ shown in equation (2.9).

   (a) Show that the normal *cdf* F relates to the standard normal *cdf* Φ by $F(y) = \Phi[(y - \mu)/\sigma]$.

   (b) From (a), show that $f(y) = (1/\sigma)\phi[(y - \mu)/\sigma]$, and show this is equation (2.8).

2.53 If Y is a standard normal random variable, with *cdf* Φ, what is the probability distribution of $X = \Phi(Y)$? Illustrate by randomly generating a million standard normal random variables, applying the *cdf* function $\Phi()$ to each, and plotting histograms of the (a) y values, (b) x values.

2.54 Review the result about the "probability integral transformation" in Section 2.5.7. For a continuous random variable Y with *cdf* F, find the probability distribution of the right-tail probability $X = 1 - F(Y)$. (We'll learn the relevance of this when Chapter 5 introduces P-values.)

2.55 Suppose that conditional on λ, the distribution of Y is Poisson with mean parameter λ, but λ itself varies among different segments of a population, with $\mu = E(\lambda)$. Use the law of iterated expectation to find $E(Y)$.

2.56 Consider the multinomial distribution (2.14) with $c = 3$ categories.

    (a) Explain why the marginal distribution of Y_1 is binomial. Based on this, report $E(Y_1)$ and var(Y_1).

    (b) Are Y_1 and Y_2 independent random variables? Why or why not?

2.57 Let $(Y_1, Y_2, \ldots, Y_c)$ denote independent Poisson random variables, with parameters $(\mu_1, \mu_2, \ldots, \mu_c)$.

    (a) Explain why the joint probability mass function for $\{Y_i\}$ is

$$\prod_{i=1}^{c} [\exp(-\mu_i)\mu_i^{y_i}/y_i!]$$

    for all nonnegative integer values $(y_1, y_2, \ldots, y_c)$.

    (b) Section 3.2.6 explains that the sum $n = \sum_i Y_i$ also has a Poisson distribution, with parameter $\sum_i \mu_i$. For independent Poisson random variables, if we condition on n, explain why $\{Y_i\}$ are no longer independent and no longer have Poisson distributions.

    (c) Show that the conditional probability of $\{y_i\}$, conditional on $\sum_i y_i = n$, is the *multinomial* (2.14), characterized by the sample size n and probabilities $\{\pi_i = \mu_i/(\sum_j \mu_j)\}$.

2.58 A balanced coin is flipped twice. Let X denote the outcome of the first flip and Y denote the outcome of the second flip, representing *head* by 1 and *tail* by 0. Suppose the flips are independent.

    (a) Let Z indicate whether both flips had the same result, with $z = 1$ for *yes* and $z = 0$ for *no*. Show that X and Z are independent.

    (b) Show that although X and Y are independent, X and Z are independent, and Y and Z are independent, X, Y, and Z are not mutually independent. So, if a set of random variables are *pairwise independent*, they are not necessarily *mutually independent*.

2.59 Explain how a board game using dice, such as "Snakes and Ladders," has a sequence of outcomes that satisfies the Markov property.

2.60 For n coin-flip bets as described in Section 2.6.7, let p_n denote the proportion of t between 1 and n for which the total winnings Y_t at time t is positive.

    (a) With $n = 100$, simulate this Markov chain a few times, each time showing a plot of $(y_1, y_2, \ldots, y_{100})$ and reporting p_n.

    (b) Now simulate this Markov chain 100,000 times. Construct a histogram of the 100,000 $\{p_n\}$ values and describe the distribution. (As n increases, p_n has a limiting beta distribution (Exercise 2.70) with $\alpha = \beta = 0.5$, so $1/2$ has the lowest density for p_n!)

2.61 Contruct an example of a Markov chain, and use simulation to randomly generate 100 values from it. Plot the sequence and describe how the Markov property affects the plot.

2.62 For independent binom$(1, \pi)$ random variables X and Y, let $U = X + Y$ and $V = X - Y$. Find the joint probability distribution of U and V. Show that U and V are uncorrelated but not independent.

2.63 Consider two random variables X and Y:

    (a) Show that var$(X + Y) =$ var$(X) +$ var$(Y) + 2$cov(X, Y).

    (b) Show that var$(X - Y) =$ var$(X) +$ var$(Y) - 2$cov(X, Y).

    (c) Show how (a) and (b) simplify when X and Y are uncorrelated.

2.64 Bounds for the correlation:

(a) Consider random variables X and Y and their standardized variables Z_x and Z_y. Using the equations from the previous exercise and the relation between the correlation and covariance, show that $\text{var}(Z_x + Z_y) \geq 0$ implies that $\text{corr}(X,Y) \geq -1$ and $\text{var}(Z_x - Z_y) \geq 0$ implies[28] $\text{corr}(X,Y) \leq +1$.

(b) When the joint distribution is such that necessarily $X = Y$, show that $\text{corr}(X,Y) = 1$.

2.65 For uncorrelated random variables U, V, and W, let $X = U + V$ and $Y = U + W$.

(a) Show that $\text{cov}(X,Y) = \text{var}(U)$ and

$$\text{corr}(X,Y) = \frac{\text{var}(U)}{\sqrt{[\text{var}(U) + \text{var}(V)][\text{var}(U) + \text{var}(W)]}}.$$

(b) For some scaling, suppose X = math achievement test score, Y = verbal achievement test score, U = intelligence (e.g., IQ), V = time studying math, W = time studying verbal. Explain how $\text{corr}(X,Y)$ changes as $\text{var}(U)$ increases, for fixed $\text{var}(V)$ and $\text{var}(W)$.

2.66 Moments of a distribution can be derived by differentiating the ***moment generating function*** (*mgf*),

$$m(t) = E(e^{tY}).$$

This function provides an alternative way to specify a distribution.

(a) Show that the kth derivative $m^{(k)}(t) = E(Y^k e^{tY})$, and hence $m'(0) = E(Y)$ and $m''(0) = E(Y^2)$.

(b) Show that the *mgf* is $m(t) = 1 + tE(Y) + \frac{t^2}{2!}E(Y^2) + \frac{t^3}{3!}E(Y^3) + \cdots$.

(c) Show that the *mgf* for the Poisson distribution is $m(t) = \exp[\mu(e^t - 1)]$. Use it to find the mean and variance.

(d) The *mgf* for the normal distribution is $m(t) = e^{\mu t + \sigma^2 t^2/2}$. Use it to find the mean and variance.

2.67 For n observations $\{y_i\}$, let $y_{(1)} \leq y_{(2)} \leq \cdots \leq y_{(n)}$ denote their ordered values, called ***order statistics***. Let q_i be the $i/(n+1)$ quantile of the standard normal distribution, for $i = 1, \ldots, n$. When $\{y_i\}$ are a random sample from a normal distribution, the plot of the points $(q_1, y_{(1)}), \ldots, (q_n, y_{(n)})$ should approximately follow a straight line, more closely so when n is large. This ***normal quantile plot*** is a special case of a ***quantile-quantile (Q-Q) plot***. The R appendix of this book presents details.

(a) Randomly generate (i) $n = 10$, (ii) $n = 100$, (iii) $n = 1000$ observations from a $N(0,1)$ distribution and construct the normal quantile plot each time, using software such as the R functions `rnorm` and `qqnorm`. Note that as n increases the points cluster more tightly along the line $y = x$, which you can add to the plot with command `abline(0, 1)`.

(b) Randomly generate 1000 observations from a $N(100, 16^2)$ distribution of IQ's and construct the normal quantile plot. What is the slope of the line approximating these points?

(c) Randomly generate 1000 observations from the (i) exponential distribution (2.2), (ii) uniform distribution over $(0, 1)$, using software such as the R functions `rexp` and `runif`. Construct the normal quantile plot in each case. Explain how they reveal the non-normality of the data.

(d) For case (ii) in (c), find appropriate uniform quantiles for which the Q-Q plot would be approximately linear. Construct the plot.

2.68 A population has F females and M males. For a random sample of size n without replacement, explain why the *pmf* for Y = number of females in the sample is

$$f(y; F, M, n) = \frac{\binom{F}{y}\binom{M}{n-y}}{\binom{F+M}{n}}, \quad \max(0, n - M) \leq y \leq \min(n, F). \tag{2.18}$$

---

[28]This also follows from the *Cauchy–Schwarz inequality* $|E(XY)| \leq \sqrt{[E(X)^2][E(Y)^2]}$.

This is called the **hypergeometric distribution**. It is an alternative to the binomial for which successive trials are not independent, because the probability of a particular outcome depends on the previous selections.

2.69 For a sequence of independent, identical binary trials, explain why the probability distribution for Y = the number of successes before failure number k occurs has probability function

$$f(y; k, \pi) = \binom{y + k - 1}{y} \pi^y (1 - \pi)^k, \quad y = 0, 1, 2, \dots . \tag{2.19}$$

This distribution, studied further in Section 7.5.2 for analyzing count data, is called the **negative binomial distribution**.

2.70 The **beta distribution** is a probability distribution over $(0, 1)$ that is often used in applications for which the random variable is a proportion. The beta *pdf* is

$$f(y; \alpha, \beta) = \frac{\Gamma(\alpha + \beta)}{\Gamma(\alpha)\Gamma(\beta)} y^{\alpha - 1} (1 - y)^{\beta - 1}, \quad 0 \le y \le 1, \tag{2.20}$$

for parameters α and β, where $\Gamma(\cdot)$ denotes the gamma function.

(a) Show that the uniform distribution is the special case $\alpha = \beta = 1$.

(b) Show that $\mu = E(Y) = \alpha/(\alpha + \beta)$.

(c) Find $E(Y^2)$. Show that $\text{var}(Y) = \alpha\beta/(\alpha + \beta)^2(\alpha + \beta + 1) = \mu(1 - \mu)/(\alpha + \beta + 1)$. For fixed $\alpha + \beta$, note that $\text{var}(Y)$ decreases as μ approaches 0 or 1.

(d) Using a function such as **dbeta** in R, plot the beta *pdf* for (i) $\alpha = \beta = 0.5, 1.0, 10, 100$, (ii) some values of $\alpha > \beta$ and some values of $\alpha < \beta$. Describe the impact of α and β on the shape and spread.

2.71 When Y has positively skewed distribution over the positive real line, statistical analyses often treat $X = \log(Y)$ as having a $N(\mu, \sigma^2)$ distribution. Then Y is said to have the **log-normal distribution**.

(a) Derive an expression for the *cdf* G of Y in terms of the *cdf* F of X, and take the derivative to obtain the *pdf* g of Y.

(b) Use the information given in Exercise 2.66 about the *mgf* of a normal random variable to show that $E(Y) = e^{\mu + \sigma^2/2}$ and $\text{var}(Y) = [e^{\sigma^2} - 1][E(Y)]^2$. As shown for the gamma distribution in Exercise 2.45, the log-normal has standard deviation proportional to the mean.

(c) Explain why the median of the distribution of Y is e^μ. What do the mean and median suggest about the skewness of the distribution?

(d) For independent observations $y_1, \dots, y_n$ from the log-normal, we could summarize the distribution by finding $\bar{x}$ for $\{x_i = \log(y_i)\}$ and then using $\exp(\bar{x})$. Show that $\exp(\bar{x}) = (\prod_i y_i)^{1/n}$, the *geometric mean* of $\{y_i\}$.

2.72 Like the gamma and log-normal distributions, the **Weibull distribution** is positively skewed over the positive real line. With shape parameter $k > 0$ and scale parameter $\lambda > 0$, its *cdf* is $F(y; \lambda, k) = 1 - e^{-(y/\lambda)^k}$ for $y > 0$.

(a) Find the *pdf*.

(b) Show that the median $= \lambda[\log(2)]^{1/k}$. (The mean and standard deviation are also proportional to λ. As k increases for fixed λ, the mean decreases toward λ and the median increases toward λ.)

(c) Plot the Weibull *pdf* for $\lambda = 1$ and $k = 1, 2, 4$ (e.g., using the **dweibull** function in R). Describe the influence of k on the shape, and explain why the mode is 0 if $k \le 1$.

(d) The Weibull is often used in reliability studies to model the life-length of a product before it fails. Over time, the failure rate of the product increases (stays the same, decreases) when $k > 1$ ($k = 1$, $k < 1$). Which distribution does the Weibull simplify to when $k = 1$?

2.73 The **Pareto distribution**, introduced by the Italian economist Wilfredo Pareto in 1909 to describe (on appropriate scales) income and wealth, is a highly positively-skewed distribution that has *pdf* $f(y;\alpha) = \alpha/y^{\alpha+1}$ for $y \geq 1$ and a parameter $\alpha > 0$.

(a) Show that f is a legitimate *pdf* (i.e., nonnegative and integrating to 1).

(b) Find $E(Y)$ for $\alpha > 1$.

(c) The **power-law distribution** is a corresponding discrete distribution that has *pmf* $f(y;\alpha) = c/y^{\alpha+1}$ for $y = 1,2,3,\ldots$, where c is the constant for which the probabilities sum to 1. Explain why no constant c exists such that $f(y) = c/y$ is a *pmf* or *pdf*. (Cases with $\alpha \approx 1$ describe many phenomena, including musical measures of success such as the number of live performances of musical compositions that have had at least one performance and the number of plays per week on a streaming service of songs played at least once.[29])

2.74 Like the gamma distribution, the log-normal distribution (Exercise 2.71), the Weibull distribution (Exercise 2.72), and the Pareto distibution (Exercise 2.73), another distribution for skewed-right variables is the **Gumbel distribution**, also called the *type I extreme-value distribution*. Often used to model the distribution of the maximum of a set of random variables (such as the highest level of a river over a period of a year), it has *cdf*

$$F(y;\theta_1,\theta_2) = \exp\{-\exp[-(y-\theta_1)/\theta_2]\}, \quad -\infty < y < \infty,$$

for parameters $\theta_2 > 0$ and $-\infty < \theta_1 < \infty$. The mode = θ_1, mean = $\theta_1 + 0.577\theta_2$, and standard deviation = $1.283\theta_2$. Plot this distribution (e.g., using the **dgumbel** function in the **VGAM** package in **R**) for various values of θ_1 with θ_2 fixed and various values of θ_2 with θ_1 fixed to illustrate that θ_1 is a *location parameter* and θ_2 is a *scale parameter* (Exercise 2.48).

[29] For details, see 2019 article by A. J. Gustar in *Empirical Musicology Review* at https://emusicology.org/article/view/7003.

3

Sampling Distributions

Chapter 2 introduced *probability distributions*, which summarize probabilities of possible values for a random variable. Before the data are gathered, any *statistic* is a random variable. It has a set of possible values, and in a study employing randomization, a probability distribution applies to them. This chapter introduces probability distributions for statistics, which are called *sampling distributions*. Chapters 4 and 5 show that sampling distributions provide the basis for evaluating how precisely statistics estimate population parameters.

The *sampling distribution of the sample mean* enables us to evaluate how close it is likely to be to the population mean. The *law of large numbers* states that the sample mean converges to the population mean as the sample size increases. The main reason for the importance of the normal distribution is the *Central Limit Theorem*, a remarkable result stating that with studies employing randomization, the sample mean has approximately a normal sampling distribution. The *delta method* shows that sampling distributions of many statistics other than the sample mean are also approximately normal.

3.1 Sampling Distributions: Probability Distributions for Statistics

The value of any particular statistic varies according to the sample chosen. The next example shows that, with randomization, a probability distribution for the possible values of a statistic enables us to evaluate how far the actual sample outcome of that statistic is likely to fall from the population parameter that it estimates.

3.1.1 Example: Predicting an Election Result from an Exit Poll

For major elections, television networks use exit polls of voters to help them predict winners well before all the votes are counted. For the 2020 Presidential election in the U.S. with Democratic candidate Joe Biden and Republican candidate Donald Trump, in an exit poll of California voters,[1] 65.5% reported voting for Biden. About 17 million people voted in California. The exit poll sampled only 2271 voters, yet based mainly on it, soon after the polls closed in California, TV networks predicted that Biden would win that state and gets its Electoral College votes (which are the votes that determines the national winner of the election). How could this exit poll of only 0.01% of all voters in California possibly give enough information to predict the winner in that state?

To judge whether 65.5% voting for Biden is sufficiently high that we can predict he will win, we might ask, "Suppose that only *half* the population of voters in California voted for Biden, and the other half voted for Trump. Would it then be very unusual that 65.5% of an

---

[1]www.cnn.com/election/2020/exit-polls shows results of exit polls conducted by Edison Research for a news consortium made up of CNN, ABC News, CBS News, and NBC News.

DOI: 10.1201/9781003159834-3

exit-poll sample would vote for Biden?" If so, we can infer that Biden received *more* than half the population votes in California. A *simulation* can help us to answer this question. The sampling method for an exit poll is much more complex than simple random sampling, but for simplicity we'll regard it as such for this example. To simulate the votes of 2271 voters randomly chosen from the population, we'll use R to perform a binomial experiment with sample size $n = 2271$ and probability $\pi = 0.50$ of voting for Biden.

```
> rbinom(1, 2271, 0.50)    # 1 binomial experiment with n = 2271, pi = 0.50
[1] 1121                   # binomial random variable outcome = 1121 Biden votes
> 1121/2271                # 0.494 = simulated proportion of Biden votes when pi = 0.50
[1] 0.4936151
```

Of the 2271 voters in the simulation, 1121 voted for Biden, a sample proportion of $1121/2271 = 0.494$, quite close to the presumed population proportion of 0.50.

We next performed this process of sampling 2271 people a million times, so we could investigate variability in the results:

```
> results <- rbinom(1000000, 2271, 0.50)/2271   # million sample proportions,
> mean(results); sd(results)                     # each having n = 2271 and pi = 0.50
[1] 0.5000219      # the mean of the million sample proportion values
[1] 0.0105048      # the standard deviation of the million sample proportions
> hist(results)    # histogram of the million sample proportions
```

Figure 3.1 shows a histogram of the million simulated sample proportion values. Nearly all fell between 0.46 and 0.54, that is, within 0.04 of the presumed population proportion of 0.50.

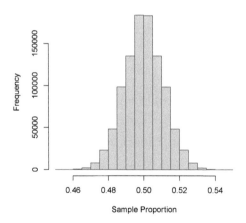

FIGURE 3.1 Histogram of one million simulations of the sample proportion favoring the Democratic candidate, for simple random samples of 2271 subjects from a population in which exactly half voted for the Democrat.

In summary, if half the population of voters had voted for Biden, we would have expected between about 46% and 54% of voters in an exit poll of size 2271 to have voted for him. So, it would have been extremely unusual to observe 65.5% voting for him, as happened in the actual exit poll. If *less than half* the population voted for Biden, it would have been even more unusual. Therefore we can predict, based on the exit poll, that Biden received more than half of the votes in California in the 2020 election.

It is possible to perform this simulation using any population proportion value. From results of the next section, for a random sample of size 2271, the sample proportion is very likely to fall within 0.04 of the population proportion regardless of its value. But we conclude this example with an important caveat: These days simple random sampling of the population of voters is not feasible in taking a sample survey about an election. It is difficult to construct a list of the population of people who plan to vote that is representative of all socioeconomic groups and political persuasions, a very high percentage of the potential respondents who are contacted by phone may refuse to participate (nearly 95% in many polls), those who do respond may be more likely to favor a particular candidate, and the likelihood that a person polled actually votes is uncertain. An exit poll cannot be conducted solely of election-day voters, as many people now choose to vote early or by mail. In Presidential elections in the U.S. in 2016 and 2020, polls in some states taken shortly before elections had errors quite a bit larger than the margins of error expected with simple random sampling.[2] How to obtain a sample that has the properties of a simple random sample of the relevant population is a strong challenge for polling organizations that aim to achieve better performance in the future.

3.1.2 Sampling Distribution: Variability of a Statistic's Value among Samples

Voter preference is a variable, varying among voters. Likewise, the sample proportion having a particular outcome or a sample mean in a survey or an experiment is a random variable: Before the sample is obtained, its value is unknown, and that value varies from sample to sample. If several random samples of size n each were selected, a certain predictable amount of variation would occur in the sample proportion or mean values. A probability distribution with appearance similar to Figure 3.1 describes the variation that occurs from repeatedly selecting random samples of a certain size n and forming a particular statistic. This distribution is called a ***sampling distribution***. It provides probabilities of the possible values of the statistic for a *single* sample of size n.

Sampling distribution

A ***sampling distribution*** of a statistic is the probability distribution that specifies probabilities for the possible values of the statistic.

For a particular design for collecting the data, each sample statistic has a sampling distribution. The sample mean has a sampling distribution, and so does the sample proportion, the sample median, and so forth. Unlike the probability distributions studied so far, a sampling distribution specifies probabilities not for individual observations but for possible values of a statistic computed from the observations. Sampling distributions are important in inferential statistics because they help us evaluate how close a statistic is likely to fall to the parameter it estimates. Figure 3.1 suggests that with a simple random sample of size 2271, the probability is close to 1.0 that a sample proportion falls within 0.04 of the population proportion, even if the population has enormous size compared with the sample.

---

[2]The sites `www.nytimes.com/2020/11/12/us/politics/election-polls-trump-biden.html` and `www.cnn.com/2020/11/02/politics/exit-polls-2020-pandemic` discussed polling issues for these elections.

3.1.3   Constructing a Sampling Distribution

It is often possible to approximate a sampling distribution by simulation, as in Figure 3.1. In practice, the form of a sampling distribution is often known theoretically or can be constructed exactly under some scenario, as the next example shows.

Consider first a random sample of $n = 4$ voters, an unrealistic but simple case. For each voter, let

$$y = 1 \text{ represent a vote for the Democratic candidate}$$
$$y = 0 \text{ represent a vote for the Republican candidate.}$$

Let (y_1, y_2, y_3, y_4) represent results for the sample. For instance, $(1, 0, 0, 1)$ represents a sample in which the first and fourth subjects voted for the Democrat and the second and third subjects voted for the Republican. The 16 possible samples are:

$$
\begin{array}{llll}
(1, 1, 1, 1) & (1, 1, 1, 0) & (1, 1, 0, 1) & (1, 0, 1, 1) \\
(0, 1, 1, 1) & (1, 1, 0, 0) & (1, 0, 1, 0) & (1, 0, 0, 1) \\
(0, 1, 1, 0) & (0, 1, 0, 1) & (0, 0, 1, 1) & (1, 0, 0, 0) \\
(0, 1, 0, 0) & (0, 0, 1, 0) & (0, 0, 0, 1) & (0, 0, 0, 0)
\end{array}
$$

If truly half the population voted for each candidate, the 16 samples are equally likely. The *proportion* of the sample that voted for the Democrat can be 0.0, 0.25, 0.50, 0.75, or 1.0. The proportion 0 occurs with only one of the 16 possible samples, $(0, 0, 0, 0)$, so its probability equals $1/16 = 0.0625$. This is merely the binomial probability of count outcome 0 when $n = 4$ and $\pi = 0.50$. The sampling distribution for the *number* voting Democrat is the binomial distribution with $n = 4$ and $\pi = 0.50$, and the sampling distribution for the *proportion* divides each possible count by 4. Figure 3.2 shows the sampling distribution for the *proportion* voting Democrat and the corresponding binomial distribution for the *number* voting Democrat. Corresponding sampling distributions and binomial distributions apply for *any* sample size n and *any* value π for the population proportion voting for the Democrat.

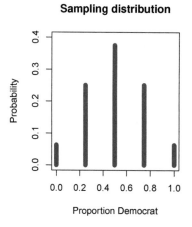
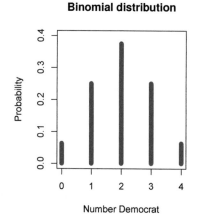

FIGURE 3.2 Sampling distribution of sample *proportion* voting Democrat for random samples of size $n = 4$ when $\pi = 0.50$, and corresponding binomial distribution of the *number* voting Democrat.

The proportion of times that 1 occurs is the sample mean of the 0 and 1 data values. For instance, for the sample (0, 1, 0, 0), the proportion voting Democrat is 1/4, and the sample mean equals $(0 + 1 + 0 + 0)/4 = 1/4 = 0.25$. The sampling distribution of a sample proportion is a special case of a sampling distribution of a sample mean.

3.1.4 Example: Simulating to Estimate Mean Restaurant Sales

In Section 3.1.1 we used simulation to construct a sampling distribution of a sample proportion. We can also do this with summary statistics for quantitative variables. We illustrate next for the sample mean and later in the chapter for the sample median.

An entrepreneur who plans to open a new restaurant would like feedback about typical per-customer sales if the restaurant uses a particular dinner menu that she has designed. She plans to sample 25 friends who she believes are comparable to a random sample of people who would attend the restaurant. She will ask each of them to look at the test version of the menu and pick the items they would order at the restaurant, keeping in mind their typical budget for eating out. She would use the sample mean of the bills for their 25 orders as an indication of typical per-customer sales. She is unsure whether a sample size of 25 is sufficient for the sample mean sales to estimate well a corresponding conceptual population mean sales μ, which is the number she'd like to know to determine whether to adopt that test menu. Before obtaining data, she surmises that μ (in U.S. dollars) would likely be about $20 to $24 and that the per-customer sales would likely be skewed to the right and vary quite a bit, from about $8 to $30 or $40.

To give her some helpful information about how precise her sample mean estimate $\overline{Y}$ from 25 friends is likely to be in estimating μ, we conduct a simulation. The sampling distribution of the sample mean provides this information. Since she expects the per-customer sales to be skewed to the right, we use the gamma distribution for the simulation. Based on her guesses about per-customer sales, we develop two scenarios: One scenario uses a lower bound of what seems likely for the mean and variability, $(\mu, \sigma) = (20, 5)$; the value of $\sigma = 5$ is based on the belief that if $\mu = 20$, about 2/3 of the time[3] the bill would be between $15 and $25. The other scenario uses an upper bound, $(\mu, \sigma) = (24, 8)$. From equation (2.11), the gamma distribution has $\mu = k/\lambda$ and $\sigma = \sqrt{k}/\lambda$ for shape parameter k and scale parameter $1/\lambda$, for which $k = (\mu/\sigma)^2$ and $1/\lambda = \sigma^2/\mu$. The two scenarios have (shape, scale) = (16, 1.25) for $(\mu, \sigma) = (20, 5)$ dollars and (shape, scale) = (9, 8/3) for $(\mu, \sigma) = (24, 8)$ dollars.

For each scenario, we randomly generate 100,000 random samples of size $n = 25$ each from the gamma distribution and find the sample mean for each sample. To do this, we randomly generate 2,500,000 gamma random variables and organize them in a matrix Y with 25 columns and 100,000 rows. Each row of the matrix contains a simulated random sample of size 25. The apply function then finds the mean within each row. At this stage, *Ymean* is a vector of 100,000 means. We then use a histogram to observe the simulated sampling distribution with the 100,000 simulated sample means, and we find their standard deviation to summarize how close they tend to be to μ.

```
> x = seq(0, 60, 0.01)
> plot(x, dgamma(x,shape=16,scale=1.25), type="l", col="red")  # gamma pdf (1st scenario)
> lines(x, dgamma(x,shape=9,scale=8/3), type="l", col="blue")  # gamma pdf (2nd scenario)
> Y1 <- matrix(rgamma(25*100000, shape=16, scale=1.25), ncol=25) # 1st scenario
> Y1mean <- apply(Y1,1,mean) # find mean of the 25 observations in each row of Y1 matrix
> mean(Y1mean); sd(Y1mean)   # in 2nd argument of apply(), use 1 for rows, 2 for columns
[1] 19.9981        # close to 1st scenario population mean of 20
[1] 1.003612       # standard deviation of the 100,000 sample means
> hist(Y1mean, freq=FALSE, xlab= "Sample mean", ylab="Relative frequency"))
```

---

[3]The actual proportion for this gamma distribution is 0.688 (Exercise 3.5(b)).

```
> Y2 <- matrix(rgamma(25*100000, shape=9, scale=8/3), ncol=25)    # 2nd scenario
> Y2mean <- apply(Y2, 1, mean)
> mean(Y2mean); sd(Y2mean)
[1] 23.9949         # close to 2nd scenario population mean of 24
[1] 1.603475        # standard deviation of the 100,000 sample means in 2nd scenario
```

Figure 3.3 shows the simulated sampling distribution of $\overline{Y}$ for the two scenarios. Even though the gamma distributions sampled are skewed right, the sampling distributions are bell-shaped. With $n = 25$, it seems likely that $\overline{Y}$ will fall within about \$2 of μ if $\sigma = 5$ but only within about \$4 of μ if $\sigma = 8$. For more precision, she may sample more people, but the challenge will be to have a sample that has characteristics truly like a random sample of people who will attend this restaurant. She may also experiment by having her sample of friends also pick items from a second test menu, and then compare results.

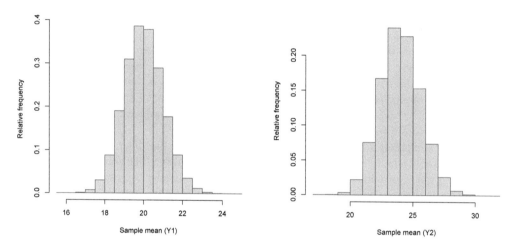

FIGURE 3.3 Simulated sampling distributions of sample mean, for random sample sizes of $n = 25$ from gamma distributions with $(\mu, \sigma) = (20, 5)$ and $(24, 8)$.

The rest of the chapter presents general results about the sampling distribution of the sample mean. We'll learn about a theoretical formula for determining the spreads of sampling distributions such as these, and we'll learn that such sampling distributions are usually well approximated by normal distributions.

3.2 Sampling Distributions of Sample Means

Sections 3.2 and 3.3 present the two key results about the sampling distribution of the sample mean. One result provides formulas for the *center* and the *spread* of the sampling distribution. The other result describes the *shape* of the sampling distribution, showing that it is often approximately normal.

3.2.1 Mean and Variance of Sample Mean of Random Variables

To find the mean and variance of the sampling distribution of the sample mean $\overline{Y}$, we first use the result (2.15) that expectations are additive. For random variables X and Y with means μ_X and μ_Y, $E(X+Y) = E(X) + E(Y) = \mu_X + \mu_Y$ and

$$
\begin{aligned}
\text{var}(X+Y) &= E[(X+Y) - (\mu_X + \mu_Y)]^2 = E[(X - \mu_X) + (Y - \mu_Y)]^2 \\
&= E(X - \mu_X)^2 + E(Y - \mu_Y)^2 + 2E[(X - \mu_X)(Y - \mu_Y)] \\
&= \text{var}(X) + \text{var}(Y) + 2\text{cov}(X,Y).
\end{aligned}
$$

More generally, when $\{Y_i\}$ have means $\{\mu_i\}$ and variances $\{\sigma_i^2\}$, $E(\sum_{i=1}^n Y_i) = \sum_{i=1}^n \mu_i$ and

$$
\begin{aligned}
\text{var}(\sum_{i=1}^n Y_i) &= E\Big[\sum_{i=1}^n Y_i - \sum_{i=1}^n \mu_i\Big]^2 = E\Big[\sum_{i=1}^n (Y_i - \mu_i)\Big]^2 \\
&= \sum_{i=1}^n E(Y_i - \mu_i)^2 + \sum_{i=1}^n \sum_{j=1}^n E[(Y_i - \mu_i)(Y_j - \mu_j)] \\
&= \sum_{i=1}^n \text{var}(Y_i) + \sum_{i=1}^n \sum_{j=1}^n \text{cov}(Y_i, Y_j).
\end{aligned}
$$

When $\{Y_i\}$ are independent, since the covariance of independent random variables is 0,

$$
\text{var}(\sum_{i=1}^n Y_i) = \sum_{i=1}^n \text{var}(Y_i).
$$

With independent observations from the same distribution, such as with simple random sampling or a randomized experiment, all $\{\mu_i\}$ are identical and all $\{\sigma_i^2\}$ are identical, that is, $\{\mu_i = \mu\}$ and $\{\sigma_i^2 = \sigma^2\}$. The n random variables are then said to be *independent and identically distributed*, abbreviated by *iid*. In this case,

$$
E(\sum_{i=1}^n Y_i) = \sum_{i=1}^n E(Y_i) = n\mu, \quad \text{var}(\sum_{i=1}^n Y_i) = \sum_{i=1}^n \text{var}(Y_i) = n\sigma^2.
$$

Then, using the result (2.5) that for any constant c, $E(cY) = c[E(Y)]$ and $\text{var}(cY) = c^2\text{var}(Y)$, the mean and variance of the sampling distribution of $\overline{Y}$ are

$$
E(\overline{Y}) = E\left[\frac{\sum_{i=1}^n Y_i}{n}\right] = \frac{1}{n} E\Big(\sum_{i=1}^n Y_i\Big) = \frac{1}{n}(n\mu) = \mu,
$$

$$
\text{var}(\overline{Y}) = \text{var}\left[\frac{\sum_{i=1}^n Y_i}{n}\right] = \frac{1}{n^2}\left[\text{var}\Big(\sum_{i=1}^n Y_i\Big)\right] = \frac{1}{n^2}(n\sigma^2) = \frac{\sigma^2}{n}.
$$

3.2.2 Standard Error of a Statistic

The spread of a sampling distribution is described by its standard deviation, which is called the **standard error**. The standard deviation of the sampling distribution of $\overline{Y}$ is called the **standard error** of $\overline{Y}$. We denote it by $\sigma_{\overline{Y}}$.

The standard error of $\overline{Y}$ describes how much $\overline{y}$ tends to vary from sample to sample of size n. The symbol $\sigma_{\overline{Y}}$ (instead of σ) and the terminology *standard error* (instead of *standard deviation*) distinguishes this measure from the standard deviation σ of the population. From the result just derived about the variance of the sampling distribution of $\overline{Y}$, when $\{Y_i\}$ are *iid*,

$$
\sigma_{\overline{Y}} = \sqrt{\text{var}(\overline{Y})} = \sqrt{\frac{\sigma^2}{n}} = \frac{\sigma}{\sqrt{n}}.
$$

This formula actually treats the population size as *infinite*. The exact formula for a finite population size is usually nearly identical to this (Exercise 3.37).

In summary, for a study employing randomization, the following result describes the center and the spread of the sampling distribution of $\overline{Y}$.

Mean and standard error of sampling distribution of $\overline{Y}$

The sampling distribution of $\overline{Y}$ specifies probabilities for the possible $\overline{y}$ values. With randomization to obtain n independent observations from a population having mean μ and standard deviation σ, the sampling distribution of $\overline{Y}$ has mean μ and standard error $\sigma_{\overline{Y}} = \sigma/\sqrt{n}$.

Error occurs when we estimate μ by $\overline{y}$, because we sampled only part of the population. This error is called the **sampling error**. The standard error is fundamental to inferential procedures that determine how large the sampling error may be in estimating a parameter. As n increases, the standard error $\sigma_{\overline{Y}} = \sigma/\sqrt{n}$ decreases. Thus, the sampling distribution gets narrower, reflecting that the sample mean tends to fall closer to μ. This agrees with our intuition that larger samples provide more precise estimates of population characteristics. Notice, however, that $\sigma_{\overline{Y}} = \sigma/\sqrt{n}$ has $\sqrt{n}$ in the denominator, not n. Since $\sqrt{4n} = 2\sqrt{n}$, the *square root law* says that *we need to quadruple n to get half as large a standard error.*

3.2.3   Example: Standard Error of Sample Mean Sales

The simulations in Section 3.1 investigated how much a sample proportion or sample mean may vary from sample to sample in surveys or experiment. Instead of conducting a simulation, we can find similar information directly by finding a standard error.

In Section 3.1.4, for estimating mean sales for a test menu, the first scenario sampled $n = 25$ subjects from a gamma distribution with $(\mu, \sigma) = (20, 5)$ dollars. The standard error of the sampling distribution of $\overline{Y}$ is then $\sigma_{\overline{Y}} = \sigma/\sqrt{n} = 5/\sqrt{25} = 1.0$. (The simulation approximated this well by 1.0036.) The histogram of the simulated $\overline{y}$ values was bell-shaped, and in Section 3.3 we shall learn that the sampling distribution of a sample mean is approximately a normal distribution. For example, with probability about 0.95, for random sampling $\overline{Y}$ falls within two standard errors of the mean per-capita sales μ for the conceptual population of all people who could attend the restaurant, that is, within $2(1.0) = 2.0$.

3.2.4   Example: Standard Error of Sample Proportion in Exit Poll

In Section 2.4.5, from the mean and variance of a binomial random variable, we found that the sample proportion $\hat{\pi}$ of n such binary observations has $E(\hat{\pi}) = \pi$ and $\text{var}(\hat{\pi}) = \pi(1-\pi)/n$. The standard error of the sampling distribution of the statistic $\hat{\pi}$ is $\sigma_{\hat{\pi}} = \sqrt{\pi(1-\pi)/n}$. This is a special case of the formula $\sigma_{\overline{Y}} = \sigma/\sqrt{n}$ with $\overline{Y} = \hat{\pi}$, because Section 2.4.3 showed that a binary random variable Y taking values 0 and 1 with $\pi = P(Y = 1)$ has $\text{var}(Y) = \pi(1 - \pi)$, and thus $\sigma = \sqrt{\pi(1 - \pi)}$. The exit poll discussed in Section 3.1.1 had $n = 2271$. If half of the population of voters in California voted for Biden, for a simple random sample of 2271 voters, the standard error is

$$\sigma_{\hat{\pi}} = \sqrt{\frac{\pi(1 - \pi)}{n}} = \sqrt{\frac{(0.50)(0.50)}{2271}} = 0.0105.$$

Since the sampling distribution is bell-shaped, with probability close to 1.0 the sample proportion falls within three standard errors of π, that is, within $3(0.0105) = 0.031$ of 0.50, or between about 0.469 and 0.531. If $\pi = 0.50$ and we could truly take a simple random sample in an exit poll, it would be surprising if fewer than 46% or more than 54% of the sample voted for the Democrat.

3.2.5 Law of Large Numbers: Sample Mean Converges to Population Mean

Because the standard error $\sigma_{\overline{Y}} = \sigma/\sqrt{n}$ decreases as n increases, $\overline{Y}$ tends to be closer to μ as n increases. The result that $\overline{Y}$ converges to μ as n grows indefinitely is called the **law of large numbers**. Here is a formal mathematical statement of this result.[4]

Law of large numbers

With n independent observations (such as in a randomized study) from a distribution with mean μ, for any $\epsilon > 0$, $P(|\overline{Y} - \mu| \geq \epsilon) \to 0$ as $n \to \infty$. Equivalently, $P(|\overline{Y} - \mu| < \epsilon) \to 1$ as $n \to \infty$.

This type of convergence involves a sequence of random variables instead of fixed values as in ordinary sequences. To reflect the randomness, the convergence is called **convergence in probability** of $\overline{Y}$ to μ, denoted by $\overline{Y} \overset{p}{\to} \mu$. When the variance $\sigma^2 < \infty$, we can show it using the Chebyshev inequality result (Section 1.4.4) that for any $k \geq 1$, the proportion of observations that fall at least k standard deviations from the mean can be no greater than $1/k^2$. By this inequality, using the standard error of $\overline{Y}$ as the standard deviation,

$$P\left[|\overline{Y} - \mu| \geq k\left(\frac{\sigma}{\sqrt{n}}\right)\right] \leq \frac{1}{k^2}.$$

For any $\epsilon > 0$, take k such that $\epsilon = k\sigma/\sqrt{n}$, that is, $k = \epsilon\sqrt{n}/\sigma$. Then, $1/k^2 = \sigma^2/\epsilon^2 n$, and

$$P(|\overline{Y} - \mu| \geq \epsilon) \leq \sigma^2/\epsilon^2 n.$$

When we let $n \to \infty$, the law of large numbers follows[5] because the upper bound $\sigma^2/\epsilon^2 n \to 0$.

Here is a simulation illustrating the convergence of $\overline{Y}$ toward μ: For a uniform distribution over $[0, 100]$, for which $\mu = 50.0$, we take simple random samples of size $n = 10$, $n = 1000$, and $n = 10,000,000$:

```
> mean(runif(10, 0, 100)); mean(runif(1000, 0, 100)); mean(runif(10000000, 0, 100))
[1] 23.58847     # sample mean for random sample of n = 10 from uniform [0, 100]
[1] 51.86637     # sample mean for n = 1000
[1] 49.99736     # sample mean for n = 10000000 (population mean = 50.0)
```

How quickly does $\overline{Y} \overset{p}{\to} \mu$ as n grows? Since the standard error is $\sigma/\sqrt{n}$, if the sampling distribution of $\overline{Y}$ is bell-shaped, the difference is rarely greater than $3\sigma/\sqrt{n}$.

3.2.6 Normal, Binomial, and Poisson Sums of Random Variables Have the Same Distribution

We've seen that the sampling distribution of $\overline{Y}$ narrows as n increases. What is its shape? Since $\overline{Y} = (\sum_i Y_i)/n$, the sampling distribution of $\sum_i Y_i$ determines its shape. *For independent observations from some families of probability distributions, the sampling distribution of $\sum_i Y_i$ falls in the same family.* Here are the most important examples:[6]

---

[4]The result stated here is sometimes called the *weak law of large numbers* to distinguish it from a *strong law of large numbers* that uses a more stringent definition of convergence, called *almost sure* convergence.

[5]The version stated above that does not require existence of σ^2 was shown by the Russian mathematician Aleksandr Khinchin in 1929.

[6]Exercise 3.45 shows how to prove these results.

1. If $\{Y_i\}$ are independent normal random variables, with $Y_i \sim N(\mu_i, \sigma_i^2)$, then $\sum_{i=1}^{n} Y_i \sim N(\sum_{i=1}^{n} \mu_i, \sum_{i=1}^{n} \sigma_i^2)$.

   The sum is also normal, with means and variances also adding.

2. If $\{Y_i\}$ are independent binomial random variables, with $Y_i \sim \text{binom}(n_i, \pi)$, then $\sum_{i=1}^{n} Y_i \sim \text{binom}(\sum_{i=1}^{n} n_i, \pi)$.

   The sum is also binomial, with number of trials adding likewise, if the success probability π is the same for each binomial.

3. If $\{Y_i\}$ are independent Poisson random variables, with $Y_i \sim \text{Pois}(\mu_i)$, then $\sum_{i=1}^{n} Y_i \sim \text{Pois}(\sum_{i=1}^{n} \mu_i)$.

   The sum is also Poisson, with means also adding.

When the binomial index for the total number of binary trials is large or when the Poisson total mean is large, these distributions are approximately normal.

   Dividing $\sum_i Y_i$ by n rescales the sampling distribution for $\sum_i Y_i$ to yield the sampling distribution of $\overline{Y}$. This has the same shape, but less spread. For these cases, therefore, the sampling distribution of $\overline{Y}$ is often approximately normal. The next section shows that this is true more generally.

3.3 Central Limit Theorem: Normal Sampling Distribution for Large Samples

Because the sample mean is used so much, and the sample proportion is also a sample mean of binary (0, 1) data, its sampling distribution merits special attention. What shape should we expect? Let's begin with a particular population—uniform over the integers 1 through 6, corresponding to rolling a balanced dice. Suppose we roll the dice 10 times and then find $\overline{Y}$. It would be surprising for $\overline{Y}$ to be at or close to 1.0, as that would require nearly every roll having the 1 outcome; likewise it would be surprising for $\overline{Y}$ to be at or close to 6.0. It would not be surprising, however, for $\overline{Y}$ to be near the middle of the range, such as between 3 and 4, because so many combinations of roll results yield such means. Thus, we might expect the sampling distribution of $\overline{Y}$ to be somewhat bell-shaped. In fact, in this section we'll learn a result with great implications for statistical inference: In studies that employ randomization, *regardless of the shape of the population distribution, the sampling distribution of $\overline{Y}$ is approximately normal.*

3.3.1 Sampling Distribution of Sample Mean Is Approximately Normal

The result that the sampling distribution of $\overline{Y}$ is approximately normal is called the **Central Limit Theorem**. Here is a rather imprecise formulation of it.

Central Limit Theorem

For a large number n of independent observations from a population distribution having mean μ and finite standard deviation σ, the sampling distribution of the sample mean $\overline{Y}$ is approximately a normal distribution with mean μ and standard error $\sigma_{\overline{Y}} = \sigma/\sqrt{n}$.

We learned about the mean and standard error of the sampling distribution of $\overline{Y}$ in the previous section, but the normality result in a general context is new. Here are some implications and interpretations of this remarkable result:

- The approximate normality of the sampling distribution applies *no matter what the shape* of the population distribution. Figure 3.4 displays sampling distributions of $\overline{Y}$ for five quite different shapes for the population distribution,[7] for simple random samples of sizes $n = 2, 5,$ and 30. As n increases, the sampling distribution has more of a bell shape.

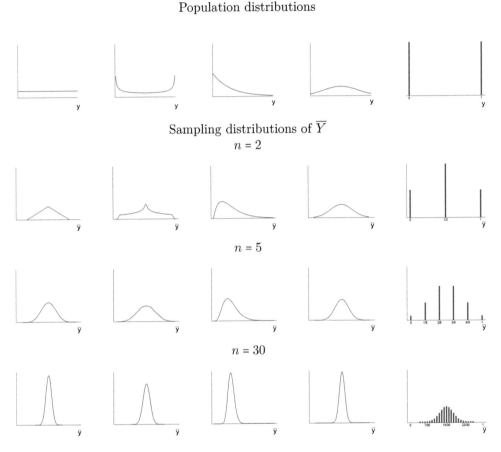

Population distributions

Sampling distributions of $\overline{Y}$

$n = 2$

$n = 5$

$n = 30$

FIGURE 3.4 Regardless of the shape of the population distribution, as n increases, the sampling distribution of $\overline{Y}$ becomes narrower and converges to a normal distribution.

- How large n must be before the sampling distribution is approximately normal depends on the skewness of the population distribution. If the population distribution is bell-shaped, then the sampling distribution is bell-shaped for *all* n. Unless the skewness is very severe, a sample size of about 30 is sufficient.[8] For studies that employ randomization, therefore, the sampling distribution is usually approximately normal.

- Knowing that the sampling distribution of $\overline{Y}$ is approximately normal helps us to find

---

[7] The five population distributions are uniform, U-shaped beta with $\alpha = \beta = 0.5$, exponential, normal, and binomial with $n = 1$ and $\pi = 0.50$.

[8] With skewness coefficient S for the population distribution, the sampling distribution of $\overline{Y}$ has skewness coefficient $S/\sqrt{n}$. Exercise 3.38 suggests that $n \geq 10S^2$ is usually sufficient for a bell shape.

probabilities for possible $\overline{Y}$ values. For instance, $\overline{Y}$ almost certainly falls within $3\sigma_{\overline{Y}} = 3\sigma/\sqrt{n}$ of μ. Reasoning of this nature is vital to inferential statistical methods.

Here is a more precise statement[9] of the Central Limit Theorem:

▶ **Central Limit Theorem**: For n independent observations from a population with mean μ and finite standard deviation σ, the *standardized* version of the sample mean (i.e., subtracting its expected value and dividing by its standard error),

$$\frac{\overline{Y} - \mu}{\sigma_{\overline{Y}}} = \frac{\overline{Y} - \mu}{\sigma/\sqrt{n}} = \frac{\sqrt{n}(\overline{Y} - \mu)}{\sigma},$$

has *cdf* that converges to the *cdf* of a standard normal distribution as $n \to \infty$.

The convergence of a sequence of *cdf*'s to a limiting *cdf* is called ***convergence in distribution***, denoted by $\overset{d}{\to}$. We denote it in this case of the standardized sample mean by

$$\frac{\sqrt{n}(\overline{Y} - \mu)}{\sigma} \overset{d}{\to} N(0,1).$$

Stating that $\sqrt{n}(\overline{Y} - \mu)/\sigma$ has an approximate $N(0,1)$ distribution is equivalent to stating that $\overline{Y}$ has an approximate normal distribution with mean μ and standard error $\sigma/\sqrt{n}$.

3.3.2 Simulations Illustrate Normal Sampling Distribution in CLT

The Central Limit Theorem (CLT) has a mathematical proof, outlined in Exercise 3.46. To aid our intuition, it helps to verify it with simulations, repeatedly selecting random samples of fixed size n from a particular distribution, calculating $\overline{y}$ for each sample, and then viewing the histogram of the $\overline{y}$-values. We can do this ourselves with software, such as we did with R for the examples in Section 3.1, or we can use various apps, such as the sampling distribution apps[10] at www.artofstat.com/web-apps.

We illustrate first using the app at that website for a continuous population distribution. With it, we can specify various shapes for the distribution, including skewed ones. Figure 3.5 is a screenshot for this app, with the choice of a population distribution that is extremely skewed to the right. With the menu, we request the app to select 10,000 simple random samples, each of size $n = 200$. The histogram under the population distribution plots the data for the last generated sample of size 200. The sample mean of 9.44 and standard deviation of 7.95 are not far from the corresponding population values, which are $\mu = 10.00$ and $\sigma = 7.75$. The third graph shown is a histogram of the 10,000 generated $\overline{y}$ values. It is bell-shaped, a consequence of the CLT, and much less spread out, with a standard deviation of only 0.545. For samples of size $n = 200$, the theoretical standard error is $\sigma_{\overline{Y}} = \sigma/\sqrt{n} = 7.75/\sqrt{200} = 0.548$.

To replicate a figure similar to Figure 3.1 for an exit poll, use the *Sampling Distribution for the Sample Proportion* app at www.artofstat.com/web-apps. Set the population proportion $\pi = 0.50$ and set $n = 2271$. Take one sample of size $n = 2271$, and the data distribution shows similar numbers of 0 and 1, and the empirical sampling distribution shows the single generated sample proportion value $\hat{\pi}$. Now draw 10,000 samples. Notice that the data distribution looks like the binary population distribution, but the sampling distribution of the sample proportion is bell-shaped and very narrow. That distribution shows that if π were 0.50, it would be very unusual to obtain $\hat{\pi} = 0.655$, as in the California exit poll.

---

[9]If we replace σ by s, the same result holds, by *Slutsky's Theorem* (Exercise 4.72).

[10]This app and others at that site were created by Bernhard Klingenberg for *Statistics: The Art and Science of Learning from Data*, by A. Agresti, C. Franklin, and B. Klingenberg (5th ed.2021, Pearson).

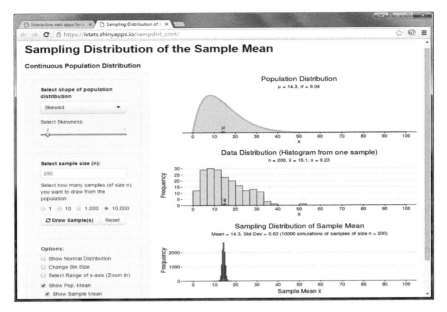

FIGURE 3.5 Screenshot of app at `www.artofstat.com` for simulating the sampling distribution of $\overline{Y}$ in random sampling from a skewed population distribution: The menu requests 10,000 simple random samples of size $n = 200$ each (the final sample being shown in the second figure) and plots the 10,000 sample mean values in the bottom figure.

3.3.3 Summary: Population, Sample Data, and Sampling Distributions

Sampling distributions are fundamental to statistical inference methodology presented in the rest of this text. Because of this, we now review and elaborate on the distinction between the sampling distribution and the two types of distributions we've previously studied—the *population* distribution and the *sample data* distribution. Here is a capsule description:

- **Population distribution**: This is the distribution from which we select the sample. Some statistical methods assume a particular family of probability distributions, such as normal or binomial. We make inferences about its characteristics, such as the mean μ or probability π.

- **Sample data distribution**: This is the distribution of the n observations in our sample. We describe it by statistics such as the sample mean $\overline{y}$ and standard deviation s. As n increases, the sample data distribution more closely resembles the population distribution.[11]

- **Sampling distribution**: This is the probability distribution for the possible values of a sample statistic, such as $\overline{y}$. A sampling distribution determines the probability that the statistic falls within a certain distance of the population parameter that it estimates.

We illustrate with the exit-poll example from Section 3.1.1, with vote Y equal to 1 for Biden and 0 for Trump or another candidate. Of the 17 million adult residents of California who voted, 63.5% voted for Biden, so the population distribution has probability 0.635 at

---

[11]See, for example, the first two plots in the Figure 3.5 screenshot.

$y = 1$ and probability 0.365 at $y = 0$. The mean of this distribution is $\mu = 0.635$, which is the population proportion π of votes for Biden. Figure 3.6 portrays this distribution, which is highly discrete (binary). It is not at all bell-shaped.

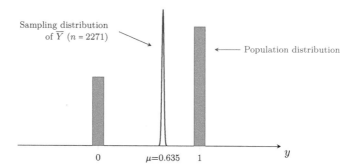

FIGURE 3.6 The population distribution for the 17 million California voters in the 2020 Presidential election ($y = 1$ is vote for Biden and $y = 0$ is vote for Trump or another candidate) and the sampling distribution of the sample proportion for $n = 2271$. The mean $\mu = 0.635$ of the binary population distribution at 0 and 1 is the California population proportion π voting for Biden.

For the exit poll of size $n = 2271$, a bar graph of the 2271 votes in the sample describes the sample data distribution. Of the 2271 voters, 65.5% said they voted for Biden (i.e., have $y = 1$) and 34.5% said they voted for Trump or another candidate ($y = 0$), so the sample data distribution very much resembles the population distribution in Figure 3.6. If the entire population is sampled, as when all the votes are counted, then the two distributions are identical.

For a random sample of size $n = 2271$, the sampling distribution of $\overline{Y}$ (which is the sample proportion $\hat{\pi}$), is approximately normal. Its mean is the population proportion 0.635, and its standard error is

$$\sigma_{\hat{\pi}} = \sqrt{\frac{\pi(1-\pi)}{n}} = \sqrt{\frac{(0.635)(0.365)}{2271}} = 0.010.$$

Figure 3.6 portrays this sampling distribution, relative to the population distribution of votes. The sampling distribution looks completely different, being much less spread out and approximately normal by the Central Limit Theorem.

3.4 Large-Sample Normal Sampling Distributions for Many Statistics*

The Central Limit Theorem is important also because a similar result holds more generally: Many sample statistics (besides the mean) used to estimate population parameters have approximately normal sampling distributions, for reasonably-sized samples in studies that employ randomization.

---

*Sections with an asterisk are optional.

3.4.1 The Delta Method

Let T be a statistic that has approximately a normal sampling distribution about a mean of θ. Most such statistics have standard errors, like $\overline{Y}$, that decrease as n increases at the rate $1/\sqrt{n}$, so suppose that T has standard error $\tau/\sqrt{n}$ for some constant τ. That is, T has an approximate $N(\theta, \tau^2/n)$ distribution, and so $\sqrt{n}(T - \theta)$ has large-sample $N(0, \tau^2)$ distribution. This setting includes the case $T = \overline{Y}$, for which $\theta = \mu$ and $\tau = \sigma$. The following derivation shows that a statistic $g(T)$ that is a smooth function of T also has an approximate normal sampling distribution.

From the Taylor series expansion for $g(t)$ in a neighborhood of $t = \theta$,

$$\sqrt{n}[g(T) - g(\theta)] \approx \sqrt{n}(T - \theta)g'(\theta)$$

for large n, where $g'(\theta)$ denotes the derivative $\partial g(t)/\partial t$ of g with respect to t evaluated at $t = \theta$. For large n, the higher-order terms in the Taylor series expansion are negligible, because as T converges toward θ, $(T - \theta)^2 g''(\theta)$ and higher-order terms tend to be small compared to $(T - \theta)g'(\theta)$. Recall that if $Y \sim N(0, \sigma^2)$, then $cY \sim N(0, c^2\sigma^2)$. By the convergence in distribution of $\sqrt{n}(T - \theta)$ to $N(0, \tau^2)$, taking $c = g'(\theta)$, we have that $\sqrt{n}[g(T) - g(\theta)] \approx \sqrt{n}(T - \theta)g'(\theta)$ implies that

$$\sqrt{n}[g(T) - g(\theta)] \xrightarrow{d} N(0, [g'(\theta)]^2 \tau^2). \tag{3.1}$$

In other words, the sampling distribution of $g(T)$ is approximately the normal distribution having mean $g(\theta)$ and variance $[g'(\theta)]^2\tau^2/n$, and thus standard error $|g'(\theta)|\tau/\sqrt{n}$. This result is called the ***delta method***, because of the role played by the derivative.

Figure 3.7 portrays the delta method.[12] Locally around θ, $g(t)$ is approximately linear, with slope $g'(\theta)$. Thus, $g(T)$ has approximately a normal distribution, because linear transformations of normal random variables are themselves normal. Its standard error depends on the rate of change of $g(t)$ at $t = \theta$. The dispersion of $g(T)$ values about $g(\theta)$ is about $|g'(\theta)|$ times the dispersion of T values about θ. For example, if the slope of g at θ is $\frac{1}{2}$, then g maps a region of T values into a region of $g(T)$ values only about half as wide, so the standard deviation of the transformed random variable is about half as large.

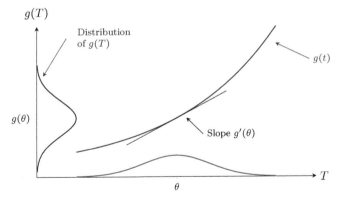

FIGURE 3.7 Depiction of delta method for a statistic $g(T)$ that is a function of a statistic T that has approximately a normal sampling distribution.

---

[12]In this figure, the distribution on the x-axis is $N(0, 1)$, the g function is $g(y) = 0.1 + \exp(y/3)$, and the normal distribution on the y-axis is the one derived by the delta method.

3.4.2   Delta Method Applied to Root Poisson Stabilizes the Variance

Historically, an early use of the delta method was to find transformations that are *variance stabilizing*, producing random variables with variances that are approximately the same for all values of a key parameter. (The reason is that some statistical methods, such as the *regression analysis* of Chapter 6, assume constant variance for the response variable.) To illustrate the delta method and variance stabilization, let Y_n be the number of nuisance calls you received on your phone in n days. Suppose that Y_n viewed over time as n increases is a *Poisson process* (Section 2.5.5), with mean $\mu = n\lambda$, for fixed $\lambda > 0$ that is the daily rate. Recall that the Poisson distribution has variance equal to the mean and is approximately normal when the mean is large. Therefore, when n is large, Y_n has approximately a normal distribution with mean $n\lambda$ and variance $n\lambda$. The scaling $T = Y_n/n$ of the Poisson random variable describes the *average number of calls per day*. It is also approximately normal, with $E(T) = (1/n)E(Y_n) = (1/n)(n\lambda) = \lambda$ and $\text{var}(T) = \text{var}(Y_n/n) = (1/n^2)\text{var}(Y_n) = (1/n^2)(n\lambda) = \lambda/n$.

Consider the transformation $g(T) = \sqrt{T}$. The derivative of $g(t) = \sqrt{t}$ is $g'(t) = 1/(2\sqrt{t})$, which evaluated at $E(T) = \lambda$ is $1/(2\sqrt{\lambda})$. By the delta method, the variance of $\sqrt{T}$ is approximately the variance of T multiplied by $[1/(2\sqrt{\lambda})]^2$. Since the variance of T is λ/n, the variance of $\sqrt{T}$ is approximately $(\lambda/n) \times [1/(2\sqrt{\lambda})]^2 = 1/4n$. So, the variance of $\sqrt{n}\sqrt{T}$ is approximately $1/4$, regardless of the value of λ. In summary, as $n \to \infty$,

$$\sqrt{n}(\sqrt{T} - \sqrt{\lambda}) \xrightarrow{d} N\left(0, \frac{1}{4}\right).$$

Since $T = Y_n/n$ is the sample Poisson daily rate, $\sqrt{n}\sqrt{T} = \sqrt{Y_n}$, the square root of the total number of nuisance calls by day n. So, the delta method implies that the square root of a Poisson random variable with a large mean has an approximate normal distribution with variance $1/4$. The approximate variance is constant, not dependent on λ or n. Even though the Poisson distribution for Y_n is more spread out as the mean increases, its square root has similar variability regardless of the value of the mean, when the mean is large.

To illustrate, we use the `rpois` function in R to generate a million independent Poisson random variables with parameter $\mu = 25$. By the delta method, the square root values have an approximate mean of $\sqrt{25} = 5$ and standard deviation of $1/4$. This holds for all large values of μ, and we illustrate also for $\mu = 100$. In such cases, the Poisson distribution itself is approximately normal, and its square root values are also, by the delta method.

```
> y <- rpois(1000000, 25) # million random observations from Poisson dist. with mean 25
> mean(y); var(y)
[1] 24.9905              # theoretical mean and variance = mu parameter = 25
[1] 24.9938
> mean(sqrt(y)); var(sqrt(y))
[1] 4.9736       # by delta method, approximate mean = root(25) = 5 and variance = 1/4
[1] 0.2541
> hist(sqrt(y)) # approximately normal distribution for square root of Poisson
> y <- rpois(1000000, 100) # now simulate from Poisson distribution with mean 100
> mean(sqrt(y)); var(sqrt(y))
[1] 9.9881
[1] 0.2507 # by delta method, variance is approximately 0.25 for all large Poisson means
```

3.4.3   Simulating Sampling Distributions of Other Statistics

Suppose we'd like to simulate the sampling distribution of some statistic other than the sample mean, assuming a random sample from a particular probability distribution. As we did in Section 3.1.4, we could use R to simulate a very large number of random samples from that distribution and then construct a histogram of the values of the statistic.

We illustrate for approximating the sampling distribution of the *sample median* for a simple random sample of size $n = 10$ from a Poisson distribution. We take the Poisson mean $\mu = 0.7$, relevant for a count variable that takes small values, such as the number of times each person sampled watched an Internet video in the previous day. Here are results of a single random sample of size 10, with its median:

```
> Y <- rpois(10, 0.7); Y        # random sample of n=10 from Poisson with mean 0.7
[1] 0 0 1 1 0 0 0 1 2 0
> median(Y)
[1] 0
```

Now we simulate 100,000 random samples of size 10 each from this Poisson distribution:

```
> Y <- matrix(rpois(10*100000, 0.7), ncol=10) # simulate Poisson rv's with mean 0.7
> Ymed <- apply(Y, 1, median)                 # find median for each sample of size 10
> hist(Ymed, freq=FALSE)                       # histogram of the 100,000 sample medians
```

Figure 3.8 shows the simulated sampling distribution. With $\mu = 0.7$, the Poisson *pmf* (2.7) has $P(Y = 0) = e^{-0.7} = 0.497$. The sample median is 0 when at least half the observations are at 0, and it is 1 when less than half are at 0 but more than half are at 0 and 1 combined.[13] Figure 3.8 also shows the simulated sampling distribution when $n = 100$ for each sample. As n increases, the outcomes 0 and 1 for the sample median are ever more likely, so the sampling distribution of the median is increasingly one with spikes at 0 and 1 instead of being bell-shaped.

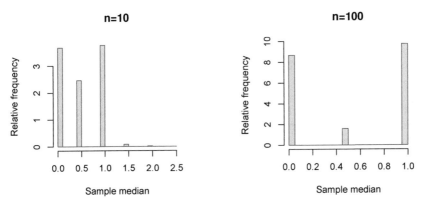

FIGURE 3.8 Simulated sampling distributions of sample median, for random sample sizes of $n = 10$ and $n = 100$ from a Poisson distribution with $\mu = 0.7$.

This example illustrates that not all statistics have approximately normal sampling distributions with all population distributions, even when n is large. In particular, in sampling from a highly discrete distribution, the sampling distribution of the sample median is also highly discrete rather than approximately normal, even as n gets very large. The R Appendix for this chapter provides a general function for generating sampling distributions of statistics. It shows that the sampling distribution of $\overline{Y}$, unlike the sample median, *is* close to normality for these cases.

In the R code for the simulation, by changing the function from the median in the `apply` command, you can simulate sampling distributions of other statistics. By changing the `rpois` argument, you can simulate sampling distributions for other probability distributions. We suggest that you simulate the sampling distributions of the sample mean and the sample median for a skewed continuous distribution, such as the exponential, in which case you'll see that both sampling distributions approach normality quickly as n increases.

---

[13]When exactly half are at 0 and half are at 1, the median is taken to be their midpoint, 0.50.

3.4.4   The Key Role of Sampling Distributions in Statistical Inference

The primary reason for the key role of the normal distribution in statistical inference is that so many statistics do have approximately normal sampling distributions. We will use this fact as we present inferential methods of statistics in the next two chapters.

3.5   Chapter Summary

A *sampling distribution* is a probability distribution of a sample statistic, such as the sample mean or sample proportion. It specifies probabilities for the possible values of the statistic for samples of the particular size n.

- The sampling distribution of the sample mean $\overline{Y}$ centers at the population mean μ, having $E(\overline{Y}) = \mu$. Its standard deviation, called the *standard error*, relates to the standard deviation σ of the population by $\sigma_{\overline{Y}} = \sigma/\sqrt{n}$. As the sample size n increases, the standard error decreases, so the sample mean tends to be closer to the population mean.

- The *Central Limit Theorem* states that for large samples obtained with randomization, *the sampling distribution of the sample mean is approximately a normal distribution.* This holds no matter what the shape of the population distribution, both for continuous and discrete variables.

- The Central Limit Theorem applies also to *proportions*, since the sample proportion is a special case of the sample mean for observations coded as 0 and 1 (such as for two candidates in an election).

- Many other statistics also have an approximately normal sampling distribution for large n. For instance, the *delta method* shows this is true for many functions of statistics that themselves have an approximate normal distribution.

The bell shape for the sampling distribution of many statistics is the main reason for the importance of the normal distribution. The next two chapters show how the Central Limit Theorem is the basis of methods of statistical inference.

Exercises

Data Analysis and Applications

3.1 In an exit poll of 2123 voters in the 2018 Senatorial election in Minnesota, 61.0% said they voted for the Democratic candidate Amy Klobuchar in her race against the Republican candidate Jim Newberger. Based on this information, if you could treat this exit poll like a simple random sample, would you be willing to predict the winner of the election? Conduct a simulation to support your reasoning.

3.2 In an exit poll of 1648 voters in the 2020 Senatorial election in Arizona, 51.5% said they voted for Mark Kelly and 48.5% said they voted for Martha McSally.

(a) Suppose that actually 50% of the population voted for Kelly. If this exit poll had the properties of a simple random sample, find the standard error of the sample proportion voting for him.

(b) Under the 50% presumption, are the results of the exit poll surprising? Why? Would you be willing to predict the election outcome? Explain by (i) conducting a simulation; (ii) using the value found in (a) for the standard error.

3.3 The 49 students in a class at the University of Florida made blinded evaluations of pairs of cola drinks. For the 49 comparisons of Coke and Pepsi, Coke was preferred 29 times. In the population that this sample represents, is this strong evidence that a majority prefers Coke? Use a simulation of a sampling distribution to answer.

3.4 The U.S. Justice Department and other groups have studied possible abuse by police officers in their treatment of minorities. One study, conducted by the American Civil Liberties Union, analyzed whether African-American drivers were more likely than others in the population to be targeted by police for traffic stops. They studied the results of 262 police car stops in Philadelphia during one week. Of those, 207 of the drivers were African-American. At that time, Philadelphia's population was 42.2% African-American. Does the number of African-Americans stopped give strong evidence of possible bias, being higher than you'd expect if we take into account ordinary random variation? Use a simulation of a sampling distribution to answer.

3.5 The example in Section 3.1.4 simulated sampling distributions of the sample mean to determine how precise $\overline{Y}$ for $n = 25$ may estimate a population mean μ.

(a) Find the theoretical standard error of $\overline{Y}$ for the scenario values of $\sigma = 5$ and 8. How do they compare to the standard deviations of the 100,000 sample means in the simulations?

(b) In the first scenario, we chose $\sigma = 5$ under the belief that if $\mu = 20$, about 2/3 of the sample values would fall between $15 and $25. For the gamma distribution with $(\mu, \sigma) = (20, 5)$, show that the actual probability between 15 and 25 is 0.688.

3.6 For the Presidential election in 2020, of an exit poll of 909 voters in the state of New York, 64% voted for Biden and 36% voted for Trump. In response to the question "Is climate change a serious problem?" 71% of those who voted for Biden responded *yes* and 28% of those who voted for Trump responded *yes*. If this sample had the characteristics of a simple random sample, what can you infer about the percentage of all Trump voters who would have responded *yes*?

3.7 In flipping a balanced coin n times, are you more likely to have (i) between 40 and 60 heads in 100 flips, or (ii) between 490 and 510 heads in 1000 flips? As n increases, explain why the *proportion* of heads converges toward 1/2 (because the standard error of a sample *proportion* decreases) but the *number* of heads need not be close to $n/2$ (because the standard deviation of a binomial *number* of successes increases).

3.8 Construct the sampling distribution of the sample proportion of heads, for flipping a balanced coin **(a)** once; **(b)** twice; **(c)** three times; **(d)** four times. Describe how the shape changes as the number of flips n increases. What would happen if n kept growing? Why?

3.9 The outcome of rolling a balanced dice has probability 1/6 for each of $\{1, 2, 3, 4, 5, 6\}$. Let (y_1, y_2) denote the outcomes for two rolls.

(a) Enumerate the 36 possible (y_1, y_2) pairs. Treating them as equally likely, construct the sampling distribution for their sample mean.

(b) Explain why the sampling distribution in (a) has relatively more probability near the middle than at the minimum and maximum values. Predict how the shape would change with additional roles of the dice.

(c) The beginning of Section 3.3 speculated about the shape of the sampling distribution of $\overline{Y}$ for 10 rolls. Use a simulation and construct a histogram to portray the sampling distribution in that case.

3.10 Refer to the previous exercise. For n rolls of the dice, let $X = \max(y_1, y_2, \ldots, y_n)$.

(a) Construct the sampling distribution of X when $n = 2$.

(b) What do you expect for the appearance of the sampling distribution of X when n is large? (If you like, conduct a simulation to investigate.) This illustrates that not every statistic has an approximately normal sampling distribution for large n.

3.11 Simulate taking a random sample of size n from a Poisson distribution with $\mu = 5$. Find $\bar{y}$ for $n = 10$, $n = 1000$, $n = 100,000$, and $n = 10,000,000$ to illustrate the law of large numbers.

3.12 Simulate random sampling from a normal population distribution with several n values to illustrate the law of large numbers.

3.13 Simulate random sampling from a uniform population distribution with several n values to illustrate the Central Limit Theorem.

3.14 On each bet in a sequence of bets, you win \$1 with probability 0.50 and lose \$1 (i.e., win $-\$1$) with probability 0.50. Let Y denote the total of your winnings and losings after 100 bets. Giving your reasoning, state the approximate distribution of Y.

3.15 According to a General Social Survey, in the United States the population distribution of $Y = $ number of good friends (not including family members) has a mean of about 5.5 and a standard deviation of about 3.9.

(a) Is it plausible that this population distribution is normal? Explain.

(b) If a new survey takes a simple random sample of 1000 people, describe the sampling distribution of $\bar{Y}$ by giving its shape and approximate mean and standard error.

(c) Suppose that actually the mean of 5.5 and standard deviation of 3.9 are not population values but are based on a sample of 1000 people. Treating results as a simple random sample, give an interval of values within which you can be very sure that the population mean falls. Explain your reasoning.

3.16 According to the U.S. Census Bureau, the number of people in a household has a mean of 2.6 and a standard deviation of 1.5. Suppose the Census Bureau instead had estimated this mean using a random sample of 225 homes, and that sample had a mean of 2.4 and standard deviation of 1.4. Describe the center and spread of the (**a**) population distribution, (**b**) sample data distribution, (**c**) sampling distribution of the sample mean for 225 homes.

3.17 At a university, 60% of the 7400 students are female. The student newspaper reports results of a survey of a simple random sample of 50 students, 18 females and 32 males, to study alcohol abuse, such as binge drinking.

(a) Set up a variable Y to represent gender, and identify its probability distribution for the population of students at this university.

(b) State the sample data distribution of gender for this sample.

(c) Describe the shape, center, and spread of the sampling distribution of the sample proportion of females for a random sample of size 50. If the sample were truly random, would it be surprising to sample only 18 females?

3.18 Sunshine City, which attracts primarily retired people, has 90,000 residents with a mean age of 72 years and a standard deviation of 12 years. The age distribution is skewed to the left. A random sample of 100 residents of Sunshine City has $\bar{y} = 70$ and $s = 11$.

(a) Describe the center and spread of the (i) population distribution, (ii) sample data distribution. What shape does the sample data distribution probably have? Why?

(b) Find the center and spread of the sampling distribution of $\bar{Y}$ for $n = 100$. What shape does it have and what does it describe?

(c) Explain why it would not be unusual to sample a person of age 60 in Sunshine City, but it would be highly unusual for the sample mean to be 60, for a random sample of 100 residents.

(d) Describe the sampling distribution of $\overline{Y}$: (i) for a random sample of size $n = 1$; (ii) if you sample all 90,000 residents.

3.19 Generate a million independent Poisson random variables with parameter (i) $\mu = 9$, (ii) $\mu = 100$, (iii) $\mu = 100000$. Show how to construct transformed values that have about the same variability in each case.

3.20 To approximate the mean μ of a probability distribution that describes a random phenomenon, you simulate n observations from the distribution and find $\overline{y}$. Explain how to assess how close $\overline{y}$ is likely to be to μ.

3.21 In your school, suppose that GPA has an approximate normal distribution with $\mu = 3.0$, $\sigma = 0.40$. Not knowing μ, you randomly sample $n = 25$ students to estimate it. Using simulation for this application, illustrate the difference between a sample data distribution and the sampling distribution of $\overline{Y}$.

Methods and Concepts

3.22 Using software, simulate forming sample proportions for simple random samples of size $n = 100$ when $\pi = 0.50$. (Alternatively, you can use an app, such as the *Sampling Distribution for the Sample Proportion* app at www.artofstat.com/web-apps.)

 (a) Simulate once and report the counts and the proportions for the two categories. Did you get a sample proportion close to 0.50? Perform this simulation of a random sample of size 100 ten times, each time observing the counts and the corresponding sample proportion of successes. Summarize.

 (b) Now simulate 10,000 times taking a random sample of size $n = 100$ and finding the sample proportion. Plot the simulated sampling distribution. How does the plot reflect results of the Central Limit Theorem?

3.23 Using software, simulate taking simple random samples from a bimodal population distribution. (Alternatively, you can use an app such as the *Sampling Distribution for the Sample Mean (Continuous Population)* app at www.artofstat.com/web-apps and select the bimodal population distribution with shape 1.)

 (a) Take 10,000 random samples of size $n = 50$ each. How does the simulated sampling distribution of sample means compare to the population distribution? What does this reflect?

 (b) Repeat the simulation, this time with $n = 2$ for each sample. Why is the sampling distribution of $\overline{Y}$ not bell-shaped?

3.24 Construct a population distribution that is plausible for Y = number of alcoholic drinks in the past day.

 (a) Simulate a single random sample of size $n = 1000$ from this population to reflect results of a typical sample survey. Summarize how the sample mean and standard deviation resemble those for the population. (Alternatively, you can do this and part (b) using an app, such as the *Sampling Distribution for the Sample Mean (Discrete Population)* app at www.artofstat.com/web-apps using the *Build Custom Distribution* option.)

 (b) Now draw 10,000 random samples of size 1000 each, to approximate the sampling distribution of $\overline{Y}$. Report the mean and standard deviation of this simulated sampling distribution, and compare to the theoretical values. Explain what this sampling distribution represents.

3.25 Simulate what would happen if everyone in a college with 1000 students flipped a fair coin 100 times and observed the proportion of heads. What do you get for the mean and the standard deviation of the 1000 proportions? What are their theoretical values?

3.26 When sample data were used to rank states by brain cancer rates, Ellenberg (2014) noted that the highest ranking state (South Dakota) and the nearly lowest ranking state (North Dakota) had relatively small sample sizes. Also, when schools in North Carolina were ranked by their average improvement in test scores, the best and the worst schools were very small schools. Explain how these results could merely reflect how the variability of sample means and proportions depends on the sample size.

3.27 Consider the standard error $\sqrt{\pi(1-\pi)/n}$ of a sample proportion $\hat{\pi}$ of successes in n binary trials.

   (a) Report the standard error when $\pi = 0$ or $\pi = 1$. Why would this value make sense to you even if you did not know the standard error formula?

   (b) For fixed n, show that the standard error is greatest when $\pi = 0.50$. In practice, what does this suggest about the precision of inferences about π when π is close to 0 or 1 (such as estimating a population proportion of adults who have at least a grade-school education) compared to when π is near 0.50 (such as predicting a close election)?

3.28 A survey is planned to estimate the population proportion π supporting more government action to address global warming. For a simple random sample, if π may be near 0.50, how large should n be so that the standard error of the sample proportion is 0.04?

3.29 Simulate for $n = 10$ and $n = 100$ the sampling distributions of the sample median for sampling from the exponential distribution (2.12) with $\lambda = 1.0$, which has $\mu = \sigma = 1.0$ and a median of 0.69. As n increases, does the sampling distribution of the sample median seem to be approximately normal?

3.30 Mimic the app display of the Central Limit Theorem in Figure 3.5 by taking 10,000 simulations of a random sample of size $n = 200$ from a gamma distribution with $\mu = 10.0$ and $\sigma = 7.75$. Plot the population distribution and the simulated sampling distribution of the 10,000 $\bar{y}$ values. Explain what your plots illustrate.

3.31 Which distribution does the sample data distribution tend to resemble more closely—the sampling distribution of the sample mean or the population distribution? Explain. Illustrate your answer for a variable Y that can take only values of 0 and 1.

Select the correct response(s) in the next three multiple-choice questions. There may be more than one correct answer.

3.32 The standard error of a statistic describes

   (a) The standard deviation of the sampling distribution of that statistic.

   (b) The standard deviation of the sample data.

   (c) How close that statistic is likely to fall to the parameter that it estimates.

   (d) The variability in values of the statistic for repeated simple random samples of size n.

   (e) The error that occurs due to nonresponse and measurement errors.

3.33 In one million tosses of a fair coin, the probability of getting exactly 500,000 heads and 500,000 tails (i.e., a sample proportion of heads exactly $= 1/2$) is

   (a) very close to 1.0, by the law of large numbers.

   (b) very close to 1/2, by the law of large numbers.

   (c) very close to 0, by the standard deviation of the binomial distribution and its approximate normality by the Central Limit Theorem.

3.34 The Central Limit Theorem implies that

   (a) All variables have approximately bell-shaped sample data distributions if a random sample contains at least about 30 observations.

   (b) Population distributions are normal whenever the population size is large.

(c) For large random samples, the sampling distribution of $\overline{Y}$ is approximately normal, regardless of the shape of the population distribution.

(d) The sampling distribution of $\overline{Y}$ looks more like the population distribution as the sample size increases.

3.35 In the previous exercise, explain what is incorrect about each option that you did not choose.

3.36 For independent observations, $\text{var}(\sum_i Y_i) = \sum_i \text{var}(Y_i)$. Explain intuitively why $\sum_i Y_i$ has a larger variance than a single observation Y_i.

3.37 The formula $\sigma_{\overline{Y}} = \sigma/\sqrt{n}$ for the standard error of $\overline{Y}$ treats the population size as *infinitely* large relative to the sample size n. With a finite population size N, separate observations are very slightly negatively correlated, so $\text{var}(\sum_i Y_i) < \sum_i \text{var}(Y_i)$, and actually

$$\sigma_{\overline{Y}} = \sqrt{\frac{N-n}{N-1}} \left(\frac{\sigma}{\sqrt{n}} \right).$$

The term $\sqrt{(N-n)/(N-1)}$ is called the **finite population correction**.

(a) In practice, n is usually small relative to N, so the correction has little influence. Illustrate for sampling $n = 300$ students from a college student body of size $N = 30,000$.

(b) If $n = N$, show that $\sigma_{\overline{Y}} = 0$. That is, if we sample the entire population, no sampling error occurs, because $\overline{Y} = \mu$.

(c) For $n = 1$, explain why the sampling distribution of $\overline{Y}$ and its standard error are identical to the population distribution and its standard deviation.

3.38 Consider n independent observations of a random variable Y that has skewness coefficient $S = E(Y-\mu)^3/\sigma^3$.

(a) Show how $E(\overline{Y}-\mu)^3$ relates to $E(Y-\mu)^3$. Based on this, show that the skewness coefficient for the sampling distribution of $\overline{Y}$ satisfies skewness$(\overline{Y}) = S/\sqrt{n}$. Explain how this result relates to the Central Limit Theorem.

(b) Suppose that we can select a value M such that we regard a unimodal distribution having $S < M$ as being "close" to bell-shaped. With simple random sampling, show that the sampling distribution of $\overline{Y}$ is then approximately normal if $n > (S/M)^2$.

(c) Plots of common unimodal distributions such as the Poisson and gamma with various values of S suggest that $S \leq M \approx 0.32$ is reasonable for giving a bell shape. For this M, show that $\overline{Y}$ has an approximate normal sampling distribution when $n \geq 10S^2$. For this guideline, how large a random sample do you need from an exponential distribution to achieve close to normality for the sampling distribution?

3.39 Explain the difference between *convergence in probability* and *convergence in distribution*. Explain how one can regard convergence in probability as a special case of convergence in distribution for which the limiting distribution has probability 1 at a single point.

3.40 For a binomial parameter π, $g(\pi) = \log[\pi/(1-\pi)]$ is called the **logit**. It is used for categorical data, as shown in Chapter 7. Let $T = \hat{\pi}$ for n independent binary trials. Use the delta method to show that

$$\sqrt{n} \left[\log\left(\frac{\hat{\pi}}{1-\hat{\pi}} \right) - \log\left(\frac{\pi}{1-\pi} \right) \right] \overset{d}{\to} N\left(0, \frac{1}{\pi(1-\pi)} \right).$$

3.41 For a binomial sample proportion $\hat{\pi}$, show that the approximate variance of $\sin^{-1}(\sqrt{\hat{\pi}})$ (with the angle being measured in radians) is $1/4n$, so this is a variance stabilizing transformation. (In reality, simulation reveals that the variance of this *arc sine transformation* is not nearly constant when π is near 0 or near 1 and n is not very large.)

3.42 Many positively-valued response variables have a unimodal distribution but with standard deviation proportional to the mean. Identify a transformation for which the variance is approximately the same for all values of the mean. Identify at least one distribution that has standard deviation proportional to the mean.

3.43 When T is a standard normal random variable, why does the delta method not imply that T^2 has a normal distribution? (*Hint*: Form the Taylor-series expansion of $g(t) = t^2$ around $g(0)$. In Section 4.4.5 we shall see that T^2 has a chi-squared distribution.)

3.44 For independent $Y_1 \sim \text{binom}(n_1, \pi_1)$ and $Y_2 \sim \text{binom}(n_2, \pi_2)$ random variables, $\hat{\pi}_1/\hat{\pi}_2$ is called the **relative risk** or **risk ratio**. This measure is often used in medical research to compare the probability of a certain outcome for two treatments.

(a) A randomized study with $n_1 = n_2 = 50$ compares the probabilities of success π_1 for a new drug and π_2 for placebo. Suppose $\pi_1 = 0.20$ and $\pi_2 = 0.10$. Simulate a million sample proportions from each treatment with $n_1 = n_2 = 50$. Construct histograms for $\hat{\pi}_1/\hat{\pi}_2$ and for $\log(\hat{\pi}_1/\hat{\pi}_2)$. Which seems to have sampling distribution closer to normality? (This shows that some statistics may require a very large sample size to have an approximate normal sampling distribution.)

(b) From a multivariate version of the delta method, a standard error for the log relative risk is $\sqrt{\frac{1-\pi_1}{n_1 \pi_1} + \frac{1-\pi_2}{n_2 \pi_2}}$. For comparing incidence of a rare disease between two populations, state the conditions for the distributions of counts to be approximately Poisson, and conclude that the standard error in terms of the Poisson means is approximately $\sqrt{\frac{1}{\mu_1} + \frac{1}{\mu_2}}$.

3.45 Refer to Exercise 2.66 and the moment generating function $m(t) = E\left(e^{tY}\right)$, an alternative to the probability function for characterizing a probability distribution. For independent random variables $Y_1, Y_2, \ldots, Y_n$, let $T = Y_1 + \cdots + Y_n$.

(a) Explain why T has *mgf* determined by the separate ones as

$$m(t) = m_1(t)m_2(t)\cdots m_n(t).$$

(b) If each $Y_i \sim N(\mu, \sigma^2)$, use the *mgf* $m(t) = e^{\mu t + \sigma^2 t^2/2}$ for each Y_i to show that T has a $N(n\mu, n\sigma^2)$ distribution, and thus conclude that $\overline{Y}$ has a $N(\mu, \sigma^2/n)$ distribution.

(c) If $Y_i \sim \text{Pois}(\mu_i)$ for $i = 1, \ldots, n$, use the *mgf* $m(t) = \exp[\mu_i(e^t - 1)]$ for Y_i to find the distribution of T.

(d) If each $Y_i \sim \text{binom}(1, \pi)$, show that $m_i(t) = [(1 - \pi) + \pi e^t]$. Explain why a $\text{binom}(n, \pi)$ distribution has *mgf* $m(t) = [(1 - \pi) + \pi e^t]^n$.

(e) If $Y_i \sim \text{binom}(n_i, \pi_i)$, for $i = 1, \ldots, n$, under what condition, if any, does T have a binomial distribution?

(f) The *mgf* of a gamma distribution (2.10) near $t = 0$ is $m(t) = [\lambda/(\lambda - t)]^k$. If each Y_i has an exponential distribution with parameter λ, show that the distribution of T is gamma with shape parameter $k = n$. What happens to this shape as n increases?

3.46 Refer to Exercise 3.45 and the *mgf* $m(t) = e^{\mu t + \sigma^2 t^2/2}$ for a normal distribution. For n independent observations $\{Y_i\}$ from an arbitrary distribution with mean μ and variance σ^2, let $m(t)$ be the *mgf* of the standardized random variable $Z_i = (Y_i - \mu)/\sigma$.

(a) Explain why the *mgf* of $\sqrt{n}(\overline{Y} - \mu)/\sigma$ is $[m(t/\sqrt{n})]^n$.

(b) Show that

$$[m(t/\sqrt{n})]^n = \left[1 + \frac{1}{n}\left(\frac{t^2}{2} + \frac{t^3 E(Z^3)}{3!\sqrt{n}} + \cdots\right)\right]^n.$$

(c) Since as $n \to \infty$, $\lim a_n = b$ implies that $\lim(1 + a_n/n)^n = e^b$, explain why the *mgf* of $\sqrt{n}(\overline{Y} - \mu)/\sigma$ converges to $e^{t^2/2}$, which is the *mgf* of a $N(0, 1)$ distribution. The sequence of *mgf*'s converging implies that the sequence of *cdf*'s converges to the $N(0, 1)$ *cdf* by a *continuity theorem*, so these steps prove the Central Limit Theorem.

4

Statistical Inference: Estimation

This chapter shows how to use sample data to estimate population parameters. The main focus is estimating population *means* for *quantitative* variables and population *proportions* for *categorical* variables. A health-care study, for example, might estimate the proportion of people who have private health insurance and the mean annual cost for those who have it. Some studies assume a particular parametric family of probability distributions for a response variable and then estimate the parameters of that distribution to fit the distribution to the data.

We first present two ways to estimate a parameter: (1) by a particular statistic, called an *estimator*, that yields a single number, called a *point estimate*; (2) by an interval of numbers, called a *confidence interval*. The classical approach obtains point estimates by maximizing a *likelihood function* that reflects assumptions about the probability distribution that generated the data. Confidence intervals are derived using the result that the sampling distribution of an estimator is usually approximately normal, regardless of the population distribution. A *bootstrap* method can find standard errors and construct confidence intervals in awkward cases in which sampling distributions are not readily available. An alternative to the classical approach to statistical inference, called *Bayesian inference*, employs probability distributions for the parameters as well as for the data. It yields *posterior* distributions for the parameters for which inference takes the form of probability statements about the parameters after observing the data.

4.1   Point Estimates and Confidence Intervals

We can use sample data in two types of ways to estimate parameters:

- A *point estimate* is the value of a statistic that predicts the parameter value.

- An *interval estimate* is an interval of numbers around the point estimate, called a *confidence interval*, within which the parameter value is believed to fall with a specified degree of confidence.

For example, the 2018 General Social Survey (GSS) asked "Do you believe there is a life after death?" For the 2123 subjects sampled, one point estimate for the *population* proportion of Americans who would respond *yes* is the *sample* proportion, which equals 0.81. A confidence interval predicts that the population proportion responding *yes* falls between 0.78 and 0.84, with 95% confidence. That is, it predicts that the point estimate of 0.81 falls within a *margin of error* of 0.03 of the true value. The confidence interval helps us gauge the probable precision of the point estimate.

The term *estimator* refers to a particular statistic used to construct a point estimate and the term *estimate* is short for its value (the *point estimate*) for a particular sample. For example, the sample proportion is an *estimator* of a population proportion. The value 0.81

DOI: 10.1201/9781003159834-4

is an *estimate* for the population proportion believing in life after death in the U.S. The estimator is a random variable, while the estimate is a particular number.

4.1.1 Properties of Estimators: Unbiasedness, Consistency, Efficiency

Let θ denote an arbitrary parameter and $\hat{\theta}$ an estimator of θ. The symbol $\hat{\ }$ over a parameter symbol is called a *caret* and read as *hat*. For example, $\hat{\theta}$ is read as *theta-hat* and represents an estimator of θ. Any parameter θ has many possible estimators. For example, when we assume a normal distribution for some population, the center of that distribution is the mean and the median, since it is symmetric. With sample data, two possible estimators of that center are the sample mean and the sample median. Another possibility is the average of the lower and upper quartiles, which like the median, is unaffected by outliers. A good estimator $\hat{\theta}$ has a sampling distribution that (1) centers around θ and (2) has as small a standard error as possible. This section introduces ways of specifying such properties.

An estimator $\hat{\theta}$ is called **unbiased** if its sampling distribution centers around the parameter, in the sense that θ is the mean of the sampling distribution of $\hat{\theta}$,

$$E(\hat{\theta}) = \theta.$$

For independent observations from a population, the sample mean $\overline{Y}$ satisfies $E(\overline{Y}) = \mu$, so $\overline{Y}$ is an unbiased estimator of the population mean μ. By contrast, the sample range is typically smaller than the population range and it cannot be larger, because the sample minimum and maximum cannot be more extreme than their population values. The sample range is a biased estimator.

A desirable property for any estimator $\hat{\theta}$ is that it tends to get closer to θ as the sample size n increases. An estimator $\hat{\theta}$ is said to be **consistent** if it converges in probability to θ; that is, for any $\epsilon > 0$,

$$P(|\hat{\theta} - \theta| \geq \epsilon) \rightarrow 0 \text{ as } n \rightarrow \infty.$$

For example, $\overline{Y}$ is a consistent estimator of μ by the law of large numbers. *All* sensible estimators are consistent.

An **efficient** estimator tends to fall *closer* to θ, on the average, than other estimators. A common way to summarize the closeness is by the **mean squared error** (MSE),

$$\text{MSE}(\hat{\theta}) = E(\hat{\theta} - \theta)^2.$$

An efficient estimator by this criterion has minimum mean squared error, uniformly for the possible values of θ. The mean squared error satisfies

$$
\begin{aligned}
\text{MSE}(\hat{\theta}) \quad &= \quad E(\hat{\theta} - \theta)^2 = E\{[\hat{\theta} - E(\hat{\theta})] + [E(\hat{\theta}) - \theta]\}^2 \\
&= \quad E[\hat{\theta} - E(\hat{\theta})]^2 + [E(\hat{\theta}) - \theta]^2 + 2[E(\hat{\theta}) - E(\hat{\theta})][E(\hat{\theta}) - \theta] \\
&= \quad E[\hat{\theta} - E(\hat{\theta})]^2 + [E(\hat{\theta}) - \theta]^2 = \text{var}(\hat{\theta}) + [E(\hat{\theta}) - \theta]^2.
\end{aligned}
$$

The *bias* of $\hat{\theta}$ is defined as $E(\hat{\theta}) - \theta$, so

$$\text{MSE}(\hat{\theta}) = \text{var}(\hat{\theta}) + (\text{bias})^2. \qquad (4.1)$$

For unbiased estimators, $E(\hat{\theta}) = \theta$, so that $\text{MSE}(\hat{\theta}) = \text{var}(\hat{\theta})$. Of the unbiased estimators, the one with smallest MSE is a *minimum variance unbiased estimator*. An estimator with minimum variance equivalently has minimum standard error. For example, for independent observations from a $N(\mu, \sigma^2)$ distribution, both $\overline{Y}$ and the sample median are unbiased and consistent estimators of μ. However, the standard error of the sample median is $1.25\sigma/\sqrt{n}$, which is 25% larger than the standard error of $\overline{Y}$. In fact, $\overline{Y}$ is the minimum variance unbiased estimator for μ for normal populations, whereas the sample median is an inefficient estimator.

4.1.2 Evaluating Properties of Estimators

Although unbiasedness seems desirable, requiring an estimator to be unbiased is too restrictive. A biased estimator may exist that has smaller MSE.[1] From (4.1), to achieve low MSE, we can sacrifice having some bias if the estimator has relatively small variance. This is called the **bias/variance tradeoff**. (Exercises 4.65 and 4.66 show examples of how the variance can decrease as the bias increases.)

Many commonly-used estimators are biased but they are **asymptotically unbiased**, the degree of bias being small and diminishing to 0 as n increases. For instance, for the random variable analog S^2 of the sample variance s^2 introduced in Section 1.4.4, we will show (Section 4.4.6) that $S^2 = [\sum_i (Y_i - \overline{Y})^2]/(n-1)$ is an unbiased estimator of σ^2 as well as being a natural estimator for use in constructing the margin of error for a confidence interval for the mean. An alternative estimator of σ^2 is $\hat{\sigma}^2 = [\sum_i (Y_i - \overline{Y})^2]/n$. It is biased, but the bias

$$E(\hat{\sigma}^2) - \sigma^2 = E\left[\left(\frac{n-1}{n}\right) S^2\right] - \sigma^2 = \left(\frac{n-1}{n}\right) E(S^2) - \sigma^2 = \left(\frac{n-1}{n}\right)\sigma^2 - \sigma^2 = \frac{-\sigma^2}{n}$$

is trivial for large n. It is asymptotically unbiased, because $E(\hat{\sigma}^2) \to \sigma^2$. In sampling from a normal population, $\hat{\sigma}^2$ has slightly smaller MSE than s^2, and it is the best estimator in terms of a criterion introduced in Section 4.2. In any case, selecting s^2 as the estimator merely because it is unbiased is silly, because to summarize variability, we more commonly use the standard deviation s, and s is a biased estimator of σ: By the concave function version of Jensen's inequality stated at the end of Section 2.3.5, $E(S) = E(\sqrt{S^2}) \le \sqrt{E(S^2)} = \sqrt{\sigma^2} = \sigma$.

Likewise, the criterion of an estimator being *efficient* is overly stringent. A good estimator is at least **asymptotically efficient**: Its MSE divided by the MSE of an efficient estimator converges toward 1 as n increases.

In summary, a good estimator $\hat{\theta}$ of θ is *consistent* and at least *asymptotically unbiased* and *asymptotically efficient*. Often the sample analog of a population parameter has such properties, but not always. For estimating a population proportion with independent observations, the sample proportion is consistent, unbiased, and efficient. For estimating a population mean μ, $\overline{Y}$ is consistent by the law of large numbers (Section 3.2.5), it is unbiased, and it is efficient for many population distributions, such as the normal. However, the sample median is not an efficient or asymptotically efficient estimator of the median of most distributions.

4.1.3 Interval Estimation: Confidence Intervals for Parameters

To be truly informative, a statistical inference should indicate how close an estimator $\hat{\theta}$ is likely to fall to the parameter θ it estimates. The precision of $\hat{\theta}$ determines the width of an *interval estimate* of θ. Because we cannot be sure that an interval estimate contains θ but merely that it does so with a certain degree of confidence, it is called a *confidence interval.*

Confidence interval

A *confidence interval* for a parameter θ is an interval of numbers within which θ is predicted to fall. The probability that the confidence interval method produces an interval that truly contains θ is called the **confidence level**. This is a number chosen to be close to 1, such as 0.95 or 0.99.

---

[1] For some parameters, no unbiased estimator even exists. Examples for the binomial distribution are the *odds* $\pi/(1-\pi)$ and the standard deviation $\sqrt{n\pi(1-\pi)}$.

We shall provide a more precise definition in Section 4.3.

One way to construct a confidence interval uses the sampling distribution of the estimator $\hat{\theta}$. Often, such as with $\hat{\theta} = \overline{Y}$, the sampling distribution is approximately normal. The normal distribution and its standard error then determines the probability that $\hat{\theta}$, which is a random variable, falls within a certain distance of θ, which is a fixed but unknown number. To construct a confidence interval, we can add and subtract from $\hat{\theta}$ some multiple of the standard error, which is the ***margin of error***. For instance, with probability about 0.95, $\hat{\theta}$ falls within two standard errors of θ, so to have "95% confidence," we take the point estimate and add and subtract a margin of error that equals about two standard errors. Sections 4.3 and 4.4 show details for mean and proportion parameters.

4.2   The Likelihood Function and Maximum Likelihood Estimation

Often in analyzing data we assume a particular parametric family of probability distributions that generated the data. We then fit the distribution to the data by estimating the parameter or parameters of that distribution. For binary trials, for instance, we estimate the probability of success parameter for the binomial distribution. Under the assumption of a particular family of probability distributions, this section introduces a way of constructing estimators that are consistent, asymptotically unbiased, and asymptotically efficient: The point estimate is *the parameter value for which the observed data would have been most likely to occur.*

4.2.1   The Likelihood Function

Let $\mathbf{y}$ denote a vector of n observations, $(y_1, \ldots, y_n)$. Let $f(\mathbf{y}; \theta)$ denote their joint probability function, according to a family with parameter θ. We substitute $\mathbf{y}$ into $f(\mathbf{y}; \theta)$ and view how it depends on θ. Expressed as a function of θ after observing $\mathbf{y}$, $f(\mathbf{y}; \theta)$ is called the ***likelihood function***.

> ### Likelihood function
>
> For the joint probability function $f(\mathbf{y}; \theta)$ of n observations $\mathbf{y} = (y_1, \ldots, y_n)$ with parameter θ, once $\mathbf{y}$ is observed, the ***likelihood function*** is the function $\ell(\theta) = f(\mathbf{y}; \theta)$ of θ. For n independent observations with probability function $f(y; \theta)$, this is $\ell(\theta) = f(y_1; \theta) \cdots f(y_n; \theta)$.

For discrete data, $\ell(\theta)$ is merely the probability of the observed data if the parameter equals the value θ.

For example, suppose that $y_1, \ldots, y_n$ are n independent binary trials with common $\pi = P(Y_i = 1)$ and $1 - \pi = P(Y_i = 0)$. Then, $f(y_i; \pi) = \pi^{y_i}(1 - \pi)^{1-y_i}$ for $y_i = 0, 1$, which is the binomial probability function (2.6) for a single trial. The joint probability function is

$$f(\mathbf{y}; \pi) = \prod_{i=1}^{n} f(y_i; \pi) = \prod_{i=1}^{n} \pi^{y_i}(1 - \pi)^{1-y_i} = \pi^{\Sigma_i y_i}(1 - \pi)^{n - \Sigma_i y_i}, \text{ for } y_i = 0, 1, \ i = 1, 2, \ldots, n.$$

After we observe the data, the likelihood function is the function of the unknown parameter value π,

$$\ell(\pi) = \pi^{\Sigma_i y_i}(1 - \pi)^{n - \Sigma_i y_i}, \ 0 \leq \pi \leq 1. \tag{4.2}$$

In $n = 10$ trials, suppose all 10 observations are $y_i = 0$, corresponding to a binomial count of $\sum_i y_i = 0$ successes in the 10 trials. The likelihood function is then $\ell(\pi) = \pi^0(1-\pi)^{10} = (1-\pi)^{10}$, for $0 \le \pi \le 1$. If $\pi = 0.40$, for example, the probability that $y = 0$ is $\ell(0.40) = (1-0.40)^{10} = 0.006$. Figure 4.1 plots this likelihood function.

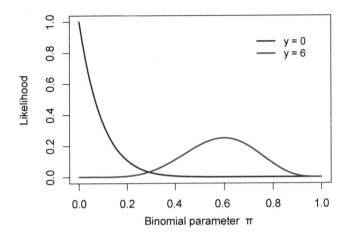

FIGURE 4.1 When we observe $y = 0$ successes in $n = 10$ trials, the binomial likelihood function displays $P(Y = 0)$ at all the possible values for π. The figure also shows the likelihood equation obtained when we observe 6 successes in 10 trials.

Although a likelihood function shows probabilities, it is not a probability distribution. The plot of the likelihood function portrays the probability of the observed data for all possible values of the parameter but would typically not integrate to 1, whereas a probability distribution shows how the total probability of 1 splits into probabilities for all the possible observations at a particular parameter value.

4.2.2 Maximum Likelihood Method of Estimation

We will use the likelihood function in various ways for statistical inference. To start, it yields an estimator that tends to perform well.

Maximum likelihood (ML) estimate

The *maximum likelihood estimate* $\hat{\theta}$ of a parameter θ, based on observed data **y**, is the value of θ at which the likelihood function $\ell(\theta)$ takes its maximum. The abbreviation **ML** symbolizes *maximum likelihood*.

That is, $\hat{\theta}$ is the θ value for which the probability of the observed data takes its greatest value. Figure 4.1 shows that the likelihood function $\ell(\pi) = (1-\pi)^{10}$ has its maximum at $\pi = 0.0$. When $n = 10$ trials have 0 successes, the ML estimate of π is $\hat{\pi} = 0.0$. The result of 0 successes in $n = 10$ trials is more likely to occur when $\pi = 0.0$ than when π equals any other value.

In general, for the binomial random variable of $Y = \sum_i Y_i$ successes in n trials, the *ML estimator* of π is $\hat{\pi} = Y/n$, the sample proportion of successes.[2] The *ML estimate* is its value for a particular sample, such as $\hat{\pi} = 6/10 = 0.60$ with $y = 6$ successes in $n = 10$ trials. Figure

---

[2]The ML estimator of a population parameter is often the sample analog, but not always. For instance,

4.1 also plots the likelihood function in this case, $\ell(\pi) = \pi^6(1-\pi)^4$. Its maximum occurs at $\hat{\pi} = 0.60$. The result $y = 6$ successes in $n = 10$ trials is more likely to occur when $\pi = 0.60$ than when π equals any other value.

To find the ML estimate $\hat{\theta}$ of a parameter θ, we need to determine the point at which the likelihood function $\ell(\theta)$ is maximized. To do this, we can differentiate the likelihood function $\ell(\theta)$ and set it equal to 0 . With n independent observations, $\ell(\theta) = f(y_1; \theta) \cdots f(y_n; \theta)$. Its logarithm $L(\theta) = \log[\ell(\theta)] = \sum_i \log[f(y_i; \theta)]$ is a summation and is simpler to differentiate, and $L(\theta)$ has maximum at the same $\hat{\theta}$ location. The log of the binomial likelihood function (4.2) is

$$L(\pi) = \log[\pi^{\sum_i y_i}(1-\pi)^{n-\sum_i y_i}] = \left(\sum_{i=1}^n y_i\right)\log(\pi) + \left(n - \sum_{i=1}^n y_i\right)\log(1-\pi).$$

Setting its derivative equal to 0 yields the *likelihood equation*

$$\frac{\partial L(\pi)}{\partial \pi} = \frac{\sum_{i=1}^n y_i}{\pi} - \frac{n - \sum_{i=1}^n y_i}{1-\pi} = 0.$$

This equation has solution $\hat{\pi} = (\sum_i y_i)/n$, the number of successes divided by the sample size, which is the sample proportion. Also,

$$\frac{\partial^2 L(\pi)}{\partial \pi^2} = -\frac{\sum_{i=1}^n y_i}{\pi^2} - \frac{n - \sum_{i=1}^n y_i}{(1-\pi)^2} < 0 \text{ for all } 0 < \pi < 1,$$

so $L(\pi)$ is a concave function and is truly maximized at $\hat{\pi}$.

4.2.3 Properties of Maximum Likelihood (ML) Estimators

ML estimators are important because they have desirable asymptotic (i.e., large n) properties:

- ML estimators are asymptotically unbiased: As n increases, any bias they have diminishes to 0.

- ML estimators are consistent: As n increases, the estimator converges toward the parameter value.

- ML estimators are asymptotically efficient: For large n, other estimators do not have smaller standard errors and tend to fall closer to the parameter.

- ML estimators have asymptotic normal sampling distributions.

Section 4.9 explains why these properties hold.

The British statistician Ronald Fisher, who is responsible for much in the way statistical science is now practiced, introduced the ML method in 1922. For n independent observations, he defined the ***information*** as

$$I(\theta) = nE\left(\frac{\partial \log f(Y; \theta)}{\partial \theta}\right)^2, \tag{4.3}$$

---

for most distributions, the ML estimator of the median differs from and is more efficient than the sample median.

with the expectation taken with respect to Y for fixed θ. The information increases as the sample size n increases. Fisher showed that the approximate normal distribution of the ML estimator $\hat{\theta}$ is

$$\hat{\theta} \sim N\left(\theta, \frac{1}{I(\theta)}\right).$$

The variance decreases as n and thus the information increase. Any estimator that has variance that simplifies to $1/I(\theta)$ for large n is asymptotically efficient. In practice, we don't know the value of θ, but we can estimate $\text{var}(\hat{\theta})$ by $1/I(\hat{\theta})$, substituting $\hat{\theta}$ for θ.

Section 4.9.1 shows that, under certain conditions, an alternative expression for the information that can also use the log-likelihood function $L(\theta)$ is

$$I(\theta) = -nE\left(\frac{\partial^2 \log f(Y;\theta)}{\partial\theta^2}\right) = -E\left(\frac{\partial^2 L(\theta)}{\partial\theta^2}\right). \tag{4.4}$$

Since the second derivative of a function describes curvature, the corresponding alternative expression $1/I(\theta)$ for the large-sample variance of $\hat{\theta}$ indicates that $\text{var}(\hat{\theta})$ is smaller when we can expect the log-likelihood function to be more highly curved.[3] In summary, the log-likelihood function is important not only to identify the $\hat{\theta}$ value that maximizes it but also to use its curvature to determine the precision of $\hat{\theta}$ as an estimator of θ.

4.2.4 Example: Variance of ML Estimator of Binomial Parameter

From Section 4.2.1, a binary random variable with $\pi = P(Y = 1)$ and $1 - \pi = P(Y = 0)$ has *pmf* $f(y;\pi) = \pi^y(1-\pi)^{1-y}$ for $y = 0, 1$, that is, the binomial *pmf* for a single trial. So,

$$\log f(y;\pi) = y\log(\pi) + (1-y)\log(1-\pi) \text{ and } \frac{\partial}{\partial\pi}[\log f(y;\pi)] = \frac{y}{\pi} - \frac{1-y}{1-\pi},$$

which combines to $(y-\pi)/[\pi(1-\pi)]$. From equation (4.3), for n independent observations,

$$I(\pi) = nE\left[\frac{\partial \log f(Y;\pi)}{\partial\pi}\right]^2 = nE\left[\frac{Y-\pi}{\pi(1-\pi)}\right]^2 = \frac{nE(Y-\pi)^2}{[\pi(1-\pi)]^2}.$$

Since $E(Y - \pi)^2$ is the binomial variance for $n = 1$, it equals $\pi(1-\pi)$ and therefore $I(\pi) = n/\pi(1-\pi)$. It follows that $\hat{\pi}$ has an approximate normal distribution around π with variance $1/I(\pi) = \pi(1-\pi)/n$. We first observed this formula for the variance of $\hat{\pi}$ in Section 2.4.5.

4.2.5 Example: Variance of ML Estimator of Poisson Mean

When $y_1, \dots, y_n$ are independent observations from a Poisson distribution with parameter $\mu > 0$, the probability mass function (2.7) is $f(y;\mu) = e^{-\mu}\mu^y/y!$ for $y = 0, 1, 2, \dots$. After observing the data, the likelihood function is

$$\ell(\mu) = \prod_{i=1}^{n} f(y_i;\mu) = \prod_{i=1}^{n} \frac{e^{-\mu}\mu^{y_i}}{y_i!} = \frac{e^{-n\mu}\mu^{\sum_{i=1}^{n} y_i}}{\prod_{i=1}^{n} y_i!}, \quad \mu > 0. \tag{4.5}$$

The log-likelihood function is

$$L(\mu) = \log[\ell(\mu)] = -n\mu + \left(\sum_{i=1}^{n} y_i\right)\log(\mu) - \log\left(\prod_{i=1}^{n} y_i!\right).$$

---

[3] The curvature of the log-likelihood function itself, $-\partial^2 L(\theta)/\partial\theta^2$, evaluated at $\theta = \hat{\theta}$, is called the ***observed information***. Its reciprocal is also sometimes used to estimate $\text{var}(\hat{\theta})$.

Differentiating the log-likelihood function, we have

$$\frac{\partial L(\mu)}{\partial \mu} = -n + \frac{\sum_{i=1}^{n} y_i}{\mu} = \frac{\sum_{i=1}^{n} y_i - n\mu}{\mu}.$$

Setting this equal to 0 yields the likelihood equation, which has solution $\hat{\mu} = (\sum_{i=1}^{n} y_i)/n = \bar{y}$. Since

$$\frac{\partial^2 L(\mu)}{\partial \mu^2} = -\frac{\sum_{i=1}^{n} y_i}{\mu^2} < 0 \text{ for all } \mu > 0,$$

$L(\mu)$ is concave and is truly maximized at $\hat{\mu}$.

From the probability mass function $f(y; \mu) = e^{-\mu} \mu^y / y!$,

$$\log f(y; \mu) = y \log(\mu) - \mu - \log(y!), \quad \text{so} \quad \frac{\partial[\log f(y; \mu)]}{\partial \mu} = \frac{y}{\mu} - 1 = \frac{y - \mu}{\mu}.$$

Using equation (4.3), since the variance $\sigma^2 = E(Y - \mu)^2 = \mu$ for the Poisson, the information is

$$I(\mu) = nE\left(\frac{\partial \log f(Y; \mu)}{\partial \mu}\right)^2 = nE\left(\frac{Y - \mu}{\mu}\right)^2 = \frac{n[\text{var}(Y)]}{\mu^2} = \frac{n\mu}{\mu^2} = \frac{n}{\mu}.$$

Or, using equation (4.4), we obtain

$$I(\mu) = -nE\left(\frac{\partial^2[\log f(y; \mu)]}{\partial \mu^2}\right) = -nE\left(\frac{\partial}{\partial \mu}\left[\frac{Y}{\mu} - 1\right]\right) = -nE\left(-\frac{Y}{\mu^2}\right) = \frac{n\mu}{\mu^2} = \frac{n}{\mu}.$$

The variance of the large-sample normal distribution of $\hat{\mu}$ is $[I(\mu)]^{-1} = \mu/n$. This is no surprise, because $\hat{\mu} = \bar{y}$, the variance of $\bar{Y}$ is σ^2/n, which is μ/n for the Poisson distribution. The corresponding estimate of $\text{var}(\hat{\mu}) = \text{var}(\bar{Y})$ is $\bar{y}/n$.

4.2.6 Sufficiency and Invariance for ML Estimates

For the most commonly-used distributions, a statistic $T(\mathbf{Y})$ exists such that the likelihood function factors as $\ell(\theta) = g[T(\mathbf{y}); \theta]h(\mathbf{y})$, that is, one function involving θ and depending on the data $\mathbf{y}$ only through $T(\mathbf{y})$ and a separate function involving $\mathbf{y}$ but not involving θ. Finding θ to maximize $\ell(\theta)$ is equivalent to finding θ to maximize $g[T(\mathbf{y}); \theta]$. So, the ML estimate of θ depends on the data only through $T(\mathbf{y})$, not each individual observation. The statistic $T(\mathbf{Y})$ is called the **sufficient statistic** for θ. Once we know its value, the data provide no further information about θ.[4] The **factorization theorem** states that when $\ell(\theta)$ factors as $g[T(\mathbf{y}); \theta]h(\mathbf{y})$, the statistic $T(\mathbf{y})$ is sufficient for estimating θ.

We illustrate for the Poisson distribution. Its likelihood function (4.5) is

$$\ell(\mu) = \frac{e^{-n\mu} \mu^{\sum y_i}}{\prod_{i=1}^{n} y_i!} = g\left(\sum y_i; \mu\right)h(\mathbf{y}),$$

where $g(\sum y_i; \mu) = e^{-n\mu} \mu^{\sum y_i}$ is the part involving μ and the data, through $T(\mathbf{y}) = \sum_i y_i$, and $h(\mathbf{y}) = 1/\prod_{i=1}^{n} y_i!$ involves the data but does not involve μ. The sufficient statistic for estimating μ is $\sum_i y_i$. For example, for $n = 3$ observations from a Poisson distribution, the samples (4, 4, 4,), (1, 4, 7), and (2, 4, 6) all provide the same information, because the sufficient statistic $\sum_i y_i = 12$ for each case.

---

[4]Formally, $T(\mathbf{Y})$ is defined as a *sufficient statistic* for θ if the conditional distribution of $\mathbf{Y} \mid T(\mathbf{y})$ does not depend on θ; that is, we get no further information about θ from the data $\mathbf{y}$ once we know $T(\mathbf{y})$. The **Rao–Blackwell Theorem** says that if $\hat{\theta}$ is *not* a function of the sufficient statistic, a more efficient estimator exists that is, obtained by conditioning on $\hat{\theta}$.

Any sensible estimator of a parameter should be a function of the data through the sufficient statistic. With huge data sets, we can reduce the dimensionality of the data by creating a much smaller data file of the sufficient statistic values and then conduct statistical analyses that depend only on sufficient statistics. Although statistical analyses are possible using only the sufficient statistics, we cannot re-create the individual observations from them. Knowing merely that $\sum_i y_i = 12$ with $n = 3$, we cannot re-create (y_1, y_2, y_3). With many sources of data, such as in medical records, privacy issues arise such that individual-level data cannot be made publicly available. Data scientists that analyze the data can report merely the sufficient statistics for the distributions used in analyzing the data, and then others can do secondary analyses without any reduction in available information and without violating privacy restrictions.

A final property of ML estimators is that they are ***invariant***: If $\hat{\theta}$ is the ML estimate of θ, then for any function g, the ML estimate of $g(\theta)$ is $g(\hat{\theta})$. For example, the skewness coefficient for a Poisson distribution is $1/\sqrt{\mu}$. Since the ML estimate of μ is $\bar{y}$, the ML estimate of the skewness coefficient is $1/\sqrt{\hat{\mu}} = 1/\sqrt{\bar{y}}$. For a normal distribution, one can show that the ML estimate of σ^2 is $\hat{\sigma}^2 = [\sum_i (y_i - \bar{y})^2]/n$. Therefore, $\sqrt{[\sum_i (y_i - \bar{y})^2]/n}$ is the ML estimate of σ.

4.3 Constructing Confidence Intervals

We next formally define a confidence interval and then present a method for constructing one.

Confidence interval

In a study employing randomization, let $T_L(\mathbf{Y})$ and $T_U(\mathbf{Y})$ be two functions of observations $\mathbf{Y} = (Y_1, \ldots, Y_n)$ such that

$$P[T_L(\mathbf{Y}) \leq \theta \leq T_U(\mathbf{Y})] = 1 - \alpha, \text{ for all possible values of } \theta.$$

Once the data $\mathbf{Y} = \mathbf{y}$ are observed, the interval $[T_L(\mathbf{y}), T_U(\mathbf{y})]$ is called a $100(1-\alpha)\%$ ***confidence interval*** for θ, with lower and upper ***confidence limits*** $T_L(\mathbf{y})$ and $T_U(\mathbf{y})$. The probability $1 - \alpha$, called the ***confidence level***, is usually chosen close to 1, such as 0.95 or 0.99,. The corresponding probability α is an ***error probability***.

A subtle distinction exists between "confidence" and "probability." Once we have observed the data, a confidence interval either does or does not contain the parameter. A probability such as 0.95 applies to the random interval $[T_L(\mathbf{Y}), T_U(\mathbf{Y})]$, with endpoints that are random variables, *before* we observe the data. Probabilities apply to random variables, not to parameter values. Section 4.7 presents an alternative inferential approach, *Bayesian statistics*, in which parameters also have probability distributions and we can legitimately say "The probability is 0.95 that θ falls between $T_L(\mathbf{y})$ and $T_U(\mathbf{y})$."

4.3.1 Using a Pivotal Quantity to Induce a Confidence Interval

We can often find confidence limits $T_L(\mathbf{y})$ and $T_U(\mathbf{y})$ using the sampling distribution of a statistic $T(\mathbf{Y})$ that is a good estimator of θ. If $T(\mathbf{Y})$ has a $N(\theta, \sigma_T^2)$ distribution, then the standardized random variable $[T(\mathbf{Y}) - \theta]/\sigma_T \sim N(0, 1)$. This ratio, which is a function of $\mathbf{Y}$ and θ but has a distribution not depending on θ, is called a ***pivotal quantity***. Now, since

95% of the standard normal distribution falls between −1.96 and 1.96,

$$P\left[-1.96 \leq \frac{T(\mathbf{Y}) - \theta}{\sigma_T} \leq 1.96\right] = 0.95.$$

But this probability is identical to

$$P\left[T(\mathbf{Y}) - 1.96\sigma_T \leq \theta \leq T(\mathbf{Y}) + 1.96\sigma_T\right].$$

Once we observe $\mathbf{y}$, the interval from $T_L(\mathbf{y}) = T(\mathbf{y}) - 1.96\sigma_T$ to $T_U(\mathbf{y}) = T(\mathbf{y}) + 1.96\sigma_T$ is a 95% confidence interval for θ.

Figure 4.2 illustrates the reasoning underlying a pivotal quantity, on the non-standardized scale. For each possible value of θ, on a horizontal axis we have a normal distribution of $T(\mathbf{Y})$ values around θ, with standard error σ_T. As θ increases, the values $T(\mathbf{y}) - 1.96\sigma_T$ and $T(\mathbf{y}) + 1.96\sigma_T$ that encompass 95% of the distribution follow the straight lines shown. Then, when we observe a value $\mathbf{y}_{obs}$ for the data, we look vertically from the observed $T(\mathbf{y}_{obs})$ to the points $T(\mathbf{y}_{obs}) - 1.96\sigma_T$ and $T(\mathbf{y}_{obs}) + 1.96\sigma_T$ on those lines. They are the endpoints of the 95% confidence interval for the unknown value of θ.

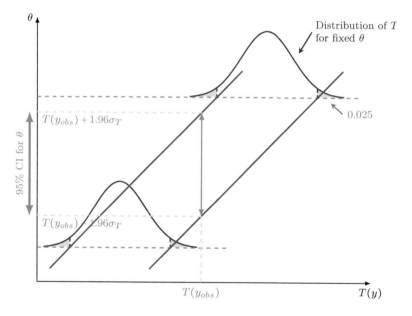

FIGURE 4.2 A statistic $T(\mathbf{y})$ with standardized version that is a pivotal quantity having a standard normal distribution induces a confidence interval (CI) for θ, here illustrated for 95% confidence.

This result has broad implications for data analysis. From the Central Limit Theorem, regardless of the population distribution, in randomized studies $\overline{Y}$ has an approximately normal sampling distribution for large n. Also, as stated in the previous section, maximum likelihood estimators typically have large-sample normal distributions, and the delta method implies that this is true for many statistics. Therefore, it is often possible to form a pivotal quantity $(\hat{\theta} - \theta)/\sigma_{\hat{\theta}}$, using an estimator $\hat{\theta}$ of θ having standard error $\sigma_{\hat{\theta}}$. This enables us to construct a confidence interval, such as $\hat{\theta} \pm 1.96\sigma_{\hat{\theta}}$ for 95% confidence.

Let z_a denote the standard normal quantile for right-tail probability equal to a, such as $z_{0.025} = 1.96$. and $z_{0.005} = 2.58$. Then, for confidence level $1 - \alpha$, the confidence interval uses quantiles with tail probabilities equal to $\alpha/2$ and has the form

$$\hat{\theta} \pm z_{\alpha/2}\sigma_{\hat{\theta}}. \tag{4.6}$$

With $\alpha = 0.05$, $\hat{\theta} \pm 1.96\sigma_{\hat{\theta}}$ is a 95% confidence interval; that is, for $\alpha = 0.05$, each tail probability is 0.025 (as shown in Figure 4.2), and $z_{\alpha/2} = z_{0.025} = 1.96$. Similarly, $\hat{\theta} \pm 2.58\sigma_{\hat{\theta}}$ is a 99% confidence interval (i.e., having $\alpha = 0.01$ and probability 0.005 in each tail). As the confidence level grows, α decreases and $z_{\alpha/2}$ increases, so that the confidence interval gets wider.

- As the confidence level increases, the confidence interval gets wider.

- As n grows, the standard error decreases, so the confidence interval gets narrower.

4.3.2 A Large-Sample Confidence Interval for the Mean

We can use the pivotal quantity approach to construct a confidence interval for a population mean μ of a quantitative variable, using n independent observations, such as in a randomized study. In practice, we usually do not know the shape of the population distribution, other than what we learn from the sample data. By the Central Limit Theorem, for large n the sampling distribution of $\overline{Y}$ is approximately normal with mean μ and standard error $\sigma_{\overline{Y}} = \sigma/\sqrt{n}$. Therefore, $Z = (\overline{Y} - \mu)/\sigma_{\overline{Y}} = (\overline{Y} - \mu)/(\sigma/\sqrt{n})$ has an approximate standard normal distribution and is a pivotal quantity. For example, as $n \to \infty$,

$$P\left[-1.96 \le \frac{\overline{Y} - \mu}{\sigma/\sqrt{n}} \le 1.96 \right] = P\left[\overline{Y} - 1.96\frac{\sigma}{\sqrt{n}} \le \mu \le \overline{Y} + 1.96\frac{\sigma}{\sqrt{n}} \right] \to 0.95.$$

Using the data, $\overline{y} \pm 1.96\sigma/\sqrt{n}$ is a 95% confidence interval for μ.

You may have noticed a glitch here. To use the formula $\overline{y} \pm 1.96\sigma/\sqrt{n}$, we need to know σ, the population standard deviation. In practice, this is rarely the case. The method is designed for large n, and then the sample standard deviation s is close to σ, so we could approximate this confidence interval by $\overline{y} \pm 1.96(s/\sqrt{n})$. However, a better approach accounts for the error introduced by substituting s for σ. Section 4.4 introduces a slight adaptation of this confidence interval formula that does this.

4.3.3 Confidence Intervals for Proportions

As explained in Section 3.3.3, since the sample proportion $\hat{\pi}$ is the sample mean $\overline{y}$ for binary $(0, 1)$ data, the sampling distribution of the random variable $\hat{\pi} = \overline{Y}$ is approximately normal, for large n. That distribution has mean π and standard error $\sigma_{\hat{\pi}} = \sqrt{\pi(1-\pi)/n}$, where π is also the parameter of the corresponding binomial distribution. The pivotal quantity

$$Z = \frac{\hat{\pi} - \pi}{\sqrt{\frac{\pi(1-\pi)}{n}}}$$

has an approximate standard normal distribution. Bounding this between standard normal percentiles,

$$P\left[-z_{\alpha/2} \le \frac{\hat{\pi} - \pi}{\sqrt{\frac{\pi(1-\pi)}{n}}} \le z_{\alpha/2} \right] \to 1 - \alpha.$$

To construct a confidence interval for π after observing the sample proportion $\hat{\pi}$, we solve the equalities

$$\hat{\pi} - \pi = \pm z_{\alpha/2} \sqrt{\frac{\pi(1-\pi)}{n}}$$

for π to get the endpoints. When we square both sides and solve the resulting equation, which is quadratic in π, we obtain the confidence interval

$$\left(\hat{\pi} + \frac{z_{\alpha/2}^2}{2n} \pm z_{\alpha/2} \sqrt{[\hat{\pi}(1-\hat{\pi}) + z_{\alpha/2}^2/4n]/n}\right) \Bigg/ \left(1 + \frac{z_{\alpha/2}^2}{n}\right), \qquad (4.7)$$

called the **score confidence interval** for a proportion.[5] Although the theory is based on large n, it performs reasonably well for any n encountered in practice.

Formula (4.7) is simple to apply with software, but it seems a bit messy. As n grows, $z_{\alpha/2}^2/n$ approaches 0, and the denominator $(1 + z_{\alpha/2}^2/n)$ for the midpoint and the margin of error approaches 1, so the confidence interval has a simple approximate formula

$$\hat{\pi} \pm z_{\alpha/2} \sqrt{\frac{\hat{\pi}(1-\hat{\pi})}{n}}. \qquad (4.8)$$

This has the pivotal-method form (4.6), but substituting an *estimated* standard error for the true one. The method of constructing a confidence interval by adding and subtracting a multiple of an *estimated* standard error from the point estimate is called the **Wald confidence interval.**

The simple Wald formula (4.8) is appealing. However, it does not perform as well as the score confidence interval (4.7), which does not require estimating the standard error. For example, the actual probability that the 95% Wald confidence interval contains the true parameter value can be much less than 0.95, especially when π is close to 0 or close to 1 (see Exercise 4.50 and Section A.4.1 of the R Appendix). Let's take a closer look at the score formula, to see what this rather messy calculation is doing. From formula (4.7), its midpoint is

$$\left(\hat{\pi} + \frac{z_{\alpha/2}^2}{2n}\right) \Bigg/ \left(1 + \frac{z_{\alpha/2}^2}{n}\right) = \hat{\pi}\left(\frac{n}{n + z_{\alpha/2}^2}\right) + \frac{1}{2}\left(\frac{z_{\alpha/2}^2}{n + z_{\alpha/2}^2}\right). \qquad (4.9)$$

This is a weighted average of $\hat{\pi}$ and $1/2$, with weight given to $\hat{\pi}$ approaching 1 as n grows. So, this midpoint shrinks $\hat{\pi}$ towards $1/2$, the shrinkage being less severe as n increases. This shrinkage is effective, because when $\hat{\pi}$ is very close to 0 or 1, it is not sensible for $\hat{\pi}$ to be the midpoint. The cases $\hat{\pi} = 0$ or 1 are especially problematic (Exercise 4.50(c)).

4.3.4   Example: Atheists and Agnostics in Europe

A 2019 Eurobarometer survey reported that the percentage of people who are atheists or agnostics varies in Western Europe between 9% in Ireland and 52% in the Netherlands.[6] Confidence intervals show the precision of such estimates. We illustrate with The Netherlands, where of the 1497 respondents, 778 reported being atheists or agnostics. The score formula (4.7) and Wald formula (4.8) are readily available in software, such as R, and apps on the Internet.[7] We obtain 95% confidence intervals, which are the default for most software, for these two methods and one other:

---

[5]Sections 4.9.1 and 5.7.3 explain the reason for the "score" name.

[6]Others include Italy 14%, Austria 16%, Denmark 22%, Finland 24%, Germany 30%, Belgium 31%, Spain 32%, UK 37%, France 40%, Sweden 50%.

[7]Such as the *Inference for a Proportion* app at `www.artofstat.com/web-apps`

```
> library(proportion)
> ciAllx(778, 1497, 0.05)              # binomial outcome, n, error probability alpha
        method   x LowerLimit UpperLimit # showing 3 of 6 confidence intervals provided
1         Wald 778  0.4943974  0.5450148
3 Likelihood 778  0.4943405  0.5449894 # uses likelihood function (discussion below)
4        Score 778  0.4943793  0.5449320
```

With this large n value, the intervals are all the same to three decimal places. From formula (4.7), the score confidence interval indicates that for $\hat{\pi} = 0.520$, the lower confidence limit of 0.494 is the value of π for which

$$z = \frac{\hat{\pi} - \pi}{\sqrt{\frac{\pi(1-\pi)}{n}}} = \frac{0.520 - 0.494}{\sqrt{\frac{0.494(0.506)}{1497}}} = 1.96,$$

and the upper confidence limit of 0.545 is the value of π for which $z = -1.96$.

The other confidence interval shown is based on a method that directly uses the likelihood function. For a parameter θ, the maximum likelihood estimate $\hat{\theta}$ is the point at which the likelihood function $\ell(\theta)$ takes its highest value. The likelihood-based confidence interval consists of the set of θ values near $\hat{\theta}$ for which $\ell(\theta)$ is not much lower than $\ell(\hat{\theta})$. For example, the 95% confidence interval consists of θ such that $\ell(\hat{\theta})/\ell(\theta)$ is no greater than about 7. This method naturally relates to a method presented in the next chapter, and we shall defer further details to Section 5.7.

4.3.5 Using Simulation to Illustrate Long-Run Performance of CIs

Having "95% confidence" means that if the confidence interval method were used in analyzing a large number of data sets, then in the long run 95% of the confidence intervals would contain the true parameter values. Figure 4.3 illustrates, showing 100 such confidence intervals $[T_L(\mathbf{y}), T_U(\mathbf{y})]$ for a parameter θ, based on 100 separate samples from some population. The intervals in red do not include θ. In the long run, 5% of the confidence intervals would provide an incorrect inference about the value of θ.

To verify the long-run performance of the method, we can simulate by taking multiple samples of a particular size when θ takes a particular value, observing the coverage and non-coverage of the confidence intervals. Or, we can use an app that does this for us. For instance, at www.artofstat.com/web-apps, click on the *Explore Coverage* app and use the *Confidence Interval for a Proportion* option. Consider a scenario such as the survey question in Section 4.3.4, for which $n = 1497$. Suppose that the true population proportion is $\pi = 0.53$. Set $\pi = 0.53$ and $n = 1497$ on the menu at the left part of the app page. The default confidence level is 95%, but it can be changed. In the method for constructing the interval, select *Wilson's Score*, which is formula (4.7). First choose 1 for the number of samples of size $n = 1497$ to draw, and click on *Draw Sample(s)*. You will then see the confidence interval constructed with that sample on the chart to the right. It has green color if it covers $\pi = 0.53$ and red color if it does not. Next reset and then select 10 separate samples, each of size $n = 1497$. Did any fail to contain $\pi = 0.53$? Do this several more times (selecting 10 samples and viewing the 10 confidence intervals), so you get a sense of how often the method fails to contain π. Reset again, now selecting 1000 separate samples, each of size $n = 1497$. You should find that approximately 95% of the confidence intervals contain the parameter value $\pi = 0.53$.

4.3.6 Determining the Sample Size before Collecting the Data

The margin of error for a confidence interval depends on the standard error of the point estimate. Thus, the basis for inferential power lies in the formulas for the standard errors.

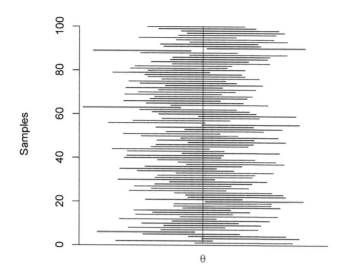

Confidence Intervals [$T_L(\mathbf{y})$, $T_U(\mathbf{y})$]

FIGURE 4.3 95% confidence intervals for a parameter θ based on 100 separate samples from a population. The confidence intervals in red are the ones that fail to include θ.

Before data collection begins, a study should determine the sample size that will provide a desired degree of precision in estimating the parameter of main interest. A relevant measure is the value of n for which the confidence interval has margin of error equal to some specified value. The key results for finding the sample size are that the margin of error depends directly on the standard error of the sampling distribution of the point estimator, and the standard error itself depends on the sample size.

4.3.7   Example: Sample Size for Evaluating an Advertising Strategy

The entrepreneur mentioned in Section 3.1.4 who plans to open a new restaurant has designed an advertisement for the restaurant that she plans to place at an Internet site and also mail to a random sample of homes in her city. The ad contains a coupon that would need to be redeemed within two weeks. To cut costs, she does not want to use a large mailing until she determines whether that method of advertising is effective, with at least about 10% of the households that receive the coupon actually using it. So, she would like to know how large a mailing she would need to determine the effectiveness. She decides to use a sample size for the mailing such that, with probability 0.95, the error in estimating the proportion π of households in that city that would redeem such a coupon would not exceed 0.04. That is, she wanted to use n such that a 95% confidence interval for π equals $\hat{\pi} \pm 0.04$.

Since the sampling distribution of $\hat{\pi}$ is approximately normal, $\hat{\pi}$ falls within 1.96 standard errors of π with probability 0.95. Thus, if n is such that 1.96 standard errors equals 0.04, then with probability 0.95, $\hat{\pi}$ falls within 0.04 units of π (see Figure 4.4). Since the true standard error is $\sigma_{\hat{\pi}} = \sqrt{\pi(1-\pi)/n}$, the equation $0.04 = 1.96\sigma_{\hat{\pi}}$ is

$$0.04 = 1.96\sqrt{\frac{\pi(1-\pi)}{n}}, \quad \text{and solving for } n, \quad n = \frac{(1.96)^2\pi(1-\pi)}{(0.04)^2}.$$

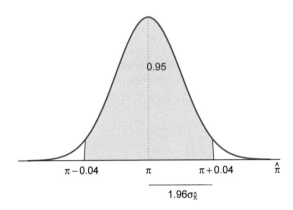

FIGURE 4.4 The sample size having error of estimation of no greater than 0.04, with probability 0.95, in using the sample proportion $\hat{\pi}$ to estimate π, is the value of n for which the sampling distribution of $\hat{\pi}$ has $0.04 = 1.96(\text{standard error})$.

Now, we face a problem. We want to determine n to estimate π, but this formula requires its value, because the standard error is a function of π. The largest possible value for $\pi(1-\pi)$ occurs when $\pi = 0.50$. The sampling distribution is more spread out, and it is more difficult to estimate π precisely, if π is close to 0.50 than if it is near 0 or 1. Thus, we could merely substitute 0.50 for π in the equation for n, yielding

$$n = \frac{(1.96)^2\pi(1-\pi)}{(0.04)^2} = \frac{(1.96)^2(0.50)(0.50)}{(0.04)^2} = 600.$$

This ensures that with confidence level 0.95, the margin of error will not exceed 0.04, no matter what the value of π. This n value is excessively large, however, if π is not near 0.50. If based on talking to colleagues who have used similar advertising mailings, she believed that π would be about 0.10, then an adequate sample size is

$$n = \frac{(1.96)^2\pi(1-\pi)}{(0.04)^2} = \frac{(1.96)^2(0.10)(0.90)}{(0.04)^2} = 216.$$

For a quantitative response, determining n so that the sampling distribution of $\bar{y}$ has a particular margin of error requires guessing the population standard deviation σ, because the standard error of $\bar{y}$ is $\sigma_{\bar{Y}} = \sigma/\sqrt{n}$. Calculators for the formulas for determining n are available on the Internet.[8]

---

[8]Such as at https://epitools.ausvet.com.au/samplesize

4.4   Confidence Intervals for Means of Normal Populations

For constructing confidence intervals for means, from Section 4.3.2, $Z = (\overline{Y} - \mu)/(\sigma/\sqrt{n})$ is a pivotal quantity for large samples, in which case it has approximately a standard normal distribution. In sampling from a normal population distribution, Z has an *exact* standard normal distribution, *for all n*. Since σ is almost always also an unknown parameter, however, we substitute the *sample* standard deviation s for σ.

4.4.1   The t Distribution

Substituting s for σ to get the *estimated* standard error, $se = s/\sqrt{n}$, introduces extra error that can be sizeable when n is small. For independent observations from a normal distribution, with S as the random variable version of s, the pivotal quantity

$$T = \frac{\overline{Y} - \mu}{S/\sqrt{n}}$$

has a sampling distribution over the entire real line that is slightly more spread out than the standard normal distribution. This distribution is called the ***t distribution***. Here are its main properties:

- The t distribution is bell-shaped and symmetric about 0.

- The *pdf* $f(y)$ of the t distribution is proportional to $1/[1 + (y^2/d)]^{(d+1)/2}$, depending on an index d called the ***degrees of freedom***, denoted by *df*. For inference about a single population mean, $df = n - 1$. When $df > 2$, the expected value of a t-distributed random variable is 0 and its standard deviation is $\sqrt{df/(df-2)}$, which is just slightly larger than 1 when *df* is large.

- The t distribution has thicker tails and is more spread out than the standard normal distribution. Different t quantile scores apply for each *df* value. The larger the *df* value, the more closely the t distribution resembles the standard normal. Figure 4.5 illustrates. When *df* is about 30 or higher, the two distributions are practically identical.

For a particular *df* value, we denote the t quantile having probability a in the right-tail (and so is the $1 - a$ quantile) by $t_{a,df}$. The t quantile scores are supplied by software and by Internet apps.[9] The R function qt gives t quantiles; pt gives t cumulative probabilities. For 95% confidence intervals, we use t quantile scores having right-tail probability of 0.025 and cumulative probability of 0.975. Here they are when $df = 1, 10, 30, 100, 1000, 10000$:

```
> qt(0.975, c(1,10,30,100,1000,10000)) # 0.975 quantiles for df values from 1 to 10000
[1] 12.706205  2.228139  2.042272  1.983972  1.962339  1.960201
> pt(1.960201, 10000) # cumulative probability at t = 1.960201 when df = 10000
[1] 0.975             # also standard normal cumulative probability = 0.975 at z = 1.96
```

In particular, $t_{0.025,10000} = 1.9602$. The corresponding normal quantile, obtained with qnorm(0.975) in R, is 1.9600. The t distribution more closely resembles the standard normal distribution as n and hence *df* increases, because s is increasingly precise as an estimate of σ in approximating the standard error $\sigma/\sqrt{n}$ by $se = s/\sqrt{n}$.

---

[9]Such as by https://istats.shinyapps.io/tdist at www.artofstat.com/web-apps

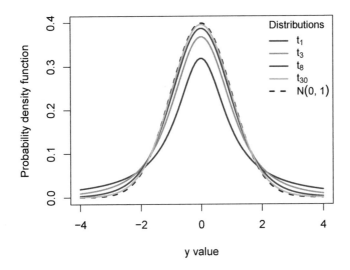

FIGURE 4.5 The t distribution, shown here with df = 1, 3, 8, and 30, has thicker tails than the standard normal distribution, but converges to it as $df \to \infty$. The two distributions are very close when $df \geq 30$.

The t distribution was discovered in 1908 by William Sealy Gosset, a British-born statistician and chemist. Gosset was employed by Guinness Breweries in Dublin, Ireland, designing experiments pertaining to the selection, cultivation, and treatment of barley and hops for the brewing process. Due to company policy forbidding the publishing of trade secrets, Gosset used the pseudonym *Student* when he wrote about his discovery. The t distribution became known as *Student's t* distribution. The method for using the t distribution to construct confidence intervals for a mean was not developed until nearly 30 years after Gosset's discovery.

4.4.2 Confidence Interval for a Mean Using the t Distribution

We use a quantile from the t distribution to construct a margin of error and a confidence interval for a mean.

Confidence interval for population mean μ

For n independent observations from a normal population distribution with sample mean $\bar{y}$, a $100(1 - \alpha)\%$ confidence interval for μ is

$$\bar{y} \pm t_{\alpha/2, n-1}\left(\frac{s}{\sqrt{n}}\right), \tag{4.10}$$

using standard error $se = s/\sqrt{n}$ and $df = n - 1$ for the t quantile score.

For instance, for a 95% confidence interval with n = 50 observations, the confidence interval is $\bar{y} \pm t_{0.025,49}(s/\sqrt{n})$, where $t_{0.025,49} = 2.0096$. We can compute t confidence intervals using software or Internet apps.[10]

Confidence intervals using the t distribution assume a normal population distribution. In practice, the population distribution may not be close to normal. We discuss the importance of this assumption later in the section.

4.4.3   Example: Estimating Mean Weight Change for Anorexic Girls

An experimental study compared three therapies for young girls suffering from anorexia, an eating disorder. For each girl, weight was measured before and after a fixed period of treatment designed to aid weight gain. For the 29 girls undergoing the cognitive behavioral (cb) therapy, the weights at the end of the study minus the weights at the beginning (in pounds) were[11]

$$1.7, 0.7, -0.1, -0.7, -3.5, 14.9, 3.5, 17.1, -7.6, 1.6, 11.7, 6.1, 1.1, -4.0, 20.9,$$
$$-9.3, 2.1, 1.4, -0.3, -3.7, -1.4, -0.8, 2.4, 12.6, 1.9, 3.9, 0.1, 15.4, -0.7$$

Let μ denote the population mean change in weight, if this therapy could be administered to the conceptual population of anorexia sufferers.

Using R to analyze the data, we obtain results for descriptive and inferential statistics:

```
> Anorexia <- read.table("http://stat4ds.rwth-aachen.de/data/Anorexia.dat", header=TRUE)
> head(Anorexia, 3)              # first 3 lines in Anorexia data file
  subject therapy before after   # before and after therapy treatment
1       1      cb   80.5  82.2    # weight change = 82.2 - 80.5 = 1.7
2       2      cb   84.9  85.6
3       3      cb   81.5  81.4    # first 29 of 72 lines in data file are cb therapy
> change <-  Anorexia$after - Anorexia$before
> summary(change[Anorexia$therapy=="cb"]) # cb is cognitive behavioral therapy
   Min. 1st Qu.  Median    Mean 3rd Qu.    Max.
 -9.100  -0.700   1.400   3.007   3.900  20.900
> sd(change[Anorexia$therapy=="cb"])       # standard deviation of weight changes
[1] 7.308504
> hist(change[Anorexia$therapy=="cb"])     # histogram of weight change values
> t.test(change[Anorexia$therapy=="cb"], conf.level=0.95)$conf.int
[1] 0.22689 5.78690                         # 95% confidence interval
> t.test(change[Anorexia$therapy=="cb"], conf.level=0.99)$conf.int
[1] -0.74328  6.75707                        # 99% confidence interval
```

The weight changes had $\bar{y} = 3.007$ pounds, with $s = 7.309$, so the estimated standard error is $se = s/\sqrt{n} = 7.309/\sqrt{29} = 1.357$. Since $n = 29$, $df = n - 1 = 28$. A 95% confidence interval for μ uses $t_{0.025,28} = 2.048$, yielding

$$\bar{y} \pm t_{0.025,28}(se) = 3.007 \pm 2.048(1.357) = 3.01 \pm 2.78, \text{ or } (0.23, 5.79).$$

With 95% confidence, we infer that the interval (0.23, 5.79) contains μ. It appears that μ is positive, but it may be very small. To be safer, we could use a 99% confidence interval. It uses $t_{0.005,28} = 2.763$, yielding

$$\bar{y} \pm 2.763(se) = 3.007 \pm 2.763(1.357), \text{ which is } (-0.74, 6.76).$$

This confidence interval is wider, the cost of having greater confidence. It contains 0, suggesting that 0 is a plausible value for μ. Another reason for caution is that this experimental

---

[10]Such as the *Inference for a Mean* app at www.artofstat.com/web-apps
[11]Courtesy of Prof. Brian Everitt, King's College, London

study used a volunteer sample, because it is not possible to identify and randomly sample a population of anorexic girls. Inferences are tentative and "95% confidence" or "99% confidence" in results may be overly optimistic. The study did employ randomization in assigning girls to three therapies (only one of which is considered here), which is reassuring for analyses conducted later that compare the therapies.

Another caveat is shown by the histogram in Figure 4.6, which reveals that the sample data distribution of weight changes is skewed to the right. The assumption of a normal population distribution may be violated—more about that below. The median weight change is only 1.40 pounds, somewhat less than the mean of 3.01 because of the skew to the right. The sample median is another indication that the size of any true effect could be quite small.

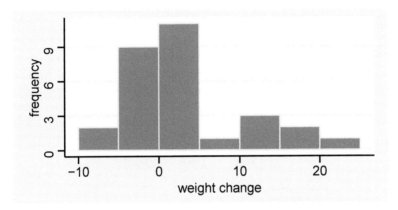

FIGURE 4.6 Histogram of weight change values (in pounds) for anorexia study.

4.4.4 Robustness for Violations of Normal Population Assumption

The t confidence interval for a mean assumes independent observations from a normal population distribution. For the anorexia study, the histogram in Figure 4.6 is not a precise portrayal of the population distribution because n is only 29, but it shows evidence of skewness. Generally, the normal population assumption seems worrisome, because variables often have population distributions that are quite far from normal.

A statistical method is said to be **robust** with respect to an assumption if it performs adequately even when that assumption is violated. The confidence interval for a mean is quite robust against violations of the normal population assumption. Even if the population is not normal, t confidence intervals still usually perform quite well, especially when n exceeds about 15. As n increases, the normal population assumption becomes less important, because of the Central Limit Theorem. The sampling distribution of $\overline{Y}$ is then bell-shaped even when the population distribution is not. The actual probability that the 95% confidence interval method generates an interval that contains μ is close to 0.95 and gets closer as n increases.

An important case when the method does not perform well is when the data are extremely skewed or contain extreme outliers. Partly this is because of the effect on the method, but also because the mean itself is not then a representative summary of the center (see Section 1.4.3). Also, the t confidence interval method is *not* robust to violations of the data-collection assumption. Like all inferential statistical methods, the method has questionable validity if the method for producing the data did not use randomization.

4.4.5 Construction of t Distribution Using Chi-Squared and Standard Normal

We next define more precisely the random variable that has a t distribution. We then show that for observations from a normal population, the pivotal quantity $T = (\overline{Y} - \mu)/(S/\sqrt{n})$ is such a random variable. To do this, we need to learn more about the *chi-squared distribution*, which Section 2.5.4 briefly introduced.

Chi-squared distribution

The ***chi-squared distribution with d degrees of freedom***, denoted by χ_d^2, is the distribution of $Z_1^2 + \cdots + Z_d^2$ for d independent standard normal random variables $Z_1, \ldots, Z_d$. It is the special case of the gamma distribution (2.10) with shape parameter $k = \frac{d}{2}$ and with $\lambda = \frac{1}{2}$ (scale parameter $= 2$).

A random variable X^2 having a χ_d^2 distribution has mean $E(X^2) = d$, variance $\text{var}(X^2) = 2d$, and skewness coefficient equal to $\sqrt{8/d}$. As d increases, the mean and variance increase but the *pdf* becomes more bell-shaped.[12] A normal approximation is reasonably good when d is at least about 30, although Figure 4.7 shows that slight skew exists even then. Section 4.4.6 and later chapters show that the chi-squared is the key distribution in statistical science for describing variability and for many inferences with discrete data.

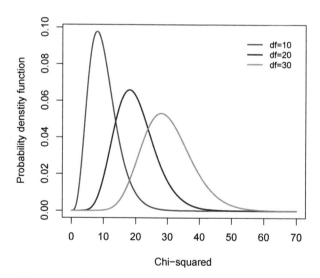

FIGURE 4.7 Chi-squared distributions with degrees of freedom (df) of 10, 20, and 30; these are gamma distributions with shape parameters = 5, 10, and 15 and scale parameter = 2.

Here is how the t distribution relates to standard normal and chi-squared random variables.

---

[12]By the Central Limit Theorem, since more terms are summed as d increases

t distribution

Let Z be a standard normal random variable and let $X^2 \sim \chi_d^2$, independent of Z. Then the probability distribution of

$$T = \frac{Z}{\sqrt{X^2/d}}$$

is the **t distribution with d degrees of freedom.**

In this definition of the T random variable, the chi-squared random variable X^2 has d degrees of freedom, so it is equivalent to the sum of d squared standard normal random variables $\{Z_i^2\}$, and X^2/d is their mean. As d increases, by the law of large numbers $(X^2/d) \xrightarrow{p} 1$, which is $E(Z_i^2) = \mathrm{var}(Z_i)$. Therefore, for large d, $T \approx Z$, a standard normal random variable.

4.4.6 Why Does the Pivotal Quantity Have the t Distribution?

A t-distributed random variable is defined with the construction $T = Z/\sqrt{X^2/d}$, with denominator containing a chi-squared random variable. The reason for this seemingly strange form is that the pivotal quantity $T = (\overline{Y} - \mu)/(S/\sqrt{n})$ that generates a confidence interval for μ has this structure. Here are the steps to show this:

- For n independent observations from a $N(\mu, \sigma^2)$ distribution,

$$\frac{(n-1)s^2}{\sigma^2} = \frac{\Sigma_i(Y_i - \overline{Y})^2}{\sigma^2} \sim \chi_{n-1}^2.$$

  We will show this result below.

- In the t-distributed random variable form, $T = Z/\sqrt{X^2/d}$, we take $Z = \sqrt{n}(\overline{Y} - \mu)/\sigma$, which has a standard normal distribution, and we take the chi-squared random variable $X^2 = (n-1)s^2/\sigma^2$, with degrees of freedom $d = n-1$. Then, if Z and X^2 are independent,

$$T = \frac{Z}{\sqrt{X^2/d}} = \frac{\sqrt{n}(\overline{Y} - \mu)/\sigma}{\sqrt{\frac{(n-1)S^2}{\sigma^2(n-1)}}} = \frac{(\overline{Y} - \mu)}{S/\sqrt{n}}$$

  has the t distribution with $df = n-1$.

- For n independent observations from a $N(\mu, \sigma^2)$ distribution, it can be shown (but is beyond our scope) that $\overline{Y}$ and S^2 are independent random variables.[13] Therefore, the numerator and denominator random variables in $T = (\overline{Y} - \mu)/(S/\sqrt{n})$ are *independent*, as is required in the definition of a t-distributed random variable.

Now let's justify the statement in the first step that $\Sigma_i(Y_i - \overline{Y})^2/\sigma^2 \sim \chi_{n-1}^2$. First, we let $Z_i = (Y_i - \mu)/\sigma$ and use from the definition of the chi-squared distribution that

$$\sum_{i=1}^{n} Z_i^2 = \sum_{i=1}^{n} \left(\frac{Y_i - \mu}{\sigma}\right)^2 = \frac{\sum_{i=1}^{n}(Y_i - \mu)^2}{\sigma^2} \sim \chi_n^2,$$

since $\{Z_i\}$ are independent standard normal random variables. Next we express

$$\frac{\Sigma_i(Y_i - \mu)^2}{\sigma^2} = \frac{\Sigma_i[(Y_i - \overline{Y}) + (\overline{Y} - \mu)]^2}{\sigma^2} = \frac{\Sigma_i(Y_i - \overline{Y})^2}{\sigma^2} + \frac{(\overline{Y} - \mu)^2}{\sigma^2/n},$$

---

[13]Independence of $\overline{Y}$ and S^2 is not true for other distributions; typically they are positively correlated when the population distribution is skewed to the right over the positive real line.

where the cross-product term is 0 because $\sum_i(Y_i - \overline{Y}) = 0$. The final term $(\overline{Y} - \mu)^2/(\sigma^2/n) \sim \chi_1^2$, since it is the square of a single standard normal random variable. Finally, we use a useful property for chi-squared random variables, shown in Exercise 4.76:

- If X_1^2 and X_2^2 are independent random variables, and if $X_1^2 \sim \chi_{d_1}^2$ and $X_1^2 + X_2^2 \sim \chi_{d_1+d_2}^2$, then $X_2^2 \sim \chi_{d_2}^2$.

In this property, we identify X_1^2 with the χ_1^2 random variable $(\overline{Y} - \mu)^2/(\sigma^2/n)$ and $X_1^2 + X_2^2$ with the χ_n^2 random variable $\sum_i(Y_i - \mu)^2/\sigma^2$. Thus, their difference, which is $\sum_i(Y_i - \overline{Y})^2/\sigma^2 = (n-1)S^2/\sigma^2$, is distributed as χ_{n-1}^2.

Incidentally, this derivation shows that using $(n-1)$ as the denominator for the sample variance s^2 is natural, because its random variable version S^2 is the estimator of σ^2 for which $(\overline{Y} - \mu)/(S/\sqrt{n})$ has a t distribution. Also, the result that $\sum_i(Y_i - \overline{Y})^2/\sigma^2$ has a χ_{n-1}^2 distribution implies that S^2 is an unbiased estimator of σ^2. Since $\sum_i(Y_i - \mu)^2 = \sum_i(Y_i - \overline{Y})^2 + n(\overline{Y} - \mu)^2$,

$$
\begin{aligned}
E\left[\sum_i(Y_i - \overline{Y})^2\right] &= E\left[\sum_i(Y_i - \mu)^2 - n(\overline{Y} - \mu)^2\right] \\
&= \sum_i E(Y_i - \mu)^2 - nE(\overline{Y} - \mu)^2 = n\sigma^2 - n(\sigma^2/n) = (n-1)\sigma^2,
\end{aligned}
$$

and it follows that $E(S^2) = E[\sum_i(Y_i - \overline{Y})^2]/(n-1) = (n-1)\sigma^2/(n-1) = \sigma^2$.

4.4.7   Cauchy Distribution: t Distribution with $df = 1$ Has Unusual Behavior

The t distribution with 1 degree of freedom is also called the **Cauchy distribution**. Its standard *pdf* over the real line is (with π as the mathematical constant 3.14159 ...)

$$
f(y) = \frac{1}{\pi(1 + y^2)}. \tag{4.11}
$$

The quartiles are -1 and $+1$, but this distribution has thick tails that die out very slowly as $|y|$ increases. If we try to find $\int yf(y)dy$ or $\int y^2 f(y)dy$, we find that the Cauchy mean and variance do not exist.

The Cauchy distribution is unusual in that many phenomena that otherwise hold quite generally do not apply for it. For instance, it does not have reduced sufficient statistics, and the Central Limit Theorem does not apply. In fact, for the Cauchy distribution, the distribution of $\overline{Y}$ is the same Cauchy distribution. Therefore, $\overline{Y}$ does not even converge in probability to 0 (the mean of the t distribution with $d > 1$ degrees of freedom) as $n \to \infty$. Because of its thick tails, the Cauchy distribution is often used to model situations that are unusual in some way. In financial applications, for instance, when a simulation uses a statistic that should have approximately a standard normal distribution under certain conditions, a Cauchy random variable is sometimes substituted to study the impact of a potential extreme event (often referred to as a *black swan*).

4.5   Comparing Two Population Means or Proportions

Most studies, rather than merely estimating a single mean or proportion, aim to compare two or more groups. To compare population means μ_1 and μ_2 for a quantitative variable, we treat $\mu_1 - \mu_2$ as a parameter and estimate it by the observed difference of sample means, $\overline{y}_1 - \overline{y}_2$. The sampling distribution of $\overline{Y}_1 - \overline{Y}_2$ has expected value $\mu_1 - \mu_2$. This section shows how to construct a confidence interval for $\mu_1 - \mu_2$ and for a difference $\pi_1 - \pi_2$ between two population proportions.

4.5.1 A Model for Comparing Means: Normality with Common Variability

Let $\{y_{i1}\}$ denote n_1 observations in the first sample and let $\{y_{i2}\}$ denote n_2 observations in the second sample. Let s_1 and s_2 denote the sample standard deviations, which estimate the corresponding population standard deviations σ_1 and σ_2. In comparing the population means, the simplest method is a special case of an inference for a statistical *model* to be introduced in Chapter 6 for comparing several means.

Model

A statistical *model* for a set of variables is a simple approximation for the true relationship among those variables in the population. A model has a framework that imposes a structure for the relationship among the variables.

Let Y_1 denote a randomly selected observation from group 1 and Y_2 a randomly selected observation from group 2. The model for the analysis assumes:

Y_1 has a $N(\mu_1, \sigma^2)$ distribution,

Y_2 has a $N(\mu_2, \sigma^2)$ distribution,

with unknown values for the parameters and with $\sigma_1^2 = \sigma_2^2 = \sigma^2$. Sampling distributions and resulting inferences are derived under the assumed model structure.

Models are convenient simplifications of reality. Population distributions will not be exactly normal with identical variances. Such model assumptions may seem worrisome. However, the confidence interval for $\mu_1 - \mu_2$ that we next present is robust against violations of this assumption, especially when $n_1 = n_2$ or they are close.[14] When the assumption of $\sigma_1^2 = \sigma_2^2$ seems to be badly violated, we'll see that an alternative version of the method is available that does not require it. When adequate, however, simpler models have benefits. They generalize directly to settings having additional variables, and inferences can be more powerful and simpler to summarize because of having fewer parameters than under more complex frameworks for the population structure.

4.5.2 A Standard Error and Confidence Interval for Comparing Means

For this model for comparing μ_1 and μ_2, we estimate the common value σ of σ_1 and σ_2 by

$$s = \sqrt{\frac{(n_1 - 1)s_1^2 + (n_2 - 1)s_2^2}{(n_1 - 1) + (n_2 - 1)}} = \sqrt{\frac{\sum_i (y_{i1} - \overline{y}_1)^2 + \sum_i (y_{i2} - \overline{y}_2)^2}{n_1 + n_2 - 2}},$$

where $\sum_i (y_{i1} - \overline{y}_1)^2$ denotes the sum of squares about the mean for observations in the first sample, and $\sum_i (y_{i2} - \overline{y}_2)^2$ denotes the sum of squares about the mean for the second sample. The *pooled estimate* s combines information from the two samples to provide a single estimate of variability. The term inside the square root is a weighted average of the two sample variances, with more weight given to the larger sample.

---

[14] Any skewness is often similar in each group, and tends to diminish for $\overline{y}_1 - \overline{y}_2$ compared with each $\overline{y}$.

From Section 3.2.1, for independent samples the variance of the difference between two random variables is the sum of the individual variances. For the common-variance model,

$$\text{var}(\overline{Y}_1 - \overline{Y}_2) = \text{var}(\overline{Y}_1) + \text{var}(\overline{Y}_2) = \frac{\sigma^2}{n_1} + \frac{\sigma^2}{n_2}.$$

With s as the estimate of σ, the estimated standard error of $\overline{Y}_1 - \overline{Y}_2$ simplifies to

$$se = \sqrt{\frac{s^2}{n_1} + \frac{s^2}{n_2}} = s\sqrt{\frac{1}{n_1} + \frac{1}{n_2}}.$$

To construct a confidence interval, we use the pivotal quantity

$$T = \frac{(\overline{Y}_1 - \overline{Y}_2) - (\mu_1 - \mu_2)}{SE} = \frac{(\overline{Y}_1 - \overline{Y}_2) - (\mu_1 - \mu_2)}{S\sqrt{\frac{1}{n_1} + \frac{1}{n_2}}},$$

where S is the random variable version of the pooled estimate s. We denote this by T rather than Z because we estimated the standard deviation. To justify that this pivotal quantity truly has a t distribution, we can express it in the defining form $T = Z/\sqrt{X^2/d}$ for a t-distributed random variable. Here, the standard normal random variable Z has the same formula as T but with σ in place of s, and the chi-squared random variable X^2 is $(n_1 + n_2 - 2)S^2/\sigma^2$, having $d = n_1 + n_2 - 2$ degrees of freedom. Therefore, the t distribution has $df = n_1 + n_2 - 2$, the sum of the df values of $(n_1 - 1)$ and $(n_2 - 1)$ for the separate inferences about μ_1 and μ_2. Bounding this pivotal quantity between two t quantiles induces a $100(1 - \alpha)\%$ confidence interval for $\mu_1 - \mu_2$,

$$(\overline{y}_1 - \overline{y}_2) \pm t_{\alpha/2, n_1 + n_2 - 2}(se), \quad \text{with} \quad se = s\sqrt{\frac{1}{n_1} + \frac{1}{n_2}}. \tag{4.12}$$

If the data show evidence of greatly different standard deviations (with, say, one being at least 50% larger than the other one), it is better to use an alternative formula. It uses the t confidence interval formula (4.12) but with the standard error of $(\overline{Y}_1 - \overline{Y}_2)$ replaced by $\sqrt{(s_1^2/n_1) + (s_2^2/n_2)}$ and df replaced by a rather messy formula designed so that the corresponding pivotal quantity has distribution closely approximated by the t distribution. The results are similar for the two approaches if s_1 and s_2 are close.

4.5.3   Example: Comparing a Therapy to a Control Group

The study described in Section 4.4.3 used a cognitive behavioral therapy to treat a sample of teenage girls who suffered from anorexia. The study, like most such studies, also had a control group that received no treatment. Then researchers analyzed how the mean weight change compared for the treatment and control groups. The girls in the study were randomly assigned to the cognitive behavioral therapy (Group 1) or to the control group (Group 2). Table 4.1 summarizes the results.

Let μ_1 and μ_2 denote the mean weight gains (in pounds) for these groups for the conceptual populations that the samples represent. The pooled estimate of the assumed common standard deviation is

$$s = \sqrt{\frac{(n_1 - 1)s_1^2 + (n_2 - 1)s_2^2}{n_1 + n_2 - 2}} = \sqrt{\frac{28(7.31)^2 + 25(7.99)^2}{29 + 26 - 2}} = 7.64.$$

TABLE 4.1 Summary of results comparing treatment group to control group for weight change (in pounds) in anorexia study.

Group	Sample Size	Mean	Standard Deviation
Treatment	29	3.01	7.31
Control	26	−0.45	7.99

Now, $\bar{y}_1 - \bar{y}_2 = 3.01 - (-0.45) = 3.46$ has an estimated standard error of

$$se = s\sqrt{\frac{1}{n_1} + \frac{1}{n_2}} = 7.64\sqrt{\frac{1}{29} + \frac{1}{26}} = 2.06.$$

With $df = n_1 + n_2 - 2 = 53$, a 95% confidence interval for $(\mu_1 - \mu_2)$ is

$$(\bar{y}_1 - \bar{y}_2) \pm t_{0.025,53}(se) = 3.46 \pm 2.006(2.06), \text{ which is } 3.46 \pm 4.14, \text{ or } (-0.68, 7.59).$$

We conclude that the mean weight change for the cognitive behavioral therapy could be as much as 0.68 pounds lower or as much as 7.59 pounds higher than the mean weight change for the control group. Since the interval contains 0, it is plausible that the population means are identical. The confidence interval is relatively wide because the sample sizes are not large.

When a confidence interval for $\mu_1 - \mu_2$ contains only positive values, we can infer that $\mu_1 > \mu_2$. One that contains only negative values suggests that $\mu_1 < \mu_2$. The identification of which is group 1 and which is group 2 is arbitrary, as is whether we estimate $\mu_1 - \mu_2$ or $\mu_2 - \mu_1$. Here is R code for constructing the confidence interval using a data file for the three groups in this study:

```
> Anor <- read.table("http://stat4ds.rwth-aachen.de/data/Anorexia.dat", header=TRUE)
> Anor
   subject therapy  before   after    # therapy = cb is cognitive behav.
1        1      cb    80.5    82.2    # therapy = c is control
2        2      cb    84.9    85.6    # therapy = f not used here
...
72      72       c    89.0    78.8
> cogbehav <- Anor$after[Anor$therapy=="cb"] - Anor$before[Anor$therapy=="cb"]
> control  <- Anor$after[Anor$therapy=="c"] - Anor$before[Anor$therapy=="c"]
> cbind(mean(cogbehav), sd(cogbehav), mean(control), sd(control))
[1]  3.006897  7.308504  -0.450000  7.988705

> t.test(cogbehav, control, var.equal=TRUE, conf.level=0.95)
95 percent confidence interval: # 95% CI for difference of cogbehav and control means
 -0.680137  7.593930
> t.test(cogbehav, control)      # not assuming equal population standard deviations
95 percent confidence interval: # 0.95 = default confidence level
 -0.7044632  7.6182563
```

The R output also shows the confidence interval for comparing the means without assuming equal population standard deviations, which is similar.[15] An advantage of assuming that $\sigma_1 = \sigma_2$, even when we know it is not exactly true, is that the method is a special case of a commonly-used method (presented in Chapter 6) that can incorporate additional variables.

Table 4.2 summarizes confidence intervals for individual means and for comparisons of two means.

---

[15]Internet apps are also available for these two methods, such as the *Comparing Two Means* app at www.artofstat.com/web-apps.

TABLE 4.2 Summary of confidence intervals for means of quantitative variables.

Setting	One Mean	Two Means
Assumptions	Random sample, normal population dist.	Random sample, normal popul. dist.'s, equal variances (*)
Parameter	μ	$\mu_1 - \mu_2$
Pivotal quantity	$T = \frac{\overline{Y} - \mu}{SE}$ with $SE = \frac{S}{\sqrt{n}}$	$T = \frac{(\overline{Y}_1 - \overline{Y}_2) - (\mu_1 - \mu_2)}{SE}$ with $SE = S\sqrt{\frac{1}{n_1} + \frac{1}{n_2}}$ for $S = \sqrt{\frac{\Sigma_i(Y_{i1} - \overline{Y}_1)^2 + \Sigma_i(Y_{i2} - \overline{Y}_2)^2}{n_1 + n_2 - 2}}$
Confidence interval	$\overline{y} \pm t_{\alpha/2}(se)$ t distribution, $df = n - 1$	$(\overline{y}_1 - \overline{y}_2) \pm t_{\alpha/2}(se)$ t distribution, $df = n_1 + n_2 - 2$

(*) Alternative method not requiring equal variances has $SE = \sqrt{(S_1^2/n_1) + (S_2^2/n_2)}$ and slightly different df.

4.5.4   Confidence Interval Comparing Two Proportions

For two groups, let π_1 and π_2 denote population proportions for a binary variable of interest. For independent samples of sizes n_1 and n_2,

$$\text{var}(\hat{\pi}_1 - \hat{\pi}_2) = \text{var}(\hat{\pi}_1) + \text{var}(\hat{\pi}_2) = \frac{\pi_1(1 - \pi_1)}{n_1} + \frac{\pi_2(1 - \pi_2)}{n_2}.$$

We can construct a confidence interval for the difference $\Delta = \pi_1 - \pi_2$ using the pivotal quantity

$$Z = \frac{(\hat{\pi}_1 - \hat{\pi}_2) - \Delta}{\sqrt{\frac{\hat{\pi}_1(\Delta)(1 - \hat{\pi}_1(\Delta))}{n_1} + \frac{\hat{\pi}_2(\Delta)(1 - \hat{\pi}_2(\Delta))}{n_2}}}.$$

Since the values of π_1 and π_2 are unknown, the standard error uses the ML estimates subject to the constraint that $\pi_1 - \pi_2 = \Delta$ (*i.e.*, $\hat{\pi}_2(\Delta) = \hat{\pi}_1(\Delta) - \Delta$), so that the denominator proportions satisfy the difference Δ in the numerator. That is, for each Δ, the standard error uses the π_1 and $\pi_2 = \pi_1 - \Delta$ values that are the ML estimates for that particular Δ. Software analyzes this for all possible Δ, and the *score confidence interval* is the set of Δ values that yield $|z| \leq z_{\alpha/2}$. More simply, we could substitute the sample proportions in the standard error formula. This yields the *Wald* confidence interval

$$(\hat{\pi}_1 - \hat{\pi}_2) \pm z_{\alpha/2}\sqrt{\frac{\hat{\pi}_1(1 - \hat{\pi}_1)}{n_1} + \frac{\hat{\pi}_2(1 - \hat{\pi}_2)}{n_2}}. \tag{4.13}$$

However, as in the single-sample case (Section 4.3.3), when sample sizes are small and $\{\pi_i\}$ are near 0 or 1, the score confidence interval has better performance. For example, the 95% score confidence interval tends to have actual coverage probability closer to 0.95 than does the 95% Wald confidence interval.

4.5.5   Example: Does Prayer Help Coronary Surgery Patients?

A study used patients at six U.S. hospitals who were to receive coronary artery bypass graft surgery.[16] The patients were randomly assigned to two groups. For one group, Christian

---

[16] H. Benson et al., *American Heart Journal*, vol. 151, pp. 934–952, 2006

volunteers were instructed to pray for a successful surgery with a quick, healthy recovery and no complications. The praying started the night before surgery and continued for two weeks. The other group did not have volunteers praying for them. The response was whether medical complications occurred within 30 days of the surgery. Table 4.3 summarizes results.

TABLE 4.3 Whether complications occurred for heart surgery patients who did or did not have group prayer.

	Complications		
Prayer	Yes	No	**Total**
Yes	315	289	604
No	304	293	597

Let π_1 denote the probability of complications for those patients who had a prayer group. Let π_2 denote the probability of complications for the patients not having a prayer group. These are population proportions for the conceptual population this sample represents. From Table 4.3, the sample proportions who had complications are

$$\hat{\pi}_1 = \frac{315}{604} = 0.522, \quad \hat{\pi}_2 = \frac{304}{597} = 0.509.$$

We can use R to construct 95% confidence intervals for $\pi_1 - \pi_2$:

```
> prop.test(c(315,304), c(604, 597), conf.level=0.95, correct=FALSE)
95 percent confidence interval:
 -0.04421536  0.06883625    # Wald 95% confidence interval for pi_1 - pi_2
sample estimates:
   prop 1    prop 2
0.5215232 0.5092127

> library(PropCIs)          # uses binomial success count and n for each group
> diffscoreci(315, 604, 304, 597, conf.level=0.95)
95 percent confidence interval:
 -0.04418699  0.06873177    # score 95% confidence interval for pi_1 - pi_2
```

With both Wald and score methods, the 95% confidence interval is $(-0.044, 0.069)$, containing 0. It indicates that the probability of complications is similar for the two groups and may be equal.

Table 4.4 summarizes confidence intervals for individual proportions and for comparisons of two proportions.

TABLE 4.4 Summary of large-sample confidence intervals for proportions.

Setting:	One Proportion	Two Proportions
Assumptions	Random sample, binary response variable	Random sample, binary group and response var's
Parameter	π	$\pi_1 - \pi_2$
Pivotal quantity	$z = \frac{\hat{\pi}-\pi}{SE}$ with $SE = \sqrt{\frac{\hat{\pi}(1-\hat{\pi})}{n}}$	$z = \frac{(\hat{\pi}_1-\hat{\pi}_2)-(\pi_1-\pi_2)}{SE}$ with $SE = \sqrt{\frac{\hat{\pi}_1(1-\hat{\pi}_1)}{n_1} + \frac{\hat{\pi}_2(1-\hat{\pi}_2)}{n_2}}$ (*)
Confidence interval (Wald)	$\hat{\pi} \pm z_{\alpha/2}(se)$	$(\hat{\pi}_1 - \hat{\pi}_2) \pm z_{\alpha/2}(se)$

(*) Alternative "score" confidence intervals use *se* evaluated at parameter value in numerator

4.6 The Bootstrap

Some statistics are too complex to have a simple standard error formula. This is often the case for statistics developed *ad hoc* to describe some situation. Even if the statistic has an approximately normal sampling distribution, without the standard error we cannot use the confidence interval formula of a point estimate plus and minus a z quantile-score multiple of an estimated standard error.

4.6.1 Computational Resampling and Bootstrap Confidence Intervals

For such cases, a computational resampling method is a simple and powerful alternative. This method, called the **bootstrap**, treats the sample distribution as if it were the true population distribution and approximates features of the unknown sampling distribution by simulation. At each step the method samples n observations, with replacement, from the sample data distribution. Each of the original n data points has probability $1/n$ of selection for each "new" observation. This new sample of size n has its own estimate of the parameter θ. The bootstrap method repeats this sampling process a very large number of times, for instance, selecting 10,000 separate samples of size n and computing 10,000 corresponding estimates $\{\hat{\theta}^{(1)}, \hat{\theta}^{(2)}, \dots, \hat{\theta}^{(10000)}\}$ of θ. Generally, for B re-samplings, the empirical distribution of $\{\hat{\theta}^{(b)}, b = 1, 2, \dots, B\}$ is the *bootstrap distribution*.

The bootstrap distribution has shape and variability similar to the actual sampling distribution of $\hat{\theta}$ around θ, but its values vary around $\hat{\theta}$ instead of around θ. That is, the sampling distribution of $\hat{\theta}^{(b)} - \hat{\theta}$ is similar to the sampling distribution of $\hat{\theta} - \theta$. Because of this, the standard deviation of the $\{\hat{\theta}^{(b)}\}$ values from the bootstrap distribution estimates a standard error for the point estimate $\hat{\theta}$ from the observed data. Also, the interval of values between the 2.5 and 97.5 percentiles of the simulated $\{\hat{\theta}^{(b)}\}$ values is a 95% confidence interval for θ. The bootstrap method is easily feasible with modern computing power. First introduced in 1979 by the statistician Bradley Efron, he and others later developed slight variations of the method.[17] For instance, the percentile-based confidence interval tends to be too narrow when n is small, and a "bias-corrected" version has coverage probabilities closer to the nominal level.

4.6.2 Example: Booststrap Confidence Intervals for Library Data

A librarian at the University of Florida recently wanted to estimate various characteristics of books in one of the university's special collections. Among the questions of interest were "How old is a typical book in the collection?" and "How long has it been since a typical book has been checked out?" She suspected that the distributions of these variables were heavily skewed to the right, so she chose the median to describe the center.

The Library data file at the book's website shows observations on P = number of years since publication of book and C = number of years since book checked out, for a simple random sample of 54 books from the collection. Figure 4.8 shows a box plot for the sample values of P. It shows several outliers at the high end. The median of 17 is more representative of the data than the mean of 22.6.

The bootstrap is available with Internet apps[18] and with software. To construct a standard error for the sample median estimate and a confidence interval for the population

---

[17]Efron won the International Prize in Statistics, granted for the second time in 2018, partly for this contribution. See www.nature.com/articles/d41586-018-07395-w.

[18]Such as the *Bootstrap* app at www.artofstat.com/web-apps

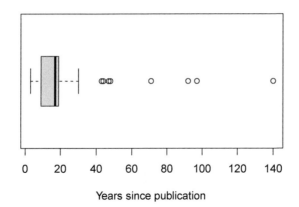

FIGURE 4.8 Box plot for number of years since publication for a sample of library books.

median, we implement the bootstrap in R. For the `boot` function, the first argument is the data, in vector, matrix, or data frame form. The second argument is a function with symbol x for the data re-sampled on the characteristic of interest and symbol b for the index for each re-sample case, and it specifies the statistic to be bootstrapped (here, the median). The third argument is the number of resamplings in the bootstrap (here, 10,000):

```
> Books <- read.table("http://stat4ds.rwth-aachen.de/data/Library.dat", header=TRUE)
> head(Books, 3)
  C  P
1 1  3
2 9  9
3 4  4
> summary(Books$P)
   Min. 1st Qu.  Median    Mean 3rd Qu.    Max.
   3.00    9.00   17.00   21.98   19.00  140.00
> boxplot(Books$P, xlab="Years since publication", horizontal=TRUE)
> library(boot)
> boot.results <- boot(Books$P, function(x,b){median(x[b])}, 10000) # function for data x
> boot.ci(boot.results)                                             # resampling case b
BOOTSTRAP CONFIDENCE INTERVAL CALCULATIONS
Level     Percentile           BCa    # showing 2 of the reported confidence intervals
95%    (11.0, 19.0)    (11.0, 18.5)   # BCa is bias-corrected bootstrap CI
> sd(boot.results$t)
[1] 2.163911 # bootstrap standard error = standard deviation of bootstrap median values
```

The sample median of 17 has a bootstrap standard error of 2.16. The percentile-based method yields a 95% confidence interval for the population median of (11.0, 19.0). The bias-corrected confidence interval, which is a bit more reliable, is (11.0, 18.5). A caveat: When n is small, the bootstrap method does not work well for the median and other statistics that depend heavily on a few observations, because of their severe discreteness.

Next we use the bootstrap to construct a confidence interval for the population standard deviation σ of the number of years since publication of the book. A simple formula exists for a confidence interval for σ based on the assumption of a normal population distribution, but it is not robust to violations of that assumption so we do not show it. The bootstrap is more reliable for this parameter. For the `Library` data file, we obtain:

```
> boot.results2 <- boot(Books$P, function(x,b){sd(x[b])}, 100000)
> boot.ci(boot.results2)
BOOTSTRAP CONFIDENCE INTERVAL CALCULATIONS
Level      Percentile                BCa
95%    (14.06, 35.73)    (17.05, 40.09)
> sd(Books$P)
[1] 25.91758 # sample standard deviation of P = years since publication
> sd(boot.results2$t)
[1] 5.599769 # bootstrap standard error = standard dev. of bootstrap standard dev. values
```

The sample standard deviation of the time since publication of the book was 25.9 years. A 95% bootstrap confidence interval for the population standard deviation is (14.1, 35.7), and the bias-corrected interval is (17.0, 40.1).

Even when a standard error exists, sometimes the confidence interval form of a sample estimate plus and minus a z or t quantile-score multiple of the standard error does not perform well. The correlation is such a case, because its sampling distribution can be quite skewed, especially when the true correlation is near -1 or $+1$. We instead use the bootstrap, illustrating for the correlation between P and C = number of years since book checked out.

```
> plot(Books$C, Books$P)              # scatterplot of C and P shows positive trend
> library(boot)
> set.seed(54321)                     # if we want to be able to reproduce results
> boot_corr = boot(cbind(Books$C, Books$P), function(x,b){cor(x[b,1],x[b,2])}, 100000)
> boot_corr
ORDINARY NONPARAMETRIC BOOTSTRAP
Bootstrap Statistics :
      original      bias     std. error
t1* 0.8121555 -0.01595873  0.09097654  # sample correlation = 0.812
> boot.ci(boot_corr, conf=0.90)
BOOTSTRAP CONFIDENCE INTERVAL CALCULATIONS
Level      Percentile              BCa
90%    ( 0.6113,  0.8944 )   ( 0.6224,  0.8973 )
> hist(boot_corr$t, xlab="Correlation", breaks="Scott")
```

Figure 4.9 shows the bootstrap distribution of the correlation. It is not symmetric, and the sample correlation of 0.81 is not the midpoint of the bias-corrected bootstrap 90% confidence interval of (0.62, 0.90).

4.7   The Bayesian Approach to Statistical Inference

The confidence intervals presented in this chapter use the classical (sometimes called *frequentist*) approach to statistical inference that treats parameter values as fixed and data as realizations of random variables having probability distributions. Probability statements refer to possible values for the data and for statistics generated from the data. Recent years have seen increasing popularity of an alternative approach that also treats parameters as random variables and assumes probability distributions for them as well. This alternative approach is called ***Bayesian statistics***, named after the British theologian Thomas Bayes (1701–1761) who presented what is now called Bayes' Theorem (Section 2.1.5), on which it is based. Statistical inferences then take the form of probability statements about the parameter values, after observing the data.

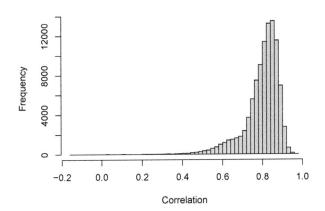

FIGURE 4.9 Bootstrap distribution of correlation between C (number of years since book checked out) and P (number of years since book's publication) for Library data.

4.7.1 Bayesian Prior and Posterior Distributions

The Bayesian approach assumes a ***prior distribution*** for the parameters, reflecting information available about the parameters before observing the data. That information might be based on other studies or it may reflect subjective prior beliefs such as opinions of "experts." Or, the prior distribution may be uninformative, so that inferential results are objective, based nearly entirely on the observed data. The prior distribution combines with the information that the data provide through the likelihood function to generate a ***posterior distribution*** for the parameters. Bayesian statistical inferences are based on the posterior distribution.

For a parameter θ, let $p(\theta)$ denote the probability function for the prior distribution. Let $f(\mathbf{y} \mid \theta)$ denote the probability function for the data, given the parameter value. Let $g(\theta \mid \mathbf{y})$ denote the probability function for the posterior distribution of θ, given the data. By *Bayes' Theorem*,

$$g(\theta \mid \mathbf{y}) = \frac{f(\mathbf{y} \mid \theta) p(\theta)}{f(\mathbf{y})},$$

where $f(\mathbf{y}) = \int_{\theta} f(\mathbf{y} \mid \theta) p(\theta) d\theta$ is the marginal distribution of the data, obtained by integrating out the parameter. In terms of θ, $g(\theta \mid \mathbf{y})$ is proportional to $f(\mathbf{y} \mid \theta) p(\theta)$. Since that product determines the posterior, we can avoid the integration to obtain $f(\mathbf{y})$ in the denominator, which can be computationally difficult. Once we observe the data, $f(\mathbf{y} \mid \theta)$ is the likelihood function $\ell(\theta)$ when we view it as a function of the parameter. So, *the posterior distribution of θ is determined by the product of the likelihood function with the probability function for the prior distribution of θ.* When the prior probability function $p(\theta)$ is relatively flat, as data analysts often choose in practice, $g(\theta \mid \mathbf{y})$ has similar shape as the likelihood function.

Except in a few simple cases, such as presented next for the binomial parameter, the posterior probability function cannot be easily calculated. Software uses simulation methods to approximate it. The primary method for doing this is called ***Markov chain Monte***

Carlo (MCMC). It is beyond our scope to discuss the technical details of how an MCMC algorithm works. In a nutshell, software simulates a very long sequence of values from a Markov chain (Section 2.6.7), the values of which approximate the posterior probability function. The data analyst takes the sequence to be long enough so that the Monte Carlo error is small in approximating summaries of $g(\theta \mid \mathbf{y})$, such as the posterior mean.

Bayesian inferences using the posterior distribution parallel classical inferences. For example, analogous to the classical 95% confidence interval for θ is an interval that contains 95% of the posterior density $g(\theta \mid \mathbf{y})$, called a **posterior interval** or **credible interval**. A simple posterior interval uses percentiles of $g(\theta \mid \mathbf{y})$. A 95% posterior interval for θ is the region between its 2.5 and 97.5 percentiles. The common Bayesian estimator of θ is the posterior mean,[19] $E(\theta \mid \mathbf{y})$.

4.7.2 Bayesian Binomial Inference: Beta Prior Distributions

To estimate a population proportion π based on independent observations in n binary trials, we regard the number of successes y as the outcome of a binomial random variable. We now label the binomial probability function $f(y; n, \pi)$ in equation (2.6) as $f(y \mid \pi; n)$ and treat it as a function of y, given the parameter value π as well as the index n. Since π is a probability, its Bayesian prior distribution is defined over the interval $[0, 1]$ of possible values for π. A common choice is the **beta distribution**. It has *pdf*

$$p(\pi; \alpha, \beta) = \frac{\Gamma(\alpha + \beta)}{\Gamma(\alpha)\Gamma(\beta)} \pi^{\alpha-1}(1 - \pi)^{\beta-1}, \quad 0 \le \pi \le 1, \tag{4.14}$$

where $\Gamma(\cdot)$ denotes the gamma function (Section 2.5.4), which provides the appropriate constant so the *pdf* integrates to 1. The distribution depends on two indices $\alpha > 0$ and $\beta > 0$, often referred to as *hyperparameters* to distinguish them from the parameter π that is the object of the inference. The mean of the beta(α, β) distribution is

$$E(\pi) = \frac{\alpha}{\alpha + \beta}.$$

The family of beta *pdfs* has a wide variety of shapes. With $\alpha = \beta$, it is symmetric around $E(\pi) = 0.50$ with var$(\pi) = 1/[4(2\alpha + 1)]$ that decreases as α increases. The *uniform distribution*, $p(\pi) = 1$ over $[0, 1]$, is the case $\alpha = \beta = 1$. The beta *pdf* has a bimodal U-shape when $\alpha = \beta < 1$ and a bell shape when $\alpha = \beta > 1$ (see Figure 4.10). It is unimodal skewed left when $\alpha > \beta > 1$ and skewed right when $\beta > \alpha > 1$.

Lack of prior knowledge about π might suggest using a uniform prior distribution. The posterior distribution then has the same shape as the binomial likelihood function. Another commonly-used prior distribution is the **Jeffreys prior**, for which prior distributions for different scales of measurement for the parameter (e.g., for π or for $\phi = \log[\pi/(1 - \pi)]$) are equivalent. The Jeffreys prior for π is the beta distribution with $\alpha = \beta = 0.5$. Although it is U-shaped rather than flat, this prior distribution is relatively uninformative, in the sense that it yields inferential results similar to those of good classical methods.

The beta distribution is the **conjugate prior distribution** for inference about a binomial parameter: When combined with the likelihood function, the posterior distribution falls in the same family as the prior, but its parameters are updated, based on the data. When we combine a binomial likelihood function with a beta(α, β) prior distribution, the posterior distribution $g(\pi \mid y) \propto f(y \mid \pi; n)p(\pi; \alpha, \beta)$, so

$$g(\pi \mid y) \propto [\pi^y(1 - \pi)^{n-y}][\pi^{\alpha-1}(1 - \pi)^{\beta-1}] = \pi^{y+\alpha-1}(1 - \pi)^{n-y+\beta-1}, \quad 0 \le \pi \le 1.$$

---

[19]Exercise 4.81 motivates this estimator as minimizing a type of *risk* or *expected loss*.

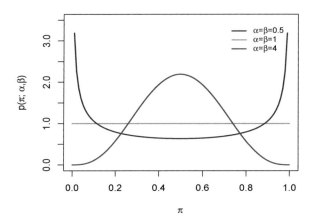

FIGURE 4.10 The *pdf* of a beta distribution with hyperparameters $\alpha = \beta$ is symmetric.

The posterior is the beta distribution indexed by hyperparameter values $\alpha^* = y + \alpha$ and $\beta^* = n - y + \beta$. The Bayesian estimate of π is the mean of this posterior distribution,

$$E(\pi \mid y) = \frac{\alpha^*}{\alpha^* + \beta^*} = \frac{y + \alpha}{n + \alpha + \beta} = \left(\frac{n}{n + \alpha + \beta}\right)\frac{y}{n} + \left(\frac{\alpha + \beta}{n + \alpha + \beta}\right)\frac{\alpha}{\alpha + \beta}.$$

This is a weighted average of the sample proportion, $\hat{\pi} = y/n$, and the mean of the prior distribution, $\alpha/(\alpha + \beta)$. With a uniform prior distribution ($\alpha = \beta = 1$), the estimate is $(y + 1)/(n + 2)$. With $\alpha = \beta$, the estimate shrinks the sample proportion toward 0.50. The weight $n/(n + \alpha + \beta)$ given to the sample proportion increases toward 1 as n increases. The amount of information in the estimate is summarized by n for the data and $\alpha + \beta$ for the prior distribution. With $c > 2$ outcome categories, the binomial distribution generalizes to the *multinomial distribution* (Exercise 2.14) and the beta prior distribution generalizes to the *Dirichlet distribution* (Exercise 4.78).

4.7.3 Example: Belief in Hell

The 2018 General Social Survey (GSS) in the U.S. asked "Do you believe in hell?" Of the 1142 respondents, 814 said *yes* and 328 said *no*. The ML estimate of π is $\hat{\pi} = 814/1142 = 0.713$, and you can check that the 95% score confidence interval (4.7) is $(0.686, 0.738)$. How does this compare to a Bayesian estimate and posterior interval?

For the Jeffreys beta(0.5, 0.5) prior distribution with $y = 814$ and $n - y = 328$, the posterior distribution is beta(α^*, β^*) with $\alpha^* = y + \alpha = 814.5$ and $\beta^* = n - y + \beta = 328.5$. The posterior mean estimate of π is $\alpha^*/(\alpha^* + \beta^*) = 814.5/(814.5 + 328.5) = 0.713$. Software reports the 95% posterior interval of $(0.686, 0.738)$. Its endpoints are the 0.025 and 0.975 quantiles of the beta posterior density. In R, the `qbeta` function provides these quantiles:

```
> qbeta(c(0.025, 0.975), 814.5, 328.5)    # quantiles, beta hyperparameters
[1] 0.686028  0.738464                     # 95% posterior interval
> library(proportion) # can find posterior intervals directly
> ciBAx(814, 1142, 0.05, 0.5, 0.5)         # y, n, error probability, beta hyperparameters
    x     LBAQx     UBAQx     LBAHx     UBAHx # 1st set is (0.025, 0.075) percentiles
1 814 0.686028 0.738464 0.686281 0.738707 # 2nd set is HPD interval (see Section 4.7.6)
> ciAllx(814, 1142, 0.05)
```

```
     method     x LowerLimit UpperLimit    # 1 of 6 confidence intervals provided
  4   Score 814  0.6858635  0.7382790       # classical score confidence interval
```

4.7.4 Interpretation: Bayesian versus Classical Intervals

In the example of estimating the probability π of belief in hell, the Bayesian estimate and posterior interval are the same, to three decimal places, as the ML estimate and classical 95% score confidence interval. This reflects that n is large and the prior distribution is highly disperse. However, the interpretations are quite different.

With the classical approach, the parameter π is fixed, not a random variable. It either *is* or *is not* in the confidence interval of (0.686, 0.738), we do not know which. Our 95% confidence refers to a probability when the data (not the parameter) are viewed as the random variable, that is, before they are observed. It has the "frequentist" interpretation that if we used this method repeatedly with separate, independent samples, in the long run 95% of the confidence intervals would contain π. The probability applies to possible data in future samples, not to the parameter. By contrast, with the Bayesian approach, the parameter π is itself a random variable that has a probability distribution. After observing the data, we can say that the probability is 0.95 that π takes value between 0.686 and 0.738.

Although their interpretations differ, Bayesian and classical approaches usually lead to the same practical conclusions, because the likelihood function is the foundation of each. The set of parameter values regarded as plausible in a classical inference are usually very similar to those regarded as plausible with Bayesian inference. The resemblance increases as n increases and the variance of the prior distribution increases, because the posterior distribution has maximum and shape increasingly similar to the likelihood function.

4.7.5 Bayesian Posterior Interval Comparing Proportions

We can also use the Bayesian approach to form a posterior interval for the difference $\pi_1 - \pi_2$ between two population proportions, based on independent binomial random variables $Y_1 \sim$ binom(n_1, π_1) and $Y_2 \sim$ binom(n_2, π_2). We illustrate with an example from Agresti (2019, p. 51) about a clinical trial with an unusual design in which the 11 patients allocated to the experimental treatment were all successes (i.e., $n_1 = y_1 = 11$) and the only patient allocated to the control treatment was a failure (i.e., $n_2 = 1$, $y_2 = 0$). When we use uniform (i.e., beta(1.0, 1.0)) prior distributions for π_1 and π_2, the posterior distribution is beta($y_1 + 1.0, n_1 - y_1 + 1.0$) = beta(12.0, 1.0) for π_1 and beta($y_2 + 1.0, n_2 - y_2 + 1.0$) = beta(1.0, 2.0) for π_2. Using R, we can simulate results for a 95% posterior interval for $\pi_1 - \pi_2$:

```
> library(PropCIs)
> diffci.bayes(11, 11, 0, 1, 1.0, 1.0, 1.0, 1.0, 0.95, nsim = 1000000)
  # arguments y1, n1, y2, n2, alpha1, beta1, alpha2, beta2, confidence, no. simulations
[1] 0.0642 0.9497 # 95% posterior interval for difference of proportions
```

The posterior probability is 0.95 that the probability of success with the experimental treatment is between 0.064 and 0.950 higher than for the control treatment. The extremely wide interval, which reflects the very small sample sizes, uses posterior quantiles with equal tail areas, 0.025 each.

4.7.6 Highest Posterior Density (HPD) Posterior Intervals

An alternative Bayesian posterior interval is the interval such that the posterior *pdf* is higher over all values in the interval than over all the values not in it. This posterior interval is called a **highest posterior density** (HPD) interval. The HPD interval for a parameter is the shortest possible interval. It is identical to the percentile-based interval when the posterior distribution is unimodal and symmetric.

The R output for the example in Section 4.7.3 shows that with the Jeffreys prior, the 95% HPD interval for estimating the population proportion in the U.S. who believe in hell is (0.6863, 0.7387), very similar to the percentile-based posterior interval of (0.6860, 0.7385). For the clinical trial example in the previous section in which the 11 patients allocated to the experimental treatment were all successes and the only patient allocated to the control treatment was a failure, uniform prior distributions implied a posterior beta(12.0, 1.0) distribution for π_1 and beta(1.0, 2.0) for π_2. We next obtain the HPD interval by intensive simulation:

```
> library(HDInterval)
> pi1 <- rbeta(10000000, 12.0, 1.0) # posterior for 11 successes, 0 failures, uniform
  prior
> pi2 <- rbeta(10000000, 1.0, 2.0)  # posterior for 0 success, 1 failure, uniform prior
> hdi(pi1 - pi2, credMass=0.95)
  lower    upper
 0.1256   0.9812                     # HPD interval for pi1 - pi2
> hist(pi1 - pi2)                    # posterior (not shown) is highly skewed to left
> plot(density(pi1 - pi2))           # density approximation for histogram (not shown)
```

The HPD interval of (0.126, 0.981) is somewhat different from the percentile-based interval (0.064, 0.950) obtained in Section 4.7.5. A histogram of the simulated posterior distribution of $\pi_1 - \pi_2$ shows that it is highly skewed to the left, so the HPD interval has tail probability above 0.025 in the left tail and below 0.025 in the right-tail.

Section A.4.6 of the R Appendix for this chapter presents cases in which the HPD interval is more appropriate than the percentile-based interval, because the posterior *pdf* takes highest value at the most extreme possible value for a parameter. However, the discussion there explains that the HPD approach can be inappropriate for interval estimation of nonlinear functions of parameters, such as the ratio π_1/π_2.

4.8 Bayesian Inference for Means

Next we consider Bayesian inference about population means of quantitative variables. Simple results occur when we assume that a sample has independent observations from a normal distribution and we use a normal prior distribution for its mean, which is the conjugate prior distribution.

4.8.1 Bayesian Inference for a Normal Mean

For independent observations from a $N(\mu, \sigma^2)$ distribution, denote the prior distribution $p(\mu; \nu, \tau)$ of μ by $N(\nu, \tau^2)$. For simplicity, we begin by treating σ as known. The posterior *pdf* is proportional to the product of the likelihood function and the prior *pdf* for μ,

$$g(\mu \mid \mathbf{y}) \propto f(\mathbf{y} \mid \mu) p(\mu; \nu, \tau) = \ell(\mu) p(\mu; \nu, \tau) \propto e^{-\frac{(\overline{y}-\mu)^2}{2\sigma^2/n}} e^{-\frac{(\mu-\nu)^2}{2\tau^2}}.$$

Combining terms in a common exponent, writing that term as quadratic in μ and then completing the square, one can show that this product is proportional to

$$e^{-\frac{1}{2\tilde{\sigma}^2}(\mu-\tilde{\mu})^2} \quad \text{with} \quad \tilde{\mu} = \frac{\overline{y}\tau^2 + \nu(\sigma^2/n)}{\tau^2 + (\sigma^2/n)} \quad \text{and} \quad \tilde{\sigma}^2 = \left[\frac{1}{\tau^2} + \frac{n}{\sigma^2}\right]^{-1}.$$

This exponential function is a constant multiple of the $N(\tilde{\mu}, \tilde{\sigma}^2)$ *pdf*, and that is the posterior distribution of μ. The posterior mean Bayes estimator $\tilde{\mu}$ of μ is a weighted average of $\bar{y}$ and the prior mean ν,

$$\tilde{\mu} = w\bar{y} + (1-w)\nu,$$

with weight $w = \tau^2/[\tau^2 + (\sigma^2/n)]$. This shrinks the sample mean toward the prior mean ν. The weight attached to $\bar{y}$ increases toward 1 as n increases. The reciprocal of a variance is a measure of information called the *precision*. The precision $1/\tilde{\sigma}^2$ of the posterior distribution equals the sum of the precision $(1/\tau^2)$ of the prior mean ν and the precision (n/σ^2) of the sample mean $\bar{y}$. For fixed n, as the prior precision $1/\tau^2 \to 0$, the posterior distribution converges to $N(\bar{y}, \sigma^2/n)$.

For comparing means of two groups, suppose we assume independent observations from a $N(\mu_i, \sigma^2)$ distribution for group $i, (i = 1, 2)$, with μ_1 and μ_2 independent from a $N(\nu, \tau^2)$ distribution. Then, the posterior mean estimate of μ_i is the weighted average $w_i\bar{y}_i + (1-w_i)\nu$, with $w_i = \tau^2/[\tau^2 + (\sigma^2/n_i)]$.

In practice, σ is also unknown, so Bayesian analyses need to include a prior distribution for it. From Section 4.4.6, treating s^2 as a random variable and σ^2 as fixed, $(n-1)s^2/\sigma^2$ has a chi-squared distribution. Now with σ^2 as the random variable, this result motivates letting the precision $1/\sigma^2$ have a gamma distribution, of which the chi-squared is a special case. The corresponding probability distribution for σ^2 itself is called the ***inverse gamma distribution***. The inverse gamma distribution for σ^2 is highly disperse when its shape and scale parameters are tiny. Then, using also a very large variance τ^2 for the prior distribution of μ, posterior Bayesian results are similar to those from classical inference. The interpretations are quite different, however, applying probability statements directly to μ and to $\mu_1 - \mu_2$.

4.8.2 Example: Bayesian Analysis for Anorexia Therapy

Section 4.4.3 obtained a confidence interval for the mean weight change of anorexic girls undergoing a cognitive behavioral therapy. Here we obtain essentially the same result from a Bayesian analysis, treating it as a special case of a model presented in Chapter 6, by taking the normal prior to have precision $1/\tau^2$ very close to 0 and by using an inverse gamma prior with tiny values for the shape and scale parameters. With 5,000,000 MCMC iterations, we obtain the following results:

```
> Anorexia <- read.table("http://stat4ds.rwth-aachen.de/data/Anorexia.dat", header=TRUE)
> change <-  Anorexia$after - Anorexia$before
> library(MCMCpack)
> fit <- MCMCregress(change[Anorexia$therapy=="cb"] ~ 1, mcmc=5000000,
>         b0=0, B0=10^{-15}, c0=10^{-15}, d0=10^{-15})
> # mean has normal prior dist. with mean b0 = 0, variance 1/B0 (std. dev. > 31 million)
> # variance has inverse gamma prior distribution (c0/2 = shape, d0/2 = scale)
> summary(fit)
1. Empirical mean and standard deviation for each variable,
            Mean    SD
(Intercept) 3.007  1.408
2. Quantiles for each variable:
             2.5%   25%    50%    75%   97.5%
(Intercept)  0.23  2.08  3.007  3.936  5.787 # posterior interval (0.23, 5.79) for mu
```

The posterior mean estimate is 3.007 (which is also the sample mean) with posterior standard deviation 1.408 (the classical standard error is 1.357). The 95% posterior interval for μ of (0.23, 5.79) is the same to two decimal places as the classical 95% confidence interval, but the interpretations differ. The Bayesian interval says that the probability is 0.95 that μ falls between 0.23 and 5.79. The classical confidence interval either does or does not contain

μ; if we used this method repeatedly with separate, independent samples, in the long run 95% of the confidence intervals would contain μ.

4.8.3 Bayesian Inference for Normal Means with Improper Priors

To eliminate the subjective element of selecting a prior distribution, we can take $f(\mu) = c$ for $-\infty < \mu < \infty$, uniform over the real line, and $f(\sigma^2) = 1/\sigma^2$ for $\sigma > 0$, for which the prior density of $\log(\sigma^2)$ is uniform over the real line. These represent *improper prior distributions*, meaning that the *pdfs* are not legitimate because their integral over the possible parameter values is infinite. An advantage of using these improper prior distributions is that the resulting posterior intervals for μ and for $\mu_1 - \mu_2$ are then identical to the classical confidence intervals using the t distribution (Sections 4.4.2 and 4.5.2).

With these improper prior distributions for μ and σ^2, a simple factorization exists for the joint posterior *pdf* of (μ, σ^2). It can be expressed as the posterior *pdf* of μ conditional on σ^2, which is $N(\bar{y}, \sigma^2/n)$, multiplied by the marginal posterior *pdf* of σ^2, which is distributed as $(n-1)S^2/X^2_{n-1}$ for variance estimator S^2 and a chi-squared random variable X^2_{n-1} with $df = n - 1$. Given the data, the marginal posterior distribution of $(\mu - \bar{y})/[s/\sqrt{n}]$ is then the t distribution with $df = n - 1$. With large n, the marginal posterior distribution of μ is essentially $N(\bar{y}, s^2/n)$. For details, see Albert (2009).

The Bayesian analysis for the anorexia data in Section 4.8.2 used a highly diffuse normal prior distribution for μ and an inverse gamma prior distribution for σ^2. We now instead use the improper priors. Using simulation for the factorization just mentioned, we generate a million random values of σ^2 from its marginal posterior distribution, and conditional on those values, generate a million random values of μ from the $N(\bar{y}, \sigma^2/n)$ distribution:

```
> y <- Anorexia$after[Anorexia$therapy=="cb"] - Anorexia$before[Anorexia$therapy=="cb"]
> n = length(y)
> S = sum((y - mean(y))^2)          # this is (n-1)s^2
> rsigma2 <- S/rchisq(1000000, n-1) # million random variables from posterior of sigma^2
> mu <- rnorm(1000000, mean=mean(y), sd=sqrt(rsigma2)/sqrt(n)) # random normal means
> cbind(n, mean(mu), sd(mu))        # mean and standard deviation of posterior distribution
     n
[1,] 29 3.006 1.408
> quantile(mu, c(0.025, 0.975)) # 95% posterior interval for population mean
    2.5%  97.5%
   0.226  5.786
```

The 95% posterior interval of (0.226, 5.786) is the same, except for simulation error, as the classical t 95% confidence interval found in Section 4.4.3, which is (0.227, 5.787).

Analogous results hold for the posterior distribution of $\mu_1 - \mu_2$ for two normal populations with common variance σ^2, when we use these improper priors. The posterior distribution of μ_i conditional on σ^2 is $N(\bar{y}_i, \sigma^2/n_i)$, $i = 1, 2$, and σ^2 has marginal posterior distributed as $(n_1 + n_2 - 2)S^2/X^2_{n_1+n_2-2}$ for the pooled variance estimator S^2 and a chi-squared random variable. The marginal posterior distribution of $\mu_1 - \mu_2$ is then very close to the $N(\bar{y}_1 - \bar{y}_2, s^2(\frac{1}{n_1} + \frac{1}{n_2}))$ distribution. We now find the posterior interval for the difference of the mean weight gains for the cognitive behavioral therapy and the control groups, for a Bayesian analysis analogous to the classical analysis in Example 4.5.3:

```
> y1 <- Anorexia$after[Anorexia$therapy=="cb"] - Anorexia$before[Anorexia$therapy=="cb"]
> y2 <- Anorexia$after[Anorexia$therapy=="c"] - Anorexia$before[Anorexia$therapy=="c"]
> n1 <- length(y1); n2 <- length(y2)
> S = sum((y1 - mean(y1))^2) + sum((y2 - mean(y2))^2) # this is [(n1-1)+(n2-1)]s^2
> rsigma2 <- S/rchisq(1000000, n1 + n2 - 2)           # random from posterior of sigma^2
> mu1 <- rnorm(1000000, mean=mean(y1), sd=sqrt(rsigma2)/sqrt(n1)) # random normal means
> mu2 <- rnorm(1000000, mean=mean(y2), sd=sqrt(rsigma2)/sqrt(n2))
```

```
> cbind(n1, n2, mean(mu1-mu2), sd(mu1-mu2))
[1,] 29 26 3.457 2.102 # mean and standard deviation of posterior distribution of mu1 - mu2
> quantile(mu1 - mu2, c(0.025, 0.975)) # 95% posterior interval for mu1 - mu2
   2.5%  97.5%
 -0.679  7.591
```

The 95% posterior interval of $(-0.679, 7.591)$ is the same, except for simulation error, as the classical t 95% confidence interval, which is $(-0.680, 7.594)$.

4.8.4 Predicting a Future Observation: Bayesian Predictive Distribution

Often one goal of a statistical analysis is to predict future observations. A Bayesian **predictive distribution** is the probability distribution for a future observation Y_f. We obtain it by averaging the probability function $p(y_f \mid \theta)$ for known θ with respect to its posterior distribution. Given the data, the predictive probability function is

$$f(y_f \mid \mathbf{y}) = \int_\theta f(y_f \mid \theta) g(\theta \mid \mathbf{y}) d\theta.$$

We can predict a future observation by the mean of this distribution.

Consider first the case of binary data. For predicting a future binary observation, $P(Y_f = 1 \mid \pi) = \pi$. Averaging this with respect to a beta posterior distribution for π yields predictive probability that is the posterior mean, $E(Y_f \mid y) = P(Y_f = 1 \mid y) = (y+\alpha)/(n+\alpha+\beta)$. For the example in Section 4.7.3, the predictive probability of belief in hell for another randomly selected person is the posterior mean for π of 0.713.

For the normal model for a mean with known variance, when we average the $N(\mu, \sigma^2)$ *pdf* for $f(y_f \mid \mu)$ with respect to the $N(\tilde{\mu}, \tilde{\sigma}^2)$ posterior *pdf* for $g(\mu \mid \mathbf{y})$, we obtain a $N(\tilde{\mu}, \sigma^2 + \tilde{\sigma}^2)$ posterior predictive distribution. The variability for the prediction adds the inherent variability σ^2 of the new observation Y_f around μ to the variability $\tilde{\sigma}^2$ reflecting posterior uncertainty about μ. With the classical approach, such integration to obtain $f(y_f \mid \mathbf{y})$ is not possible, because θ is not a random variable with its own distribution. Except in a few cases (such as presented in Section 6.4.5), making probabilistic predictions about future observations is not straightforward. With large n, a simple approximation uses $f(y_f \mid \hat{\theta})$ as a predictive distribution, acting as if θ equals its ML estimate $\hat{\theta}$.

4.8.5 The Bayesian Perspective, and Empirical Bayes and Hierarchical Bayes Extensions

Historically, some statisticians have disliked the Bayesian approach because of the necessity of selecting a prior distribution and the subjective aspect it adds to a statistical analysis. Proponents of the Bayesian approach do not see that as problematic. They note that classical methods need to select a probability distribution for the data, which determines the likelihood function, and such assumptions are subjective and never exactly true. The Bayesian approach can use a highly disperse prior, so that posterior results rely mainly on the likelihood function. Proponents of the Bayesian approach also argue that it is more natural to interpret a posterior interval, making a probability statement about the parameter, than a confidence interval, with the probability applying before observing the data or to the long-run proportion of times the method captures the parameter. Finally, the Bayesian approach applies naturally to predicting future observations and to updating beliefs as we obtain more data at several stages. The posterior distribution following any stage serves as the prior distribution for the next stage.

Some methodologists who otherwise like the Bayesian approach find it unappealing to need to select values for the hyperparameters in prior distributions. This is unnecessary with two alternative ways of implementing the Bayesian approach. The **empirical Bayes** approach uses the data to estimate the hyperparameters of the prior distribution. The name "empirical Bayes" refers to this method's use of the data to estimate the hyperparameters. The **hierarchical Bayes** approach quantifies the uncertainty about the hyperparameters by letting those hyperparameters have their own prior distribution. Using uninformative distributions for the hyperparameters reduces the impact of the choice of prior distribution. The analysis may then be more robust, with the subjectivity reduced because posterior results are averaged over a family of prior distributions. For details of these two approaches, see Carlin and Louis (2008).

4.9 Why Maximum Likelihood and Bayes Estimators Perform Well *

Section 4.2.3 introduced maximum likelihood estimators and their properties and explained why they are so important. This section provides explanations of why the properties are true. The discussion is necessarily rather technical, so this is a starred section. Please be patient and willing to read lightly at first and then more closely as you become more familiar with the ideas presented.

We consider only the case of a scalar parameter θ. The results require certain regularity conditions. Key ones are that the possible values for y do not depend on θ (e.g., unlike the uniform distribution over $[0, \theta]$) and that the true value of θ does not fall on the boundary of the parameter space (e.g., unlike the binomial distribution with $\theta = \pi = 0.0$ or 1.0). We need to be able to differentiate $\log f(Y; \theta)$ with respect to θ at least twice and take the derivative inside an integral (Leibniz's rule). The conditions hold for the *exponential family* of distributions introduced in Exercise 4.75, which includes most common distributions, including the binomial, Poisson, normal, and gamma.

4.9.1 ML Estimators Have Large-Sample Normal Distributions

Maximum likelihood estimators fall in the class of **best asymptotically normal** (BAN) estimators, meaning that for large n they have approximately normal sampling distributions and are asymptotically efficient. From Section 4.2.3, the large-sample normal distribution of an ML estimator $\hat{\theta}$ is $N(\theta, 1/I(\theta))$ distribution, where the *information* $I(\theta)$ has two equivalent expressions,

$$I(\theta) = nE\left(\frac{\partial \log f(Y;\theta)}{\partial \theta}\right)^2 = -nE\left(\frac{\partial^2 \log f(Y;\theta)}{\partial \theta^2}\right). \tag{4.15}$$

We next present a heuristic explanation of why $\hat{\theta}$ has a large-sample normal distribution, followed by showing that these two expressions for $I(\theta)$ are equal.

For the log-likelihood function $L(\theta)$, the Taylor series expansion of the first derivative $L'(\theta) = \partial L(\theta)/\partial \theta$, evaluated at $\hat{\theta}$, is

$$L'(\hat{\theta}) \approx L'(\theta) + (\hat{\theta} - \theta)L''(\theta).$$

For regular cases in which $L(\theta)$ evaluated at its maximum $\hat{\theta}$ satisfies $L'(\hat{\theta}) = 0$,

$$(\hat{\theta} - \theta) \approx \frac{L'(\theta)}{L''(\theta)} = \frac{L'(\theta)/n}{L''(\theta)/n}. \tag{4.16}$$

---

*Sections with an asterisk are optional.

For data $\mathbf{y} = (y_1, \ldots, y_n)$, we denote the derivative of the log-likelihood function by

$$U(\mathbf{y}; \theta) = L'(\theta) = \frac{\partial L(\theta)}{\partial \theta} = \frac{\partial}{\partial \theta} \log[\ell(\theta)] = \frac{\partial}{\partial \theta} \log[\prod_i f(y_i; \theta)] = \sum_{i=1}^n \frac{\partial[\log f(y_i; \theta)]}{\partial \theta}. \quad (4.17)$$

We refer to $U(\mathbf{y}, \theta)$ as the **score function**.[20] For instance, for binary data $\{y_i\}$ and estimating a proportion π, from Section 4.2.4 with $f(y; \pi) = \pi^y (1 - \pi)^{1-y}$ for $y = 0, 1$, we have $\log[f(y; \pi)] = y \log(\pi) + (1 - y) \log(1 - \pi)$,

$$\frac{\partial[\log f(y_i; \pi)]}{\partial \pi} = \frac{y_i}{\pi} - \frac{1 - y_i}{1 - \pi} = \frac{y_i - \pi}{\pi(1 - \pi)},$$

so that the score function is

$$U(\mathbf{y}; \pi) = \sum_{i=1}^n \frac{\partial[\log f(y_i; \pi)]}{\partial \pi} = \frac{\sum_i (y_i - \pi)}{\pi(1 - \pi)} = \frac{n(\hat{\pi} - \pi)}{\pi(1 - \pi)}.$$

The ML estimate $\hat{\pi} = (\sum_i y_i)/n$ is derived by solving $U(\mathbf{y}; \pi) = 0$.

When Y is a continuous random variable, considering the distribution of Y for fixed θ,

$$E\left[\frac{\partial[\log f(Y; \theta)]}{\partial \theta}\right] = \int \left[\left(\frac{1}{f(y; \theta)}\right) \frac{\partial f(y; \theta)}{\partial \theta}\right] f(y; \theta) dy = \frac{\partial}{\partial \theta}\left[\int f(y; \theta) dy\right] = \frac{\partial}{\partial \theta}[1] = 0,$$

and likewise for discrete random variables. Thus,

$$U(\mathbf{Y}; \theta) = \sum_{i=1}^n \frac{\partial[\log f(Y_i; \theta)]}{\partial \theta} \quad \text{has} \quad E(U) = 0.$$

For fixed value θ, the variance of U is

$$E(U^2) = E\left[\sum_{i=1}^n \frac{\partial[\log f(Y_i; \theta)]}{\partial \theta}\right]^2 = nE\left[\frac{\partial[\log f(Y; \theta)]}{\partial \theta}\right]^2,$$

because each term in the sum that is squared has expectation 0 and covariance 0 with other terms due to the independence of observations. From the first expression in equation (4.15), the variance of U is the information $I(\theta)$. Also, $(1/n)U(\mathbf{Y}; \theta)$, being a sample mean, by the Central Limit Theorem has approximately a normal distribution with mean 0 and variance $I(\theta)/n^2$. Now, from expression (4.16), the approximate denominator of $(\hat{\theta} - \theta)$ is

$$\frac{L''(\theta)}{n} = \frac{1}{n} \sum_{i=1}^n \frac{\partial^2}{\partial \theta^2}[\log f(y_i; \theta)].$$

By the law of large numbers, this converges in probability to $E[\partial^2 \log f(Y; \theta)/\partial \theta^2]$, which from the second expression in equation (4.15) is $-I(\theta)/n$. Thus, since

$$(\hat{\theta} - \theta) \approx \frac{L'(\theta)/n}{L''(\theta)/n} = \frac{U/n}{L''(\theta)/n},$$

and since $\text{var}(U) = I(\theta)$, overall $(\hat{\theta} - \theta)$ is approximately a normal random variable with mean 0 and variance $I(\theta)/n^2$ divided by $-I(\theta)/n$. That is, the distribution of $(\hat{\theta} - \theta)$ is approximately $-[n/I(\theta)]N(0, I(\theta)/n^2)$, which is $N(0, 1/I(\theta))$.

---

[20]For fixed $\mathbf{y}$, since we find $\hat{\theta}$ by equating the score function to 0 and solving for θ, the *likelihood equation* for θ is also called the *score equation*.

The approximate normality is reflected, for regular cases, by the log-likelihood function being concave and increasingly parabolic as n increases. For a normal distribution, the log-likelihood $L(\mu)$ is exactly parabolic (Exercise 4.42). The closer the log-likelihood function is to parabolic, the closer to normality is the sampling distribution of the ML estimator.

We next show why the two formulas presented for $I(\theta)$ in (4.15), $nE(\partial[\log f(Y;\theta)]/\partial\theta)^2$ and $-nE(\partial^2[\log f(Y;\theta)]/\partial\theta^2)$, are equivalent. For every value of θ, $E(\partial[\log f(Y;\theta)]/\partial\theta) = 0$, so

$$0 = \frac{\partial}{\partial\theta}\left[E\left(\frac{\partial\log f(Y;\theta)}{\partial\theta}\right)\right] = \frac{\partial}{\partial\theta}\left[\int_y\left(\frac{\partial}{\partial\theta}\log f(y;\theta)\right)f(y;\theta)dy\right].$$

Then, using the rule for differentiating a product of terms and noting that $(\partial/\partial\theta)[f(y:\theta)]$ is the same as $(\partial/\partial\theta)[\log f(y;\theta)]f(y;\theta)$, this becomes

$$0 = \int\left[\frac{\partial^2}{\partial\theta^2}\log f(y;\theta)\right]f(y:\theta)dy + \int\left[\frac{\partial}{\partial\theta}\log f(y;\theta)\right]^2 f(y;\theta)dy,$$

and these two integrals are $E(\partial^2[\log f(Y;\theta)]/\partial\theta^2)$ and $E(\partial[\log f(Y;\theta)]/\partial\theta)^2$.

In passing, we mention that the "score" name for a score confidence interval relates to theory that derives it using the score function U. The $100(1-\alpha)\%$ score confidence interval for a parameter θ is defined to be the set of θ for which

$$-z_{\alpha/2} \le \frac{U(\mathbf{y};\theta)}{\sqrt{I(\theta)}} \le z_{\alpha/2}.$$

Treating the *score statistic* $U(\mathbf{Y};\theta)/\sqrt{I(\theta)}$ as approximately standard normal is based on the results we found above that $U(\mathbf{Y};\theta)$ has a large-sample normal distribution with mean 0 and $\mathrm{var}(U) = I(\theta)$. For instance, for estimating a population proportion π, we found above that $U(\mathbf{Y};\pi) = n(\hat{\pi} - \pi)/\pi(1-\pi)$, and from Section 4.2.4, $I(\pi) = n/[\pi(1-\pi)]$, so this ratio is

$$\frac{U(\mathbf{Y},\pi)}{\sqrt{I(\pi)}} = \frac{n(\hat{\pi}-\pi)/\pi(1-\pi)}{\sqrt{n/\pi(1-\pi)}} = \frac{\hat{\pi}-\pi}{\sqrt{\pi(1-\pi)/n}}.$$

This is the pivotal quantity that we used to derive the score confidence interval (4.7) in Section 4.3.3.

4.9.2 Asymptotic Efficiency of ML Estimators Same as Best Unbiased Estimators

From Section 4.2.3, ML estimators are asymptotically efficient: As n grows, other estimators do not have smaller variance than the variance $1/I(\theta)$ of an ML estimator.

▶ In fact, under weak regularity conditions, the minimum possible variance for an unbiased estimator of θ is $1/I(\theta)$.

To show this, let $T = T(Y_1,\ldots,Y_n)$ be an unbiased estimator of θ. Since the correlation (2.16) can be no greater than 1 in absolute value,

$$|\mathrm{corr}(T,U)| = \frac{|\mathrm{cov}(T,U)|}{\sqrt{\mathrm{var}(T)\mathrm{var}(U)}} \le 1 \quad \text{implies} \quad \mathrm{var}(T) \ge \frac{[\mathrm{cov}(T,U)]^2}{\mathrm{var}(U)}.$$

For $U(\mathbf{Y};\theta) = \sum_{i=1}^n \partial[\log f(Y_i;\theta)]/\partial\theta$, we have just noted that $E(U) = 0$, so $\mathrm{cov}(T,U) = E(TU)$, and since $\mathrm{var}(U) = I(\theta)$, $\mathrm{var}(T) \ge [\mathrm{cov}(T,U)]^2/I(\theta)$. Since T is unbiased,

$$E(T) = \theta = \int\cdots\int T(y_1,\ldots,y_n)[\prod_i f(y_i;\theta)]dy_1\cdots dy_n.$$

Differentiating with respect to θ, we have

$$1 = \int \cdots \int T(y_1,\ldots,y_n)\Big[\sum_i f'(y_i;\theta)\Big(\prod_{j\neq i} f(y_j;\theta)\Big)\Big]dy_1\cdots dy_n$$

$$= \int \cdots \int T(y_1,\ldots,y_n)\Big[\sum_i \Big(\frac{f'(y_i;\theta)}{f(y_i;\theta)}\Big)\Big]\Big[\prod_i f(y_i;\theta)\Big]dy_1\cdots dy_n$$

$$= \int \cdots \int T(y_1,\ldots,y_n)\Big[\sum_i \frac{\partial\log f(y_i;\theta)}{\partial\theta}\Big]\Big[\prod_i f(y_i;\theta)\Big]dy_1\cdots dy_n = E(TU).$$

In summary for unbiased estimators, since $\text{cov}(T,U) = E(TU)$, and since $E(TU) = 1$ and $\text{var}(U) = I(\theta)$,

$$\text{var}(T) \geq \frac{[\text{cov}(T,U)]^2}{\text{var}(U)} = \frac{[E(TU)]^2}{\text{var}(U)} = \frac{1}{I(\theta)}.$$

The expression $1/I(\theta)$ for the minimum possible variance[21] for an unbiased estimator of θ is also called the **Cramér–Rao lower bound**, in honor of the statisticians who derived it in the early 1940s.

4.9.3 Bayesian Estimators Also Have Good Large-Sample Performance

The large-sample properties of maximum likelihood estimators extend to Bayesian estimators. As n increases, the posterior distribution of θ is mainly affected by the likelihood function. The posterior distribution often looks much like a likelihood function re-scaled to integrate to 1, so the behavior of the likelihood function determines the behavior of Bayesian estimators.

An exception to this is in applications that have a huge number of parameters, sometimes more than observations. Even if you use a very diffuse prior distribution, the posterior results may depend strongly on that prior. Maximum likelihood estimation also performs poorly in such situations. We discuss this further in Section 7.7.

4.9.4 The Likelihood Principle

A statistical method satisfies the **likelihood principle** if it is based solely on the likelihood function in terms of how the data and the design for collecting them provide evidence about a parameter θ. Then, if two entirely different experiments produce likelihood functions that are proportional to each other (as functions of θ), then the conclusions about θ are the same for both experiments. Because maximum likelihood and Bayesian estimation use the data only through the likelihood function, they satisfy the likelihood principle.

We illustrate for estimating a binomial parameter π. In one case, an experiment is designed with $n = 10$ independent trials. The experiment observes $y = 8$ successes. In the second case, the experiment is designed to keep observing trials until observing two failures. That failure occurs on the 10th trial. Then in each case the likelihood function is proportional to $\pi^8(1-\pi)^2$ and the maximum likelihood estimator is $\hat{\pi} = y/n = 8/10$. If we use the same prior distribution in each case, we will obtain the same posterior distribution in each, even though the sampling procedures were quite different. Inference is then the same. This is not the case for classical methods that do not rely solely on the likelihood function but also on the design for obtaining the data. For instance, the unbiased estimator of π is $y/n = 8/10 = 0.80$ in the first case and $y/(y+1) = 8/9$ in the second case.[22]

---

[21] A more general result allowing $E[T(\mathbf{Y})] = b(\theta)$ states that $\text{var}(T) \geq [\partial b(\theta)/\partial\theta]^2/I(\theta)$.
[22] The number of successes until failure k has the negative binomial distribution (Exercise 2.69), for which the best unbiased estimator of π is $Y/(Y+k-1)$, which is $8/9$ when $y = 8$ and $k = 2$.

4.10 Chapter Summary

This chapter presented methods of estimation, focusing on population means for quantitative variables and population proportions for categorical variables. A *point estimate* is a value of a statistic that predicts the parameter value. An *interval estimate*, called a *confidence interval*, is an interval of numbers within which the parameter is believed to fall with a specified degree of confidence.

Point estimators:

- A good estimator is *unbiased* (having expected value equal to the parameter) or *asymptotically unbiased* (having bias decreasing toward 0 as n increases), *consistent* (converging toward the parameter as n increases), and *asymptotically efficient* (having the smallest possible standard error).

- The *maximum likelihood estimator*, which is the parameter value for which the data would have highest value for their probability function, has these properties and has an approximately normal sampling distribution for large n.

- The maximum likelihood (ML) estimator maximizes the *likelihood function*, which regards the probability function for the data as a function of the unknown parameter, after we observe the data.

Confidence intervals:

- Confidence intervals assume randomization for obtaining the data. For a population mean, a population proportion, and a difference between two population means or two population proportions, they have the form

  point estimate ± *margin of error*, with *margin of error* = score×(*se*),

  where *se* is the estimated standard error.

- Confidence intervals for proportions require no assumption about the population distribution, because the Central Limit Theorem implies approximate normality of the sampling distribution of the sample proportion estimator. The score that multiplies the *se* is a z-quantile from the standard normal distribution.

- Confidence intervals for the mean assume a normal population distribution, but use the t distribution because of needing to replace the population standard deviation σ by an estimate s in the *se*. The score that multiplies the *se* is a t-quantile. The method is *robust* to violations of the normality assumption.

- The t *distribution* is centered at 0 but has spread determined by its *degrees of freedom* (df). Its variability decreases as df increases, and for large df the t distribution looks nearly identical to the standard normal distribution.

- The probability that the confidence interval method yields an interval that contains the parameter, called the *confidence level*, is controlled by the choice of the z or t quantile in the margin of error. Increasing the confidence level results in a wider interval.

- Larger sample sizes produce smaller *se* values and narrower confidence intervals and greater precision of estimation.

Table 4.2 at the end of Section 4.5.3 summarizes confidence intervals for individual means and for comparisons of two means. Table 4.4 at the end of Section 4.5.5 summarizes confidence intervals for individual proportions and for comparisons of two proportions.

The **bootstrap** is a resampling method that takes a very large number of samples of size n (with replacement) from the sample data distribution and calculates the point estimate for each sample. It then uses the variability of those estimates around the ML estimate to approximate the spread of the sampling distribution of the ML estimator around the unknown parameter value. The bootstrap distribution yields standard errors and confidence intervals for measures, such as the median and the correlation, for which simple *se* formulas are not available.

The **Bayesian** approach to statistical inference applies probabilities to parameters as well as data. It assumes a **prior distribution** for the parameters that combines with the information that the data provide through the likelihood function to generate a **posterior distribution** for the parameters. Bayesian statistical inferences are based on the posterior distribution, such as a *posterior interval* that is an analog of a confidence interval. With it, one can make a statement such as "The probability is 0.95 that the population proportion π falls between 0.52 and 0.58," whereas the corresponding classical inference that "We are 95% confident that π falls between 0.52 and 0.58" means that if we used this method repeatedly with independent samples, in the long run 95% of the confidence intervals formed would truly contain the parameter.

Exercises

Data Analysis and Applications

4.1 For a point estimate of the mean of a population that is assumed to have a normal distribution, a data scientist decides to use the average of the sample lower and upper quartiles for the $n = 100$ observations, since unlike the sample mean $\bar{Y}$, the quartiles are not affected by outliers. Evaluate the precision of this estimator compared to $\bar{Y}$ by randomly generating 100,000 samples of size 100 each from a $N(0,1)$ distribution and comparing the standard deviation of the 100,000 estimates with the theoretical standard error of $\bar{Y}$.

4.2 For a sequence of observations of a binary random variable, you observe the geometric random variable (Section 2.2.2) outcome of the first success on observation number $y = 3$. Find and plot the likelihood function.

4.3 Plot the log-likelihood function $L(\pi)$ corresponding to the binomial likelihood function $\ell(\pi)$ shown in Figure 4.1 with $y = 6$ for $n = 10$ (e.g., in R by taking `pi` (π) as a sequence between 0 and 1 and then taking L as the log of `dbinom(6, 10, pi)`). Identify $\hat{\pi}$ in the plot and explain why maximization occurs at the same point as in the plot of $\ell(\pi)$ itself.

4.4 For the **Students** data file (Exercise 1.2 in Chapter 1) and corresponding population, find the ML estimate of the population proportion believing in life after death. Construct a Wald 95% confidence interval, using its formula (4.8). Interpret.

4.5 The General Social Survey has asked respondents, "Do you think the use of marijuana should be made legal or not?" View results at the most recent cumulative datafile at **sda.berkeley. edu/archive.htm** by entering the variables GRASS and YEAR.

   (a) Describe any trend you see since 1973 in the percentage favoring legalization.

   (b) In the 2018 survey, 938 of 1447 were in favor of legalization. Use a Wald or score confidence interval to determine if this provides sufficient evidence to conclude whether a majority or a minority of the population support legalization.

4.6 In a random sample of 25 people to estimate the extent of vegetarianism in a society, 0 people were vegetarian. Construct a 99% Wald confidence interval for the population proportion of vegetarians. Explain the awkward issue in doing this, and find and interpret a more reliable confidence interval. (As Section 4.3.3 mentioned and Exercise 4.50 shows, Wald methods perform poorly when π may be close to 0 or 1, especially when n is not large.)

4.7 A social scientist wanted to estimate the proportion of school children in Boston who live in a single-parent family. She decided to use a sample size such that, with probability 0.95, the error would not exceed 0.05. How large a sample size should she use, if she has no idea of the size of that proportion?

4.8 To estimate the proportion of traffic deaths in California last year that were alcohol related, determine the necessary sample size for the estimate to be accurate to within 0.04 with probability 0.90. Based on results of studies reported by the National Highway Traffic Safety Administration (www.nhtsa.gov), we expect the proportion to be about 0.30.

4.9 A study investigates the distribution of annual income for heads of households living in public housing in Chicago. For a random sample of size 30, the annual incomes (in thousands of dollars) are in the Chicago data file at the text website.

   (a) Based on a descriptive graphic, describe the shape of the sample data distribution. Find and interpret point estimates of the population mean and standard deviation.

   (b) Construct and interpret a 95% confidence interval for μ, using (i) formula (4.10), (ii) software.

4.10 A recent General Social Survey asked male respondents how many female partners they have had sex with since their 18th birthday. For the 131 males between the ages of 23 and 29, the median = 6 and mode = 1 (16.8% of the sample). Software summarizes other results:

Variable	n	Mean	StDev	SE Mean	95.0% CI
NUMWOMEN	131	10.53	15.36	1.34	(8.0, 13.1)

Interpret the reported confidence interval. For the results shown, state a statistical factor that might make you skeptical about its usefulness.

4.11 The observations on number of hours of daily TV watching for the 10 subjects in the 2018 GSS who identified themselves as Islamic were 0, 0, 1, 1, 1, 2, 2, 3, 3, 4.

   (a) Construct and interpret a 95% confidence interval for the population mean.

   (b) Suppose the observation of 4 was incorrectly recorded as 24. What would you obtain for the 95% confidence interval? What does this suggest about potential effects of outliers on confidence intervals for means?

4.12 The Income data file at the book's website shows annual incomes in thousands of dollars for subjects in three racial-ethnic groups in the U.S.

   (a) Use a graphic such as a side-by-side box plot (Section 1.4.5) to compare incomes of Black, Hispanic, and White subjects.

   (b) Treating the sample as random and assuming equal population variances, construct and interpret a 90% confidence interval for the difference between the population mean incomes of Blacks and Whites.

   (c) Use software to construct the interval without the equal variance assumption, and compare results.

4.13 Sections 4.4.3 and 4.5.3 analyzed data from a study about anorexia. The Anorexia data file at the text website contains results for the cognitive behavioral and family therapies and the control group. Using data for the 17 girls who received the family therapy:

   (a) Conduct a descriptive statistical analysis using graphs and numerical summaries.

   (b) Construct a 95% confidence interval for the population mean change in weight.

(c) Construct a 95% confidence interval for the difference between the population mean weight changes for the family therapy and the control. Interpret.

4.14 Using the **Students** data file, for the corresponding population, construct a 95% confidence interval (**a**) for the mean weekly number of hours spent watching TV; (**b**) to compare females and males on the mean weekly number of hours spent watching TV. In each case, state assumptions, including the practical importance of each, and interpret results.

4.15 In the 2018 General Social Survey, when asked whether they believed in life after death, 1017 of 1178 females said *yes*, and 703 of 945 males said *yes*. Construct 95% confidence intervals for the population proportions of females and males that believe in life after death and for the difference between them. Interpret.

4.16 The **Substance** data file at the book's website shows a contingency table formed from a survey that asked a sample of high school students whether they have ever used alcohol, cigarettes, and marijuana. Construct a 95% Wald confidence interval to compare those who have used or not used alcohol on whether they have used marijuana, using (**a**) formula (4.13); (**b**) software. State assumptions for your analysis, and interpret results.

4.17 Randomly generate 10,000 observations from a t distribution with $df = 3$ and construct a normal quantile plot (Exercise 2.67). How does this plot reveal non-normality of the data in a way that a histogram does not?

4.18 A standardized variable Y dealing with a financial outcome is considered to take an unusually extreme value if $y > 3$. Find $P(Y > 3)$ if (**a**) Y is modeled as having a standard normal distribution $Y \sim N(0,1)$, (**b**) Y instead behaves like a ratio of standard normal random variables, in which case Y has the standard Cauchy distribution (4.11). What do you observe?

4.19 With the data on the number of years since a book was checked out (variable C) in the **Library** data file at the text website, use the bootstrap to find and interpret the 95% (**a**) percentile confidence interval for the median, (**b**) percentile and bias-corrected confidence intervals for the standard deviation.

4.20 To illustrate how sampling distribution of the correlation can be highly skewed when the the true correlation is near −1 or +1, construct and plot the bootstrap distribution for the correlation between *GDP* and *CO2* for the **UN** data. (This is merely for illustration, because this data set is not a random sample of nations).

4.21 The ***trimmed mean*** calculates the sample mean after excluding a small percentage of the lowest and highest data points, to lessen the impact of outliers. For example, with the function **mean(y, 0.05)** applied to a variable y, R finds the *10% trimmed mean*, excluding 5% at each end. For a heavy-tailed symmetric distribution, the trimmed mean is often more efficient than the sample mean in estimating center. To illustrate, randomly generate 1000 observations from the standard Cauchy distribution (4.11), for which $E(Y)$ does not exist but the median and trimmed mean are 0.

(a) Use the bootstrap to find a 95% confidence interval using the 10% trimmed mean. Compare with the ordinary 95% confidence interval (4.10) for the mean.

(b) Use the bootstrap to find a 95% confidence interval for the median. Compare to those for the mean and trimmed mean. What does this suggest about these estimators for heavy-tailed distributions?

4.22 In a 2016 Pew Research survey (www.pewresearch.org), the percentage who favored allowing gays and lesbians to marry legally was 84% for liberal Democrats and 24% for conservative Republicans. Suppose $n = 300$ for each group. Using uniform prior distributions,

(a) Construct 95% posterior intervals for the population proportions.

(b) Compare the interpretation of the Bayesian posterior interval for liberal Democrats with the classical confidence interval.

(c) Construct and interpret a 95% posterior interval for the difference between the population proportions for liberal Democrats and conservative Republicans.

4.23 You want to estimate the proportion of students at your school who answer *yes* when asked whether governments should do more to address global warming. In a random sample of 10 students, every student says *yes*. Give a point estimate of the probability that the next student interviewed will answer *yes*, if you use (a) ML estimation, (b) Bayesian estimation with a uniform prior distribution.

4.24 Refer to the vegetarian survey result in Exercise 4.6, with $n = 25$ and no vegetarians.

 (a) Find the Bayesian estimate of π using a beta prior distribution with $\alpha = \beta$ equal (i) 0.5, (ii) 1.0, (iii) 10.0. Explain how the choice of prior distribution affects the posterior mean estimate.

 (b) If you were planning how to take a larger survey from the same population, explain how you can use the posterior results of the previous survey with $n = 25$ based on the prior with $\alpha = \beta = 1$ to form the prior distribution to use with the new survey results.

4.25 Refer to the previous exercise, regarding estimating π when $y = 0$ in $n = 25$ trials.

 (a) With uniform prior distribution, find the 95% highest posterior density (HPD) interval, and compare with the 95% equal-tail posterior interval, using the 2.5 and 97.5 percentiles. Why are they different?

 (b) When $y = 0$, explain why the lower Bayesian equal-tail posterior interval limit for π cannot be 0, unlike the Bayesian HPD interval. Why is the HPD interval more sensible in this case? (See also the discussion in Section A.4.6 of the R Appendix.)

4.26 Refer to the clinical trial example in Section 4.7.5. Using the Jeffreys prior for π_1 and for π_2, simulate and plot the posterior distribution of $\pi_1 - \pi_2$. Find the HPD interval. What does that interval reflect about the posterior distribution?

4.27 Refer to Exercise 4.13. Consider Bayesian inference for the population mean weight change μ for the family therapy.

 (a) Select diffuse prior distributions for μ and σ^2 and find the posterior mean estimate and a 95% posterior interval for μ.

 (b) Construct the classical 95% confidence interval for μ. Explain the difference in the interpretations of the Bayesian and classical intervals.

4.28 Refer to the previous exercise. Conduct Bayesian methods with improper priors to obtain a posterior interval for the population mean weight change for the family therapy and the difference between the population means for that therapy and the control condition. For the difference, explain the difference in the interpretations of the Bayesian and classical intervals.

4.29 A study that Section 7.3.2 discusses about endometrial cancer analyzed how a histology grade response variable (HG = 0, low; HG = 1, high) relates to three risk factors, including NV = neovasculation (1 = present, 0 = absent). Using the **Endometrial** data file at the book's website, conduct classical or Bayesian statistical inference that compares the probability of HG being high for those with and without neovasculation. Prepare a short report in which you show results and interpret them.

4.30 When a 2015 Pew Research survey (www.pewresearch.org) asked Americans whether there is solid evidence of global warming, 92% of Democrats who identified themselves as liberal said *yes* whereas 38% of Republicans who identified themselves as conservative said *yes*. Suppose $n = 200$ for each group. If we wanted to compare responses for Democrats and Republicans, how could we do so inferentially? Prepare a short report that conducts an analysis, including assumptions and interpretations.

4.31 The **Houses** data file at the book's website lists, for 100 home sales in Gainesville, Florida, several variables, including the selling price in thousands of dollars and whether the house is new (1 = yes, 0 = no). Prepare a short report in which, stating all assumptions including the relative importance of each, you conduct descriptive and inferential statistical analyses to compare the selling prices for new and older homes.

4.32 The `Afterlife` data file at the book's website shows data from the 2018 General Social Survey on postlife = belief in the afterlife (1 = yes, 2 = no) and religion (1 = Protestant, 2 = Catholic, 3 = Jewish, other categories excluded). Analyze these data with methods of this chapter. Summarize results in a short report, including edited software output as an appendix.

Methods and Concepts

4.33 Take $n = 100$ observations from a standard normal distribution and find the sample mean and median. Do this 100,000 times and plot their estimated sampling distributions. Estimate their mean squared errors around the common population mean and median of 0. Which seems to be a better estimator? (For theoretical results about this, see Exercise 4.37.)

4.34 Using simulation, conduct an investigation of whether the sample mean or median is a better estimator of the common value for the mean and median of a uniform distribution.

4.35 Is the following statement true or false? If $\hat{\theta}$ is an unbiased estimator for θ, then for any function g, $g(\hat{\theta})$ is an unbiased estimator for $g(\theta)$. If true, explain why. If false, give a counter-example.

4.36 Section 4.4.6 showed that $E(s^2) = \sigma^2$. For independent sampling from a $N(\mu, \sigma^2)$ distribution, $\hat{\sigma}^2 = [\sum_i (Y_i - \overline{Y})^2]/n$ is the ML estimator and $\tilde{\sigma}^2 = [\sum_i (Y_i - \overline{Y})^2]/(n+1)$ is the estimator having minimum MSE.

   (a) Show that $\tilde{\sigma}^2$ is an asymptotically unbiased estimator of σ^2.

   (b) Show that $\hat{\sigma}^2$ is a consistent estimator of σ^2. (*Hint*: Apply the law of large numbers to $[\sum_i (Y_i - \mu)^2]/n$ and show that its difference from $\hat{\sigma}^2$ goes to 0 as n increases.)

4.37 When f is a continuous *pdf* with median M, for simple random sampling the sample median $\widehat{M}$ has approximately a $N(M, 1/4[f(M)]^2 n)$ sampling distribution.

   (a) Consider sampling from a normal population, for which $\mu = M$. Using formula (2.8), show that $\widehat{M}$ has asymptotic standard error $\sqrt{\pi/2}(\sigma/\sqrt{n})$ (for $\pi = 3.14...$).

   (b) Show that the ratio of variances of $\overline{Y}$ and $\widehat{M}$ is $2/\pi$, so $\overline{Y}$ is a much more efficient estimator, since $\overline{Y}$ achieves the same standard error as $\widehat{M}$ with only $100(2/\pi) = 63.7\%$ as much data.

   (c) Find the ratio of variances of $\overline{Y}$ and $\widehat{M}$ for simple random samples from a uniform distribution (2.4) over $[0, \theta]$, and interpret.

4.38 For independent observations $y_1, \ldots, y_n$ having the geometric distribution (2.1):

   (a) Find a sufficient statistic for π.

   (b) Derive the ML estimator of π.

4.39 For independent observations $y_1, \ldots, y_n$ from the exponential *pdf* $f(y; \lambda) = \lambda e^{-\lambda y}$ for $y \geq 0$, for which $\mu = \sigma = 1/\lambda$:

   (a) Find the log-likelihood function $L(\lambda)$.

   (b) Find the ML estimator $\hat{\lambda}$ of λ.

   (c) Suppose $\overline{y} = 10$. Plot $L(\lambda) - L(\hat{\lambda})$ between $\lambda = 0.01$ and $\lambda = 4.00$ if $n =$ (i) 1, (ii) 5, (iii) 10. How does the shape of $L(\lambda)$ change as n increases? What are the implications of the narrowing log-likelihood? (Also, when the log-likelihood is closer to parabolic, the distribution of the ML estimator is closer to normality.)

   (d) Find the information $I(\lambda)$ using equation (4.3) and using equation (4.4). Specify the asymptotic distribution of $\hat{\lambda}$.

4.40 Exercise 2.73 introduced the *Pareto distribution*, which has *pdf* $f(y; \alpha) = \alpha/y^{\alpha+1}$ for $y \geq 1$ and a parameter $\alpha > 0$. A study uses this family to model n independent observations on income. Find the likelihood function and the ML estimator of α and its asymptotic variance.

4.41 For n independent observations $\{y_i\}$ from the gamma *pdf* (2.10), with shape parameter k known (such as with the exponential distribution special case):

(a) Find the likelihood function and show that the ML estimator of λ is $\hat{\lambda} = k/\bar{Y}$.

(b) What is the ML estimator of $E(Y) = k/\lambda$?

(c) Show that the large-sample variance of $\hat{\lambda}$ is λ^2/kn.

4.42 Consider n independent observations from a $N(\mu, \sigma^2)$ distribution.

(a) Focusing on μ, find the likelihood function. Show that the log-likelihood function is a concave, parabolic function of μ. Find the ML estimator $\hat{\mu}$.

(b) Considering σ^2 to be known, find the information using (i) equation (4.3), (ii) equation (4.4). Use them to show that the large-sample variance of $\hat{\mu}$ is σ^2/n. Explain why $\hat{\mu}$ is the minimum variance unbiased estimator.

(c) Show that the ML estimator $\hat{\sigma}$ of σ is $\sqrt{[\sum_i (Y_i - \bar{Y})^2]/n}$. Show that the large-sample variance of $\hat{\sigma}$ is $\sigma^2/2n$.

4.43 Exercise 2.71 mentioned that when Y has positively skewed distribution over the positive real line, statistical analyses often treat $\log(Y)$ as having a $N(\mu, \sigma^2)$ distribution. Then Y has the *log-normal distribution*, which has *pdf* for $y > 0$,

$$f(y; \mu, \sigma) = [1/y(\sqrt{2\pi}\sigma)] \exp\{-[\log(y) - \mu]^2/2\sigma^2\}.$$

(a) For n independent observations $\{y_i\}$, find the ML estimates of μ and σ^2.

(b) Find the estimated standard error for the ML estimator $\hat{\mu}$.

(c) Using the invariance property of ML estimators, find the ML estimates of the mean and variance of the distribution, which are $E(Y) = e^{\mu + \sigma^2/2}$ and $\text{var}(Y) = (e^{\sigma^2} - 1)[E(Y)]^2$.

4.44 Refer to the previous two exercises. Consider the selling prices (in thousands of dollars) in the **Houses** data file mentioned in Exercise 4.31.

(a) Fit the normal distribution to the data by finding the ML estimates of μ and σ for that distribution.

(b) Fit the log-normal distribution to the data by finding the ML estimates of its parameters.

(c) Find and compare the ML estimates of the mean and standard deviation of selling price for the two distributions.

(d) Superimpose the fitted normal and log-normal distributions on a histogram of the data. Which distribution seems to be more appropriate for summarizing the selling prices?

4.45 The Hardy–Weinberg formula for the genetic variation of a population at equilibrium states that with probability π of the A allele, the probabilities of genotypes (AA, Aa, aa) are $(\pi^2, 2\pi(1-\pi), (1-\pi)^2)$. Assume a multinomial distribution (Section 2.6.4) for n observations with counts (y_1, y_2, y_3) of (AA, Aa, aa).

(a) Express the log-likelihood function for the multinomial and find the ML estimate of π.

(b) Using equation (4.4), find $I(\pi)$ and the approximate large-sample standard error of $\hat{\pi}$.

(c) Explain how you could use the large-sample normality of ML estimators and the result in (b) to construct a 95% confidence interval for π.

4.46 Explain what is meant by a *pivotal quantity*.

4.47 Explain why confidence intervals are narrower with (**a**) smaller confidence levels, (**b**) larger sample sizes.

4.48 For a simple random sample of n subjects, explain why it is about 95% likely that the sample proportion has error no more than $1/\sqrt{n}$ in estimating the population proportion. (*Hint*: To show this "$1/\sqrt{n}$ rule," find two standard errors when $\pi = 0.50$, and explain how this compares to two standard errors at other values of π.) Using this result, show that $n = 1/M^2$ is a safe sample size for estimating a proportion to within M with 95% confidence.

4.49 Explain the reasoning behind the following statement: Studies about more diverse populations require larger sample sizes. Illustrate for estimating mean income for all medical doctors compared to estimating mean income for all entry-level employees at McDonald's restaurants.

4.50 Use simulation or an app, such as the *Explore Coverage* app at www.artofstat.com/web-apps, to explore the performance of confidence intervals for a proportion when n is not very large and π may be near 0 or 1, by repeatedly generating random samples and constructing the confidence intervals. Take the population proportion $\pi = 0.06$, $n = 20$, and confidence level 95%.

(a) Use the Wald confidence interval (formula (4.8)). Choose 10 samples of size $n = 20$. Now draw another 10. How many of the 20 Wald intervals contained the true value, $\pi = 0.06$? How many would you expect to contain it? To see that this is not a fluke, simulate by drawing 1000 random samples of size $n = 20$ and constructing 1000 confidence intervals. What percentage contain $\pi = 0.06$? What does this suggest?

(b) Using simulation or an app, such as the *Sampling Distribution of the Sample Proportion* app at www.artofstat.com/web-apps, let $\pi = 0.06$ and draw 10,000 random samples of size 20 each. Look at the simulated sampling distribution of $\hat{\pi}$, which is highly discrete. Is it bell-shaped and symmetric? Use this to help explain why the Wald confidence interval performs poorly in this case.

(c) When $\hat{\pi} = 0$, show that the Wald confidence interval is $(0, 0)$. As π approaches 0, explain why $P(\hat{\pi} = 0)$ approaches 1, and thus the actual probability that the Wald interval contains π approaches 0.

(d) Now use the Wilson's score interval (formula (4.7)) with simulation or in the *Explore Coverage* app. Draw 1000 samples of size 20 each when $\pi = 0.06$. What percentage of the 95% confidence intervals actually contained π? Explain how this relates to the interpretation for confidence intervals.

4.51 Select the correct response: The reason we use a $z_{\alpha/2}$ normal quantile score in constructing a confidence interval for a proportion is that:

(a) For large random samples, the sampling distribution of the sample proportion is approximately normal.

(b) The population distribution is approximately normal.

(c) For large random samples, the sample data distribution is approximately normal.

(d) If in doubt about the population distribution, it is safest to assume that it is the normal distribution.

4.52 Select the correct response: Other things being equal, quadrupling the sample size causes the width of a confidence interval for a population mean or proportion to (**a**) double, (**b**) halve, (**c**) be one quarter as wide.

4.53 Based on responses of 1467 subjects in a General Social Survey, a 95% confidence interval for the mean number of close friends equals (6.8, 8.0). Identify which of the following interpretations is (are) correct, and indicate what is wrong with the others.

(a) We can be 95% confident that $\bar{y}$ is between 6.8 and 8.0.

(b) We can be 95% confident that μ is between 6.8 and 8.0.

(c) In this sample, ninety-five percent of the values of y = number of close friends are between 6.8 and 8.0.

(d) If random samples of size 1467 were repeatedly selected, then in the long run 95% of the confidence intervals formed would contain the true value of μ.

(e) If random samples of size 1467 were repeatedly selected, then in the long run 95% of the $\bar{y}$ values would fall between 6.8 and 8.0.

4.54 Consider n independent observations from an exponential *pdf* $f(y; \lambda) = \lambda e^{-\lambda y}$ for $y \geq 0$, with parameter $\lambda > 0$ for which $E(Y) = 1/\lambda$.

(a) Find the sufficient statistic for estimating λ.

(b) Find the maximum likelihood estimator of λ and of $E(Y)$.

(c) One can show that $2\lambda(\sum_i Y_i)$ has a chi-squared distribution with $df = 2n$. Explain why $2\lambda(\sum_i Y_i)$ is a pivotal quantity, and use it to derive a 95% confidence interval for λ.

4.55 Using the definition of the chi-squared distribution in Section 4.4.5, prove its *reproductive property*: If X_1^2 and X_2^2 are independent chi-squared random variables with $X_1^2 \sim \chi_{d_1}^2$ and $X_2^2 \sim \chi_{d_2}^2$, then $X_1^2 + X_2^2 \sim \chi_{d_1+d_2}^2$.

4.56 In the T pivotal quantity for comparing two means, explain why $X^2 = (n_1 + n_2 - 2)S^2/\sigma^2$ has a chi-squared distribution with $d = n_1 + n_2 - 2$ degrees of freedom.

4.57 Let Y denote a standard Cauchy random variable, that is, a t-distributed random variable with $df = 1$.

(a) From the definition of the t distribution in Section 4.4.5, show that Y can be expressed as a ratio of two independent standard normal random variables.

(b) Simulate (i) 1, (ii) 100, (iii) 10,000, (iv) 100,000, (v) 1,000,000, (vi) 10,000,000 standard Cauchy random variables, each time finding the sample mean. Does the sample mean seem to be converging, as the law of large numbers predicts? Why or why not? For the $n = 10,000,000$ case, construct a boxplot and report the five-number summary to show how some observations can be very far from the quartiles of -1.0 and 1.0. Do the sample median and quartiles seem to converge to the true values as n increases?

4.58 A random sample of 50 records yields a 95% confidence interval for the mean age at first marriage of women in a certain county of 23.5 to 25.0 years. Explain what is wrong with each of the following interpretations.

(a) If random samples of 50 records were repeatedly selected, then 95% of the time the sample mean age at first marriage for women would be between 23.5 and 25.0 years.

(b) Ninety-five percent of the ages at first marriage for women in the county are between 23.5 and 25.0 years.

(c) We can be 95% confident that $\bar{y}$ is between 23.5 and 25.0 years.

(d) If we repeatedly sampled the entire population, then 95% of the time the population mean would be between 23.5 and 25.0 years.

4.59 Refer to the previous exercise. Suppose that the Bayesian 95% posterior interval is (23.5, 25.0). Interpret, and compare to the proper interpretation of a classical 95% confidence interval.

4.60 For a binom(n, π) observation y, consider the Bayes estimator of π using a beta(α, β) prior distribution.

(a) For large n, show that the posterior distribution of π has approximate mean $\hat{\pi} = y/n$. (It also has approximate variance $\hat{\pi}(1 - \hat{\pi})/n$.) Interpret, and relate to classical inference.

(b) Show that the ML estimator is a limit of Bayes estimators, for a certain sequence of $\alpha = \beta$ values.

4.61 Suppose $y_1, \ldots, y_n$ are independent observations from a Poisson distribution with mean parameter μ. With a Bayesian approach, we use a gamma(k, λ) prior distribution for μ. Then, find the posterior distribution for μ and give its approximate mean for large n. (The gamma is the conjugate prior distribution for estimating the Poisson parameter.)

4.62 For the bootstrap method, explain the similarity and difference between the true sampling distribution of $\hat{\theta}$ and the empirically-generated bootstrap distribution in terms of its center and its spread.

4.63 For n independent observations $\{y_i\}$ from a Poisson distribution with mean μ:

(a) Find the score statistic $U(\mathbf{y}, \mu)$ and the information $I(\mu)$.

(b) Show how to find a score confidence interval for μ.

4.64 *Bias-variance tradeoff*: For a binomial parameter π, consider the Bayesian estimator $(Y + 1)/(n + 2)$ that occurs with a uniform prior distribution.

   (a) Derive its bias and its variance. Compare these with the bias and variance of the ML estimator $\hat{\pi} = Y/n$.

   (b) Show that its MSE $= [n\pi(1-\pi) + (1-2\pi)^2]/(n+2)^2$. For $n = 10$ and for $n = 1000$, plot this and the MSE of the ML estimator as a function of π. Describe the π values for which the MSE is smaller for the Bayes estimator. Explain how this reflects its shrinkage toward $1/2$ and the bias/variance tradeoff.

4.65 *Bias-variance tradeoff 2*: Some statistical methods discussed in Chapters 7 and 8 use a "shrinkage" or "smoothing" of the ML estimator, such that as the amount of shrinkage increases, the bias increases but the variance decreases. To illustrate how this can happen, for $Y \sim \text{binom}(n, \pi)$, let $\tilde{\pi} = (Y + c)/(n + 2c)$ be an estimator of π for a constant $c \geq 0$.

   (a) Show that $\tilde{\pi}$ is a weighted average of $\hat{\pi} = Y/n$ and $1/2$, thus shrinking the ML estimator $\hat{\pi}$ toward $1/2$, with greater shrinkage as c increases.

   (b) Find the bias of $\tilde{\pi}$ and var($\tilde{\pi}$). Show that as c increases, the |bias| increases and the variance decreases.

   (c) Explain how the estimate $\tilde{\pi} = (y + c)/(n + 2c)$ results from a Bayesian approach to estimation. Explain the influence of n on the extent of shrinkage toward $1/2$.

4.66 *Bias-variance tradeoff 3*: For n independent weight changes in an anorexia study, a researcher believes it plausible that $\mu = 0$ and to estimate μ decides to use the estimator $\tilde{\mu} = c\overline{Y}$ for a constant c with $0 \leq c \leq 1$.

   (a) Show that as c decreases from 1 to 0, |bias| increases but var($\tilde{\mu}$) decreases.

   (b) Find MSE. Suppose $\mu = \sigma = n = 1$. For c between 0 and 1, plot (bias)^2, var($\tilde{\mu}$), and MSE($\tilde{\mu}$). Find c to minimize MSE and describe how this would change as n increases.

   (c) Explain how the estimate $\tilde{\mu} = c\overline{y}$ results from a Bayesian approach to estimation. Explain the influence of n on the extent of shrinkage toward 0.

4.67 Show that with y successes in n binary trials, the 95% score confidence interval (4.7) for π:

   (a) Has midpoint (4.9) that is approximately $\tilde{\pi} = (y+2)/(n+4)$, that is, the sample proportion after we add two successes and two failures to the data set.

   (b) Has square of the coefficient of $z_{\alpha/2}$ in the term that is added to and subtracted from this midpoint to form the confidence interval approximately equal to

$$\frac{1}{n+4}\left[\hat{\pi}(1 - \hat{\pi})\left(\frac{n}{n+4}\right) + \left(\frac{1}{2}\right)\left(\frac{1}{2}\right)\left(\frac{4}{n+4}\right)\right].$$

This is a weighted average, with weight $n/(n+4)$ for the variance of a sample proportion when $\pi = \hat{\pi}$ and weight $4/(n+4)$ for the variance of a sample proportion when $\pi = 1/2$, using $n + 4$ in place of the usual sample size n in the denominator of each variance. (The Wald confidence interval $\hat{\pi} \pm z_{\alpha/2}\sqrt{\hat{\pi}(1 - \hat{\pi})/n}$ with $\hat{\pi}$ replaced by $(y + 2)/(n + 4)$ and n replaced by $(n+4)$ is called the **Agresti–Coull confidence interval**. It performs similarly to the score interval and much better than the Wald confidence interval (4.8).)[23]

4.68 In a diagnostic test for a disease, as in Section 2.1.4 let D denote the event of having the disease, and let + denote a positive diagnosis by the test. Let the *sensitivity* $\pi_1 = P(+ \mid D)$, the *false positive rate* $\pi_2 = P(+ \mid D^c)$, and the *prevalence* $\rho = P(D)$. Relevant to a patient who has received a positive diagnosis is $P(D \mid +)$, the *positive predictive value*.

---

[23]For comparing two proportions, the Wald confidence interval found after adding four observations, one success and one failure to each sample, is called the *Agresti–Caffo confidence interval*. These improvements of the Wald confidence interval are also called *plus four confidence intervals*.

(a) Show that $P(D \mid +) = \pi_1 \rho / [\pi_1 \rho + \pi_2 (1 - \rho)]$.

(b) Assuming independent $Y_i \sim \text{binom}(n_i, \pi_i)$, $i = 1, 2$, with $n_1 = n_2 = 100$, suppose $y_1 = 95$ and $y_2 = 5$. Assuming that $\rho = 0.005$, simulate to obtain a 95% posterior interval for $P(D \mid +)$ based on independent uniform priors for π_1 and π_2. Do this by randomly generating 10,000 π_1 and π_2 from their posterior distributions and then finding the relevant percentiles of the 10,000 corresponding generated values of $P(D \mid +)$. (Classical confidence intervals for $P(D \mid +)$ are considerably more complex.)

(c) Repeat (b) for $\rho = 0.05$ and $\rho = 0.50$ to show the influence of ρ on the likely values for $P(D \mid +)$.

4.69 In estimating the probability π of the *yes* response on a sensitive question, the method of **randomized response** can be used to encourage subjects to make responses. The subject is asked to flip a coin, in secret. If it is a head, the subject tosses the coin once more and reports the outcome, head or tails. If, instead, the first flip is a tail, the subject reports instead the response to the sensitive question, reporting *head* if the true response is *yes* and reporting *tail* if the true response is *no*.

(a) Explain why the values in Table 4.5 are the probabilities of the four possible outcomes.

(b) Let $\tilde{\pi}$ denote the sample proportion of subjects who report *head* for the second response. Explain why $2\tilde{\pi} - 0.5$ estimates π.

(c) Using this approach, 200 subjects are asked whether they have ever knowingly cheated on their income tax. Report the estimate of π if the number of reported heads equals (i) 50, (ii) 100.

TABLE 4.5 Joint probabilities for randomized response outcomes.

	Second Response	
First Coin	Head	Tail
Head	0.25	0.25
Tail	$\pi/2$	$(1 - \pi)/2$

4.70 Long before Ronald Fisher proposed the maximum likelihood method in 1922, in 1894 Karl Pearson proposed the **method of moments**. This expresses the mean of the probability distribution in terms of the parameter and equates it to the sample mean. For two parameters, you equate the first two moments. Let $Y_1, \ldots, Y_n$ be n independent random variables from the uniform distribution (2.4) over $(0, \theta)$.

(a) Show that the method of moments estimate is $\tilde{\theta} = 2\bar{y}$.

(b) Let $y_{(1)} \le y_{(2)} \le \cdots \le y_{(n)}$ denote the ordered observations, called **order statistics**. Explain why the likelihood function is $\ell(\theta) = 1/\theta^n$ for $\theta \ge y_{(n)}$. Explain why the ML estimate $\hat{\theta} = y_{(n)}$.

(c) Report the two estimates for the sample data $\{1, 2, 9\}$. Explain why the method of moments estimate does not make sense. (For distributions for which ML and method of moments estimators differ, Fisher showed that the ML estimator is more efficient.)

(d) This is a rare case in which the ML estimator $\hat{\theta}$ does not have a large-sample normal distribution, because of violating the regularity condition that the possible values for y cannot depend on the value of θ. Show that for $0 < y < \theta$, the cdf of $\hat{\theta}$ is $F(y) = (y/\theta)^n$ and its pdf is $f(y) = (ny^{n-1})/\theta^n$.

(e) Show that the method of moments estimator $\tilde{\theta}$ is unbiased but $E(\hat{\theta}) = [n/(n+1)]\theta$, illustrating that an unbiased estimator need not be better than a biased estimator.

(f) If you were to use the bootstrap with the ML estimator $\hat{\theta} = Y_{(n)}$, describe the likely appearance of the bootstrap distribution. How would the percentile-based confidence interval perform for estimating θ?

4.71 Use the Markov inequality (Exercise 2.50) to show that as $n \to \infty$:

(a) If $\hat{\theta}$ is *mean-squared-error consistent* in the sense that $E(\hat{\theta} - \theta)^2 \to 0$, then $\hat{\theta} \xrightarrow{p} \theta$.

(b) If $E(\hat{\theta}) \to \theta$ and $\text{var}(\hat{\theta}) \to 0$, then $\hat{\theta} \xrightarrow{p} \theta$. (Here, use $\text{MSE}(\hat{\theta}) = \text{var}(\hat{\theta}) + (\text{bias})^2$.)

4.72 Theory exists that justifies substituting the estimated standard error for the true one in forming a pivotal quantity. Here we show this for a proportion.

(a) The **continuous mapping theorem** states that continuous functions preserve limits even if their arguments are sequences of random variables. In particular, if $X_n \xrightarrow{p} c$ and if $g()$ is a continuous function at c, then $g(X_n) \xrightarrow{p} g(c)$. Using this, explain why $\sqrt{\pi(1-\pi)/\hat{\pi}(1-\hat{\pi})} \xrightarrow{p} 1$.

(b) **Slutsky's Theorem** states that if $Z_n \xrightarrow{d} Z$ and if $X_n \xrightarrow{p} c$, then $X_n Z_n \xrightarrow{d} cZ$. Apply this with $Z_n = (\hat{\pi} - \pi)/\sqrt{\pi(1-\pi)/n}$ and $X_n = \sqrt{\pi(1-\pi)/\hat{\pi}(1-\hat{\pi})}$ to justify that $(\hat{\pi} - \pi)/\sqrt{\hat{\pi}(1-\hat{\pi})/n}$ has a large-sample standard normal distribution.

4.73 Refer to the definitions of chi-squared and T random variables in Section 4.4.5.

(a) From the representation $(Z_1^2 + \cdots + Z_d^2)$ with standard normals, explain why the χ_d^2 distribution has mean d.

(b) From the representation $T = Z/\sqrt{X^2/d}$, explain why the t distribution converges to the standard normal as $d \to \infty$. (*Hint*: Apply the weak law of large numbers inside the square root, and then apply Slutzky's Theorem, stated in the previous exercise.)

4.74 Let Z denote a standard normal random variable, which has *pdf* $\phi(z) = (1/\sqrt{2\pi})\exp(-z^2/2)$ and *cdf* Φ. Recall that $Y = Z^2$ has a χ_1^2 distribution.

(a) Explain why the *cdf* of Y for $y \geq 0$ is $F(y) = \Phi(\sqrt{y}) - \Phi(-\sqrt{y})$.

(b) Taking the derivative, show that the *pdf* of Y is[24]

$$f(y) = (1/\sqrt{y})[\phi(\sqrt{y}) + \phi(-\sqrt{y})] = (1/\sqrt{2\pi y})e^{-y/2}, \quad y \geq 0.$$

Using $\Gamma(1/2) = \sqrt{\pi}$, this is the gamma *pdf* (2.10) with $\lambda = 1/2$ and $k = 1/2$.

4.75 The family of probability distributions having *pdf* of form

$$f(y; \theta) = B(\theta)h(y)\exp[Q(\theta)R(y)]$$

is called the **exponential family**. The **natural exponential family** is the special case $Q(\theta) = \theta$ and $R(y) = y$, with θ called the **natural parameter**.

(a) Show that the binomial distribution is in the natural exponential family with natural parameter $\theta = \log[\pi/(1-\pi)]$, the *logit*. (Other distributions in this family include the Poisson, gamma and exponential with parameter λ, geometric, normal with parameter μ; ones not in the family include the uniform with support $[0, \theta]$ and the Cauchy with median θ, $f(y; \theta) = 1/\{\pi[1 + (y - \theta)^2]\}$.)

(b) For independent $\{y_i\}$ from a natural exponential family, find the likelihood function. Show that a sufficient statistic for θ is $\sum_i Y_i$. (Its distribution is also in the exponential family.)[25]

4.76 The moment generating function of a χ_d^2 random variable is $m_d(t) = (1 - 2t)^{-d/2}$ for $t < 1/2$. Suppose that U and V are independent, with $U \sim \chi_{d_1}^2$ and $U + V \sim \chi_{d_1+d_2}^2$. From Exercise 3.45, $m_{U+V}(t) = m_U(t)m_V(t)$. Show that $V \sim \chi_{d_2}^2$.

---

[24]This method of finding a *pdf* by deriving its *cdf* and then taking the derivative is called the *cdf method*.
[25]If a distribution has possible y values not dependent on θ, useful sufficient statistics exist only if the distribution is in the exponential family.

4.77 For a continuous distribution, explain why the number of observations that fall below the population median has a binom$(n, 0.50)$ distribution. If we order the observations in magnitude, giving the *order statistics* $Y_{(1)} \le Y_{(2)} \le \cdots \le Y_{(n)}$, explain why the probability is about 0.95 that the interval $(Y_{(a)}, Y_{(b)})$ contains the median, where $a \approx n/2 - 1.96\sqrt{n/4}$ and $b \approx n/2 + 1.96\sqrt{n/4}$. So, $(Y_{(a)}, Y_{(b)})$ is an approximate 95% confidence interval for the median. For the library example in Section 4.6.2, find this interval for the median of the distribution of P.

4.78 For the multinomial distribution (2.14) with counts $\{y_j\}$ in c categories satisfying $\sum_j y_j = n$, Bayesian methods often use the **Dirichlet distribution** as a prior distribution for $(\pi_1, \ldots, \pi_c)$,

$$p(\pi_1, \ldots, \pi_c; \alpha_1, \ldots, \alpha_c) \propto \pi_1^{\alpha_1 - 1} \pi_2^{\alpha_2 - 1} \cdots \pi_c^{\alpha_c - 1}, \quad 0 \le \pi_j \le 1, \quad \sum_j \pi_j = 1,$$

for hyperparameters $\{\alpha_j > 0\}$. This distribution has $E(\pi_j) = \alpha_j / (\sum_k \alpha_k)$.

(a) Which values for $\{\alpha_j\}$ yield a uniform distribution over the probability simplex?

(b) Show that the posterior distribution is also the Dirichlet, so the Dirichlet is the conjugate prior.

(c) Show that the posterior mean of π_j is $(y_j + \alpha_j)/(n + \sum_k \alpha_k)$. With the uniform prior, explain why the estimates are sample proportions after adding a single observation to each category.

4.79 Explain how using a standard normal pivotal quantity in the form

$$P\left[-\infty \le \frac{T(\mathbf{Y}) - \theta}{\sigma_T} \le 1.645\right] = 0.95 \quad \text{or} \quad P\left[-1.645 \le \frac{T(\mathbf{Y}) - \theta}{\sigma_T} \le \infty\right] = 0.95$$

would lead to a *one-sided* 95% confidence interval for θ. Use this idea to get a Wald 95% lower confidence bound for the population proportion supporting legalization of marijuana in Exercise 4.5.

4.80 A point estimator $\hat{\theta}$ is **location invariant** if for all possible data and all constants c, when we add c to each observation, the estimator increases by c. It is **scale invariant** if when we multiply each observation by $c > 0$, the estimator multiplies by c.

(a) Show that $\overline{Y}$ is location invariant and S is scale invariant.

(b) Is the Bayes estimator of the mean of a normal distribution location invariant? Why or why not?

4.81 A basic element in **statistical decision theory** is the *loss function* for a statistical decision. In the context of estimation, a common loss function for an estimator $\hat{\theta}$ of a parameter θ is the squared-error loss,

$$\text{L}(\theta, \hat{\theta}) = (\hat{\theta} - \theta)^2.$$

The loss function refers to a single sample, and to evaluate $\hat{\theta}$, we use the expected loss,

$$R(\theta, \hat{\theta}) = E[\text{L}(\theta, \hat{\theta})] = \int \text{L}(\theta, \hat{\theta}(\mathbf{y})) f(\mathbf{y}; \theta) d\mathbf{y},$$

called the *risk function*. For the squared-error loss function, this is the mean squared error (MSE). In a Bayesian framework, the overall evaluation of $\hat{\theta}$ is based on the *Bayesian risk*

$$r_p(\hat{\theta}) = E[R(\theta, \hat{\theta})] = \int \int \text{L}(\theta, \hat{\theta}(\mathbf{y})) f(\mathbf{y}; \theta) p(\theta) d\mathbf{y} d\theta,$$

which averages the risk function with respect to the prior distribution $p(\theta)$ for θ. An estimator that minimizes the Bayes risk is called a *Bayes estimator*. It can be proved that a Bayesian estimator minimizes the *posterior expected loss*

$$E[\text{L}(\theta, \hat{\theta}) \mid \mathbf{y}] = \int \text{L}(\theta, \hat{\theta}(\mathbf{y})) g(\theta \mid \mathbf{y}) d\theta.$$

Show that for the squared-error loss function, the Bayes estimator of θ is the posterior mean, $\hat{\theta} = E(\theta \mid \mathbf{y}) = \int \theta g(\theta \mid \mathbf{y}) d\theta$.

4.82 Refer to the previous exercise. For the absolute-error loss function

$$L(\theta, \hat{\theta}) = |\theta - \hat{\theta}|,$$

show that the Bayes estimator of θ is the median of the posterior distribution.

5

Statistical Inference: Significance Testing

A goal of many research studies is to use data to check certain predictions. The predictions, which usually result from previous studies or from theory that drives the research, are *hypotheses* about the study population.

> ### Hypothesis
>
> In statistics, a ***hypothesis*** is a statement about a population distribution. It takes the form of a prediction about the distribution, such as that a particular parameter has the same value for two groups being compared.

Examples of hypotheses are the following: "For all the employees of a fast-food chain, the mean salary is the same for women and for men." "For all college students in the U.S., there is no correlation between weekly number of hours spent studying and and number of hours spent partying." "Only half of adults in the United Kingdom are satisfied with their national health service." The hypotheses are investigated with reference to *alternative hypotheses*, such as "For all the employees of a fast-food chain, the mean salary is *higher* for men than for women."

A statistical ***significance test***, called a *test* for short, uses data to summarize the evidence about a hypothesis by comparing a point estimate of the parameter of interest to the value predicted by the hypothesis. After listing the elements that all significance tests have in common, we present significance tests about population proportions and population means, both for a single sample and for comparing two groups. We then show how to control the probability of an incorrect decision about a hypothesis. Connections exist between significance tests and confidence intervals. We'll explain the limitations of significance tests and show that confidence intervals can be more informative than tests for learning about the size of an effect. Tests for means use the t distribution and assume a normal population distribution, but we also introduce *nonparametric tests* that apply regardless of the population distribution or the sample size.

5.1 The Elements of a Significance Test

We use an example to illustrate the elements of significance tests.

5.1.1 Example: Testing for Bias in Selecting Managers

A supermarket chain in the southeastern U.S. periodically selects employees to receive management training. A group of women employees recently asserted that the company selects males at a disproportionally high rate for such training. The company denied this claim. In past years, similar claims of gender bias have been made about promotions and pay for women who work for various companies.[1]

Suppose the employee pool for potential management training is large and has 40% males and 60% females. The company's claim of a lack of gender bias is a hypothesis that, other things being equal, at each choice the probability of selecting a male equals 0.40 and the probability of selecting a female equals 0.60. The women's claim is an alternative hypothesis that the probability of selecting a male exceeds 0.40. Suppose that in the latest selection of employees for management training, 9 of the 10 chosen were male. We might be inclined to believe the women's claim. However, even if selected at random from the employee pool, due to sampling variation, not exactly 40% of those chosen need be male and perhaps 9 males of 10 chosen is quite possible. To evaluate this, we should analyze whether this selection result would be unlikely, if there were *no* gender bias. We next introduce a statistical framework to do this as a way of testing the women's claim.

5.1.2   Assumptions, Hypotheses, Test Statistic, *P*-Value, and Conclusion

Each significance test has four elements: (1) *Assumptions*, (2) *Hypotheses*, (3) *Test statistic*, and (4) *P-value and conclusion*.

(1) Assumptions

Like other statistical methods, each significance test makes certain assumptions or has certain conditions to be valid. These pertain to:

- *Type of data*: Each significance test applies for either quantitative or categorical data.

- *Randomization*: Each significance test assumes that the data gathering employed randomization, such as a simple random sample or a randomized experiment.

- *Population distribution*: Some significance tests assume that the variable has population distribution in a particular family of probability distributions, such as the normal or binomial.

- *Sample size*: Some significance tests, such as those based on the Central Limit Theorem, are valid only when the sample size is sufficiently large.

(2) Hypotheses

Significance tests have two hypotheses about population distributions, usually expressed in terms of parameters of those distributions.

Null hypothesis, Alternative hypothesis

The *null hypothesis*, denoted by H_0, is a statement that a parameter takes a particular value. The *alternative hypothesis*, denoted by H_a, states that a parameter takes value in some alternative range. Usually the value in H_0 corresponds, in a certain sense, to *no effect*. The values in H_a then represent a particular type of effect.

The hypotheses are formulated *before* analyzing the data. The alternative hypothesis is usually a research hypothesis that the investigator believes to be true.

---

[1]For example, see http://now.org/blog/walmart-and-sex-discrimination

In a company's selection of management trainees, let π denote the probability that any particular selection is a male. The company's claim that $\pi = 0.40$ is an example of a null hypothesis, *no effect* referring to a lack of gender bias. The alternative hypothesis reflects the women employees' belief that this probability exceeds 0.40. These hypotheses are H_0: $\pi = 0.40$ and H_a: $\pi > 0.40$. Whereas H_0 has a *single* value, H_a has a range of values.

A significance test analyzes whether the data contradict H_0 and suggest that H_a is true, using the indirect route of *proof by contradiction*. H_0 is presumed to be true. Under this presumption, if the observed data would be very unusual, the evidence supports H_a. In testing potential gender bias, we presume that H_0: $\pi = 0.40$ is true and analyze whether a sample proportion of males of 9/10 would be unusual, under this presumption. If so, we may be inclined to believe the women's claim. If the difference between the sample proportion 9/10 and the H_0 value of 0.40 could easily be due to ordinary sampling variability, however, we conclude that the company's claim of a lack of gender bias is plausible.

(3) Test Statistic

The parameter to which the hypotheses refer has a point estimate. The **test statistic** summarizes how far that point estimate falls from the parameter value in H_0, such as by the *number of standard errors* between them.

(4) *P*-value and Conclusion

Different significance tests use different test statistics, and simpler interpretations result from transforming from the test-statistic scale to a *probability* summary of the evidence against H_0. To do this, we use the sampling distribution of the test statistic, under the presumption that H_0 is true. The farther the test statistic falls out in a tail of the sampling distribution in a direction predicted by H_a, the stronger the evidence against H_0. We can summarize how far out in the tail it falls by the tail probability of that test statistic value and of more extreme values. These test statistic values provide *at least as much evidence against H_0 as the observed test statistic*, in the direction predicted by H_a. Their probability is called the **P-value**.

P-value

The **P-value** is the probability, presuming that H_0 is true, that the test statistic equals the observed value or a value even more extreme in the direction predicted by H_a.

A small *P*-value, such as 0.01, means that the observed data would have been unusual, if H_0 were true. A moderate to large *P*-value, such as 0.26 or 0.83, means the data are consistent with H_0; if H_0 were true, the observed data would not be unusual. *Smaller P-values reflect stronger evidence against H_0.*

For testing H_0: $\pi = 0.40$ against H_a: $\pi > 0.40$ for the managerial trainee selections, one possible test statistic is the number of standard errors that the sample proportion $\hat{\pi}$ falls from the H_0 value. We'll use this test statistic in the next section for cases with large n, but with n only 10 it is sufficient to use the sample count itself, $y = 9$, treating it as the outcome of a binomial random variable. The y values that provide this much or even more extreme evidence against H_0: $\pi = 0.40$ and in favor of H_a: $\pi > 0.40$ are the right-tail values ≥ 9, that is, 9 or 10 males out of the 10 selected. From the binomial distribution (2.6), the probability of 9 or 10 males in 10 selections from a large population of possible trainees when $\pi = 0.40$ is[2]

$$P(Y \geq 9) = \binom{10}{9}(0.4)^9(0.6)^1 + \binom{10}{10}(0.4)^{10}(0.6)^0 = 0.0017,$$

and this is the *P*-value. If the selections truly were random with respect to gender, the probability of such an extreme sample result is only 0.0017, providing strong evidence against H_0: $\pi = 0.40$ and supporting H_a: $\pi > 0.40$.

Sometimes it is necessary to make a decision about the validity of H_0. If the *P*-value is sufficiently small, we reject H_0 and accept H_a. Research studies require small *P*-values, such as ≤ 0.05, in order to reject H_0. Results are then said to be *significant at the 0.05 level*. We defer discussion of decisions and their probabilities of error until Section 5.5. Table 5.1 summarizes the elements of a significance test.

TABLE 5.1 The elements of a statistical significance test.

(1)	**Assumptions**
	Type of data, randomization, population distribution, sample size condition
(2)	**Hypotheses**
	Null hypothesis, H_0 (parameter value for "no effect")
	Alternative hypothesis, H_a (range of alternative parameter values)
(3)	**Test statistic**
	Compares point estimate of parameter to its H_0 value
(4)	**P-value and conclusion**
	P-value is probability, under H_0, of observed data or more extreme results
	If decision needed, "reject H_0" if *P*-value is sufficiently small

5.2 Significance Tests for Proportions and Means

The simplest significance tests deal with a proportion or a mean from a single sample. This section presents these tests, and then the following two sections deal with the more common situation in which we use a significance test to compare proportions or to compare means of two groups.

5.2.1 The Elements of a Significance Test for a Proportion

For categorical variables, the parameters are the population proportions for the categories. The binary case (two categories) has only a single parameter π, since the proportion in the other category is $1 - \pi$.

(1) Assumptions

As usual for statistical inference, we assume that the data are obtained using randomization. The sample size should be sufficiently large that the sampling distribution of $\hat{\pi}$ is

---

[2]In R, this is `dbinom(9, 10, 0.4)` + `dbinom(10, 10, 0.4)`. If the population size is not much larger than n, π is not the same for each selection and the *hypergeometric distribution* (Exercise 2.68) is more appropriate. For example, if the employee pool had 40 men and 60 women, the *P*-value for this example would be, in R, `dhyper(9, 40, 60, 10)` + `dhyper(10, 40, 60, 10)` = 0.0010.

approximately normal. This is satisfied when the expected number of observations is at least 10 for both categories. For example, to test H_0: $\pi = 0.50$, we need at least about $n = 20$, because then we expect $20(0.50) = 10$ observations in one category and $20(1-0.50) = 10$ in the other category. For H_0: $\pi = 0.90$ or H_0: $\pi = 0.10$, we need $n \geq 100$. Obtaining a symmetric bell shape for the sampling distribution of $\hat{\pi}$ requires larger n when π is near 0 or 1 than when π is near 0.50. With small n or for greater precision, we can use the binomial distribution directly instead of a normal sampling distribution, such as shown in the Section 5.1.2 example of gender-bias in hiring with $n = 10$.

(2) Hypotheses

The null hypothesis of a test about a population proportion has form

$$H_0 : \pi = \pi_0$$

where π_0 denotes a particular value between 0 and 1, such as H_0: $\pi = 0.50$. The most common alternative hypothesis is

$$H_a : \pi \neq \pi_0, \quad \text{such as} \quad H_a : \pi \neq 0.50.$$

This alternative hypothesis is called **two-sided**, because it contains values both below and above the value listed in H_0.

(3) Test Statistic

The sampling distribution of $\hat{\pi}$ is approximately normal with mean π and standard error $\sqrt{\pi(1-\pi)/n}$ (Section 3.2). When H_0: $\pi = \pi_0$ is true, the standard error is $se_0 = \sqrt{\pi_0(1-\pi_0)/n}$. The notation se_0 indicates that this is the standard error under the presumption that H_0 is true. The evidence about H_0 is summarized by the number of standard errors that $\hat{\pi}$ falls from π_0. The test statistic[3] is

$$Z = \frac{\hat{\pi} - \pi_0}{se_0}, \quad \text{where} \quad se_0 = \sqrt{\frac{\pi_0(1-\pi_0)}{n}}. \tag{5.1}$$

When H_0 is true, its sampling distribution is approximately the standard normal distribution.

(4) *P*-value and Conclusion

Under the presumption that H_0 is true, the *P*-value is the probability that the Z test statistic equals the observed value or a *more extreme value* that provides *even stronger evidence* against H_0 and in favor of H_a. For H_a: $\pi \neq \pi_0$, the more extreme z values are the ones even farther out in the two tails of the standard normal distribution, and the *P*-value is the two-tail probability that $|Z|$ is at least as large as the observed $|z|$. This is also the probability that $\hat{\pi}$ falls at least as far from π_0 *in either direction* as the observed value of $\hat{\pi}$.

Figure 5.1 shows the sampling distribution of the Z test statistic for testing H_0: $\pi = 0.50$, when H_0 is true. Suppose that we observe $z = 1.26$, as in the next example, which means that $\hat{\pi}$ falls 1.26 standard errors above $\pi_0 = 0.50$. The *P*-value is the probability that $Z \geq 1.26$ or $Z \leq -1.26$ (i.e., $|Z| \geq 1.26$). The probability in one tail above 1.26 is 0.104, so the two-tail probability is $2(0.104) = 0.208$, which is the *P*-value.

---

[3]This test is referred to as a *score test*, because like confidence interval (4.7), it can be derived using the *score function* introduced in Section 4.9.1. We explain this further in Section 5.7.3.

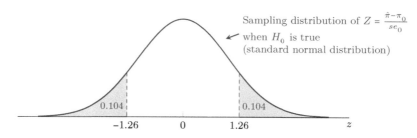

FIGURE 5.1 *P*-value for testing H_0: $\pi = 0.50$ against H_a: $\pi \neq 0.50$ is the two-tail probability of a test statistic at least as extreme as the observed $z = 1.26$, which is $2(0.104) = 0.208$.

5.2.2 Example: Climate Change a Major Threat?

A Fox News poll asked a random sample of 1008 Americans in 2019 whether they thought climate change was a major threat to the stability of the United States. Let π denote the population proportion who would say *yes*. To analyze whether this is a minority of the population ($\pi < 0.50$) or a majority ($\pi > 0.50$), we test H_0: $\pi = 0.50$ against H_a: $\pi \neq 0.50$. Presuming H_0: $\pi = 0.50$ is true, the standard error of $\hat{\pi}$ is

$$se_0 = \sqrt{\frac{\pi_0(1 - \pi_0)}{n}} = \sqrt{\frac{(0.50)(0.50)}{1008}} = 0.0157.$$

In the poll, 52.0% (524 of the 1008) said *yes*. With $\hat{\pi} = 0.520$, the test statistic equals

$$z = \frac{\hat{\pi} - \pi_0}{se_0} = \frac{0.520 - 0.50}{0.0157} = 1.26.$$

The two-sided *P*-value is 0.208. This *P*-value is not very small, so the evidence against H_0 is not strong. It is plausible that $\pi = 0.50$. There is insufficient evidence to determine whether a majority or minority of the population believes that climate change is a major threat.

We can conduct the test using software or an Internet app,[4] such as shown here with R:

```
> prop.test(524, 1008, p=0.50, alt="two.sided", conf.level=0.95, correct=FALSE)
data:  524 out of 1008, null probability 0.5
p-value = 0.20771,  alternative hypothesis: true p is not equal to 0.5
95 percent confidence interval: 0.48898 0.55055 # Sec. 5.5 explains connection with test
sample estimates:  p  0.5198
```

Round the *P*-value, such as to 0.21, before reporting it. Stating the *P*-value with many decimal places makes it seem as if more accuracy exists than actually does. The sampling distribution is only *approximately* the standard normal distribution.

5.2.3 One-Sided Significance Tests

A different alternative hypothesis predicts a deviation from H_0 in a particular direction. It has form

$$H_a : \pi > \pi_0 \quad \text{or} \quad H_a : \pi < \pi_0.$$

---

[4]Such as the *Inference for a Proportion* app at www.artofstat.com/web-apps. In the R code, the *correct=FALSE* option suppresses a *continuity correction*, which better approximates the *P*-value found using the binomial distribution but has conservative performance and does not have the connection with confidence intervals presented in Section 5.6.

These hypotheses are called *one-sided*. For H_a: $\pi > \pi_0$, the *P*-value is the probability, presuming H_0 to be true, of a test statistic Z falling *above* the observed z test statistic value. It is the *right-tail* probability under the standard normal curve. These z-scores provide more extreme evidence than the observed value in favor of H_a: $\pi > \pi_0$. A z test statistic of 1.26 has a *P*-value of 0.104 for this alternative. For H_a: $\pi < \pi_0$, the *P*-value is the *left-tail* probability *below* the observed z test statistic value. Then, $z = 1.26$ has a *P*-value of $1 - 0.104 = 0.896$, and $z = -1.26$ has a *P*-value of 0.104.

An example of a one-sided H_a is H_a: $\pi > 0.40$ used in the gender-bias in hiring case to predict that the probability π of selecting a male was higher than claimed by the company. To find the *P*-value of $P(Y \geq 9) = 0.0017$ with that one-sided H_a, we used the binomial sampling distribution at $\pi = 0.40$, so H_0 has a single value as it does in the two-sided case. That is, we express H_0 as H_0: $\pi = 0.40$ rather than H_0 $\pi \leq 0.40$, because we need a particular value for π to find the binomial probabilities. Now, suppose $\pi = 0.20$. Then $P(Y \geq 9)$ would be even smaller than 0.0017, because $y = 9$ men when $n = 10$ is even less likely when $\pi = 0.20$ than when $\pi = 0.40$. Using a *P*-value of 0.0017 to conclude that it is implausible that $\pi = 0.40$ implicitly indicates that the broader null hypothesis of H_0: $\pi \leq 0.40$ is implausible.

In most research articles, significance tests use two-sided *P*-values. Partly this reflects an objective approach to research that recognizes that an effect could go in either direction. In using two-sided *P*-values, researchers avoid the suspicion that they chose H_a when they saw the direction in which the data occurred, which is not ethical. Two-sided tests coincide with the usual approach in estimation. Confidence intervals are two-sided, often obtained by adding and subtracting a margin of error from the point estimate, and we'll show a strong connection between confidence intervals and two-sided tests in Section 5.6. One-sided confidence intervals are also possible,[5] for instance having 95% confidence that a population proportion is *no greater than* 0.546 (*i.e.*, between 0.0 and 0.546), but are not commonly used.

5.2.4 The Elements of a Significance Test for a Mean

For quantitative variables, significance tests usually refer to population means. The elements of a significance test for a mean resemble those for a proportion, except for using the t distribution instead of the standard normal for the sampling distribution of the test statistic.

(1) Assumptions

Significance tests for means assume that the data are obtained using randomization. The test presented in this section assumes a normal population distribution. This assumption is mainly relevant for small sample sizes and one-sided H_a, because otherwise the test is *robust* (Section 4.4.4), performing adequately even when that assumption is violated.

(2) Hypotheses

The null hypothesis about a population mean μ has the form

$$H_0 : \mu = \mu_0$$

for a particular value μ_0. This hypothesis usually refers to *no effect* or *no change* compared to some standard. For example, in Section 4.4.3 we estimated the population mean weight

---

[5] See Exercise 4.79

change μ for a therapy for anorexia. The hypothesis that the therapy has *no effect* is a null hypothesis, H_0: $\mu = 0$.

The most common alternative hypothesis is

$$H_a : \mu \neq \mu_0, \quad \text{such as} \quad H_a : \mu \neq 0.$$

For the anorexia study, H_a: $\mu \neq 0$ states that the therapy has *some effect*, the population mean equaling some value other than 0. The one-sided alternatives

$$H_a : \mu > \mu_0 \quad \text{and} \quad H_a : \mu < \mu_0$$

predict a deviation in a certain direction from the H_0 value, and are less common.

(3) Test Statistic

In a study employing randomization, when the population distribution is normal, the sampling distribution of the sample mean $\bar{Y}$ is normal about μ. The evidence in the data about H_0 is summarized by the number of standard errors that the observed $\bar{y}$ falls from μ_0. The standard error is $\sigma_{\bar{Y}} = \sigma/\sqrt{n}$, for population standard deviation σ. As in Chapter 4, because σ is unknown, we substitute the sample standard deviation s for σ and use an *estimated* standard error, $se = s/\sqrt{n}$. The test statistic is

$$T = \frac{\bar{Y} - \mu_0}{SE} \quad \text{where} \quad SE = \frac{S}{\sqrt{n}}. \tag{5.2}$$

Its null sampling distribution is the *t distribution* (Section 4.4.1), with $df = n - 1$. The t distribution applies instead of the standard normal because of substituting s for σ.

(4) *P*-value and Conclusion

The *P*-value is the probability, presuming H_0, that the test statistic T equals the observed value t or a more-extreme value that provides even stronger evidence against H_0. For H_a: $\mu \neq \mu_0$, the *P*-value is the two-tail probability that T is at least as large in absolute value as the observed t, which is the probability that $\bar{Y}$ falls at least as far from μ_0 *in either direction* as its observed value. For one-sided alternatives, the *P*-value is a one-tail probability. As usual, the smaller the *P*-value, the more strongly the data contradict H_0 and support H_a.

Figure 5.2 shows the sampling distribution of the T test statistic when H_0 is true. In testing H_0: $\mu = 0$, suppose we observe $t = 1.283$ for $n = 369$ observations, as in the next example. That is, $\bar{y}$ falls 1.283 estimated standard errors above $\mu_0 = 0$. The *P*-value is the probability that $T \geq 1.283$ or $T \leq -1.283$. The probability in one tail above 1.283 is 0.10, so the two-tail probability is $2(0.10) = 0.20$.

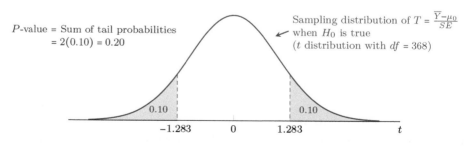

FIGURE 5.2 *P*-value for testing H_0: $\mu = 0$ against H_a: $\mu \neq 0$ is the two-tail probability of a test statistic T at least as extreme as the observed $t = 1.283$, which is $2(0.10) = 0.20$.

TABLE 5.2 Responses on a scale of political ideology, by race.

	Race		
Political ideology	Hispanic	Black	White
1. Extremely liberal	5	16	73
2. Liberal	49	52	209
3. Slightly liberal	46	42	190
4. Moderate, middle of road	155	182	705
5. Slightly conservative	50	43	260
6. Conservative	50	25	314
7. Extremely conservative	14	11	84
n	369	371	1835

5.2.5 Example: Significance Test about Political Ideology

On the average, how politically conservative or liberal are U.S. citizens? We can study political ideology by analyzing an item on the General Social Survey that has a seven-point scale of political views ranging from 1 = extremely liberal to 7 = extremely conservative. Table 5.2 shows the scale and the distribution of responses among the levels for a recent GSS, with subjects classified by race.

Political ideology is an ordinal scale. It is sometimes informative to treat ordinal data in a quantitative manner by assigning scores to the categories, in order to use the mean to summarize the responses. For the category scores in Table 5.2, a mean below 4 shows a propensity toward liberalism and a mean above 4 shows a propensity toward conservatism. To test whether the data show much evidence of either of these, we conduct a significance test[6] about how the population mean μ compares to the moderate value of 4, with hypotheses

$$H_0 : \mu = 4.0, \quad H_a : \mu \neq 4.0.$$

H_0 states that, on the average, the population response is politically "moderate, middle of road." H_a states that the mean falls in the liberal direction ($\mu < 4.0$) or in the conservative direction ($\mu > 4.0$).

We'll illustrate the t test by conducting it for the Hispanic sample.[7] The 369 Hispanic observations in Table 5.2 have $\bar{y} = 4.089$, $s = 1.339$, and estimated standard error

$$se = \frac{s}{\sqrt{n}} = \frac{1.339}{\sqrt{369}} = 0.0697.$$

The observed value of the test statistic is

$$t = \frac{\bar{y} - \mu_0}{se} = \frac{4.089 - 4.0}{0.0697} = 1.283,$$

with $df = 369 - 1 = 368$. The sample mean falls 1.283 estimated standard errors above the H_0 value. The P-value is the two-tail probability, presuming H_0 is true, that T would exceed 1.283 in absolute value, which is 0.20. If the population mean ideology μ for Hispanics were

---

[6]The sampling is more complex than simple random sample, but treated as such here to illustrate the test.

[7]Results for the entire sample are in Section 5.6.2.

4.0, then the probability equals 0.20 that $\overline{Y}$ for 369 subjects would fall at least as far from 4.0 as the observed $\bar{y}$ of 4.089; the observed data would not be unusual. It is plausible that μ was 4.0, not in the conservative or liberal direction.

We can conduct the t test using software or an Internet app.[8] Here are results using R with the Hispanic sub-sample:

```
> Polid <- read.table("http://stat4ds.rwth-aachen.de/data/Polid.dat", header=TRUE)
> Polid
          race ideology
1      hispanic        1
2      hispanic        1
...
2575      white        7

> t.test(Polid$ideology[Polid$race=="hispanic"], mu=4.0, alt="two.sided")
# Replace "two.sided" by "greater" or "less" for one-sided alternatives
t = 1.2827, df = 368, p-value = 0.2004
alternative hypothesis: true mean is not equal to 4
95 percent confidence interval:
 3.952333 4.226528            # like the test, suggests that mu = 4.0 is plausible
```

Round the reported P-value, such as from 0.2004 to to 0.20, before reporting it. The sampling distribution is only *approximately* the t distribution.

The t test assumes that the population distribution is normal, to ensure that the T test statistic has the t distribution. This seems inappropriate here, because the measurement of political ideology is discrete. As n increases in a study with randomization, however, this assumption becomes less important; an approximate normal sampling distribution occurs for $\overline{Y}$ (and a t null distribution for the T test statistic) regardless of the population distribution, by the Central Limit Theorem. *Two-sided* inferences for a mean using the t distribution are robust against violations of the normal population assumption. The test does not perform well for a one-sided test when n is small and the population distribution is highly skewed. Section 5.8 presents *nonparametric* tests that are better suited for that case.

5.3 Significance Tests Comparing Means

In practice, inferences about means or proportions usually involve comparisons for different groups. This section presents significance tests for comparing means for a quantitative response variable, and the following section shows how to compare proportions for a categorical response variable.

5.3.1 Significance Tests for the Difference between Two Means

To compare the population means μ_1 and μ_2 of two groups, we test H_0: $\mu_1 = \mu_2$. For the difference $\mu_1 - \mu_2$ parameter that we estimated with a confidence interval in Section 4.5.2, this hypothesis is H_0: $\mu_1 - \mu_2 = 0$, *no difference*, or *no effect*.

As in Section 4.5.2 on confidence intervals for $\mu_1 - \mu_2$, a standard method assumes that the population standard deviations satisfy $\sigma_1 = \sigma_2$. The significance test is then a special case of an inference for a statistical *model*[9] introduced in the next chapter. Let Y_1 denote a randomly selected observation from group 1 and Y_2 a randomly selected observation from group 2. The hypotheses can be expressed as the model,

---

[8]Such as the *Inference for a Mean* app at www.artofstat.com/web-apps
[9]The linear model with an indicator variable for the groups, and equivalently, the "analysis of variance"

H_0: Both Y_1 and Y_2 have a $N(\mu, \sigma^2)$ distribution

H_a: $Y_1 \sim N(\mu_1, \sigma^2)$, $Y_2 \sim N(\mu_2, \sigma^2)$, with $\mu_1 \neq \mu_2$.

We estimate the common value σ of σ_1 and σ_2 by the pooled estimate s introduced in Section 4.5.1. Models are merely convenient simplifications of the true structure in the population. We do not expect the probability distributions for the groups to be *exactly* normal with *exactly* equal variances. In this case, two-sided tests are robust against violations of the assumptions of normality with common variance, especially when the sample sizes are similar and not extremely small.

To test H_0: $\mu_1 = \mu_2$ (i.e., $\mu_1 - \mu_2 = 0$), the test statistic is

$$T = \frac{(\overline{Y}_1 - \overline{Y}_2) - 0}{SE}, \qquad (5.3)$$

where the standard error is estimated by using the pooled standard deviation estimate,

$$se = \sqrt{\frac{s^2}{n_1} + \frac{s^2}{n_2}} = s\sqrt{\frac{1}{n_1} + \frac{1}{n_2}}.$$

Under H_0, the T test statistic has a t distribution with $df = n_1 + n_2 - 2$.

If the data show evidence of greatly different standard deviations (with, say, one being at least 50% larger than the other one), it is better to use an alternative t test that does not assume $\sigma_1 = \sigma_2$, called the **Welch t-test**. It uses the same form $T = (\overline{Y}_1 - \overline{Y}_2)/SE$ for the test statistic, but the standard error is estimated by $se = \sqrt{(s_1^2/n_1) + (s_2^2/n_2)}$ and df is replaced by a value designed so that T has null distribution closely approximated by the t distribution. When approximately valid, we prefer the test that assumes $\sigma_1 = \sigma_2$, because this method relates to modeling methods of the next chapter with additional variables and because H_0 then more completely specifies "no effect." In particular, in experimental studies with randomization, "no effect" naturally corresponds to the entire distributions being identical, rather than merely the means.

Table 5.3 summarizes significance tests for means for one and two samples. The summaries refer to two-sided alternative hypotheses, which are much more common in practice than one-sided. Section 5.8 presents *nonparametric* tests that do not have the normality assumption.

5.3.2 Example: Comparing a Therapy to a Control Group

Section 4.5.3 used a confidence interval to compare mean weight changes in conceptual populations of anorexic girls receiving cognitive behavioral therapy or a control. We now test H_0: $\mu_1 = \mu_2$ against H_a: $\mu_1 \neq \mu_2$. If the therapy truly has no effect relative to the control, the weight changes for the two populations would have equal means and equal standard deviations. From Section 4.5.3, the sample standard deviations are 7.31 for the cognitive behavioral therapy and 7.99 for the control, the pooled standard deviation estimate is $s = 7.64$, and $\overline{y}_1 - \overline{y}_2 = 3.01 - (-0.45) = 3.46$ has $se = 2.06$.

For testing H_0: $\mu_1 = \mu_2$, the observed value of the T test statistic is

$$t = \frac{\overline{y}_1 - \overline{y}_2}{se} = \frac{3.01 - (-0.45)}{2.06} = 1.68,$$

with $df = n_1 + n_2 - 2 = 29 + 26 - 2 = 53$. From software or an Internet app,[10] the two-sided P-value is 0.10, only weak evidence of different population means. Here is R output:

---

[10]Such as the *Comparing Two Means* app at www.artofstat.com/web-apps

TABLE 5.3 Summary of two-sided significance tests for means of quantitative variables.

Parameter	One Mean	Two Means
Assumptions	Random sample, normal population dist.,	Random sample, binary group variable, normal population dist. each group with equal variances $(^*)$
Hypotheses	$H_0: \mu = \mu_0$ $H_a: \mu \neq \mu_0$	$H_0: \mu_1 = \mu_2$ $H_a: \mu_1 \neq \mu_2$
Test statistic	$T = \frac{\overline{Y} - \mu_0}{SE}$ with $SE = \frac{S}{\sqrt{n}}$	$T = \frac{\overline{Y}_1 - \overline{Y}_2}{SE}$ with $SE = S\sqrt{\frac{1}{n_1} + \frac{1}{n_2}}$ for $S = \sqrt{\frac{\sum_i (Y_{i1} - \overline{Y}_1)^2 + \sum_i (Y_{i2} - \overline{Y}_2)^2}{n_1 + n_2 - 2}}$
P-value	Two-tail prob. in t distribution $df = n - 1$	Two-tail prob. in t distribution $df = n_1 + n_2 - 2$

$(^*)$ Welch t test does not require assuming equal variances, has slightly different df.

```
> Anor <- read.table("http://stat4ds.rwth-aachen.de/data/Anorexia.dat", header=TRUE)
> cogbehav <- Anor$after[Anor$therapy=="cb"] - Anor$before[Anor$therapy=="cb"]
> control  <- Anor$after[Anor$therapy=="c"] - Anor$before[Anor$therapy=="c"]
> t.test(cogbehav, control, var.equal=TRUE)
t = 1.676, df = 53, p-value = 0.09963
alternative hypothesis: true difference in means is not equal to 0

> t.test(cogbehav, control)
        Welch Two Sample t-test # not assuming equal population standard deviations
t = 1.6677, df = 50.971, p-value = 0.1015
```

The output also shows the Welch t-test for comparing the means without assuming $\sigma_1 = \sigma_2$. It gives a similar result, with the same P-value (0.10) to two decimal places. Many textbooks present and most software can find a statistic denoted by F for testing $H_0: \sigma_1 = \sigma_2$. That test also assumes that the population distributions are normal. It is not appropriate to conduct this test to determine which t method to use. In fact, unless strong evidence exists that the distributions are close to normal, we do not recommend this test even if the main purpose is to compare variability of two groups. It is *not* robust to violations of the normality assumption.

With several groups and a null hypothesis of equal population means, the t distribution no longer applies. Tests comparing several means use a F statistic that is based on a ratio of chi-squared statistics. We'll consider that case in Section 6.4.1, as it pertains to a model studied in the next chapter.

5.3.3 Effect Size for Comparison of Two Means

In this example, is the estimated difference of 3.46 between the mean weight gains for the two groups large, or small, in practical terms? As will be explained in Section 5.6.2, the P-value does not answer this question. A standardized way to describe $\overline{y}_1 - \overline{y}_2$ divides it by the pooled standard deviation estimate. This is called the ***effect size***. We obtain the same effect size if we measure the weight gain in different units, such as kilograms or ounces. It is not sensitive to the sample sizes, unlike the standard error and P-value. Whether a particular effect size is small, medium, or large depends on the substantive context, but an effect size of about 0.2 or less in absolute value is usually not practically important. An effect is considered to be large if the effect size is about 1, or larger, in absolute value.

With sample means of 3.01 and −0.45 pounds and a pooled standard deviation of $s = 7.64$ pounds, the effect size is

$$\text{Effect size} = \frac{\bar{y}_1 - \bar{y}_2}{s} = \frac{3.01 - (-0.45)}{7.64} = 0.45.$$

The difference between the sample means is a bit less than half a standard deviation, which is a moderate difference.

5.3.4 Bayesian Inference for Comparing Two Means

The Bayesian inference method (Section 4.7) that treats parameters as well as observations as random variables can be used for analogs of significance tests. For Bayesian inference about a population mean μ, the basic model assumes independent observations from a $N(\mu, \sigma^2)$ distribution and treats μ also as a random variable. It is common to use a $N(\nu, \tau^2)$ prior distribution for μ, typically with $\nu = 0$ and large τ so the prior is uninformative relative to the likelihood function. To compare two groups, the model assumes that observations have a $N(\mu_1, \sigma^2)$ distribution in group 1 and a $N(\mu_2, \sigma^2)$ distribution in group 2, with $N(\nu, \tau^2)$ prior distributions for both μ_1 and μ_2 since they are equal under H_0. The $N(\mu_i, \sigma^2)$ distributions describe the *within-group* variability, and the $N(\nu, \tau^2)$ distribution describes the *between-group* variability.

With continuous prior distributions, the posterior distribution is continuous and the posterior probability of any single value for μ or for $\mu_1 - \mu_2$ is zero. This accords with intuition in most applications that H_0 conditions such as $\mu = 0$ or $\mu_1 - \mu_2 = 0$ *exactly* are implausible. It is more relevant to summarize the evidence that $\mu < 0$ versus $\mu > 0$ or that $\mu_1 > \mu_2$ versus $\mu_1 < \mu_2$, by reporting posterior tail probabilities such as $P(\mu > 0)$ and $P(\mu_1 > \mu_2)$ or $P(\mu_1 > \mu_2 + d)$ for some relevant practically significant difference d. Ways exist of setting prior distributions that are a mixture of continuous and discrete so that conditions such as $\mu_1 = \mu_2$ have positive posterior probability. But the posterior probabilities of $\mu_1 = \mu_2$, $\mu_1 < \mu_2$, and $\mu_1 > \mu_2$ can then depend strongly on the choice of prior. With continuous prior distributions, when neither posterior $P(\mu_1 > \mu_2)$ or $P(\mu_1 < \mu_2)$ is close to 0, we realize that $\mu_1 = \mu_2$ is plausible.

In practice, σ is also unknown, so a Bayesian analysis includes a prior distribution for it. Most common is a highly disperse inverse gamma distribution. Another possibility is the improper prior $f(\sigma^2) \propto 1/\sigma^2$. With prior distributions that are flat relative to the likelihood function, a posterior tail probability is similar to a classical one-sided P-value.

5.3.5 Example: Bayesian Comparison of Therapy and Control Groups

Section 5.3.2 compared mean weight changes for therapy and control groups of anorexic girls. The following R output first shows the classical analysis, using a modelling approach from the next chapter. It models the weight changes as a function of an indicator for whether the group is the cognitive behavioral (*cb*) therapy, deleting observations 30 through 46 which refer to a third group not considered here. The estimated difference of means between the groups is 3.457 with $se = 2.063$, for a test statistic of $t = 1.676$, as we obtained in Section 5.3.2. The one-sided P-value for the alternative of a higher mean for the cognitive behavioral therapy is $0.0996/2 = 0.0498$. We observe similar results if we use a Bayesian analysis with highly disperse prior distributions for the parameters. The posterior $P(\mu_1 \geq \mu_2)$ tends to be similar to the classical one-sided P value for testing $H_0: \mu_1 = \mu_2$ against $H_a: \mu_1 < \mu_2$, for which the implicit null hypothesis is $H_0: \mu_1 \geq \mu_2$.

```
> Anor <- read.table("http://stat4ds.rwth-aachen.de/data/Anorexia.dat", header=TRUE)
> fit <- lm(after-before ~ factor(therapy), data=Anor[-(30:46),]) # deleting obs's 30-46
> summary(fit)                                    # classical approach
                 Estimate Std. Error t value Pr(>|t|)
(Intercept)        -0.450      1.498  -0.300   0.7650
factor(therapy)cb   3.457      2.063   1.676   0.0996   # one-sided P-value=0.0498
---
Residual standard error: 7.637 on 53 degrees of freedom   # pooled estimate s = 7.637

> library(MCMCpack)
> fit.bayes <- MCMCregress(after - before ~ factor(therapy), mcmc=10000000,
+             b0=0, B0=10^{-15}, c0=10^{-15}, d0=10^{-15}, data=Anor[-(30:46),])
> # mean has normal prior dist. with mean b0 = 0, variance 1/B0 (std. dev. > 31 million)
> # variance has highly disperse inverse gamma prior distribution (tiny c0 and d0)
> summary(fit.bayes)
1. Empirical mean and standard deviation for each variable,
                   Mean     SD
(Intercept)      -0.449  1.526
factor(therapy)cb  3.456  2.102  # posterior estimate of difference of means = 3.456

> mean(fit.bayes[,2] <= 0)       # posterior probability that 2nd model parameter <= 0
[1] 0.0498                       # corresponds to P(H0) for one-sided Ha: mu1 < mu2
```

For an analog of a one-sided *P*-value, we can find the posterior probability that the mean weight change is less for the cognitive behavioral group than the control group (i.e., that the parameter for the *cb* term, which is the `fit.bayes[,2]` second parameter in the R code above, is negative). This equals 0.0498, similar to the classical result but with a simpler interpretation: The Bayesian analysis concludes that the probability is 0.0498 that the population mean weight change is smaller for the cognitive behavioral group. The classical analysis concludes that if the population mean changes were equal, the probability would be 0.0498 that the difference in sample means between cognitive behavioral therapy and control would be at least as large as observed (3.457).

5.4 Significance Tests Comparing Proportions

This section presents significance tests for comparing groups in terms of their proportions on a categorical response variable. We first consider two groups with binary response variables and then more general cases.

5.4.1 Significance Test for the Difference between Two Proportions

To compare two groups on the population proportions π_1 and π_2 having a particular outcome, we test $H_0: \pi_1 = \pi_2$. For the difference $\pi_1 - \pi_2$ parameter that we estimated with a confidence interval in Section 4.5.4, this hypothesis is $H_0: \pi_1 - \pi_2 = 0$, *no difference*, or *no effect*. We assume independent samples of sizes n_1 and n_2, with success counts Y_1 and Y_2 having binomial distributions and yielding sample proportion estimates $\hat{\pi}_1 = y_1/n_1$ and $\hat{\pi}_2 = y_2/n_2$.

For studies employing randomization, the estimator $\hat{\pi}_1 - \hat{\pi}_2$ of $\pi_1 - \pi_2$ has an approximately normal sampling distribution, with variance

$$\text{var}(\hat{\pi}_1 - \hat{\pi}_2) = \text{var}(\hat{\pi}_1) + \text{var}(\hat{\pi}_2) = \frac{\pi_1(1-\pi_1)}{n_1} + \frac{\pi_2(1-\pi_2)}{n_2}.$$

The values π_1 and π_2 are not known, but under the presumption for H_0 that $\pi_1 = \pi_2$, we estimate their common value by the *pooled estimate*. This is the sample proportion $\hat{\pi}$ after pooling together the binomial counts y_1 and y_2 and the sample sizes, $\hat{\pi} = (y_1 + y_2)/(n_1 + n_2)$. The standard error is then estimated by

$$se_0 = \sqrt{\frac{\hat{\pi}(1-\hat{\pi})}{n_1} + \frac{\hat{\pi}(1-\hat{\pi})}{n_2}} = \sqrt{\hat{\pi}(1-\hat{\pi})\left(\frac{1}{n_1} + \frac{1}{n_2}\right)}.$$

The test statistic measures the number of standard errors between the estimator $\hat{\pi}_1 - \hat{\pi}_2$ and the H_0 value of 0 for $\pi_1 - \pi_2$,

$$Z = \frac{\text{Estimator} - H_0 \text{ value}}{\text{Standard error}} = \frac{(\hat{\pi}_1 - \hat{\pi}_2) - 0}{SE_0} = \frac{\hat{\pi}_1 - \hat{\pi}_2}{\sqrt{\hat{\pi}(1-\hat{\pi})\left(\frac{1}{n_1} + \frac{1}{n_2}\right)}}. \tag{5.4}$$

The *P*-value is a two-tail or one-tail probability from the standard normal distribution, according to whether H_a is two-sided, H_a: $\pi_1 \neq \pi_2$, or one-sided, H_a: $\pi_1 > \pi_2$ or H_a: $\pi_1 < \pi_2$.

This *z*-test is valid when each sample has at least 10 outcomes of each type.[11] The data can be summarized in a 2×2 contingency table, with rows for the two groups and columns for the two outcome categories. Some software for the test reports a *chi-squared statistic* for that contingency table. It is the square of the *z* test statistic, and thus its degrees of freedom are *df* = 1. That χ_1^2 statistic is a special case of a chi-squared statistic to be presented in Section 5.4.4 for categorical variables with several categories or several groups.

5.4.2 Example: Comparing Prayer and Non-Prayer Surgery Patients

For the research investigation of the efficacy of prayer in Section 4.5.5, we found a confidence interval for $\pi_1 - \pi_2$. Table 5.4 shows the data in contingency table form. The proportion suffering complications after heart surgery was $\hat{\pi}_1 = y_1/n_1 = 315/604 = 0.522$ for the patients who had a prayer group and $\hat{\pi}_2 = y_2/n_2 = 304/597 = 0.509$ for the patients not having a prayer group.

TABLE 5.4 Whether complications occurred for heart surgery patients who did or did not have group prayer.

Prayer	Complications Yes	No	Total
Yes	315	289	604
No	304	293	597

The pooled estimate of the H_0 value of $\pi_1 = \pi_2$ is

$$\hat{\pi} = (315 + 304)/(604 + 597) = 0.515.$$

The standard error estimate for the significance test is

$$se_0 = \sqrt{\hat{\pi}(1-\hat{\pi})\left(\frac{1}{n_1} + \frac{1}{n_2}\right)} = \sqrt{0.515(0.485)\left(\frac{1}{604} + \frac{1}{597}\right)} = 0.0288.$$

The test statistic for H_0: $\pi_1 = \pi_2$ is

$$z = \frac{\hat{\pi}_1 - \hat{\pi}_2}{se_0} = \frac{0.522 - 0.509}{0.0288} = 0.43.$$

---

[11] At least 5 of each type in each sample is adequate for the two-sided H_a. *Fisher's exact test* handles small-sample cases (Agresti 2019, p. 46).

The two-sided P-value equals 0.67. It is plausible that the probability of complications is the same for the prayer and non-prayer conditions.

You can use software or Internet apps[12] to conduct significance tests comparing proportions. The `prop.test` function in R reports a χ_1^2 test statistic that is the square of the z statistic. Here, $z = 0.43$ has $z^2 = 0.18$ (denoted X^2 in R, which is the notation for a chi-squared statistic introduced in Section 5.4.4). The P-value is that[13] for $H_a\colon \pi_1 \neq \pi_2$.

```
> prop.test(c(315, 304), c(604, 597), correct=FALSE)      # data c(y1, y2), c(n1, n2)
X-squared = 0.18217, df = 1, p-value = 0.6695   # X-squared = square of z test statistic
alternative hypothesis: two.sided                # X-squared does not show direction
```

5.4.3   Bayesian Inference for Comparing Two Proportions

For a Bayesian comparison of proportions for two independent binomial random variables $Y_1 \sim \text{binom}(n_1, \pi_1)$ and $Y_2 \sim \text{binom}(n_2, \pi_2)$, a simple analysis uses beta prior distributions for π_1 and π_2. The posterior distributions for π_1 and π_2 are then also beta distributions and induce a posterior distribution for $\pi_1 - \pi_2$ that enables us to find posterior probabilities such as $P(\pi_1 > \pi_2)$. A simple way to do this is by direct simulation: Generate a very large number of beta random variables from the posterior beta densities of π_1 and π_2 and approximate the posterior $P(\pi_1 > \pi_2)$ by the proportion of the simulated joint distribution for which $\pi_1 > \pi_2$.

For the prayer and heart surgery example, we use uniform prior distributions, which are beta(1,1). With $\hat{\pi}_1 = y_1/n_1 = 315/604$ for the patients who had a prayer group and $\hat{\pi}_2 = y_2/n_2 = 304/597$ for patients not having a prayer group, the posterior beta distribution for π_1 has beta hyperparameters $\alpha_1 = 315 + 1 = 316$ and $\beta_1 = (604 - 315) + 1 = 290$, and the posterior beta distribution for π_2 has beta hyperparameters $\alpha_1 = 304 + 1 = 305$ and $\beta_1 = (597 - 304) + 1 = 294$. Here are results with a simulation using 10 million draws from each posterior beta density:

```
> pi1 = rbeta(10000000, 316, 290); pi2 = rbeta(10000000, 305, 294)
> quantile(pi1 - pi2, c(0.025, 0.975))
      2.5%        97.5%
-0.04411204  0.06865900  # approximate posterior interval for difference of proportions
> mean(pi1 < pi2); mean(pi1 > pi2)   # approximate posterior P(pi1 < pi2), P(pi1 > pi2)
[1] 0.3347936
[1] 0.6652064
```

The posterior probability that complications are less likely with prayer is 0.33 and the posterior probability that complications are more likely with prayer is 0.67. Neither is exceptionally high, so it is plausible that $\pi_1 = \pi_2$.

In the classical approach, the two-sided P-value equals 0.670. So, for the one-sided alternative $\pi_1 > \pi_2$ that agrees with the direction in the sample data, for which $\hat{\pi}_1 > \hat{\pi}_2$, the P-value is $0.670/2 = 0.335$. This is essentially the same as the posterior $P(\pi_1 \leq \pi_2)$, that is, the posterior probability of the null-hypothesis complement of that alternative. When prior distributions are flat relative to likelihood functions, a posterior tail probability takes similar value as a P-values for a one-sided test. The interpretations are quite different, however. The classical approach says that if $\pi_1 = \pi_2$, then the probability would be 0.335 of the sample result or even more extreme results that favor the prayer group even less. The Bayesian approach provides explicit probability estimates for the two cases.

---

[12]Such as the *Comparing Two Proportions* app at www.artofstat.com/web-apps

[13]For a one-sided H_a, take $z = \pm\sqrt{X^2}$ with negative sign if $\hat{\pi}_1 - \hat{\pi}_2 < 0$ and positive sign if $\hat{\pi}_1 - \hat{\pi}_2 > 0$; the P-value is then half that reported if the data support the direction predicted in H_a.

5.4.4 Chi-Squared Tests for Multiple Proportions in Contingency Tables

Significance tests comparing two proportions are common in many application areas, such as comparing success rates of a new drug and placebo in a medical clinical trial. Sometimes the response variable has more than two categories or the comparison involves more than two treatments or groups, such as in comparing (placebo, low dose, high dose) of a drug on the response outcomes (better, same, worse). A natural null hypothesis is then that the probability distribution of the response variable is the same for each group, that is, the response variable is *independent* of the explanatory variable (Section 2.6.6). For a categorical response variable Y and a categorical explanatory variable X, this is

$$H_0 : P(Y = j \mid X = i) = P(Y = j) \quad \text{for all} \quad i, j.$$

That is, the *conditional distributions* of Y given X (Section 2.6.3) are *homogeneous*. When both X and Y are response variables, their *joint distribution* (Section 2.6.1) has cell probabilities $\{\pi_{ij}\}$. In that case, we can express H_0: X and Y are independent as

$$H_0 : \pi_{ij} = P(X = i, Y = j) = P(X = i)P(Y = j) \quad \text{for all } i \text{ and } j.$$

Let $\{y_{ij}\}$ denote cell counts in the contingency table that cross classifies X and Y, with $\{\mu_{ij} = E(Y_{ij})\}$ and total sample size n. We denote the number of rows in the table by r and the number of columns by c. With $c > 2$, the *multinomial distribution* (Section 2.6.4) generalization of the binomial applies to the c counts in row i having the conditional probabilities $\{P(Y = 1 \mid X = i), \ldots, P(Y = c \mid X = i)\}$, for $i = 1, \ldots, r$. Let $\{y_{i+} = \sum_j y_{ij}\}$ denote the row totals and $\{y_{+j} = \sum_i y_{ij}\}$ denote the column totals of the sample *marginal distributions*. The proportion y_{+j}/n of the observations fall in column category j, and under H_0, we expect each row to have this same proportion in that category. That is, in row i, we expect the proportion y_{+j}/n of the y_{i+} observations to fall in the cell in column j, so we estimate the expected frequency μ_{ij} in that cell by $\hat\mu_{ij,0} = y_{i+}(y_{+j}/n) = (y_{i+}y_{+j})/n$. When both X and Y are response variables, the ML estimate of $P(X = i)$ is y_{i+}/n, the ML estimate of $P(Y = j)$ is y_{+j}/n, and the ML estimate of $\mu_{ij} = n\pi_{ij} = nP(X = i)P(Y = j)$ is again

$$\hat\mu_{ij,0} = n\hat\pi_{ij} = n\hat P(X = i)\hat P(Y = j) = n\left(\frac{y_{i+}}{n}\right)\left(\frac{y_{+j}}{n}\right) = \frac{y_{i+}y_{+j}}{n}.$$

The test statistic for H_0: independence summarizes differences between observed counts $\{y_{ij}\}$ and estimated expected frequencies $\{\hat\mu_{ij,0}\}$, using

$$X^2 = \sum_{i=1}^{r}\sum_{j=1}^{c} \frac{(y_{ij} - \hat\mu_{ij,0})^2}{\hat\mu_{ij,0}} = \sum_{i=1}^{r}\sum_{j=1}^{c} \frac{[y_{ij} - (y_{i+}y_{+j})/n]^2}{(y_{i+}y_{+j})/n}.$$

For random counts $\{Y_{ij}\}$, the statistic can be expressed alternatively as a sum of squares of statistics having standard normal distributions, so its sampling distribution is the *chi-squared distribution*. Introduced in 1900 by the British statistician Karl Pearson, it is called the **Pearson chi-squared statistic**. Greater differences $\{|y_{ij} - \hat\mu_{ij,0}|\}$ produce larger X^2 values and stronger evidence against H_0, so the P-value is the right-tail probability from the chi-squared distribution above the observed value. The chi-squared approximation improves as n increases, and it is usually adequate when $\{\hat\mu_{ij,0} \geq 5\}$.

When a chi-squared test refers to multiple parameters, the degrees of freedom is the difference between the number of needed parameters under H_a and under H_0. When both X and Y are response variables and have a joint distribution, H_a has $rc - 1$ parameters, since $\{\pi_{ij}\}$ sum to 1 over the rc cells. Under H_0, since $\pi_{ij} = P(X = i)P(Y = j)$ for all i

and j with $\sum_{i=1}^{r} P(X = i) = 1$ and $\sum_{j=1}^{c} P(Y = j) = 1$, H_0 has $(r-1)+(c-1)$ parameters. Therefore, this chi-squared test has[14] $df = [(rc-1)-(r-1)-(c-1)]=(r-1)(c-1)$. The same formula holds when only Y is a response variable and H_0 is homogeneity of the conditional distributions (Exercise 5.46).

5.4.5 Example: Happiness and Marital Status

In their 2018 random sample[15] of Americans, the General Social Survey queried subjects about their happiness and their marital status. We use R to form the contingency table of counts $\{y_{ij}\}$ cross classifying happiness and marital status from the Happy data file at the text website. We then construct the sample conditional distribution of happiness for each marital status, find the estimates $\{\hat{\mu}_{ij,0}\}$ of the expected frequencies for testing H_0: independence of happiness and marital status (equivalently, homogeneity of the population conditional distributions of happiness), and conduct the chi-squared test:

```
> Happy <- read.table("http://stat4ds.rwth-aachen.de/data/Happy.dat", header=TRUE)
# To construct contingency tables, define variables as factors
> Happiness <- factor(Happy$happiness); Marital <- factor(Happy$marital)
> levels(Happiness) <- c("Very happy", "Pretty happy", "Not too happy")
> levels(Marital) <- c("Married", "Divorced/Separated", "Never married")
> table(Marital, Happiness)          # forms contingency table
                  Happiness
Marital            Very happy Pretty happy Not too happy
  Married              432         504           61
  Divorced/Separated    92         282          103
  Never married        124         409          135
> prop.table(table(Marital,Happiness), 1) # proportions within rows (each row total = 1)
                  Happiness               # conditional distributions on happiness
Marital            Very happy Pretty happy Not too happy
  Married           0.43329990   0.50551655    0.06118355
  Divorced/Separated 0.19287212  0.59119497    0.21593291
  Never married     0.18562874   0.61227545    0.20209581
> chisq.test(Marital, Happiness)$expected # expected frequencies under H0: independence
                  Happiness
Marital            Very happy Pretty happy Not too happy
  Married            301.6134    556.2162     139.17040
  Divorced/Separated 144.3025    266.1134      66.58403
  Never married      202.0840    372.6704      93.24556
> chisq.test(Marital, Happiness)         # chi-squared test of independence
          Pearson's Chi-squared test
X-squared = 197.41, df = 4, p-value < 2.2e-16
```

The Pearson chi-squared statistic is $X^2 = 197.4$. With $r = c = 3$, the $df = (r-1)(c-1) = 4$. The chi-squared distribution is concentrated on the nonnegative real line with mean $= df$ and standard deviation $= \sqrt{2df}$, so a value of 197.4 has P-value essentially 0, which we can report as $P < 0.0001$. The evidence is extremely strong that happiness and marital status are not independent.

Table 5.5 summarizes significance tests for proportions for two-sided alternative hypotheses. Section 5.7 presents another test for proportions based directly on the likelihood-function.

---

[14]Pearson incorrectly stated that $df = rc-1$, but R. A. Fisher found the correct formula in 1922. Exercise 5.66 presents an alternative chi-squared statistic for H_0, based on theory introduced in Section 5.7.

[15]The sampling is more complex than simple random sample, but treated as such here for simplicity of exposition. The data for the widowed category of marital status are not used here.

TABLE 5.5 Summary of two-sided significance tests for proportions (R.s.: Random sample).

Parameter	One Proportion	Two Proportions	Multiple Proportions
Assumptions	R.s., binary response variable, $n \geq 10$ each category	R.s., binary group and binary response variable, $n \geq 5$ each group category	R.s., two categorical var's, one or two response var's, expected freq's ≥ 5
Hypotheses	$H_0: \pi = \pi_0$ $H_a: \pi \neq \pi_0$	$H_0: \pi_1 = \pi_2$ $H_a: \pi_1 \neq \pi_2$	H_0: var's independent H_a: var's dependent
Test statistic	$Z = \frac{\hat{\pi} - \pi_0}{se_0}$ with $se_0 = \sqrt{\frac{\pi_0(1-\pi_0)}{n}}$	$Z = \frac{\hat{\pi}_1 - \hat{\pi}_2}{SE_0}$ with $SE_0 = \sqrt{\hat{\pi}(1-\hat{\pi})\left(\frac{1}{n_1} + \frac{1}{n_2}\right)}$ $\hat{\pi} = (Y_1 + Y_2)/(n_1 + n_2)$	$X^2 = \sum_{i=1}^r \sum_{j=1}^c \frac{(Y_{ij} - \hat{\mu}_{ij,0})^2}{\hat{\mu}_{ij,0}}$ with $\hat{\mu}_{ij,0} = \frac{Y_{i+}Y_{+j}}{n}$ $(*)$
P-value	Two-tail probability in $N(0,1)$	Two-tail probability in $N(0,1)$	Right-tail chi-sq. prob., $df = (r-1)(c-1)$

$(*)$ When $r = c = 2$, the X^2 test is equivalent to the two proportions test, with $X^2 = z^2$, $df = 1$.

5.4.6 Standardized Residuals: Describing the Nature of an Association

A large chi-squared statistic provides strong evidence of an association between two variables, but it tells us nothing about the nature of that association. From the expected frequency estimates in the R output, we see that more married people were very happy than we would expect if the variables were independent, whereas fewer divorced/separated and never married people were very happy than we'd expect. One way to summarize the difference in each cell is to divide it by its null standard error, giving its ***standardized residual***,

$$\text{standardized residual} = \frac{y_{ij} - \hat{\mu}_{ij,0}}{se_0} = \frac{y_{ij} - \hat{\mu}_{ij,0}}{\sqrt{\hat{\mu}_{ij,0}[1 - (y_{i+}/n)][1 - (y_{+j}/n)]}}.$$

When H_0 is true, the standardized residual of a random cell count Y_{ij} has a large-sample standard normal distribution, so values larger than about 3 in absolute value give strong evidence of a true difference in that cell in the population. We can use R to find them:

```
> stdres <- chisq.test(Marital, Happiness)$stdres; stdres # standardized residuals
                    Happiness
Marital             Very happy Pretty happy Not too happy
  Married             12.295576    -4.554333      -9.770639
  Divorced/Separated  -5.913202     1.661245       5.457032
  Never married       -7.928512     3.411881       5.619486
```

For instance, the count of 432 married subjects who are very happy is 12.3 standard errors *above* the 301.6 expected if happiness were independent of marital status, whereas the count of 124 never married who are very happy is 7.9 standard errors *below* the 202.1 expected.

A ***mosaic plot*** displays the cells of the contingency table as rectangles having areas proportional to the observed frequencies, with large standardized residuals displayed:

```
> levels(Happiness) <- c("Very", "Pretty", "Not too")
> levels(Marital) <- c("Married", "Div/Sep", "Never")
> library(vcd)
> mosaic(table(Marital, Happiness), gp=shading_Friendly, residuals=stdres,
+             residuals_type="Standardized\nresiduals", labeling=labeling_residuals)
```

Figure 5.3 shows this plot. Darker blue (red) colored cells have standardized residuals exceeding 4.0 (less than −4.0) and contain considerably more (fewer) people than expected under independence. The alignment and size of the areas is informative about the association. The married subjects clearly were more likely to be very happy and less likely to be not too happy than the other subjects. This plot and the sample conditional distributions indicate that the never married and divorced/separated were similar in their happiness distributions. To follow-up the test, we could also construct confidence intervals for individual proportions or for differences between pairs of marital status groups on the proportion making a particular response.

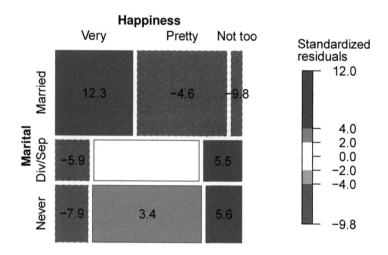

FIGURE 5.3 Mosaic plot for contingency table cross-classifying marital status and happiness, with cells showing observed frequencies by their size and standardized residuals comparing them to frequencies expected under H_0: independence.

A chi-squared test also applies to the generalization of the test of H_0: $\pi = \pi_0$ about a binomial parameter to a test of H_0: $\pi_1 = \pi_{10}, \ldots, \pi_c = \pi_{c0}$ that the parameters of a multinomial distribution for a c-category variable take particular values. An example of such a hypothesis is H_0: $\pi_1 = \pi_2 = \cdots = \pi_6 = 1/6$ that the six sides of a dice are equally likely. Details are summarized in Exercise 5.65.

5.5   Significance Test Decisions and Errors

Significance tests report the P-value to summarize the evidence against H_0. When useful, a test can include a formal decision, rejecting H_0 if the P-value is sufficiently small. This section introduces the types of errors that can occur in making a decision and shows how to find their probabilities.

5.5.1 The α-level: Making a Decision Based on the P-Value

Before we observe the data, the P-value is a random variable. When H_0 is true, the P-value has approximately a uniform distribution between 0 and 1.[16] When H_0 is false, the P-value is more likely to be near 0 than near 1. Researchers do not regard the evidence against H_0 as strong unless the P-value is very small, say, ≤ 0.05 or ≤ 0.01. We can base a decision about whether to reject H_0 on whether the P-value falls below a pre-specified cutoff point, called the α-*level*.

α-level (significance level)

The α-*level*, also called the *significance level*, is a number α between 0 and 1 such that we reject H_0 if the P-value $\leq \alpha$. In practice, common α-levels are 0.05 and 0.01.

Table 5.6 summarizes the possible decisions when the α-level = 0.05. Like the choice of a confidence level for a confidence interval, the choice of α reflects how cautious you want to be. The smaller the α-level, the stronger the evidence must be to reject H_0. To avoid bias in the decision-making process, α is selected *before* analyzing the data.

TABLE 5.6 Possible decisions in a significance test with α-level = 0.05.

	Decision	
P-Value	H_0	H_a
P-value ≤ 0.05	Reject	Accept
P-value > 0.05	Do not reject	Do not accept

In practice, it is better to report the P-value than to indicate merely whether H_0 is rejected. The P-values of 0.049 and 0.001 both result in rejecting H_0 when $\alpha = 0.05$, but the second case provides much stronger evidence. P-values of 0.049 and 0.051 provide, in practical terms, the same amount of evidence about H_0. Most research articles report the P-value rather than a decision about H_0. From the P-value, readers can view the strength of evidence against H_0 and make their own decision, if they want to.

5.5.2 Never "Accept H_0" in a Significance Test

The example in Section 5.2.2 about climate change tested H_0: $\pi = 0.50$ about the population proportion π who thought it is a major threat to stability. The P-value of 0.21 was not small, so H_0 is plausible. In this case, as Table 5.6 suggests, the conclusion is sometimes reported as "Do not reject H_0," since the data do not contradict H_0. It is not appropriate to say "Accept H_0." The population proportion has many plausible values besides the number in H_0. For instance, the R output reported a 95% confidence interval for π of $(0.49, 0.55)$. Even though insufficient evidence exists to conclude that $\pi \neq 0.50$, it is improper to conclude that $\pi = 0.50$.

Null hypotheses such as H_0: $\pi = 0.50$, H_0: $\mu = 0$, H_0: $\pi_1 - \pi_2 = 0$, and H_0: $\mu_1 - \mu_2 = 0$, contain a single value for the parameter. When the P-value is larger than the α-level, saying "Do not reject H_0" instead of "Accept H_0" emphasizes that this single value is merely one of *many* plausible values, because of the inherent sampling variability. The terminology "accept H_a" is permissible because when the P-value is sufficiently small, all the plausible values fall within the infinite range of values that H_a specifies.

---

[16]It is *exactly* uniform when the test statistic is a *continuous* random variable; see Exercise 5.73. In the discrete case, approximate uniformity holds for the *mid P-value*; see Exercise 5.74.

5.5.3 Type I and Type II Errors

Because of sampling variability, decisions in tests always have some uncertainty. A decision could be erroneous. The two potential errors are called *Type I error* and *Type II error*.

Type I error, Type II error

When H_0 is true, a *Type I error* occurs when H_0 is rejected.
When H_0 is false, a *Type II error* occurs when H_0 is not rejected.

The two possible decisions cross-classified with the two possibilities for whether H_0 is true generate four possible results, shown in Table 5.7.

TABLE 5.7 The four possible results of making a decision in a significance test: Type I and Type II errors are the incorrect decisions.

	Decision	
	Reject H_0	Do not reject H_0
H_0 true	Type I error	Correct decision
H_0 false	Correct decision	Type II error

When we make a decision with α-level = 0.05, we reject H_0 when the *P*-value ≤ 0.05. When H_0 is true, for any test statistic that has a continuous distribution, the *P*-value has a uniform distribution over $[0, 1]$. Therefore, when H_0 is true, the probability that the *P*-value ≤ 0.05 and we thus incorrectly reject H_0 is 0.05.

P(Type I error) and α-level

When H_0 is true, P(Type I error) is the α-level for the test.

We can control P(Type I error) by the choice of α. The more serious the consequences of a Type I error, the smaller α should be. In practice, α = 0.05 is common, just as a confidence level of 0.95 is common with confidence intervals. When a Type I error has serious implications, it is safer to use α = 0.01. When we make a decision, we do not know whether we have made an error, just as we do not know whether a particular confidence interval truly contains the parameter value. However, we can control the probability of an incorrect decision for either type of inference.

The collection of test statistic values for which a significance test rejects H_0 is called the *rejection region*. For example, for two-sided tests about a proportion π with α = 0.05, the *P*-value is ≤ 0.05 whenever the test statistic $|z| \geq 1.96$. For a one-sided test with $H_a\colon \pi > \pi_0$, the rejection region is $z \geq 1.645 = z_{0.05}$. The cutoff point for the rejection region is called the *critical value*. With α = 0.05, the probability of the values in the rejection region under the standard normal curve that applies for the sampling distribution of z when H_0 is true is 0.05, reflecting that the probability of Type I error (i.e., rejecting H_0 when it is true) is exactly the α-level of 0.05.

5.5.4 As P(Type I Error) Decreases, P(Type II Error) Increases

Depending on the nature of the application, one type of error may be considered more serious than the other. When we make a decision for which a Type I error would be especially harmful, why not use an extremely small P(Type I error), such as α = 0.0000001? Consider this in the context of a criminal legal trial. Let H_0 represent defendant innocence and H_a represent guilt. The jury rejects H_0 and judges the defendant to be guilty if the evidence is sufficient to convict. A Type I error, rejecting a true H_0, occurs in convicting a defendant who is actually innocent. We don't make it nearly impossible to convict someone who is innocent, because we would then be unlikely to convict many defendants who are truly guilty. This reasoning reflects the fundamental relation:

▶ *When P(Type I error) decreases, P(Type II error) increases.*

Figure 5.4 illustrates why this relation holds. The left curve is the sampling distribution of $\overline{Y}$ when H_0: $\mu = \mu_0$ is true. The right curve is the sampling distribution when a particular value μ_1 from H_a is the actual value of μ. The rejection region consists of $\overline{y}$ values above some critical value c, where c depends on our selection for $\alpha = P(\text{Type I error})$, which is the probability under the left curve to the right of c (i.e., the blue-shaded area in the figure). The $P(\text{Type II error})$ is the probability to the left of the critical value c under the right curve (i.e., the red-shaded area in the figure). When we make α smaller, we move the critical value c to the right, but then $P(\text{Type II error})$ increases.

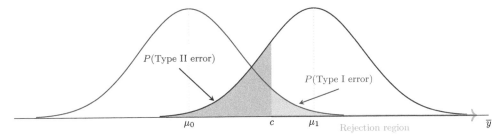

FIGURE 5.4 Probability of Type I error for testing H_0: $\mu = \mu_0$ against H_a $\mu > \mu_0$ and probability of Type II error for a particular value $\mu_1 > \mu_0$. The rejection region is $\overline{Y} > c$ for the critical value c.

For a fixed $P(\text{Type I error})$, $P(\text{Type II error})$ has more than one value, because H_a contains a range of possible values for μ_1. As μ_1 moves farther away from μ_0 in Figure 5.4, the right curve moves to the right, and the probability under that curve to the left of the critical value c decreases. The farther that μ_1 falls from μ_0, the less likely a Type II error. For a fixed $P(\text{Type I error})$, $P(\text{Type II error})$ also depends on the sample size. As n increases, the curves in Figure 5.4 are narrower, and a Type II error is less likely. Keeping both $P(\text{Type I error})$ and $P(\text{Type II error})$ at low levels requires using a relatively large n unless the parameter falls quite far from the H_0 value.

In summary, for fixed values of other factors,

▶ *P(Type II error) decreases as*

   – *P(Type I error) increases.*

   – *the true parameter value is farther from the value in H_0.*

   – *the sample size n increases.*

In practice, we usually fix $P(\text{Type I error})$ by taking α to be very small (e.g., 0.05 or 0.01) and then use a test method (such as the z test for proportions and t test for means) for which $P(\text{Type II error})$ is as small as possible.

5.5.5 Example: Testing Whether Astrology Has Some Truth

One scientific test[17] of the pseudo-science astrology used the following experiment: For each of 116 adult subjects, an astrologer prepared a horoscope based on the positions of the planets and the moon at the moment of the person's birth. Each subject also filled out a California Personality Index survey. For each adult, his or her birth data and horoscope were shown to an astrologer with the results of the personality survey for that adult and for two other adults randomly selected from the experimental group. The astrologer was asked which personality chart of the three subjects was the correct one for that adult, based on their horoscope. Let π denote the probability of a correct prediction. If the predictions are no different from random guessing, then $\pi = 1/3$. To test this against the alternative that the predictions are better than random guessing, we test H_0: $\pi = 1/3$ against H_a: $\pi > 1/3$. The National Council for Geocosmic Research, which supplied the astrologers for the experiment, claimed π would be 0.50 or higher. Let's find $P(\text{Type II error})$ if actually $\pi = 0.50$, for an $\alpha = 0.05$-level test.

We first find the $\hat{\pi}$ values for which we would not reject H_0. Under H_0: $\pi = 1/3$, the sampling distribution of $\hat{\pi}$ is the curve shown on the left in Figure 5.5. With $n = 116$, this curve has standard error

$$se_0 = \sqrt{\frac{\pi_0(1 - \pi_0)}{n}} = \sqrt{\frac{\left(\frac{1}{3}\right)\left(\frac{2}{3}\right)}{116}} = 0.0438.$$

For H_a: $\pi > 1/3$, the P-value (right-tail probability) equals 0.05 if the test statistic $z = 1.645$, which is the critical value. We *fail to reject* H_0, getting a P-value *above* 0.05, if $z < 1.645$, that is, if $\hat{\pi}$ falls less than 1.645 standard errors above $1/3$,

$$\hat{\pi} < 1/3 + 1.645(se_0) = 1/3 + 1.645(0.0438) = 0.405,$$

which is the critical value on the sample proportion scale. Therefore, the right-tail probability above 0.405 is $\alpha = 0.05$ for the curve on the left in Figure 5.5.

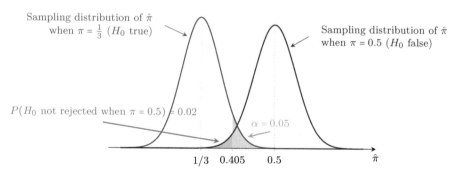

FIGURE 5.5 For testing H_0: $\pi = 1/3$ against H_a: $\pi > 1/3$ at $\alpha = 0.05$ level when $\pi = 0.50$, a Type II error occurs if $\hat{\pi} < 0.405$, since then the P-value > 0.05 even though H_0 is false.

To find $P(\text{Type II error})$ if $\pi = 0.50$, we must find $P(\hat{\pi} < 0.405)$ based on the sampling distribution of $\hat{\pi}$ when $\pi = 0.50$. This is the left-tail probability *below* the critical value of 0.405 for the curve on the right in Figure 5.5. Its standard error is $\sqrt{[(0.50)(0.50)]/116} = 0.0464$. (This differs a bit from se_0 for the test statistic, which uses $1/3 = \pi_0$ instead of 0.50 for π.) For the normal distribution with mean $\pi = 0.50$ and $se = 0.0464$, $\hat{\pi} = 0.405$ has

$$z = \frac{0.405 - 0.50}{0.0464} = -2.04.$$

---

[17]S. Carlson, *Nature*, vol. 318 (1985), pp. 419–425

Then, $P(\hat{\pi} < 0.405)$ is the probability that a standard normal random variable falls below −2.04, which equals 0.02. If astrologers truly had the predictive power they claimed, the chance of failing to detect this with this experiment[18] would have been only about 0.02.

Recall that as $\alpha = P(\text{Type I error})$ decreases, $P(\text{Type II error})$ increases. If the astrology study used $\alpha = 0.01$, when $\pi = 0.50$ you can verify that $P(\text{Type II error}) = 0.08$, compared to $P(\text{Type II error}) = 0.02$ when $\alpha = 0.05$. Recall also that $P(\text{Type II error})$ increases when π is closer to H_0. You can check that when π decreases from 0.50 to 0.40, with $\alpha = 0.05$, $P(\text{Type II error})$ increases from 0.02 to 0.55. Figure 5.6 plots $P(\text{Type II error})$ for the $\pi > 1/3$ values in H_a.

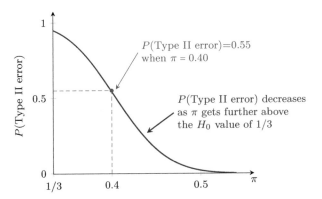

FIGURE 5.6 Probability of Type II error for testing H_0: $\pi = 1/3$ against H_a: $\pi > 1/3$ at $\alpha = 0.05$ level, plotted for the parameter values in H_a: $\pi > 1/3$.

For other significance tests in this book, we shall not show calculations for $P(\text{Type II error})$, as they are beyond our scope. For means and proportions, you can find $P(\text{Type II error})$ with software or an Internet app.[19] For other cases, $P(\text{Type II error})$ can be approximated by simulation.

5.5.6 The Power of a Test

When H_0 is false, the probability of (correctly) rejecting H_0 is called the **power** of the test. For a particular value of the parameter from within the H_a range,

$$\text{Power} = 1 - P(\text{Type II error}).$$

In the astrology example, since the test of H_0: $\pi = 1/3$ has $P(\text{Type II error}) = 0.02$ at $\pi = 0.50$, the power of the test equals $1 - 0.02 = 0.98$. Since $P(\text{Type II error})$ decreases as the parameter value gets farther from the H_0 value, the power increases. For means and proportions, power calculations are available with software and Internet apps.[20] For instance:

```
> library(pwr)
> pwr.p.test(ES.h(0.5, 1/3), n=116, sig.level=0.05, alt="greater")
      power = 0.978 # power of alpha=0.05 test of H0:pi=1/3 when pi=0.5
```

Before granting financial support for a planned study, research agencies expect investigators to show that reasonable power (usually, at least 0.80) exists at parameter values

---

[18]To see what actually happened, see Exercise 5.5.

[19]Such as the excellent *Errors and Power* app at www.artofstat.com/web-apps.

[20]Such as at www.powerandsamplesize.com and the power.t.test and power.prop.test functions and pwr package in R

that are practically important. When you read that results of a study are *not* statistically significant, be skeptical if no information is given about the power. The power may be low, especially if n is small or the effect size is not large.

5.5.7   Making Decisions versus Reporting the P-Value

The hypothesis-testing framework that incorporates a formal decision with a fixed P(Type I error) was developed by the statisticians Jerzy Neyman and Egon Pearson[21] in the late 1920s and early 1930s. This approach formulates H_0 and H_a, selects an α-level for the P(Type I error), uses a test statistic that minimizes P(Type II error) for that fixed α, determines the rejection region of test statistic values, and then makes a decision about whether to reject H_0 according to whether the observed test statistic falls in that rejection region. The alternative approach of finding a P-value and using it to summarize evidence against H_0 is mainly due to R. A. Fisher. He advocated merely reporting the P-value, rather than making a formal decision about H_0. Over time, this approach has become much more popular in practice, especially since software can now report precise P-values for a wide variety of significance tests.

5.6   Duality between Significance Tests and Confidence Intervals

Conclusions using two-sided significance tests are consistent with conclusions using confidence intervals. If a significance test concludes that a particular value is plausible for the parameter, then so does a confidence interval having the same error rate. This section amplifies this connection. We then explain the limitations of significance tests. For most purposes, inferential statistical analyses should mainly focus on results of confidence intervals.

5.6.1   Connection between Two-Sided Tests and Confidence Intervals

The significance test of H_0: $\mu = \mu_0$ versus H_a: $\mu \neq \mu_0$ rejects H_0 at the $\alpha = 0.05$ level when the observed value of the test statistic $t = (\bar{y} - \mu_0)/se$ is greater in absolute value than $t_{0.025}$; that is, when $\bar{y}$ falls more than $t_{0.025}(se)$ from μ_0. But if this happens, then the 95% confidence interval for μ, which is $\bar{y} \pm t_{0.025}(se)$, does not contain μ_0. Figure 5.7 illustrates. These two inference procedures are consistent.

> ### Significance test decisions and confidence intervals
>
> In testing H_0: $\mu = \mu_0$ against H_a: $\mu \neq \mu_0$, when H_0 is rejected at the α-level, the $100(1 - \alpha)\%$ confidence interval for μ does not contain μ_0. For example, when the two-sided test of H_0: $\mu = 0$ has P-value < 0.05, the 95% confidence interval for μ does not contain 0. Analogous results hold for comparing means and for proportions.

    A test decision at a particular α-level relates to a confidence interval with the same error probability. The α-level is P(Type I error) for the test and the probability that the confidence interval method yields an interval that does not contain the parameter. In the Section 5.2.5 example about political ideology, the P-value for testing H_0: $\mu = 4.0$ against H_a: $\mu \neq 4.0$ was 0.20. At the $\alpha = 0.05$ level, we do not reject H_0: $\mu = 4.0$. The R output

---

[21]The son of Karl Pearson, whose contributions included chi-squared tests and a correlation estimate

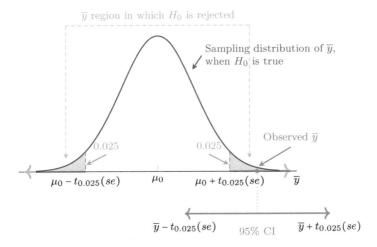

FIGURE 5.7 When $\bar{y}$ falls more than $t_{0.025}(se)$ from μ_0, the two-sided significance test of H_0: $\mu = \mu_0$ has P-value < 0.05, and the 95% confidence interval $\bar{y} \pm t_{0.025}(se)$ does not contain μ_0.

for the example showed that a 95% confidence interval for μ is (3.95, 4.23), which contains $\mu_0 = 4.0$.

Results of the confidence interval for comparing two means in Section 4.5.2 are equivalent to results of the significance test of H_0: $\mu_1 = \mu_2$ in Section 5.3.1. The confidence interval is based on the pivotal quantity

$$T = \frac{(\overline{Y}_1 - \overline{Y}_2) - (\mu_1 - \mu_2)}{SE} = \frac{(\overline{Y}_1 - \overline{Y}_2) - (\mu_1 - \mu_2)}{S\sqrt{\frac{1}{n_1} + \frac{1}{n_2}}}.$$

When $\mu_1 - \mu_2 = 0$, this is the T test statistic for H_0: $\mu_1 = \mu_2$, and observing $|t| > t_{0.025}$ is equivalent to 0 not falling in the 95% confidence interval for $\mu_1 - \mu_2$.

Similarly, results of two-sided tests about proportions relate to corresponding confidence intervals. For example, the confidence interval (4.7) for π in Section 4.3.3 and the significance test for π in Section 5.2.1 are both based on the pivotal quantity

$$Z = \frac{\hat{\pi} - \pi}{\sqrt{\frac{\pi(1-\pi)}{n}}}.$$

A 95% confidence interval is the set of π such that $|z| \leq 1.96$. A significance test of H_0: $\pi = \pi_0$ substitutes π_0 for π and obtains a two-sided P-value > 0.05 if $|z| < 1.96$, in which case π_0 falls in the confidence interval.

5.6.2 Effect of Sample Size: Statistical versus Practical Significance

In Section 5.2.5 we analyzed a 7-point scale of political ideology, with level 4 for moderate. For the 369 Hispanic Americans, $\bar{y} = 4.089$. We now analyze the entire General Social Survey sample, combining the race categories, to illustrate the effect of sample size on results of a test. The $n = 2575$ observations have $\bar{y} = 4.108$ and $s = 1.425$. Political ideology had a similar mean for the entire sample as for Hispanics alone.[22]

---

[22]It also is stable over time, equaling 4.13 in 1980, 4.16 in 1990, and 4.10 in 2000.

We test H_0: $\mu = 4.0$ against H_a: $\mu \neq 4.0$ to analyze whether the population mean differs from the moderate ideology score of 4.0:

```
> Polid <- read.table("http://stat4ds.rwth-aachen.de/data/Polid.dat", header=TRUE)
> t.test(Polid$ideology, mu=4.0, alternative="two.sided")
t = 3.8456, df = 2574, p-value = 0.0001232
95 percent confidence interval:
  4.052911 4.163012
```

With $se = s/\sqrt{n} = 1.425/\sqrt{2575} = 0.028$, the observed value of the T test statistic is

$$t = \frac{\bar{y} - \mu_0}{se} = \frac{4.108 - 4.0}{0.028} = 3.85,$$

and the two-sided P-value is 0.0001. The test provides *very* strong evidence that $\mu > 4.0$, that is, that μ falls on the conservative side of moderate. On a scale of 1.0 to 7.0, however, $\bar{y} = 4.108$ is close to 4.0. Although the difference of 0.108 between $\bar{y}$ and $\mu_0 = 4.0$ is highly significant statistically, it is small in practical terms. The difference is highly *statistically significant* but not *practically significant*. The 95% confidence interval for μ is (4.05, 4.16). By contrast, if $\bar{y}$ had been 6.108 instead of 4.108, the 95% confidence interval of (6.05, 6.16) would indicate a substantial practical difference from 4.0.

The analysis for the $n = 369$ Hispanic Americans with $\bar{y} = 4.1$ has P-value = 0.20, not much evidence against H_0, but now with $\bar{y} = 4.1$ for $n = 2575$, the P-value = 0.0001. A particular difference between an estimate and the H_0 value has a larger test statistic and a smaller P-value as n increases, because the standard error in the denominator of the test statistic decreases. The larger n is, the more certain we can be that sample deviations from H_0 are indicative of true population deviations. Even a small difference can yield a small P-value, however, if n is sufficiently large. For large samples, *statistical significance does not imply practical significance*. A tiny P-value, such as 0.0001, does not imply an *important* finding in any practical sense. The tiny P-value merely means that if H_0 were true, the observed data would be highly unusual. It does not mean that the parameter falls far from H_0 in practical terms.

To summarize practical significance, we can report an analog of the *effect size* measure introduced in Section 5.3.3. For a single sample, the effect size is $(\bar{y} - \mu_0)/s$. For the entire sample of size $n = 2575$, the estimated effect size is $(4.108 - 4.0)/1.425 = 0.08$, which is tiny.[23]

5.6.3 Significance Tests Are Less Useful than Confidence Intervals

In most fields of application, the usual null hypotheses that have a single value in H_0, such as H_0: $\mu = 0$ or H_0: $\mu_1 - \mu_2 = 0$, are rarely true. That is, rarely is the parameter *exactly* equal to the value listed in H_0. With sufficiently large samples, so that a Type II error is unlikely, these hypotheses will normally be rejected. Then, of main relevance is the *direction* of the effect (e.g., whether $\mu_1 > \mu_2$ or $\mu_2 > \mu_1$) and whether the parameter is sufficiently different from the H_0 value to be of practical importance. Although P-values are useful for summarizing the evidence against H_0, significance tests are overemphasized in much research. We learn more from confidence intervals. A test merely indicates whether the particular value in H_0 is plausible. The confidence interval, by contrast, displays the entire set of plausible values. It shows the extent to which reality may differ from H_0 by showing whether the values in the interval are far from H_0. Thus, it helps us to determine whether rejection of H_0 has practical importance.

When a P-value is not small but the confidence interval is quite wide, this forces us to realize that the parameter might well fall far from H_0 even though we cannot reject H_0. This also supports why it does not make sense to "accept H_0," as discussed in Section 5.5.2.

---

[23]By contrast, $\bar{y} = 6.108$ has effect size 1.48.

5.6.4 Significance Tests and *P*-Values Can Be Misleading

We've seen that it is improper to "accept H_0." We've also seen that statistical significance does not imply practical significance. Here is a summary of other important points about significance tests:

- **It is misleading to report test results only if they are statistically significant.** Some research journals have the policy of publishing results of a research study only if the *P*-value ≤ 0.05. Here's a danger of this policy: Suppose there truly is no effect, but 20 researchers independently conduct studies. We would expect about $20(0.05) = 1$ of them to obtain significance at the 0.05 level merely by chance. (When H_0 is true, about 5% of the time we get a *P*-value below 0.05 anyway.) If that researcher then submits results to a journal but the other 19 researchers do not, the article published will be a Type I error, reporting an effect that actually does not exist. *Publication bias* occurs when results of some studies never appear in print because they did not obtain a small enough *P*-value to seem important.[24]

- **Some tests may be statistically significant just by chance.** In a research study, it is inappropriate to search for results in software output that are statistically significant and report only them. In every 100 tests, even if all the null hypotheses are correct, you expect *P*-values ≤ 0.05 about $100(0.05) = 5$ times. Be skeptical of reports of significance that might merely reflect ordinary random variability. When multiple inferences are conducted, methods exist (such as presented in Section 6.5.4 of the next chapter) for adjusting *P*-values and confidence intervals so they apply to the entire set of inferences rather than to each individual one.

- **Be wary of confirmation bias.** Those who pay attention only to results that agree with their personal beliefs, such as a *P*-value below 0.05 for particular hypotheses, are guilty of *confirmation bias*. Information is embraced that confirms a view but ignored or rejected if it casts doubt on it. A *meta-analysis* is a proper, unbiased statistical summary of all the research studies conducted on a topic.[25]

- **True effects are often smaller than reported estimates.** Even if a statistically significant result is a true effect, the actual effect size is often much smaller than reported. When several researchers perform similar studies, the result that receives the most attention is often the most extreme one, well out in the tail of the sampling distribution of all the possible results and having a very small *P*-value (see Figure 5.8). As a consequence, be skeptical when you hear about a research study that reports important effects, such as a medical advance. The true effect may be weaker than reported, or even nonexistent.

- **Replication of studies can reveal Type I errors.** Because some tests are statistically significant just by chance, many "discoveries" that make it into print are spurious.[26] Ideally, other researchers would conduct follow-up studies to see if the same effects occur. This is called *replication*. It is not done as often as it should. It can be difficult to get funding for replication research, and journals tend not to publish replication studies, because the results are less interesting to readers than the original discovery.

---

[24]A *New York Times* investigation (January 17, 2008) reported that 94% of medical studies with positive results found their way into print, whereas only 14% of those with disappointing or uncertain results did.

[25]For instance, see *Introduction to Meta-Analysis* by M. Borenstein *et al.* (Wiley, 2011).

[26]See article by J. Ioannidis in `https://doi.org/10.1371/journal.pmed.0020124`. Exercise 5.35 shows how to estimate the percentage of reported medical "discoveries" that could actually be Type I errors.

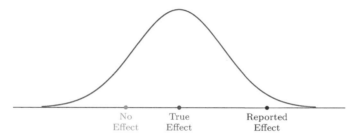

FIGURE 5.8 Sampling distribution showing how possible sample effects vary around the true effect: With many studies about an effect, the result reported by popular media often overestimates the true effect, because a study with a relatively large sample effect and a small P-value receives more attention.

- **It is incorrect to interpret the P-value as the probability that H_0 is true.**
  The P-value is P(test statistic takes a value like that observed or even more extreme), presuming that H_0 is true. It is not $P(H_0$ true). Classical statistical methods calculate probabilities about random variables and statistics (such as test statistics) that vary randomly from sample to sample, not about parameters. Statistics have sampling distributions, parameters do not. In reality, H_0 is not a matter of probability. It is either true or not true. We just don't know which is the case. By contrast, with the *Bayesian* approach, probability statements *are* possible about parameters. Posterior tail probabilities such as $P(\mu > 0)$ and $P(\mu_1 > \mu_2)$ are easier to understand and interpret than P-values.

Because of the ways that P-values can be misunderstood and misused, in 2016 the American Statistical Association released a statement[27] about them. It emphasized many points made in this chapter, in particular that a P-value does not measure the size or the importance of an effect, and thus scientific conclusions and business or policy decisions should not be based only on whether a P-value falls below a particular α-level such as 0.05.

Finally, because of the issues just discussed about significance tests and their potential misuse and misinterpretation, ***reproducibility*** *is important in scientific research.* Authors should make their data available at a site so others can access them, and they should document the statistical methods used to obtain their results. Then, others can reproduce the analysis and check the validity of the conclusions.

5.7 Likelihood-Ratio Tests and Confidence Intervals *

We have formed confidence intervals and test statistics for significance tests using a pivotal quantity. This section introduces an alternative method that applies more generally, such as to parameters of probability distributions that may not refer to means or proportions. It uses the *likelihood function* directly to formulate significance tests and corresponding confidence intervals. This method assumes a particular family of distributions for the data, since the likelihood function derives from the joint distribution of the observations.

---

[27] See www.amstat.org/newsroom/pressreleases/P-ValueStatement.pdf
*Sections with an asterisk are optional.

5.7.1 The Likelihood-Ratio and a Chi-Squared Test Statistic

For a generic parameter θ, the test of H_0: $\theta = \theta_0$ uses the likelihood function $\ell(\theta)$ through the ratio of (1) the maximum $\ell(\hat{\theta})$ of $\ell(\theta)$ over all possible θ values, which is its value at the maximum likelihood (ML) estimate $\hat{\theta}$, (2) the value $\ell(\theta_0)$ when H_0 is true. Then, $\ell(\hat{\theta})$ is always at least as large as $\ell(\theta_0)$, because $\ell(\hat{\theta})$ refers to maximizing over the entire parameter space rather than just at θ_0. The ***likelihood-ratio* test statistic** equals

$$2\log[\ell(\hat{\theta})/\ell(\theta_0)] = 2[L(\hat{\theta}) - L(\theta_0)],$$

where $L(\hat{\theta}) = \log[\ell(\hat{\theta})]$ and $L(\theta_0) = \log[\ell(\theta_0)]$ are the log-likelihood function values at $\hat{\theta}$ and at θ_0. This test statistic is nonnegative. Larger values of $\ell(\hat{\theta})/\ell(\theta_0)$ yield larger values of $2\log[\ell(\hat{\theta})/\ell(\theta_0)]$ and stronger evidence against H_0.

The reason for taking the log transform and doubling is that, under H_0: $\theta = \theta_0$, for large samples $2\log[\ell(\hat{\theta})/\ell(\theta_0)]$ has approximately a *chi-squared* distribution with $df = 1$. From Section 4.4.5, the chi-squared distribution is skewed to the right with support over the positive real line. With $df = 1$, the χ_1^2 distribution has mean 1 and is the distribution[27] of Z^2 for a standard normal random variable Z. Since larger values of the test statistic provide stronger evidence against H_0, the P-value is the right-tail probability from the χ_1^2 distribution of values at least as large as the observed test statistic. The right-tail probability for the chi-squared distribution above a point x equals the two-tail probability for the standard normal below $-\sqrt{x}$ and above $\sqrt{x}$. A one-sided chi-squared P-value is a two-sided normal P-value.

The likelihood-ratio test has a corresponding confidence interval. The 95% confidence interval for θ is the set of θ_0 values for H_0: $\theta = \theta_0$ such that the P-value in the test is larger than 0.05. With multiple parameters, it is called a *profile likelihood confidence interval*, because it *profiles* out the other parameters by using their values that maximize the likelihood at any fixed value θ_0 for the main parameter of interest.

5.7.2 Likelihood-Ratio Test and Confidence Interval for a Proportion

We illustrate likelihood-ratio tests and confidence intervals for a population proportion π. This is the parameter of a binomial distribution, and we assume that the data result from a binomial experiment (Section 2.4.1), with probability π of success on each trial. For observation y_i that is 0 or 1 for $i = 1, \ldots, n$, $f(y_i; \pi) = \pi^{y_i}(1-\pi)^{1-y_i}$. For $0 \le \pi \le 1$, the likelihood function is $\ell(\pi) = \pi^{\Sigma_i y_i}(1-\pi)^{n-\Sigma_i y_i} = \pi^y(1-\pi)^{n-y}$, for number of successes $y = \Sigma_i y_i$. Under H_0: $\pi = \pi_0$, this is $\ell(\pi_0) = \pi_0^y(1-\pi_0)^{n-y}$. From Section 4.2.2, the ML estimate of π is $\hat{\pi} = y/n$, so under H_a: $\pi \ne \pi_0$, the maximum of $\ell(\pi)$ is $\ell(\hat{\pi}) = \hat{\pi}^y(1-\hat{\pi})^{n-y}$. The likelihood-ratio test statistic equals

$$2\log\left[\frac{\ell(\hat{\pi})}{\ell(\pi_0)}\right] = 2\log\left[\frac{\hat{\pi}^y(1-\hat{\pi})^{n-y}}{\pi_0^y(1-\pi_0)^{n-y}}\right]$$

$$= 2y\log(\hat{\pi}/\pi_0) + 2(n-y)\log[(1-\hat{\pi})/(1-\pi_0)].$$

The 95% confidence interval consists of the set of π_0 values for which this test statistic is smaller than the 0.95 quantile[28] of the χ_1^2 distribution, which is the critical value for the likelihood-ratio test using $\alpha = 0.05$.

---

[27]When $df = 1$, the signed square root of the likelihood-ratio statistic, with sign the same as that of $(\hat{\theta} - \theta_0)$, has a null $N(0,1)$ distribution.

[28]From the connection with squaring a standard normal, this quantile is $(1.96)^2 = 3.84$.

For the example in Section 5.2.2, with π the population proportion who think that climate change is a major threat, $\hat{\pi} = 524/1008 = 0.52$. The test used there had test statistic $z = 1.26$, which is equivalent to a chi-squared statistic of $z^2 = 1.59$. This is a *score test*, as explained below and shown with a corresponding *Wald test* that gives the same result to two decimal places. The two-sided P-value for either test is 0.21. The following R code shows that the likelihood-ratio statistic is also 1.59 (to two decimal places), with a P-value of 0.21. The R output shows that the 95% confidence interval for π is (0.489, 0.551) using the Wald confidence interval (4.8), the score confidence interval (4.7), and the confidence interval based on the likelihood-ratio test. When n is large, the methods tend to give similar results.

```
> prop.test(524, 1008, p=0.50, "two.sided", correct=FALSE)   # X-squared is square of
X-squared = 1.5873, df = 1, p-value = 0.2077                  # score test statistic (5.1)
> pihat <- 524/1008
> Wald <- (pihat - 0.50)/sqrt(pihat*(1 - pihat)/1008); Wald^2 # square of Wald test stat.
[1] 1.589805                                                  # discussed below
> LRStat <- 2*524*log(pihat/0.50) + 2*(1008-524)*log((1-pihat)/(1-0.50)); LRStat
[1] 1.5877184                 # using formula for likelihood-ratio test statistic
> 1 - pchisq(LRTestStat, 1) # P-value = chi-squared right-tail probability for df=1
[1] 0.20765                   # = P-value for two-sided Ha for proportion

> library(proportion)
> ciAllx(524, 1008, 0.05)    # showing 3 of 6 confidence intervals provided
       method    x LowerLimit UpperLimit
1        Wald 524    0.48900    0.55068 # Wald CI; formula (4.8)
3 Likelihood 524    0.48897    0.55062 # likelihood-ratio test-based CI
4       Score 524    0.48898    0.55055 # "score" CI; formula (4.7)
```

5.7.3 Likelihood-Ratio, Wald, Score Test Triad

For testing H_0: $\theta = \theta_0$ about a parameter θ, three types of test statistics exist:

- The **likelihood-ratio test statistic**,[29] $2[L(\hat{\theta}) - L(\theta_0)]$.

- The **Wald test statistic**,[30] $(\hat{\theta} - \theta_0)/se$, where the standard error is estimated at $\hat{\theta}$, that is, $se = 1/\sqrt{I(\hat{\theta})}$ for the information $I(\theta)$ (see equation (4.15)) evaluated at $\hat{\theta}$.

- The **score test statistic**,[31] $U(\mathbf{y}, \theta_0)/\sqrt{I(\theta_0)}$, where $U(\mathbf{y}; \theta)$ is the score function from equation (4.17), $U(\mathbf{y}; \theta) = \partial L(\theta)/\partial \theta = \sum_{i=1}^{n} \partial[\log f(y_i; \theta)]/\partial \theta$ and the information $I(\theta)$ is evaluated at θ_0.

Like the likelihood-ratio test statistic, for random $\mathbf{Y}$ and estimator $\hat{\theta}$, the squares of the Wald and score test statistics have null chi-squared distributions with $df = 1$. For statistical methods that assume a normal distribution for the response variable, the three tests provide identical test statistics and P-values. For other distributions, the three test statistics differ but have similar behavior when n is large and H_0 is true. A marked divergence in their values, such as often happens when n is small and $\hat{\theta}$ is near the boundary of the parameter space, indicates that the sampling distribution of $\hat{\theta}$ may be far from normality. Each significance test method has a corresponding confidence interval consisting of the θ_0 values not rejected in the test of H_0: $\theta = \theta_0$. For instance, the 95% score confidence interval for a parameter θ is the set of θ_0 for which $|U(\mathbf{y}, \theta_0)|/\sqrt{I(\theta_0)} \leq 1.96$.

---

[29]First proposed by the statistician Sam Wilks in 1938
[30]Proposed by the statistician Abraham Wald in 1943
[31]Proposed by the statistician Calyampudi Radhakrishna Rao in 1948

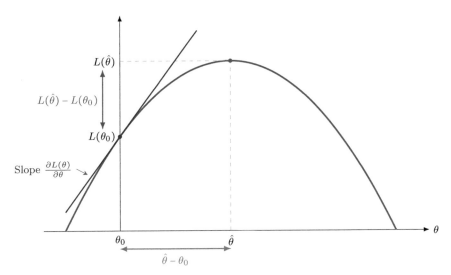

FIGURE 5.9 Elements of the log-likelihood function $L(\theta)$ used in tests of H_0: $\theta = \theta_0$: The likelihood-ratio test statistic equals twice the *vertical* distance $[L(\hat{\theta}) - L(\theta_0)]$ at $\hat{\theta}$ and at θ_0. The Wald test statistic uses the *horizontal* distance $(\hat{\theta} - \theta_0)$. The score test statistic uses the *slope* of the line drawn tangent to $L(\theta)$ at θ_0.

Figure 5.9 shows a generic plot of a log-likelihood function $L(\theta)$ for a parameter θ, to illustrate graphically the three tests. The ML estimate $\hat{\theta}$ is the point at which $L(\theta)$ takes its highest value. The likelihood-ratio statistic $2[L(\hat{\theta}) - L(\theta_0)]$ is twice the *vertical* distance between values of $L(\theta)$ at $\hat{\theta}$ and at θ_0. The Wald test utilizes the *horizontal* distance $(\hat{\theta} - \theta_0)$, with se derived based on the curvature of $L(\theta)$ at $\hat{\theta}$. (Recall the discussion about the information in Section 4.2.3.) The score test uses the tangent *slope* $U(\mathbf{y}, \theta_0) = \partial L(\theta)/\partial\theta$ at the H_0 value θ_0, with se based on the curvature of $L(\theta)$ at θ_0.

We illustrate the three test statistics for the test of H_0: $\pi = \pi_0$ about a proportion. We just found the likelihood-ratio test statistic. For each binary observation y_i,

$$\log f(y_i; \pi) = \log\left[\pi^{y_i}(1-\pi)^{1-y_i}\right] = y_i\log(\pi) + (1-y_i)\log(1-\pi),$$

$$\frac{\partial\log f(y_i; \pi)}{\partial\pi} = \frac{y_i}{\pi} - \frac{1-y_i}{1-\pi} = \frac{y_i - \pi}{\pi(1-\pi)},$$

$$\text{and } U(\mathbf{y}; \pi) = \sum_{i=1}^{n}\frac{\partial[\log f(y_i; \pi)]}{\partial\pi} = \frac{\sum_i y_i - n\pi}{\pi(1-\pi)} = \frac{n(\hat{\pi} - \pi)}{\pi(1-\pi)}.$$

From equation (4.3),

$$I(\pi) = nE\left(\frac{\partial[\log f(Y_i; \pi)]}{\partial\pi}\right)^2 = \frac{nE(Y_i - \pi)^2}{[\pi(1-\pi)]^2} = \frac{n\pi(1-\pi)}{[\pi(1-\pi)]^2} = \frac{n}{\pi(1-\pi)}.$$

It follows that the score test statistic is $U(\mathbf{y}, \pi_0)/\sqrt{I(\pi_0)} = (\hat{\pi} - \pi_0)/\sqrt{\pi_0(1-\pi_0)/n}$, which is the test statistic (5.1) used in Section 5.2.1 for a test about a proportion and is the pivotal quantity used in Section 4.3.3 to get a score confidence interval for π. By contrast, the Wald test statistic uses $se = 1/\sqrt{I(\hat{\pi})} = \sqrt{\hat{\pi}(1-\hat{\pi})/n}$ and equals $(\hat{\pi} - \pi_0)/\sqrt{\hat{\pi}(1-\hat{\pi})/n}$. The score test is preferable to the Wald test, because its standard error, $se_0 = \sqrt{\pi_0(1-\pi_0)/n}$, does not require estimating π.

The test statistic (5.4) that we used in Section 5.4.1 to test H_0: $\pi_1 = \pi_2$ is also a score statistic, evaluating the standard error under H_0. The chi-squared test of independence introduced in Section 5.4.4 is a generalized form of score statistic for multiple parameters. For that hypothesis, a likelihood-ratio test is also commonly used (Exercise 5.66). Section 6.4.6 introduces a likelihood-ratio statistic for a test about mean parameters in several normal distributions.

5.8   Nonparametric Tests *

For comparing two means, the significance test method presented in Section 5.3.1 assumes that the population distributions are normal, with the same variance. Although the two-sided case is robust to violations of this assumption, in some cases we might prefer to compare groups without it. One such case is when the method is not robust, such as for one-sided tests with small samples when the population distribution is highly skewed. With small n, it is difficult to judge the shape of a population distribution. Also, if that distribution may be highly skewed, the mean is less relevant as a summary measure, but we may still want to test the hypothesis that two groups have identical population distributions.

This section introduces three such tests. They are examples of ***nonparametric statistical methods***, which are inferential statistical methods that do not assume a particular family of probability distributions for the population. For these significance tests, H_0 states that the population distributions are identical for the two groups, without specifying their shape. The tests assume independent observations from the two groups, obtained with randomization.

5.8.1   A Permutation Test to Compare Two Groups

A ***permutation test*** derives the sampling distribution of a statistic such as the difference between the sample medians or sample means by evaluating all possible permutations for how the $n_1 + n_2$ observations in the two samples could have been allocated to the two groups, with n_1 observations in the first group and n_2 in the second. When H_0 of identical population distributions is true, all such permutations are equally likely. The P-value is the proportion of them for which the chosen statistic is at least as extreme as observed, with the more extreme values based on whether the test has a one-sided or two-sided alternative.

As n_1 and n_2 increase, it is computationally more demanding to evaluate all possible permutations, but software and apps can generate a very large random sample (say, a million) of them. The proportion of those simulated permutations that are at least as extreme as the observed samples in terms of the chosen statistic serves as a close approximation for the exact permutation P-value.

5.8.2   Example: Petting versus Praise of Dogs

In a study to determine whether dogs prefer petting or vocal praise,[33] the researchers randomly placed 14 dogs into two groups of 7 each. In group 1 the owner would pet the dog. In group 2 the owner would provide vocal praise. The response variable is the time, in seconds, that the dog interacted with its owner. Those times were 114, 203, 217, 254, 256,

---

[*]Sections with an asterisk are optional.

[33]Discussed on pp. 540–543 of Agresti, Franklin, and Klingenberg (2021), with data shown in the *Permutation Test* app at www.artofstat.com/web-apps

284, 296 in group 1 and 4, 7, 24, 25, 48, 71, 294 in group 2. The lowest value in group 1 and the highest value in group 2 seem to be outliers. As the true distributions are potentially highly skewed, we focus on the median, which is 254 seconds in group 1 and 25 seconds in group 2.

We test the null hypothesis of identical population distributions against the one-sided alternative that the population median is higher for petting. For the test statistic, we use the difference between the two sample medians. The number of ways to partition the 14 dogs into two groups of 7 each is $\binom{14}{7} = 3432$. The P-value for the permutation test is the proportion of those partitions for which the difference between the two sample medians is at least $254 - 25 = 229$. In R, a function in the EnvStats package can conduct this test, but it uses the exact distribution only when $n_1 + n_2 \leq 10$, and otherwise uses simulation. Here are results for this example, using one million simulations:

```
> library(EnvStats)
> petting <- c(114, 203, 217, 254, 256, 284, 296)
> praise  <- c(4, 7, 24, 25, 48, 71, 294)
> test <- twoSamplePermutationTestLocation(petting, praise,          # compare medians
+          fcn="median", alternative="greater", exact=FALSE, n.permutations=1000000)
> test$p.value
[1] 0.01752 # simulated P-value for Ha: higher median for petting
> test <- twoSamplePermutationTestLocation(petting, praise, fcn="mean", # compare means
+          alternative="greater", exact=FALSE, n.permutations=1000000)
> test$p.value
[1] 0.0038  # simulated P-value for Ha: higher mean for petting
```

The evidence is quite strong that the population median is higher for petting, and this is true also for the population means, as shown in the output. Alternatively, we can obtain exact P-values without simulation using the *Permutation Test* app at www.artofstat.com/web-apps. That app shows that the sampling distribution (under H_0) for the difference between the sample medians is far from normal, having a large gap between about –100 and +100. The app indicates that 60 of the 3432 permutations had a sample median difference of at least 229, so the exact P-value is $60/3432 = 0.01748$.

As always, estimation is more informative than significance testing. To allow potentially greatly skewed population distributions, we focus on estimating the difference between the population medians. We first use the bootstrap, which is simple but highly approximate because of the small samples and the bootstrapped sampling distribution of the difference of medians being highly discrete:

```
> library(simpleboot)
> b <- two.boot(petting, praise, median, R=100000)
> library(boot)
> boot.ci(b)
Level   Percentile           BCa # Sample difference of medians = 254 - 25 = 229
95%     (132, 260 )      (146, 260 )
```

Another method is available when we specify H_a more fully than merely about how the population medians (or means) differ. This H_a states that one distribution is a location shift of the other, with the second distribution having the same shape but shifting down or up compared with the first. This alternative can also be one-sided or two-sided. For this approach, H_0 states that the population distributions are identical when the first distribution is shifted down by some particular fixed value. The $100(1 - \alpha)\%$ confidence interval then consists of all possible values for the shift such that the P-value for the two-sided permutation test is greater than α. The function shown in the above output from the EnvStats package can specify non-zero values for the shift. One can apply this by trial and error to find this confidence interval. Using 86 or lower values for the shift gives a P-value below 0.05.

```
> test <- twoSamplePermutationTestLocation(petting, praise, fcn="median",
+ alternative="two.sided", mu1.minus.mu2=87, n.permutations=1000000)
> test$p.value # P-value for H0: dist. for praise = dist. for petting shifted down by 87
[1] 0.0583     # Since P-value > 0.05, 87 is in the confidence interval
> test <- twoSamplePermutationTestLocation(petting, praise, fcn="median",
+ alternative="two.sided", mu1.minus.mu2=86, n.permutations=1000000)
> test$p.value # P-value for H0: dist. for praise = dist. for petting shifted down by 86
[1] 0.0351     # Since P-value < 0.05, 86 is not in the confidence interval
```

Likewise, using 270 or higher values gives a P-value below 0.05, so the 95% confidence interval for the difference between the medians for the conceptual population is (87, 269), quite a bit wider than the bootstrap interval. But this interval is also a bit shaky in justification, as the outliers for the two groups being in different tails makes us question the location-shift model for this study. With such a small n, we have little information about the true shapes of the population distributions.

5.8.3　Wilcoxon Test: Comparing Mean Ranks for Two Groups

Many nonparametric statistical methods use the *rankings* of the observations, taking the $n_1 + n_2$ observations and ranking them in magnitude from 1 to $n_1 + n_2$. Observations having the same values, said to be *tied*, are assigned the average of the ranks that would have been given without the ties. An advantage of using ranks is that outlying observations are no longer outliers when converted to ranks and are not so highly influential on measures such as the mean.

The best known rank-based significance test for comparing two groups is the **Wilcoxon test**.[34] For it, H_0 states that the two population distributions are identical and H_a states that one distribution is a location shift of the other. Again, this alternative can be one-sided or two-sided. The evidence about H_0 is summarized by the difference between the mean ranks for the two groups.

For a study using randomization, the P-value is the probability, under H_0, of a difference between the sample mean ranks like the observed difference or even more extreme, in terms of favoring H_a. To find the P-value, software enumerates all possible ways of partitioning the observations, n_1 in the first group and n_2 in the second, and finds the proportion of the partitionings for which the difference between the sample mean ranks is at least as extreme as observed. When it is not feasible to generate all the permutations, software can closely approximate the exact P-value by taking a very large random sample of them. For large n_1 and n_2, the sampling distribution of the difference between the sample mean ranks is approximately normal, and some software bases the P-value on tail probabilities for this normal approximation.

For the study about dog petting and praise, the times that the dog interacted with the owner are (114, 203, 217, 254, 256, 284, 296) seconds in group 1 (petting) and (4, 7, 24, 25, 48, 71, 294) seconds in group 2 (praise). We use the one-sided H_a of a higher distribution for petting than for vocal praise. Starting the ranks with the lowest times, the ranks for group 1 are (7, 8, 9, 10, 11, 12, 14), for a sum of ranks of 71. The smallest value it can possibly take is $n_1(n_1 + 1)/2 = 7(8)/2 = 28$. A higher sum of ranks for the petting group, and equivalently a greater difference between sample mean ranks for petting and for praise, give more evidence in favor of petting. Here is R code for doing this analysis:

```
> petting <- c(114, 203, 217, 254, 256, 284, 296)
> praise  <- c(4, 7, 24, 25, 48, 71, 294)
> wilcox.test(petting, praise, alternative="greater", exact=TRUE)
```

---

[34]It was devised in 1945 by a chemist-turned-statistician, Frank Wilcoxon. It is equivalent to an alternative nonparametric test called the *Mann–Whitney test*.

```
W = 43, p-value = 0.008741 # exact P-value for Ha favoring petting
alternative hypothesis: true location shift is greater than 0
```

The W statistic reported is the sum of ranks for group 1 minus its smallest possible value, $W = 71 - 28 = 43$. The P-value gives strong evidence in favor of a higher distribution of times for petting.[35]

5.8.4 Comparing Survival Time Distributions with Censored Data

When a study observes the time until some event, the event may not have occurred by the end of the observation period for the study. We illustrate with a study that observed how long advanced-stage lung-cancer patients live with a new drug treatment compared with a control condition. During a study period of 3 years, patients were randomly assigned to a group. At the end of the study, the survival times (in months) for the 20 patients in each group were:

Drug: $0, 1+, 2, 2, 4, 4+, 5, 6, 8+, 10, 13, 14, 17, 20, 24, 30, 32+, 36+, 36+, 36+$

Control: $0, 0, 0, 1, 1, 1, 1+, 2, 2, 3, 4, 5, 5+, 6, 7, 7+, 9, 12, 17, 36+$

The observations with the + notation indicates subjects still alive at the end of the study or at the end of the time at which they were observed. For instance, an observation 4+ indicates that the subject lived for at least 4 months, but we don't know how much longer. Such an observation is said to be ***censored***.

We now show a way to compare two distributions when samples have *right-censored* observations, the unknown true value being to the right on the real number line of the reported value, such as in this example. At each observation time, we compare the number of deaths for the drug group to the number expected if the true distributions were identical, and then we sum that information over all the observation times. Table 5.8 shows the observations summarized at the end of the first month and at the end of the second month of observation. During the initial month of observation, 1 of the 20 subjects in the drug group died (i.e., had survival time = 0), and 3 of the 20 control subjects died. Under H_0: identical population distributions of survival times, of the 4 subjects who died, we would have expected $4(20/40) = 2.0$ of them to be from the drug group.[36] During the second month of observation, 0 of the 19 remaining subjects in the drug group died, and 3 of the remaining 17 control subjects died, as summarized in the second panel of Table 5.8. Under H_0: identical population distributions of survival times, of the 3 subjects who died, we would have expected $3(19/36) = 1.58$ deaths in the drug group. If a survival time is censored after a particular month of observation, that individual is considered to be at risk of dying in that month but not in subsequent ones.

In month j of observation, let y_j denote the number of deaths in the drug group, and let μ_j denote the expected number under H_0, conditional on the numbers at risk in each group and the total number that died in that period. We can summarize results over all the periods of observation with the test statistic

$$X^2 = \left[\frac{\sum_j (Y_j - \mu_j)}{se_0} \right]^2,$$

---

[35] The *Permutation Test* app at www.artofstat.com/web-apps can also conduct the Wilcoxon test.

[36] As in testing independence in Sec. 5.4.4, expected frequency = (row total)×(column total)/sample size.

TABLE 5.8 Comparison of drug and control groups for survival through initial two periods of observation.

	Death in Month 1			Death in Month 2		
Group	Yes	No	**Total**	Yes	No	**Total**
Drug	1	19	20	0	19	19
Control	3	17	20	3	14	17
Total	4	36	40	3	33	36

where se_0 is the standard error[37] of $\sum_j Y_j$ under H_0. The greater the magnitude of X^2 for this test, which is a score test, the greater the evidence against H_0. Assuming that censoring occurs at random in the same way in the two groups, as the sample sizes increase with the number of possible values for X^2 increasing, the null sampling distribution of X^2 is less highly discrete and converges to an approximate null chi-squared distribution with $df = 1$.

With software, we can conduct this test with a data file that lists, for each subject, their group, their observed survival time, and whether the observation is censored. Here are results using R for this test:

```
> Survival <- read.table("http://stat4ds.rwth-aachen.de/data/Survival.dat", header=TRUE)
> Survival
    group time status # status is 1 for observed outcome, 0 for censored outcome
1      1    0      1 # group = 1 for drug, 0 for control
2      1    1      0 # time is number of months until death or censoring
...
39     0   17      1
40     0   36      0
> library(survival)
> survdiff(Surv(time, status) ~ group, data=Survival) # function for test comparing
           N Observed Expected (O-E)^2/E (O-E)^2/V    # survival distributions
group=0 20       16     9.98      3.63      6.25      # with censored data
group=1 20       13    19.02      1.90      6.25
 Chisq=6.3 on 1 degree of freedom, p=0.01 # tests H0: identical survival distributions
```

For these data, the chi-squared statistic equals 6.25. The P-value is 0.01 for the two-sided alternative of some difference between the two survival distributions.

We can describe the survival responses graphically and by estimating the median time of survival. For graphical comparison of the two groups, we can plot their estimated probabilities of survival beyond time t as a function of t. We illustrate for the drug group. In the first month, 1 of 20 people in that group died, so the probability of having survival time T longer than 0 months is $S(0) = P(T > 0) = 19/20$. The next death for the drug group was in month 3, when 18 were still at risk (one other removed by censoring after month 1) and 2 died, so the estimated conditional probability of surviving from the end of period 0 to the end of month 2 is 16/18. The estimated survival function at time 2 takes value

$$\hat{S}(2) = \hat{P}(T > 2) = \hat{P}(T > 2 \text{ and } T > 0) = P(T > 2 \mid T > 0)P(T > 0) = \frac{16}{18} \times \frac{19}{20} = 0.844.$$

In a particular group, if y_j people died of the r_j at risk at time j, then $(r_j - y_j)$ survived and $\hat{P}(T > j \mid T > j - 1) = (r_j - y_j)/r_j$ for $j = 0, 1, 2, \ldots$. The estimated survival function at t is

$$\hat{S}(t) = \left(\frac{r_0 - y_0}{r_0}\right)\left(\frac{r_1 - y_1}{r_1}\right)\cdots\left(\frac{r_t - y_t}{r_t}\right).$$

---

[37]For the n_j subjects for observation j, conditional on r_j at risk in group 1 and $n_j - r_j$ at risk in group 2 and d_j total number of deaths, Y_j has a hypergeometric distribution (Exercise 2.68) with $\text{var}(Y_j) = r_j(n_j - r_j)d_j(n_j - d_j)/[n_j^2(n_j - 1)]$, and $se_0^2 = \text{var}(\sum_j Y_j) = \sum_j \text{var}(Y_j)$. In the notation of Exercise 2.68, $F = r_j$, $M = n_j - r_j$, and the number sampled is $n = d_j$.

When plotted against t, $\hat{S}(t)$ is a decreasing step function. It is referred to as the **Kaplan–Meier estimate** of the true survival function, named after two statisticians who proposed it in 1959. Figure 5.10 shows the estimated survival functions for the two groups. The function for the drug group is always higher, indicating that at every time t we estimate a higher probability of survival past time t for that group.

Here is R code for finding and plotting these functions:

```
> fit <- survfit(Surv(time, status) ~ group, data=Survival)
> fit
          n events median 0.95LCL 0.95UCL
group=0 20     16      4       2      17 # control median survival = 4 months
group=1 20     13     14       6      NA # drug median survival = 14 months
> plot(fit, xlab="Time", ylab="Estimated P(survival)") # Kaplan-Meier plot
```

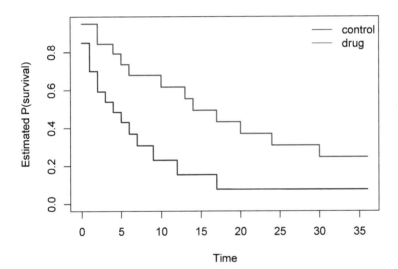

FIGURE 5.10 Kaplan–Meier estimators of survival functions for drug and control groups, giving estimated probabilities of survival as a function of time.

We cannot calculate means with censored data, but using the estimated survival curve we can estimate the median as the smallest time t for which $\hat{S}(t) \leq 0.50$. The R output gives estimated median survival times of 14 months for the drug group and 4 months for the control group.

The chi-squared test for comparing distributions of survival times with censored data is sometimes referred to as the *Mantel–Haenszel test*, named after two statisticians who in 1959 designed a generalization of the chi-squared test of independence to test conditional independence for multiple contingency tables that are stratified by levels of a third variable, with Mantel considering this particular application in a 1966 article. The test statistic depends on their survival or censoring times only through their ranks rather than the actual times. It is also referred to as the *log-rank test*. When no observations are censored, the z statistic form of the test[38], the signed square root of X^2, has a null $N(0,1)$ distribution.

---

[38] That is, $z = [\sum_j (y_j - \mu_j)]/se_0$

It is equivalent to the z statistic used in the large-sample version of the Wilcoxon test for comparing mean ranks.

5.9   Chapter Summary

Chapter 4 and this chapter have introduced two methods for using sample data to make inferences about populations. A **confidence interval** provides a range of plausible values for a parameter. A **significance test** judges whether a particular value for the parameter is plausible. Significance tests ("tests" for short) for *means* with quantitative variables and for *proportions* with categorical variables have four parts:

1. **Assumptions:**

   - Tests assume *randomization*, such as a random sample from the population.
   - Large-sample tests about proportions require no assumption about the population distribution, because the Central Limit Theorem implies approximate normality of the sampling distribution of the sample proportion.
   - Tests for means assume that the population distribution is normal but use the t distribution because of needing to replace the population standard deviation σ by an estimate s in the standard error. In practice, two-sided tests (like confidence intervals) are *robust* to violations of the normality assumption.

2. **Null and alternative hypotheses** about the parameter: The null hypothesis has form H_0: $\mu = \mu_0$ for a mean and H_0: $\pi = \pi_0$ for a proportion. The most common alternative hypothesis is *two-sided*, such as H_a: $\pi \neq 0.50$. Hypotheses such as H_a: $\pi < 0.50$ and H_a: $\mu > 0$ are *one-sided*, designed to detect departures from H_0 in a particular direction. Tests for comparing groups use H_0: $\mu_1 = \mu_2$ and H_0: $\pi_1 = \pi_2$.

3. **Test statistic**: The Z statistic for proportions and T statistic for means measure the number of standard errors that the point estimate falls from the H_0 value.

4. The **P-value** describes the evidence about H_0 in probability form.

   - Under the presumption that H_0 is true, the P-value equals the probability that the test statistic takes the observed value or a more extreme value. The more extreme results are determined by H_a. For two-sided H_a, the P-value is a two-tail probability.
   - Small P-values result when the point estimate falls far from the H_0 value, so that the test statistic is large and it would be unusual to observe such data if H_0 were true. The smaller the P-value, the stronger the evidence against H_0.

When we need to make a decision, we reject H_0 when the P-value is less than or equal to a fixed α-level (such as $\alpha = 0.05$). Two types of errors can occur:

- When H_0 is true, a **Type I error** results if we reject it.
- When H_0 is false, a **Type II error** results if we fail to reject it.

Decreasing the $P(\text{Type I error})$ causes the $P(\text{Type II error})$ to increase. The α-level is also $P(\text{Type I error})$. For fixed α, $P(\text{Type II error})$ decreases when the parameter is farther from the H_0 value or as the sample size increases.

Table 5.3 at the end of Section 5.3.1 summarizes significance tests for means and for comparisons of two means for two-sided alternative hypotheses. Table 5.5 at the end of Section 5.4.5 summarizes significance tests for proportions.

A 95% confidence interval for a parameter consists of all values for which a corresponding two-sided significance test has P-value > 0.05. It is more informative, showing all plausible values for the parameter. **Likelihood-ratio tests** use the *likelihood function* directly to formulate test statistics for significance tests and corresponding confidence intervals. **Nonparametric tests**, such as tests based on all possible permutations of the observed data or on rankings of the observations, enable inferences without assuming a particular probability distribution for the population.

Exercises

Data Analysis and Applications

5.1 Introducing notation for a parameter, state the following hypotheses in terms of the parameter values and indicate whether it is a null hypothesis or an alternative hypothesis.

   (a) The proportion of all adults in the UK who favor legalized gambling equals 0.50.

   (b) The correlation for Australian adults between smoking (number of cigarettes per day) and blood pressure is positive.

   (c) The mean grade point average this year of all college graduates in the U.S. is the same for females and males.

5.2 When a government does not have enough money to pay for the services that it provides, it can raise taxes or it can reduce services. When the Florida Poll asked a random sample of 1200 Floridians which they preferred, 52% (624 of the 1200) chose *raise taxes* and 48% chose *reduce services*. Let π denote the population proportion of Floridians who would choose raising taxes. Analyze whether this is a minority of the population ($\pi < 0.50$) or a majority ($\pi > 0.50$) by testing $H_0 : \pi = 0.50$ against $H_a: \pi \neq 0.50$. Interpret the P-value. Is it appropriate to "accept H_0? Why or why not?

5.3 Same-sex marriage was legalized across Canada by the Civil Marriage Act enacted in 2005. Is this supported by a majority, or a minority, of the Canadian population? In a 2017 survey of 3402 Canadians (https://sondage.crop.ca), 73% supported the act. Analyze the results with a significance test, stating any assumptions, and interpret the P-value

5.4 The example in Section 5.2.2 could not determine whether a majority or minority of Americans consider climate change to be a major threat. However, this is clearer for particular groups. A survey by Pew Research Center in March 2020 reported that 88% of the 487 Democrats and Democrat-leaning Independents and 31% of the 429 Republicans and Republican-leaning Independents consider climate change a major threat. Software shows the following results for Republicans or those leaning that way:

```
Test of proportion = 0.5 vs not = 0.5
   n    Sample prop      95% CI       z-Value  P-Value
  429     0.311      (0.268, 0.355)    7.870    0.0000
```

Specify the parameter and the hypotheses tested. Explain how to interpret results of the test. Explain what we learn from the confidence interval reported that we do not learn from the significance test.

5.5 In the scientific test of astrology discussed in Section 5.5.5, the astrologers were correct with 40 of their 116 predictions. Test $H_0: \pi = 1/3$ against $H_a: \pi > 1/3$ to analyze whether their predictions were better than expected merely by chance. Find the P-value, make a decision using $\alpha = 0.05$, and interpret.

5.6 Before a Presidential election, polls are taken in two swing states. The Republican candidate was preferred by 59 of the 100 people sampled in state A and by 525 of 1000 sampled in state B. Treat these as independent binomial samples, where the parameter π is the population proportion voting Republican in the state.

    (a) If we can treat these polls as if the samples were random, use significance tests of H_0: $\pi = 0.50$ against H_a: $\pi > 0.50$ to determine which state has greater evidence supporting a Republican victory. Explain your reasoning.

    (b) Conduct a Bayesian analysis to answer the question in (a) by finding in each case the posterior $P(\pi < 0.50)$, corresponding to the P-value in (a). Use beta(50, 50) priors, which have standard deviation 0.05 and reflect the pollster's strong prior belief that π almost surely is between 0.35 and 0.65. Explain any differences between conclusions.

5.7 You want to know whether adults in your country think the ideal number of children is equal to 2, on the average, or higher or lower than that.

    (a) Defining notation, state H_0 and H_a for investigating this.

    (b) Software shows these results for responses in a recent GSS to the question, "What do you think is the ideal number of children to have?":

```
Test of mu = 2.0 vs mu not = 2.0
Variable    n     Mean    StDev    SE Mean    T       P-value
Children   1302   2.490   0.850    0.0236     20.80   0.0000
```

    Show how to obtain the test statistic from other values reported. Explain what the P-value represents, and interpret its value.

5.8 For the **Students** data file at the text website, analyze political ideology.

    (a) Test whether the population mean μ differs from 4.0, the moderate response. Report the P-value, and interpret. Make a conclusion using α-level = 0.05.

    (b) Construct the 95% confidence interval for μ. Explain how results relate to those of the test in (a).

5.9 The output of a t significance test reports a P-value of 0.4173545. In summarizing the test, explain why it is more sensible to report P-value = 0.42 than P-value = 0.4173545.

5.10 A study of sheep mentioned in Exercise 1.27 analyzed whether the sheep survived for a year from the original observation time (1 = yes, 0 = no) as a function of their weight (kg) at the original observation. Stating any assumptions including the conceptual population of interest, use a t test with the data in the **Sheep** data file at the text website to compare mean weights of the sheep that survived and did not survive. Interpret the P-value.

5.11 Use descriptive statistics and significance tests to compare the population mean political ideology for each pair of groups in Table 5.2 using the **Polid** data file. Summarize results using P-values and using a non-technical explanation.

5.12 The example in Section 3.1.4 described an experiment to estimate the mean sales with a proposed menu for a new restaurant. In a revised experiment to compare two menus, on Tuesday of the opening week the owner gives customers menu A and on Wednesday she gives them menu B. The bills average \$22.30 for the 43 customers on Tuesday ($s = 6.88$) and \$25.91 for the 50 customers on Wednesday ($s = 8.01$). Under the strong assumption that her customers each night are comparable to a random sample from the conceptual population of potential customers, show how to compare the mean sales for the two menus based on (a) the P-value of a significance test, (b) a 95% confidence interval. Which is more informative, and why? (When used in an experiment to compare two treatments to determine which works better, a two-sample test is often called an *A/B test*.) .

5.13 From GSS results at **sda.berkeley.edu/archive.htm**, political ideology (POLVIEWS, with 1 = extremely liberal and 7 = extremely conservative) had mean and standard deviation by political party identification (PARTYID) (3.74, 1.39) for the 229 strong Democrats in 1974, (4.76, 1.29) for the 103 strong Republicans in 1974, (2.79, 1.38) for the 368 strong Democrats in

2018, and (5.66, 1.11) for the 252 strong Republicans in 2018. Use the methods of this and the previous chapter to summarize the rather dramatic change over time in the difference between strong Republicans and strong Democrats in their mean political ideology. Explain how you learn more from the confidence intervals than the significance tests.

5.14 The `Income` data file at the book's website shows annual incomes in thousands of dollars for subjects in three racial-ethnic groups in the U.S.

   (a) Stating all assumptions including the relative importance of each, show all steps of a significance test for comparing population mean incomes of Blacks and Hispanics. Interpret.

   (b) Conduct a Bayesian analysis with disperse priors. Find the posterior probability of a higher population mean income for Blacks, and show that it is similar to a one-sided P-value for the test in (a).

5.15 A recent report[39] estimated mean adult heights in the U.S. of 175.4 *cm* (69.1 inches) for men and 161.7 *cm* (63.7 inches) for women, with standard deviation about 7 *cm* for each group. For all finishers in the Boston Marathon since 1972, the time to finish has a mean of 221 minutes for men and 248 minutes for women, each with a standard deviation of about 40 minutes. According to the effect size, is the difference between men and women greater for height or for marathon times? Explain.

5.16 An experiment[40] used a sample of college students to investigate whether cell phone use impairs drivers' reaction times. On a machine that simulated driving situations, at irregular periods a target flashed red or green. Participants were instructed to press a brake button as soon as possible when they detected a red light. Under the cell phone condition, each student carried out a conversation on a cell phone with someone in a separate room. In the control condition, the same students listened to a radio broadcast. The `CellPhone` data file records the students' mean response times (in milliseconds) over several trials for each condition, $\{y_{i1}\}$ for the cell phone condition and $\{y_{i2}\}$ for control.

   (a) The comparisons of means or proportions in this chapter assume independent samples for the two groups. Explain why the samples for these two conditions are *dependent* rather than independent.

   (b) To compare μ_1 and μ_2, you can use $\{d_i = y_{i1} - y_{i2}, \ i = 1, \ldots, n\}$, here with $n = 8$. Specify the parameter μ_d and H_0 for doing this, and explain why $\mu_d = \mu_1 - \mu_2$.

   (c) State the assumptions and test statistic, explain why it has a t distribution with $df = n-1$. Report the P-value with two-sided H_a, and interpret. (The test is called a *matched-pairs t test*. Matched-pairs analyses also are possible with confidence intervals, as Section 4.4.3 did in comparing weights of anorexic girls before and after a period of treatment by analyzing the mean difference in weights.)

5.17 Ideally, results of a statistical analysis should not depend greatly on a single observation. In a *sensitivity study*, we re-do the analysis after deleting an outlier from the data set or changing its value to a more typical value and checking whether results change much. For the anorexia data analysis in Section 5.3.2, the weight change of 20.9 pounds for the *cb* group was a severe outlier. Suppose this observation was actually 2.9 pounds but recorded incorrectly. Find the P-value for testing $H_0: \mu_1 = \mu_2$ against $H_a: \mu_1 \neq \mu_2$ with and without that observation. Summarize its influence.

5.18 Using the `Anorexia` data file at the text website:

   (a) Test $H_0: \mu_1 = \mu_2$ against $H_a: \mu_1 \neq \mu_2$ for the weight changes with the family and cognitive behavioral therapies. Report and interpret the P-value, and give the decision for $\alpha = 0.05$. If the decision is in error, what type of error is it?

---

[39]See `www.cdc.gov/nchs/data/nhsr/nhsr122-508.pdf` and `https://doi.org/10.1371/journal.pone.0212797` for results for this exercise.
[40]For results of such an experiment, see D. Strayer and W. Johnston, *Psych. Science*, **21**: 462–466 (2001).

(b) Show how the test result relates to the 95% confidence interval for the difference of means. Explain how the confidence interval is more informative.

(c) In the context of this study, what would be a (i) Type I error, (ii) Type II error?

5.19 In the 2018 General Social Survey, when asked whether they believed in life after death, 1017 of 1178 females said *yes*, and 703 of 945 males said *yes*. Test that the population proportions are equal for females and males. Report and interpret the *P*-value.

5.20 Refer to the previous exercise. Using uniform prior distributions, find the posterior probability that the population proportion believing in life after death is higher for females than for males.

5.21 In Exercise 5.4, 133 of the 429 identifying as Republicans and 429 of the 487 identifying as Democrats stated climate change is a major threat. Show how to display the results in a contingency table, and use chi-squared to test whether opinion is independent of political party. Interpret.

5.22 The **Substance** data file at the book's website shows a contingency table formed from a survey that asked a sample of high school students whether they have ever used alcohol, cigarettes, and marijuana. Find the *P*-value for testing whether a difference exists between those who have used or not used alcohol on whether they have used marijuana, using (**a**) formula (5.4); (**b**) software. State assumptions for your analysis, and interpret results.

5.23 Use the **Happy** data file from the 2018 General Social Survey at the text website to form a contingency table that cross classifies happiness with gender. For H_0: independence between happiness and gender:

(a) Conduct and interpret the chi-squared test.

(b) Show the estimated expected frequencies and standardized residuals, and form a mosaic plot. Explain how they are consistent with the result of the chi-squared test.

5.24 For the example in Section 5.4.5, interpret the standardized residuals for the *not too happy* category.

5.25 With the data in the example in Section 5.4.5, conduct and interpret the Pearson chi-squared test (**a**) comparing divorced/separated with never married on happiness; (**b**) comparing married with divorced/separated and never married combined. (The sum of the two X^2 statistics, with $df = 2 + 2 = 4$, approximately equals X^2 for the full table as analyzed in Section 5.4.5, showing that chi-squared statistics and their df values partition.)

5.26 Using the **GSS2018** data file, cross classify the 2016 vote for President (**PRES16**, with 1 = Clinton, 2 = Trump, 3 = Other, 4 = Never) by sex (1 = male, 2 = female).

(a) Form the contingency table and report the conditional distributions on the vote.

(b) Conduct the chi-squared test, show the estimated expected frequencies, report the standardized residuals, and form a mosaic plot. Interpret results.

5.27 For the data in the **PartyID** data file at the book's website, use significance testing and estimation methods to analyze the relationship between political party affiliation and race.

5.28 The **Afterlife** data file at the book's website shows data from the 2018 General Social Survey on postlife = belief in the afterlife (1 = yes, 2 = no), religion (1 = Protestant, 2 = Catholic, 3 = Jewish, other categories excluded), and gender (1 = male, 2 = female). Analyze these data with methods of estimation and significance testing. Summarize results in a short report, including edited software output as an appendix.

5.29 A study of 100 women suffering from excessive menstrual bleeding considers whether a new analgesic provides greater relief than the standard analgesic. Of the women, 40 reported greater relief with the standard analgesic and 60 reported greater relief with the new one. Test the hypothesis that the probability of greater relief with the standard analgesic is the same as the probability of greater relief with the new analgesic. Report and interpret the *P*-value for the two-sided alternative. (*Hint*: The samples are *dependent*, not independent. Express the hypotheses in terms of a single parameter. A test to compare matched-pairs responses in terms of which is better is called a *sign test*.)

5.30 The 2018 General Social Survey asked 1136 subjects whether they believe in heaven and whether they believe in hell. Of them, 804 said *yes* to both, 209 said *no* to both, 113 said *yes* to heaven and *no* to hell, and 10 said *no* to heaven and *yes* to hell.

    (a) Show the data in a 2×2 contingency table. Denote the population proportions saying *yes* by π_1 for heaven and π_2 for hell. Find $\hat{\pi}_1$ and $\hat{\pi}_2$. Explain why the samples are *dependent* rather than independent, so the test of $H_0: \pi_1 = \pi_2$ in Section 5.4.1 is not valid.

    (b) Explain why $H_0: \pi_1 = \pi_2$ is equivalent to $H_0: \pi_{12} = \pi_{21}$, where π_{ij} denotes the population proportion for the cell in row i and column j of the contingency table. Show how to use a one-sample test for a proportion to test H_0 for these data, using the data in two of the four cells of the contingency table.[41]

5.31 A study[42] compared population dynamics of the threatened species Sooty Falcon on Fahal Island and the Daymaniyat islands in the Sea of Oman during 2007-2014. The clutch sizes had mean and standard deviation 2.660 and 0.618 on Fahal Island (n = 100) and 2.920 and 0.787 on the Daymaniyat islands (n = 53). The percentage of nests that failed were 1 of 108 nests on Fahal Island and 29 of 118 nests on the Daymaniyat islands. Stating any assumptions including the conceptual population of interest, use inferential methods to compare results in the two locations. Summarize the results of your analyses in a short report.

5.32 Section 5.5.5 mentioned a study about whether astrologers can predict the correct personality chart for a given horoscope better than by random guessing.

    (a) In the words of that study, what would be a (i) Type I error? (ii) Type II error?

    (b) If we decrease α from 0.05 to 0.01, to what value does $P(\text{Type II error})$ increase?

5.33 Jones and Smith separately conduct studies to test $H_0: \pi = 0.50$ against $H_a: \pi \neq 0.50$, each with $n = 400$. Jones gets $\hat{\pi} = 220/400 = 0.550$. Smith gets $\hat{\pi} = 219/400 = 0.5475$.

    (a) Show that the P-value is 0.046 for Jones and 0.057 for Smith. Using $\alpha = 0.05$, indicate in each case whether the result is "statistically significant." Using this, explain the misleading aspect of reporting the test result as "P-value ≤ 0.05" versus "P-value > 0.05," or as "reject H_0" versus "Do not reject H_0", without reporting the P-value.

    (b) Use confidence intervals to show that, in practical terms, the two studies had very similar results.

5.34 Jones and Smith separately conduct studies to test $H_0: \mu = 500$ against $H_a: \mu \neq 500$, each with $n = 1000$. Jones gets $\bar{y} = 519.5$, with $se = 10.0$. Smith gets $\bar{y} = 519.7$, with $se = 10.0$.

    (a) Show that the P-value is 0.051 for Jones and 0.049 for Smith. Using $\alpha = 0.050$, for each study indicate whether the result is "statistically significant." Using this example, explain the misleading aspects of not reporting the actual P-value.

    (b) Use confidence intervals to show that, in practical terms, the two studies had very similar results.

5.35 Are many medical "discoveries" actually Type I errors? In medical research, suppose[43] that an actual population effect exists only 10% of the time and that when an effect truly exists, the chance of making a Type II error and failing to detect it (perhaps because of insufficient sample size) is 0.50. Given that a test is significant at the 0.05 level, use Bayes theorem to show that 47% of such studies are actually reporting Type I errors.

---

[41]The test comparing dependent proportions is often called *McNemar's test*.
[42]By M. J. McGrady et al., *Ibis*, **159**: 828–840 (2017); thanks to Prof. M. K. Oli for showing me this study.
[43]These hypothetical percentages were used in an article about this issue by J. Sterne, G. Smith, and D. R. Cox, BMJ, **322**: 226–231 (2001).

5.36 For an $\alpha = 0.05$-level likelihood-ratio test of H_0: $\theta = \theta_0$ using the likelihood function values $\ell(\hat{\theta})$ and $\ell_0 = \ell(\theta_0)$, explain why the corresponding 95% confidence interval for θ is the set of θ_0 for which $\ell(\hat{\theta})/\ell(\theta_0) \leq \exp(3.84/2) = 6.8$, where 3.84 is the 0.95 quantile for a chi-squared distribution with $df = 1$. Illustrate by finding this ratio for the endpoints of the likelihood-based confidence interval shown for the climate change example in Section 5.7.2.

5.37 Section 5.3.2 used a t test to compare cognitive behavioral and control groups for anorexia patients. Using simulation with software or with the *Permutation Test* app at www.artofstat. com/web-apps, conduct the analogous permutation test comparing (a) means, (b) mean ranks (Wilcoxon test). State hypotheses, interpret P-values, and compare results with the t test.

5.38 Refer to the petting versus praise of dogs example in Section 5.8.2.

(a) For the 14 times observed, show the partitioning of the values to the two groups for which the P-value would be smallest. What is that P-value?

(b) For this partitioning, use the bootstrap to construct a 95% confidence interval for the difference between the population medians. Explain how this is more informative than the significance test.

5.39 The Houses data file at the book's website lists, for 100 home sales in Gainesville, Florida, several variables, including the selling price (in thousands of dollars) and whether the house is new (1 = yes, 0 = no).

(a) Based on graphical or numerical descriptive statistics, use an appropriate method with the t distribution to find the P-value for comparing the mean selling prices for new and older homes. Interpret. Make a decision using $\alpha = 0.05$ and show the relation to the 95% confidence interval for the comparison.

(b) Since the distribution of selling price seems skewed right, conduct a permutation test to compare the population medians. Interpret.

5.40 For the example in Section 5.8.4, the subject taking the drug who was censored after 4 months is now found to have had a survival time of 11 months.

(a) Conduct a significance test of identical survival distributions. Interpret the P-value.

(b) Give an example of an additional change in the data that would have no further effect on the test result.

5.41 A book[44] on methods for modeling survival times discussed an example comparing times of remission (in weeks) of leukemia patients taking a drug or control. The data, with censored observations indicated by the "+" sign, are:

Treatment: $6+, 6, 6, 6, 7, 9+, 10+, 10, 11+, 13, 16, 17+, 19+, 20+, 22, 23, 25+, 32+, 32+, 34+, 35+$

Control: $1, 1, 2, 2, 3, 4, 4, 5, 5, 8, 8, 8, 8, 11, 11, 12, 12, 15, 17, 22, 23$

The associated data file is Survival_Cox_Oakes at the book's website. Conduct a significance test of identical survival distributions. Interpret the P-value. Graphically portray the sample survival distributions using Kaplan–Meier curves, and estimate the median remission times for the two groups.

Methods and Concepts

5.42 Small P-values indicate strong evidence against H_0, because the data would then be unusual if H_0 were true. Why does it not make sense to define a P-value as the probability that the test statistic equals the *observed result* (when H_0 is true) rather than as the tail probability that the test statistic equals the *observed result or a value even more extreme* in the direction predicted by H_a?

[44] *Analysis of Survival Data*, by D. Cox and D. Oakes, Chapman and Hall (1984).

5.43 Explain why the terminology "do not reject H_0" is preferable to "accept H_0."

5.44 Construct two scenarios of independent samples of four men and four women with y = number of hours spent on Internet in past week having $\bar{y}_1 = 5$ and $\bar{y}_2 = 10$, such that for testing $H_0 :$ $\mu_1 = \mu_2$ against $H_a : \mu_1 \ne \mu_2$, (a) P-value < 0.05, (b) P-value > 0.05. How do the within-groups variability differ in the two cases?

5.45 For the Bayesian model for comparing means in Section 5.3.4, explain why the prior and posterior $P(\mu_1 = \mu_2) = 0$.

5.46 For testing H_0: $P(Y = j \mid X = i) = P(Y = j)$ for all i and j, that is, *homogeneity* of the conditional distributions of a c-category response variable at the r categories of an explanatory variable, compare the number of parameters under H_a and under H_0 to find df for the chi-squared test.

5.47 Results of 99% confidence intervals for means are consistent with results of two-sided tests with which α-level? Explain the connection.

Select the correct response(s) in the next two exercises. (More than one may be correct.)

5.48 We analyze whether the discharge of arsenic in the liquid effluent from an industrial plant exceeds the company claim of a mean of 10 *mg* per liter. For the decision in the one-sided test using $\alpha = 0.05$:

  (a) If truly $\mu = 10$, with probability 0.05 we will conclude that they are exceeding the limit.

  (b) If truly $\mu = 10$, the probability that the sample mean equals the observed value equals 0.05.

  (c) If the plant is exceeding the limit, the probability that we will conclude that they are not exceeding the limit is 0.05.

  (d) If we reject H_0, the probability that it is actually true is 0.05.

5.49 Let β denote P(Type II error). For an $\alpha = 0.05$-level test of H_0: $\mu = 0$ against H_a: $\mu > 0$ with $n = 30$ observations, $\beta = 0.36$ at $\mu = 4$. Then:

  (a) At $\mu = 5$, $\beta > 0.36$.

  (b) If $\alpha = 0.01$, then at $\mu = 4$, $\beta > 0.36$.

  (c) If $n = 50$, then at $\mu = 4$, $\beta > 0.36$.

  (d) The power of the test is 0.64 at $\mu = 4$.

  (e) This must be false, because necessarily $\alpha + \beta = 1$.

5.50 A random sample of size 40 has $\bar{y} = 120$. The P-value for testing H_0: $\mu = 100$ against H_a: $\mu \ne 100$ is 0.057. Explain what is incorrect about each of the following interpretations of this P-value, and provide a proper interpretation.

  (a) The probability that H_0 is correct equals 0.057.

  (b) The probability that $\bar{y} = 120$ if H_0 is true equals 0.057.

  (c) The probability of Type I error equals 0.057.

  (d) We can accept H_0 at the $\alpha = 0.05$ level.

5.51 Refer to the previous exercise and the P-value of 0.057.

  (a) Explain why the P-value is the smallest α-level at which H_0 can be rejected.

  (b) Explain why the 94.3% confidence interval is the narrowest confidence interval for μ that contains $\mu_0 = 100$.

5.52 For a matched-pairs t test (Exercise 5.16), let $\sigma^2 = \mathrm{var}(Y_{i1}) = \mathrm{var}(Y_{i2})$ and $\rho = \mathrm{corr}(Y_{i1}, Y_{i2})$. Using the result from Exercise 2.63 that for two random variables Y_1 and Y_2, $\mathrm{var}(Y_1 - Y_2) = \mathrm{var}(Y_1) + \mathrm{var}(Y_2) - 2\mathrm{cov}(Y_1, Y_2)$, show that $\mathrm{var}(\bar{Y}_1 - \bar{Y}_2) = \mathrm{var}(\bar{d}) = 2\sigma^2(1-\rho)/n$. Explain how this indicates that precision for estimating $\mu_1 - \mu_2$ can be much better for highly positively correlated dependent samples than for independent samples.

5.53 Criminal defendants are convicted if the jury finds them to be guilty "beyond a reasonable doubt." A jury interprets this to mean that if the defendant is innocent, the probability of being found guilty should be only 1 in a billion. Describe any disadvantage this strategy has.

5.54 Medical tests for diagnosing conditions such as breast cancer are fallible, just like decisions in significance tests. Identify (H_0 true, H_0 false) with disease (absent, present), and (Reject H_0, Do not reject H_0) with diagnostic test (positive, negative). In this context, explain the difference between Type I and Type II errors, and explain why decreasing P(Type I error) increases P(Type II error).

5.55 Use the *Errors and Power* app at `www.artofstat.com/web-apps` to investigate the performance of significance tests. Set the hypotheses as H_0: $\pi = 0.50$ and H_a: $\pi > 0.50$ with sample size 100, and set P(Type I error) $= \alpha = 0.05$. The app shows the null sampling distribution of $\hat{\pi}$ and the actual sampling distribution of $\hat{\pi}$ for various true values of π. Click on *Show Type II error*, and it also displays P(Type II error).

    (a) Set the true value of the proportion to be (i) 0.55, (ii) 0.60, (iii) 0.65, (iv) 0.70. Report P(Type II error) in each case and summarize the impact of π getting farther from the H_0 value of 0.50.

    (b) Report P(Type II error) for π = (i) 0.53, (ii) 0.52, (iii) 0.51. Explain why P(Type II error) approaches $1 - \alpha = 0.95$ as π gets closer to the H_0 value of 0.50.

    (c) Set π = 0.60. Report P(Type II error) for n equal to (i) 50, (ii) 100, (iii) 200, and summarize the impact of n on P(Type II error).

5.56 For testing H_0: $\mu = 0$ against H_a: $\mu > 0$ with $\alpha = 0.05$, use Figure 5.4 to explain why P(Type II error) increases toward 0.95 as μ decreases toward 0.

5.57 You plan to test H_0: $\mu_1 = \mu_2$. When your research hypothesis is that $\mu_1 > \mu_2$, if you are correct, explain why you will have greater power if you use H_a: $\mu_1 > \mu_2$ instead of H_a: $\mu_1 \neq \mu_2$.

5.58 A researcher conducts a significance test every time she analyzes a new data set. Over time, she conducts 100 significance tests, each at the 0.05 level. If H_0 is true in every case, what is the probability distribution of the number of times she rejects H_0, and how many times would we expect H_0 to be rejected?

5.59 A research study conducts 40 significance tests. Of these, only two are significant at the 0.05 level. The authors write a report about those two results, not mentioning the other 38 tests. Explain what is misleading about their report.

5.60 In an evaluation of 32 schools in a county over the past five years according to the mean score of senior students on a standardized achievement test, only one school performed above the median in all five years. Explain what is misleading about a conclusion that that school performed better than the others. Relate your discussion to significance testing and to searching for significance in multiple inferences.

5.61 Some journals publish research results only if they achieve statistical significance at the 0.05 α-level. Explain *publication bias* and its dangers.

5.62 When articles in the mass media about medical studies report large dangers of certain agents (e.g., coffee drinking), later research often suggests that the effects are smaller than first believed, or may not even exist. Explain why.

5.63 A data analyst assumes that the n independent observations in a data file come from a Poisson distribution.

    (a) Derive the likelihood-ratio statistic for testing H_0: $\mu = \mu_0$ against H_a: $\mu \neq \mu_0$.

    (b) Simulate the exact distribution of the test statistic in (a) for n = 25, when μ_0 = 3.0. (Section A.5.2 of the R Appendix shows code to do this.) Compare graphically to the limiting chi-squared distribution.

    (c) For n = 25, suppose $\bar{y}$ = 4.0. Find the 95% confidence interval for μ based on likelihood-ratio tests.

(d) Derive the likelihood-ratio test of H_0: $\mu_1 = \mu_2$ for independent Poisson samples of sizes n_1 and n_2.

5.64 Derive the likelihood-ratio test of H_0: $\pi_1 = \pi_2$ for independent $Y_1 \sim \text{binom}(n_1, \pi_1)$ and $Y_2 \sim \text{binom}(n_2, \pi_2)$.

5.65 For a c-category variable, consider testing H_0: $\pi_1 = \pi_{10}, \ldots, \pi_c = \pi_{c0}$ when counts $(y_1, \ldots, y_c)$ have a multinomial distribution (2.14) with $n = \sum_j y_j$.

(a) Using the result that the ML estimate of π_j is the jth sample proportion y_j/n, show that the likelihood-ratio statistic for testing H_0 is

$$2 \sum_j y_j \log(y_j/n\pi_{j0}),$$

with $df = c-1$ for the large-sample chi-squared distribution. (The corresponding Pearson statistic is $X^2 = \sum_j [(y_j - n\pi_{j0})^2]/(n\pi_{j0})$.)

(b) For testing that the six sides of a dice are equally likely, we roll the dice 100 times and obtains counts (15, 20, 13, 14, 17, 21) for outcomes (1, 2, 3, 4, 5, 6). Conduct the likelihood-ratio test and interpret the P-value.

(c) Simulate the exact sampling distribution of the likelihood-ratio statistic in (b), and use it to precisely approximate the exact P-value of the test for the data shown.

5.66 For two categorical variables X and Y, let $\pi_{ij} = P(X = i, Y = j)$, $i = 1, \ldots, r$, $j = 1, \ldots, c$. Consider H_0: $\pi_{ij} = P(X = i)P(Y = j)$ for all i and j with n observations having cell counts $\{y_{ij}\}$. Using the multinomial distribution for $\{y_{ij}\}$ and the ML estimate for π_{ij} of $\hat{\pi}_{ij,0} = (y_{i+}/n)(y_{+j}/n)$ under H_0 and $\hat{\pi}_{ij} = y_{ij}/n$ under H_a, show that the likelihood-ratio statistic for testing H_0 is

$$2 \sum_i \sum_j y_{ij} \log(y_{ij}/\hat{\mu}_{ij,0}),$$

for $\hat{\mu}_{ij,0} = n\hat{\pi}_{ij,0}$. Specify its large-sample distribution.

5.67 For a large number n of independent Poisson random variables $\{Y_i\}$, with $\mu = E(Y_i)$, consider testing H_0: $\mu = \mu_0$.

(a) Show that the score test statistic is $Z = \sqrt{n}(\bar{Y} - \mu_0)/\sqrt{\mu_0}$.

(b) Show that the Wald test statistic is $Z = \sqrt{n}(\bar{Y} - \mu_0)/\sqrt{\bar{Y}}$. Under H_0, why would you expect the normal distribution approximation to be better for the score test statistic?

(c) Show that the value of the likelihood-ratio test statistic for observed data $\{y_i\}$ is

$$2(L_1 - L_0) = 2[n(\mu_0 - \bar{y}) + n\bar{y}\log(\bar{y}/\mu_0)].$$

(d) Explain how these tests can be used to construct confidence intervals. Illustrate for the Wald and score confidence intervals, and explain why you would expect the score method to perform better.

5.68 Explain why the confidence interval based on the Wald test of H_0: $\theta = \theta_0$ is symmetric around $\hat{\theta}$ (i.e., having center exactly equal to $\hat{\theta}$. This is not true for the confidence intervals based on the likelihood-ratio and score tests.) Explain why such symmetry can be problematic when θ and $\hat{\theta}$ are near a boundary, using the example of a population proportion that is very close to 0 or 1 and a sample proportion that may well equal 0 or 1.

5.69 Explain the logic underlying the permutation test to compare two distributions. Compare its assumptions with those of the two-sample t test.

5.70 Refer to Exercise 5.44 and its scenario of $n_1 = n_2 = 4$ with $\bar{y}_1 = 5$ and $\bar{y}_2 = 10$.

(a) Construct two scenarios such that the two-sided permutation test comparing means would have (i) P-value < 0.05, (ii) P-value > 0.05.

(b) Create a scenario such that the P-value for the permutation test would be the minimum possible but the P-value for the t test would be even smaller.

5.71 Explain the logic underlying inverting permutation tests to obtain a confidence interval for the difference between two population means. Illustrate the method by finding the 95% confidence interval for the difference between mean interaction times for petting and praise of dogs using the data in Section 5.8.2. Compare with results from a t confidence interval and bootstrap interval.

5.72 Explain what is meant by *censored* data. Give an example of a situation in which some observations would be (a) right-censored, (b) left-censored.

5.73 From Section 2.5.7, if T is a continuous random variable with *cdf* F, then $F(T)$ has the uniform distribution over $[0, 1]$.

(a) In significance testing with a test statistic T, explain why $F(T)$ and $1 - F(T)$ correspond to one-sided P-values. Explain why $1 - F(T)$ also has a uniform distribution under H_0. (Uniformity also holds for two-sided P-values under H_0.)

(b) Suppose H_0: $\pi = 0.50$ is true. Generate 1,000,000 random samples, each of size $n = 1500$, and for H_a: $\pi > 0.50$ find the P-value for each sample. Plot a histogram or density estimate using the 1,000,000 P-values. Relate it to the result in (a).

5.74 For a discrete distribution and a test statistic T with observed value t_{obs} and one-sided H_a such that large T contradicts H_0,

$$\text{mid } P\text{-value} = \frac{1}{2}P(T = t_{obs}) + P(T > t_{obs}).$$

(a) Suppose that $P(T = t_j) = \pi_j$, $j = 1, \ldots c$. Show that $E(\text{mid } P\text{-value}) = 0.50$. (*Hint:* Show that $\sum_j \pi_j[(\pi_j/2) + \pi_{j+1} + \cdots + \pi_c] = (\sum_j \pi_j)^2/2$. The mid P-value has null distribution closer to uniform (which is the distribution of the P-value for a test statistic having a continuous distribution) than the ordinary P-value.

(b) For the results in Section 5.1.1 on testing for bias in selecting managers, find the mid P-value. Find the P-value for these data with the z-test of Section 5.2.1, even though n is small. (For discrete data, P-values for large-sample tests are usually more similar to mid P-values than to ordinary P-values using exact distributions.)

5.75 A family of distributions $f(y; \theta)$ is said to have *monotone likelihood ratio* (MLR) if a statistic $T(\mathbf{y})$ exists such that whenever $\theta' < \theta$, $\ell(\theta)/\ell(\theta')$ is a nondecreasing function of T. For any such family, the most powerful test of H_0: $\theta = \theta_0$ against H_a: $\theta > \theta_0$ forms P-values from values of T at least as large as observed.

(a) Show that any distribution in the exponential family $f(y; \theta) = B(\theta)h(y)\exp[Q(\theta)R(y)]$ (see Exercise 4.75) that has $Q(\theta)$ monotone increasing in θ has MLR with $T = \sum_i R(y_i)$.

(b) Show that the binomial distribution satisfies (a) with $Q(\pi) = \log[\pi/(1-\pi)]$ and $T = \sum y_i$.

6

Linear Models and Least Squares

Statistical methods for multiple variables typically analyze how the outcome on a *response variable* is associated with or can be predicted by the values of the *explanatory variables*. For instance, a study might analyze how the annual amount contributed to charity is associated with explanatory variables such as a person's annual income, number of years of education, religiosity, age, and gender. For statistical inference, the methods assume a probability distribution for the response variable, at each combination of values of the explanatory variables. No assumption is needed about the distributions of the explanatory variables.

This chapter presents methods for quantitative response variables, with inference assuming that the conditional distribution of the response variable, given the explanatory variables, is a normal distribution. The following chapter extends the methods to handle discrete data and alternative response distributions, such as the binomial for categorical responses, the Poisson for count responses, and the gamma for skewed positively-valued responses. We use statistical **models** as the basis of analyses. From Section 4.5.1, *a model for a set of variables is a simple approximation for the true relationship among those variables in the population.* A model uses a framework that incorporates assumptions about the random variability in observations of those variables and imposes a structure for describing and making inferences about relationships. Sampling distributions and statistical inferences are derived under the assumed model structure. Reality is more complex and never perfectly described by a model, but a model is a tool for making our perception of reality clearer.

6.1 The Linear Regression Model and Its Least Squares Fit

For a quantitative response variable Y, we begin with a single explanatory variable x, and the following sections extend to multiple explanatory variables. We treat Y as a random variable, observed at various values for x, so we use upper-case notation for it.

The straight-line formula $Y = \beta_0 + \beta_1 x$ is a simple possible model for the relationship . This is a *deterministic model*: Subjects who have the same x-value necessarily have the same Y-value. A *statistical model*, allowing for variability in Y at each value of x, is more realistic in real-life situations. For example, for x = number of years of education and Y = annual income, a conditional distribution describes how annual income varies for individuals with any particular education x. We next present a statistical model in which $\beta_0 + \beta_1 x$ represents the *mean* of the conditional distribution of Y for subjects having that value of x.

6.1.1 The Linear Model Describes a Conditional Expectation

A basic statistical model with a single explanatory variable has equation

$$E(Y) = \beta_0 + \beta_1 x$$

DOI: 10.1201/9781003159834-6

describing the relation between x and the mean μ of the conditional distribution of Y at each value of x. For Y = annual income (in thousands of dollars) and x = number of years of education, suppose $E(Y) = -5 + 3x$. Then, those having a high school education ($x = 12$) have a mean income of $E(Y) = -5 + 3(12) = 31$ thousand dollars. At $x = 13$ this increases to $-5 + 3(13) = 34$ thousand dollars.

Because the formula $E(Y) = \beta_0 + \beta_1 x$ describes the mean of a *conditional* distribution, alternative notation is $E(Y \mid x)$, as we are actually modeling a *conditional expectation*. The equation $E(Y) = \beta_0 + \beta_1 x$ is an example of a **linear model**. Here, *linear* refers to the equation being *linear in the parameters*, β_0 and β_1. The explanatory variable x itself can be a nonlinear function of the originally-measured variable u, such as $x = u^2$ or $x = \log(u)$. When we plot this equation on a graph with horizontal x and vertical y axes, the *y-intercept* β_0 represents the value of $E(Y)$ when $x = 0$. Whether this is relevant[1] depends on whether 0 is a plausible value for x. The parameter β_1 is the *slope*. For the equation $E(Y) = -5 + 3x$, we might say, "If a person attains one more year of education, we expect his or her income to increase by 3 thousand dollars." For this interpretation to be valid, we'd need to conduct an experiment that adds a year of education for each person and then observes the results. Otherwise, a higher mean income at a higher education level could at least partly reflect the correlation of several other variables with both income and educational attainment, such as the person's achievement motivation. A more appropriate interpretation, although less concise, is "When we compare those having a certain number of years of education with those having one fewer year, the difference in the means of their incomes is 3 thousand dollars."

6.1.2   Describing Variation around the Conditional Expectation

The linear model is completed by specifying a conditional probability distribution for the variation in Y around the conditional expectation $E(Y) = \beta_0 + \beta_1 x$ at each value of x. The standard model uses the normal distribution, for some variance σ^2 that is also a parameter. Let (x_i, Y_i) denote the values of x and Y for observation i, with $\mu_i = E(Y_i)$, $i = 1, \ldots, n$. The probability distribution for Y_i is assumed to be $N(\beta_0 + \beta_1 x_i, \sigma^2)$, with $\beta_0 + \beta_1 x_i = \mu_i$, where the conditional variance σ^2 is the same for all observations.

An alternative formulation for the model expresses Y_i, rather than $E(Y_i)$, in terms of x_i. The alternative model formula is

$$Y_i = \beta_0 + \beta_1 x_i + \epsilon_i,$$

where ϵ_i is the deviation of Y_i from $E(Y_i) = \beta_0 + \beta_1 x_i$. In it, ϵ_i is called the **error** term, since it represents the error that results from using the conditional expectation of Y at x_i to predict the individual observation. Each observation has its own ϵ_i, its sign reflecting whether the observation is above or below the conditional expected value. See Figure 6.1, which shows ϵ_i as the vertical distance between the point for observation i and the line for the linear model.

With sample data $\{(x_i, y_i)\}$, we do not know $\{\epsilon_i\}$, because we do not know the parameter values and the equation $\beta_0 + \beta_1 x_i$. We use the data to find a **prediction equation** $\hat{\mu}_i = \hat{\beta}_0 + \hat{\beta}_1 x_i$. This equation provides an estimate $\hat{\mu}_i$ of $E(Y_i)$ at each x_i value, called a **fitted value**. For it, let e_i be such that

$$y_i = \hat{\beta}_0 + \hat{\beta}_1 x_i + e_i = \hat{\mu}_i + e_i.$$

That is, $e_i = y_i - \hat{\mu}_i$. This difference between observed and fitted values of Y is called a

---

[1] Exercise 6.29 shows model parameterizations for which the intercept *is* necessarily meaningful.

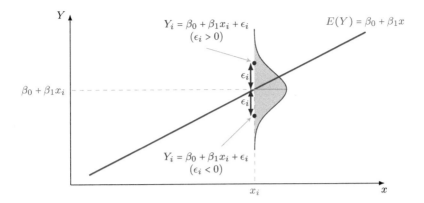

FIGURE 6.1 In the model formula $Y_i = \beta_0 + \beta_1 x_i + \epsilon_i$, when $\epsilon_i > 0$, observation y_i falls above the mean of the conditional distribution (which falls on the line); when $\epsilon_i < 0$, observation y_i falls below the mean of the conditional distribution. For a particular observation, the distribution of the random response Y_i is normal with mean $E(Y_i) = \beta_0 + \beta_1 x_i$.

residual. Since $y_i = \beta_0 + \beta_1 x_i + \epsilon_i = \hat{\beta}_0 + \hat{\beta}_1 x_i + e_i$, the residual e_i estimates ϵ_i, which is a *population residual*.

In summary, we can express the basic linear model either as

$$E(Y_i) = \beta_0 + \beta_1 x_i \quad \text{or as} \quad Y_i = \beta_0 + \beta_1 x_i + \epsilon_i \quad \text{for } i = 1, \dots, n.$$

We mainly use the first equation, because it connects better with models in the next chapter for discrete response variables.

6.1.3 Least Squares Model Fitting

To analyze the data, the first step plots the n observations. We show the observation (x_i, y_i) for subject i as a point on a graph with x and y axes. A *scatterplot* of the n data points $\{(x_i, y_i)\}$ shows whether the linear model $E(Y_i) = \beta_0 + \beta_1 x_i$ is sensible. The data points should follow roughly a straight-line trend, except for random variability around that trend. We'll see in this chapter that outlying observations can be quite influential. To find estimates $\hat{\beta}_0$ and $\hat{\beta}_1$ of the model parameters and the prediction equation that yields fitted values $\{\hat{\mu}_i = \hat{\beta}_0 + \hat{\beta}_1 x_i\}$, we use the *least squares method*.

Least squares

For the linear model $E(Y_i) = \beta_0 + \beta_1 x_i$, with a sample of n observations the **least squares method** determines the values of $\hat{\beta}_0$ and $\hat{\beta}_1$ that minimize

$$\sum_{i=1}^{n}(y_i - \hat{\mu}_i)^2 = \sum_{i=1}^{n}\left[y_i - (\hat{\beta}_0 + \hat{\beta}_1 x_i)\right]^2 = \sum_{i=1}^{n} e_i^2,$$

the sum of the squared residuals.

As a function of the model parameters (β_0, β_1), the expression

$$S(\beta_0, \beta_1) = \sum_{i}(y_i - \mu_i)^2 = \sum_{i}[y_i - (\beta_0 + \beta_1 x_i)]^2$$

is quadratic in β_0 and β_1. We can minimize it by equating

$$\frac{\partial S}{\partial \beta_0} = -\sum_{i=1}^{n}[y_i - (\beta_0 + \beta_1 x_i)] = 0,$$

and

$$\frac{\partial S}{\partial \beta_1} = -\sum_{i=1}^{n} x_i[y_i - (\beta_0 + \beta_1 x_i)] = 0.$$

We rewrite these equations as

$$\sum_{i=1}^{n} y_i = n\beta_0 + \beta_1 \sum_{i=1}^{n} x_i, \qquad \sum_{i=1}^{n} x_i y_i = \beta_0\Big(\sum_{i=1}^{n} x_i\Big) + \beta_1 \sum_{i=1}^{n} x_i^2.$$

Simultaneous solution of the two equations yields the least squares estimates, which are unique. They are

$$\hat{\beta}_1 = \frac{\sum_{i=1}^{n}(x_i - \overline{x})(y_i - \overline{y})}{\sum_{i=1}^{n}(x_i - \overline{x})^2} = \frac{s_{xy}}{s_x^2}, \quad \hat{\beta}_0 = \overline{y} - \hat{\beta}_1 \overline{x}, \tag{6.1}$$

where

$$s_x = \sqrt{\frac{\sum_i (x_i - \overline{x})^2}{n-1}} \quad \text{and} \quad s_{xy} = \frac{\sum_i (x_i - \overline{x})(y_i - \overline{y})}{n-1}.$$

Here, s_x is the sample standard deviation of x values and s_{xy} is the sample covariance between x and y. The sample covariance s_{xy} is a sample analog of the covariance $\text{cov}(X, Y) = E[(X - \mu_X)(Y - \mu_Y)]$ defined in Section 2.7.1 for two random variables. From the solution for $\hat{\beta}_0$, the least squares fitted equation satisfies $\overline{y} = \hat{\beta}_0 + \hat{\beta}_1 \overline{x}$. At $x = \overline{x}$, $\hat{\mu} = \overline{y}$. That is, the line passes through the point $(\overline{x}, \overline{y})$, which is the *center of gravity* of the data.

The least squares method does not require any assumption about the conditional probability distribution of Y. However, under the added assumption of normality with constant variance, the least squares estimates are also *maximum likelihood* (ML) estimates. From equation (2.8) for the normal *pdf*, the logarithm of the likelihood function for independent observations $\{Y_i \sim N(\mu_i, \sigma^2)\}$ is, in terms of $\{\mu_i = \beta_0 + \beta_1 x_i\}$,

$$\log\left[\prod_{i=1}^{n}\left(\frac{1}{\sqrt{2\pi}\sigma}e^{-(y_i - \mu_i)^2/2\sigma^2}\right)\right] = \text{constant} - (1/2\sigma^2)\sum_{i=1}^{n}(y_i - \mu_i)^2.$$

We maximize the log-likelihood function by minimizing $\sum_i(y_i - \mu_i)^2$. With the added assumption of normality, we refer to the model as a ***normal linear model***.

6.1.4 Example: Linear Model for Scottish Hill Races

Each year the Scottish Hill Runners Association publishes a list of hill races in Scotland for the year.[2]. Table 6.1 shows the record times for men and for women for some of the races, as of January 2021. Explanatory variables listed are the distance of the race and the climb in elevation. In this chapter we model the record times for women, using the data for the 68 races in the ScotsRaces data file. Exercises 6.1 and 6.20 ask you to model the men's record times.

Here are some summary statistics:

```
> Races <- read.table("http://stat4ds.rwth-aachen.de/data/ScotsRaces.dat", header=TRUE)
> head(Races, 3)                              # timeM for men, timeW for women
                   race  distance  climb  timeM  timeW
```

---

[2]See https://scottishhillrunners.uk

TABLE 6.1 Record time to complete Scottish hill race (in minutes), by distance and climb in elevation of the course (in kilometers).

Race	Distance	Climb	Record Time Men	Record Time Women
Ben Lomond	12.0	0.97	62.27	71.95
Craig Dunain	9.0	0.27	39.23	45.76
Greenmantle	3.2	0.20	15.10	18.75
Highland Fling	85.0	1.20	439.15	490.05
Isle of Jura	28.0	2.37	185.23	218.72
Lairig Ghru	43.0	0.64	178.17	212.63

The data for all 68 races are in the `ScotsRaces` data file at the book's website.

```
1          AnTeallach      10.6  1.062   74.68   89.72
2          ArrocharAlps    25.0  2.400  187.32  222.03
3     BaddinsgillRound     16.4  0.650   87.18  102.48

> matrix(cbind(mean(Races$timeW), sd(Races$timeW), mean(Races$climb), sd(Races$climb),
+             mean(Races$distance), sd(Races$distance)), nrow=2)
          [,1]    [,2]     [,3]
[1,] 100.722   0.887  16.634  # timeW mean = 100.7, standard deviation = 72.6 minutes
[2,]  72.587   0.538  11.819  # distance mean = 16.6, standard deviation = 11.8 km
> pairs(~timeW + distance + climb, data=Races) # scatterplot matrix (Figure 6.2)
```

Figure 6.2 is a *scatterplot matrix*. It portrays two scatterplots for each pair of variables, interchanging which is on the x axis and which is on the y axis. The scatterplot for record time and distance reveals a strong linear trend. The scatterplot of record time and climb shows a rather severe outlier, discussed later.

We first fit the linear model using distance as the explanatory variable for predicting

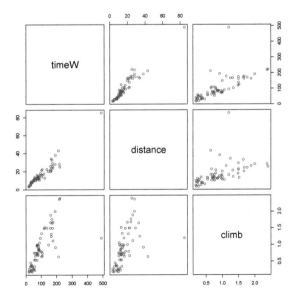

FIGURE 6.2 Scatterplot matrix for record time for women, distance of course, and climb in elevation of course, for Scottish hill races data.

record time.[3] Here is edited R output using the lm function for *linear modeling* with least squares:

```
> fit.d <- lm(timeW~distance, data=Races) # model E(timeW) as linear function of distance
> summary(fit.d)
              Estimate
(Intercept)   3.1076
distance      5.8684 # slope estimate for effect of distance on E(timeW)
```

The model fit $\hat{\mu} = 3.11 + 5.87x$ indicates that the predicted women's record time increases by 5.87 minutes for every additional kilometer of distance.

6.1.5 The Correlation

For the n observations, the sample *correlation* between x and y describes their association.[4]

Correlation

For n observations $\{(x_i, y_i)\}$ of two quantitative variables, the **correlation** is

$$r = \frac{s_{xy}}{s_x s_y} = \frac{\sum_{i=1}^{n}(x_i - \bar{x})(y_i - \bar{y})}{\sqrt{[\sum_{i=1}^{n}(x_i - \bar{x})^2][\sum_{i=1}^{n}(y_i - \bar{y})^2]}}. \tag{6.2}$$

With the sample standard deviations s_x of x and s_y of y and sample covariance s_{xy}, r is a sample analog of the correlation (2.16) defined in Section 2.7.1 for two random variables, which divides the *covariance* by the product of standard deviations. The formula for r is symmetric in x and y, so r has the same value when x predicts y as when y predicts x. The correlation satisfies $-1 \leq r \leq 1$, with $|r| = 1$ when all n data points fall exactly in a straight-line pattern. Larger values of $|r|$ correspond to a stronger *linear* association.

Alternatively, we can express the correlation as

$$r = \frac{\sum_i(x_i - \bar{x})(y_i - \bar{y})}{\sqrt{[\sum_i(x_i - \bar{x})^2][\sum_i(y_i - \bar{y})^2]}} = \frac{1}{n-1}\sum_{i=1}^{n}\left(\frac{x_i - \bar{x}}{s_x}\right)\left(\frac{y_i - \bar{y}}{s_y}\right).$$

That is, the correlation is approximately the average cross-product of the z-score for x times the z-score for y, where the z-scores measure the number of standard deviations from the mean. From this formula, the correlation does not depend on the units of measurement, since the z-scores are unit-free. From (6.2) and formula (6.1) for the estimated slope $\hat{\beta}_1$ of the linear model,

$$r = \hat{\beta}_1\left(\frac{s_x}{s_y}\right). \tag{6.3}$$

Therefore, r has the same sign as $\hat{\beta}_1$, and $r = 0$ when $\hat{\beta}_1 = 0$. Moreover, $r = \hat{\beta}_1$ when both variables have the same standard deviation, such as when x and y are standardized and $s_x = s_y = 1$. In this sense, *the correlation is a standardized slope.*

Software can display a *correlation matrix* showing the correlation between each pair of variables in a data set:

```
> cor(Races[, c("timeW", "distance", "climb")]) # correlation matrix
          timeW distance climb # symmetric around "main diagonal" correlation = 1.0
```

---

[3]To instead constrain $\beta_0 = 0$, since time = 0 when distance = 0, see Exercise 6.40 and Section 6.2.7.
[4]This estimate is sometimes called the *Pearson correlation*, because the British statistician Karl Pearson proposed it in 1895, but the concept of correlation was introduced by Francis Galton in the late 1880s.

```
timeW     1.0000 0.9555 0.6853 # correlation = 0.9555 between time and distance
distance 0.9555 1.0000 0.5145
climb     0.6853 0.5145 1.0000 # correlation = 0.6853 between climb and time
```

Not surprisingly, distance has a very strong positive correlation with the record time. The correlation between a variable and itself is necessarily and obviously 1.0.

When the sample size is not very large, a single observation can be influential in the least squares fit and in the correlation. For instance, the scatterplot between record time and climb in elevation shows that the race with much greater record time than the others (race 41, the Highland Fling) is a severe outlier for its modest climb value. When we remove this observation, the correlation between time and climb increases from 0.69 to 0.85. Besides being influenced by *outliers*, the correlation depends on the *range* of x-values analyzed. When we analyze a portion of the data that has a restricted range of variation in x, the magnitude of the correlation tends to decrease. For instance, the scatterplot between record time and distance shows that observation 41, although having much greater distance than the other 67 observations, falls in the general trend of the others. However, when we remove this observation, the correlation between record time and distance decreases from 0.96 to 0.92. Here are correlation results without observation 41:

```
> cor(cbind(Races[-41,]$timeW, Races[-41,]$distance, Races[-41,]$climb))
         [,1]    [,2]    [,3]    # correlations after remove outlying observation 41
[1,] 1.0000 0.9205 0.8516
[2,] 0.9205 1.0000 0.6617
[3,] 0.8516 0.6617 1.0000
```

The correlation of 0.96 between record time and distance decreases to 0.80 if we use only races with distances between the lower and upper quartiles of distance.

6.1.6   Regression toward the Mean in Linear Regression Models

Here is an important implication of the relation (6.3) between r and $\hat{\beta}_1$: Consider increasing the x-value from $x = \bar{x}$ to $x = \bar{x} + s_x$. With this increase of s_x in the x direction, the $\hat{\mu}$ values differ by $\hat{\beta}_1 s_x$. But since $r = \hat{\beta}_1(s_x/s_y)$, we have $\hat{\beta}_1 s_x = r s_y$. So, an increase from the mean in x of a standard deviation corresponds to a change in the predicted value of y of r standard deviations. This equation relates to the phenomenon of **regression toward the mean**, first noted by the British scientist Francis Galton in 1886: When $|r| < 1$, a standard deviation increase in x corresponds to a predicted change of *less* than a standard deviation in y. Because of this property, the linear model is also called a **linear regression model** and $E(Y) = \beta_0 + \beta_1 x$ is called a **regression line**. Empirically, Galton noted the regression effect by observing that very tall (very short) parents tended to have tall (short) children, but on the average not quite so tall (short).[5] For all fathers who are 6 1/2 feet tall, perhaps their sons average 6 1/4 feet tall. For all mothers who are 5 feet tall, perhaps their daughters average 5 feet, 2 inches. For correlated variables, extreme observations on one variable tend to correspond to less-extreme observations on the other.

The implications of regression toward the mean are profound. Many effects that might be regarded as causal may merely reflect regression toward the mean. For example, suppose that a particular university course has correlation $r = 0.50$ between $x =$ score on midterm exam and $y =$ score on final exam, and both exams have a mean of 70 and standard deviation of 10. Then, the very poorly-performing students who scored 40 on the midterm would average about 55 on the final exam. That is, we predict that students who were 3 standard deviations

---

[5]Likewise, reversing x and y in the model, very tall (very short) children on average have somewhat shorter (taller) parents than themselves.

below the mean on the midterm average $(0.5)3 = 1.5$ standard deviations below the mean on the final exam. If a special tutoring project raises poorly-performing students by half the distance to the mean, on the average, we should not be impressed. This would happen by chance alone when at most a moderate positive correlation exists between midterm and final exam scores.

6.1.7   Linear Models and Reality

A linear model merely *approximates* the true relationship between $E(Y)$ and x. No sensible researcher who uses a normal linear model expects the actual relationship to be *exactly* a straight line, with *exactly* normal conditional distributions for Y having *identical* variances at each x. As explained by the British statistician Sir David Cox,[6] "The very word *model* implies simplification and idealization. The idea that complex physical, biological or sociological systems can be exactly described by a few formulae is patently absurd. The construction of idealized representations that capture important stable aspects of such systems is, however, a vital part of general scientific analysis."

Plots of the data and other diagnostics presented in this chapter may suggest an improvement over the simple linear model that we've used so far. For example, a scatterplot may show a *nonlinear* trend. Figure 6.3 plots total counts of Covid-19 cases in the U.S. by day for a month[7] and suggests that y = total number of cases might be approximately an exponential function of x = day number. A linear model then fits better when applied to $\{\log(y_i)\}$ values (Exercise 6.5). Figure 6.3 also shows the scatterplot for the log-transformed values, for which the straight-line model fits much better.

For any data set, a proposed model can be fitted, checked, perhaps modified somewhat and checked again or used with another data set of similar nature, and so on. Especially with multiple explanatory variables, model building is an iterative process. Its goals are to find a realistic model that is adequate for describing the relationship and making predictions but that is reasonably simple to interpret.

---

[6] A comment in *Journal of the Royal Statistical Society* **A 158**: 455–456 (1995)
[7] From https://www.cdc.gov/coronavirus

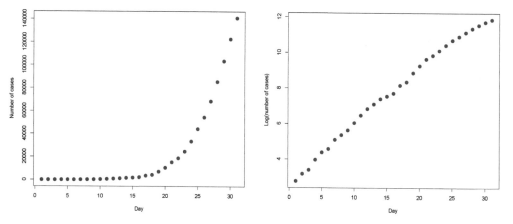

FIGURE 6.3 Scatterplot of total number of Covid-19 cases in the U.S., between February 28 and March 29, 2020, from `Covid19` data file at text website.

6.2 Multiple Regression: Linear Models with Multiple Explanatory Variables

The linear regression model with a single explanatory variable extends to include multiple explanatory variables. For subject i in the sample, let x_{ij} denote the value of explanatory variable j. The linear model with p explanatory variables, called the **multiple regression model**, is

$$E(Y_i) = \beta_0 + \beta_1 x_{i1} + \cdots + \beta_p x_{ip},$$

where here $E(Y_i)$ represents the *conditional expectation* of the response variable at the values $(x_{i1}, \ldots, x_{ip})$ of the explanatory variables. The standard linear model assumes that Y has constant variance σ^2 at each combination of values of the explanatory variables. In practice, usually p is much smaller than n. When instead p is large, in some areas of application potentially even larger than n and with perhaps many $\{\beta_j = 0\}$, it is better to fit the model using *regularization* methods presented in Section 7.7 rather than least squares.

6.2.1 Interpreting Effects in Multiple Regression Models

How do we interpret $\{\beta_j\}$ in the multiple regression model? Suppose y_i is a young adult's attained education (in number of years), and we fit the linear model having x_{i1} = mother's attained education, x_{i2} = father's attained education, x_{i3} = age, and x_{i4} = high school GPA, yielding the least squares fit

$$\hat{\mu}_i = \hat{\beta}_0 + \hat{\beta}_1 x_{i1} + \hat{\beta}_2 x_{i2} + \hat{\beta}_3 x_{i3} + \hat{\beta}_4 x_{i4}.$$

Since $\hat{\beta}_1 = \partial \hat{\mu}_i / \partial x_{i1}$, we might say, "The estimated difference between the mean attained education of those adults having a certain mother's attained education and those having one fewer year equals $\hat{\beta}_1$, when we keep constant the father's attained education and the subject's age and high school GPA." Controlling variables is possible in designed experiments. But it is unnatural and possibly inconsistent with the data for many observational studies to envision increasing one explanatory variable while keeping all the others fixed. For example, x_1 and x_2 are undoubtedly positively correlated, so increases in x_1 naturally tend to occur with increases in x_2. Some data sets might not even have a 1-unit range in an explanatory variable when all the others are held constant. A better interpretation is this: "The estimated difference between the mean attained education of adults with a certain mother's attained education and adults with one fewer year equals $\hat{\beta}_1$, when both groups have the same value for $\hat{\beta}_2 x_{i2} + \hat{\beta}_3 x_{i3} + \hat{\beta}_4 x_{i4}$." More concisely we say, "The estimated effect of mother's attained education on a person's attained education equals $\hat{\beta}_1$, *adjusting* for father's education, age, and high school GPA."

Depending on the units of measurement, an effect may be more relevant when expressed with changes other than one unit. For example, to compare two groups that differ in x_1 by 4 years (such as college graduates and high school graduates), adjusting for the other explanatory variables, the estimated effect is $4\hat{\beta}_1$.

An effect β in the linear model with a sole explanatory variable x_1 is usually not the same as the effect β_1 of the same variable x_1 in a model with multiple explanatory variables. The effect β is a *marginal* effect, *ignoring* all other potential explanatory variables, whereas β_1 is a *conditional* effect, *adjusting* for the other explanatory variables.

6.2.2   Example: Multiple Regression for Scottish Hill Races

For the Scottish hill races data, we next use both distance of the course and climb in elevation as explanatory variables for the women's record time:

```
> fit.dc <- lm(timeW ~ distance + climb, data=Races)
> summary(fit.dc)
               Estimate
(Intercept)   -14.5997
distance        5.0362
climb          35.5610
```

The model fit $\hat{\mu} = -14.60 + 5.04(\text{distance}) + 35.56(\text{climb})$ indicates that (1) adjusted for climb, the predicted record time increases by 5.04 minutes for every additional kilometer of distance; (2) adjusted for distance, the predicted record time increases by 35.56 minutes for every additional kilometer of climb. The estimated *conditional* distance effect of 5.04 differs from the estimated *marginal* effect of 5.87 found in Section 6.1.4 with distance as the sole explanatory variable, because distance and climb are positively correlated. With the climb in elevation fixed, distance has less of an effect than when the model ignores climb so that it also tends to increase as distance increases.

6.2.3   Association and Causation

Causality is central to the scientific endeavor. We know, for instance, that being exposed to a virus can cause the flu and that smoking can cause lung cancer. If we suspect that one variable is causally explained by another, how do we analyze whether it actually is? A relationship between two variables must satisfy three criteria to be considered causal:

• Existence of association between the variables

• An appropriate time order of the variables

• The elimination of alternative explanations for the association

Association by itself cannot establish causality.

▶ *Association does not imply causation!*

The two variables must have the appropriate *time order*, with the cause preceding the effect. For instance, race, age, and gender exist prior to current attitudes or achievements, so any causal association must treat them as causes rather than effects. When two variables do not have a time order but are measured together over time, they may be associated merely because they both have a time trend. For example, for recent annual data there is a correlation of 0.993 between divorce rate in Maine and per capita consumption of margarine.[8] They both have a decreasing trend over time, so they have a strong positive correlation, with higher divorce rates occurring in years that have higher consumption of margarine. Each variable would be strongly negatively correlated with all variables that have a positive time trend, such as the percentage of people who use smart phones.

For an association to reflect causality, it must not have an *alternative explanation*. We may think we've found a causal relationship, but we may merely not have thought of a particular reason that can explain the association. With observational data, it is easy to find associations, but those associations are often explained by other variables that may not have been measured in a study. For example, some medical studies have found associations

---

[8]See www.tylervigen.com/spurious-correlations.

between coffee drinking and various responses, such as the likelihood of a heart attack or the mean blood pressure level. But after taking into account other variables associated with the extent of coffee drinking, such as extent of smoking, country of residence, occupation, and levels of stress, such associations have disappeared or weakened considerably. Because of this, *observational studies can never prove that one variable is a cause of another.*

In a randomized experiment, when we observe an association between the group variable and the response variable, we do not expect another variable to provide an alternative explanation for the association. With randomized assignment to groups, the two groups should have similar distributions for variables not observed but which may be associated with the response variable. So, the association is not due to an association between the group variable and an alternative variable. In addition, when a research study is experimental, the time order is fixed. The outcome for a subject is observed *after* the group is assigned, so the time order is certain. Because of these factors, *it is easier to assess causality with randomized experiments than with observational studies.*

In a study designed to compare two groups, each subject has a *potential outcome* if they are in Group 1 and another potential outcome if they are in Group 2, but we can observe only one of those. When we compare the mean blood pressure for n_1 subjects who drink coffee with the mean blood pressure for n_2 subjects who do not, we cannot observe the potential outcomes if the n_1 coffee drinkers instead did not drink coffee and if the n_2 non-drinkers did drink it. These are called the *counterfactual* outcomes. If we could also observe the counterfactual outcomes, we could better estimate the true difference in expected values using $n_1 + n_2$ observations for each group. We can obtain an unbiased estimate of this true difference with a randomized experiment but not with an observational study.

Since we cannot observe the counterfactual outcomes, in an observational study we can use regression models to investigate results of *statistical control*, adjusting for relevant variables as we analyze the effect for the primary variable of interest. For instance, in considering whether an alternative explanation for an association between Y and X_1 is due to their associations with a variable X_2, we compare the estimated marginal effect $\hat{\beta}$ in the linear model with x_1 as the sole explanatory variable to the estimated conditional effect $\hat{\beta}_1$ of x_1 in the model that also contains x_2. When X_1 and X_2 both are correlated with Y but are also correlated with each other, the marginal effect differs from the conditional effect.

6.2.4 Confounding, Spuriousness, and Conditional Independence

When the marginal effect of an explanatory variable differs from the conditional effect after adjusting for another explanatory variable, the discrepancy is called ***confounding***. It is not possible to determine whether either variable truly has a causal relationship with Y, because one variable's effect could be at least partly due to its association with the other variable. In observational studies, the explanatory variables almost always exhibit some correlation, and typically many lurking variables exist that are associated both with Y and with the explanatory variables. The size of the effect of any variable often depends strongly on which other explanatory variables are in the model. By contrast, in randomized experiments, the design can set the values of the explanatory variables at which Y is observed so that they are uncorrelated. Then, marginal and conditional effects are the same.

An important special case of confounding is a ***spurious association***: An association between Y and X_1 is due to a third variable X_2 that has a causal influence on each of them, such that the association between Y and X_1 disappears when we add X_2 to the model. When an association is observed between two variables, later studies often attempt to determine whether that association might be spurious, by adjusting for variables that could be a common cause. For example, some studies of mortality rates in the U.S. found that states having more income inequality tend to have higher mortality rates, but this association disappeared after adjusting for the percentage of a state's residents that had at least a high school education. Perhaps the association was spurious, with education having a causal influence on both income inequality and mortality. Other possible explanations include a *chain relationship*, with education having a causal influence on income inequality, which itself has a causal influence on the mortality rate. Merely from analyzing associations, we do not know which provides a better explanation.

With a spurious or a chain relationship, the corresponding random variables Y and X_1 are **conditionally independent**,[9] given X_2. That is, Y and X_1 are independent at each value x_2 of X_2. Figure 6.4 depicts these possibilities. In practice, when X_1 and X_2 are strongly correlated, the conditional effect of X_1 is much weaker than its marginal effect but it does not completely disappear.

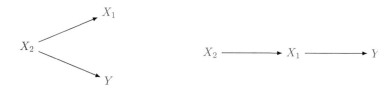

FIGURE 6.4 Graphical depiction of a spurious association and a chain relationship. When X_2 causally affects both X_1 and Y, the association between Y and X_1 disappears when we adjust for X_2; that is, Y and X_1 are *conditionally independent*, given X_2.

In analyzing the effect of an explanatory variable of key interest, if a study neglects to observe a confounding variable that explains a major part of that effect, the results and conclusions will be biased. Such bias is called **omitted variable bias**. Confounding and omitted variable bias are constant worries in research studies. They are the main reason it is difficult to study many issues of importance, such as what causes crime or what causes the economy to improve or what causes students to succeed in school.

6.2.5   Example: Modeling the Crime Rate in Florida

The `Florida` data file at the book's website has data from the 67 Florida counties on *crime rate* (annual number of crimes per 1000 residents), median *income* per resident (in thousands of dollars), *education* (percentage with at least a high school education, of those aged at least 25), and *urbanization* (percentage living in an urban environment). Surprisingly, a positive correlation exists (0.47) between crime rate and education. The crime rate tends to *increase* as education increases. Could this relationship be spurious, explained by urbanization? Perhaps as urbanization increases, both education and crime tend to increase. Let's estimate the effect of education, marginally and conditional on urbanization:

```
> Florida <- read.table("http://stat4ds.rwth-aachen.de/data/Florida.dat", header=TRUE)
> head(Florida, 2)
    County Crime Income   HS Urban # HS = percentage with at least high school education
1  ALACHUA   104   22.1 82.7  73.2
2    BAKER    20   25.8 64.1  21.5
> cor(Florida$Crime, Florida$HS)
[1] 0.4669119
> summary(lm(Crime ~ HS, data=Florida))
            Estimate  Std. Error
(Intercept)  -50.8569    24.4507
HS             1.4860     0.3491 # marginal effect of HS education > 0
```

---

[9]Section 2.6.7 introduced *conditional independence* in the context of Markov chains.

```
---
> summary(lm(Crime ~ HS + Urban, data=Florida))
             Estimate  Std. Error
(Intercept)  59.1181      28.3653
HS           -0.5834       0.4725 # conditional effect of HS education < 0
Urban         0.6825       0.1232
---
> cor(Florida$HS, Florida$Urban)  # urbanization strongly positively correlated
[1] 0.790719                      # with both crime rate and HS education
> cor(Florida$Crime, Florida$Urban)
[1] 0.6773678
```

Adjusting for urbanization, the effect of education does not disappear, but it changes sign! Adjusting for urbanization, the crime rate tends to *decrease* as education increases. Urbanization has a correlation of 0.79 with education and 0.68 with the crime rate. More highly-urbanized counties tend to have both higher education levels and higher crime rates.

Figure 6.5 shows how a positive association between crime rate and education can change to negative when we adjust for urbanization, where in this figure the urbanization quantitative variable is measured simply as rural and urban. This phenomenon of association reversal between marginal and conditional associations is called ***Simpson's paradox***.[10]

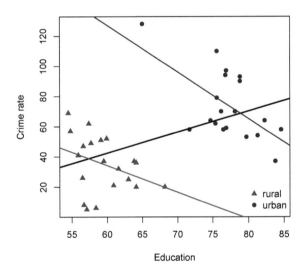

FIGURE 6.5 Illustration of *Simpson's paradox*, showing a negative correlation between crime rate and education conditionally at each level of urbanization (represented by the red and blue lines), yet a positive marginal correlation when we ignore urbanization (represented by the black line).

6.2.6 Equations for Least Squares Estimates in Multiple Regression

To find the least squares estimates of the parameters in a multiple regression model, we minimize

$$S(\beta_0, \beta_1, \ldots, \beta_p) = \sum_i (y_i - \mu_i)^2 = \sum_i [y_i - (\beta_0 + \beta_1 x_{i1} + \cdots + \beta_p x_{ip})]^2$$

---

[10]Named after the British statistician E. H. Simpson, who studied the phenomenon in a 1951 article.

with respect to the parameters. Differentiating with respect to each parameter, we obtain

$$\frac{\partial S}{\partial \beta_0} = -\sum_{i=1}^{n}[y_i - (\beta_0 + \beta_1 x_{i1} + \cdots + \beta_p x_{ip})] = 0$$

$$\frac{\partial S}{\partial \beta_j} = -\sum_{i=1}^{n} x_{ij}[y_i - (\beta_0 + \beta_1 x_{i1} + \cdots + \beta_p x_{ip})] = 0, \quad j = 1, \ldots, p.$$

Evaluated at the least squares estimates, the first equation tells us

$$\sum_{i=1}^{n}[y_i - (\hat{\beta}_0 + \hat{\beta}_1 x_{i1} + \cdots + \hat{\beta}_p x_{ip})] = \sum_{i=1}^{n}(y_i - \hat{\mu}_i) = \sum_{i=1}^{n} e_i = 0.$$

The residuals $\{e_i\}$ sum to 0 and thus have a mean of 0. The second equation tells us

$$\sum_{i=1}^{n} x_{ij} y_i = \sum_{i=1}^{n} x_{ij} \hat{\mu}_i. \quad j = 1, \ldots, p.$$

The first equation also has this form by setting $x_{i0} = 1$. In fact, for the normal linear model $\{\sum_{i=1}^{n} x_{ij} y_i, j = 0, 1, \ldots, p\}$ are the *sufficient statistics* for the model parameters (Section 4.2.6). The least-squares equations equate the sufficient statistics to the estimates of their expected values.

To find the least squares estimates, software solves these $p+1$ equations in $p+1$ unknowns. This can be done using matrix algebra, as Section 6.7 shows.

6.2.7   Interaction between Explanatory Variables in Their Effects

The equation $E(Y_i) = \beta_0 + \beta_1 x_{i1} + \cdots + \beta_p x_{ip}$ assumes that the relationship between $E(Y)$ and each x_j is linear and that *the slope β_j of that relationship is identical at all values of the other explanatory variables*. The model implies a parallelism of lines relating the two variables, at fixed values of the other variables. Figure 6.6 illustrates, for the case $p = 2$. This model containing only so-called *main effects* is sometimes too simple. The effect of x_1 on y may change as the value of x_2 changes, referred to as *interaction* between x_1 and x_2 in their effects.

Interaction

Two explanatory variables exhibit ***interaction*** in their effects on the response variable Y when the effect of one variable changes as the value of the other variable changes.

A common approach for allowing interaction introduces *cross-product terms* of the explanatory variables in the model. With two explanatory variables, the model is

$$E(Y_i) = \beta_0 + \beta_1 x_{i1} + \beta_2 x_{i2} + \beta_3 x_{i1} x_{i2}.$$

This is a special case of the model with three explanatory variables, in which x_3 is the cross-product $x_3 = x_1 x_2$ of the two primary explanatory variables. To analyze how $E(Y)$ relates to x_1, at different values for x_2, we rewrite the equation in terms of x_1 as

$$E(Y_i) = (\beta_0 + \beta_2 x_{i2}) + (\beta_1 + \beta_3 x_{i2}) x_{i1} = \beta_0^* + \beta_1^* x_{i1},$$

where $\beta_0^* = \beta_0 + \beta_2 x_{i2}$ and $\beta_1^* = \beta_1 + \beta_3 x_{i2}$. For fixed x_2, $E(Y)$ changes linearly as a function of x_1. The slope of the relationship is $\beta_1^* = (\beta_1 + \beta_3 x_{i2})$, so as x_2 changes, the slope for the effect of x_1 changes.

When the number of explanatory variables exceeds two, a model allowing interaction

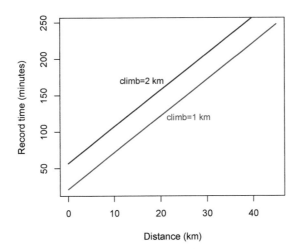

FIGURE 6.6 The multiple regression model $E(Y) = \beta_0 + \beta_1 x_1 + \beta_2 x_2$ implies parallel lines relating $E(Y)$ and x_1 at fixed values of x_2. This plot shows the equation $\hat{\mu} = -14.60 + 5.04(\text{distance}) + 35.56(\text{climb})$ at climb values of 1 *km* and 2 *km*.

can contain cross-product terms for any pair of the explanatory variables. When a model includes an interaction term, it should have the *hierarchical* model structure by which it also contains the main effect terms that go into that interaction. If instead a model contains an $x_1 x_2$ term but not a x_1 main effect, then it forces the effect of x_1 to be 0 when $x_2 = 0$, which is usually not sensible.

For the Scottish hill races, it is plausible that the effect of distance on record time is greater when the climb in elevation is greater. To allow the effect of distance to depend on the climb, we add an interaction term:

```
> summary(lm(timeW ~ distance + climb + distance:climb, data=Races))
                 Estimate
(Intercept)       -5.0162
distance           4.3682
climb             23.9446
distance:climb     0.6582
```

A bit unsatisfactory here is the negative predicted time when distance = climb = 0. This is not a fatal flaw, as none of the races have values close to these values, but we can make the fit a bit more realistic by constraining the intercept term to equal 0:

```
> summary(lm(timeW ~ -1 + distance + climb + distance:climb, data=Races)) # -1 constrains
                 Estimate                                                  # intercept = 0
distance           4.0898
climb             18.7128
distance:climb     0.9124 # distance:climb denotes cross-product term for interaction
```

For a fixed climb value, the coefficient of distance in the prediction equation is $4.090 + 0.912(\text{climb})$. Between the minimum climb of 0.185 *km* and the maximum climb of 2.40 *km*, the effect on record time of a 1 *km* increase in distance changes from $4.090 + 0.912(0.185) = 4.26$ minutes to $4.090 + 0.912(2.40) = 6.28$ minutes.

6.2.8 Cook's Distance: Detecting Unusual and Influential Observations

For a particular model, various ways exist to check how well the model fits and to search for inadequacies. One way highlights observations that fall far from the model fit. An observation may not seem unusual when we look at each scatterplot between y and an explanatory variable, but it may be very unusual if we could view its location in the multidimensional space with an axis for y and for each x_j. We can *plot residuals* to detect observations that fall far from the trend generated by the model. The R Appendix (Section A.6.2) and Python Appendix (Section B.6.3) illustrate residual plots, the latter focusing on the Scottish hill races data.

Another way to check a model is to inspect numerical measures that detect observations that highly influence the model fit. The **leverage** is a measure of an observation's potential influence on the fit. We define this in terms of a matrix representation of the model in Section 6.7.3. For now, we mention that the leverage measures how far the explanatory variable values fall from their means, and it takes values between 0 and 1. Observations for which explanatory variables are far from their means have greater *potential* influence on the least squares estimates. For an observation to actually be influential, it must have both a relatively large leverage and a relatively large residual. **Cook's distance** is a diagnostic[11] that uses both, based on the change in $\{\hat{\beta}_j\}$ when the observation is removed from the data set. For the residual e_i and leverage h_i for observation i, Cook's distance is

$$D_i = \frac{e_i^2 h_i}{(p+1)s^2(1-h_i)^2},$$

where s^2 is an estimate of the conditional variance σ^2 introduced in the next section. This diagnostic is nonnegative, with a relatively large D_i occurring when both e_i and h_i are relatively large. You can plot them (see the R Appendix and Python Appendix) and further investigate ones that are substantially larger than the others, especially if they are larger than about 1.

For the model with main effects for distance and climb fitted to the Scottish hill runners data (Section 6.2.2), a highly influential observation is the Highland Fling, the race having much greater distance than the others but not an extreme climb. For this observation, the following R output shows that the residual is 490.05 − 456.15 = 33.90. The leverage (called the "hat value" in the R output) is 0.63, the largest for the 68 observations, the next largest being 0.14. Cook's distance is 9.07, which is 42 times the next largest value.

```
> fit.dc <- lm(timeW ~ distance + climb, data=Races)
> res <- residuals(fit.dc); fitval <- fitted(fit.dc); leverage <- hatvalues(fit.dc)
> cooks.ds <-cooks.distance(fit.dc); tail(sort(cooks.ds), 3)
        55            2           41          # observ. with three largest Cook's distances
0.1392402 0.2162927 9.0682767                 # largest Cook's distance for observation 41
> hist(res)                                   # Histogram display of residuals (not shown)
> plot(cooks.ds)                              # Plot of Cook's distance values (not shown)
> out <- cbind(race, timeW, fitval, res, leverage, cook.ds, rank(cook.ds))
> out[c(1,41,68),]              # print output for the 1st, 41th and 68th observations
       race            timeW     fitval    res       leverage   cook.ds
1  "AnTeallach"       "89.72"   "76.55"  "13.17"   "0.0256"   "0.0080"  "46"
41 "HighlandFling"    "490.05"  "456.15" "33.90"   "0.6304"   "9.0683"  "68" # **
68 "Yetholm"          "71.55"   "76.89"  "-5.34"   "0.0164"   "0.0008"  "21"
#  ** largest Cook's distance = 9.07 has rank 68 of 68 observations
> fit.dc2 <- lm(timeW ~ distance + climb, data=Races[-41,]) # re-fit without observ. 41
> summary(fit.dc2)
                Estimate
(Intercept)      -8.931
```

---

[11] Named after the American statistician R. Dennis Cook, who introduced it in 1977.

distance	4.172
climb	43.852

When we remove Highland Fling from the data file, the estimated effects change from 5.04 to 4.17 for *distance* and from 35.56 to 43.85 for *climb*. However, we found in Section 6.2.7 that models allowing interaction provide a fuller description of the effects. You can check that the Highland Fling race is also influential for those models, having Cook's distance of 7.88 for the basic model and 9.13 for the model without an intercept term. After removing that observation, the interaction models give a similar fit as the model containing only main effects.

Section A.6.2 of the R Appendix and Section B.6.3 of the Python Appendix discuss additional diagnostics that you can use to check modeling assumptions. These include plots of the residuals against fitted values and against each explanatory variable and Q-Q plots for checking normality. In practice, with several potential explanatory variables and potential interaction terms, selecting an appropriate model is not simple. Section 7.1.6 and Section A.7.3 of the R Appendix discuss issues in model selection.

6.3 Summarizing Variability in Linear Regression Models

The variance σ^2 of the conditional distribution of Y in linear regression models is also an unknown parameter. To distinguish σ^2 from other variances, such as marginal variances of individual variables and squared standard errors, we refer to it as the **error variance**. This name refers to σ^2 also being the variance of the error term (ϵ_i), for the model formulated as $Y_i = \beta_0 + \beta_1 x_{i1} + \cdots + \beta_p x_{ip} + \epsilon_i$. This section shows its estimate and introduces a way to decompose the marginal variability of Y into the error variance and the variability *explained* by the explanatory variables.

Estimating the Error Variance: The Residual Mean Square

An unbiased estimator of the error variance in a linear model having an intercept and p explanatory predictors (i.e., $p+1$ parameters in the linear predictor) is

$$S^2 = \frac{\sum_{i=1}^{n}(Y_i - \hat{\mu}_i)^2}{n - (p+1)}. \tag{6.4}$$

This adjusted average of the squared residuals is called the **residual mean square**.

The sum of squares in the numerator of s^2 is abbreviated by *SSE*, for **sum of squared errors**, and is also called the **residual sum of squares**.

As Section 4.1.2 explained, it is adequate for an estimator to be *asymptotically unbiased*, rather than exactly unbiased. In fact, $S = \sqrt{S^2}$, which is a more relevant measure for interpreting variability, is a biased but asymptotically unbiased estimator of σ. Both S and S^2 occur naturally in distribution theory for linear models, as Section 6.4 shows. In particular, the standard errors for $\{\hat{\beta}_j\}$ used in confidence intervals and significance tests are proportional to the sample value s of S.

6.3.1   The Error Variance and Chi-Squared for Linear Models

Statistical inference for a mean μ in Sections 4.4 and 5.2 did not take into account any explanatory variables (i.e., $p = 0$). The corresponding linear model has only an intercept,

$$E(Y_i) = \beta_0,$$

where $\beta_0 = \mu$. This model is called the **null model.** For it, each $\hat{\mu}_i = \overline{Y}$. The numerator of S^2 is then $\sum_{i=1}^{n}(Y_i - \overline{Y})^2$, and the estimator (6.4) of σ^2 with $p = 0$ in the denominator $n - (p + 1)$ is

$$S^2 = \frac{\sum_{i=1}^{n}(Y_i - \overline{Y})^2}{n - 1}.$$

Section 4.4.6 showed that this estimator is unbiased. For sample $\{y_i\}$ values, the corresponding estimate s^2 is the sample variance s_y^2 which estimates the variance σ_Y^2 of the marginal distribution of Y.

The magnitudes of the sum of squared errors $SSE = \sum_i (Y_i - \hat{\mu}_i)^2$ and of S^2 in equation (6.4) depend on the units of measurement for Y. For statistical inferences to be introduced in Section 6.4, normal linear models use the ratio (SSE/σ^2), which does not depend on the units of measurement and has a *chi-squared distribution*. From Section 4.4.5, the chi-squared distribution has mean that is the *degrees of freedom (df)*. Since $S^2 = SSE/[n - (p + 1)]$ is an unbiased estimator of σ^2, $E(SSE/[n - (p + 1)]) = \sigma^2$ and so $E(SSE/\sigma^2) = n - (p + 1)$. Thus, (SSE/σ^2) has the chi-squared distribution with $df = n - (p + 1)$.

6.3.2   Decomposing Variability into Model Explained and Unexplained Parts

The decomposition of each residual for the null model,

$$(y_i - \overline{y}) = (\hat{\mu}_i - \overline{y}) + (y_i - \hat{\mu}_i),$$

yields the sum of squares decomposition

$$\sum_i (y_i - \overline{y})^2 = \sum_i (\hat{\mu}_i - \overline{y})^2 + \sum_i (y_i - \hat{\mu}_i)^2, \tag{6.5}$$

since the cross-product term sums to 0 (Exercise 6.51). We abbreviate this decomposition of the marginal variability in y as

$$TSS = SSR + SSE,$$

for the *total sum of squares TSS*, the *sum of squares due to the regression model SSR*, and the *sum of squared errors SSE*. Figure 6.7 portrays the differences $(y_i - \overline{y})$ and $(y_i - \hat{\mu}_i)$ used in TSS and SSE, with the areas of the shaded squares in the figures equaling the squared values in the sums.

Here, using $(y_i - \overline{y})$ in the decomposition corresponds to adjusting y_i by including an intercept term before investigating effects of the explanatory variables, so TSS summarizes the sum of squared residuals after fitting the null model.[12] The SSE component represents the variation in y "unexplained" by the full model, that is, the sum of squared residuals summarizes prediction error remaining after fitting that model. The SSR component represents the variation in y "explained" by the full model, that is, the reduction in variation from TSS to SSE resulting from adding explanatory variables to a model that contains only an intercept term. It is called[13] the **regression sum of squares.**

---

[12] For the null model $E(Y_i) = \beta_0$, least squares yields $\hat{\mu}_i = \overline{y}$; TSS is also called the *corrected* total sum of squares because of subtracting $\overline{y}$ before summing the squares.
[13] Some software calls it the **model sum of squares.**

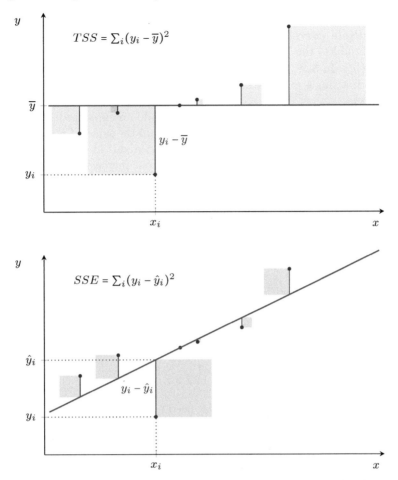

FIGURE 6.7 Graphical representation of differences that are squared and summed to get the *total sum of squares* $TSS = \sum_i (y_i - \bar{y})^2$ and the *sum of squared errors* $SSE = \sum_i (y_i - \hat{\mu}_i)^2$ for the fit of a regression model. Each squared difference in a sum of squares is equal to the area of the corresponding shaded square in the figure.

6.3.3 *R*-Squared and the Multiple Correlation

For a particular data set and its TSS value, the larger the value of SSR relative to SSE, the more effective the explanatory variables are in predicting the response variable. A summary of this predictive power is called *R-squared*.

R-squared

For a linear model with response observations $\{y_i\}$ and fitted values $\{\hat{\mu}_i\}$,

$$R^2 = \frac{SSR}{TSS} = \frac{TSS - SSE}{TSS} = \frac{\sum_i (y_i - \bar{y})^2 - \sum_i (y_i - \hat{\mu}_i)^2}{\sum_i (y_i - \bar{y})^2}.$$

Since $SSR = TSS - SSE$ measures the reduction in the sum of squared prediction errors after adding the explanatory variables to the null model, R^2 measures the *proportional reduction in error*. It falls between 0 and 1.

The sample correlation between $\{y_i\}$ and $\{\hat{\mu}_i\}$ is a related measure of predictive power, called the **multiple correlation**. Of the possible linear prediction equations that use the explanatory variables, the least squares solution yields $\{\hat{\mu}_i\}$ that have the maximum correlation with $\{y_i\}$. In fact, this correlation equals $+\sqrt{R^2}$. The multiple correlation satisfies $0 \leq R \leq 1$. With a single explanatory variable, $R = |r|$, where r is the bivariate correlation between x and y.

The least squares fit minimizes SSE. When we add an explanatory variable to a model, SSE cannot increase, because we could at worst obtain the same SSE value by setting $\hat{\beta}_j = 0$ for the new variable. Since TSS depends only on $\{y_i\}$ and is identical for every model fitted to a particular data set, $SSR = TSS - SSE$ is monotone increasing as the set of explanatory variables grows. Thus, when explanatory variables are added to a model, R^2 and R are monotone increasing.

When n is not large and a model has several explanatory variables, R^2 tends to overestimate the corresponding population value, which compares the marginal and conditional variances by the proportional reduction in variance. An **adjusted R-squared** is designed to reduce this bias. It is the proportional reduction in variance based on the unbiased variance estimates, s_y^2 for $\text{var}(Y)$ in the marginal distribution and s^2 for the variance in the conditional distributions; that is,

$$\text{Adjusted } R^2 = \frac{s_y^2 - s^2}{s_y^2} = 1 - \frac{s^2}{s_y^2} = 1 - \frac{SSE/[n-(p+1)]}{TSS/(n-1)}$$

$$= 1 - \frac{n-1}{n-(p+1)}\left(\frac{SSE}{TSS}\right) = 1 - \frac{n-1}{n-(p+1)}(1-R^2).$$

It is slightly smaller than ordinary R^2, and it need not monotonically increase as explanatory variables are added to a model.

6.3.4   Example: R-Squared for Modeling Scottish Hill Races

We now view some additional information for models fitted to the Scottish Hill Runners data, without the highly influential Highland Fling observation. For the model that assumes a lack of interaction:

```
> fit.dc2 <- lm(timeW ~ distance + climb, data=Races[-41,])
> summary(fit.dc2)              # for Races data file without Highland Fling
            Estimate
(Intercept)   -8.931
distance       4.172
climb         43.852
---
Residual standard error: 12.23 on 64 degrees of freedom # This is s
Multiple R-squared:  0.952,     Adjusted R-squared:  0.9505
> cor(Races[-41,]$timeW, fitted(fit.dc2)) # multiple correlation = correlation between
[1] 0.9757                       # observed and fitted record times
> (sigma(fit.dc2))^2; (sd(Races[-41,]$timeW))^2
[1]   149.4586 # estimate of error variance = square of residual standard error
[1] 3017.798  # estimate of marginal variance of women's record times
```

In the output, the *residual standard error* of 12.23 minutes is the estimated conditional standard deviation s of record times, at fixed values of distance and climb. From Section 6.3.1, the error variance estimate $s^2 = (12.23)^2 = 149.46$ averages the squared residuals, with denominator $[n-(p+1)]$, which is here $df = 67 - (2+1) = 64$. The sample marginal variance for the record times is $s_y^2 = 3017.80$, considerably larger than s^2. In fact, $R^2 = 0.952$ indicates a reduction of 95.2% in the sum of squared errors from using this prediction equation instead of $\bar{y}$ to predict the record times. (By contrast, R^2 is 0.847 with distance as the sole predictor and 0.725 with climb as the sole predictor.) The adjusted $R^2 = 0.9505$. We estimate that the conditional variance for record times is only 5% of the marginal variance. The multiple correlation $R = \sqrt{0.952} = 0.976$ equals the correlation between the 67 observed values $\{y_i\}$ and corresponding fitted values $\{\hat{\mu}_i\}$.

When we fit this model using the `glm` function in R as a normal linear model, the output states:

```
      Null deviance: 199174.6  on 66  degrees of freedom
  Residual deviance:   9565.4  on 64  degrees of freedom
```

We introduce the *deviance* in the next chapter. For now, we mention that for the normal linear model, the null deviance is TSS and the residual deviance is SSE. Thus, $R^2 = (TSS - SSE)/TSS = (199174.6 - 9565.4)/199174.6 = 0.952$. The difference $199174.6 - 9565.4 = 189609.2$ is the regression sum of squares (SSR) for the model.

6.4 Statistical Inference for Normal Linear Models

We now introduce confidence intervals and significance tests for linear models. The inferences apply to the *normal linear model*, which assumes that the conditional distribution of Y is normal with constant variance. Chapter 7 shows how inferences can assume other distributions, such as the gamma distribution. A key assumption in each case is that observations are *independent*. In some studies this is not true, such as when groups being compared consist of the same subjects rather than separate sets of individuals or when observations within units that contribute to a sample, such as families or classrooms in schools, are correlated. When we assume the observations are independent but they are not, standard errors can be poorly estimated and resulting inferences are more likely to be in error.[14]

Inferential methods for a single parameter in a normal linear model use the t distribution. Significance tests about multiple parameters use the F distribution, which is introduced next.

6.4.1 The F Distribution: Testing That All Effects Equal 0

Software for fitting normal linear models reports results of a significance test for the *global null hypothesis* $H_0: \beta_1 = \cdots = \beta_p = 0$ that *none* of the explanatory variables in the model have an effect on y. This compares the model's fit to the fit of the *null model* that has only an intercept term.

The observed sums of squared residuals are $SSE = \sum_i (y_i - \hat{\mu}_i)^2$ for the fitted model and $TSS = \sum_i (y_i - \bar{y})^2$ for the null model. Larger values for $(TSS - SSE)$ give stronger evidence against H_0. When H_0 is true so the models are identical, the positive value for $(TSS - SSE)$ merely reflects sampling variability and the $\{\hat{\beta}_j\}$ not equaling 0 even though $\{\beta_j = 0\}$. The magnitude of $(TSS - SSE)$ depends on the units of measurement for y, with its value tending to be larger when the error variance σ^2 is larger. The expression

$$TSS = SSR + SSE = (TSS - SSE) + SSE$$

decomposes TSS into two independent parts, and, for random variables $\{Y_i\}$,

$$(TSS - SSE)/\sigma^2 \quad \text{and} \quad SSE/\sigma^2$$

---

[14]Section A.7.4 of the R Appendix briefly introduces more appropriate methods for correlated observations.

are also independent random variables with distributions not depending on the units of measurement.

Section 6.3.1 stated that for a normal linear model with p explanatory variables, SSE/σ^2 has a chi-squared distribution with $df = n - (p + 1)$. For the null model ($p = 0$), TSS/σ^2 has a chi-squared distribution with $df = n - 1$, a result shown in Section 4.4.6. In fact, under H_0: $\beta_1 = \cdots = \beta_p = 0$, TSS/σ^2 partitions into independent chi-squared random variables $(TSS - SSE)/\sigma^2$ and SSE/σ^2, with the degrees of freedom for TSS/σ^2 partitioning into

$$n - 1 = p + [n - (p + 1)].$$

For testing H_0, to eliminate the unknown parameter σ^2, we form the ratio of the independent chi-squared components,

$$\frac{(TSS - SSE)/\sigma^2}{SSE/\sigma^2} = \frac{(TSS - SSE)}{SSE}.$$

In the first expression, the numerator chi-squared has $df = p$ and the denominator chi-squared has $df = n - (p + 1)$. So that the numerator and denominator both have expected value 1 under H_0, we divide each by their df value. This yields the test statistic

$$F = \frac{(TSS - SSE)/p}{SSE/[n - (p + 1)]}. \tag{6.6}$$

The sampling distribution of this statistic is called[15] the *F distribution*. It has two degrees of freedom values, which are the df values of the constituent chi-squared components, $df_1 = p$ and $df_2 = n - (p + 1)$.

F distribution

For two independent chi-squared random variables U and V with df values df_1 and df_2, the ratio

$$F = \frac{U/df_1}{V/df_2}$$

has the *F* **distribution** with df_1 and df_2 degrees of freedom.

Like chi-squared random variables, an F random variable can take only nonnegative values. When H_0: $\beta_1 = \cdots = \beta_p = 0$ is true, F test statistic values tend to fluctuate around 1, which is the approximate mean of the distribution.[16] For that H_0, larger $(TSS - SSE)$ values yield larger F test statistic values and stronger evidence against H_0, so the P-value is the right-tail probability above the observed value. An equivalent statistic uses R^2, with larger R^2 values giving stronger evidence against H_0 (Exercise 6.52). It is also possible to derive this F test as a likelihood-ratio test (Section 6.4.6).

6.4.2   Example: Normal Linear Model for Mental Impairment

Table 6.2 shows some data from a study with a random sample of adults in Alachua County, Florida, that investigated the relationship between certain mental health indices and several explanatory variables.[17] The response variable is an index of mental impairment, which incorporates various dimensions of psychiatric symptoms, including aspects of anxiety and

---

[15] In honor of the British statistician, R. A. Fisher, who proposed a closely-related distribution in 1924
[16] The mean of the F distribution is $df_2/(df_2 - 2)$. This is close to 1 for large n, since $df_2 = n - (p + 1)$.
[17] The data file and example are based on a much larger survey conducted by Dr. Charles Holzer.

depression. This measure ranged from 17 to 41 for the 40 observations in the data file, with $\bar{y} = 27.30$ and $s_y = 5.46$. The explanatory variables are x_1 = life events score and x_2 = socioeconomic status (SES, denoted in the data file by ses). The life events score is a composite measure of both the number and severity of life events the subject experienced within the past three years, such as a death in the family or losing a job. It ranged from 3 to 97 in the sample, with $\bar{x}_1 = 44.42$ and $s_{x_1} = 22.62$. The SES score is a composite index based on occupation, income, and education. It ranged from 0 to 100, with $\bar{x}_2 = 56.60$ and $s_{x_2} = 25.28$.

TABLE 6.2 Part of Mental data file at the text website with y = mental impairment, x_1 = life events, and x_2 = socioeconomic status (ses).

impair	life	ses	impair	life	ses	impair	life	ses
17	46	84	26	50	40	30	44	53
19	39	97	26	48	52	31	35	38
20	27	24	26	45	61	31	95	29

The following R output shows results of viewing the data and fitting a linear model with the life events and SES explanatory variables as main effects:

```
> Mental <- read.table("http://stat4ds.rwth-aachen.de/data/Mental.dat", header=TRUE)
> Mental
    impair life ses
1      17   46  84
...
40     41   89  75
> attach(Mental)
> pairs(~impair + life + ses)    # scatterplot matrix for variable pairs (not shown)
> cor(cbind(impair, life, ses)) # correlation matrix
          impair     life      ses
impair   1.00000  0.37222  -0.39857 # corr(impair, life) > 0, corr(impair, ses) < 0
life     0.37222  1.00000   0.12334
ses     -0.39857  0.12334   1.00000
> summary(lm(impair ~ life + ses, data=Mental))
             Estimate  Std. Error  t value  Pr(>|t|)
(Intercept)  28.22981     2.17422   12.984  2.38e-15
life          0.10326     0.03250    3.177   0.00300
ses          -0.09748     0.02908   -3.351   0.00186
---
F-statistic: 9.495 on 2 and 37 DF,  p-value: 0.0004697
```

The F statistic for testing H_0: $\beta_1 = \beta_2 = 0$ is 9.495 with $df_1 = 2$ and $df_2 = 37$, for a P-value of 0.0005. The evidence is very strong that at least one explanatory variable is associated with mental impairment.

6.4.3 t Tests and Confidence Intervals for Individual Effects

A small P-value in testing H_0: $\beta_1 = \cdots = \beta_p = 0$ is not surprising, if we've chosen variables wisely, but it does justify evaluating effects of individual explanatory variables. We next present significance tests and confidence intervals.

Let SE_j denote the standard error of $\hat{\beta}_j$. The significance test of H_0: $\beta_j = 0$ has test statistic

$$T = \frac{\hat{\beta}_j - 0}{SE_j},$$

which is the number of standard errors that $\hat{\beta}_j$ falls from the H_0 value of 0. Its null t

distribution has $df = n - (p + 1)$. To form a confidence interval, we construct a pivotal quantity for a t test of H_0: $\beta_j = \beta_{j0}$ about potential values for β_j and then invert it. This more general test statistic is

$$T = \frac{\hat{\beta}_j - \beta_{j0}}{SE_j}.$$

The $100(1 - \alpha)\%$ confidence interval for β_j is the set of all β_{j0} values for which the test has P-value $> \alpha$, that is, for which $|t| < t_{\alpha/2, n-(p+1)}$. The 95% confidence interval for β_j is therefore

$$\hat{\beta}_j \pm t_{0.025, n-(p+1)}(se_j).$$

We illustrate by investigating the effect of life events for the study of mental impairment. The hypothesis that mental impairment is independent of life events, adjusting for SES, is H_0: $\beta_1 = 0$. From the R output in Section 6.4.2, the observed test statistic is $t = \hat{\beta}_1/se_1 = 0.103/0.032 = 3.18$, with $df = n - (p+1) = 40 - 3 = 37$. The P-value is 0.003, strong evidence of an effect in the population. A 95% confidence interval for β_1 is

$$\hat{\beta}_1 \pm t_{0.025, 37}(se_1) = 0.103 \pm 2.026(0.032), \quad \text{which is} \quad (0.04, 0.17).$$

Adjusting for SES, we are 95% confident that the change in mean mental impairment per one-unit increase in life events falls between 0.04 and 0.17, or equivalently, between 4 and 17 over a range of life-events values from 0 to 100. Since the confidence interval contains only positive numbers, we infer that the association between mental impairment and life events is positive, adjusting for SES.

6.4.4   Multicollinearity: Nearly Redundant Explanatory Variables

A global F test that provides strong evidence that at least one $\beta_j \neq 0$ does not imply that at least one of the t inferences reveals a statistically significant individual effect. In observational studies, the explanatory variables often "overlap" considerably. Each explanatory variable may be nearly redundant, in the sense that it can be predicted well using the others, and so the effects in the multiple regression model may not be statistically significant even if highly significant marginally.

Let R_j^2 denote R^2 from regressing x_j on the other explanatory variables from the model. Then, the estimated variance of $\hat{\beta}_j$ can be expressed as

$$\text{var}(\hat{\beta}_j) = (se_j)^2 = \frac{1}{1 - R_j^2}\left[\frac{s^2}{(n-1)s_{x_j}^2}\right],$$

where $s_{x_j}^2$ denotes the sample variance of x_j. The *variance inflation factor* $VIF_j = 1/(1-R_j^2)$ represents the multiplicative increase in $\text{var}(\hat{\beta}_j)$ due to x_j being correlated with the other explanatory variables. When the VIF values are large, standard errors are relatively large and statistics such as $t = \hat{\beta}_j/se_j$ may not be large even when the global F test is highly significant. This condition is called *multicollinearity*.

Statistical inference is not relevant with the Scottish hill races data, because the races are not a random sample of all such races. However, we can use the strong correlation between timeW and timeM for these data to illustrate multicollinearity, by predicting the climb in elevation of a race by using the women's record time and then using also the men's record time:

```
> summary(lm(climb ~ timeW, data=Races))
             Estimate  Std. Error  t value  Pr(>|t|)
(Intercept)  0.375956    0.082231    4.572  2.18e-05
```

```
timeW         0.005076    0.000664    7.645   1.15e-10
---
Multiple R-squared:  0.4696
> summary(lm(climb ~ timeW + timeM, data=Races))
              Estimate  Std. Error  t value  Pr(>|t|)
(Intercept)   0.345481    0.085152    4.057   0.000136
timeW         0.014440    0.007280    1.984   0.051528 .
timeM        -0.010752    0.008324   -1.292   0.201060
---
Multiple R-squared:  0.4829
F-statistic: 30.35 on 2 and 65 DF,  p-value: 4.912e-10
> cor(Races$timeM, Races$timeW)
[1] 0.9958732
```

The P-value of the timeW effect is essentially 0 when it is the sole explanatory variable. When we add timeM as a predictor, the *se* for the timeW effect increases from 0.0007 to 0.0073. Although the F statistic for testing H_0: $\beta_1 = \beta_2 = 0$ is very large (30.35) and has P-value essentially 0, the P-value of the timeW effect then exceeds 0.05, and the estimated timeM effect is surprisingly negative and has P-value 0.20. The dramatic change in the *se* for timeW and the lack of statistical significance for the conditional effects is due to the very high correlation (0.996) between timeW and timeM.

When multicollinearity occurs in multiple regression modeling, usually we can attain nearly as large an R^2 value in predicting Y with a reduced set of explanatory variables. In this example, for instance, R^2 is 0.48 using both predictors, but we obtain $R^2 = 0.47$ solely by using timeW. We run the risk of *overfitting* the data if we try to use several highly intercorrelated explanatory variables, one impact being that estimates of individual effects can have large standard errors and can be quite poor.

6.4.5 Confidence Interval for $E(Y)$ and Prediction Interval for Y

Besides estimating effects of explanatory variables, we can use a model to estimate $E(Y)$ at particular settings of the explanatory variables. At a fixed setting $(x_{01}, \ldots, x_{0p})$ for the p explanatory variables, $\hat{\mu}_0 = \hat{\beta}_0 + \hat{\beta}_1 x_{01} + \cdots + \hat{\beta}_p x_{0p}$ estimates $E(Y_0) = \beta_0 + \beta_1 x_{01} + \cdots + \beta_p x_{0p}$. We can construct a confidence interval for $E(Y_0)$, centered at $\hat{\mu}$. We illustrate this for the model $E(Y) = \beta_0 + \beta_1 x$, which we refer to as the **bivariate model** because it models two variables. At a particular value x_0 for x, the estimator $\hat{\mu}_0 = \hat{\beta}_0 + \hat{\beta}_1 x_0$ has

$$\text{var}(\hat{\mu}_0) = \sigma^2 \left[\frac{1}{n} + \frac{(x_0 - \bar{x})^2}{\sum_{i=1}^{n}(x_i - \bar{x})^2} \right]. \tag{6.7}$$

At $x_0 = \bar{x}$, $\hat{\mu}_0 = \bar{y}$ and $\text{var}(\hat{\mu}_0) = \text{var}(\bar{Y}) = \sigma^2/n$. The variance increases in a symmetric manner as x_0 moves away from $\bar{x}$. A $100(1 - \alpha)\%$ confidence interval for $E(Y_0)$ is

$$(\hat{\beta}_0 + \hat{\beta}_1 x_0) \pm t_{\alpha/2, n-(p+1)} s \sqrt{\frac{1}{n} + \frac{(x_0 - \bar{x})^2}{\sum_{i=1}^{n}(x_i - \bar{x})^2}}. \tag{6.8}$$

The formula with multiple predictors is beyond our scope but available in software with the fits of linear models.

We can also construct an interval that is designed to contain a future observation Y_f of Y. This is called a **prediction interval**. For the bivariate model, the prediction interval at $x = x_0$ is

$$(\hat{\beta}_0 + \hat{\beta}_1 x_0) \pm t_{\alpha/2, n-(p+1)} s \sqrt{1 + \frac{1}{n} + \frac{(x_0 - \bar{x})^2}{\sum_{i=1}^{n}(x_i - \bar{x})^2}}.$$

At $x_0 = \bar{x}$, $\hat{\mu}_0 = \bar{y}$, and the variance of the prediction error $(\hat{\mu}_0 - Y_f)$ is $\text{var}(\bar{Y} - Y_f) = \text{var}(\bar{Y}) + \text{var}(Y_f) = \sigma^2/n + \sigma^2$, so the variance for the prediction interval is $\sigma^2(1 + 1/n)$. The standard error is estimated by $s\sqrt{1 + 1/n}$ at $x_0 = \bar{x}$, and it increases as x_0 moves away from $\bar{x}$. The variability for the prediction interval adds[18] the inherent variability of an observation to the variability reflecting uncertainty because of estimating μ by $\hat{\mu}$. As n increases at any x_0, the variance of the prediction has σ^2 as its lower bound, whereas the variance (6.7) of the estimated mean $\hat{\mu}$ for the confidence interval for $E(Y_0)$ decreases toward 0. Even if we can estimate nearly perfectly the regression line, we are limited in how accurately we can predict any future observation.

We illustrate these intervals for the mental impairment study introduced in Section 6.4.2. At the mean values of 44.42 for life events and 56.60 for SES, the following R output displays a 95% confidence interval for the mean impairment and a 95% prediction interval for a future impairment value, first for the model containing only life events as predictor and then both life events and SES:

```
> newdata <- data.frame(life=44.42, ses=56.60) # mean values of life events and SES
> fit1 <- lm(impair ~ life, data=Mental)
> predict(fit1, newdata, interval="confidence")
       fit      lwr      upr # lwr = lower bound, upr = upper bound
1 27.29955 25.65644 28.94266 # 95% CI for E(Y) is (25.7, 28.9)
> predict(fit1, newdata, interval="predict")
       fit      lwr      upr # 95% prediction interval for Y is (16.8, 37.8)
1 27.29955 16.77851 37.82059
> fit2 <- lm(impair ~ life + ses, data=Mental)
> predict(fit2, newdata, interval="confidence")
       fit      lwr      upr
1 27.29948  25.83974  28.75923 # 95% CI for E(Y) is (25.8, 28.8)
> predict(fit2, newdata, interval="predict")
       fit      lwr      upr
1 27.29948  17.95257  36.64639 # 95% prediction interval for Y is (18.0, 36.6)
```

The intervals are slightly narrower when we use both predictors. Figure 6.8 portrays the confidence interval and the prediction interval as a function of x_0 for the model with solely life events as a predictor.

A caveat: We should have considerable faith in a model before forming prediction intervals. Even if we do not truly believe the model, which is usually the case, a confidence interval for $E(Y)$ at various predictor values is useful for describing the best fit of the model in the population of interest. If the model fails, however, either in its description of the population mean as a function of the explanatory variables or in its assumptions of normality with constant variance, then the actual percentage of many future observations that fall within the limits of 95% prediction intervals may be very different from 95%.

6.4.6   The F Test That All Effects Equal 0 is a Likelihood-Ratio Test *

We finish this section by showing that the global F test of $H_0: \beta_1 = \cdots = \beta_p = 0$ introduced in Section 6.4.1 is equivalent to the *likelihood-ratio test* of this hypothesis. For the normal linear model, the likelihood function is the product of the normal *pdf*'s for the n independent observations. As a function of $(\beta_0, \beta_1, \ldots, \beta_p)$ and σ, with $\mu_i = \sum_{j=0}^{p} \beta_j x_{ij}$ for $x_{i0} = 1$, the

---

[18]Section 4.8.4 showed a similar sum of two sources of variability in Bayesian prediction for a future observation.

*Sections with an asterisk are optional.

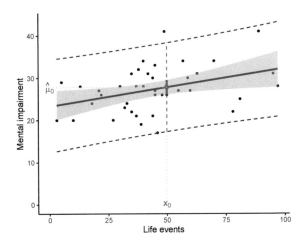

FIGURE 6.8 Portrayal of confidence intervals for the mean mental impairment, $E(Y_o) = \beta_0 + \beta_1 x_0$, and the wider prediction intervals for a future observation Y_f, at various x_0 values for life events. For $x_0 = 50$, these are marked by the green vertical linear segments (dashed for the prediction interval).

likelihood function is

$$\ell(\beta_0, \beta_1, \ldots, \beta_p, \sigma) = \prod_{i=1}^{n}\left(\frac{1}{\sigma\sqrt{2\pi}}\right)e^{-\left[\frac{1}{2\sigma^2}\left(y_i - \sum_{j=0}^{p}\beta_j x_{ij}\right)^2\right]}.$$

$$= \left(\frac{1}{\sigma\sqrt{2\pi}}\right)^n e^{\left[-\frac{1}{2\sigma^2}\sum_{i=1}^{n}(y_i - \sum_{j=0}^{p}\beta_j x_{ij})^2\right]}.$$

The log-likelihood function is

$$L(\beta_0, \beta_1, \ldots, \beta_p, \sigma) = -(n/2)\log(2\pi) - n\log(\sigma) - \frac{1}{2\sigma^2}\sum_{i=1}^{n}\left(y_i - \sum_{j=0}^{p}\beta_j x_{ij}\right)^2.$$

Differentiating with respect to $\{\beta_j\}$ and equating these partial derivatives to 0 yields the likelihood equations, and the least squares estimates are their solutions. Differentiating with respect to σ yields

$$\frac{\partial L}{\partial \sigma} = -\frac{n}{\sigma} + \frac{\sum_{i=1}^{n}(y_i - \sum_{j=0}^{p}\beta_j x_{ij})^2}{\sigma^3}.$$

Setting this equal to 0 and solving for σ^2 and substituting the least squares estimates for $\{\beta_j\}$, we obtain the ML estimator

$$\hat{\sigma}^2 = \frac{\sum_{i=1}^{n}(Y_i - \sum_{j=1}^{p}\hat{\beta}_j x_{ij})^2}{n} = \frac{SSE}{n}.$$

This estimator is the multiple $[n-(p+1)]/n$ of the unbiased estimator S^2. Substituting the ML estimates, the maximized likelihood function simplifies to

$$\ell(\hat{\beta}_0, \hat{\beta}_1, \ldots, \hat{\beta}_p, \hat{\sigma}) = \left(\frac{1}{\hat{\sigma}\sqrt{2\pi}}\right)^n e^{-n/2}.$$

The likelihood-ratio test (Section 5.7.1) uses the ratio of the maximized likelihood functions in general and under H_0. As just seen, the maximum depends on $\hat{\sigma}$ for the model but otherwise not on $\{\hat{\beta}_j\}$. For the null model, the fitted values are all $\bar{y}$, and the ML estimator of the variance is TSS/n. Denote the ML variance estimates by $\hat{\sigma}_0^2 = TSS/n$ for the null model and by $\hat{\sigma}_1^2 = SSE/n$ for the full model. The likelihood ratio is

$$\left[\left(\frac{1}{\hat{\sigma}_1\sqrt{2\pi}}\right)^n e^{-n/2}\right]\bigg/\left[\left(\frac{1}{\hat{\sigma}_0\sqrt{2\pi}}\right)^n e^{-n/2}\right] = \left(\frac{\hat{\sigma}_0^2}{\hat{\sigma}_1^2}\right)^{n/2}$$

$$= \left(\frac{TSS}{SSE}\right)^{n/2} = \left(1 + \frac{TSS - SSE}{SSE}\right)^{n/2} = \left(1 + \frac{p}{n-(p+1)}F\right)^{n/2}$$

for the F test statistic (6.6) stated above. A large value of the likelihood-ratio, and thus strong evidence against H_0, corresponds to a large value of the F statistic. The likelihood-ratio test leads to the same analysis as the F test.

6.5   Categorical Explanatory Variables in Linear Models

Linear models can contain categorical as well as quantitative explanatory variables. Categorical explanatory variables are also called **factors**. For a nominal-scale variable, the categories do not represent different magnitudes, so we cannot enter the variable in the linear predictor using a βx term with numerical values for the categories.

6.5.1   Indicator Variables for Categories

We represent the c categories of a categorical variable by $c - 1$ indicator variables, each one indicating whether the observation is in a particular category. For example, suppose racial-ethnic status has $c = 3$ categories, (Black, Hispanic, White). For subject i, let $x_{i1} = 1$ for Hispanic and 0 otherwise, and let $x_{i2} = 1$ for White and 0 otherwise. Then, x_{i1} indicates whether subject i is Hispanic, and x_{i2} indicates whether subject i is White. When $x_{i1} = x_{i2} = 0$, subject i is Black, so that category does not need a separate indicator. With racial-ethnic status as explanatory variable, the model has linear predictor

$E(Y_i) = \beta_0 + \beta_1 x_{i1} + \beta_2 x_{i2}$ for $x_{i1} =$ Hispanic (1=yes, 0=no), $x_{i2} =$ White (1=yes, 0=no).

For Blacks, since $x_{i1} = x_{i2} = 0$, $E(Y_i) = \beta_0$. For Hispanics, $x_{i1} = 1$ and $x_{i2} = 0$, so $E(Y_i) = \beta_0 + \beta_1$. For Whites, $x_{i1} = 0$ and $x_{i2} = 1$, so $E(Y_i) = \beta_0 + \beta_2$. The difference between $E(Y)$ values for two groups is β_1 for Hispanics and Blacks, β_2 for Whites and Blacks, and $\beta_1 - \beta_2$ for Hispanics and whites.

It is redundant to include an indicator for Blacks in the linear predictor. Suppose we did so, adding $x_{i3} = 1$ for Blacks and 0 otherwise, and expressing the model as $E(Y_i) = \beta_0 + \beta_1 x_{i1} + \beta_2 x_{i2} + \beta_3 x_{i3}$. Then $E(Y)$ is $\beta_0 + \beta_1$ for Hispanics, $\beta_0 + \beta_2$ for Whites, and $\beta_0 + \beta_3$ for Blacks. The model has 4 parameters for 3 means, so the parameters are not uniquely defined. For example, suppose $(\mu_1, \mu_2, \mu_3) = (30, 25, 40)$. An infinite number of $(\beta_0, \beta_1, \beta_2, \beta_3)$ values yield these means, such as $(0, 30, 25, 40)$, $(30, 0, -5, 10)$, and $(40, -10, -15, 0)$. We cannot estimate the parameters uniquely, no matter how much data we have.

Identifiability

In a linear model, $\{\beta_j\}$ are **identifiable** if whenever $\{\beta_j\}$ take different values, the set of $E(Y)$ values generated by the model also differs.

Equivalently, if you know all the means satisfying a particular linear model, then those means determine $\{\beta_j\}$, because only one set of parameter values can generate them through the linear model. The parameters are not identifiable when we use 4 of them to describe 3 means.

To obtain identifiability in a model with a c-category factor, we exclude the parameter for one category, called the *reference* category. Some software, such as R, does this using the first-category-reference parameterization, constructing indicators for categories $2, \ldots, c$. An observation is in category 1 when all those indicators equal 0, and the parameter coefficients provide *contrasts*[19]. with category 1. Some software, such as SAS, does this using the last-category-reference parameterization, constructing indicators for categories $1, \ldots, c-1$. The parameter coefficients provide contrasts with category c. All possible choices of $c-1$ indicators for c categories are equivalent, having the same model fit and the same results for inferences about the population means. The interpretations of $\{\beta_j\}$ depend on the choice of reference category, but the differences $\beta_j - \beta_k$ used to compare groups are identical for each possible choice.[20]

6.5.2 Example: Comparing Mean Incomes of Racial-Ethnic Groups

For a sample of adult Americans aged over 25, Table 6.3 shows some data on y = annual income and x = number of years of education, for three racial-ethnic groups. The complete data file of $n = 80$ observations exhibit patterns of a much larger sample taken by the U.S. Bureau of the Census. We first model income in terms of racial-ethnic group, and later we add education to the model.

TABLE 6.3 Observations on y = annual income (thousands of dollars) and x = number of years of education for three racial-ethnic groups (Black, Hispanic, White).

Black		Hispanic		White	
y	x	y	x	y	x
16	10	32	16	30	14
18	7	16	11	48	14
26	9	20	10	40	7

Note: The complete data are in the **Income** data file at the book's website.

Here is some R output from fitting the linear model with indicator variables for the racial-ethnic groups:

```
> Income <- read.table("http://stat4ds.rwth-aachen.de/data/Income.dat", header=TRUE)
> Income
     income education  race
1       16         10     B
...
80      56         20     W
> summary(lm(income ~ race, data=Income))
            Estimate  Std. Error  t value  Pr(>|t|)
(Intercept)   27.750       4.968    5.586  3.37e-07
raceH          3.250       7.273    0.447    0.6562
raceW         14.730       5.708    2.581    0.0118
---
F-statistic: 4.244 on 2 and 77 DF,  p-value: 0.01784
```

---

[19]Technically, a *contrast* is a linear combination $\sum_j a_j \mu_j$ with $\sum_j a_j = 0$. Here, $\beta_j = \mu_j - \mu_1$ is the contrast with $a_j = 1$, $a_1 = -1$, and $a_k = 0$ for $k \neq 1, j$

[20]Yet another choice available with most software is to use c parameters but with the constraint that $\sum_j \beta_j = 0$, in which case β_k is the difference between μ_k and the average of $\{\mu_j\}$.

The `lm` function automatically treats race as a factor, because that variable has character rather than numerical values in the data file. If the data file had the labels (1, 2, 3) for the categories, we should replace `race` by `factor(race)` in the model statement. Since R uses a first-category-reference parameterization, the first race category (alphabetically) of Blacks does not have an indicator, and the output shows indicators `raceH` for Hispanics and `raceW` for Whites. We denote these by H and W. The fit of the linear model is

$$\hat{\mu} = 27.75 + 3.25H + 14.73W.$$

The estimated differences of means are 3.25 thousand dollars between Hispanics and Blacks, 14.73 thousand dollars between Whites and Blacks, and $14.73 - 3.25 = 11.48$ thousand dollars between Whites and Hispanics.

The R output also shows an F statistic. This refers to the global F test introduced in Section 6.4.1. In this case, it is a test of H_0: $\beta_H = \beta_W = 0$ for the model $E(Y) = \beta_0 + \beta_1 H + \beta_2 W$. Since $\beta_1 = \mu_H - \mu_B$ and $\beta_2 = \mu_W - \mu_B$, this is equivalently a test of equality of the three population means. Here $F = 4.24$ has a P-value of 0.018. We next give more details of the significance test for comparing several population means.

6.5.3 Analysis of Variance (ANOVA): An F Test Comparing Several Means

Many research studies have the central goal of comparing response distributions for different groups. The previous two chapters presented inference methods for comparing *two* means. More general analyses to compare *several* population means are easily formulated in the context of linear models with indicator variables. We regard the groups as categories of a factor. For c groups of independent observations, the corresponding linear model has $c - 1$ indicator variables. For the test of H_0: $\mu_1 = \cdots = \mu_c$, in the linear model H_0 corresponds to H_0: $\beta_1 = \cdots = \beta_{c-1} = 0$ for the parameters that are the coefficients of the indicator variables. The global F test introduced in Section 6.4.1 yields a test of H_0.

Let y_{ij} denote response observation i in group j, for $j = 1, \ldots, c$ and $i = 1, \ldots, n_j$. For this linear model with indicator explanatory variables, the total sum of squares is a sum over groups and over observations within a group,

$$TSS = \sum_{j=1}^{c} \sum_{i=1}^{n_j} (y_{ij} - \overline{y})^2,$$

where $\overline{y}$ is the sample mean of the overall sample of $n = (n_1 + \cdots + n_c)$ observations. The fitted value in group j is the sample mean $\overline{y}_j$ of the n_j observations in group j, so the sum of squares decomposition (6.5) of TSS into regression and error sums of squares becomes

$$TSS = \sum_{j=1}^{c} n_j (\overline{y}_j - \overline{y})^2 + \sum_{j=1}^{c} \sum_{i=1}^{n_j} (y_{ij} - \overline{y}_j)^2.$$

The second term, which is SSE, summarizes variability *within* the c groups. It is called a *within-groups* sums of squares. Since it refers to a linear model with c parameters, its residual *df* equal $n - c$. The first term describes variability among the c sample means. It is a *between-groups* sum of squares. It is the amount by which SSE increases when we take out the $c-1$ indicator variables and use the null model by which all c population means are identical. The within-groups sum of squares divided by its *df* value of $n - c$ is the *residual mean square* for the linear model (Section 6.3), which estimates the error variance of the model. The between-groups sum of squares divided by its degrees of freedom of $c - 1$ is a *groups mean square.* Under H_0, the sums of squares are independent chi-squared random variables, so the ratio of the mean squares

$$F = \frac{\text{Groups mean square}}{\text{Residual mean square}} = \frac{\sum_{j=1}^{c} n_j (\overline{Y}_j - \overline{Y})^2 / (c-1)}{\sum_{j=1}^{c} \sum_{i=1}^{n_j} (Y_{ij} - \overline{Y}_j)^2 / (n-c)}$$

is a test statistic having an F distribution for testing equality of the c population means, with $df_1 = c - 1$ and $df_2 = n - c$. Its sample value tends to be larger when $\{\overline{y}_j\}$ vary more.

This significance test is a special case of what is called **analysis of variance** (**ANOVA**).[21] The name refers to the fact that, although the main purpose of the test is to compare means, the information we need to do so depends on the two types of variability—between-groups and within-groups. The F distribution naturally arises as a sampling distribution for ratios of sample variances (Exercise 6.54). In this case, the residual mean square of the F statistic (based on SSE) is the unbiased estimator of the error variance σ^2 for the linear model. The numerator is an alternative estimator of σ^2 that tends to be too large when H_0 is false, so the F ratio then tends to exceed 1.

The data structure $\{y_{ij}, \ i = 1, \ldots, n_j, \ j = 1, \ldots, c\}$ for observing responses in c categories of a factor is called the **one-way layout**. An example is a comparison of mean incomes by categories of racial-ethnic status. Groups that are the cross classification of *two* factors form a *two-way layout*, such as in evaluating how mean income varies by racial-ethnic status and gender, and so forth for additional factors. In experimental settings, one can evaluate two or more factors with a single experiment using linear models with multiple factors. This is more efficient than designing a separate experiment for each factor and permits investigating interaction between factors in their effects on the response.

For the example in Section 6.5.2 comparing mean incomes of three racial-ethnic groups, The F test of H_0: $\mu_B = \mu_H = \mu_W$ had test statistic value $F = 4.24$ with $df_1 = 2$ and $df_2 = 77$ and a P-value of 0.018. Here is corresponding ANOVA output, which shows the groups mean square and residual mean square that have ratio that is the F statistic:

```
> anova(lm(income ~ race, data=Income)) # analysis of variance comparing mean
Analysis of Variance Table               # income by group, for group = race
Response: income
          Df   Sum Sq  Mean Sq  F value  Pr(>F) # F = 4.24 = ratio of mean squares
race       2   3352.5  1676.23  4.2444   0.01784 # groups mean square = 1676.23
Residuals 77  30409.5   394.93                   # residual mean square = 394.93
```

The reported residual mean square of 394.93 is the error variance estimate for the linear model. This is the square of the "residual standard error" of 19.87 reported in the earlier R output for the linear model. The large F ratio of the mean squares and the P-value of 0.018 suggests that at least two population means differ. Follow-up confidence intervals help us determine which pairs differ and by how much.

6.5.4 Multiple Comparisons of Means: Bonferroni and Tukey Methods

Using confidence intervals to evaluate differences between means for all $c(c-1)/2$ pairs of c groups can entail many inferences. Even if each inference has a small error probability, unless c is small, the probability may be substantial that *at least one* inference is in error. We can construct the inferences so that the error probability applies to the entire *family* of inferences rather than to each individual one. A simple way[22] to conduct multiple inferences while controlling the overall error rate is based on an inequality:

---

[21] Proposed by the British statistician R. A. Fisher in 1925.
[22] Shown by the British mathematician George Boole in 1854.

Boole's inequality: For t events $E_1, E_2, \ldots, E_t$ in a sample space, the probability $P(E_1 \cup E_2 \cup \cdots \cup E_t)$ that at least one occurs satisfies

$$P(E_1 \cup E_2 \cup \cdots \cup E_t) \leq P(E_1) + P(E_2) + \cdots + P(E_t).$$

A Venn diagram illustrates the simple proof of this inequality (Exercise 6.59).

In the context of multiple confidence intervals, let E_j (for $j = 1, \ldots, t$) denote the event that interval j is in error, not containing the relevant parameter value. If each confidence interval has error probability α/t and confidence coefficient $(1 - \alpha/t)$, then the (a priori) probability that at least one of the t intervals is in error is bounded above by $t(\alpha/t) = \alpha$. So, the family-wise confidence coefficient for the set of the t intervals is at least $1 - \alpha$. If we compare each pair of $c = 5$ means with confidence level 99% for each of the 10 pairwise comparisons, then the overall confidence level is at least 90% (i.e., here $\alpha = 0.10$ and $t = 10$). This method for constructing simultaneous confidence intervals is called[23] the **Bonferroni method**.

For the modeling in Section 6.5.2 of income for three racial-ethnic groups, for a family-wise error probability of $\alpha = 0.05$, we use $0.05/3$ as the error probability for each of the three intervals comparing means, so each one has confidence level $1 - 0.05/3 = 0.9833$. Each interval can use the t distribution, with df equal to the total sample size minus the number of parameters, here $df = 80 - 3 = 77$. The t quantile score with right-tail probability $(0.05/3)/2$ and $df = 77$ is 2.447. For comparing Whites and Blacks, the R output in Section 6.5.2 for the linear model, shown again next, reports that the estimated difference of 14.73 has a standard error of 5.708, so the confidence interval is $14.73 \pm 2.447(5.708)$, which is $(0.76, 28.70)$:

```
> Income <- read.table("http://stat4ds.rwth-aachen.de/data/Income.dat", header=TRUE)
> fit <- lm(income ~ race, data=Income)
> summary(fit)
            Estimate  Std. Error  t value  Pr(>|t|)
(Intercept)   27.750       4.968    5.586  3.37e-07
raceH          3.250       7.273    0.447    0.6562
raceW         14.730       5.708    2.581    0.0118
> confint(fit, level = 1 - 0.05/3) # confidence level 0.9833 instead of 0.95
                0.833 %  99.167 %
raceH       -14.5492476  21.04925 # Bonferroni CI comparing H and B
raceW         0.7601417  28.69986 # Bonferroni CI comparing W and B
```

We infer that the population mean is higher for Whites, but with the small sample sizes (16 Blacks and 50 Whites), the confidence interval is wide. The confidence intervals for the other two comparisons both contain 0. The original output did not show the result comparing H and W, but we can obtain this by re-fitting the model with one of them as the reference category:

```
> race2 <- factor(Income$race, levels=c("H","B","W")) # re-code so H is reference
> confint(lm(income ~ race2, data=Income), level = 1 - 0.05/3)
               0.833 %  99.167 %
race2B      -21.049248  14.54925 # Bonferroni CI comparing B and H
race2W       -3.226387  26.18639 # Bonferroni CI comparing W and H
```

An advantage of the Bonferroni method is its generality. It applies for any probability-based inferences for any distribution, not just confidence intervals for a normal linear model. A disadvantage is that the method is *conservative*: If we want overall 95% confidence (say), the method ensures that the actual confidence level is *at least* 0.95. As a consequence, the

---

[23]It relies on Boole's inequality but cites the Italian probabilist/mathematician Carlo Bonferroni, who in 1936 generalized Boole's inequality in various ways and applied them to statistical matters.

intervals are wider than ones that would produce *exactly* or *approximately* that confidence level. The **Tukey multiple comparison method**[24] is designed for the special case of comparing means from normal distributions. It is exact when sample sizes are equal and only slightly conservative otherwise. With equal $\{n_j = n\}$, the Tukey method is based on the sampling distribution, called the *studentized range distribution*, of the maximum standardized difference between pairs of sample means, $(\bar{y}_{max} - \bar{y}_{min})/\sqrt{2s^2/n}$. Here are the results we get using his method:

```
> fit.aov <- aov(income ~ race, data=Income) # analysis of variance function
> TukeyHSD(fit.aov, conf.level=0.95)
  Tukey multiple comparisons of means, 95% family-wise confidence level
$race
       diff        lwr      upr
H-B    3.25  -14.130754  20.63075
W-B   14.73    1.088600  28.37140 # compare to Bonferroni CI (0.76, 28.70)
W-H   11.48   -2.880612  25.84061
```

The intervals are slightly shorter than obtained with the Bonferroni method.

6.5.5 Models with Both Categorical and Quantitative Explanatory Variables

Linear models can contain both quantitative and categorical explanatory variables. For example, suppose observation i measures an individual's annual income y_i, racial-ethnic status with indicators H_i for Hispanics and W_i for Whites, and a quantitative measure x_i of the number of years of education. The linear model with these variables as main effects is

$$E(Y_i) = \beta_0 + \beta_1 H_i + \beta_2 W_i + \beta_3 x_i.$$

For the effect of education, this implies the relation $E(Y_i) = (\beta_0 + \beta_1) + \beta_3 x_i$ for Hispanics, $E(Y_i) = (\beta_0 + \beta_2) + \beta_3 x_i$ for Whites, and $E(Y_i) = \beta_0 + \beta_3 x_i$ for Blacks. For the Income data file introduced in Section 6.5.2, here is R output:

```
> fit2 <- lm(income ~ race + education, data=Income)
> summary(fit2)
              Estimate  Std. Error  t value  Pr(>|t|)
(Intercept)   -26.5379      8.5124   -3.118   0.00257
raceH           5.9407      5.6702    1.048   0.29809
raceW          10.8744      4.4730    2.431   0.01741
education       4.4317      0.6191    7.158   4.42e-10
---
F-statistic: 21.75 on 3 and 76 DF,  p-value: 2.853e-10
```

The first panel in Figure 6.9 is a scatterplot showing the prediction equations for the three groups. The lines relating estimated mean income to education for the three groups are parallel, because they each have the same slope, 4.43, for the effect of education. The parallelism reflects the lack of interaction terms for this model. The coefficient 5.941 of the indicator for Hispanics represents the difference ($5,941) between the estimated annual mean income for Hispanics and for Blacks, adjusting for education. Likewise, $10,874 is the difference between the estimated annual mean income for Whites and for Blacks, adjusting for education. The second panel in Figure 6.9 is a scatterplot showing the prediction equations for a more complex model introduced in Section 6.5.7 that allows interaction by permitting the three groups to have different slopes.

---

[24] Proposed in 1953 by John Tukey, best known for methods of exploratory data analysis

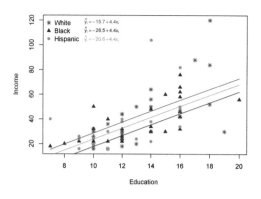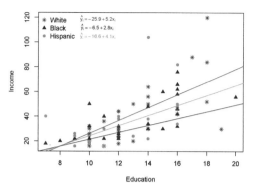

FIGURE 6.9 Plot of prediction equations for linear model with a quantitative explanatory variable and a 3-category factor: For the three categories, the relation between the quantitative variables has the same slope for the *main effects model* in the first figure but different slopes for the *interaction model* in the second figure.

6.5.6 Comparing Two Nested Normal Linear Models

In statistical model-building, we often need to compare a model to a more complex one that has additional parameters or to a simpler one that eliminates some parameters. An example is analyzing whether a model needs a set of interaction terms. Denote the simpler model by M_0 and the more complex model by M_1. The model M_0 is said to be **nested** in model M_1. Denote the numbers of explanatory variables by p_0 for M_0 and by p_1 for M_1. A relevant inference for comparing the models is a significance test of

$$H_0 : M_0 \quad \text{against} \quad H_a : M_1,$$

that is, a test that the $p_1 - p_0$ parameters in M_1 but not M_0 are all 0.

Denote the sum of squared residuals for the two models by SSE_0 and SSE_1. As explanatory variables are added to a model, SSE is necessarily nonincreasing, and larger values for $(SSE_0 - SSE_1)$ give more evidence that M_1 is better than M_0. A derivation similar to that in Section 6.4.1 for the global F test yields the test statistic

$$F = \frac{(SSE_0 - SSE_1)/(p_1 - p_0)}{SSE_1/[n - (p_1 + 1)]}. \tag{6.9}$$

When H_0 is true, its sampling distribution is the F distribution with $df_1 = p_1 - p_0$ and $df_2 = n - (p_1 + 1)$. The P-value is the right-tail probability above the observed F value. The test can be derived as a likelihood-ratio test.

We illustrate this F test for comparing nested normal linear models with the example just mentioned of modeling annual income using education and racial-ethnic status, as

$$E(Y_i) = \beta_0 + \beta_1 H_i + \beta_2 W_i + \beta_3 x_i.$$

To test that racial-ethnic status has no effect on annual income, adjusting for education, we test $H_0: \beta_1 = \beta_2 = 0$. The next R output shows that $F = 3.06$ has a P-value of 0.053.

```
> fit2 <- lm(income ~ race + education, data=Income)
> library(car)
> Anova(fit2) # tests effects of explanatory variables
```

```
Response: y
            Sum Sq  Df  F value    Pr(>F)
race        1460.6   2   3.0556   0.05292    # t = 7.158 for testing education effect
education  12245.2   1  51.2346  4.422e-10   # is square root of F = 51.2346
```

To test that education has no effect on annual income, adjusting for racial-ethnic status, we test H_0: $\beta_3 = 0$. The R output shows that $F = 51.23$, which has a P-value essentially 0. In this case, H_0 has only one parameter, so we could also use the corresponding t test with test statistic $T = \hat{\beta}_3/SE_3$. From the previous R output, this has observed value $t = 7.16$. In fact, this statistic is the signed square root of the F statistic. This relates to the following result.

T^2 has the F distribution

The square of a statistic T that has a a t distribution has an F distribution with $df_1 = 1$ and df_2 equal to the df for the t distribution.

In this case, the square of $t = 7.16$ is $F = 51.23$.

Another examples of the F test for comparing nested models is the global F test of H_0: $\beta_1 = \cdots = \beta_p = 0$. In this special case, M_0 is the null model with $p_0 = 0$ explanatory variables and M_1 is the full model having p parameters. Then, $(SSE_0 - SSE_1) = (TSS - SSE)$ and $df_1 = p_1 - p_0 = p$.

6.5.7 Interaction with Categorical and Quantitative Explanatory Variables

In modeling income using education and racial-ethnic group, if the effect of education is not the same for each racial-ethnic group, then interaction occurs between them. We allow interaction by taking the cross-product of each categorical indicator with the quantitative variable:

```
> fit3 <- lm(income ~ race + education + race:education, data=Income)
> summary(fit3)
                 Estimate  Std. Error  t value  Pr(>|t|)
(Intercept)       -6.536      14.980    -0.436   0.6639
raceH            -10.069      26.527    -0.380   0.7053
raceW            -19.333      18.293    -1.057   0.2940
education          2.799       1.182     2.368   0.0205
raceH:education    1.290       2.193     0.588   0.5582
raceW:education    2.411       1.418     1.700   0.0933 .
---
F-statistic:  13.8 on 5 and 74 DF,  p-value: 1.618e-09

> Anova(fit3) # tests individual effects of explanatory variables
Response: y    # with Anova function in car package
                Sum Sq  Df  F value    Pr(>F)
race            1460.6   2    3.093   0.05128 .
education      12245.2   1   51.862  4.131e-10
race:education   691 8   2    1.465   0.23769
```

Using the model parameter estimates, we can recover prediction equations relating income to education for each of the three racial-ethnic groups. The estimated slopes for the education effect are $2.80 + 1.29 = 3.09$ for Hispanics, $2.80 + 2.41 = 5.21$ for Whites, and 2.80 for Blacks. The F test shown for the interaction term is the test comparing the full model to the one with only the main effects. It shows that the evidence of interaction is not strong (P-value $= 0.24$), so the simpler model containing only the main effects is adequate.

For testing explanatory variable effects, the default analysis with the `Anova` function in the `car` package in R reports *Type II sums of squares*. For the main effects, these are the same as the variability explained partially by each (adjusting for the others) in the model without the interaction term. This is sensible, since the main effect terms are relevant on their own only when the model does not contain interaction terms. For the interaction term, the Type II sum of squares is the variability explained *after* the main effects are already in the model, since interaction terms are relevant only when a model also has main effects. These are all *partial sum of squares*, the ones for race and education being for the main-effects model and the one for the interaction term being for the interaction model.

Models with several quantitative and categorical explanatory variables can potentially have interaction terms for any pair of the variables. An interaction term for two categorical factors has cross-products of indicators from the separate variables.

6.6   Bayesian Inference for Normal Linear Models

Bayesian methods for normal linear models can make probability statements directly about the model parameters, instead of probability statements only about data under various conditions for the parameters. This section presents Bayesian analogs of classical inference for the normal linear model.

6.6.1   Prior and Posterior Distributions for Normal Linear Models

The normal linear model states that $\{Y_i\}$ are independent and for $i = 1, \ldots, n$, Y_i has a $N(\mu_i, \sigma^2)$ distribution with $\mu_i = \sum_{j=0}^{p} \beta_j x_{ij}$ (for $x_{i0} = 1$ as the coefficient of β_0). The Bayesian approach adds prior distributions for $\{\beta_j\}$ to this structure. It is common to treat them as independent $N(\lambda, \tau^2)$ random variables, usually with $\lambda = 0$. When τ is large, the posterior distribution mainly reflects the likelihood function. When τ is not large, to have the effects be comparable in their prior magnitude, we can use standardized versions of the explanatory variables. Section 6.7.6 shows that the posterior mean estimate $\tilde{\beta}_j$ of β_j is a weighted average of the least squares estimate $\hat{\beta}_j$ and the prior mean. The weight that $\hat{\beta}_j$ receives increases as n increases and as τ increases.

The error variance σ^2 requires its own prior distribution. With a highly disperse inverse gamma distribution for it and very large τ in the prior distributions for $\{\beta_j\}$. the posterior results closely resemble classical inference with the t distribution. The marginal posterior distribution of β_j around $\hat{\beta}_j$ has the same shape as the sampling distribution of $\hat{\beta}_j$ around β_j. A posterior interval for β_j is then nearly identical to the classical t confidence interval. The Bayesian approach, however, can assert that the probability is 0.95 that β_j is in the 95% posterior interval. By contrast, a classical confidence level refers to a probability before observing data (i.e., with the observations, not the parameters, as random variables), and consequently to long-run performance of the classical method for constructing confidence intervals.

6.6.2   Example: Bayesian Linear Model for Mental Impairment

For the study of mental impairment (Section 6.4.2), we next show a Bayesian analysis that gives essentially the same results as the least squares fit of the linear model with main effects of life events and SES. We use the `MCMCregress` function in the `MCMCpack` package in R, selecting normal priors for $\{\beta_j\}$ with mean 0 and precision $1/\tau^2 = 10^{-10}$, for which the standard deviation $\tau = 100{,}000$. The function uses an inverse gamma prior distribution for σ^2 (Section 4.8.1), specified by parameters c_0 and d_0 that relate to shape and scale. The improper prior $f(\sigma^2) \propto 1/\sigma^2$ is approximated by taking tiny values for c_0 and d_0. Here are results:

```
Mental <- read.table("http://stat4ds.rwth-aachen.de/data/Mental.dat", header=TRUE)
> summary(lm(impair ~ life + ses, data=Mental)) # least squares
               Estimate   Std. Error   t value   Pr(>|t|)
(Intercept)    28.2298      2.1742      12.984    2.38e-15
life            0.1033      0.0325       3.177    0.00300 # one-tail 0.0015
ses            -0.0975      0.0291      -3.351    0.00186 # one-tail 0.0009
---

> library(MCMCpack)
> fit.bayes <- MCMCregress(impair ~ life + ses, mcmc=5000000,
+            b0=0, B0=10^(-10), c0=10^(-10), d0=10^(-10), data=Mental)
> summary(fit.bayes) # normal priors with means = b0, variances = 1/B0
1. Empirical mean and standard deviation for each variable
              Mean      SD      Naive SE    Time-series SE
(Intercept) 28.2280   2.2354   9.997e-04       1.000e-03
life         0.1033   0.0334   1.495e-05       1.495e-05
ses         -0.0975   0.0299   1.338e-05       1.338e-05
sigma2      21.9461   5.4044   2.417e-03       2.613e-03
2. Quantiles for each variable: # quantiles of posterior distributions
               2.5%      25%       50%       75%      97.5%
(Intercept) 23.8252   26.7448   28.2278   29.7095   32.6336
life         0.0374    0.0811    0.1033    0.1254    0.1692
ses         -0.1564   -0.1173   -0.0975   -0.0777   -0.0385

> mean(fit.bayes[,2] <= 0); mean(fit.bayes[,3] >= 0)
[1] 0.001507  # posterior prob(2nd parameter <= 0) for life events effect
[1] 0.000927  # posterior prob(3rd parameter >= 0) for SES effect
```

The posterior means reported are approximations for the actual values and have greater accuracy as the number of Markov Chain Monte Carlo (MCMC) iterations increases. The code shown uses a chain of length 5,000,000, and the approximations are good. The naive standard error (SE) refers to the standard deviation of the simulation error if the observations in the Markov chain were independent, and the time series SE accounts for the positive correlation that typically occurs for successive values in the chain. For instance, the reported posterior mean of 0.1033 for life events has a simulation SE of 0.000015, so it is safe to report it as 0.1033.

The Bayesian approach can also generate posterior probabilities, such as $P(\beta_j \leq 0)$ as an analog of a one-sided P-value that is simpler to interpret. The R analysis, by finding the indicator for whether each of the 5,000,000 elements in the Markov chain for generating the posterior distribution of β_1 is less than 0 and then finding their mean, reports $P(\beta_1 \leq 0) = 0.0015$; that is, 0 is the 0.0015 quantile of the marginal posterior distribution of β_1. This is the same as the classical one-sided P-value for testing H_0: $\beta_1 = 0$ (and implicitly H_0: $\beta_1 \leq 0$) against H_a: $\beta_1 > 0$. Similarly, the posterior $P(\beta_2 \geq 0) = 0.0009$ is also the classical P-value for testing H_0: $\beta_2 = 0$ (and implicitly H_0: $\beta_2 \geq 0$) against H_a: $\beta_2 < 0$.

6.6.3 Bayesian Approach to the Normal One-Way Layout

The Bayesian results for a mean and for comparing two means (Section 4.8.1) extend directly to a set of means for several groups. As in ordinary ANOVA for the one-way layout, we assume that response Y_{ij} for subject i in group j has a $N(\mu_j, \sigma^2)$ distribution. We treat observerations as independent within groups and between groups and use $N(\lambda, \tau^2)$ prior distributions for $\{\mu_j\}$. The $N(\mu_j, \sigma^2)$ distribution describes the *within-groups* variability, and the $N(\lambda, \tau^2)$ distribution describes the *between-groups* variability.

With this structure and known σ^2, the posterior mean of μ_j is

$$\tilde{\mu}_j = w\bar{y}_j + (1-w)\lambda \quad \text{with} \quad w = \tau^2/[\tau^2 + (\sigma^2/n_j)],$$

a weighted average of $\bar{y}_j$ and the prior mean. The Bayesian estimator shrinks the least squares estimate $\bar{y}_j$ toward λ. Less shrinkage occurs as n_j increases, for fixed τ, and as τ increases, for fixed n_j. With an improper or highly disperse prior also for σ^2, the weighted average expression applies approximately with s^2 substituting for σ^2 in the weight.

6.7   Matrix Formulation of Linear Models *

This final section of the chapter assumes some familiarity with matrix algebra. For the normal linear model, we show expressions for least squares and Bayesian estimates and their standard errors.

6.7.1   The Model Matrix

We list the n observations on the response variable in a vector $y = (y_1,\ldots,y_n)^T$. The superscript ^{T} on a vector or matrix denotes the transpose, so y is a $n \times 1$ column vector. A $n \times 1$ vector μ contains $E(Y_i)$ for $i = 1,2,\ldots,n$. A $(p+1) \times 1$ vector $\beta = (\beta_0, \beta_1, \beta_2, \ldots, \beta_p)^T$ contains the linear model parameters. A $n \times (p+1)$ **model matrix** X contains values of the explanatory variables, one row for each subject, as in a data file. The value x_{ij} of explanatory variable j for subject i occurs in row i and column j of X. A quantitative explanatory variable has a single column in X, showing its n values. A categorical factor with c categories requires $c-1$ columns, one for each indicator variable (Section 6.5.1). The first column of the model matrix consists of a vector of 1 values, which are the coefficients of the intercept parameter β_0.

The n equations $\mu_i = E(Y_i) = \sum_j \beta_j x_{ij}$ for $i = 1,\ldots,n$ that specify the linear model for the n subjects have the matrix form

$$\mu = X\beta.$$

We illustrate for $n = 6$ observations and two explanatory variables, the first of which (x_1) is quantitative and the second of which is a factor with three categories, when observations 1 and 2 are from category 1, 3 and 4 are from category 2, and 5 and 6 are from category 3. With a first-category reference category, such as R uses, the linear model is

$$\begin{pmatrix} \mu_1 \\ \mu_2 \\ \mu_3 \\ \mu_4 \\ \mu_5 \\ \mu_6 \end{pmatrix} = \begin{pmatrix} 1 & x_{11} & 0 & 0 \\ 1 & x_{21} & 0 & 0 \\ 1 & x_{31} & 1 & 0 \\ 1 & x_{41} & 1 & 0 \\ 1 & x_{51} & 0 & 1 \\ 1 & x_{61} & 0 & 1 \end{pmatrix} \begin{pmatrix} \beta_0 \\ \beta_1 \\ \beta_2 \\ \beta_3 \end{pmatrix}.$$

For example, for observation 3, taking the third row of X times the parameter vector yields

$$\mu_3 = 1(\beta_0) + x_{31}(\beta_1) + 1(\beta_2) + 0(\beta_3) = \beta_0 + \beta_1 x_{31} + \beta_2.$$

*Sections with an asterisk are optional.

6.7.2 Least Squares Estimates and Standard Errors

To estimate β using least squares, Section 6.2.6 showed that minimizing $\sum_i (y_i - \hat{\mu}_i)^2$ with $\hat{\mu}_i = \sum_j \hat{\beta}_j x_{ij}$ corresponds to solving $(p+1)$ linear equations for the $(p+1)$ elements of $\hat{\beta}$,

$$\sum_{i=1}^{n} x_{ij} y_i = \sum_{i=1}^{n} x_{ij} \hat{\mu}_i. \quad j = 0, 1, \ldots, p. \tag{6.10}$$

In matrix form, the equations are $\boldsymbol{X}^T \boldsymbol{y} = \boldsymbol{X}^T \hat{\boldsymbol{\mu}}$, and since $\hat{\boldsymbol{\mu}} = \boldsymbol{X}\hat{\beta}$, we can express them in terms of $\hat{\beta}$ as

$$\boldsymbol{X}^T \boldsymbol{y} = \boldsymbol{X}^T \boldsymbol{X}\hat{\beta}. \tag{6.11}$$

Here, $\boldsymbol{X}^T \boldsymbol{y}$ takes the inner product of each row of $\boldsymbol{X}^T$ (i.e., each column of $\boldsymbol{X}$) with the response-data vector. When the square matrix $(\boldsymbol{X}^T \boldsymbol{X})$ is nonsingular,

$$\hat{\beta} = (\boldsymbol{X}^T \boldsymbol{X})^{-1} \boldsymbol{X}^T \boldsymbol{y}. \tag{6.12}$$

The least squares estimate is a linear function of the response observations $\boldsymbol{y}$.

For the normal linear model and a random vector response $\boldsymbol{Y}$, since the $\hat{\beta}$ estimator is a linear function of $\boldsymbol{Y}$, $\hat{\beta}$ has a multivariate normal distribution.[25] For a matrix of constants $\boldsymbol{A}$, generalizing the univariate formula, $E(aY) = aE(Y)$,

$$E(\boldsymbol{AY}) = \boldsymbol{A}E(\boldsymbol{Y}).$$

Letting $\boldsymbol{I}$ denote an *identity matrix* that has 1 for each main-diagonal element and 0 otherwise, the mean of the least squares estimator is

$$E(\hat{\beta}) = E[(\boldsymbol{X}^T \boldsymbol{X})^{-1} \boldsymbol{X}^T \boldsymbol{Y}] = (\boldsymbol{X}^T \boldsymbol{X})^{-1} \boldsymbol{X}^T E(\boldsymbol{Y}) = (\boldsymbol{X}^T \boldsymbol{X})^{-1} \boldsymbol{X}^T \boldsymbol{X}\beta = \boldsymbol{I}\beta = \beta,$$

so $\hat{\beta}$ is unbiased.

For a random vector $\boldsymbol{Y}$, the *covariance matrix* has $\{\sigma_i^2 = \text{var}(Y_i)\}$ on the main diagonal (from top left to bottom right) and has $\{\text{cov}(Y_i, Y_k)\}$ for the off-diagonal pairs. We denote it by $\text{var}(\boldsymbol{Y})$. Since the linear model assumes that $\{Y_i\}$ are independent with common variance σ^2, it has $\text{var}(\boldsymbol{Y}) = \sigma^2 \boldsymbol{I}$ for an $n \times n$ identity matrix $\boldsymbol{I}$. That is, $\sigma^2 \boldsymbol{I}$ has the value σ^2 at each main-diagonal element and 0 for each pair off that diagonal. The univariate formula, $\text{var}(aY) = a^2 \text{var}(Y)$, generalizes to

$$\begin{aligned}\text{var}(\boldsymbol{AY}) &= E\{[\boldsymbol{AY} - E(\boldsymbol{AY})][\boldsymbol{AY} - E(\boldsymbol{AY})]^T\} \\ &= \boldsymbol{A}\{E[\boldsymbol{Y} - E(\boldsymbol{Y})][\boldsymbol{Y} - E(\boldsymbol{Y})]^T\}\boldsymbol{A}^T = \boldsymbol{A}\text{var}(\boldsymbol{Y})\boldsymbol{A}^T.\end{aligned}$$

Therefore, the covariance matrix of $\hat{\beta} = (\boldsymbol{X}^T \boldsymbol{X})^{-1} \boldsymbol{X}^T \boldsymbol{y}$ is

$$\begin{aligned}\text{var}(\hat{\beta}) &= (\boldsymbol{X}^T \boldsymbol{X})^{-1} \boldsymbol{X}^T [\text{var}(\boldsymbol{Y})] \boldsymbol{X}(\boldsymbol{X}^T \boldsymbol{X})^{-1} = (\boldsymbol{X}^T \boldsymbol{X})^{-1} \boldsymbol{X}^T (\sigma^2 \boldsymbol{I}) \boldsymbol{X}(\boldsymbol{X}^T \boldsymbol{X})^{-1} \\ &= \sigma^2 (\boldsymbol{X}^T \boldsymbol{X})^{-1} \boldsymbol{X}^T \boldsymbol{X}(\boldsymbol{X}^T \boldsymbol{X})^{-1} = \sigma^2 (\boldsymbol{X}^T \boldsymbol{X})^{-1}.\end{aligned} \tag{6.13}$$

The main diagonal of this matrix contains the variances of $(\hat{\beta}_0, \hat{\beta}_1, \ldots, \hat{\beta}_p)$. The standard errors are their square roots, substituting s for σ.

---

[25] This extends to the multivariate normal the comment in Section 2.5.2 that any linear transformation of a normal random variable has a normal distribution. The multivariate normal *pdf* with mean μ and covariance matrix $\boldsymbol{\Sigma}$ is proportional to $\exp\{-\frac{1}{2}[(\boldsymbol{y}-\mu)^T \boldsymbol{\Sigma}^{-1}(\boldsymbol{y}-\mu)]\}$. Section 2.7.4 shows it for a bivariate normal distribution.

6.7.3   The Hat Matrix and the Leverage

The fitted values $\hat{\mu}$ for a linear model are also a linear transformation of y,

$$\hat{\mu} = X\hat{\beta} = X(X^T X)^{-1} X^T y = Hy,$$

with $H = X(X^T X)^{-1} X^T$. The $n \times n$ matrix H is called the **hat matrix** because it linearly transforms y to $\hat{\mu} = Hy$. The hat matrix H is an example of a **projection matrix**. It projects y to $\hat{\mu}$ in the model space of possible mean vectors for the model matrix X. Each specified linear model has its unique projection matrix.

The element h_{ii} in row i and column i of the hat matrix H is the **leverage** of observation i. For the bivariate linear model $E(Y_i) = \beta_0 + \beta x_i$,

$$h_{ii} = \frac{1}{n} + \frac{(x_i - \bar{x})^2}{\sum_{k=1}^{n}(x_k - \bar{x})^2}.$$

For it, $\sum_{i=1}^{n} h_{ii} = 2$. With p explanatory variables and an intercept term, $0 < h_{ii} \le 1$ with $\sum_{i=1}^{n} h_{ii} = p + 1$. An observation that falls far from the mean on the explanatory variables has a relatively large leverage. It can strongly influence the least squares fit if its residual is also large, as summarized by Cook's distance.

6.7.4   Alternatives to Least Squares: Robust Regression and Regularization

Why use least squares to fit regression models? Other criteria are possible, such as minimizing $\sum_i |y_i - \hat{\mu}_i|$ instead of minimizing $\sum_i (y_i - \hat{\mu}_i)^2$. One reason is historical: It is simple to use calculus to find the least squares estimates. Other criteria have no closed-form solution and require iterative numerical methods. This is less problematic in this modern computing age. Software now exists for other criteria that are more robust, being less sensitive to influential observations.

With least squares, minimizing $\sum_i e_i^2$ with $e_i = (y_i - \hat{\mu}_i)$, observations are influential that have both a large residual and large leverage. So that such observations have less influence, **robust regression** methods (also called *M-estimation*) minimize a function $\sum_i \rho(e_i)$ that gives less weight to observations that have large $|e_i|$. The *Huber* robust regression implementation, which tends to be more efficient than using $\rho(e) = |e|$, takes $\rho(e) = |e|^2$ for small $|e|$ and a linear function of $|e|$ beyond that point. Another approach, **quantile regression**, models the *median* (or another quantile) of the response variable, conditional on the values of the explanatory variables. Such methods are now available in software.[26]

Alternative *regularization methods* modify least squares to give sensible answers in unstable situations. An important such case is very large p, possibly even larger than n, in which case some formulas given in this chapter (such as for regression parameter estimates) fail. Section 7.7 presents one such method (the *lasso*) in the context of a generalization of the linear model for possibly non-normal response distributions.

6.7.5   Restricted Optimality of Least Squares: Gauss–Markov Theorem

When we assume normality for the conditional distribution of Y, a justification for least squares estimates is that they are also the maximum likelihood estimates. So, when the conditional distribution is truly close to normal, least squares estimators are more efficient

---

[26]For instance, in R with **robustreg** and **quantreg** packages

(having smaller standard errors) than those obtained using another criterion, such as mini-mizing $\sum_i |y_i - \hat{\mu}_i|$. Even without the normality assumption, least squares provides the best possible estimator of β, in a certain restricted sense.

Gauss–Markov Theorem

Suppose $E(\mathbf{Y}) = \mathbf{X}\beta$, where $\mathbf{X}$ has full rank, and $\text{var}(\mathbf{Y}) = \sigma^2 \mathbf{I}$. The least squares estimator $\hat{\beta} = (\mathbf{X}^T\mathbf{X})^{-1}\mathbf{X}^T\mathbf{Y}$ is the *best linear unbiased estimator* (BLUE) of β, in this sense: Of the estimators of β_j that are linear in $\mathbf{Y}$ and unbiased, $\hat{\beta}_j$ has minimum variance, for each j. For any linear combination $\sum_j c_j \beta_j$ of $\{\beta_j\}$, such as $\beta_j - \beta_k$, the estimator $\sum_j c_j \hat{\beta}_j$ is best linear unbiased.

With the added assumption of normality for the distribution of $\mathbf{Y}$, $\hat{\beta}_j$ is the minimum variance unbiased estimator (MVUE) of β_j. Here, the restriction is still unbiasedness, but not linearity in $\mathbf{Y}$.

At first glance, the Gauss–Markov Theorem is impressive, the least squares estimator being declared *best*. However, the restriction to estimators that are both linear and unbiased is severe. ML estimators for parameters in models for non-normal responses, such as introduced in the next chapter, usually satisfy neither property. ML estimators, even though they are often slightly biased, are asymptotically unbiased, consistent, and asymptotically efficient: They converge to the parameter and tend to be closer to it than other estimators (Section 4.2.3).

6.7.6 Matrix Formulation of Bayesian Normal Linear Model

Section 6.6.1 introduced the Bayesian approach for the normal linear model by which $\{\beta_j\}$ have independent $N(\lambda, \tau^2)$ distributions, that is,

$$(\mathbf{Y} \mid \beta, \sigma^2) \sim N(\mathbf{X}\beta, \sigma^2 \mathbf{I}), \quad (\beta \mid \lambda, \tau^2) \sim N(\lambda \mathbf{1}, \tau^2 \mathbf{I}).$$

With σ^2 treated as known, the posterior *pdf* of β is proportional to the product of the likelihood function with the prior density,

$$g(\beta \mid \mathbf{y}, \sigma^2) \propto \exp\left\{ -\frac{1}{2}[\sigma^{-2}(\mathbf{y} - \mathbf{X}\beta)^T(\mathbf{y} - \mathbf{X}\beta) + \tau^{-2}(\beta - \lambda \mathbf{1})^T(\beta - \lambda \mathbf{1})] \right\}.$$

Now, completing the quadratic form in β in the exponent, with some algebra one can show that $g(\beta \mid \mathbf{y}, \sigma^2)$ is the multivariate normal *pdf* with mean $\tilde{\beta}$ and covariance matrix $\tilde{\Sigma}$, with

$$\tilde{\beta} = \tilde{\Sigma}[\sigma^{-2}\mathbf{X}^T\mathbf{y} + \tau^{-2}\lambda \mathbf{1}], \quad \tilde{\Sigma} = (\sigma^{-2}\mathbf{X}^T\mathbf{X} + \tau^{-2}\mathbf{I})^{-1}.$$

The posterior mean $\tilde{\beta}$ is

$$\tilde{\beta} = \tilde{\Sigma}[\sigma^{-2}\mathbf{X}^T\mathbf{y} + \tau^{-2}\lambda \mathbf{1}] = (\sigma^{-2}\mathbf{X}^T\mathbf{X} + \tau^{-2}\mathbf{I})^{-1}[\sigma^{-2}(\mathbf{X}^T\mathbf{X})\hat{\beta} + \tau^{-2}\lambda \mathbf{1}],$$

where $\hat{\beta} = (\mathbf{X}^T\mathbf{X})^{-1}\mathbf{X}^T\mathbf{y}$ is the ordinary least squares estimate. The coefficients of $\hat{\beta}$ and of $\lambda \mathbf{1}$ sum to $\mathbf{I}$, so $\tilde{\beta}$ is a weighted average of $\hat{\beta}$ and the prior mean. As $\tau \to \infty$, $\tilde{\beta}$ converges to $\hat{\beta}$, $\tilde{\Sigma}$ converges to $\sigma^2(\mathbf{X}^T\mathbf{X})^{-1}$, and $g(\beta \mid \mathbf{y}, \sigma^2)$ converges to a $N[\hat{\beta}, (\mathbf{X}^T\mathbf{X})^{-1}\sigma^2]$ distribution. The classical probability distribution of the estimator $\hat{\beta}$ is $N[\beta, (\mathbf{X}^T\mathbf{X})^{-1}\sigma^2]$, so the two inferential approaches then merely interchange the roles of β and $\hat{\beta}$. With σ^2 unknown, using the improper prior distribution $f(\sigma^2) \propto 1/\sigma^2$ yields analogous results with a t distribution and S substituting for σ.

6.8 Chapter Summary

This chapter dealt with linear models for quantitative response variables.

- The **linear regression equation** $E(Y) = \beta_0 + \beta_1 x$ uses a straight line for the relationship between the mean of the conditional distribution of Y and the explanatory variable x.

- **Least squares** estimates provide the prediction equation closest to the data, minimizing the sum of squared *residuals* (differences between observed and predicted values).

- The **correlation** describes the *strength* of the linear association. It is a standardized slope, having the same sign but falling between −1 and +1.

- A t test of H_0: $\beta_1 = 0$ uses test statistic $T = \hat{\beta}_1/SE_1$. A confidence interval estimates β_1.

When we study effects of multiple explanatory variables on Y, to demonstrate a **causal relationship**, we must show *association* between variables with proper *time order* and *eliminate alternative explanations*. This is possible for randomized experiments, but eliminating alternative explanations for an association is a challenge for observational studies. For instance, the association between Y and X_1 is **spurious** if a variable X_2 jointly affects both Y and X_1 and their association disappears when we adjust for X_2.

A **multiple regression model** relating Y to a set of p explanatory variables,

$$E(Y) = \beta_0 + \beta_1 x_1 + \beta_2 x_2 + \cdots + \beta_p x_p,$$

enables us to analyze effects while adjusting for other variables.

- β_j is the change in $E(Y)$ for a one-unit increase in x_j, adjusting for the other variables.

- **Statistical interaction** occurs when the effect of an explanatory variable on Y varies according to the value of another explanatory variable. We can allow this by adding cross-products of explanatory variables to the model.

- R^2 falls between 0 and 1 and represents the *proportional reduction in error* from predicting y using the prediction equation instead of $\bar{y}$. It equals the square of the **multiple correlation**, which is the correlation between the observed and predicted y-values.

- An F **statistic** tests H_0: $\beta_1 = \beta_2 = \cdots = \beta_p = 0$ that none of the explanatory variables have an effect on Y. The F values are nonnegative and have two df values. A large F test statistic and small P-value suggest that the response variable is correlated with at least one of the explanatory variables.

- Individual t tests and confidence intervals for $\{\beta_j\}$ analyze the effect of each explanatory variable, adjusting for the other variables in the model.

Table 6.4 summarizes the basic properties and inference methods for bivariate and multiple regression models.[27]

▶ Multiple regression models can also have *categorical* explanatory variables, called **factors**.

---

[27]For a broad and in-depth presentation of statistical models, beyond Chapters 6 and 7 of this book, we recommend Davison (2003).

TABLE 6.4 Summary of Bivariate and Multiple Regression Models.

	BIVARIATE REGRESSION	MULTIPLE REGRESSION	
Model:	$E(Y) = \beta_0 + \beta_1 x$	$E(Y) = \beta_0 + \beta_1 x_1 + \cdots + \beta_p x_p$	
Prediction:	$\hat{y} = \hat{\beta}_0 + \hat{\beta}_1 x$	$\hat{y} = \hat{\beta}_0 + \hat{\beta}_1 x_1 + \cdots + \hat{\beta}_p x_p$	

	Overall effect of x	Simultaneous effect	Partial effects
Measures	$\hat{\beta}_1$ = slope r = correlation $-1 \le r \le 1$	R^2 = (TSS–SSE)/TSS R = Multiple corr. $0 \le R \le 1$	$\hat{\beta}_j$ = partial slope
Tests of no effect	$H_0: \beta_1 = 0$ No effect of x on Y	$H_0: \beta_1 = \cdots = \beta_p = 0$ No effect of $x_1, \ldots, x_p$ on Y	$H_0: \beta_j = 0$ No effect of x_j on Y adjusting for others
Test statistic	$T = \frac{\hat{\beta}_1}{SE_1}$ $df = n - 2$	$F = \frac{(TSS-SSE)/p}{SSE/[n-(p+1)]}$ $df_1 = p,\ df_2 = n - (p+1)$	$T = \frac{\hat{\beta}_j}{SE_j}$ $df = n - (p+1)$

- An ***indicator variable*** represents a group, taking value 1 for observations from the group and 0 otherwise.
- An ***analysis of variance*** (ANOVA) F test compares several groups according to their means on a quantitative response variable.
- ***Multiple comparison*** methods, such as the *Bonferroni* and *Tukey* methods, provide simultaneous confidence intervals for differences between pairs of means, while controlling the overall error probability.

▶ To inferentially ***compare regression models***, a *complete* model and a simpler *reduced* model, an F test compares the sum of squared error (SSE) values.

Exercises

Data Analysis and Applications

6.1 For the Scottish hill races data, a linear model can predict men's record times from women's record times.

    (a) Show the scatterplot and report the prediction equation. Predict the men's record time for the Highland Fling, for which timeW = 490.05 minutes.

    (b) Find and interpret the correlation.

    (c) We could impose the natural constraint that when timeW = 0, then timeM = 0. Fit the model $E(Y_i) = \beta x_i$. (In R, you can use a command such as `lm(timeM ~ -1 + timeW, data=Races)`.) Interpret the estimated slope.

6.2 For advanced industrialized nations, the **Firearms** data file at the text website shows annual homicide rates (per million population) and the number of firearms (per 100 people), with data taken from Wikipedia and `smallarmssurvey.org`.

(a) Construct a scatterplot and highlight any observations that fall apart from the general trend.

(b) Find the correlation with and without the outlying observation. Why is it so different in the two cases?

(c) Fit the linear regression model with and without the outlying observation, and note how influential an outlier can be on the fit.

6.3 The `Firearms2` data file at the text website shows U.S. statewide data on x = percentage of people who report owning a gun and y = firearm death rate (annual number of deaths per 100,000 population), from `www.cdc.gov`. Identify a potentially influential observation from the scatterplot and from Cook's distance values. Show how the correlation changes when you remove this observation from the data file.

6.4 In the 2000 Presidential election in the U.S. with Democratic candidate Al Gore and Republican candidate George W. Bush, some political analysts thought that most of the votes in Palm Beach County, Florida, for the Reform party candidate, Pat Buchanan, may have actually been intended for Gore (whose name was next to Buchanan's on the ballot) but wrongly cast for Buchanan because of the design of the "butterfly ballot" used in that county, which many voters found confusing. The `BushGore` data file contains the Florida county-wide votes for the Reform party candidates in 2000 (Buchanan) and in 1996 (Ross Perot).

(a) Construct a scatterplot for predicting the Buchanan vote in 2000 based on the Perot vote in 1996. Are there any apparent outliers for a linear regression model?

(b) Fit the linear model to (i) all observations, (ii) all but the observation for Palm Beach county. Does the outlier have an impact on the results? Find the residual for that observation with fit (ii) and interpret.[28]

(c) In the scatterplot, why is the top point, but not each of the two rightmost points, influential in determining the regression fit? For the model fitted to all the data, use Cook's distance to highlight this influential observation.

6.5 For the `Covid19` data file at the text website:

(a) Construct the two scatterplots shown in Figure 6.3.

(b) Find and interpret the correlation between time and (i) cases, (ii) log(cases).

(c) Fit the linear model for the log-transformed counts and report the prediction equation.[29] Explain why the predicted count at day $x+1$ equals the predicted count at day x multiplied by $\exp(\hat{\beta}_1) = 1.36$.

6.6 Refer to the study of mental impairment in Section 6.4.2.

(a) Sketch a figure to illustrate an association between impairment and life events that is spurious, explain by SES. Fit two models to investigate whether this is the case, and summarize.

(b) Section 6.4.2 showed inference for the conditional effect of life events on mental impairment. Conduct corresponding inference for the conditional effect of SES.

6.7 For the model permitting interaction between distance and climb in their effect on women's record times for the Scottish hill races, analyze whether any observation is influential in the least squares fit. How does the parameter estimate for the interaction term change when you analyze the data without it?

---

[28] Bush won the state by 537 votes and, with it, the Electoral College and the election. Other factors that played a role were 110,000 disqualified "overvote" ballots in which people mistakenly voted for more than one presidential candidate — with Gore marked on 84,197 ballots and Bush on 37,731 — often because of confusion from names being listed on more than one page of the ballot, and 61,000 "undervotes" caused by factors such as "hanging chads" from manual punch-card machines.

[29] Some lack of fit the last few days reflects the impact of increasing "social distancing."

6.8 Refer to the example in Section 6.2.5 of the crime rate in Florida counties.

(a) Explain what it means when we say these data exhibit *Simpson's paradox*. What could cause this change in the direction of the association between crime rate and education when we adjust for urbanization?

(b) Using the **Florida** data file, construct the scatterplot between x = education (**HS**) and y = income (**Income**), for which the correlation is 0.79. If we had data at the individual level as well as aggregated for a county, sketch a scatterplot to show that at that level the correlation could be much weaker. So, predictions about individuals based on the behavior of aggregate groups, known as the *ecological fallacy*, can be quite misleading.

(c) Refer to (b), in which x falls between 54.5 and 84.9. Is it sensible to use the least squares line to predict a county's median income if $x = 0$? Sketch a hypothetical true relationship between x and $E(Y)$ to show the danger of *extrapolation*, using a fitted line to predict $E(Y)$ far from the observed x values.

6.9 Exercise 1.49 gave a link to 2020 U.S. statewide data on x = percentage of people wearing masks in public and y = percentage of people who know someone with Covid-19 symptoms. Interpret the value of r^2 for the data, which is 0.724, and report the correlation.

6.10 The **Students** data file shows responses on variables summarized in Exercise 1.2.

(a) Fit the linear model using *hsgpa* = high school GPA, *tv* = weekly hours watching TV, and *sport* = weekly hours participating in sports as predictors of *cogpa* = college GPA. Report the prediction equation. What do the P-values suggest?

(b) Summarize the estimated effect of *hsgpa*.

(c) Report and interpret R^2, adjusted R^2, and the multiple correlation.

6.11 Refer to the model fitted in the previous exercise to predict college GPA.

(a) Test H_0: $\beta_1 = \beta_2 = \beta_3 = 0$. Report the P-value and interpret.

(b) Show how to conduct a significance test about the individual effect of *hsgpa*, adjusting for *tv* and *sport*, using $\alpha = 0.05$. Interpret.

(c) Is the effect in (b) significant at the $\alpha = 0.05$ level if we use the Bonferroni approach to test the family of three individual effects? Explain.

(d) Are the effects of *tv* and *sport* significant? Propose an alternative model.

6.12 For the **UN** data file at the book's website (see Exercise 1.24), construct a multiple regression model predicting Internet using all the other variables. Use the concept of multicollinearity to explain why adjusted R^2 is not dramatically greater than when GDP is the sole predictor. Compare the estimated GDP effect in the bivariate model and the multiple regression model and explain why it is so much weaker in the multiple regression model.

6.13 For the **Polid** data file summarized in Table 5.2, conduct an ANOVA to analyze whether mean political ideology varies by race. Use a follow-up multiple comparison method with overall confidence level 0.95 to estimate differences of means between pairs of races on political ideology. Interpret results.

6.14 The data set[30] **Crabs2** at the book's website comes from a study of factors that affect sperm traits of male horseshoe crabs. A response variable, *SpermTotal*, is the log of the total number of sperm in an ejaculate. It has $\bar{y} = 19.3$ and $s = 2.0$. The two explanatory variables used in the R output are the horseshoe crab's *carapace width* (CW, mean 18.6 *cm*, standard deviation 3.0 *cm*), which is a measure of its size, and *color* (1 = dark, 2 = medium, 3 = light), which is a measure of adult age, darker ones being older.

---

[30]Thanks to Jane Brockmann and Daniel Sasson for making these data available.

```
> summary(lm(SpermTotal ~ CW + factor(Color), data=Crabs2))
                Estimate  Std. Error  t value  Pr(>|t|)
(Intercept)       11.366       0.638   17.822   < 2e-16
CW                 0.391       0.034   11.651   < 2e-16
factor(Color)2     0.809       0.246    3.292   0.00114
factor(Color)3     1.149       0.271    4.239   3.14e-05
---

F-statistic: 55.06 on 3 and 254 DF,  p-value: < 2.2e-16
> library(car)
> Anova(lm(SpermTotal ~ CW + factor(Color) + CW:factor(Color), data=Crabs2))
Anova Table (Type II tests)
                  Sum Sq  Df  F value    Pr(>F)
CW                341.25   1 136.3607 < 2.2e-16
factor(Color)      47.93   2   9.5757 9.812e-05
CW:factor(Color)    7.61   2   1.5198   0.2207
Residuals         630.65 252
```

(a) Using the results shown, write the prediction equation and interpret the parameter estimates.

(b) Explain the differences in what is tested with the F statistic (i) for the overall model, (ii) for the factor(Color) effect, (iii) for the interaction term. Interpret each.

6.15 Table 6.5 shows observations on home sales in Gainesville, Florida, from the Houses data file at the book's website for 100 homes. Variables listed are selling price (thousands of dollars), size of house (square feet), annual property tax bill (dollars), number of bedrooms, number of bathrooms, and whether the house is new. For illustrative purposes, treat the data as a simple random sample of a conceptual population of home sales in this market and model Y = selling price using x_1 = size of house and x_2 = whether the house is new (1 = yes, 0 = no).

TABLE 6.5 Selling prices and related characteristics for home sales.

Home	Selling price	Size	Taxes	Bedrooms	Bathrooms	New
1	419.85	2048	3104	4	2	no
2	219.75	912	1173	2	1	no
3	365.55	1654	3076	4	2	no

(a) Summarize the data with a scatterplot between y and x_1, using separate symbols for the two categories of x_2.

(b) Fit the model $E(Y_i) = \beta_0 + \beta_1 x_{i1} + \beta_2 x_{i2}$. Interpret the estimated effects.

(c) Report and interpret R^2 for summarizing the global predictive power.

(d) Conduct a significance test for the effect of whether the house is new, adjusting for size. Interpret.

(e) At the mean size of the new homes, find and interpret a 95% confidence interval for the mean selling price of new homes and a 95% prediction interval for the selling price of a new home.

(f) Using Cook's distance, identify the most influential observation for the model fit. Analyze the effect of fitting the model without it. (We'll see that this observation is not influential or even unusual when we consider an alternative model in Section 7.1.3 that allows the variability of selling price to increase as its mean increases.)

6.16 Refer to the previous example. The data exhibit a strong positive correlation of 0.84 between selling price and the tax bill. Might this be a spurious association, with the size of the home causally affecting both of them? Sketch a figure to reflect the potential spurious relationship. Analyze how the effect of taxes on selling price changes after adjusting for size of home.

6.17 For 72 young girls suffering from anorexia, the `Anorexia.dat` file at the book's website shows their weights before and after an experimental period. The girls were randomly assigned to receive cognitive behavioral therapy (cb). family therapy (f), or be in a control group (c).

(a) Conduct an ANOVA to compare the mean weight changes for the three therapies. Interpret the P-value.

(b) Use a multiple comparison method to form confidence intervals comparing the mean weight changes, with family-wise confidence level 0.95. Interpret.

(c) Regarding weight after the experimental period as the sole response, fit a linear model with the initial weight and the therapy as explanatory variables. Interpret the therapy estimates. Conduct inference comparing the therapies while adjusting for the initial weight. (The test comparing groups while adjusting for a quantitative covariate is called *analysis of covariance*).

6.18 A pharmaceutical clinical trial[31] randomly assigned 24 patients to three treatment groups (drug A, drug C, placebo) and compared them on a measure of respiratory ability (FEV1 = forced expiratory volume in 1 second, in liters) after 1 hour of treatment. For the `FEV` data file at the book's website, fit the linear model for *fev* with explanatory variables *base* (the baseline measurement prior to administering the drug) and *drug* (categorical with labels A, C, P). Show the fitted equations between fev and base for each drug, show how to conduct an overall test for drug, and show individual tests comparing each pair of drugs.

6.19 Conduct Bayesian fitting of the linear model for the Scottish hill races, using climb and distance predictors of women's record times without the outlying Highland Fling race observation. Compare the posterior mean estimates of the parameters to the least squares estimates, as you vary the spread of the normal prior distributions.

6.20 Use linear modeling to analyze the record times for men in the Scottish hill races, with distance and climb as explanatory variables, (a) with least squares, (b) with Bayesian methods. Prepare a report, including highly edited software output in an appendix.

6.21 For the Scottish hills races data, model the record time simultaneously for men and women by using distance, climb, and gender as explanatory variables. Prepare a report of at most 300 words, including highly edited software output in an appendix. For the final model chosen, interpret parameter estimates, find and interpret R^2, and investigate the effects of any influential observations.

6.22 Refer to the mental impairment example in Sections 6.4.2 and 6.6.2.

(a) The example in Section 6.6.2 used highly disperse priors. Let's compare results to informative priors based on subjective beliefs that β_1 and β_2 are not vary large. With the `MCMCregress` function in R, we can specify different prior variances for these effects than for the intercept parameter by specifying a covariance matrix of the parameters. For instance, to take prior standard deviation $\tau = 0.2$ for β_1 and β_2 (and thus precision $1/(0.20)^2 = 25$) yet have a highly disperse prior for β_0 (e.g., precision $= 10^{-10}$), we can specify a 3×3 matrix A to use for the precision B_0, where the values on the main diagonal are the precisions for $(\beta_0, \beta_1, \beta_2)$:

```
> A = diag(c(10^(-10), 25, 25))
> fit.bayes <- MCMCregress(impair ~ life + ses, data=Mental, mcmc=5000000,
+                          b0=0, B0=A, c0=10^(-10), d0=10^(-10))
```

Conduct a Bayesian analysis using prior standard deviation $\tau = 0.1$ for the effects of life events and SES and compare results with highly disperse normal priors having $\tau = 10.0$. Explain how the posterior means for β_1 and β_2 depend on τ.

(b) In (a), suppose you also used $\tau = 0.1$ for the prior distribution for β_0. Show that shrinking β_0 far from the least squares estimate of 28.2 toward 0 also forces dramatic changes in the other Bayesian posterior mean estimates.

---

[31] Described by R. Littell, J. Pendergast, and R. Natarajan, *Statist. Med.* **19**: 1793–1819 (2000). Thanks to Ramon Littell for making these data available.

(c) With $\tau = 10$ and similar results as with least squares, explain differences between the interpretations of the Bayesian posterior $P(\beta_1 \le 0)$ and the classical P-value for testing $H_0: \beta_1 = 0$ against $H_a: \beta_1 > 0$.

6.23 The `Hare` data file at the book's website[32] has data for 550 hares on body mass (grams) and hind foot length (mm), by gender of the hare. Use regression models with body mass as the response variable, interpreting carefully any effects or interactions. Prepare a report of at most 300 words, including highly edited software output in an appendix.

Methods and Concepts

6.24 Construct a scatterplot with 5 points that have a correlation close to +1, and then add a single point that changes the correlation to a strong negative value.[33] Explain why this single outlying observation has so much influence.

6.25 The Internet site `www.artofstat.com/web-apps` has a *Guess the Correlation* app. Play the *Correlation Game* 10 times. Show the table of guesses and actual values and find the correlation between them.

6.26 The statistician George Box, who had an illustrious academic career at the University of Wisconsin, is often quoted as saying, "All models are wrong, but some models are useful." Why do you think that, in practice, **(a)** all models are wrong, **(b)** some models are *not* useful.

6.27 Show that for the null model $E(Y_i) = \beta_0$, least squares yields $\hat{\beta}_0 = \bar{y}$.

6.28 Show that the correlation between a variable and itself is necessarily 1.0.

6.29 An alternative parameterization of the bivariate regression model centers x around its mean and expresses the model as
$$E(Y) = \beta_0 + \beta_1(x - \mu_x).$$

(a) For this parameterization, explain how to interpret β_0. How does this differ from the interpretation for the model without centering?

(b) If you replace μ_x in this expression by $x_0 = \min(\{x_i\})$, how do you interpret β_0?

6.30 When the values of y are multiplied by a constant c, from their formulas, show that s_y and $\hat{\beta}_1$ in the bivariate linear model are also then multiplied by c. Thus, show that $r = \hat{\beta}_1(s_x/s_y)$ does not depend on the units of measurement.

6.31 When observations on both x and y are standardized, show that the bivariate prediction equation has the form $\hat{\mu}_i = rx_i$, where r is the sample correlation.

6.32 With least squares for the bivariate linear model, equation (6.1) states that $\hat{\beta}_0 = \bar{y} - \hat{\beta}_1\bar{x}$.

(a) Using this formula, show that an alternative expression for the fitted line is $(\hat{\mu}_i - \bar{y}) = \hat{\beta}_1(x_i - \bar{x})$.

(b) For data on $y =$ final exam score and $x =$ midterm score, suppose $r = 0.70$ and $s_x = s_y$. Show that $(\hat{\mu}_i - \bar{y}) = 0.70(x_i - \bar{x})$. Explain how a score on the final exam is predicted to regress toward its mean relative to the distance between the midterm exam score and its mean.

6.33 A healthy systolic blood pressure is 120 mm Hg or less. A study took a volunteer sample of subjects with high-blood pressure and asked them to walk for 30 minutes at lunch time each day. After one month, their mean systolic blood pressure fell from 150 to 140. Explain how this could merely reflect regression toward the mean.

---

[32]Thanks to Dr. Madan K. Oli and Dr. Charles J. Krebs for these unpublished data.
[33]The Internet site `www.artofstat.com/web-apps` has an *Explore Linear Regression* app that does this, with the *Draw Your Own* option.

6.34 For the *bivariate normal distribution* (Section 2.7.4) with correlation ρ, in 1886 Francis Galton showed that the conditional distribution of $(Y \mid X = x)$ is $N[\mu_Y + \rho(\sigma_Y / \sigma_X)(x - \mu_x), \sigma_Y^2(1 - \rho^2)]$. Show that

$$\frac{E(Y \mid X = x) - \mu_Y}{\sigma_Y} = \rho\left(\frac{x - \mu_X}{\sigma_X}\right),$$

and use it to explain the concept of regression toward the mean.

6.35 In bivariate modeling, suppose we treat X also as a random variable, with (X, Y) having a bivariate normal distribution with correlation ρ. Regression analysis estimates the equation $E(Y \mid X = x) = \mu_Y + \rho(\sigma_Y / \sigma_X)(x - \mu_X)$.

  (a) State the equation estimated if we instead use Y to predict X.

  (b) If $E(Y) = \beta_0 + \beta_1 x$ and $E(X) = \beta_0^* + \beta_1^* y$, show that the two separate regressions satisfy $\beta_1/(1/\beta_1^*) = \rho^2$, so $\beta_1 = 1/\beta_1^*$ only when $|\rho| = 1$.

6.36 Let β_1 denote the effect of x in the regression equation using x to predict y and let β_1^* denote the effect of y in the regression equation using y to predict x. Show that the correlation r is the geometric mean (Exercise 1.44) of $\hat{\beta}_1$ and $\hat{\beta}_1^*$.

6.37 For Y = income (thousands of dollars) and x = education (years), randomly generate $n = 100$ observations when X has a uniform distribution over the integers 10 to 17 and, conditional on $X = x$, Y has a $N(-25.0 + 6.0x, 15^2)$ distribution. Use software to find the least squares fit of the linear model to these data. Plot the data, and overlay the regression equation and its least squares fit. Explain how this plot would change as you let n grow indefinitely.

6.38 The distribution of X = heights (*cm*) of women in the U.K. is approximately $N(162, 7^2)$. Conditional on $X = x$, suppose Y = weight (*kg*) has a $N(3.0 + 0.40x, 8^2)$ distribution. Simulate a million observations from this distribution. Approximate the correlation. Approximate the regression equation for predicting X using y.

6.39 Section 6.1.5 showed that a single outlying Scottish race observation influences whether the correlation between women's record time and climb is 0.69 or 0.85. Section 5.8.3 showed that in comparing groups, it can be more robust to use ranks. Transform the time and climb values to their ranks and find the correlation with and without the outlier. (The correlation between rank scores is called the **Spearman correlation**.)

6.40 For the Scottish hill races data with y = women's record time, we could impose the natural constraint that when x = distance = 0, $E(Y) = 0$.

  (a) For the model $E(Y_i) = \beta x_i$, derive the least squares estimate of β.

  (b) Fit the model to the data. (In R, you can use `lm(timeW ~ -1 + distance, data=Races)`.) Interpret and compare results to the ordinary model.

6.41 For the model $E(Y_i) = \beta_0 + \beta_1 x_i$, consider the expression for $\hat{\beta}_1$ in equation (6.1).

  (a) Specify the sampling distribution of $\hat{\beta}_1$ and show that $E(\hat{\beta}_1) = \beta_1$ and $\text{var}(\hat{\beta}_1) = \sigma^2/[\sum_i(x_i - \bar{x})^2]$.

  (b) From the variance formula, explain why more precise estimation of β_1 is possible when the data have (i) more variation in x; (ii) less variation in y given x; (iii) more observations.

6.42 You can fit the quadratic equation $E(Y) = \beta_0 + \beta_1 x + \beta_2 x^2$ by fitting a multiple regression model with $x_1 = x$ and $x_2 = x^2$.

  (a) Simulate 100 independent observations from the model $Y = 40.0 - 5.0x + 0.5x^2 + \epsilon$, where X has a uniform distribution over $[0, 10]$ and $\epsilon \sim N(0, 1)$. Plot the data and fit the quadratic model. Report how the fitted equation compares with the true relationship.

  (b) Find the correlation between x and y and explain why it is so weak even though the plot shows a strong relationship with a large R^2 value for the quadratic model.

6.43 A ten-year study[34] of elderly people found that those who played at least one round of golf every week were more likely to be alive a decade later. Explain how this could be spurious by describing potential associations between another variable and both mortality and frequency of playing golf.

6.44 A research article states that subjects who exercise regularly reported only half as many serious illnesses per year, on the average, as those who do not exercise regularly. The results section states, "We next analyzed whether age was a confounding variable affecting this association."

(a) Explain what confounding means in this context, and explain how age could potentially explain the association.

(b) For this study, explain what is meant by *potential outcomes* and *counterfactuals*.

6.45 A study found that children who regularly eat breakfast get better math grades than those who do not eat breakfast. This result was based on the association between X = whether eat breakfast (yes, no) and Y = grade in last math course taken. Suggest a possible lurking variable and explain how to check whether the association is spurious because of the nature of the effects of the lurking variable on X and Y.

6.46 For recent U.S. presidential elections, in each state wealthier voters tend to be more likely to vote Republican, yet states that are wealthier in an aggregate sense tend to have smaller proportions voting for the Republican.[35] Sketch a plot of statewide values of x = median income against y = percent voting Republican showing an overall negative trend. For several individuals in two of the states, add to the plot their values of income against their stated probability that they would vote for a Republican presidential candidate, showing a positive trend and illustrating how this instance of Simpson's paradox could occur.

6.47 For uncorrelated random variables U, V, and W, let $X = U + V$ and $Y = U + W$. (a) What happens to the correlation between X and Y when we condition on U by keeping it fixed; (b) Explain how a spurious association can occur.

6.48 Explain why conditional independence between Y and X_1, given X_2, does not imply marginal independence between Y and X_1. To illustrate this, sketch a hypothetical scatterplot between y and x_1 values at different values of x_2.

6.49 Using how r^2 for the bivariate model is based on the marginal variability of y and the conditional variability of y given x, explain why for a particular trend, we'd expect r^2 (and $|r|$) to be larger when the range of x-values sampled is larger.

6.50 From Section 6.1.5 and Exercise 6.31, the correlation is a *standardized slope*. When we fit a multiple regression model to standardized versions of y and the explanatory variables, the estimated regression parameters are called *standardized regression coefficients*.

(a) Explain how to interpret the standardized coefficient for x_j.

(b) To compare effects of variables with very different units (e.g., cholesterol level, systolic blood pressure, weight, age, and number of years of education), explain why it is more meaningful to compare the standardized than the ordinary regression coefficients.

6.51 Use the equations in Section 6.2.6 that are solved to find the least squares estimates to show that the least squares fit of a multiple regression model satisfies

$$\sum_i (y_i - \bar{y})^2 = \sum_i (\hat{\mu}_i - \bar{y})^2 + \sum_i (y_i - \hat{\mu}_i)^2.$$

6.52 F statistics have alternate expressions in terms of R^2 values.

(a) Show that for testing $H_0: \beta_1 = \cdots = \beta_p = 0$,

$$F = \frac{(TSS - SSE)/p}{SSE/[n - (p + 1)]} \quad \text{is equivalently} \quad \frac{R^2/p}{(1 - R^2)/[n - (p + 1)]}.$$

Explain why larger values of R^2 yield larger values of F.

---

[34]See https://fullfact.org/health/golf-heart-attacks
[35]See Section 14.2 of Gelman and Hill (2006).

(b) Show that for comparing nested linear models,

$$F = \frac{(SSE_0 - SSE_1)/(p_1 - p_0)}{SSE_1/[n - (p_1 + 1)]} = \frac{(R_1^2 - R_0^2)/(p_1 - p_0)}{(1 - R_1^2)/[n - (p_1 + 1)]}.$$

6.53 Using the definitions of T and F random variables, show that if T has a t distribution, then T^2 has an F distribution with $df = 1$ and df_2 equal df for the t distribution.

6.54 For independent random samples of sizes n_1 and n_2 from normal populations with common variance σ^2, using Section 4.4.6 and the definition of the F distribution in Section 6.4.1, explain why S_1^2/S_2^2 has an F distribution with $df_1 = n_1 - 1$ and $df_2 = n_2 - 1$.

6.55 Consider the confidence interval (6.8) for $E(Y)$ in the bivariate model.

(a) Show that at $x_0 = \bar{x}$, the interval is the same as the interval $\bar{y} \pm t_{\alpha/2,n-1}(s/\sqrt{n})$ in the formula (4.10) for the marginal distribution of y, except for the t quantile score.

(b) At $x_0 \neq \bar{x}$, explain why you can estimate $E(Y)$ more precisely when $\{x_i\}$ are more spread out.

6.56 (a) Explain intuitively why a prediction interval for Y is much wider than a confidence interval for $E(Y)$.

(b) Explain how prediction intervals for Y at various values of x would likely be in substantial error if (i) the variability in Y tends to increase as x increases, (ii) Y is highly discrete, such as Y = number of children in a family.

6.57 Suppose that the population correlation ρ is close to 1.

(a) What shape would you expect the sampling distribution of r to have? Why?

(b) In 1915, R. A. Fisher showed that with simple random sampling,

$$T(r) = (1/2)\log_e[(1+r)/(1-r)]$$

has an approximate $N[T(\rho), 1/(n-3)]$ distribution. Using this, explain how to construct a confidence interval for ρ.

6.58 Illustrate how between-groups and within-groups variability affect the result of the ANOVA F test of $H_0: \mu_1 = \mu_2 = \mu_3$ by constructing two scenarios, each with $n_1 = n_2 = n_3 = 4$ and $\bar{y}_2 = 10$, $\bar{y}_2 = 12$, $\bar{y}_2 = 14$, such that one scenario has a relatively large P-value and one has a relatively small P-value.[36]

6.59 To show Boole's inequality (Section 6.5.4), let

$$B_1 = E_1, \quad B_2 = E_1^c \cap E_2, \quad B_3 = E_1^c \cap E_2^c \cap E_3, \ldots$$

Explain why $P(\cup_j E_j) = P(\cup_j B_j) = \sum_j P(B_j) \leq \sum_{j=1}^{t} P(E_j)$.

6.60 In conducting a large number of significance tests, the **false discovery rate** (FDR) is the expected proportion of the rejected null hypotheses that are erroneously rejected. A simple algorithm can ensure FDR $\leq \alpha$ when applied with t independent tests and is especially useful when a small proportion of the null hypotheses are expected to be false. Let $P_{(1)} \leq P_{(2)} \leq \cdots \leq P_{(t)}$ denote the ordered P-values. The method rejects hypotheses (1), ..., (j^*), where j^* is the maximum j for which $P_{(j)} \leq j\alpha/t$.

(a) Explain why the FDR and Bonferroni make the same decision for the most significant test, but otherwise the FDR method rejects in at least as many cases as the Bonferroni method.

(b) The statisticians (Yoav Benjamini and Yosef Hochberg) who introduced this method in 1995 illustrated the FDR for a study about myocardial infarction. For the 15 hypotheses tested in the study, the ordered P-values $(P_{(1)}, P_{(2)}, \ldots, P_{(15)})$ were

---

[36]You can use the *ANOVA* app at www.artofstat.com/web-apps to do this.

$$0.0001, 0.0004, 0.0019, 0.0095, 0.020, 0.028, 0.030,$$
$$0.034, 0.046, 0.32, 0.43, 0.57, 0.65, 0.76, 1.00.$$

With $\alpha = 0.05$, indicate which hypotheses are rejected with the FDR method and with the Bonferroni method.

6.61 Derive the F test in Section 6.5.6 for comparing nested normal linear models as a likelihood-ratio test, using an argument like the one in Section 6.4.6 for the global F test.

6.62 The linear model for the one-way layout generalizes for two or more factors. For the two-way $r \times c$ layout with factors A and B:

   (a) Write the linear model formula that assumes a lack of interaction. Explain how to construct an F statistic for testing that the A main effects are zero.

   (b) Write the linear model permitting interaction, for the case $r = 2$ and $c = 3$. Explain how to construct an F statistic to test the set of interaction effects.

6.63 To summarize the interaction between quantitative x and binary z, suppose we center x at its mean and express the model as

$$E(Y) = \beta_0 + \beta_1(x - \mu_x) + \beta_2 z + \beta_3(x - \mu_x) \times z.$$

Explain how to interpret β_2. How does this differ from the interpretation for the model without centering?

6.64 Show the model matrix for 12 observations and three explanatory variables, the first of which is quantitative, the second is binary, and the third has three categories, such that each combination of the categorical variables has two observations.

6.65 Using formula 6.13, explain heuristically why $\text{var}(\hat{\beta}_j)$ tends to decrease as n increases.

6.66 With quantitative x and y, it can be informative to plot the data and show a smoothing of the relationship without assuming linearity or some other functional form. With an Internet search, read about the *lowess* (locally weighted scatterplot smoothing) method for this. Explain the method, with an example, in a report of at most 300 words.

7

Generalized Linear Models

Chapter 6 introduced linear models, which assume a linear relationship between the mean of the response variable Y and a set of explanatory variables, with inference assuming that Y has a normal conditional distribution with constant variance. *The **generalized linear model** permits distributions for Y other than the normal and permits modeling nonlinear functions of the mean.* This generalization enables us to model, in a unified framework, response variables that are categorical, counts, or continuous but that badly violate assumptions of the normal linear model.

We first introduce the three components of a generalized linear model (GLM). We then present GLMs for binary response variables, such as *favor* and *oppose* for a question in a sample survey about legalized same-sex marriage. The most popular model, which assumes a *binomial* distribution for the response variable, is called the *logistic regression model* (Section 7.2). We also present Bayesian inference for logistic regression models (Section 7.3). This approach is especially useful with certain patterns of binary data in which maximum likelihood (ML) estimates of some model parameters are infinite, whereas Bayesian fitting provides finite estimates. We then introduce GLMs for count data responses, such as a question in the survey about the total number of friends the respondent has who are gay (Sections 7.4 and 7.5). The models assume that the response variable has a *Poisson* distribution, or a *negative binomial* distribution to permit variability greater than the Poisson allows, that is, so-called *overdispersion* (Section 2.4.7). We then present an algorithm that software uses to fit GLMs and obtain standard errors of model parameter estimates (Section 7.6.1). Finally, we introduce *regularization* methods for modifying ML estimates with high-dimensional data and other situations in which the ML estimates are unstable or do not even exist (Section 7.7).

All methods presented in this chapter assume independent observations. Further generalizations exist for modeling correlated observations, such as occur in studies that observe the response variable for each subject repeatedly, at several times or under various conditions. Section A.7.4 of the R Appendix outlines the main types of these generalized linear models for correlated observations.

7.1 Introduction to Generalized Linear Models

Generalized linear models (GLMs) extend normal linear models to encompass non-normal response distributions and equating linear predictors to nonlinear functions of the mean. They provide a unified theory of modeling that includes the most important models for continuous and discrete response variables.

7.1.1 The Three Components of a Generalized Linear Model

GLMs have three components:

DOI: 10.1201/9781003159834-7

- **Response variable**: This component specifies the response variable Y and its probability distribution. The n observations $(y_1, \ldots, y_n)$ of Y are assumed to be realizations of independent random variables.

- **Explanatory variables**: This component specifies the p explanatory variables for a *linear predictor* $\beta_0 + \beta_1 x_{i1} + \cdots + \beta_p x_{ip}$, where x_{ij} is the value of explanatory variable j for observation i.

- **Link function**: This component is a function g applied to the *conditional expectation* $\mu_i = E(Y_i \mid x_{i1}, \ldots, x_{ip})$ of the response variable at explanatory variable values $(x_{i1}, \ldots, x_{ip})$, relating it to the linear predictor,

$$g(\mu_i) = \beta_0 + \beta_1 x_{i1} + \cdots + \beta_p x_{ip}.$$

The link function $g(\mu_i) = \mu_i$ is called the **identity link function**. Through $\mu_i = \beta_0 + \beta_1 x_{i1} + \cdots + \beta_p x_{ip}$, it equates the linear predictor directly to $E(Y_i)$, as in the linear models introduced in the previous chapter. We shall see that nonlinear link functions provide flexibility that is especially useful for categorical and count response variables. Each possible probability distribution for Y in a GLM has a **canonical link function** for which technical aspects simplify, such as simple likelihood equations for the ML estimates of $\{\beta_j\}$. GLM software uses the canonical link function by default, although other choices are possible. The most popular GLMs for practical application use the canonical link function, and we next introduce three of them.

7.1.2 GLMs for Normal, Binomial, and Poisson Responses

For continuous response variables, the most important GLMs are *normal linear models*. Such models assume independent response observations $Y_i \sim N(\mu_i, \sigma^2)$ for $i = 1, \ldots, n$, and use the identity link function, for which $\mu_i = \beta_0 + \beta_1 x_{i1} + \cdots + \beta_p x_{ip}$. This is the canonical link function for a normal response. Other distributions and link functions are possible. For instance, the *gamma distribution* is useful when observations on Y are necessarily nonnegative and show variability that increases as the mean increases.

For a categorical response variable, we model the probability that the outcome falls in a particular category. When the response variable is binary, representing the "success" and "failure" outcomes by 1 and 0, observation i has probabilities $P(Y_i = 1) = \pi_i$ and $P(Y_i = 0) = 1 - \pi_i$. This is the special case of the *binomial* distribution with $n_i = 1$ trial, for which $\mu_i = \pi_i$. The probability π_i is not compatible with the linear predictor $\beta_0 + \beta_1 x_{i1} + \cdots + \beta_p x_{ip}$, because it falls between 0 and 1 whereas the linear predictor can take any real-number value. Models for categorical data use a link function to transform probabilities so that they can also take any real number value. In the binary case, the canonical link function for $\mu_i = \pi_i$ is $\log[\mu_i/(1 - \mu_i)]$, called the **logit**. Like the linear predictor, the logit can take any real number value. GLMs using the logit link function have the form

$$\log\left(\frac{\mu_i}{1 - \mu_i}\right) = \beta_0 + \beta_1 x_{i1} + \cdots + \beta_p x_{ip}, \quad i = 1, \ldots, n.$$

They are called **logistic regression models**.

When the response variable has counts for the outcomes, the simplest probability distribution for Y is the *Poisson*. The *log* function is then the most common link function and is the canonical link function. The mean of a count response variable must be nonnegative, and its log can take any real number value, like a linear predictor. A GLM using the log link function

$$\log \mu_i = \beta_0 + \beta_1 x_{i1} + \cdots + \beta_p x_{ip}, \quad i = 1, \ldots, n,$$

is called a **loglinear model**. With the assumption that Y has a Poisson distribution, it is called a **Poisson loglinear model**. The **negative binomial loglinear model** permits *overdispersion*, a common situation with count data in which var(Y) exceeds $E(Y)$ at each setting of the explanatory variables.

To use software for GLMs, we specify (1) the response variable Y and its probability distribution, (2) the explanatory variables in the linear predictor, and (3) the link function. For example, since the normal linear model is a GLM for a normal response, we can fit it with GLM software as well as linear model software. In R, we use the `glm` function, for which the family of normal distributions is referred to as *gaussian*, and we specify the identity link function. An advantage of using the `glm` function instead of the `lm` function is that other link functions are also possible, which an example in Section 7.1.8 shows can be very helpful.

7.1.3 Example: GLMs for House Selling Prices

The `Houses` data file at the book's website has observations on 100 home sales in Gainesville, Florida. Variables listed include y = selling price (in thousands of dollars), x_1 = size (in square feet), and x_2 = whether the house is new (1 = yes, 0 = no). For illustrative purposes, we treat the data as a simple random sample of a conceptual population of home sales in this market. Figure 7.1 shows a scatterplot between y and x_1, distinguishing between the 11 new homes and 89 older ones.

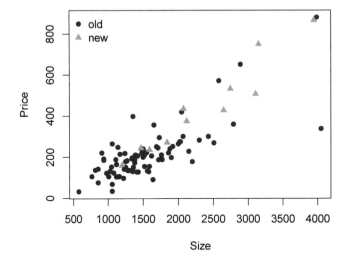

FIGURE 7.1 Scatterplot of house selling price by size and whether the house is new. Can you identify the outlier that does not follow the overall trend?

We first fit a normal GLM, permitting interaction in the effects to allow the effect of size to differ for new homes and older homes:

```
> Houses <- read.table("http://stat4ds.rwth-aachen.de/data/Houses.dat", header=TRUE)
> head(Houses, 2)
  case  price size new taxes bedrooms baths
```

```
  1    1 419.85 2048   0  3104        4    2
  2    2 219.75  912   0  1173        2    1
> fit1 <- glm(price ~ size + new + size:new, family=gaussian(link=identity), data=Houses)
>                                    # gaussian is family of normal distributions
> summary(fit1)                      # link=identity is default for gaussian family
            Estimate  Std. Error  t value  Pr(>|t|)
(Intercept)  -33.3417    23.2817    -1.43    0.1554
size           0.1567     0.0141    11.08    <2e-16 # size effect 0.157 when new=0
new         -117.7913    76.5115    -1.54    0.1270
size:new       0.0929     0.0325     2.86    0.0053 # size effect 0.157+0.093 when new=1
---
    Null deviance: 2284086  on 99  degrees of freedom # total sum of squares
Residual deviance:  584022  on 96  degrees of freedom # residual sum of squares
AIC: 1161                            # AIC is explained in Section 7.1.6
```

The interaction is highly significant. From the size effect and the interaction term, the estimated effect on selling price of a square-foot increase in size is 0.157 (i.e., \$157) for older homes and 0.157 + 0.093 = 0.250 (i.e., \$250) for newer homes. Figure 7.1 shows that one older home (observation 64) is a clear outlier, having a very large size but relatively low selling price. This observation is influential according to Cook's distance, which equals 1.02. The interaction is still significant without it, but the estimated size effect for older homes then increases from \$157 to \$185.

The scatterplot, however, suggests that the variability in Y could be greater when its mean is higher, at higher house sizes, violating the ordinary linear model assumption of constant variability in Y. We could instead assume that the conditional distribution of Y is the *gamma distribution* (Section 2.5.4), because it is a positively-skewed distribution over positive y values for which the standard deviation is proportional to the mean. The standard deviation satisfies $\sigma = \mu/\sqrt{k}$, for the shape parameter k. Software that fits gamma GLMs refers to $1/k$ as the *dispersion parameter*, reflecting that the dispersion as measured by the variance (i.e., $\sigma^2 = \mu^2/k$) increases as $1/k$ increases. Here is the fit of the corresponding gamma GLM:

```
> fit2 <- glm(price ~ size + new + size:new, family=Gamma(link=identity), data=Houses)
> summary(fit2)
            Estimate  Std. Error  t value  Pr(>|t|)
(Intercept)  -11.1783    19.4608    -0.57    0.57
size           0.1417     0.0151     9.40    2.9e-15
new         -116.8550    96.8741    -1.21    0.23
size:new       0.0974     0.0551     1.77    0.08 .
---
(Dispersion parameter for Gamma 0.11021) # shape parameter = 1/dispersion = 1/0.1102 = 9.2
    Null deviance: 31.940 on 99 degrees of freedom
Residual deviance: 10.563 on 96 degrees of freedom # see Section 7.1.4
AIC: 1129                                 # AIC explained in Section 7.1.6
```

Unlike the normal GLM, the interaction is not significant at the 0.05 level. The outlying observation is much less influential for the gamma GLM, because this model expects more variability in y when its mean is larger. Without that observation, the estimated size effect for older homes changes only from \$142 to \$146. The dispersion parameter estimate is $1/\hat{k} = 0.1102$, so the estimated standard deviation $\hat{\sigma}$ of the conditional distribution of Y relates to the estimated mean selling price $\hat{\mu}$ by $\hat{\sigma} = \hat{\mu}/\sqrt{\hat{k}} = \sqrt{0.1102}\hat{\mu} = 0.332\hat{\mu}$. For example, when the estimated mean selling price is \$100,000, $\hat{\sigma} = \$33,200$, whereas when it is \$500,000, $\hat{\sigma} = 5(\$33,200) = \$166,000$. By contrast, for the normal GLM, $\hat{\sigma}$ is constant at \$78,000.

This example shows that in modeling, it is not sufficient to focus on how $E(Y)$ depends on the explanatory variables. The assumption about how $\text{var}(Y)$ depends on $E(Y)$, through the choice of probability distribution for Y, can affect inferential conclusions and decisions about whether particular observations fall outside the scope of a model. We'll observe another example of this, for count data, in Section 7.5.3.

7.1.4 The Deviance

The GLM outputs just shown report a "null deviance" and "residual deviance." For the normal linear model, the residual deviance is the residual sum of squares, $SSE = \sum_i (y_i - \hat{\mu}_i)^2$. The null deviance is the residual sum of squares for the null model, containing only an intercept. For it, all $\hat{\mu}_i = \bar{y}$, and $SSE = \sum_i (y_i - \bar{y})^2$, which we labeled as the total sum of squares (TSS) for linear models in Section 6.3.2. This section introduces the *deviance* in a GLM context.

With observations $\mathbf{y} = (y_1, \ldots, y_n)$ and means $\boldsymbol{\mu} = (\mu_1, \ldots, \mu_n)$, let $L(\boldsymbol{\mu}; \mathbf{y})$ denote the log-likelihood function for the model. This reflects the probability distribution assumed for the response variable Y and is a function of $\{\beta_j\}$ through how the link function g relates $\boldsymbol{\mu}$ to them; that is, since $g(\mu_i) = \beta_0 + \beta_1 x_{i1} + \cdots + \beta_p x_{ip}$, μ_i is a function of $\{\beta_j\}$ through the inverse function, $\mu_i = g^{-1}(\beta_0 + \beta_1 x_{i1} + \cdots + \beta_p x_{ip})$ such as $\mu_i = \exp(\beta_0 + \beta_1 x_{i1} + \cdots + \beta_p x_{ip})$ for a GLM that uses the log link function. Let $L(\hat{\boldsymbol{\mu}}; \mathbf{y})$ denote the maximized log-likelihood evaluated at its fitted values $\{\hat{\mu}_i\}$ for the ML fit of the GLM. Of possible GLMs, the most general one has a separate parameter for each observation and provides the perfect fit, $\{\hat{\mu}_i = y_i\}$. That model attains the maximum achievable log-likelihood, which is $L(\mathbf{y}; \mathbf{y})$. This perfectly-fitting model is called the **saturated model**. A perfect fit sounds good, but the saturated model has residual $df = 0$ and does not smooth the data or have the advantages of parsimony that a simpler model has, such as better estimation of the true relation. However, it serves as a baseline for constructing a likelihood-ratio statistic that compares it to the chosen (simpler) model,

$$D(\mathbf{y}; \hat{\boldsymbol{\mu}}) = 2\log\left[\frac{\text{maximum likelihood for saturated model}}{\text{maximum likelihood for chosen model}}\right]$$
$$= 2\big[L(\mathbf{y}; \mathbf{y}) - L(\hat{\boldsymbol{\mu}}; \mathbf{y})\big].$$

This statistic, which describes model lack of fit, is called the **scaled deviance**. Since the saturated model is more general than the chosen model, $L(\mathbf{y}; \mathbf{y}) \geq L(\hat{\boldsymbol{\mu}}; \mathbf{y})$, and therefore always $D(\mathbf{y}; \hat{\boldsymbol{\mu}}) \geq 0$. The greater the value of $D(\mathbf{y}; \hat{\boldsymbol{\mu}})$, the poorer the fit. For a particular GLM, *maximizing the likelihood corresponds to minimizing the scaled deviance*.

We illustrate for a GLM with normal random component, for which equation (2.8) shows the *pdf*. The log-likelihood function is the log of the product of *pdf* terms for the n observations,

$$L(\boldsymbol{\mu}; \mathbf{y}) = \log\left[\prod_{i=1}^{n}\left(\frac{1}{\sqrt{2\pi}\sigma}e^{-(y_i - \mu_i)^2/2\sigma^2}\right)\right] = -n\log(\sqrt{2\pi}\sigma) - \frac{\sum_{i=1}^{n}(y_i - \mu_i)^2}{2\sigma^2}.$$

Similarly, $L(\hat{\boldsymbol{\mu}}; \mathbf{y})$ is this expression with $\{\hat{\mu}_i\}$ substituted for $\{\mu_i\}$, where with the identity link function, $\hat{\mu}_i = \hat{\beta}_0 + \hat{\beta}_1 x_{i1} + \cdots + \hat{\beta}_p x_{ip}$. For the saturated model, the first term in $L(\mathbf{y}; \mathbf{y})$ is the same as in $L(\hat{\boldsymbol{\mu}}; \mathbf{y})$, but the second term equals 0, because each $\hat{\mu}_i = y_i$. Therefore,

$$D(\mathbf{y}; \hat{\boldsymbol{\mu}}) = 2\big[L(\mathbf{y}; \mathbf{y}) - L(\hat{\boldsymbol{\mu}}; \mathbf{y})\big] = \left(\frac{1}{\sigma^2}\right)\sum_{i=1}^{n}(y_i - \hat{\mu}_i)^2.$$

In practice, we do not observe the scaled deviance for normal GLMs, because σ^2 is unknown. The numerator of the scaled variance is called the **deviance**. For normal linear models, this is SSE. The discrete-data models introduced in this chapter do not have a separate variance parameter, and the *deviance* and *scaled deviance* are identical.

7.1.5   Likelihood-Ratio Model Comparison Uses Deviance Difference

A primary use of the deviance is for inferential comparisons of models. Much as we compare SSE values to compare two normal linear models (Section 6.5.6), we use the difference between deviances to compare two GLMs. For two nested models, with M_0 a special case of M_1, suppose M_0 has p_0 explanatory variables and fitted values $\hat{\boldsymbol{\mu}}_0$ and M_1 has p_1 explanatory variables and fitted values $\hat{\boldsymbol{\mu}}_1$. Since the parameter space for M_0 is contained in that for M_1, $L(\hat{\boldsymbol{\mu}}_0; \boldsymbol{y}) \le L(\hat{\boldsymbol{\mu}}_1; \boldsymbol{y})$ and

$$D(\boldsymbol{y}; \hat{\boldsymbol{\mu}}_1) = 2\big[L(\boldsymbol{y}; \boldsymbol{y}) - L(\hat{\boldsymbol{\mu}}_1; \boldsymbol{y})\big] \le 2\big[L(\boldsymbol{y}; \boldsymbol{y}) - L(\hat{\boldsymbol{\mu}}_0; \boldsymbol{y})\big] = D(\boldsymbol{y}; \hat{\boldsymbol{\mu}}_0).$$

Simpler models have larger deviances.

Consider the null hypothesis that model M_0 holds, in the sense that the true relationship satisfies model M_0, conditional on the alternative hypothesis that the true relationship satisfies model M_1. The likelihood-ratio test uses the test statistic

$$
\begin{aligned}
2[L(\hat{\boldsymbol{\mu}}_1; \boldsymbol{y}) - L(\hat{\boldsymbol{\mu}}_0; \boldsymbol{y})] &= 2[L(\hat{\boldsymbol{\mu}}_1; \boldsymbol{y}) - L(\boldsymbol{y}; \boldsymbol{y})] - 2[L(\hat{\boldsymbol{\mu}}_0; \boldsymbol{y}) - L(\boldsymbol{y}; \boldsymbol{y})] \\
&= D(\boldsymbol{y}; \hat{\boldsymbol{\mu}}_0) - D(\boldsymbol{y}; \hat{\boldsymbol{\mu}}_1). \qquad\qquad (7.1)
\end{aligned}
$$

This statistic is larger when M_0 fits more poorly, compared with M_1. For discrete-data models, differences between deviance statistics $D(\boldsymbol{Y}; \hat{\boldsymbol{\mu}}_0) - D(\boldsymbol{Y}; \hat{\boldsymbol{\mu}}_1)$ often have large-sample chi-squared null distributions (i.e., when M_0 holds), with $df = p_1 - p_0$.

Testing H_0: $\beta_j = 0$ is an example of a model comparison, in which M_0 deletes the effect of explanatory variable j, and $df = 1$ for comparing the models. In this case, an alternative to the likelihood-ratio test statistic is $Z = \hat{\beta}_j / SE_j$. This is an example of the *Wald statistic* (Section 5.7.3). Since ML estimators have approximate normal sampling distributions, Z has an approximate standard normal null distribution. This statistic is an analog of the t test statistic used in normal linear models. Squaring the Wald statistic also yields a chi-squared statistic with $df = 1$. For discrete-data GLMs, the likelihood-ratio test is often slightly more powerful.[1]

7.1.6   Model Selection: AIC and the Bias/Variance Tradeoff

In practice, with several potential explanatory variables, selecting an appropriate subset of them for a model is not a trivial task. We now recall some key points previously made, and see Section A.7.3 of the R Appendix for further discussion. In selecting a model through some process, one should not conclude that the chosen model is the "correct" one. Any model is a simplification of reality. For example, an explanatory variable will not truly have *exactly* a linear effect on the link-function scale. A simple model that fits adequately, however, has the advantages of simple interpretation and model parsimony.[2]

In selecting a model, a fundamental tradeoff occurs between bias and variance. We explained this tradeoff in Section 4.1.2 in the context of estimating a parameter. For a model, measures of bias and variance apply to estimators of characteristics such as the model parameters and the conditional response mean $E(Y)$ at any particular values of the explanatory variables. For example, consider comparing a simple model and a more complex model in terms of using a GLM fitted value $\hat{\mu} = g^{-1}(\hat{\beta}_0 + \hat{\beta}_1 x_1 + \cdots + \hat{\beta}_p x_p)$ to estimate the true value of $E(Y)$ at particular values of the explanatory variables. Because the more complex model can describe a wider variety of relationships, the *expected value* of $\hat{\mu}$ for that model will tend to be *closer* to the true $E(Y)$ than the expected value of $\hat{\mu}$ for the simpler

---

[1]It also is valid when Wald statistics are inappropriate, such as when $\hat{\beta}_j$ is infinite (Sec. 7.2.6).

[2]In a more general context, *Occam's razor* is the principle that of the many possible models that can adequately describe some situation, "simpler is better."

model. Since the bias is the difference between $E(\hat{\mu})$ and the true $E(Y)$, the more complex model has less bias. However, the estimator $\hat{\mu}$ for the more complex model will have greater variance than the estimator $\hat{\mu}$ for the simpler model, because of its greater number of model parameters.

▶ As the model complexity increases, the ML estimator of a characteristic such as the true conditional mean $E(Y)$ at particular values of the explanatory variables has less bias but greater variance.

Because of this, the estimator $\hat{\mu}$ for the simpler model may actually tend to be *closer* to the true $E(Y)$ than the estimator $\hat{\mu}$ for the more complex model, because of its smaller variance.

From equation (4.1), *the mean squared error (MSE) of an estimator equals the variance plus the squared bias.* Therefore, an increase in bias with a simpler model is not problematic if the variance decreases sufficiently. Figure 7.2 illustrates the tradeoff in terms of estimating a particular characteristic such as a response mean or a parameter describing some effect. The most complex of a set of models is not necessarily preferable, even though it has the smallest deviance and perhaps fits best in terms of statistical significance. Overfitting the data, using more predictor terms than we need, also results in poorer effects of individual predictors because of multicollinearity (Section 6.4.4).

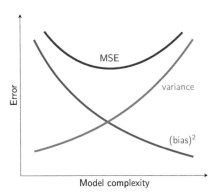

FIGURE 7.2 The bias/variance tradeoff in using a model to estimate a characteristic such as a response mean: Compared with an overly complex model, a sensible model adds some bias to reduce variance and to achieve mean squared error (MSE) near the minimum.

To illustrate this, we randomly generated $n = 20$ observations, with X having a uniform distribution over $[0, 100]$, and conditional on $X = x$, Y having a normal distribution and a quadratic relationship with x, $E(Y) = 40 + 4.0x - 0.1x^2$, and with $\sigma = 5.0$. Figure 7.3 shows the data, the true relationship, and the fits of three models: The null model $E(Y) = \beta_0$, the straight-line model $E(Y) = \beta_0 + \beta_1 x$, and a fifth-degree polynomial $E(Y) = \beta_0 + \beta_1 x + \beta_2 x^2 + \beta_3 x^3 + \beta_4 x^4 + \beta_5 x^5$. The polynomial model allows lots of flexibility, with straight-line and quadratic models being special cases as well as "wiggly" relationships in which the shape changes from concave to convex or the reverse a few times. The SSE decreases as the model complexity increases: 1761.3 for the null model, 403.5 for the straight-line model, and 237.2 for the polynomial, but the null model has high bias and the polynomial model has high variance. Suppose that we repeatedly took random samples with this structure. The fit of the null model would not vary much from sample to sample, but its large bias would be reflected by its fitted values always tending to fall far from the true means, no matter how large the sample size n. By contrast, the fit of the polynomial model would vary greatly from sample to sample, but it has good bias characteristics (e.g., the fit would gradually converge toward the true quadratic relationship as n increases). The polynomial model contains the true quadratic model as a special case, which the straight-line model does not. For these data, however, by utilizing the bias/variance tradeoff, the straight-line model has fit that is closer overall to the true relationship. The sum of squares of the model fitted values around the means from the true relationship is 180.7 for the polynomial model and 55.5 for the straight-line model. The straight-line model also has much simpler interpretation.

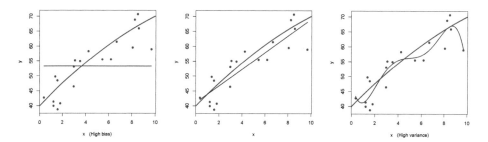

FIGURE 7.3 Fits of (i) null model, (ii) straight-line model, (iii) fifth-degree polynomial model, in each case showing (in blue) the true relationship $E(Y) = 40+4.0x-0.1x^2$. The data were randomly generated with X uniform over $[0, 100]$ and Y having a normal conditional distribution around $E(Y)$ with $\sigma = 5$.

Because of the bias/variance tradeoff and the advantages of parsimonious models, other criteria besides statistical significance tests can help in selecting a model. The best known is the ***Akaike information criterion*** (AIC). It judges a model by how close its fitted values tend to be to the true expected values, as summarized by a certain expected distance between the two. For maximized log-likelihood function $L(\hat{\mu}; y)$ and p explanatory variables ($p + 1$ parameters), a good model by this criterion has a relatively small value of

$$\text{AIC} = -2(\text{log likelihood}) + 2(\text{number of parameters in model}) = -2L(\hat{\mu}; y) + 2(p + 1).$$

For a particular log-likelihood value, AIC increases as the number of parameters ($p + 1$) increases. Because smaller AIC is better, the AIC penalizes a model for having many parameters.[3] Even though a simpler model necessarily has smaller log likelihood (and larger deviance) than a more complex model, its estimates may tend to be closer to the true expected values. For a set of potential models, the ones having AIC within about 2.0 of the minimum AIC for those models have substantial support and are worthy of consideration for the goal of having fitted values near true expected values. For modeling house selling prices, from the outputs in Section 7.1.3, AIC = 1161 for the normal GLM and AIC = 1129 for the gamma GLM. These indicate a clear preference for the gamma GLM.[4]

An alternative criterion, called BIC, replaces 2 by $\log(n)$ in the penalty multiple of the number of parameters in the AIC formula. It penalizes a model more strongly for having many parameters. Derived from a Bayesian viewpoint, it regards a model as better if its posterior probability is higher, based on equal prior probabilities for the possible models and uninformative priors on the model parameters. Minimizing BIC can yield a more parsimonious model than AIC. When n is very large, this is often desirable, because a model regarded as optimal according to AIC can have effects that are statistically significant but not *practically* significant.

---

[3]Corrections of AIC apply when a model has a very large number of parameters or when overdispersion exists for discrete data. See Burnham and Anderson (2002, Section 2.4 and 2.5).

[4]These models do not differ in structure but their probability distributions differ. Model selection in such cases can also be based on AIC. See Burnham and Anderson (2002, Section 6.7).

7.1.7 Advantages of GLMs versus Transforming the Data

Before GLMs were developed, a common way for statisticians to model response variables that badly violated the ordinary linear model assumptions of a normal distribution with constant variance was to use a transformation $g(y)$ of the response that better satisfies those assumptions and then constructing linear models for $E[g(Y)]$. For example, with count data that have a Poisson distribution, the distribution is skewed to the right with $\text{var}(Y) = E(Y)$. Section 3.4.2 showed that the transformation $g(Y) = \sqrt{Y}$ has a more bell-shaped distribution with variance approximately $1/4$. For most data, however, it is challenging to find a transformation that provides both approximate normality and constant variance. With GLMs, it is not necessary to have normality or constant variance, because the fitting process maximizes the likelihood function for the choice of probability distribution for Y, and that choice is not restricted to normality. Also, the GLM with link function g then describes $g[E(Y)]$, rather than $E[g(Y)]$. As a consequence we'll see in this chapter that GLMs provide information about $E(Y)$ on the original scale, which makes interpretation more direct than in modeling $E[g(Y)]$.

Although the transformed data approach has fallen out of favor as GLMs have become more popular, it is still useful in some situations. Modeling the mean on the original scale may be misleading when the response distribution is extremely skewed and has many outliers. A transformed response such as $\log(Y)$ can then be a more meaningful and stable measure, in which case it is sensible to construct models for that transformed response. Linear models for log-transformed responses are also often used when Y tends to grow exponentially as a function of x, to make a straight-line predictor appropriate. GLMs can also handle exponential relationships, using the log link function and an appropriate distribution for Y.

7.1.8 Example: Normal and Gamma GLMs for Covid-19 Data

Figure 6.3 in Section 6.1.7 plotted total counts of Covid-19 cases in the U.S. in March 2020. The plot showed that y = total number of cases was approximately an exponential function of x = day number during the early days of the pandemic. The $\{\log(y_i)\}$ values, also shown in Figure 6.3, more closely follow a linear pattern, having a correlation of $r = 0.997$ with x. Section 7.4 introduces models for count data, but here the counts have such a large number of possible values that we can treat y as continuous. Fitting a normal linear model to those log-transformed values, with $E[\log(Y_i)] = \beta_0 + \beta_1 x_i$, assumes that $\log(Y)$ has a normal distribution, for each day. The corresponding distribution with support on the positive real line for Y itself is the *log-normal distribution* (Exercise 2.71). Like the gamma distribution, it has standard deviation proportional to the mean, so it permits Y to vary more when $E(Y)$ is higher, which is common in practice for nonnegative Y.

By contrast, rather than modeling $E[\log(Y)]$, a GLM applies the log link function to $E(Y)$,

$$\log[E(Y_i)] = \beta_0 + \beta_1 x_i.$$

An advantage is that this induces a model for $E(Y)$ itself, as $E(Y_i) = \exp(\beta_0 + \beta_1 x_i)$. The GLM that assumes a normal distribution for Y assumes a constant variance for Y at all x. The GLM that assumes a gamma distribution for Y permits the standard deviation to be proportional to the mean, as is true for the log-normal distribution. Because of this common relation between the standard deviation and the mean, using the gamma GLM with log link tends to give results similar to those based on assuming the log-normal distribution for Y (i.e., using a linear model for $\log(Y)$).

The following R output shows results for (1) the linear model for a log-normal response, (2) the GLM using the log link for a normal response, (3) the GLM using the log link for a gamma response. Results for (1) and (3) are similar, since both allow the variability of Y to grow as $E(Y)$ grows, whereas model (2) assumes constant variance. Of the two GLMs, the AIC is lower for model (3), suggesting that the gamma GLM fit is better.

```
> Covid <- read.table("http://stat4ds.rwth-aachen.de/data/Covid19.dat", header=TRUE)
> Covid
  day   cases
  1        16
 ...
  31    140904
 # (1) normal linear model for log(count); models E[log(Y)] with log(Y) ~ normal
> fit1 <- glm(log(cases) ~ day, family=gaussian(link=identity), data=Covid)
> summary(fit1) # equivalent to using fit1 <- lm(log(cases) ~ day, data=Covid)
             Estimate  Std. Error  t value  Pr(>|t|)
(Intercept)  2.843852   0.084012    33.85    <2e-16
day          0.308807   0.004583    67.38    <2e-16
---

 # (2) normal GLM with log link applied to mean; models log[E(Y)] with Y ~ normal
> fit2 <- glm(cases ~ day, family=gaussian(link=log), data=Covid)
> summary(fit2)
             Estimate  Std. Error  t value  Pr(>|t|)
(Intercept)  5.315921   0.167679    31.70    <2e-16
day          0.212920   0.005741    37.09    <2e-16
---
AIC: 596.08
 # (3) gamma GLM with log link; models log[E(Y)] with Y ~ gamma
> fit3 <- glm(cases ~ day, family=Gamma(link=log), data=Covid)
> summary(fit3)
             Estimate  Std. Error  t value  Pr(>|t|)
(Intercept)  2.857252   0.077281    36.97    <2e-16
day          0.309405   0.004216    73.39    <2e-16
---
AIC: 481.37
```

The gamma GLM has fit $\log(\hat{\mu}_i) = 2.857 + 0.309x_i$. We can obtain the estimated mean by exponentiating both sides, yielding $\hat{\mu}_i = \exp(2.857 + 0.309x_i) = 17.41(1.36)^{x_i}$. When we use the log link function, model effects are *multiplicative*. The estimated mean on day $x + 1$ equals the estimated mean on day x multiplied by 1.36; that is, the mean increases by 36%.

7.2   Logistic Regression Model for Binary Data

GLMs for binary responses assume a *binomial* distribution for the response variable. The most common link function for binomial GLMs is the *logit*, which is the canonical link function and for which the model itself is *logistic regression*. Early uses were in biomedical studies, such as to model the effects of cholesterol level, blood pressure, and smoking on the presence or absence of heart disease. Recent years have seen substantial use in social science research for modeling behaviors and opinions (e.g., whether the government should provide a basic income to low-income families having children), in marketing applications for modeling consumer decisions (e.g., the choice between two brands of a particular product), and in finance for modeling credit-related outcomes (e.g., whether a credit card bill is paid on time).

7.2.1 Logistic Regression: Model Expressions

For binary data, each observation y_i takes value 0 or 1. Then, $\mu_i = E(Y_i) = P(Y_i = 1)$, denoted by π_i. Let $\text{logit}(\pi_i)$ denote $\log[\pi_i/(1-\pi_i)]$. The **logistic regression model** with p explanatory variables is

$$\text{logit}(\pi_i) = \log\left(\frac{\pi_i}{1-\pi_i}\right) = \beta_0 + \beta_1 x_{i1} + \cdots + \beta_p x_{ip}, \quad i = 1,\ldots,n. \tag{7.2}$$

An expression for the probability itself is

$$P(Y_i = 1) = \pi_i = \frac{\exp(\beta_0 + \beta_1 x_{i1} + \cdots + \beta_p x_{ip})}{1 + \exp(\beta_0 + \beta_1 x_{i1} + \cdots + \beta_p x_{ip})}. \tag{7.3}$$

The function $F(z) = e^z/(1 + e^z)$ is the *cdf* of a standard **logistic distribution**.[5] This distribution has a bell-shaped *pdf*, symmetric around 0, but with thicker tails than the standard normal distribution. Formula (7.3) for π_i substitutes $\beta_0 + \beta_1 x_{i1} + \cdots + \beta_p x_{ip}$ for z in this formula. This is the reason for the name, *logistic* regression.

7.2.2 Parameter Interpretation: Effects on Probabilities and Odds

We next consider interpretation of model parameters in logistic regression. To simplify notation, we focus on the case of a single quantitative explanatory variable x, then mentioning generalizations to multiple quantitative and/or categorical explanatory variables. For the model $\text{logit}[P(Y = 1)] = \beta_0 + \beta_1 x$, for which

$$P(Y = 1) = \frac{\exp(\beta_0 + \beta_1 x)}{1 + \exp(\beta_0 + \beta_1 x)} \quad \text{and} \quad P(Y = 0) = 1 - P(Y = 1) = \frac{1}{1 + \exp(\beta_0 + \beta_1 x)},$$

the curve for $P(Y = 1)$ is monotone in x: When $\beta_1 > 0$, $P(Y = 1)$ increases as x increases; when $\beta_1 < 0$, $P(Y = 1)$ decreases as x increases (see Figure 7.4). When $\beta_1 = 0$, the logistic curve flattens to a horizontal line. As x changes, $P(Y = 1)$ approaches 1 at the same rate that it approaches 0. The model has $P(Y = 1) = 0.50$ when $\text{logit}[P(Y = 1)] = \log(0.50/0.50) = \log(1) = 0 = \beta_0 + \beta_1 x$, which occurs at $x = -\beta_0/\beta_1$. With multiple explanatory variables, $P(Y = 1)$ is monotone in each explanatory variable according to the sign of its coefficient. The rate of climb or descent increases as $|\beta_j|$ increases. When $\beta_j = 0$, Y is conditionally independent of x_j, given the other explanatory variables.

We can also interpret the magnitude of β_1. A straight line drawn tangent to the curve at any particular value describes the rate of change in $P(Y = 1)$ at that point. Using the logistic regression formula for $P(Y = 1)$, this slope is

$$\frac{\partial P(Y = 1)}{\partial x} = \frac{\partial}{\partial x}\left[\frac{\exp(\beta_0 + \beta_1 x)}{1 + \exp(\beta_0 + \beta_1 x)}\right] = \beta_1 \frac{\exp(\beta_0 + \beta_1 x)}{[1 + \exp(\beta_0 + \beta_1 x)]^2} = \beta_1 P(Y = 1)[1 - P(Y = 1)].$$

The slope is steepest, and equals $\beta_1/4$, when $P(Y = 1) = 1/2$. The slope decreases toward 0 as $P(Y = 1)$ moves toward 0 or 1. With multiple explanatory variables, the rate of change in $P(Y = 1)$ as a function of explanatory variable j, adjusting for the other explanatory variables, is $\beta_j P(Y = 1)[1 - P(Y = 1)]$. Alternatively, to summarize an effect we can use equation (7.3) to compare $P(Y = 1)$ at relevant values of x_j, such as its maximum and minimum or its upper and lower quartiles, with other explanatory variables set at their means.

---

[5]A general logistic family, replacing z by $(y - \mu)/\tau$ for $\tau > 0$, permits arbitrary mean and standard deviation $\sigma = \tau\pi/\sqrt{3}$ (for $\pi = 3.14\ldots$), like the normal family.

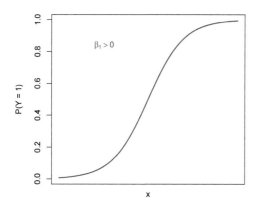 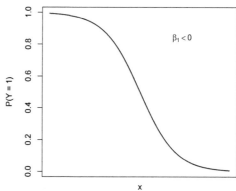

FIGURE 7.4 The logistic regression curve with a single quantitative explanatory variable is monotone increasing or monotone decreasing according to the sign of β_1.

An alternative interpretation for β_1 uses the **odds** of success,

$$\text{odds} = \frac{P(Y=1)}{P(Y=0)}.$$

The odds can take any nonnegative value. With an odds of 3, for instance, we expect 3 successes for every failure; with an odds of $1/3$, we expect 1 success for every 3 failures. The log of the odds is the logit. From the logistic regression formulas for $P(Y=1)$ and $P(Y=0)$, the odds with this model are

$$\frac{P(Y=1)}{P(Y=0)} = \frac{\exp(\beta_0 + \beta_1 x)/[1 + \exp(\beta_0 + \beta_1 x)]}{1/[1 + \exp(\beta_0 + \beta_1 x)]} = \exp(\beta_0 + \beta_1 x) = e^{\beta_0}(e^{\beta_1})^x. \qquad (7.4)$$

The odds have an exponential relationship with x. A 1-unit increase in x has a multiplicative impact of e^{β_1}: The odds at $x = u+1$ equals the odds at $x = u$ multiplied by e^{β_1}. Equivalently, e^{β_1} is the *ratio* of the odds at $x+1$ divided by the odds at x, which is called an **odds ratio**.[6] For a logistic regression model with multiple explanatory variables, the odds are

$$\frac{P(Y=1)}{P(Y=0)} = \exp(\beta_0 + \beta_1 x_1 + \ldots + \beta_j x_j + \ldots + \beta_p x_p) = e^{\beta_0}(e^{\beta_1})^{x_1} \ldots (e^{\beta_j})^{x_j} \ldots (e^{\beta_p})^{x_p}.$$

If x_j is quantitative or binary, e^{β_j} is a *conditional odds ratio*. That is, e^{β_j} equals the odds at $x_j = u+1$ divided by the odds at $x_j = u$, adjusting for the other explanatory variables.

7.2.3   Example: Dose–Response Study for Flour Beetles

The `Beetles` data file at the book's website contains data from one of the first studies[7] to use a binary regression model, in 1935. For 481 adult flour beetles, the study observed the number that died after five hours of exposure to gaseous carbon disulfide at eight distinct

---

[6]British statistician George Udny Yule promoted this measure for categorical data in several articles between 1900 and 1912, one of which showed that *conditional* odds ratios, adjusting for other variables, can be very different from *marginal* odds ratios. This result is a special case of Simpson's paradox.

[7]The data were first reported in an article by C. Bliss, *Ann. Appl. Biol.* **22**: 134–167 (1935).

dosages (in $mg/$liter). At each value of $x = \log_{10}(\text{dose})$, we treat $y =$ number dead as a binomial random variable for the number of beetles n at that dose. Figure 7.5 plots the sample proportion killed against x. The proportion jumps up at about $x = 1.81$, and it is close to 1 above there.

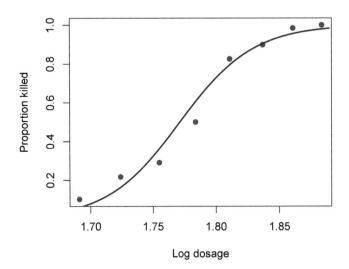

FIGURE 7.5 Proportion of dead beetles versus log dosage of gaseous carbon disulfide, with fit of logistic regression model.

Using R, we can fit a logistic regression model with the `glm` function, specifying a binomial distribution with logit link function, which is the canonical default for the binomial:

```
> Beetles <- read.table("http://stat4ds.rwth-aachen.de/data/Beetles.dat", header=TRUE)
> Beetles
  logdose live dead  n
1   1.691   53    6 59      # for 59 beetles at lowest dosage, 6 died, 53 survived
2   1.724   47   13 60
3   1.755   44   18 62
4   1.784   28   28 56
5   1.811   11   52 63
6   1.837    6   53 59
7   1.861    1   61 62
8   1.884    0   60 60
> fit <- glm(dead/n ~ logdose, weights=n, family=binomial(link=logit), data=Beetles)
 # number dead treated as binomial, "weights=n" specifies binomial number of trials
 # can omit (link=logit), which is default canonical link function for binomial response
> summary(fit)
            Estimate  Std. Error  z value  Pr(>|z|)
(Intercept)  -60.740       5.182   -11.72    <2e-16
logdose       34.286       2.913    11.77    <2e-16
----

    Null deviance: 284.202  on 7  degrees of freedom
Residual deviance:  11.116  on 6  degrees of freedom

> fitted(fit) # estimated P(Y = 1) at the 8 values of logdose
      1       2       3       4       5       6       7       8
0.05938 0.16367 0.36162 0.60491 0.79440 0.90406 0.95547 0.97926
> exp(0.01*confint(fit))
```

```
          2.5%   97.5%     # 95% profile-likelihood CI for multiplicative
  x      1.3347 1.4966     # effect on odds, exp[(0.01)beta_1]
```

Figure 7.5 also shows the fit of the model.[8] As x increases from the lowest dosage of 1.691 to the highest dosage of 1.884, $\hat{P}(Y = 1)$ increases from 0.059 to 0.979, with value 0.50 at $x = -\hat{\beta}_0/\hat{\beta}_1 = 60.74/34.29 = 1.77$. The effect is substantial.

Here, log-dosage has a range of only $1.884 - 1.691 = 0.19$, so it is not sensible to consider the effect for a 1-unit change in x. For each 0.01 increase in the log dosage, the estimated odds of death multiply by $e^{0.01(34.286)} = 1.41$. The 95% Wald confidence interval for 0.01β is $0.01[34.286 \pm 1.96(2.913)]$, which is $(0.286, 0.400)$. A 95% confidence interval for this odds ratio is $(e^{0.286}, e^{0.400})$, which is $(1.33, 1.49)$. Applying the `confint` function in R to a GLM model fit yields the profile-likelihood confidence interval (based on inverting results of likelihood-ratio tests) shown in the output, which is similar.

The difference between the null and residual deviances, $284.20 - 22.12 = 273.09$, is the likelihood-ratio statistic for testing $H_0: \beta_1 = 0$. The P-value, which is the right-tail probability above 273.09 for the χ_1^2 distribution, is essentially 0. An alternative test statistic is the Wald statistic, $z = \hat{\beta}_1/se = 34.286/2.913 = 11.77$ or its corresponding χ_1^2 statistic of $(\hat{\beta}_1/se)^2 = 138.5$. Either chi-squared statistic provides extremely strong evidence of an effect in the conceptual population.

7.2.4 Grouped and Ungrouped Binary Data: Effects on Estimates and Deviance

When all explanatory variables are discrete, data files for binary data have two possible formats. When each observation y_i refers to a single subject, and thus equals 0 or 1, the data are said to be *ungrouped*. The ungrouped data file for the beetle dose–response study has 481 lines of data, where for each beetle, $y = 1$ for death and $y = 0$ for survival:

```
> Beetles <- read.table("http://stat4ds.rwth-aachen.de/data/Beetles_ungrouped.dat",
+                       header=TRUE)
> Beetles
          x  y       # y=1 for death, y=0 for survival
1      1.691  1      # 481 lines of data in ungrouped data file
2      1.691  1
...
481    1.884  1
```

Figure 7.6 plots the data in ungrouped form. When many data points have exactly or nearly exactly the same position, such as when observations are discrete or are rounded, it is often helpful to plot the data after *jittering*, which is the action of adding a small amount of random noise to the data. Adding values generated randomly according to a uniform distribution over an interval $[-a, a]$ to x and to y for each of the observations makes it easier to see where most of the observations fall. The constant a chosen for the maximum amount added depends on the scaling of the variables. You can try various separate values for x and y to improve clarity of the plot. Figure 7.6 shows scatterplots obtained without jittering and with jittering, with $a = 0.008$ for the x jitter and $a = 0.1$ for the y jitter. Here is the code to do this:

```
> plot(Beetles$x, Beetles$y, xlab="x", ylab="y") # no jittering
> plot(jitter(Beetles$x, amount=0.008), jitter(Beetles$y, amount=0.1))
```

The jittered plot shows that $y = 0$ is more common when x is small and $y = 1$ is more common when x is large. Caution is needed with jittering, since adding too much random noise can weaken the visual impact of a relationship.

---

[8]In the R Appendix, Section A.7.2 shows how to plot the curve.

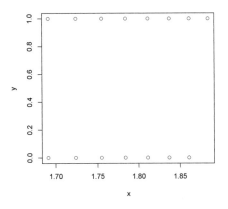 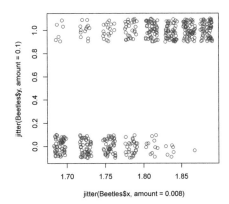

FIGURE 7.6 Scatterplot without jittering (left) and with jittering (right) for the beetles dose–response study, which has a binary response variable and a discrete explanatory variable taking only 8 values.

For *grouped data*, sets of observations have the same value for each explanatory variable. For the beetle mortality example, the previous R output showed the data in grouped form (8 lines of data, one for each of the 8 dosage levels). This is adequate, because the sufficient statistic (Section 4.2.3) for a binomial sample with a particular number of trials is the number of successes. So, the data can be summarized in that form without losing any information. We obtain the same ML estimates and standard errors in logistic regression with the grouped and the ungrouped data. Here are corresponding logistic regression results on beetle mortality with the ungrouped data file:

```
> Beetles <- read.table("http://stat4ds.rwth-aachen.de/data/Beetles_ungrouped.dat",
+                            header=TRUE)
> fit <- glm(y ~ x, family = binomial(link=logit), data=Beetles) # weights not needed
> summary(fit)                                                    # for ungrouped data
             Estimate  Std. Error  z value  Pr(>|z|)
(Intercept)  -60.740      5.182     -11.72    <2e-16
x             34.286      2.913      11.77    <2e-16
----
     Null deviance: 645.44  on 480  degrees of freedom # different from grouped data,
 Residual deviance: 372.35  on 479  degrees of freedom # but same difference
```

For a particular model for binary data, *the residual and null deviance differ for the grouped and ungrouped data files*, because the saturated model differs in the two cases. For the ungrouped binary data in this example, the saturated model has fitted probability $\tilde{\pi}_i = y_i$, with $y_i = 0$ or 1 $(i = 1, \ldots, 481)$. For the grouped binary data, y_i is the number of deaths for n_i beetles at dosage i, and the saturated model has fitted probability estimate $\tilde{\pi}_i = y_i/n_i$ that is the same for all n_i observations at a particular dosage $(i = 1, \ldots, 8)$. Comparing to the fitted probabilities $\{\hat{\pi}_i\}$ for the chosen model, the deviance $D(\boldsymbol{y}; \hat{\boldsymbol{\pi}})$ for n binary ungrouped observations is

$$2\big[L(\tilde{\boldsymbol{\pi}}; \boldsymbol{y}) - L(\hat{\boldsymbol{\pi}}; \boldsymbol{y})\big] = 2\left\{ \log\left[\prod_{i=1}^{n} \tilde{\pi}_i^{y_i}(1 - \tilde{\pi}_i)^{1-y_i} \right] - \log\left[\prod_{i=1}^{n} \hat{\pi}_i^{y_i}(1 - \hat{\pi}_i)^{1-y_i} \right] \right\}$$

$$= 2\sum_{i=1}^{n} y_i \log\left(\frac{y_i}{\hat{\pi}_i}\right) + 2\sum_{i=1}^{n}(1 - y_i)\log\left(\frac{1 - y_i}{1 - \hat{\pi}_i}\right).$$

For k grouped binomial observations, one can show that the deviance is

$$2\sum_{i=1}^{k} y_i \log\left(\frac{y_i}{n_i\hat{\pi}_i}\right) + 2\sum_{i=1}^{k}(n_i - y_i)\log\left(\frac{n_i - y_i}{n_i - n_i\hat{\pi}_i}\right). \tag{7.5}$$

From the second R output for the beetles data, with $n = 481$ ungrouped observations, the deviance equals 372.35 for the fitted model and 645.44 for the null model. These differ from the residual and null deviance values of 11.12 and 284.20 in the first R output for fitting the model to the grouped data file of $k = 8$ binomial observations. Both the ungrouped and grouped data cases have the same *difference of deviances* of 273.09, which is the likelihood-ratio statistic for testing the dosage effect. This happens because equation (7.1) showed that the log-likelihood for the saturated model cancels when we form the difference of deviances.

7.2.5 Example: Modeling Italian Employment with Logit and Identity Links

Like ordinary regression models, logistic regression models can contain categorical as well as quantitative explanatory variables, and better fits are sometimes possible by permitting interaction terms. To illustrate, we fitted models to a data file having results summarized in Table 7.1. The table refers to 72,200 people with age under 65, out of a random sample of 100,000 people taken in 2015 from the Tuscany region of Italy, using administrative sources collected and organized by Istituto Nazionale di Statistica (Istat). We model Y = whether the subject is employed, in terms of being present in any administrative source (1 = yes, 0 = no). Explanatory variables are G = gender (1 = female, 0 = male), I = whether an Italian citizen (1 = yes, 0 = no), and P = whether receiving a pension (1 = yes, 0 = no).

TABLE 7.1 Data for Istat sample and fitted values for models with logit and identity links for predicting whether employed using gender (G; 1 = female, 0 = male), whether Italian (I; 1 = yes, 0 = no), and whether receiving a pension (P; 1 = yes, 0 = no). The models have (i) main effects, (ii) main effects and an interaction between I and P.

			Sample proportion	(i) Main effects model		(ii) Main effects + I×P interaction	
				Logit	Identity	Logit	Identity
G	I	P	(Sample size) $\hat{P}(Y=1)$	$\hat{P}(Y=1)$	$\hat{P}(Y=1)$	$\hat{P}(Y=1)$	$\hat{P}(Y=1)$
1	1	1	0.199 (3400)	0.188	0.192	0.184	0.177
1	1	0	0.597 (27700)	0.601	0.600	0.601	0.602
1	0	1	0.220 (100)	0.103	0.041	0.215	0.212
1	0	0	0.434 (5200)	0.427	0.449	0.424	0.433
0	1	1	0.288 (3800)	0.305	0.331	0.301	0.317
0	1	0	0.745 (27500)	0.741	0.739	0.742	0.742
0	0	1	0.337 (100)	0.179	0.180	0.343	0.352
0	0	0	0.572 (4400)	0.587	0.587	0.584	0.573

Source: Roberta Varriale, Istat, Rome Italy. The sample sizes were not the actual ones but are rounded to the nearest hundred, for Istat confidentiality reasons.

Using indicator variables for the binary explanatory variables, the next output shows that the logistic regression model fit is

$$\text{logit}(\hat{\pi}_i) = \log\left[\frac{\hat{P}(Y_i = 1)}{\hat{P}(Y_i = 0)}\right] = 0.351 - 0.644G_i + 0.701I_i - 1.873P_i.$$

```
> Employ <- read.table("http://stat4ds.rwth-aachen.de/data/Employment.dat", header=TRUE)
> head(Employ, 2)
  subject female italian pension employed
1       1      0       0       0        1
2       2      0       0       0        1
> fit <- glm(employed ~ female + italian + pension, family = binomial, data = Employ)
> summary(fit) # logit is the default link with binomial response
            Estimate  Std. Error  z value  Pr(>|z|)
(Intercept)  0.35077    0.02237     15.68   <2e-16
female      -0.64449    0.01613    -39.95   <2e-16 # estimated P(employed) lower
italian      0.70130    0.02248     31.20   <2e-16 # for females than males
pension     -1.87323    0.02881    -65.03   <2e-16
```

For instance, adjusting for whether an Italian citizen and whether receiving a pension, the odds that a woman is employed are estimated to be $e^{-0.644} = 0.52$ times the odds that a man is employed.

As a function of a particular explanatory variable, the logistic regression curve for $P(Y = 1)$ is close to a straight line when $P(Y = 1)$ falls between 0.20 and 0.80. Therefore, the logistic regression model has fit resembling an ordinary linear model when all fitted probabilities are within that range. For those of age under 65 in the Italian survey, the sample proportions employed in the eight cases that cross classify the three explanatory variables fell between 0.20 and 0.75, so we illustrate this closeness by fitting the model with the identity link function. The GLM for binary data with identity link function is called a *linear probability model*. The next ouput shows that its fit[9] is

$$\hat{P}(Y_i = 1) = 0.587 - 0.139G_i + 0.152I_i - 0.408P_i.$$

```
> fit2 <- glm(employed ~ female + italian + pension,
              family=quasi(link=identity, variance="mu(1-mu)"), data=Employ)
> summary(fit2) # glm does not permit identity link function for binomial family
            Estimate  Std. Error  t value  Pr(>|t|)
(Intercept)  0.58728    0.00522    112.42   <2e-16
female      -0.13888    0.00345    -40.19   <2e-16 # estimated P(employed) is 0.139
italian      0.15176    0.00521     29.14   <2e-16 # lower for females than males
pension     -0.40836    0.00522    -78.23   <2e-16
```

This model has the advantage of simplicity of interpretation, because a model parameter estimate is merely a difference in estimated probabilities for a 1-unit increase in the explanatory variable. For instance, adjusting for whether an Italian citizen and whether receiving a pension, the probability that a woman is employed is estimated to be 0.139 lower than the probability that a man is employed.

Table 7.1 shows that the fitted proportions are quite similar for the two models. Both models show lack of fit for the non-Italians with a pension, but these are only 200 of the 72,200 cases. Table 7.1 also shows fitted values for the models that add an interaction term between the Italian citizen and pension variables. For that fit (not shown here), the gender main effect changes only from −0.1389 to −0.1397.

7.2.6 Complete Separation and Infinite Logistic Parameter Estimates

With certain data configurations, the log-likelihood function for logistic regression does not have a maximum but is monotone in a parameter β_j, so the ML estimate $\hat{\beta}_j$ is infinite. In such cases, however, the log-likelihood function looks quite flat at a very large value for $\hat{\beta}_j$.

---

[9]The `glm` function in R does not permit identity link function for a binomial response, so to get this fit we use an alternative family for which we can specify the binomial variance to obtain the fit.

The iterative process that software uses to fit the model determines that the maximum of the log-likelihood is at such a value and reports it as the ML estimate. Because the log-likelihood function is nearly flat at the reported value and because $\text{var}(\hat{\beta}_1)$ is determined by the curvature of the log likelihood, software reports a huge standard error for the estimated effect.

We illustrate with a simple toy example, and the following section shows actual data for which this happens. We fit a logistic regression model to six observations, shown in Figure 7.7: $y = 0$ at $x = 1, 2, 3$ and $y = 1$ at $x = 4, 5, 6$. A step function with $\hat{\pi}_i = 0$ for $x \leq 3.5$ and $\hat{\pi}_i = 1$ for $x > 3.5$ gives a perfect fit. When $\hat{\beta}_1 \to \infty$ and, for fixed $\hat{\beta}_1$, $\hat{\beta}_0 = -3.5\hat{\beta}_1$, this sequence of estimates has ever-increasing value of the likelihood function that comes successively closer to giving this perfect fit.[10]

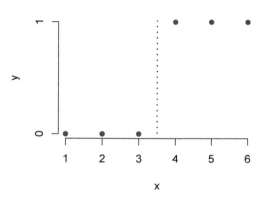

FIGURE 7.7 Complete separation of explanatory variable values, such as $y = 0$ when $x < 3.5$ and $y = 1$ when $x > 3.5$, causes an infinite ML effect estimate in logistic regression.

Here are result using R to fit the logistic regression model to these data:

```
> x <- c(1,2,3,4,5,6);  y <- c(0,0,0,1,1,1)  # complete separation
> fit <- glm(y ~ x, family = binomial(link = logit))
Warning message: glm.fit: fitted probabilities numerically 0 or 1
> summary(fit)
            Estimate Std. Error z value Pr(>|z|)
(Intercept) -165.32  407521.44       0        1
x             47.23  115264.41       0        1 # before rounding, z=0.0004, P-value=0.9997
----                                            # true ML estimate = infinity, not 47.23
    Null deviance: 8.3178e+00  on 5  degrees of freedom # residual deviance = 0 indicates
Residual deviance: 2.2152e-10  on 4  degrees of freedom # model has perfect fit
Number of Fisher Scoring iterations: 25 # unusually large; default max = 25; can increase,
                                        # e.g., use control=list(maxit=50) in glm command
```

The reported ML estimate of $\hat{\beta}_1 = 47.23$ has $se = 115264.4$. The Wald test statistic for H_0: $\beta_1 = 0$ is $z = 47.23/115264.4 = 0.0004$, with P-value = 0.9997. For these data, the true $\hat{\beta}_1 = \infty$. In such a case, Wald inference is useless, but likelihood-ratio tests are still available. The log-likelihood function $L(\beta)$ has a maximized value as $\hat{\beta} \to \infty$, so you can compare it with the maximized $L(\beta)$ value when β_1 has a fixed value such as 0. In the R output, the likelihood-ratio test statistic for H_0: $\beta_1 = 0$ equals the difference between the null and

---

[10]Note $\hat{\pi} = 0.50$ at $x = 3.5$ when $\text{logit}(\hat{\pi}) = \hat{\beta}_0 + \hat{\beta}_1(3.5) = 0$; i.e., when $\hat{\beta}_0 = -3.5\hat{\beta}_1$.

residual deviances, which is 8.32. This statistic has a chi-squared (for $df = 1$) P-value $=$ 0.004, very different from the Wald test and strong evidence that actually $\beta_1 > 0$.

For logistic regression, infinite estimates occur when the space of explanatory variable values exhibits **complete separation**, in which a plane (or a line in the case of a single explanatory variable, as in Figure 7.7) can perfectly separate cases having $y = 1$ from cases having $y = 0$. A weaker condition, called **quasi-complete separation**, occurs when separation occurs except at a boundary at which cases exist with both outcomes, such as occurs if we add an observation at $x = 3$ that has $y = 1$. Quasi-complete separation is not uncommon with explanatory factors. If any category has either no cases with $y = 0$ or no cases with $y = 1$, quasi-complete separation occurs when that variable is entered as a factor in the model.

For example, suppose that a randomized clinical trial comparing a new drug ($x = 1$) to placebo ($x = 0$) has 10 successes in 10 trials for the new drug and 5 successes in 10 trials for placebo. Table 7.2 shows the results for the binary response y (1 = success, 0 = failure). This 2×2 contingency table shows quasi-complete separation, because all observations are successes for the drug but both types of outcome occur for placebo. For the logistic regression model, $\text{logit}[P(Y = 1)]) = \beta_0 + \beta_1 x$, e^{β_1} is the odds ratio comparing drug to placebo. For the table showing the grouped data, $\hat{\beta}_1$ is the sample log odds ratio. For Table 7.2, this is $\log[(10 \times 5)/(0 \times 5)] = \infty$.

TABLE 7.2 A 2×2 contingency table comparing two groups on a binary response variable for which logistic regression has an infinite ML effect estimate because of quasi-complete separation.

	y	
Group (x)	1	0
Drug ($x = 1$)	10	0
Placebo ($x = 0$)	5	5

7.3 Bayesian Inference for Generalized Linear Models

As with normal linear models, Bayesian inference for GLMs provides a posterior distribution for $\{\beta_j\}$ that combines the likelihood function with their prior distribution. The posterior mean estimates shrink the ML estimates $\{\hat{\beta}_j\}$ toward the mean of the prior distribution.

7.3.1 Normal Prior Distributions for GLM Parameters

A relatively uninformative prior structure takes $\{\beta_j\}$ to be independent $N(0, \sigma^2)$ random variables with a very large σ. The posterior distribution using such priors has similar shape as the likelihood function. Unlike the normal linear model, most GLMs do not have closed form for posterior distributions. Software uses Markov Chain Monte Carlo (MCMC) methods to approximate them.

We next illustrate with logistic regression. With independent $N(0, \sigma^2)$ prior distributions, even if the data exhibit complete or quasi-complete separation, the posterior mean estimate of each β_j is finite.

7.3.2   Example: Logistic Regression for Endometrial Cancer Patients

A study about endometrial cancer with 79 patients analyzed how a histology grade response variable (HG = 0, low; HG = 1, high) relates to three risk factors: NV = neovasculation (1 = present, 0 = absent), PI = pulsatility index of arteria uterina (ranging from 0 to 49), and EH = endometrium height (ranging from 0.27 to 3.61). Table 7.3 shows some of the data.

TABLE 7.3 Part of endometrial cancer data set[a].

HG	NV	PI	EH	HG	NV	PI	EH	HG	NV	PI	EH
0	0	13	1.64	0	0	16	2.26	0	0	8	3.14
...				...				...			
1	1	21	0.98	1	0	5	0.35	1	1	19	1.02

[a] HG = histology grade, NV = neovasculation, PI = pulsatility index, EH = endometrium height. *Source:* Data courtesy of E. Asseryanis, G. Heinze, and M. Schemper, from article by Heinze and Schemper, *Statist. Medic.* **21**: 2409–2419 (2002). Complete data ($n = 79$) in `Endometrial` data file at book's website.

For these data, when NV = 0, both HG response outcomes occur, but for all 13 patients having NV = 1, the outcome is HG = 1. The data exhibit quasi-complete separation.

```
> Endo <- read.table("http://stat4ds.rwth-aachen.de/data/Endometrial.dat", header=TRUE)
> Endo
  NV PI    EH HG  # HG is histology grade binary response variable
1  0 13 1.64  0
...
79 0 33 0.85  1
> xtabs(~NV + HG, data=Endo)     # contingency table for NV and HG
    HG
NV   0  1
  0 49 17        # quasi-complete separation:
  1  0 13        # when NV=1, no HG=0 cases occur
```

In fitting models with these data, we use standardized versions of the two quantitative variables, PI and EH. This enables us to compare effects of explanatory variables with very different units (Exercise 6.50). For instance, a 1-unit change in PI, which has a standard deviation of 10.00, is tiny compared to a 1-unit change in EH, which has a standard deviation of 0.66. For a standardized explanatory variable, an effect (called a *standardized coefficient*) refers to a one-standard-deviation change in the original variable. For the binary explanatory variable NV, instead of the usual (0, 1) coding for an indicator, we let it take values –0.5 and 0.5. Then the NV parameter still has the usual interpretation of a conditional log odds ratio and the ML estimate of the NV effect is the same, but for Bayesian inference each NV group then contributes the same prior variability to the linear predictor. First we view R results for the ML fit:

```
> Endo$PI2 <- scale(Endo$PI); Endo$EH2 <- scale(Endo$EH)      # standardized variables
> Endo$NV2 <- Endo$NV - 0.5  # rescale from (0, 1) to (-0.5, 0.5), for Bayesian fitting
> fit <- glm(HG ~ NV2 + PI2 + EH2, family=binomial, data=Endo)
> summary(fit)                          # maximum likelihood fit of main effects model
            Estimate  Std. Error  z value  Pr(>|z|)
(Intercept)   1.7408    282.3389    0.006    0.9951
NV2           6.7859    640.2315    0.011    0.9915   # true ML estimate is infinite
PI2          -0.4217      0.4432   -0.952    0.3413   # huge standard error for NV2
EH2          -1.9219      0.5599   -3.433    0.0006   # is warning sign
> library(car)
> Anova(fit) # likelihood-ratio tests are valid even with infinite ML estimates
```

```
Response: HG
      LR Chisq  Df  Pr(>Chisq)
NV2   9.3576    1   0.00222      # P-value = 0.002 gives strong evidence of NV effect,
PI2   0.9851    1   0.32093      # unlike P-value of 0.99 in Wald test
EH2   19.7606   1   8.777e-06

> library(profileModel)          # use to get profile likelihood confidence intervals
> confintModel(fit, objective="ordinaryDeviance", method="zoom", endpoint.tolerance=1e-08)
           Lower     Upper   # 95% profile likelihood confidence intervals
NV2      1.28411       Inf   # NV effect on log odds has lower bound of 1.284
PI2     -1.37047   0.38176   # Wald CI not possible when ML estimate is infinite
EH2     -3.16891  -0.95108
```

Because of the quasi-complete separation, the ML estimate of the NV effect is $\hat{\beta}_1 = \infty$. Unlike the Wald test with its P-value of 0.99, the likelihood-ratio test shows strong evidence of a NV effect on the histology grade (P-value = 0.002). The 95% profile likelihood confidence interval (Section 5.7.1) indicates that all β_1 values between 1.284 and ∞ have values for the log-likelihood function $L(\beta)$, when maximized with respect to the other parameters, that are close enough to $L(\hat{\beta})$ to be plausible. We conclude that the NV effect is strong, with a conditional odds ratio between NV and HG of at least $e^{1.284} = 3.61$. The likelihood-ratio test also shows very strong evidence of a EH effect on HG but not of a PI effect. Because we are using standardized variables, we can observe that the EH effect may be much stronger than the PI effect.

When a logistic regression model has an infinite ML estimate, alternative estimates are finite. Some methods, such as the Bayesian approach used next and the "penalized likelihood" approach described in Section 7.7, shrink the ML estimates toward 0. Many data analysts prefer such estimates when it is implausible that any β_j is truly infinite. For the Bayesian analysis, we use $N(0, \sigma^2)$ prior distributions for all components of $\{\beta_j\}$. To reflect a lack of information about the effect sizes, we took these distributions to be diffuse, with $\sigma = 10$. Here are some R results, based on an MCMC process with 10,000,000 iterations:

```
> library(MCMCpack)
> fitBayes <- MCMClogit(HG ~ NV2 + PI2 + EH2, mcmc=10000000,
+              b0=0, B0=0.01, data=Endo) # prior mean = b0, prior variance = 1/B0
> summary(fitBayes)
1. Empirical mean and standard deviation: # posterior distribution
               Mean      SD   Naive SE  Time-series SE
(Intercept)   3.213   2.560
NV2           9.115   5.093   0.00161          0.0054  # NV effect posterior mean = 9.1,
PI2          -0.473   0.454   0.00014          0.0006  # compared to infinite ML estimate
EH2          -2.138   0.593   0.00019          0.0009
2. Quantiles for each variable:
               2.5%     25%      50%      75%    97.5%
(Intercept)  -0.342   1.271    2.722    4.687    9.346
NV2           2.108   5.234    8.128   12.048   21.331  # 95% posterior interval (2.1, 21.3)
PI2          -1.414  -0.767   -0.455   -0.159    0.366
EH2          -3.403  -2.515   -2.101   -1.722   -1.082
> mean(fitBayes[,2] <= 0) # probability that 2nd model parameter (NV effect) <= 0
[1] 0.000223
```

Table 7.4 shows posterior means and standard deviations and the 95% equal-tail posterior interval for β_1 as well as corresponding results for the ML analysis. With such a long MCMC process, the Monte Carlo standard errors for the approximations to the Bayes estimates were negligible — about 0.005 for the NV effect and much less for the others. From the posterior mean, the Bayesian estimated odds of the higher-grade histology when neovasculation is present are $\exp(\hat{\beta}_1) = \exp(9.12) = 9136$ times the estimated odds when neovasculation is absent. The 95% equal-tail posterior interval for β_1 is (2.1, 21.3), indicating that $\beta_1 > 0$ and that the effect is strong. The estimated effect size is imprecise, because the

TABLE 7.4 Results of Bayesian and maximum likelihood (ML) fitting of models to the endometrial cancer data (partly shown in Table 7.3).

Analysis	$\hat{\beta}_1$ (SD)	Interval[a] for β_1	$\hat{\beta}_2$ (SD)	$\hat{\beta}_3$ (SD)	$P(\beta_1 \leq 0)$[b]
ML	∞ (—)	$(1.28, \infty)$	−0.42 (0.44)	−1.92 (0.56)	0.0011
Bayes, $\sigma = 100$	18.33 (9.08)	(3.2, 33.5)	−0.49 (0.46)	−2.12 (0.59)	0.00006
Bayes, $\sigma = 10$	9.12 (5.10)	(2.1, 21.3)	−0.47 (0.45)	−2.14 (0.59)	0.0002
Bayes, $\sigma = 1$	1.65 (0.69)	(0.3, 3.0)	−0.22 (0.33)	−1.77 (0.43)	0.0068

[a]Profile likelihood confidence interval and Bayes equal-tail posterior interval
[b]In ML row, this is classical one-sided P-value for likelihood-ratio test of $H_a: \beta_1 > 0$

log-likelihood function is so flat in the β_1 dimension and the prior distribution is relatively flat. However, the upper bound for the interval is not ∞, as it is for the profile likelihood confidence interval. Inferences about β_2 and β_3 were substantively the same as with the ML analysis.

The classical P-value for testing $H_0: \beta_1 = 0$ against $H_a: \beta_1 > 0$ evaluates evidence that $\beta_1 \leq 0$ versus $\beta_1 > 0$. For the likelihood-ratio test, from the output in the previous section for the ML analysis, this one-sided P-value is $0.0022/2 = 0.0011$. The Bayesian analysis provides the posterior $P(\beta_1 \leq 0) = 0.0002$; that is, 0.0 is the 0.0002 quantile of the posterior distribution. This also provides very strong evidence that $\beta_1 > 0$.

Because of the relatively flat log-likelihood function, posterior results for β_1 are highly dependent on the value for σ in the prior distribution. This is illustrated by results shown in Table 7.4 for $\sigma = 1$, reflecting a strong prior belief that the effects are not very strong, and $\sigma = 100$, an even less informative prior distribution than using $\sigma = 10$. The highly informative prior yields the 95% posterior interval of (0.3, 3.0), not overlapping at all with the corresponding interval of (3.2, 33.5) obtained with the uninformative prior. These both contrast with classical inference, which in not assuming prior information about β_1 and not observing any cases with response $HG = 0$ when $NV = 1$, regards *all* β_1 values from 1.28 to ∞ as plausible.

7.4 Poisson Loglinear Models for Count Data

Many response variables have counts as their possible outcomes. A criminal justice study, for instance, might observe the number of times each person in the sample has ever been arrested. A sample survey might ask "How many devices do you own that can access the Internet (laptops, smart cell phones, tablets, etc.)?" or "How many children do you expect to have in your lifetime?" Counts also occur as entries in cells of contingency tables that cross-classify categorical variables, such as the number of people in a survey who are female, college educated, and agree that their government should do more to address climate change.

7.4.1 Poisson Loglinear Models

Counts $\{y_i\}$ have positive means. Although a GLM can model a positive mean using the identity link, it is more common to model the *log* of the mean. The **loglinear model** is

$$\log \mu_i = \beta_0 + \beta_1 x_{i1} + \cdots + \beta_p x_{ip}, \quad i = 1, \ldots, n.$$

The **Poisson loglinear model** assumes that the counts are independent Poisson random variables. The log is the canonical link function for the Poisson.

For loglinear models, the mean satisfies the exponential relation

$$\mu_i = \exp(\beta_0 + \beta_1 x_{i1} + \cdots + \beta_p x_{ip}).$$

The mean of Y at $x_{ij} + 1$ equals the mean at x_{ij} multiplied by e^{β_j}, adjusting for the other explanatory variables.

7.4.2 Example: Modeling Horseshoe Crab Satellite Counts

Table 7.5 shows some data from a study of $n = 173$ female horseshoe crabs[11] on an island off the coast of Florida in the Gulf of Mexico. During spawning season, a female migrates to the shore to breed. With a male attached to her posterior spine, she burrows into the sand and lays clusters of eggs. The eggs are fertilized externally, in the sand beneath the pair. During spawning other male crabs, called *satellites*, may cluster around the pair and also fertilize the eggs. The response outcome for each female crab is y = number of satellites. Explanatory variables are the female crab's color (1 = medium light; 2 = medium; 3 = medium dark; 4 = dark), spine condition (1 = both good; 2 = one worn or broken; 3 = both worn or broken), carapace width (*cm*), and weight (*kg*). Color is a surrogate for the age of the crab, as older crabs tend to have a darker color.

TABLE 7.5 Data for female horseshoe crabs on number of male satellites, color, spine condition, carapace width, and weight.

sat	color	spine	width	weight	sat	color	spine	width	weight
8	2	3	28.3	3.05	0	3	3	22.5	1.55
4	3	3	26.0	2.60	0	2	3	23.8	2.10
0	3	3	25.6	2.15	0	3	3	24.3	2.15
0	4	2	21.0	1.85	14	2	1	26.0	2.30

Source: Data courtesy of Jane Brockmann, University of Florida, from study described in *Ethology* **102**: 1–21 (1996). Complete data ($n = 173$) are in Crabs data file at text website.

Here, we use only the horseshoe crab's weight and color as explanatory variables, as width is highly correlated with weight and model-building does not reveal any effects for spine condition. At first, we ignore the ordinality of the color categories, treating it as a nominal-scale factor. We express the model as

$$\log(\mu_i) = \beta_0 + \beta_1 w_i + \beta_2 c_{i2} + \beta_3 c_{i3} + \beta_4 c_{i4},$$

using indicator variables for colors 2, 3, and 4. An alternative modeling approach, more sensitive to a trend across ordered categories, treats color as quantitative by assigning scores to the color categories (Exercise 7.21). Here are some results:

```
> Crabs <- read.table("http://stat4ds.rwth-aachen.de/data/Crabs.dat", header=TRUE)
> fit <- glm(sat ~ weight + factor(color), family=poisson(link=log), data=Crabs)
> summary(fit)
             Estimate  Std. Error  z value  Pr(>|z|)
(Intercept)  -0.04978     0.23315   -0.214    0.8309
```

---

[11] See en.wikipedia.org/wiki/Horseshoe_crab and horseshoecrab.org for details about horseshoe crabs, including pictures of their mating.

```
weight              0.54618    0.06811    8.019  1.07e-15
factor(color)2     -0.20511    0.15371   -1.334   0.1821
factor(color)3     -0.44980    0.17574   -2.560   0.0105
factor(color)4     -0.45205    0.20844   -2.169   0.0301
---

    Null deviance: 632.79  on 172  degrees of freedom
Residual deviance: 551.80  on 168  degrees of freedom
AIC: 917.1
> library(car)
> Anova(fit)                       # likelihood-ratio tests of explanatory variable effects
             LR Chisq  Df  Pr(>Chisq)
weight         57.334   1    3.677e-14        # testing weight effect, adjusted for color
factor(color)   9.061   3    0.02848          # testing color effect, adjusted for weight
> exp(confint(fit))   # profile-likelihood CI for odds ratio with 1 kg increase in weight
                2.5 %     97.5 %
weight      1.5076222  1.9689147
```

In R, the *factor* command requests indicator variables, using the first category as the reference to achieve identifiability. For example, since $\hat{\beta}_2 = -0.205$ for color category 2, the estimated mean for crabs of color 2 is $e^{-0.205} = 0.81$ times the estimated mean for crabs of color 1, adjusting for weight. The estimates $(0, \hat{\beta}_2 = -0.205, \hat{\beta}_3 = -0.450, \hat{\beta}_4 = -0.452)$ for the four color categories suggest that the expected number of satellites decreases as color gets darker, adjusting for weight. The estimated weight effect $\hat{\beta}_1 = 0.546$ indicates that the expected number of satellites increases as weight increases, adjusting for color; for instance, the estimated expected number of satellites multiplies by $e^{0.546} = 1.73$ for each *kg* increase in weight. The Wald 95% confidence interval is $e^{0.546 \pm 1.96(0.068)}$, which is (1.51, 1.97) and is also the profile-likelihood confidence interval shown in the output. The P-values for the likelihood-ratio tests are small both for testing $H_0: \beta_1 = 0$ for the weight effect and for testing $H_0: \beta_2 = \beta_3 = \beta_4 = 0$ for the color effect.

From Section 7.1.6, AIC judges a model by how close its fitted values tend to be to the true expected values, with smaller AIC being preferable. This model has AIC = 917.1. the model with weight alone has AIC = 920.2 and the model with color alone has AIC = 972.4. Using weight alone does almost as well, but using color alone is clearly insufficient. We could also consider permitting interaction, but we will not do further modeling here because Section 7.5.3 shows that the assumption that Y has a Poisson distribution seems inappropriate.

7.4.3   Modeling Rates: Including an Offset in the Model

Often the expected value of a response count is proportional to an index t. For instance, in modeling annual murder counts $\{y_i\}$ for cities, t_i might be the population size of city i. In modeling regional counts $\{y_i\}$ of an animal or plant species, t_i might be the spatial area of region i. A sample count y_i corresponds to a *rate* of y_i/t_i, with expected value μ_i/t_i.

With explanatory variables, a loglinear model for the expected rate is

$$\log(\mu_i/t_i) = \beta_0 + \beta_1 x_{i1} + \cdots + \beta_p x_{ip}.$$

Because $\log(\mu_i/t_i) = \log \mu_i - \log t_i$, the model makes the adjustment $-\log t_i$ to the log link of the mean. The adjustment term is called an ***offset***. The expected response count satisfies

$$\mu_i = t_i \exp(\beta_0 + \beta_1 x_{i1} + \cdots + \beta_p x_{ip}).$$

The mean has a proportionality coefficient for t_i that depends on the values of the explanatory variables.

TABLE 7.6 Number of deaths from lung cancer, with months of time at risk for the sample of patients, by stage of disease and follow-up time interval.

Follow-up time interval:	0–2 months			2–4 months			4–6 months		
Stage of disease:	1	2	3	1	2	3	1	2	3
Number of deaths:	15	17	89	5	11	56	13	13	29
Time at risk:	255	227	443	224	191	271	203	168	175

Source: Based on data presented by T. Holford, *Biometrics* **36**: 299–305 (1980); the complete data are in the `Cancer` data file at the text website.

7.4.4 Example: Lung Cancer Survival

Table 7.6 shows death counts for males diagnosed with lung cancer. The prognostic factor is stage of disease, with observations grouped into seven two-month intervals of follow-up time after the diagnosis, the final one containing months 12 and higher. Table 7.6 shows data for the first three time intervals, and the `Cancer` data file at the book's website contains the complete data for 539 subjects, 353 of whom died during the study. For each particular follow-up time interval and stage of disease, the table also shows the time at risk, which is the number of months of observation of subjects still alive during that follow-up interval. We treat the death counts in the table as observations of independent Poisson random variables.

Let μ_{ij} denote the expected number of deaths and t_{ij} the total time at risk for those patients alive during follow-up time interval j who had stage of disease i. The Poisson loglinear model for the death rate,

$$\log(\mu_{ij}/t_{ij}) = \beta_0 + \beta_i^S + \beta_j^T,$$

treats stage of disease and the follow-up time interval as factors. The superscript notation shows the classification labels, with parameters β_1^S and β_2^S that are coefficients of indicator variables for 2 of the 3 levels of stage of disease and $\{\beta_j^T\}$ that are coefficients of indicator variables for 6 of the 7 levels of time interval. (In R, $\hat{\beta}_1^S = \hat{\beta}_1^T = 0$ for identifiability.) Here is output for the model fit:

```
> Cancer <- read.table("http://stat4ds.rwth-aachen.de/data/Cancer.dat", header=TRUE)
> Cancer
    time stage deaths risktime
1    1    1    15      255
2    2    1    5       224
...
21   7    3    6       46
> logrisktime = log(Cancer$risktime)
> fit <- glm(deaths ~ factor(stage) + factor(time), family = poisson(link=log),
+            offset = logrisktime, data=Cancer)    # can omit (link=log) Poisson default
> summary(fit)
                 Estimate  Std. Error  z value  Pr(>|z|)
(Intercept)      -2.9414   0.1582      -18.587   < 2e-16
factor(stage)2   0.4722    0.1744      2.708     0.00678
factor(stage)3   1.3288    0.1500      8.859     < 2e-16 # stage of disease has 3 categories
factor(time)2    -0.1303   0.1491      -0.874    0.38185
factor(time)3    -0.0841   0.1635      -0.515    0.60667
factor(time)4    0.1092    0.1708      0.639     0.52257
factor(time)5    -0.6810   0.2604      -2.615    0.00892
factor(time)6    -0.3600   0.2433      -1.480    0.13900
```

```
factor(time)7  -0.1873      0.2496   -0.750   0.45309 # 7 time intervals
---
> library(car)
> Anova(fit)                      # likelihood-ratio tests of explanatory variable effects
            LR Chisq  Df  Pr(>Chisq)
factor(stage)  104.826   2    < 2e-16
factor(time)    11.765   6    0.06741
> exp(confint(fit)) # profile likelihood CI's
              2.5 %  97.5 %
factor(stage)2  1.1413  2.2650 #  multiplicative effects on death rate compared to stage 1
factor(stage)3  2.8354  5.1103
```

The implicit value of $\beta_1^S = 0$ for the reference category together with the estimates $\hat{\beta}_2^S = 0.472$, and $\hat{\beta}_3^S = 1.329$ show the progressively worsening death rate as the stage of disease advances. The estimated death rate at stage 3 is $\exp(1.329) = 3.78$ times that at stage 1, adjusting for follow-up time and histology. A profile likelihood 95% confidence interval for this effect is $(2.84, 5.11)$.

Models such as this one that assume a lack of interaction between follow-up time interval and stage of disease have the same effects of stage of disease in each time interval. A ratio of death rates for two groups is the same at all times t. This is an example of a property called *proportional hazards*. This property occurs in models for times until some event, such as survival times for lung cancer patients. The rate of occurrence of the event, called the *hazard rate*, is modeled as a function of time t by

$$\log h(t) = \alpha(t) + \beta_1 x_1 + \cdots + \beta_p x_p,$$

where the intercept $\alpha(t)$ can vary with time. For example, if x_1 is gender (1 = female, 0 = female), the ratio of hazard rates for females and males is $\exp(\beta_1)$ at all times. Analyses of survival times have the complication that some data are *censored*: Some patients were still alive at the end of the study and we do not observe their death in one of the observed time intervals.[12] The modeling above for the lung cancer study used death counts for the 353 subjects who died. The survival times were censored for the 186 subjects who did not die during the study, but they were used in the analysis through contributing to the times at risk needed for forming death rates. For details about proportional hazards models and other models for survival times or times to some event, see Allison (2014).

7.5   Negative Binomial Models for Overdispersed Count Data *

For the Poisson distribution, the variance equals the mean. However, count observations often exhibit *overdispersion* (Section 2.4.7), variability exceeding that predicted by the Poisson. A common reason for overdispersion is heterogeneity, with $E(Y)$ varying according to values of unobserved variables. Perhaps Y has a Poisson distribution if all the variables that are correlated with Y are fixed in value. Because some variables are unobserved, however, the population at fixed values of the observed variables is a mixture of several Poisson populations, each having its own $E(Y)$. This heterogeneity results in an overall response distribution that has greater variation than the Poisson.

---

[12]Section 5.8.4 showed how to deal with censored data in comparing survival times for two groups.
*Sections with an asterisk are optional.

7.5.1 Increased Variance Due to Heterogeneity

Suppose Y is a random variable with variance $\text{var}(Y \mid \lambda)$ when a parameter λ is fixed, but λ itself varies because of unobserved variables. The unconditional means and variances then relate to the conditional values by the *law of iterated expectation*[13]

$$E(Y) = E_\lambda[E(Y \mid \lambda)], \quad \text{var}(Y) = E_\lambda[\text{var}(Y \mid \lambda)] + \text{var}_\lambda[E(Y \mid \lambda)],$$

where the inside conditional expectation and conditional variance relate to Y as the random variable, for fixed λ, and the outside expectations and variance treat λ as the random variable. For instance, at any fixed setting of the entire set of explanatory variables that are associated with Y, suppose that the conditional distribution of Y is Poisson with parameter λ (so, it has mean λ and variance λ), but that λ itself varies as values vary for explanatory variables that are not observed, with $\mu = E(\lambda)$. Then the overall distribution of Y has

$$E(Y) = E[E(Y \mid \lambda)] = E(\lambda) = \mu,$$

$$\text{var}(Y) = E[\text{var}(Y \mid \lambda)] + \text{var}[E(Y \mid \lambda)] = E(\lambda) + \text{var}(\lambda) = \mu + \text{var}(\lambda) > \mu.$$

Although $\text{var}(Y) = E(Y)$ when all relevant variables that are associated with Y take fixed values, $\text{var}(Y) > E(Y)$ when some are fixed but others vary in their values. The extent to which $\text{var}(Y)$ exceeds $E(Y)$ increases as $\text{var}(\lambda)$ increases.

Overdispersion is not an issue in normal linear models, because the normal distribution has a separate parameter (σ^2) to describe variability. Overdispersion is common in Poisson modeling of counts, however, because of the lack of a separate parameter for variability. When the model has the correct link function and linear predictor, but the true response distribution has more variability than the Poisson, the ML estimators of $\{\beta_j\}$ assuming a Poisson distribution for Y are still valid. Standard errors, however, are too small. We next introduce a distribution that has more flexibility in handling count data, because it has an extra parameter to account for variability.

7.5.2 Negative Binomial: Gamma Mixture of Poisson Distributions

A *mixture model* is a flexible way to account for overdispersion in the setting just described in which Y has a Poisson distribution when its mean λ is fixed, but λ varies with its own mean μ as unobserved variables vary. For fixed λ, the Poisson *pmf* with $E(Y) = \lambda$ is

$$f(y \mid \lambda) = \frac{e^{-\lambda}\lambda^y}{y!}, \quad 0, 1, 2, \dots.$$

Since $\lambda > 0$, mixture models use a distribution for λ that has positive real numbers for the support. The gamma distribution has two parameters and provides a wide variety for this. We use here the alternative parameterization for the gamma *pdf* in terms of the shape parameter $k > 0$ and mean $\mu > 0$, shown in formula (2.17) in Exercise 2.45. Treating λ as a random variable, we replace y in that formula by λ; that is, λ varies according to the *pdf*

$$g(\lambda; k, \mu) = \frac{(k/\mu)^k}{\Gamma(k)} e^{-k\lambda/\mu} \lambda^{k-1}, \quad \lambda > 0. \tag{7.6}$$

For this parameterization, the gamma distribution has $E(\lambda) = \mu$ and $\text{var}(\lambda) = \mu^2/k$. To find the overall *pmf* of Y, we take its Poisson *pmf* $f(y \mid \lambda)$ for a fixed λ value and average it with respect to the gamma *pdf* $g(\lambda; k, \mu)$ for λ. That is, $p(y, \lambda; \mu, k) = f(y \mid \lambda)g(\lambda; k, \mu)$ is

---

[13] For proofs, see Casella and Berger (2002, pp. 164, 167–168). See also Exercise 7.40.

the joint distribution for y and λ (for particular parameter values μ and k for the gamma distribution), and integrating over λ yields the marginal *pmf* for y,

$$p(y;\mu,k) = \int_0^\infty p(y,\lambda;\mu,k)d\lambda = \int_0^\infty f(y\mid\lambda)g(\lambda;\mu,k)d\lambda = \int_0^\infty \left[\frac{e^{-\lambda}\lambda^y}{y!}\right]\left[\frac{(k/\mu)^k}{\Gamma(k)}e^{-k\lambda/\mu}\lambda^{k-1}\right]d\lambda$$

The part of the integrand involving λ is

$$e^{-\lambda}\lambda^y e^{-k\lambda/\mu}\lambda^{k-1} = e^{-[(k+\mu)/\mu]\lambda}\lambda^{k+y-1}.$$

Taking $k^* = k+y$ and $\mu^* = \mu(k+y)/(k+\mu)$, we can express this function of λ as $e^{-k^*\lambda/\mu^*}\lambda^{k^*-1}$, which is the kernel of a gamma *pdf* with parameters k^* and μ^*. So, from (7.6), this part of the integrand, when multiplied by

$$\frac{(k^*/\mu^*)^{k^*}}{\Gamma(k^*)} = \frac{[(k+\mu)/\mu]^{k+y}}{\Gamma(k+y)},$$

integrates out to 1. It follows that taking the original integrand above and multiplying and dividing by that constant yields

$$p(y;\mu,k) = \frac{\Gamma(y+k)}{\Gamma(k)\Gamma(y+1)}\left(\frac{\mu}{\mu+k}\right)^y\left(\frac{k}{\mu+k}\right)^k, \quad y = 0,1,2,\dots, \tag{7.7}$$

the *pmf* of the **negative binomial distribution.**

The negative binomial distribution has

$$E(Y) = \mu, \quad \text{var}(Y) = \mu + \mu^2/k.$$

The value of the gamma shape parameter k determines how much the variance exceeds the value μ that applies with the Poisson distribution. For the negative binomial distribution, the index $1/k$ is a *dispersion parameter*: As it increases, the dispersion as measured by the variance increases, and the greater is the overdispersion relative to the Poisson. By contrast, as the dispersion parameter $1/k$ decreases toward 0 (i.e., k increases indefinitely), the variance μ^2/k of the gamma distribution for λ decreases toward 0, and the negative binomial variance of $\mu + \mu^2/k$ decreases toward the Poisson variance, which is μ, and the negative binomial distribution converges to the Poisson.

The negative binomial distribution has much greater scope than the Poisson. For example, the Poisson is unimodal with mode equal to the integer part of the mean, so the mode = 0 only when $\mu < 1$. The negative binomial is also unimodal, but the mode can be 0 for any μ. In practice, many discrete variables have modes of 0 but means that are possibly much larger—e.g., in the previous year for some population, the number of times working out at a gym or the number of times having sex.

Like Poisson loglinear models, negative binomial GLMs commonly use the log link. For simplicity, the model can let the dispersion parameter be the same constant for all n observations but treat it as unknown, much like the error variance in normal linear models.

7.5.3   Example: Negative Binomial Modeling of Horseshoe Crab Data

For the study of $n = 173$ mating female horseshoe crabs introduced in Section 7.4.2, the response variable is Y = number of male satellites. Let's investigate the marginal distribution of Y.

```
> mean(Crabs$sat); var(Crabs$sat)      # sat = number of crab satellites
[1] 2.9191
[1] 9.9120 # much larger than mean suggests overdispersion for Poisson
> hist(Crabs$sat, breaks=c(0:16)-0.5) # Histogram with sufficient bins
```

The mode of 0, mean of 2.92, and variance of 9.91 suggest overdispersion relative to the Poisson. Strong evidence of overdispersion also occurs when we fit loglinear models to the data.

We next fit a negative binomial GLM with weight and categorical color predictors:

```
> library(MASS)  # contains glm.nb for negative binomial modelling
> fit <- glm.nb(sat ~ weight + factor(color), link=log, data=Crabs)
> summary(fit)   # log link is default for glm.nb, identify link sometimes also useful
               Estimate  Std. Error  z value  Pr(>|z|)
(Intercept)     -0.4263      0.5382   -0.792    0.428
weight           0.7121      0.1615    4.410  1.04e-05
factor(color)2  -0.2527      0.3486   -0.725    0.468
factor(color)3  -0.5218      0.3799   -1.373    0.170
factor(color)4  -0.4804      0.4282   -1.122    0.262
---

    Null deviance: 220.01  on 172  degrees of freedom
Residual deviance: 196.56  on 168  degrees of freedom
AIC: 757.94
Theta: 0.960  Std. Err.: 0.175 # theta=k (shape parameter) in our notation
                                # 1/theta = 1.04 = estimated dispersion parameter
> library(car)
> Anova(fit)          # likelihood-ratio tests of explanatory variable effects
              LR Chisq Df Pr(>Chisq)
weight         17.4542  1  2.943e-05
factor(color)   2.7368  3     0.434
```

The fit describes the tendency of the mean response to increase with weight, adjusting for color. However, unlike the results for the Poisson loglinear model in Section 7.4.2, the color effect is no longer significant. The weight effect has standard error that increases from 0.068 in the Poisson model to 0.161 in the negative binomial model. The estimated negative binomial dispersion parameter is $1/0.960 = 1.04$. This estimate that is well above 0 results in the much larger standard error values for the negative binomial model. These larger and more realistic standard error values and the much smaller AIC value compared to the corresponding Poisson model suggest that assuming a Poisson response distribution is not appropriate for these data.

7.6   Iterative GLM Model Fitting *

The likelihood equations for most GLMs are nonlinear functions of $\{\hat{\beta}_j\}$. Unlike the equations (6.11) for the ordinary linear model, they do not have an explicit solution. To solve them, software uses an iterative method. To describe this method, we use matrix algebra,[14] which is useful also for expressing the covariance matrix of $\{\hat{\beta}_j\}$.

7.6.1   The Newton–Raphson Method

The ***Newton–Raphson method*** approximates the log-likelihood function $L(\beta)$ of the model parameters $\beta = (\beta_0, \beta_1, \ldots, \beta_p)$ in a neighborhood of an initial approximation for the ML estimate $\hat{\beta}$ of β by a second-degree polynomial (i.e., a parabolic function), because it is straightforward to find its maximum. The second approximation for $\hat{\beta}$ is the location of that polynomial's maximum value. It then repeats this step, successively using

---

*Sections with an asterisk are optional.

[14]Without matrix algebra, Exercise 7.47 shows the single-parameter version of the method.

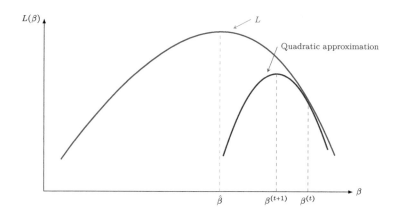

FIGURE 7.8 Illustration of a cycle of the Newton–Raphson method: At the approximation $\beta^{(t)}$ for $\hat{\beta}$ at step t, a parabolic approximation to the log-likelihood function $L(\beta)$ has maximum at the approximation $\beta^{(t+1)}$ for $\hat{\beta}$ at step $t+1$.

second-degree polynomials to generate a sequence of approximations for $\hat{\beta}$. Figure 7.8 illustrates a cycle of the method, showing the parabolic approximation at a given step t.

The details about the Newton–Raphson method follow: Let

$$\boldsymbol{u} = \left(\frac{\partial L(\boldsymbol{\beta})}{\partial \beta_0}, \frac{\partial L(\boldsymbol{\beta})}{\partial \beta_1}, \ldots, \frac{\partial L(\boldsymbol{\beta})}{\partial \beta_p} \right)^T$$

be the score function (Section 4.9.1). Let $\boldsymbol{H}$ denote the matrix $\partial \boldsymbol{u}(\boldsymbol{\beta})/\partial \boldsymbol{\beta}$ having entries $h_{jk} = \partial^2 L(\boldsymbol{\beta})/\partial \beta_j \partial \beta_k$, called a *Hessian matrix*. Let $\boldsymbol{u}^{(t)}$ and $\boldsymbol{H}^{(t)}$ be $\boldsymbol{u}$ and $\boldsymbol{H}$ evaluated at $\boldsymbol{\beta}^{(t)}$, approximation t for $\hat{\boldsymbol{\beta}}$. Step t in the iterative process $(t = 0, 1, 2, \ldots)$ approximates $L(\boldsymbol{\beta})$ near $\boldsymbol{\beta}^{(t)}$ by the second-order Taylor series expansion,

$$L(\boldsymbol{\beta}) \approx L(\boldsymbol{\beta}^{(t)}) + \boldsymbol{u}^{(t)T}(\boldsymbol{\beta} - \boldsymbol{\beta}^{(t)}) + \left(\frac{1}{2}\right)(\boldsymbol{\beta} - \boldsymbol{\beta}^{(t)})^T \boldsymbol{H}^{(t)}(\boldsymbol{\beta} - \boldsymbol{\beta}^{(t)}).$$

Solving $\partial L(\boldsymbol{\beta})/\partial \boldsymbol{\beta} \approx \boldsymbol{u}^{(t)} + \boldsymbol{H}^{(t)}(\boldsymbol{\beta} - \boldsymbol{\beta}^{(t)}) = \boldsymbol{0}$ for $\boldsymbol{\beta}$ yields

$$\boldsymbol{\beta}^{(t+1)} = \boldsymbol{\beta}^{(t)} - (\boldsymbol{H}^{(t)})^{-1}\boldsymbol{u}^{(t)}, \tag{7.8}$$

when $\boldsymbol{H}^{(t)}$ is nonsingular.

Iterations proceed until changes in $L(\boldsymbol{\beta}^{(t)})$ between successive cycles are sufficiently tiny. The ML estimator is the limit of $\boldsymbol{\beta}^{(t)}$ as $t \to \infty$, but the sequence could converge to an incorrect value if $L(\boldsymbol{\beta})$ has other local maxima at which $\boldsymbol{u}(\boldsymbol{\beta}) = \boldsymbol{0}$. For commonly used GLMs, such as logistic regression and Poisson loglinear models, the log-likelihood function is concave and the convergence of $\boldsymbol{\beta}^{(t)}$ to $\hat{\boldsymbol{\beta}}$ is usually rapid.

7.6.2 Newton–Raphson Fitting of Logistic Regression Model

We illustrate by applying the Newton–Raphson method for logistic regression models. For binary data in ungrouped form, the joint probability mass function is proportional to the product of n binomial functions, each based on a single trial,

$$\prod_{i=1}^{n} \pi_i^{y_i}(1-\pi_i)^{1-y_i} = \left\{\prod_{i=1}^{n}\left(\frac{\pi_i}{1-\pi_i}\right)^{y_i}\right\}\left\{\prod_{i=1}^{n}(1-\pi_i)\right\} = \left\{\prod_{i=1}^{n}\exp\left[\log\left(\frac{\pi_i}{1-\pi_i}\right)^{y_i}\right]\right\}\left\{\prod_{i=1}^{n}(1-\pi_i)\right\}$$

$$= \left\{\exp\left[\sum_{i=1}^{n} y_i \log\left(\frac{\pi_i}{1-\pi_i}\right)\right]\right\}\left\{\prod_{i=1}^{n}(1-\pi_i)\right\}.$$

Since the logit for observation i is $\sum_{j=0}^{p}\beta_j x_{ij}$ with $x_{i0} = 1$, the exponential term equals $\exp\left[\sum_{i=1}^{n} y_i\left(\sum_{j=0}^{p}\beta_j x_{ij}\right)\right] = \exp\left[\sum_{j=0}^{p}\left(\sum_{i=1}^{n} y_i x_{ij}\right)\beta_j\right]$. Also, since $(1-\pi_i) = \left[1 + \exp\left(\sum_{j=0}^{p}\beta_j x_{ij}\right)\right]^{-1}$, the log of the likelihood function in terms of $\boldsymbol{\beta} = (\beta_0, \beta_1, \ldots, \beta_p)$ equals

$$L(\boldsymbol{\beta}) = \sum_{j=0}^{p}\left(\sum_{i=1}^{n} y_i x_{ij}\right)\beta_j - \sum_{i=1}^{n}\log\left[1 + \exp\left(\sum_{j=0}^{p}\beta_j x_{ij}\right)\right].$$

This depends on the binary data $\{y_i\}$ only through $\{\sum_{i=1}^{n} y_i x_{ij}\}$, $j = 0, 1, \ldots, p$, which are the sufficient statistics for the parameters in the logistic regression model.

Next,

$$\frac{\partial L(\boldsymbol{\beta})}{\partial \beta_j} = \sum_{i=1}^{n} y_i x_{ij} - \sum_{i=1}^{n} x_{ij}\frac{\exp\left(\sum_{k=0}^{p}\beta_k x_{ik}\right)}{1 + \exp\left(\sum_{k=0}^{p}\beta_k x_{ik}\right)} = \sum_{i=1}^{n} y_i x_{ij} - \sum_{i=1}^{n}\pi_i x_{ij}.$$

The likelihood equations result from setting $\partial L(\boldsymbol{\beta})/\partial \beta_j = 0$ for $j = 0, 1, \ldots, p$. The likelihood equations are nonlinear in $\{\hat{\beta}_j\}$ and we use the Newton–Raphson method to solve them.

From the expression for $\partial L(\boldsymbol{\beta})/\partial \beta_j$,

$$u_j^{(t)} = \left.\frac{\partial L(\boldsymbol{\beta})}{\partial \beta_j}\right|_{\boldsymbol{\beta}^{(t)}} = \sum_{i=1}^{n}(y_i - \pi_i^{(t)})x_{ij} \quad \text{and} \quad \boldsymbol{u}^{(t)} = \boldsymbol{X}^T(\boldsymbol{y} - \boldsymbol{\pi}^{(t)}).$$

Here $\boldsymbol{\pi}^{(t)}$, approximation t for $\hat{\boldsymbol{\pi}}$, is obtained from $\boldsymbol{\beta}^{(t)}$ through

$$\pi_i^{(t)} = \frac{\exp\left(\sum_{j=0}^{p}\beta_j^{(t)} x_{ij}\right)}{1 + \exp\left(\sum_{j=0}^{p}\beta_j^{(t)} x_{ij}\right)}. \tag{7.9}$$

Taking the partial derivative $\partial u_b(\boldsymbol{\beta})/\partial \beta_a$, we can also derive that

$$\frac{\partial^2 L(\boldsymbol{\beta})}{\partial \beta_a \partial \beta_b} = -\sum_{i=1}^{n}\frac{x_{ia}x_{ib}\exp\left(\sum_{j=0}^{p}\beta_j x_{ij}\right)}{\left[1 + \exp\left(\sum_{j=0}^{p}\beta_j x_{ij}\right)\right]^2} = -\sum_i x_{ia}x_{ib}\pi_i(1-\pi_i). \tag{7.10}$$

Therefore, the elements of the approximation for the Hessian matrix are

$$h_{ab}^{(t)} = \left.\frac{\partial^2 L(\boldsymbol{\beta})}{\partial \beta_a \partial \beta_b}\right|_{\boldsymbol{\beta}^{(t)}} = -\sum_{i=1}^{n} x_{ia}x_{ib}\pi_i^{(t)}(1-\pi_i^{(t)}).$$

Using $\boldsymbol{u}^{(t)}$ and $\boldsymbol{H}^{(t)}$ with formula (7.8) yields the next value, $\boldsymbol{\beta}^{(t+1)}$.

For the ungrouped data, we express the model with $\boldsymbol{\ell} = [\text{logit}(\pi_1), \ldots, \text{logit}(\pi_n)]^T$, a model matrix $\boldsymbol{X}$, and a column vector $\boldsymbol{\beta}$ as

$$\boldsymbol{\ell} = \boldsymbol{X}\boldsymbol{\beta}.$$

Letting $\boldsymbol{D}^{(t)}$ denote the diagonal matrix with elements $\{\pi_i^{(t)}(1-\pi_i^{(t)})\}$ on the main diagonal.

The Hessian matrix takes the inner product of the column of X for parameter β_a times the column of X for parameter β_b times the diagonal elements of $D^{(t)}$, that is, $H^{(t)} = -X^T D^{(t)} X$. The Newton–Raphson process has the iterative steps

$$\beta^{(t+1)} = \beta^{(t)} - (H^{(t)})^{-1} u^{(t)} = \beta^{(t)} + \left[X^T D^{(t)} X \right]^{-1} X^T (y - \pi^{(t)}), \qquad (7.11)$$

where we can express the vector of elements $\pi_i^{(t)}$ in (7.9) as

$$\pi^{(t)} = \frac{\exp\left(X \beta^{(t)} \right)}{1 + X \beta^{(t)}}, \qquad (7.12)$$

with the division done element-wise with the two vectors. With an initial guess $\beta^{(0)}$, (7.12) yields $\pi^{(0)}$, and for $t > 0$ the iterations proceed using (7.11) and (7.12). In the limit, $\pi^{(t)}$ and $\beta^{(t)}$ converge to the ML estimates $\hat{\pi}$ and $\hat{\beta}$.

7.6.3   Covariance Matrix of Parameter Estimators and Fisher Scoring

From Section 4.2.3, the ML estimator $\hat{\theta}$ of a scalar parameter θ with log-likelihood function $L(\theta)$ has large-sample $\text{var}(\hat{\theta}) = 1/I(\theta)$, where $I(\theta) = -E[\partial^2 L(\theta)/\partial\theta^2]$ is the *information*. Similarly, for a vector of GLM parameters β, the ML estimator $\hat{\beta}$ has a covariance matrix that can be approximated using the expected curvature of the log-likelihood function. The $(p+1) \times (p+1)$ matrix with elements

$$-E\left[\frac{\partial^2 L(\beta)}{\partial\beta_j \partial\beta_k} \right],$$

called the **information matrix**, generalizes the univariate information. This depends on β and is estimated by substituting the ML estimates. Its inverse is the estimated covariance matrix of $\hat{\beta}$. For logistic regression, for instance, the Hessian matrix is $\left[-X^T D X \right]$, where D is diagonal with elements $\{\pi_i(1-\pi_i)\}$ on the main diagonal. This is the same as its expected value, so the estimated covariance matrix of $\hat{\beta}$ is $\left[X^T \hat{D} X \right]^{-1}$, in which we substitute the ML estimates to get $\hat{D}$.

   Fisher scoring is an alternative iterative method for solving likelihood equations.[15] It uses the information matrix evaluated at $\beta^{(t)}$ in adjusting $\beta^{(t)}$ in (7.8), whereas Newton–Raphson uses the matrix with elements $-\partial^2 L(\beta)/\partial\beta_j \partial\beta_k$ (i.e., without the expected value) at $\beta^{(t)}$. That matrix evaluated at $\hat{\beta}$ is called the *observed information* matrix. Each iteration of the Fisher scoring method can be expressed as a weighted version of least squares, in which observations having smaller estimated response variance receive greater weight.

   Most software for GLMs uses Fisher scoring. For GLMs that use the canonical link function, the observed and expected information are identical. In such cases, the Newton–Raphson method is equivalent to Fisher scoring. When the methods are not equivalent, they both yield the ML estimate, but standard errors are slightly different because of being based on the two types of information matrix.

7.6.4   Likelihood Equations and Covariance Matrix for Poisson GLMs

We next find the likelihood equations and the covariance matrix for a Poisson loglinear model that does not have an offset term. The likelihood function for n independent

---

[15]Technically, this approach applies for the *exponential family* of probability distributions (Exercise 4.75).

observations, using formula (2.7) for the Poisson *pmf*, is

$$\prod_{i=1}^{n} \frac{e^{-\mu_i}(\mu_i)^{y_i}}{y_i!} = \frac{e^{-\Sigma_i \mu_i} \prod_i(\mu_i)^{y_i})}{\prod_i y_i!}.$$

In terms of the Poisson parameters $\mu = (\mu_1, \ldots, \mu_n)$, the log-likelihood function is

$$L(\mu) = \sum_{i=1}^{n} y_i \log(\mu_i) - \sum_{i=1}^{n} \mu_i.$$

Substituting the loglinear model formula yields the log-likelihood function in terms of $\{\beta_j\}$,

$$L(\beta) = \sum_{i=1}^{n} y_i \left(\sum_{j=0}^{p} \beta_j x_{ij} \right) - \sum_{i=1}^{n} \exp\left(\sum_{j=0}^{p} \beta_j x_{ij} \right)$$

$$= \sum_{j=0}^{p} \beta_j \left(\sum_{i=1}^{n} y_i x_{ij} \right) - \sum_{i=1}^{n} \exp\left(\sum_{j=0}^{p} \beta_j x_{ij} \right).$$

Differentiating with respect to β_j, we obtain

$$\frac{\partial L(\beta)}{\partial \beta_j} = \sum_{i=1}^{n} y_i x_{ij} - \sum_{i=1}^{n} x_{ij} \exp\left(\sum_{k=0}^{p} \beta_k x_{ik} \right) = \sum_{i=1}^{n} y_i x_{ij} - \sum_{i=1}^{n} \mu_i x_{ij}. \qquad (7.13)$$

Setting this equal to 0 gives the likelihood equations, which can be solved using the Newton–Raphson method.

To obtain the covariance matrix for $\hat{\beta}$, we express the Poisson loglinear model as $\log \mu = X\beta$ for a vector of means μ and a model matrix X. From the expression for $\partial L(\beta)/\partial \beta_j$, an element of the Hessian matrix is

$$\frac{\partial^2 L(\beta)}{\partial \beta_j \partial \beta_k} = -\sum_{i=1}^{n} x_{ij} x_{ik} \exp\left(\sum_{h=0}^{p} \beta_h x_{ih} \right) = -\sum_{i=1}^{n} x_{ij} x_{ik} \mu_i.$$

This element is constant with respect to the response Y and thus is identical to its expected value. Since it does not depend on Y, the observed and expected information matrices are the same. This Hessian matrix takes the inner product of the column of X for parameter β_j times the column of X for parameter β_k times the elements of μ. The corresponding expression for the entire information matrix is $X^T D X$, where D is the diagonal matrix with elements $\{\mu_i\}$. The estimated asymptotic covariance matrix of $\hat{\beta}$ is $\left[X^T \hat{D} X\right]^{-1}$. The standard errors are the square roots of the diagonal terms of this matrix. They tend to be smaller when the $\{\hat{\mu}_i\}$ are larger and when the number of observations increases, so that X has more rows and the terms $\{\sum_{i=1}^{n} x_{ij}^2 \hat{\mu}_i, j = 0, 1, \ldots, p\}$ on the main diagonal of $[X^T \hat{D} X]$ are larger.

7.7 Regularization with Large Numbers of Parameters *

Some data sets are high-dimensional, having a very large number p of explanatory variables and potential model parameters. Such data are increasingly common in application areas such as genomics, biomedical imaging, market basket data, and portfolio allocation in finance. In genomics, statistical analyses pertain to classifying tumors and predicting a clinical prognosis using microarray gene expression data, and detecting differential expression

---

*Sections with an asterisk are optional.

(change between two or more conditions) in many thousands of genes. For model fitting, high-dimensional data are not well handled by classical ML methods.

When p is very large, sometimes even with $p > n$, a vital issue for model-building is selection of explanatory variables. The ML estimates of GLM parameters can be highly unstable or not even exist, such as when binary data exhibit complete separation. *Regularization methods* are ways of estimating effects under the assumption that the true model is *sparse*, with most of the explanatory variables expected to have no effect or a practically insignificant effect on the response. Such methods yield estimates that can be more appropriate than the ML estimates in such situations. With regard to model selection criteria, AIC can lead to variable-selection bias in a high-dimensional setup. Corrected versions are available, such as the `AICc` function in the `gamlr` R package, which is preferred when $n < 40p$. Also corrected versions[16] of BIC, such as an extended BIC (EBIC) are more appropriate than BIC, since the model prior assumed by BIC is not suitable in high-dimensional settings.

7.7.1   Penalized Likelihood Methods

The *penalized likelihood* method adds a term to the log-likelihood function such that the values that maximize it are smoothings of the ordinary ML estimates, typically shrinking them toward 0, like Bayesian estimates. For a model with log-likelihood function $L(\beta)$, the method maximizes

$$L^*(\beta) = L(\beta) - s(\beta),$$

where s is a function such that $s(\beta)$ decreases as elements of β are smoother in some sense. The penalized log-likelihood is expressed in terms of standardized versions of the variables, so that the smoothing function treats each variable in the same way and the degree of smoothing does not depend on the choice of scaling.

Among the positive features of penalized likelihood methods are sensible estimates when the ML estimate may not exist or is badly affected by multicollinearity. They are especially effective for logistic regression models. The ML estimator in logistic regression is biased away from 0, and a penalized likelihood correction[17] reduces the bias. The smoothing function utilized to do this gives estimates similar to Bayesian estimates with a *Jeffreys prior distribution* that is beyond our scope, being more complex than a normal prior distribution. Here is how this method handles quasi-complete separation for the endometrial cancer data analyzed in Sections 7.3.2:

```
> library(logistf) # implements Firth's penalized likelihood method
> fit.pen <- logistf(HG ~ NV2 + PI2 + EH2, family=binomial, data=Endo)
> summary(fit.pen)
Confidence intervals and p-values by Profile Likelihood # penalized likelihood
               coef  se(coef)  lower 0.95 upper 0.95  Chisq        p
(Intercept)  0.3080   0.8006     -0.9755     2.7888   0.17    0.681
NV2          2.9293   1.5508      0.6097     7.8546   6.80    9.12e-03
PI2         -0.3474   0.3957     -1.2443     0.4045   0.75    3.87e-01
EH2         -1.7243   0.5138     -2.8903    -0.8162  17.76    2.51e-05
```

Compare the penalized-likelihood estimates with the ML estimates in Table 7.4. The penalized likelihood estimate for β_1 of 2.93 and the 95% profile penalized likelihood confidence interval of $(0.61, 7.85)$ shrink the ML estimate $\hat{\beta}_1 = \infty$ and the ordinary profile likelihood interval of $(1.28, \infty)$ considerably toward 0, but still suggest that the NV effect may be very strong.

---

[16]R packages that perform high-dimensional variable selection based on EBIC include `bestglm` and `BeSS`.
[17]Proposed by the statistician David Firth in 1993 and identified in software as the Firth method.

7.7.2 Penalized Likelihood Methods: The Lasso

When p is very large, often only a few $\{\beta_j\}$ are practically different from 0. For such cases, a popular smoothing function for penalized likelihood methods is

$$s(\beta) = \lambda \sum_{j=1}^{p} |\beta_j|$$

for some *smoothing parameter* $\lambda \geq 0$. This method is called the **lasso**, which is an acronym for *least absolute shrinkage and selection operator*. The lasso penalizes an effect $|\hat{\beta}_j|$ for being large, and the method is equivalent to maximizing $L(\beta)$ subject to the constraint that $\sum_j |\hat{\beta}_j|$ is below some cutoff. With this method, many $\{\hat{\beta}_j\}$ may equal 0. The choice of λ reflects the bias/variance tradeoff. Ordinary ML estimates result from $\lambda = 0$. Increasing λ results in greater shrinkage of $\{\hat{\beta}_j\}$ toward 0, potentially reducing the variance but increasing the bias. A plot of the lasso estimates as λ increases summarizes how $\{\hat{\beta}_j\}$ reach 0 and corresponding explanatory variables drop out of the linear predictor.

The smoothing parameter λ is usually chosen with cross-validation: For each λ value in a grid, software fits the model to part of the data and then checks the goodness of the predictions for y in the remaining data, using some measure of prediction error. With k-fold cross-validation, this is done k times (for k typically about 10), each time leaving out the fraction $1/k$ of the data and predicting those y values using the model fit from the remaining data. The summary measure of prediction error is the sample mean prediction error for the k runs. A possible selection for λ is the value that has the lowest sample mean prediction error. At each λ, however, the sample mean prediction error is itself a random variable. An alternative choice is a larger value of λ that has mean prediction error one standard error above the minimum, which moves the estimates in the direction of greater regularization. This approach, called the *one-standard-error rule*, is less likely to overfit the model.

The lasso method is appealing but it has disadvantages. It can overly penalize β_j that are truly large. The lasso estimators do not have approximate normal sampling distributions and can be highly biased, making statistical inference difficult. Standard errors are potentially misleading with such highly biased estimates. An alternative regularization method, called **ridge regression**,[18] uses smoothing function $s(\beta) = \lambda \sum_{j=1}^{p} \beta_j^2$. It shrinks estimates toward 0 but does not completely remove variables from predictions. Ridge regression is especially helpful for reducing the impact of multicollinearity.

7.7.3 Example: Predicting Opinions with Student Survey Data

The Students data file at the book's website shows responses to a questionnaire by 60 social science graduate students in an introductory Statistics course at the University of Florida. The variables are summarized in Exercise 1.2 in Chapter 1. Here we use the 14 binary and quantitative variables to predict a subject's opinion about whether abortion should be legal in the first three months of a pregnancy (1 = yes, 0 = no).

When we use all 14 explanatory variables as main effects in a logistic regression model, the likelihood-ratio test has strong evidence against H_0: $\beta_1 = \cdots = \beta_{14} = 0$, with P-value $= 0.00016$, but only two explanatory variables are significant at the 0.05 level in Wald tests and likelihood-ratio tests. Four explanatory variables (*news, ideol, relig, affirm*) show significance when used as the sole predictor.

```
> Students <- read.table("http://stat4ds.rwth-aachen.de/data/Students.dat", header=TRUE)
```

---

[18]The name refers to replacing the least squares estimate $\hat{\beta} = (\boldsymbol{X}^T\boldsymbol{X})^{-1}\boldsymbol{X}^T\boldsymbol{y}$ of β in (6.12) by $\tilde{\beta} = (\boldsymbol{X}^T\boldsymbol{X} + k\boldsymbol{I})^{-1}\boldsymbol{X}^T\boldsymbol{y}$, thus adding a diagonal ridge to the matrix inverted.

```
> fit <- glm(abor ~ gender + age + hsgpa + cogpa + dhome + dres + tv + sport + news +
+             aids + veg + ideol + relig + affirm, family=binomial, data=Students)
> summary(fit)
            Estimate Std. Error  z value  Pr(>|z|)
(Intercept)  10.1014    10.8914    0.927    0.3537
gender        1.0022     1.8655    0.537    0.5911
age          -0.0783     0.1275   -0.615    0.5389
hsgpa        -3.7344     2.8093   -1.329    0.1837
cogpa         2.5113     3.7399    0.671    0.5019
dhome         0.0006     0.0007    0.821    0.4116
dres         -0.3388     0.2954   -1.147    0.2514
tv            0.2660     0.2532    1.051    0.2934
sport         0.0272     0.2551    0.107    0.9151
news          1.3869     0.6987    1.985    0.0471 # Likelihood-ratio test P-value=0.0003
aids          0.3967     0.5664    0.700    0.4837
veg           4.3213     3.8615    1.119    0.2631
ideol        -1.6378     0.7892   -2.075    0.0380 # Likelihood-ratio P-value=0.0010
relig        -0.7246     0.7821   -0.926    0.3542
affirm       -2.7481     2.6899   -1.022    0.3069
---
    Null deviance: 62.719  on 59  degrees of freedom
Residual deviance: 21.368  on 45  degrees of freedom
> 1 - pchisq(62.719 - 21.368, 59 - 45) # LR test that all 14 betas = 0
[1] 0.0001566
```

We next use the lasso, implemented in R with the **glmnet** package, which operates on the standardized variables:

```
> attach(Students)
> x <- cbind(gender, age, hsgpa, cogpa, dhome, dres, tv, sport, news,
+            aids, veg, ideol, relig, affirm) # explanatory variables for lasso
> library(glmnet)
> fit.lasso <- glmnet(x, abor, alpha=1, family="binomial") # alpha=1 selects lasso
> plot(fit.lasso, "lambda")
> set.seed(1) # a random seed to implement cross-validation
> cv <- cv.glmnet(x, abor, alpha=1, family="binomial", type.measure="class")
  cv$lambda.min # best lambda by 10-fold cross-validation
  [1] 0.06610251 # a random variable, changes from run to run
  cv$lambda.1se # lambda suggested by one-standard-error rule, a random variable
  [1] 0.1267787
> coef(glmnet(x, abor, alpha=1, family="binomial", lambda=0.1268))
                s0 # using lambda from one-standard-error rule
(Intercept)  2.3668 # all 12 lasso estimates that are not shown equal 0
ideol       -0.2599 # ML estimate is -1.638
relig       -0.1830 # ML estimate is -0.725
> coef(glmnet(x, abor, alpha=1, family="binomial", lambda=0.0661))
                s0 # using lambda minimizing CV mean prediction error
(Intercept)  2.6969
news         0.1400 # news effect much less than ML estimate of 1.387
ideol       -0.4239 # ideol and relig effects not shrunk as much toward 0
relig       -0.3603 # as when use one-standard-error rule
```

The fit using the smoothing parameter value of $\lambda = 0.1268$ suggested with the one-standard-error rule has only *ideol* (political ideology, higher values being more conservative) and *relig* (how often you attend religious services) as explanatory variables, with estimated negative effects -0.260 and -0.183 on favoring legalized abortion. The value $\lambda = 0.0661$ that has the minimum cross-validated mean prediction error adds *news* as a predictor, and then *ideol* and *relig* are not shrunk quite as much toward 0.

Figure 7.9 shows how the lasso estimates change as the smoothing parameter λ increases, on the log scale. The values at the left end of the plot, with the smallest shown value for $\log(\lambda)$, are very close to the ML estimates, for which $\lambda = 0$. The *ideol* estimate shrinks toward 0 from the ML value of −1.638, becoming 0 when $\log(\lambda) \geq -1.5$ (i.e., $\lambda \geq 0.22$). The ML estimate of −0.725 for *relig* decreases to 0 when $\log(\lambda) \geq -1.7$ (i.e., $\lambda \geq 0.18$).

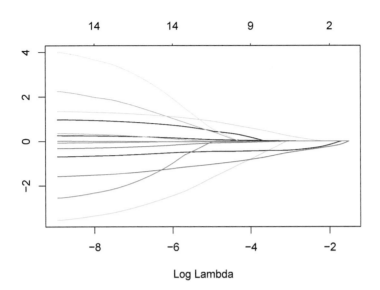

FIGURE 7.9 Plot of lasso model parameter estimates for predicting opinion on legalized abortion using student survey data, as function of $\log(\lambda)$ smoothing parameter. Above the plot are the number of non-zero coefficients for various $\log(\lambda)$ values.

For any data set, different lasso runs yield different results, because the chosen λ is a random variable that depends on the data-splitting for the cross-validation. When we used the lasso again for these data, the one-standard-error rule suggested $\lambda = 0.2215$, for which *ideol* was the sole predictor, with an effect of only −0.00018. You can use the set.seed function, as shown in the above output, so that results are reproducible.

7.7.4 Why Shrink ML Estimates toward 0?

To methodologists who commonly use estimators that are unbiased or approximately so, the strong shrinkage of $\{\hat{\beta}_j\}$ toward 0 that occurs with penalized likelihood methods can seem counterintuitive. Why can such shrinkage be effective? In studies having a very large number of explanatory variables, often most of them have no effect or very minor effects. An example is genetic association studies, which simultaneously consider each of possibly thousands of genes for the association between the genetic expression levels and the response of whether a person has a particular disease. Unless n is very large, by ordinary sampling variability, the ML estimates $\{\hat{\beta}_j\}$ tend to be much larger in absolute value than the true values. This tendency is exacerbated when we consider only statistically significant values.

Shrinkage toward 0 tends to move the ML estimates closer to the true values. This is yet another example of the bias/variance tradeoff. Introducing a penalty function sometimes increases bias but can benefit from reduced variance. For further details about regularization methods, see Hastie et al. (2009, Chap. 3) and James et al. (2021, Chap. 6).

7.7.5 Dimension Reduction: Principal Component Analysis

The lasso is a type of *dimension-reduction* method: It reduces the number of explanatory variables by removing more of them from the linear predictor as the smoothing parameter increases. An alternative approach, called **principal component analysis**, creates a few new variables directly from the standardized original set $\{x_j\}$, summarizing them without losing much information. The first principal component is the linear combination $\sum_j w_j x_j$, with weights satisfying $\sum_j w_j^2 = 1$, that has the largest possible variance. Each successive component has the highest variance while being orthogonal to preceding components. In many applications, a few principal components explain most of the variability. The interpretation of each component may be rather unclear in terms of the original context, but may reflect the original variables to which it gives the highest weights. This method is beyond the scope of this book. James et al. (2021, Sec. 12.2) give details.

7.7.6 Bayesian Inference with a Large Number of Parameters

Dealing with a large number of parameters is also challenging for Bayesian inference. The impact of forming prior distributions for a very large number of parameters may differ from what you intuitively expect. Even if you pick a very diffuse prior, the effect may depend strongly on which prior you choose and the data themselves may have relatively little influence on the posterior distribution.

We illustrate for the example of a multinomial response distribution (2.14) with a very large number c of outcome categories[19] having probabilities $\{\pi_j\}$ and observed counts $\{y_j\}$ with $n = \sum_j y_j$. The conjugate prior distribution for multinomial parameters is the *Dirichlet distribution* (Exercise 4.78). With hyperparameters $\{\alpha_j = \alpha\}$ for the c categories, the Dirichlet posterior density has posterior mean for π_j of $(y_j + \alpha)/(n + c\alpha)$. The impact of the prior is to add α observations to each category before forming a sample proportion. The value $\alpha = 1$ corresponds to a uniform prior distribution over the probability simplex. This seems diffuse, but the impact of adding c observations overall is considerable when c is large, especially when c is much larger than n.

For example, suppose we observe which in a list of $c = 1000$ books is selected as the favorite book by each of $n = 100$ people. With uniform prior, the posterior mean of π_j is $(y_j+1)/(n+c) = (y_j+1)/(100+1000)$. When book j receives $y_j = 1$ of the 100 observations, the posterior mean estimate for that book is $2/1100 = 0.002$, shrinking the sample proportion of 0.010 for the book toward the equi-probability value of 0.001. But if book j receives all 100 observations, the posterior mean estimate is $101/1100 = 0.092$. This shrinks much more from the sample proportion value of 1.0 than seems sensible. Even though the prior distribution is quite diffuse, it has a stronger impact on the posterior results than the data themselves. Much more diffuse priors can be more effective, yielding posterior results for each parameter that are more similar to what we would obtain if c were small. For instance, taking $\alpha = 1/c$, which corresponds to adding an overall total of 1 to the cells instead of c, simplifies with $c = 2$ to the Jeffreys prior for a proportion (Section 4.7.2).

7.7.7 Huge n: Handling Big Data

We have focused in this section on dealing with a large number p of explanatory variables in a model. An alternative challenge arises from the advent of *big data* in terms of a huge number n of observations. Such data are becoming more common, with large-scale administrative data from public and private sectors as well as types of data (e.g., imaging records, digital

---

[19]Here, similar issues arise when c has any size but the number of explanatory variables in a GLM, such as the multinomial models introduced in Exercises 7.56 and 7.57, is large.

records from brain or heart monitors or satellite climate recorders, microwave transmission data, network cybersecurity data) that do not have the format of a traditional data file. Statistical analyses with the traditional form of data file such as we've used throughout this book are often infeasible because of computer memory and storage limitations.

For huge data files, the *Divide and Recombine* approach analyzes the data for separate data subsets independently using fast parallel computation and then combines results over the subanalyses.[20] The subsets are stored in objects with the same data structure. The recombination can summarize results, such as by averaging model coefficient estimates, or yield a new and smaller dataset for further analyses. When privacy issues are paramount, the subanalyses can use sufficient statistics for the parameters of interest,[21] and sufficiency is also of use for reducing the dimensionality of the data. This is currently an active area of development and beyond our scope here, but see `DeltaRho.org` for information about software for divide and recombine analyses that uses `R` on the front end.

7.8 Chapter Summary

Generalized linear models, which apply to discrete as well as continuous response variables, enable us to assume distributions other than the normal for the response variable and to model functions of the mean through a *link function*.

- For binary response variables, the *logistic regression* model describes how the probability of a particular category depends on explanatory variables. Assuming a binomial distribution for the response variable, it uses a linear model for the *logit* transform of the probability, which is the log of the *odds* $= P(Y = 1)/P(Y = 0)$. For a quantitative explanatory variable, an S-shaped curve describes how the probability changes as the explanatory variable changes.

- The antilog of a parameter estimate in logistic regression is a multiplicative effect on the odds for the response variable. Thus, for logistic regression the *odds ratio* comparing two values for an explanatory variable is a natural measure of the nature and strength of an effect on the response variable or of an association.

- Bayesian methods are available for GLMs. They are especially useful for logistic regression when complete or quasi-complete separation of explanatory variable values causes some ML estimates of parameters to be infinite.

- For response variables that are counts, GLMs assume that the response variable has a *Poisson* distribution, or a *negative binomial* distribution to permit overdispersion. Such models usually use the *log* link function and are called *loglinear models*.

- The Newton–Raphson method is an algorithm that software can use, based on parabolic approximations for the log-likelihood function, to maximize the log-likelihood function to fit a GLM and to obtain standard errors of model parameter estimates.

---

[20]See `https://www.routledgehandbooks.com/doi/10.1201/b19567-6` for a survey of this approach.

[21]See `https://www.tandfonline.com/doi/full/10.1080/00031305.2016.1255659` for an example of such an approach using a Gamma–Poisson model for which the Poisson component uses individual-level explanatory variables for estimating effects on an event rate and the gamma component incorporates area-to-area variation in such effects.

- *Regularization* methods modify maximum likelihood estimates for high-dimensional data and other situations in which the ML estimates are unstable or do not even exist. The *lasso* method constrains the sum of absolute values of parameter estimates to be small, and the impact is to reduce dimensionality by forcing many of the parameter estimates to equal 0.

Exercises

Data Analysis and Applications

7.1 For the Houses data file described in Section 7.1.3, consider Y = selling price, x_1 = tax bill (in dollars), and x_2 = whether the house is new.

  (a) Form the scatterplot of y and x_1. Does the normal GLM structure of constant variability in y seem appropriate? If not, how does it seems to be violated?

  (b) Using the identity link function, fit the (i) normal GLM, (ii) gamma GLM. For each model, interpret the effect of x_2.

  (c) For each model, describe how the estimated variability in selling prices varies as the mean selling price varies from 100 thousand to 500 thousand dollars.

  (d) Which model is preferred according to AIC?

7.2 For the Scottish hill races data (Section 6.1.4) in the ScotsRaces data file, it is plausible that the record times are more variable at higher values of distance and climb.

  (a) Using the identity link function, fit the gamma GLM to the women's record times with distance and climb as explanatory variables. Describe how the estimated conditional standard deviation of the response relates to the estimated mean. Specify how it changes between the minimum and maximum estimated mean values for this sample. Is it close to constant, like the normal model assumes?

  (b) According to AIC, which is the preferred model with identity link, the gamma GLM or the normal GLM?

  (c) Fit the gamma GLM permitting interaction between distance and climb in their effects. Describe how the effect on record time of a 1 *km* increase in distance changes between the minimum and maximum climb values of 0.185 and 2.40 *km*.

7.3 Refer to the simulation in Section 7.1.6. Randomly sample 6 observations from the same uniform/normal structure. Fit the null model, the straight-line model, and the fifth-degree polynomial. For each model fit, find SSE and find the sum of squared errors around the true means. Explain what this shows.

7.4 Analogously to the previous exercise, randomly sample 30 X observations from a uniform in the interval (-4,4) and conditional on $X = x$, 30 normal observations with $E(Y) = 3.5x^3 - 20x^2 + 0.5x + 20$ and $\sigma = 30$. Fit polynomial normal GLMs of lower and higher order than that of the true relationship. Which model would you suggest? Repeat the same task for $E(Y) = 0.5x^3 - 20x^2 + 0.5x + 20$ (same σ) several times. What do you observe? Which model would you suggest now?

7.5 A study of sheep mentioned in Exercise 1.27 analyzed whether the sheep survived for a year from the original observation time (1 = yes, 0 = no) as a function of their weight (*kg*) at the original observation.

  (a) Does the survival of the sheep seem to depend on their weight? If so, how does the weight of a sheep affect its probability of survival? Answer by fitting a generalized linear model for the survival probability.

(b) For what weight values do the sheep have more than a 50% chance of survival?

7.6 Use the following toy data to illustrate effects of grouped versus ungrouped binary data on the estimates and the deviance for logistic regression modeling:

```
x     Number of trials    Number of successes
0            4                     1
1            4                     2
2            4                     4
```

Denote by M_0 the null model and by M_1 the model $logit(\pi_i) = \beta_0 + \beta_1 x_i$.

(a) Create a data file in two ways, entering the data as (i) ungrouped: $n_i = 1$, $i = 1, \ldots, 12$, (ii) grouped: $n_i = 4$, $i = 1, 2, 3$. Fit M_0 and M_1 for each data file. Compare their estimates and *se* values.

(b) Show that the deviances for M_0 and M_1 with the grouped data are different with the ungrouped data. Why is this?

(c) Show that the difference between the residual deviances for M_0 and M_1 is the same for the grouped and ungrouped data. Why is this? What is this difference used for?

7.7 The **Afterlife** data file at the book's website shows data from the 2018 General Social Survey on belief in the afterlife (postlife = 1, yes; postlife = 2, no), religion (1 = Protestant, 2 = Catholic, 3 = Jewish, other categories excluded), and gender (1 = male, 2 = female). Analyze these data by fitting a logistic regression model using classical or Bayesian methods. Report the fitted equation and summarize effects.

7.8 The **Soybeans** data file at the book's website shows results of an experiment[22] to compare the proportions of soybean seeds that have healthy radicle of at least 2 *mm* after being wrapped with wet germinating paper under treatment A of 25 degrees Celsius for 24 hours and under treatment B of 20 degrees Celsius for 48 hours. The data file has results from a private lab and a public lab (National Institute of Agricultural Technology in Argentina) of the number of successes y out of $n = 50$ seeds for 4 replicates and 12 cultivars for each treatment.

(a) Stating assumptions, fit a GLM with identity link function to model the probability of success in terms of treatment and lab. Interpret the estimated treatment effect.

(b) Show that significant interaction exists when we use the logit link function but not with the identity link. (So, it is plausible that the two labs have the same difference in success probabilities between the treatments but not the same odds ratio; see Exercise 7.33)

7.9 The **SoreThroat** data file at the book's website contains data from from a study[23] about $Y =$ whether a patient having surgery had a sore throat on waking (1 = yes, 0 = no) as a function of $D =$ duration of the surgery (in minutes) and $T =$ type of device used to secure the airway (1 = tracheal tube, 0 = laryngeal mask airway).

(a) Fit a GLM using both explanatory variables as main effects. Interpret effects.

(b) Fit a GLM permitting interaction between the explanatory variables. Interpret the effect of D at each category of T.

7.10 For indictments in cases with multiple murders in Florida during a 12-year period, the death penalty was given in 53 of 467 cases in which a White killed a White, in 0 of 16 cases in which a White killed a Black, in 11 of 48 cases in which a Black killed a White, and in 4 of 143 cases in which a Black killed a Black.[24]

---

[22] Thanks to Cristina Cuesta, Carina Gallo, and Luciana Magnano for these data.
[23] Described in "Binary Data" by D. Collett, *Encyclopedia of Biostatistics*, 2nd ed. (Wiley, 2005), pp. 439–446.
[24] [*Source*: M. Radelet and G. Pierce, *Florida Law Review* **43**: 1–34 (1991)

(a) Construct the three-way contingency table relating y = death penalty verdict to d = defendant's race and v = victim's race. Compare the percentages of Blacks and Whites getting the death penalty, both marginally and conditionally on the category of v. Explain what causes the marginal association to have different direction from the conditional association (the phenomenon called *Simpson's paradox*).

(b) Construct a data file and use logistic regression to model the effects of d and v on y. Interpret the effect estimate for defendant's race.

7.11 For first-degree murder convictions in East Baton Rouge Parish, Louisiana, between 1990 and 2008, the death penalty was given in 3 of 25 cases in which a White killed a White, in 0 of 3 cases in which a White killed a Black, in 9 of 30 cases in which a Black killed a White, and in 11 of 132 cases in which a Black killed a Black.[25] Construct a data file, letting y = death penalty verdict (1 = yes, 0 = no), d = 1 (d = 0) for Black (White) defendants and v = 1 (v = 0) for Black (White) victims, and fit a logistic regression model. Prepare a short report of about 100 words summarizing what you learn from the model fit.

7.12 Fit the interaction model referred to in Section 7.2.5 for Italian employment in the **Employment** data file, using logit and identity link functions. In each case, explain how to interpret the estimated gender effect.

7.13 For the Italian survey introduced in Section 7.2.5, results for the 27,775 subjects having age over 65 are in the **Employment2** data file at the book's website. Sample proportions employed at the various combinations of values of explanatory variables suggest that the gender effect may be larger for Italian citizens than for non-citizens. Fit a logistic regression model to check for this, and use it to describe the gender effect for citizens and for non-citizens.

7.14 "Stand your ground" (SYG) laws empower individuals to use any force necessary to defend themselves against anyone they believe to be an imminent threat. For court trials in which the defendant claimed SYG, logistic regression was used to analyze the probability of conviction.[26] The study found that for cases of domestic violence, the log odds changed in a statistically significant way by 1.8 when the victim was White instead of non-White, −1.9 when the defendant was White instead of non-White, and −2.7 when the defendant was male instead of female. Set up indicator variables and a model for which parameter estimates would be these values, and explain how to interpret them.

7.15 Comparison of *odds ratio* with *ratio of proportions*:

(a) According to **ourworldindata.org**, in 2017 the proportion of the population that died due to suicides done by firearms was 0.00006291 (i.e., about 6.29 per 100,000) in the United States and 0.00000168 (i.e., about 0.17 per 100,000) in the United Kingdom. Use these to find an *odds ratio* comparing the nations, and interpret. Compare them also by the *risk ratio*, which is the ratio of the proportions of deaths that were suicides due to firearms. Explain why this is close to the odds ratio when both proportions are close to 0.

(b) A Pew Research Report (February 13, 2020) reported results of a survey in which 78% of Democrats and 21% of Republicans in the U.S. stated that dealing with climate change should be a top priority for the President and Congress. Compare the political parties by the odds ratio and by the risk ratio. (When proportions exceed 0.2, unlike the result in (a), the odds ratio is better approximated by the *square* of the risk ratio than by the risk ratio itself.[27])

(c) Formulate a logistic regression model for the comparison in (b), and report $\hat{\beta}$ for the stated results.

7.16 For the clinical trials data mentioned in Section 7.2.6 of 10 successes in 10 trials for the new drug and 5 successes in 10 trials for placebo, fit the logistic regression model.

[25] From G. Pierce and M. Radelet, *Louisiana Law Review* **71**: 647–673 (2011).
[26] Article by J. Murphy, *Social Science Quarterly*, **99**: 439–452 (2018).
[27] See article by T. J. VanderWeele, *Biometrics* **76**: 746–752 (2019).

(a) What does software report for $\hat{\beta}_1$? What is the actual value?

(b) Give the result of the Wald test of H_0: $\beta_1 = 0$? Compare with the result of the likelihood-ratio test. Which is more appropriate for such data?

(c) Conduct a Bayesian analysis for these data, and interpret.

7.17 Suppose $y = 0$ at $x = 10, 20, 30, 40$ and $y = 1$ at $x = 60, 70, 80, 90$.

(a) What is the true ML estimate $\hat{\beta}$ for logistic regression? Report the estimate and standard error provided by your software. Why is the reported standard error so large?

(b) Use a Bayesian method or the Firth penalized likelihood method to fit the model. Compare results to ML for point and interval estimates.

7.18 Refer to the analyses of the endometrial cancer data in Section 7.3.2.

(a) Explain the difference between the interpretations of the classical one-sided P-value of 0.0011 and the Bayesian posterior $P(\beta_1 \leq 0) = 0.0002$ that we obtain using $\sigma = 10.0$ for the prior distributions.

(b) To conduct a Bayesian analysis with uninformative priors, use $\sigma = 100$ in the Bayesian analysis, verifying results such as shown in Table 7.4. Compare what you learn about the effect of NV with this prior and with the highly informative prior having $\sigma = 1$.

7.19 In a tennis match with players a and b, let Π_{ab} be the probability that a defeats b. The *Bradley–Terry model* is

$$\log(\Pi_{ab}/\Pi_{ba}) = \beta_a - \beta_b,$$

with an identifiability constraint, such as $\beta_c = 0$ for player c. For T players, this models $T(T-1)/2$ probabilities by $(T-1)$ parameters. Fit the model to the `Tennis` data file at the book's website, which shows results for Djokovic, Federer, Murray, Nadal, and Wawrinka between January 2014 and January 2018. (Each line of the data file shows the numbers of wins and losses for matches between the player with indicator +1 and the player with indicator −1. Using an R model statement in the format `glm(won/(won+lost) ~ -1 + Djokovic + ... + Wawrinka, ...)` suppresses the intercept term.) Estimate the probability that Federer beats Murray and compare it with the sample proportion.

7.20 In the `Crabs` data file introduced in Section 7.4.2, the variable y indicates whether a female horseshoe crab has at least one satellite (1 = yes, 0 = no).

(a) Fit a main-effects logistic model using weight and categorical color as explanatory variables. Conduct a significance test for the color effect, and construct a 95% confidence interval for the weight effect.

(b) Fit the model that permits interaction between color as a factor and weight in their effects, showing the estimated effect of weight for each color. Test whether this model provides a significantly better fit.

(c) Use AIC to determine which models seem most sensible among the models with (i) interaction, (ii) main effects, (iii) weight as the sole predictor, (iv) color as the sole predictor, and (v) the null model.

7.21 Refer to the Poisson loglinear model in Section 7.4.2 for the horseshoe crabs, with weight and color as explanatory variables.

(a) When you view a scatterplot, identify an unusual observation. Re-fit the Poisson GLM without it and describe how the estimate of the weight effect changes.

(b) Fit the Poisson loglinear model with weight and color predictors in which color is treated quantitatively with scores (1, 2, 3, 4). Compare to the categorical-color model fitted in Section 7.4.2 (i) by describing the color effect for each, (ii) by comparing AIC values. Which model do you prefer? Why?

(c) Fit the models permitting interaction, with color as quantitative. Is this model preferred to the corresponding main-effects model according to either statistical significance or AIC?

(d) Repeat (b) and (c) using negative binomial modeling. Of the various models, which would you select for these data? Why?

7.22 Refer to the previous example. Using all four explanatory variables in the data file as potential predictors, and considering color and spine condition as quantitative, select a model using AIC or BIC. Interpret its effects.

7.23 A question in a GSS asked subjects how many times they had sexual intercourse in the preceding month. The sample means were 5.9 for males and 4.3 for females; the sample variances were 54.8 and 34.4. The mode for each gender was 0. Would a Poisson GLM with an indicator variable for gender be suitable for these data? Why or why not?

7.24 For the study of lung cancer survival described in Section 7.4.4, the `Cancer2` data file at the book's website contains an expanded data set that also gives the disease histology as a prognostic factor.

(a) Include histology with stage of disease and time interval in the model for the death rate. Interpret the estimates of the stage of disease effects for this model and show results of the likelihood-ratio test of the effect of stage of disease.

(b) The study had 539 subjects, of whom 353 died. Does the analysis use the sample size 539 in any way? Explain.

7.25 A county's highway department keeps records of the number of automobile accidents reported each working day on a superhighway that runs through the county. Describe factors that are likely to cause the distribution of this count over time to show overdispersion relative to the Poisson.

7.26 A headline in *The Gainesville Sun* (Feb. 17, 2014) proclaimed a worrisome spike in shark attacks in the previous two years. The reported total number of shark attacks in Florida per year from 2001 to 2013 were 33, 29, 29, 12, 17, 21, 31, 28, 19, 14, 11, 26, 23. Are these counts consistent with a null Poisson model? Explain, and compare aspects of the Poisson model and negative binomial model fits.

7.27 For the data analyzed in Sections 7.3.2 and 7.7.1 on risk factors for endometrial cancer, compare the classical, uninformative Bayesian, and penalized likelihood results for the NV effect with those you obtain with the lasso by selecting λ using cross-validation with (a) lowest sample mean prediction error, (b) the one-standard-error rule.

7.28 For the `Students` data file, model y = whether you are a vegetarian with the 14 binary and quantitative explanatory variables.

(a) For ordinary logistic regression, show that this model fits better than the null model, but no Wald tests are significant.

(b) Use the lasso, with λ to minimize the sample mean prediction error in cross-validation. Compare estimates to those from ordinary logistic regression.

(c) Specify the range of λ values for which the lasso smoothing generates the null model.

7.29 Using the `Happy` data file from the 2018 General Social Survey at the book's website has data on happiness (1 = very happy, 2 = pretty happy, 3 = not too happy), marital status (1 = married, 2 = divorced or separated, 3 = never married), and gender. To analyze the effects of marital status and gender on whether one reports being *very happy*, specify a GLM and fit it using classical or Bayesian methods. Summarize your analyses in a short report, including interpretations and highly-edited software output.

7.30 In a 3-year study of the effects of AZT in slowing the development of AIDS symptoms,[28] veterans whose immune symptoms were beginning to falter after infection with HIV were

---

[28]Reported in *The New York Times*, Feb. 15, 1991.

randomly assigned to receive AZT immediately or wait until their T cells showed severe immune weakness. Of those who received AZT, 11 of 63 Black subjects and 14 of 107 White subjects developed AIDS symptoms. Of those who did not receive AZT, 12 of 55 Black subjects and 32 of 113 White subjects developed AIDS symptoms. Formulate an appropriate GLM for the study. Fit it and report and interpret and conduct classical or Bayesian inference about the AZT effect.

Methods and Concepts

7.31 The transformed-data approach uses a linear predictor for $E[g(Y)]$ whereas a GLM uses a linear predictor for $g[E(Y)]$. Explain why these are not the same, and state an advantage of the GLM approach if we are truly interested in modeling $E(Y)$.

7.32 For nested GLMs M_0 and M_1, with M_0 a special case of M_1, explain why their log-likelihood functions satisfy $L(\hat{\boldsymbol{\mu}}_0; \boldsymbol{y}) \le L(\hat{\boldsymbol{\mu}}_1; \boldsymbol{y})$.

7.33 Refer to Exercise 7.8 and modeling the probability of success in terms of two treatments and two labs. In the conceptual population, suppose that the main effects model with identity link function holds with nonzero effects. Explain why the main effects model would *not* then hold with the logit link. Illustrate with a set of four probabilities that satisfy the main effects model with identity link function. (Generally, when a GLM holds with one link function, it does not necessarily hold with a different link function; this has limited relevance in practice, because no model holds exactly.)

7.34 For the population having binary response Y, suppose the conditional distribution of X given $Y = y$ is $N(\mu_y, \sigma^2)$, $y = 0, 1$.

(a) Using Bayes' theorem, show that $P(Y = 1 \mid x)$ satisfies the logistic regression model with $\beta_1 = (\mu_1 - \mu_0)/\sigma^2$.

(b) Adult heights (in *cm*) in the U.S. have approximately a $N(161.7, 7^2)$ distribution for women and $N(175.4, 7^2)$ distribution for men. Let X = height and Y = gender (0 = woman, 1 = man). For each value of Y, randomly generate 100,000 observations on X. Fit the logistic regression model to Y given x. Compare $\hat{\beta}_1$ to the theoretical value of β_1.

7.35 For a logistic model, show that the average estimated rate of change in $P(Y = 1)$ as a function of explanatory variable j, adjusting for the others, satisfies $\partial \hat{\pi}_i / \partial x_{ij} = \hat{\beta}_j[\hat{\pi}_i(1 - \hat{\pi}_i)]$, and thus

$$\frac{1}{n}\sum_{i=1}^{n}\left(\frac{\partial \hat{\pi}_i}{\partial x_{ij}}\right) = \left(\frac{1}{n}\right)\hat{\beta}_j \sum_{i=1}^{n}[\hat{\pi}_i(1 - \hat{\pi}_i)].$$

Explain why $\hat{\beta}_j/4$ is an upper bound for the size of this effect at any observation.

7.36 For grouped binary data, with $Y_i \sim \text{binom}(n_i, \pi_i)$, $i = 1, \ldots, k$, construct the likelihood function. Show that the deviance is as shown in equation (7.5).

7.37 For a contingency table of arbitrary dimensions with cell counts $\{y_i\}$ and fitted values $\{\hat{\mu}_i\}$, where $\sum_i y_i = \sum_i \hat{\mu}_i = n$, the *dissimilarity index*

$$D = \sum |y_i - \hat{\mu}_i|/2n$$

is a summary measure of lack of fit. It takes values between 0 and 1, with smaller values representing a better fit.

(a) Explain how D could help us to judge whether a complex model that fits better than a simpler model in terms of statistical significance also fits better in terms of practical significance.

(b) Find D for the two logistic models fitted to the grouped-data version of the Italian employment data summarized in Table 7.1. Does the interaction model fit much better in terms of (i) statistical significance? (ii) practical significance?

7.38 Just as the Poisson sometimes does not permit sufficient variability, the same is true of the binomial distribution. Suppose n binary trials have $P(Y_i = 1) = \pi$ but are correlated, with $\text{corr}(Y_i, Y_j) = \rho$ whenever $i \neq j$. Show that $\text{var}(Y_i) = \pi(1-\pi)$, $\text{cov}(Y_i, Y_j) = \rho\pi(1-\pi)$, and

$$\text{var}\left(\sum_{i=1}^{n} Y_i\right) = n[1 + \rho(n-1)]\pi(1-\pi).$$

For what values of ρ does overdispersion occur? (In observing a data file of binomials, note that overdispersion cannot occur if each $n = 1$.)

7.39 A mixture model that is sometimes used when grouped binary data exhibit overdispersion relative to the binomial specifies that $(Y \mid \pi) \sim \text{binom}(n, \pi)$, but π itself has a beta distribution. The overall distribution for Y is called the **beta-binomial**. Describe an application in which such a mixture model might be relevant.

7.40 For two random variables with joint *pdf* $f(x,y)$, $E(Y) = \int\int yf(x,y)dxdy$. Using $f(x,y) = f(y \mid x)f_1(x)$ with f_1 the marginal *pdf* of X, show the law of the iterated expectation result (Sections 2.6.3 and 7.5.1) that $E(Y) = E[E(Y \mid X)]$.

7.41 Suppose that $(Y \mid \lambda)$ is Poisson with mean λ, but λ has the gamma distribution (7.6). Apply the formulas $E(Y) = E[E(Y \mid \lambda)]$ and $\text{var}(Y) = E[\text{var}(Y \mid \lambda)] + \text{var}[E(Y \mid \lambda)]$, and relate it to the mean and variance of a negative binomial distribution.

7.42 For modeling the horseshoe crab satellite counts, the *se* values for the Poisson model output in Section 7.4.2 are less than half the *se* values for the negative binomial model output in Section 7.5.3. Does this imply that the Poisson model is preferable? Explain.

7.43 For count variables for some activities, some subjects may have a 0 observation by chance whereas some will necessarily have a 0 (e.g., number of times going to a gym in the past week). Then, data may show more zeroes than could be generated by a Poisson or negative binomial model. Specify a model for such **zero-inflated data**, by a mixture of a distribution concentrated at 0 and an ordinary discrete distribution. Give an example of another variable that is likely to have zero-inflated data.[29]

7.44 For a sequence of independent binary trials, Exercise 2.69 showed the probability distribution of Y = the number of successes before the kth failure. Show that this distribution is a special case of the negative binomial distribution (7.7), for $\pi = \mu/(\mu + k)$. (The *geometric distribution* is the special case $k = 1$.)

7.45 If you are modeling count data, explain why it is not sufficient to analyze ordinary raw residuals, $(y_i - \hat{\mu}_i)$, to highlight observations not well described for the model, as you would for ordinary linear models.

7.46 For n independent Poisson random variables $\{Y_i\}$ with $E(Y_i) = \lambda$, consider Bayesian inference for λ with prior distribution $\lambda \sim \text{gamma}(\mu, k)$ as in equation (2.17) with y replaced by λ, for which $E(\lambda) = \mu$.

(a) Show that the posterior distribution of λ is the gamma distribution, where in the parameterization form (2.10) the shape parameter is $k' = \sum_{i=1}^{n} y_i + k$ and the rate parameter (reciprocal of the scale parameter) is $\lambda' = n + k/\mu$. (So, the gamma prior distribution is a conjugate prior.)

(b) Show that the posterior mean is a weighted average of the sample mean $\bar{y}$ and the prior mean μ. Explain how the weights change as n increases. (When n is very large, the posterior distribution has approximate mean $\bar{y}$ and approximate variance $\bar{y}/n$.)

7.47 Let's use the Newton–Raphson method to find the value $\hat{\beta}$ that maximizes a function $L(\beta)$, such as a log-likelihood function. Using $L'(\hat{\beta}) = L'(\beta^{(0)}) + (\hat{\beta} - \beta^{(0)})L''(\beta^{(0)}) + \cdots$, argue that for an initial approximation $\beta^{(0)}$ close to $\hat{\beta}$, approximately $0 = L'(\beta^{(0)}) + (\hat{\beta} - \beta^{(0)})L''(\beta^{(0)})$. Solve this equation to obtain an approximation $\beta^{(1)}$ for $\hat{\beta}$. Letting $\beta^{(t)}$ denote approximation t for $\hat{\beta}$, $t = 0, 1, 2, \ldots$ justify that the next approximation is

$$\beta^{(t+1)} = \beta^{(t)} - L'(\beta^{(t)})/L''(\beta^{(t)}).$$

[29] Agresti (2015, Section 7.5) used such a model for the horseshoe crab satellite counts.

7.48 Use software to write a program to conduct the Newton–Raphson method for a logistic regression model. Check it by fitting the model to the ungrouped beetle data in Section 7.2.4.

7.49 Refer to the log-likelihood function for the logistic regression model in Section 7.6.2.

(a) Explain why $\sum_{i=1}^{n} y_i x_{ij}$ for $j = 0, 1, \ldots, p$ are the sufficient statistics for the model.

(b) From the expression for $\partial L(\beta)/\partial \beta_j$, show that the likelihood equations have the expression

$$\sum_{i=1}^{n} y_i x_{ij} - \sum_{i=1}^{n} \pi_i x_{ij} = 0. \quad j = 0, 1, \ldots, p.$$

Explain why these equations equate the sufficient statistics to their expected values. (This was also the case for the equations (6.10) for normal linear models. In fact, the sufficient statistics and likelihood equations that equate them to their estimated expected values are identical for all GLMs that use the canonical link function.)

(c) For the null model, all $\mu_i = \pi$ for a single binomial parameter that equals $e^{\beta_0}/(1 + \beta_0)$. Explain why the likelihood equation then simplifies to $\sum_{i=1}^{n} y_i = n\pi$, so $\hat{\pi} = \bar{y}$, the overall sample proportion.

7.50 Construct the log-likelihood function for the model $\text{logit}(\pi_i) = \beta_0 + \beta_1 x_i$ with independent binomial outcomes of y_1 successes in n_1 trials at $x_1 = 1$ and y_2 successes in n_2 trials at $x_2 = 0$. Derive the likelihood equations, and show that $\hat{\beta}_1$ is the sample log odds ratio.

7.51 Refer to the likelihood equations for Poisson loglinear models derived in Section 7.6.4.

(a) For Poisson GLMs, show that $L(\hat{\mu}; y) = \sum_{i=1}^{n} [y_i \log(\hat{\mu}_i) - \hat{\mu}_i - \log(y_i!)]$.

(b) Show that the deviance equals $D(y; \hat{\mu}) = 2 \sum_{i=1}^{n} [y_i \log(y_i/\hat{\mu}_i) - y_i + \hat{\mu}_i]$.

(c) When a model with log link contains an intercept term, explain why the likelihood equation implied by that parameter is $\sum_i y_i = \sum_i \hat{\mu}_i$ and the deviance simplifies to

$$D(y; \hat{\mu}) = 2 \sum_{i=1}^{n} y_i \log(y_i/\hat{\mu}_i).$$

(For Poisson and for binomial GLMs with deviance shown in Exercise 7.36, the deviance has the form $2 \sum \text{observed}[\log(\text{observed}/\text{fitted})]$. The Poisson case sums over the n counts, whereas the binomial case sums over the n success indicators and the n failure indicators or the corresponding grouped totals.)

7.52 For Poisson loglinear models, consider the log-likelihood function shown in Section 7.6.4.

(a) Explain why the sufficient statistics for the model parameters are $\sum_{i=1}^{n} y_i x_{ij}$, $j = 0, 1, \ldots, p$, as in logistic regression models and normal linear models.

(b) From equation (7.13), show that the likelihood equations have the form

$$\sum_{i=1}^{n} y_i x_{ij} = \sum_{i=1}^{n} \mu_i x_{ij}, \quad j = 0, 1, \ldots, p,$$

which occur for any GLM that uses the canonical link function.

(c) For the null model, show that the likelihood equation implies that $\hat{\beta}_0 = \log(\bar{y})$.

7.53 Refer to the Poisson loglinear model likelihood equations in the previous exercise. For a model that contains an intercept, use the likelihood equation for $j = 0$ to show that the average estimated rate of change in the mean as a function of explanatory variable j satisfies $\frac{1}{n} \sum_i (\partial \hat{\mu}_i/\partial x_{ij}) = \hat{\beta}_j \bar{y}$.

7.54 Using the estimated covariance matrix for a Poisson loglinear model derived in Section 7.6.3, show that an estimated standard error for $\hat{\beta}_0$ in the null model $\log(\mu_i) = \beta_0$, $i = 1, \ldots, n$, is $\sqrt{1/n\bar{y}}$.

7.55 For the logistic regression model, from Section 7.6.3, the estimated covariance matrix of $\hat{\boldsymbol{\beta}}$ is $\left[\boldsymbol{X}^T \hat{\boldsymbol{D}} \boldsymbol{X}\right]^{-1}$. From this expression, explain why the standard errors of $\{\hat{\beta}_j\}$ **(a)** tend to be smaller as you obtain more data and **(b)** tend to be larger if $\{\hat{\pi}_i\}$ tend to fall close to 0 or close to 1.

7.56 For a multinomial response variable with c categories, the standard model pairs each category with a baseline category, such as category c, and forms a logistic model. For the response Y_i of subject i, the ***multinomial logit model***

$$\log\left[\frac{P(Y_i = j)}{P(Y_i = c)}\right] = \beta_{j0} + \beta_{j1}x_{i1} + \beta_{j2}x_{i2} + \cdots + \beta_{jp}x_{ip}, \quad j = 1, 2, \ldots, c-1,$$

has a separate set of effect parameters for each of the $c-1$ logit equations.

(a) Show that these $c-1$ equations imply equations for all $c(c-1)/2$ pairs of categories by finding the expression for $\log[P(Y_i = a)/P(Y_i = b)]$ for an arbitrary pair of categories a and b.

(b) Give two applications in which such a model would be appropriate to consider.

7.57 The model in the previous exercise treats the response variable as nominal-scale. When it is ordinal-scale, we can utilize the ordinality by forming logits of cumulative probabilities,

$$\log\left[\frac{P(Y_i \leq j)}{P(Y_i > j)}\right] = \beta_{j0} + \beta_1 x_{i1} + \beta_2 x_{i2} + \cdots + \beta_p x_{ip}, \quad j = 1, 2, \ldots, c-1,$$

called a ***cumulative logit model***.

(a) This model has the same effect parameters for each logit, called *proportional odds* structure. Sketch a plot of the model for $P(Y_i \leq j)$ for $j = 1, 2, 3$ with $c = 4$ and $p = 1$ that reflects the order of the three cumulative probabilities. Explain why a more general model with the effect β_1 of x_1 replaced by β_{j1} may violate that ordering.

(b) Give two applications in which such a model would be appropriate to consider.

7.58 For a joint distribution $\{\pi_{ij}\}$ for two categorical variables X and Y, Section 5.4.4 presented a chi-squared test for H_0: $\pi_{ij} = P(X = i, Y = j) = P(X = i)P(Y = j)$ for all i and j. For n independent observations from this distribution, let $\{\mu_{ij} = n\pi_{ij}\}$.

(a) Express H_0 as a loglinear model with main effects for X and Y.

(b) The Pearson statistic X^2 for testing H_0 is a goodness-of-fit statistic for the loglinear model, with H_0: independence of the variables being H_0: the loglinear model of independence holds. The corresponding likelihood-ratio statistic for testing independence (Exercise 5.66) is the residual deviance for that model. By treating the counts for the example in Section 5.4.5 on happiness and marital status as independent Poisson random variables (for which Exercise 2.57 showed that the conditional distribution, given n, is multinomial), fit the loglinear model and report and interpret the residual deviance.

7.59 Another use of loglinear models is for modeling cell counts in multi-dimensional contingency tables that cross-classify several categorical response variables. Table 7.7 comes from a survey that asked a sample of high school students whether they have ever used alcohol, cigarettes, and marijuana. Here are results of fitting a loglinear model for the expected cell counts in the joint distribution, using an interaction term for each pair of the three variables:

```
> Drugs <- read.table("http://stat4ds.rwth-aachen.de/data/Substance.dat", header=TRUE)
> Drugs
  alcohol cigarettes marijuana count # 8 rows, for 8 cell counts
1    yes       yes       yes    911
...
8     no        no        no    279
> A <- Drugs$alcohol; C <- Drugs$cigarettes; M <- Drugs$marijuana
> fit <- glm(count ~ A + C + M + A:C + A:M + C:M, family=poisson, data=Drugs)
```

```
> summary(fit)
              Estimate  Std. Error  z value  Pr(>|z|)
(Intercept)    5.6334     0.0597     94.36   < 2e-16
Ayes           0.4877     0.0758      6.44   1.22e-10
Cyes          -1.8867     0.1627    -11.60   < 2e-16
Myes          -5.3090     0.4752    -11.17   < 2e-16
Ayes:Cyes      2.0545     0.1741     11.80   < 2e-16  # AC log odds ratio = 2.0545
Ayes:Myes      2.9860     0.4647      6.43   1.31e-10
Cyes:Myes      2.8479     0.1638     17.38   < 2e-16
---
Residual deviance:    0.37399   on 1   degrees of freedom
```

TABLE 7.7 Alcohol (A), Cigarette (C), and Marijuana (M) use for high school seniors.

Alcohol Use	Cigarette Use	Marijuana Use Yes	No
Yes	Yes	911	538
	No	44	456
No	Yes	3	43
	No	2	279

Source: Thanks to Prof. Harry Khamis, Wright State Univ., for these data.

(a) Define indicator variables as shown in the output and show the formula for the loglinear model fitted there.

(b) Using the loglinear formula, form the AC conditional log odds ratio and show it is the AC interaction parameter. That is, the coefficients of the interaction terms in the model fit are estimated conditional log odds ratios.

(c) Suppose you instead use M as a response and A and C as explanatory variables. Construct an appropriate data file with 4 binomial observations, fit the logistic model, and find its residual deviance and the estimated conditional log odds ratios between M and each of A and C. This shows how effects in loglinear models equate with effects in certain logistic models.[30]

7.60 For a quantitative response variable, a generalization of a GLM replaces $\beta_j x_j$ in the linear predictor by an unspecified smooth function $s(x_j)$. With an Internet search, read about *generalized additive models*. Explain the method, with an example, in a report of at most 300 words.

---

[30] Agresti (2019, Chapter 7) and Kateri (2014, Chapter 8) showed details about such loglinear models and their connection with logistic models.

8

Classification and Clustering

The analyses in Chapters 6 and 7 for investigating the relationship between a response variable and explanatory variables have utilized *models*. This chapter presents alternative ways of analyzing data, by (1) using an algorithm for predicting Y that need not specify a functional form for the relationship with the explanatory variables, or (2) clustering similar observations.

We first introduce two methods for *classification* of observations into categories of a binary response variable based on their explanatory variable values. *Linear discriminant analysis* yields a linear predictor formula that is similar to that from logistic regression but is more efficient when the explanatory variables have a normal distribution. A graphical *classification tree* portrays how a simple partitioning of values of explanatory variables can provide classification predictions. We then briefly describe two algorithms for classification— *k-nearest neighbors* and *neural networks*. These methods and graphical trees can also predict quantitative and multiple-category response variables.

Cluster analysis groups observations on multiple variables into clusters of similar observations. The response variable is unknown for which the clusters are its categories. In botany and zoology, for example, cluster analysis methods can be the basis of taxonomy, using values of many observed variables to classify plants or classify animals into groups sharing certain similarities. Clustering methods are sometimes referred to as *unsupervised learning*, as they attempt to discover structure in the data without knowing the categories that provide the structure. By contrast, logistic regression and the classification methods introduced in the next section are *supervised learning* methods, for which the response categories are known in advance.

Contrasting the methods of this chapter with the modeling methods of Chapters 6 and 7 suggests the existence of two quite different cultures for data analysis—statistical modeling and algorithms.[1] The statistical modeling approach is more useful for describing effects of explanatory variables on response variables and making inferences about which effects exist and are substantively important. Algorithms instead focus on prediction of a response rather than analyzing and interpreting effects of explanatory variables. Algorithms can be more effective than models for complex, non-linear relationships, as well as for applications with other types of data, such as analysis of images and speech, especially with data files that are very large.

---

[1] Highlighted in the article "Statistical modeling: The two cultures" by Leo Breiman, *Statistical Science*, **16**: 199–231. (2001), available by search at `https://projecteuclid.org`.

DOI: 10.1201/9781003159834-8

8.1   Classification: Linear Discriminant Analysis and Graphical Trees

Section 7.2 showed how logistic regression models a binary response variable in terms of explanatory variables. Using the model fit we can predict that $Y = 1$, which we denote by $\hat{Y} = 1$, whenever the explanatory variable values are such that $\hat{P}(Y = 1)$ exceeds some cutpoint, such as 0.50. This section presents alternative ways to predict Y, based on partitioning the explanatory variable values into two sets: In one set, the method yields prediction $\hat{Y} = 1$, and $\hat{Y} = 0$ in the other set.

8.1.1   Classification with Fisher's Linear Discriminant Function

Linear discriminant analysis, like logistic regression, makes predictions using a linear predictor. Unlike logistic regression, the method treats the explanatory variables as random variables, so we denote them by upper-case $\boldsymbol{X} = (X_1, \ldots, X_p)$. Assuming a common covariance matrix for $\boldsymbol{X}$ within each Y category, in 1936 R. A. Fisher derived the linear predictor of explanatory variables such that its observed values when $y = 1$ were separated as much as possible from its values when $y = 0$, relative to the variability of the linear predictor values within each y category. The linear predictor is called *Fisher's linear discriminant function*. Its coefficients relate to those of the prediction equation for the least squares fit of the linear model with an indicator variable for Y. This model,

$$E(Y \mid \boldsymbol{x}) = P(Y = 1 \mid \boldsymbol{x}) = \beta_0 + \beta_1 x_1 + \cdots + \beta_p x_p,$$

is the *linear probability model* (Section 7.2.5).

With the additional assumption of multivariate normality for the probability distribution of $\boldsymbol{X}$ at each value of y and the specification of a prior probability for $P(Y = 1)$, Bayes Theorem yields posterior probability estimates, $\hat{P}(Y = 1 \mid \boldsymbol{x})$ and $\hat{P}(Y = 0 \mid \boldsymbol{x})$. For example, letting $\hat{f}(\boldsymbol{x} \mid y)$ denote the estimated normal *pdf* of $\boldsymbol{X}$ when $Y = y$,

$$\hat{P}(Y = 1 \mid \boldsymbol{x}) = \frac{\hat{f}(\boldsymbol{x} \mid y = 1) P(Y = 1)}{\hat{f}(\boldsymbol{x} \mid y = 1) P(Y = 1) + \hat{f}(\boldsymbol{x} \mid y = 0) P(Y = 0)}.$$

The prior probability $\pi_0 = P(Y = 1)$ is usually set as 0.50 or as the sample proportion of cases with $y = 1$. The prediction $\hat{y}$ is the category with higher posterior probability. For example, suppose that a single explanatory variable x has sample means $\bar{x}_0$ when $y = 0$ and $\bar{x}_1 > \bar{x}_0$ when $y = 1$, and we set $\pi_0 = 0.50$. Then $\hat{y} = 1$ if $x > (\bar{x}_1 + \bar{x}_0)/2$ and $\hat{y} = 0$ if $x < (\bar{x}_1 + \bar{x}_0)/2$, that is, $\hat{P}(Y = 1 \mid x) > 0.50$ if x is closer to $\bar{x}_1$ than to $\bar{x}_0$.

8.1.2   Example: Predicting Whether Horseshoe Crabs Have Satellites

Section 7.4.2 used Poisson regression to model counts of male "satellites," for a sample of 173 mating female horseshoe crabs. We shall illustrate linear discriminant analysis by predicting the binary response Y of whether a female crab has any satellites (1 = yes, 0 = no), using as explanatory variables the female crab's wt = weight (in kg), w = carapace width (in cm), c = color, and s = spine condition. We use the quantitative scoring (1, 2, 3, 4) for the levels of color and (1, 2, 3) for the levels of spine condition, both of which are ordinal variables with $c = 4$ the darkest color and $s = 3$ the worst spine condition. The R output shown next reports

$$\text{linear discriminant function} = 0.683wt + 0.256w - 0.650c + 0.315s.$$

As we explain below, the method predicts $\hat{y} = 1$ when the value of the linear discriminant function is above some value.

```
> Crabs <- read.table("http://stat4ds.rwth-aachen.de/data/Crabs.dat", header=TRUE)
> library(MASS)
> fit.lda <- lda(y ~ weight + width + color + spine, data=Crabs) # linear discrim. anal.
> fit.lda
Prior probabilities of groups:    # can use prior=c(0.5,0.5) or other in fit.lda command
     0        1                    # y = whether crab has satellites (1=yes, 0=no)
0.35838 0.64162   # sample proportions with y=0 and with y=1 (default)
Group means:     # crabs with y=1 have higher mean weight, width, lower mean color
     weight      width      color     spine
0 2.139113   25.16935   2.725806   2.516129
1 2.603685   26.92973   2.279279   2.468468
Coefficients of linear discriminants:
                LD1 # linear discriminant function is
weight   0.6829109 # 0.683wt + 0.256w - 0.650c + 0.315s
width    0.2564224
color   -0.6500500
spine    0.3148502
```

The least squares fit[2] of the linear probability model is $\hat{P}(Y = 1 \mid x) = -0.832 + 0.132wt + 0.050w - 0.126c + 0.061s$. Its coefficients equal those in the linear discriminant function divided by 5.16. Here is R output for that model and for the logistic regression model:

```
> summary(lm(y ~ weight + width + color + spine, data=Crabs)) # least squares fit of
              Estimate  Std. Error  t value  Pr(>|t|)          # linear probability model
(Intercept) -0.83172     0.67274    -1.236   0.21807
weight       0.13230     0.12533     1.056   0.29266
width        0.04968     0.03432     1.448   0.14962
color       -0.12594     0.04596    -2.740   0.00681
spine        0.06100     0.04371     1.395   0.16473
---
> fit.logistic <- glm(y ~ weight + width + color + spine, family=binomial, data=Crabs)
> summary(fit.logistic) # ML fit of logistic regression model
              Estimate  Std. Error  z value  Pr(>|z|)
(Intercept) -7.5994      3.7542     -2.024   0.0429
weight       0.7949      0.6917      1.149   0.2505
width        0.2733      0.1893      1.443   0.1489
color       -0.5915      0.2417     -2.447   0.0144
spine        0.2717      0.2410      1.127   0.2597
```

With a prior value π_0 for $P(Y = 1)$ and an assumption of multivariate normality for the explanatory variables, which is at best very approximate here because of the discrete nature of color and spine condition, the method yields the posterior $P(Y = 1 \mid x)$. The method predicts $\hat{y} = 1$ when $P(Y = 1 \mid x) > 0.50$, which corresponds to the linear discriminant function taking a sufficiently large value.[3] Here are R results, using the predict function to display posterior probabilities and the predicted response category (class). We first show posterior probabilities with π_0 as the sample proportion (0.6416) and then with $\pi_0 = 0.50$, with the first case also showing the predicted class:

```
> fit.lda <- lda(y ~ weight + width + color + spine, data=Crabs)
> lda.predict<-predict(fit.lda)$posterior # posterior prob's depend on prior pi_0 in lda
> head(cbind(lda.predict, Crabs$y), 2)     # default pi_0 = sample proportion
```

---

[2] Section 7.2.5 showed how R can obtain the ML fit. Unlike it, the least squares fit has no restriction on $E(Y)$. With ML, we need $0 \leq E(Y) \leq 1$ because $E(Y) = P(Y = 1) = \pi$ is the binomial parameter.

[3] James et al. (2021, Section 4.4.2) shows the rather complex formula for the linear discriminant function and its boundary for predictions. With $\pi_0 = 0.50$, the prediction boundary is $\hat{P}(Y = 1 \mid x) > 0.50$ for the linear probability model fit only when the sample proportion with $y = 1$ is 0.50.

```
            0         1
1 0.1018824 0.8981176 1  # crab 1 has posterior P(Y=1 | wt, w, c, s) = 0.898 and y=1
2 0.7547380 0.2452620 0  # crab 2 has posterior P(Y=1 | wt, w, c, s) = 0.245 and y=0
> predict(fit.lda)$class # predicted y=1 when posterior P(Y=1 | wt, w, c, s) > 0.50
   [1] 1 0 1 0 1 1 1 0 0 1 0 1 1 0 1 1 1 1 0 1 0 1 0 1 0 0 1 1 1 1 1 1 1 1 0 1 1 0
  [40] 1 1 1 1 1 1 1 1 1 1 1 0 1 1 0 1 1 1 1 1 0 1 0 1 1 1 1 1 0 1 1 0 0 1 0 0 0 1
  [79] 0 1 0 1 0 0 1 0 1 0 0 0 1 1 0 1 0 1 1 1 0 1 1 1 1 1 0 1 1 1 1 1 1 1 1 1 1 0 1
 [118] 0 1 1 0 1 1 1 1 1 1 0 1 1 1 1 1 0 1 1 1 1 1 1 1 1 1 0 1 0 1 1 0 1 1 1 0 0 0 1
 [157] 1 1 0 1 1 1 1 0 1 1 0 1 1 1 1 1 1
> fit.lda2 <- lda(y ~ weight + width + color + spine,  prior=c(0.5, 0.5), data=Crabs)
> lda.predict2 <- predict(fit.lda2)$posterior # pi_0=0.50 instead of sample proportion
> head(cbind(lda.predict2, Crabs$y), 2)
            0         1
1 0.1688098 0.8311902 1 # crab 1 now has P(Y=1 | wt, w, c, s) = 0.831 instead of 0.898
2 0.8463739 0.1536261 0
```

Those crabs predicted to have satellites are ones with relatively high weight and carapace width and relatively light color and poorer spine condition. The *P*-values for the corresponding logistic regression model reveal a significant effect only of color. As in ordinary regression modeling, we may do just as well and possibly even better using fewer explanatory variables. Here, weight and carapace width have a correlation of 0.887, and you can check that if we included only one of them in such a model, it would be much more highly significant than color or spine condition.

Section A.8.1 of the R Appendix and Section B.8.1 of the Python Appendix show ways of visualizing the data and the predictions from a linear discriminant analysis. We next show ways of summarizing how well the method predicts the binary response variable.

8.1.3 Summarizing Predictive Power: Classification Tables and ROC Curves

A ***classification table*** cross-classifies the observed binary outcome y with the prediction $\hat{y}$, for predictions based on linear discriminant analysis, logistic regression, or any other classification method. For any classification method, the true misclassification probabilities tend to be underestimated by predicting the response category using the same observations used to implement the method. We get less biased estimates using *leave-one-out cross-validation*,[4] for which the classification for a particular observation uses the prediction based on applying the method to the other $n-1$ observations. Thus, in implementing leave-one-out cross-validation, the classification method is applied n times.

As the prior value π_0 increases, the set of observations for which $\hat{y} = 1$ (i.e., $\hat{P}(Y_i = 1 \mid x_i) > 0.50$) gets larger. The next R output shows a classification table following leave-one-out cross-validation, for predictions based on posterior probabilities from the linear discriminant analysis with the prior value $\pi_0 = 0.50$:

```
> fit.lda <- lda(y ~ width + color, prior=c(0.5, 0.5), CV=TRUE, data=Crabs)
> xtabs(~Crabs$y + fit.lda$class) # classification table with cross-validation (CV=TRUE)
          fit.lda$class
Crabs$y  0  1
      0 43 19
      1 35 76
```

The classification table indicates that the prediction sensitivity[5] is $\hat{P}(\hat{Y} = 1 \mid y = 1) = 76/(35 + 76) = 0.685$ and the prediction specificity is $\hat{P}(\hat{Y} = 0 \mid y = 0) = 43/(43 + 19) = $

---

[4]This is the special case with $k = n$ of the k-fold cross-validation introduced in Section 7.7.2 that each time leaves out the fraction $1/k$ of the data.

[5]See Section 2.1.4 for definitions of sensitivity and specificity.

0.694. The overall proportion of correct predictions is $(43 + 76)/173 = 0.688$. This is not especially impressive, as one obtains 0.64 proportion correct merely by predicting that all crabs have satellites (i.e., using $\pi_0 = 1.0$). Section A.8.2 of the R Appendix discusses other cross-validation methods, such as *model training*, which randomly partitions the data frame into a training sample and a test sample, uses linear discriminant analysis or fits a model on the training sample, and checks its accuracy when applied to the test sample.

Classification tables have limitations: Since they collapse continuous predicted probabilities into binary ones, results are sensitive to the choice of the prior value π_0 and to the relative numbers of cases with $y = 1$ and $y = 0$. A ***receiver operating characteristic*** (ROC) curve is a plot that shows the prediction sensitivity $\hat{P}(\hat{Y} = 1 \mid y = 1)$ and specificity $\hat{P}(\hat{Y} = 0 \mid y = 0)$ for *all* the possible π_0. The ROC curve plots sensitivity on the vertical axis versus $(1 - \text{specificity})$ on the horizontal axis. When π_0 is near 1, almost all predictions are $\hat{y} = 1$; then, sensitivity is near 1, specificity is near 0, and the point for $(1 - \text{specificity}, \text{sensitivity})$ has coordinates near $(1, 1)$. When π_0 is near 0, almost all predictions are $\hat{y} = 0$; then, sensitivity is near 0, specificity is near 1, and the point for $(1 - \text{specificity}, \text{sensitivity})$ has coordinates near $(0, 0)$. The ROC curve usually has a nearly concave shape connecting the points $(0, 0)$ and $(1, 1)$. Figure 8.1 shows the ROC curve for linear discriminant analysis for the horseshoe crabs using weight, width, color, and spine condition as predictors for whether the crab has at least one satellite.

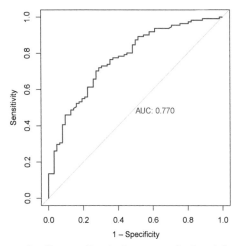

FIGURE 8.1 ROC curve for linear discriminant analysis with weight, width, color, and spine condition predictors of whether female horseshoe crabs have male satellites. The area under the curve (AUC = 0.770) summarizes the predictive power.

For a particular specificity value, better predictive power corresponds to higher sensitivity and a higher value for the ROC curve. Because of this, the ***area under the ROC curve*** is a summary of the predictive power. The greater the area, the better the predictive power. This measure of predictive power is called the ***concordance index***. Consider all pairs of observations (i, j) such that $y_i = 1$ and $y_j = 0$. The concordance index estimates the probability that the predictions and the outcomes are *concordant*, which means that the observation with $y = 1$ has the larger $\hat{P}(Y = 1 \mid \boldsymbol{x})$. A concordance value of 0.50 means predictions were no better than random guessing. That value occurs for the null model, having only an intercept term. Its ROC curve is a straight diagonal line connecting the points $(0, 0)$ and $(1, 1)$.

For predicting the presence of satellites with the horseshoe crab data, here is R code for an ROC curve and the area under it, first for the linear discriminant analysis and then for the fit of the logistic regression model:

```
> library(pROC); library(MASS)
> fit.lda <- lda(y ~ weight + width + color + spine, data=Crabs)
> lda.predict <- predict(fit.lda)$posterior
> rocplot <- roc(y ~ lda.predict[,2], data=Crabs, plot=TRUE, legacy.axes=T, print.auc=T)
> auc(rocplot)              # auc = area under ROC curve = concordance index
Area under the curve: 0.7704 # concordance index for linear discriminant analysis
---
 # logistic regression fit, ROC curve, and area under ROC curve
> fit.logistic <- glm(y ~ weight + width + color + spine, family=binomial, data=Crabs)
> rocplot2 <- roc(y ~ fitted(fit.logistic), data=Crabs, plot=TRUE, legacy.axes=TRUE)
> auc(rocplot2)
Area under the curve: 0.7701 # concordance index for logistic regression
```

The areas under the ROC curve are close for the two methods. However, we can do essentially as well with fewer explanatory variables. You can check, for example, that the area under the ROC curve is 0.761 when we use only weight and color in the linear discriminant function. It is 0.738 when we use solely weight, merely predicting the presence of satellites whenever a crab's weight is above a particular value.

Linear discriminant analysis generalizes in various ways. If we remove the assumption of equal covariance matrices for X within each y category, the optimal discriminant function is *quadratic*, containing not only each explanatory variable but also their squares and cross products. It seems inviting to remove that assumption, but the method then has many more parameters and need not perform better unless n is very large. Linear discriminant analysis also extends to multiple-category classification. For details about these and other generalizations, see James et al. (2021, Chapter 4) and Tutz (2011).

8.1.4   Classification Trees: Graphical Prediction

In recent years, non-model-based methods have been developed for predicting response variables using a set of explanatory variables. These methods are often referred to with the terms ***statistical learning*** or ***machine learning***. Rather than relying on a formula such as a linear predictor to summarize effects of explanatory variables on the response variable, such methods are algorithm-driven. Using various criteria, they provide a way of "learning" from the available information on all the variables to estimate the unknown, possibly very complex, relationship between $E(Y)$ and the explanatory variables x. This yields an algorithm for predicting y for other observations based solely on values of x. The effectiveness of the algorithm is evaluated by its prediction error rate for these other observations.

For binary response variables, a ***classification tree*** provides a graphical depiction of a decision process that uses a sequential set of questions about the x values to partition them into the values that yield each prediction for y. The classification tree summarizes binary splits on variables at various stages to determine the prediction. At the node for a particular stage, a splitting criterion that describes the *impurity* of the node is used to decide which variable gives the best split and how that split is done. The default is to minimize the *Gini* impurity index. For probabilities $\{\pi_j\}$ in c classes, this is $1 - \sum_j \pi_j^2$, which is the probability that two randomly selected observations are in different classes. Minimizing an alternative impurity index, *entropy* $= -\sum_j \pi_j \log(\pi_j)$, usually gives the same results. The set of x values for which $\hat{y} = 1$ consists of a set of rectangular regions that are easily summarized without a linear predictor or other formula.

For using the horseshoe crab data to predict the presence of satellites, Figure 8.2 shows two possible classification trees. Of the four explanatory variables available for constructing

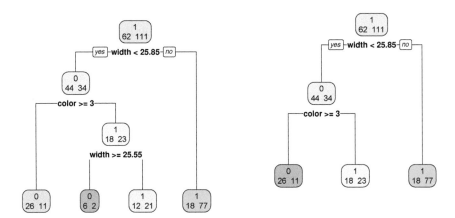

FIGURE 8.2 Two classification trees for predicting whether female horseshoe crabs have satellites: Each node shows the number of crabs with $y = 0$ (no satellites) followed by the number of crabs with $y = 1$. The terminal nodes at the bottom show whether $\hat{y} = 1$ or $\hat{y} = 0$ at that node by the number at the top of the box.

a classification tree, the plots use only the female horseshoe crab's carapace width and color to predict whether the crab has satellites.

In the first plot in Figure 8.2, the first split predicts that all horseshoe crabs of width ≥ 25.85 *cm* have satellites; of them, 77 actually do and 18 do not. Of those having width < 25.85 *cm*, the second split predicts that those of color ≥ 3 (the darker crabs) do not have satellites; of them, 26 do not but 11 do. Of those having width < 25.85 *cm* and color < 3, the third split predicts that those of width ≥ 25.55 *cm* do not have satellites and those of width < 25.55 *cm* have satellites. In summary, the horseshoe crabs predicted to have satellites were all those of width ≥ 25.85 *cm* and those of width < 25.55 *cm* with the two lightest colors (1 and 2). This classification tree, without cross-validation, has prediction sensitivity $\hat{P}(\hat{y} = 1 \mid y = 1) = (77 + 21)/111 = 0.883$ and prediction specificity $\hat{P}(\hat{y} = 0 \mid y = 0) = (26 + 6)/62 = 0.517$. The overall proportion of correct predictions is $130/173 = 0.751$. Here is the R code that created this classification tree:

```
> library(rpart) # or use tree package described by James et al. (2021, Section 8.3.1)
> fit <- rpart(y ~ weight + width + color + spine, method="class", data=Crabs)
>              # method="class" for categorical y
> plotcp(fit)   # plots error rate by cp=complexity parameter for pruning
> p.fit <- prune(fit, cp=0.056) # prune with particular value for cp
> library(rpart.plot)
> rpart.plot(p.fit, extra=1, digits=4, box.palette="auto") # pruned tree
```

The algorithm for constructing a classification tree can keep creating branches until each distinct set of x values has its own node, but this is overfitting. A classification tree performs better for new predictions when some branches are eliminated by **pruning**. The choice of a *complexity parameter* λ determines the extent of pruning, much like a smoothing parameter describes the extent of pruning of explanatory variables with the lasso method (Section 7.7.2). With $\lambda = 0$, the tree is the most complex possible, and increasing λ results in more pruning and a simpler tree. The choice of λ reflects the tradeoff between bias and variance. Fitting the data well (small λ and many nodes) has relatively low bias, whereas having a parsimonious tree (large λ and few nodes) has relatively low variance.

The first plot in Figure 8.2 used the complexity parameter value $\lambda = 0.056$ suggested from the results of the `plotcp` command[6] in the `rpart` package in R. However, its results are a bit counter-intuitive: The horseshoe crabs of the lightest two colors that are predicted to have satellites were those of width < 25.55 *cm* or ≥ 25.85 *cm*, whereas logistic regression modeling does not suggest evidence of nonmonotonicity for the width or weight effects, adjusting for color. The second plot in Figure 8.2 used greater pruning, with $\lambda = 0.07$ yielding only 3 nodes. This highly-pruned tree is simpler to interpret. The horseshoe crabs predicted to have satellites were all those of width ≥ 25.85 *cm* and those of smaller width with the two lightest colors (1 and 2). It has results in accord with those of logistic regression and linear discriminant analysis, which indicated that crabs that were lighter in color and larger in width (or weight) were more likely to have satellites. It has prediction sensitivity $\hat{P}(\hat{y} = 1 \mid y = 1) = (77 + 23)/111 = 0.90$ and prediction specificity $\hat{P}(\hat{y} = 0 \mid y = 0) = 26/62 = 0.42$, with overall proportion of correct predictions $126/173 = 0.728$ not much less than with the more complex tree.

Classification trees can also be formed for quantitative responses, with nodes of the tree showing the predicted mean of Y for rectangular regions of explanatory variable values. Such a tree is called a **regression tree**. For details about classification and regression trees, including ways of choosing λ and the role of cross-validation, see James et al. (2021, Chapter 8) and Tutz (2011, Chapter 11).

8.1.5 Logistic Regression versus Linear Discriminant Analysis and Classification Trees

Logistic regression model fitting makes no assumption about the distribution of the explanatory variables. Its likelihood function is based merely on assuming a binomial distribution for Y at each set of x values. By contrast, the linear discriminant function also treats X as a random variable and is derived based on assuming a common covariance matrix for X within each category for y. If this is true and if X have a joint normal distribution, then the linear discriminant analysis is a more efficient method for making predictions, potentially considerably more as the groups become more widely separated. It does not require the assumption that X has a normal distribution, but when that is the case, linear discriminant analysis is optimal for classifying observations. Often, however, the distribution of X is far from normal, such as when at least one explanatory variable is categorical. Also, severe outliers on x can have a large effect on linear discriminant analysis, as in ordinary linear modeling. Outliers have little impact on logistic regression, which is more robust and has broader scope because it makes no assumption about a distribution for X. Also, logistic regression has the advantage of providing direct ways of summarizing effects of x, through measures such as odds ratios.

Classification trees provide a simple mechanism for using answers to a set of questions to predict y. A person can view the tree and easily see which subjects have $\hat{y} = 1$. Compared with logistic regression and linear discriminant analysis, this method clearly shows which regions of the explanatory variables make each prediction. Since the trees do not require assumptions about the functional relationship between Y and x, it is easier to detect complex interaction structure. A disadvantage of a classification tree is the lack of smoothness, due to the region of explanatory variable values having $\hat{y} = 1$ being a set of rectangular regions. If a linear structure truly describes the effect of x on Y, as in a logistic regression model

---

[6]$\lambda = 0.056$ is the greatest pruning for which the cross-validated total error is less than one standard error above its minimum.

having only main effects, the tree will not help us discover this structure. Finally, the classification tree method can have low bias but high variance. Classification trees produced by different random samples from a common population can be very different, partly because of its hierarchical nature. Two samples that have a different initial split may end up with very different trees because of the influence of the initial split on the way the tree evolves.[7]

In summary, (1) if it seems reasonable to assume that X is approximately normally distributed with common covariance when $y = 0$ and when $y = 1$, linear discriminant analysis is a good choice for classification; (2) if X may be far from normally distributed but a logistic regression model seems to fit well, it is a good choice for classification; (3) if X may interact in unknown ways to determine y but simple rectangular regions are desired for classification, then classification trees are natural.

8.1.6 Other Methods for Classification: k-Nearest Neighbors and Neural Networks *

Other methods are available for classification (and regression), but beyond our scope as they lie more in the realm of data science algorithms than classical statistical science. Like tree-based prediction, compared to modeling, the other methods do not require constraining assumptions such as linearity and can be successful even when the boundary between explanatory variable values where $P(Y = 1 \mid x) > 1/2$ and where $P(Y = 1 \mid x) < 1/2$ is highly irregular.

An example of a very simple classification method is the **k-nearest neighbors** algorithm. At any particular point in the space of explanatory variable values, using some distance measure, such as the Euclidean distance defined in Section 8.2.1, the algorithm finds the k observations that are closest. One should implement the method on standardized versions of the variables, so that distances are comparable in each dimension. At any setting for the explanatory variables, the estimated conditional $P(Y = 1)$ is the proportion of those nearest neighbors having $y = 1$. The classification prediction for whether $Y = 1$ or $Y = 0$ is the outcome that is more common in the k nearest neighbors. An option is to weight the contributions of those neighbors, so nearer neighbors contribute more to the prediction. For instance, one could give weight $1/d$ to a neighbor having distance d, and then predict the category with highest total weight.

A good value for the number of neighbors k depends on the bias/variance tradeoff. With relatively small values for k, such as $k = 1$, the nearest-neighbor classifier has low bias but large variance because the prediction is so dependent on few observations. Larger values for k can reduce variability but make the decision boundary less distinct. A very large k is ineffective because the prediction then has little dependence on the explanatory variables. For high-dimensional data, standard distance measures are less meaningful because of the curse of dimensionality, in which case no neighbors are especially close. It is then better to reduce the dimensionality before employing the method or use a more complex type of distance measure.[8]

The k-nearest neighbors method also can be used in a regression context to estimate values of continuous response variables. Like classification and regression trees, a disadvantage compared to modeling is that the method is not designed to determine which of the explanatory variables are important or to provide summaries of their effects, because of not having model coefficients. An advantage is improved performance with large n and small p when the decision boundary is highly nonlinear.

---

[7]Generalized classification-tree methods aim to reduce the high variability, such as by averaging many trees. See *random forests* and *bagging* in James et al. (2021, Section 8.2).

*Sections with an asterisk are optional.

[8]For instance, see Hastie et al. (2009, Sec. 13.3 and 13.4).

The prediction aspect of the k-nearest neighbor method is available with the `knn` function in the `class` package of R. For a random partition of the data into a training sample and a test sample, for each observation in the test sample, the function finds the majority class for the k nearest neighbors in the training sample. (For a binary response, selecting k to be an odd number avoids ties.) A classification table can then summarize the accuracy of the method as applied to the test sample. We illustrate with $k = 1$, $k = 3$, and $k = 5$ nearest neighbors for predicting the presence of satellites for the female horseshoe crabs.

```
> Crabs.std <- scale(Crabs[, 4:7]) # standardize weight, width, color, spine
> y <- Crabs$y                # columns 4, 5, 6, 7 of Crabs data file
> Crabs2 <- data.frame(cbind(y, Crabs.std))
> head(Crabs2, 1)
    y    weight      width      color      spine
1 1  1.0620147  0.9488375 -0.5478090  0.6231873
> train_index <- sample(nrow(Crabs), (2/3)*nrow(Crabs))
> Crabs_train <- Crabs2[train_index, ]          # 2/3 of data in training sample
> Crabs_test <- Crabs2[-train_index, ]          # 1/3 of data in test sample
> target_cat <- Crabs2[train_index, 1] # actual y values for training set
> test_cat <- Crabs2[-train_index, 1]  # actual y values for test set
> library(class) # package needed for knn function
> pr1 <- knn(Crabs_train, Crabs_test, cl=target_cat, k=1) # using k=1 neighbor
> table(pr1, test_cat) # classification table for 58 crabs in test sample
    test_cat            # results differ when repeat analysis, because
pr1  0   1              # training and test samples randomly selected
  0 14   0
  1  3  41
> pr3 <- knn(Crabs_train, Crabs_test, cl=target_cat, k=3) # using k=3 neighbors
> table(pr3, test_cat)
    test_cat
pr1  0   1
  0 12   2
  1  5  39
> pr5 <- knn(Crabs_train, Crabs_test, cl=target_cat, k=5) # using k=5 neighbors
> table(pr5, test_cat)
    test_cat
pr5  0   1
  0 13   3
  1  4  38
```

For these data, this simple method does incredibly well using only a single neighbor. For more details about nearest-neighbor methods, see James et al. (2021, Sec. 2.2.3, 3.5, and 4.7.6).

By contrast with the simplicity of k-nearest neighbors, an example of a very complex method for classification and regression is the one that uses a ***neural network***.[9] Increasingly popular in practice, this is a nonlinear, potentially multi-layered process consisting of the input variables, the output prediction function, and *hidden layers* in between. Each hidden layer contains hidden units, each of which mimics the functions of a nucleus in a human brain. A hidden unit receives a weighted sum of its inputs, with weights iteratively calculated to minimize some error function. That hidden unit yields an output that is propagated to other hidden units in the next hidden layer and then eventually to the output prediction function. The neural network method is a nonlinear generalization of the linear model that has broad scope. With multiple hidden layers, it is a type of method called *deep learning*. In the context of making predictions about outcomes on a single response variable, it is an alternative to linear models or GLMs or classification methods discussed in this section. The method has been applied to a much wider variety of settings, however, including complex applications such as image classification and automatic speech recognition.

---

[9]The type of neural network presented here is called an *artificial neural network*.

The fitting of a neural network is a black-box method that uses an algorithm, called *back-propagation*, that is much more complex than simple algorithms for maximizing a likelihood function for a logistic regression model or finding binary splits of predictors to minimize prediction error for a classification tree or using responses of near neighbors. The algorithm compares the prediction that a network produces with the actual response outcome and uses the difference to modify the weights of the connections between units in the network, working backward. For any method, as we increase complexity or the number of parameters, we expect the predictions to be closer to the observed data. Performance is better assessed by testing the obtained prediction function on other data, such as with cross-validation. The method is commonly applied by randomly partitioning the data into a training sample and a test sample, performing the neural network analysis on the training sample, and checking its accuracy when applied to the test sample. This training approach is explained in Section A.8.2 in the R Appendix for classification methods. We illustrate with a neural network for predicting the presence of satellites for the female horseshoe crabs:

```
> train_index <- sample(nrow(Crabs), (2/3)*nrow(Crabs))
> Crabs_train <- Crabs[train_index, ]          # train with 2/3 of data
> Crabs_test <- Crabs[-train_index, ]          # test with 1/3 of data
> library(neuralnet)
> nn <- neuralnet(y=="1" ~ weight + width + color + spine, Crabs_train, linear.output=F)
> pred.nn <- predict(nn, Crabs_test)           # results differ when repeat analysis,
> cbind(head(Crabs_test$y, 3), head(pred.nn, 3))  # because test sample randomly selected
    [,1]      [,2]
1     1 0.8587442
2     0 0.3002590
5     1 0.8349790
> classtab <- table(Crabs_test$y=="1", pred.nn[, 1] > 0.64) # using sample proportion cutoff
> classtab
        FALSE TRUE # classification table for 58 crabs in test sample
  FALSE    12   12
  TRUE      8   26
> sum(diag(classtab))/nrow(Crabs_test)          # proportion of correct classification
[1] 0.65517
> plot(nn, information = F)                      # plots the neural network
> plot(Crabs_test$weight, pred.nn, pch=as.character(Crabs_test$color)) # (not shown here)
```

Using code such as this, with such a modest sample size you can check that repeated submissions can have highly variable results. Figure 8.3 shows the neural network for this analysis, to illustrate how the input layer of explanatory variables propagate to hidden layers (here, a single one, with a single hidden unit) which itself propagate to output predictions. It is beyond our scope to explain the equations or the numerical values of the weights shown for the input variables or for the input circles labeled by "1" that represent intercept terms for prediction equations. Plotting the predicted values against weight (not shown here) reveals that, for each color, the neural network method yields a sigmoidal curve between weight and the predicted response probability. Alternatively, the **nnet** function in the **nnet** package of R allows one to control the number of units in the hidden layer. Neural networks can also be plotted by the **plotnet** function in the **NeuralNetTools** package.

This method and the k-nearest neighbor method are less relevant for these data than the other classification methods we've discussed, because n is relatively small and the focus of the horseshoe crab study was on investigating which explanatory variables have an effect on the response and describing those effects.

The neural network method, being a black box, focuses on prediction rather than describing effects, and its predictive power can be more effectively exploited with a much larger n than in this example. It is likely to be increasingly used in applications for which the training set can be extremely large and interpretability of effects is not especially

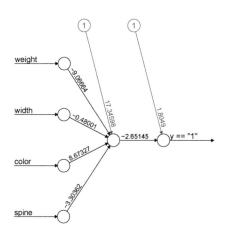

FIGURE 8.3 A neural network with a hidden layer for predicting whether female horseshoe crabs have satellites.

important. For details about the neural network method, see James et al. (2021, Chapter 10) and Chollet and Allaire (2018) with focus on R; see Rashid (2016) and `https://www.coursera.org/learn/neural-networks-deep-learning` with focus on Python.

8.2   Cluster Analysis

Linear discriminant analysis and classification trees resemble logistic regression in using explanatory-variable values to classify observations into well-defined groups that are the categories of a response variable. Some applications do not have such well identified groups, but it is still relevant to sort observations into ***clusters*** of similar observations. For example, in "market basket data," a person's observation is a long list of binary indicators in which a particular component indicates whether the person purchased a particular item, and a company might identify clusters of customers that have similar buying behavior. A company that sells products over the Internet might recommend products to people based on a cluster *affinity analysis* that takes into account their purchase history and the history of other people who have bought the same items. Clustering methods have even been used in evaluations of Scotch whiskies to group together brands with similar characteristics[10] and in archaeology for clustering ancient ceramics.[11]

This section presents clustering methods for a data file that consists of n observations of p variables. The goal is to group the n observations into clusters of observations that are similar. The number of clusters may itself be unknown. The variables can be categorical or quantitative. We illustrate for binary variables, and Section A.8.4 of the R Appendix describes cluster analysis for quantitative variables.

---

[10]F.-J. Lapointe and P. Legendre, *Applied Statistics* **43**: 237–257 (1994).
[11]I. Papageorgiou, M. J. Baxter, and M. A. Cau, *Archaeometry* **43**: 571–588 (2001).

Cluster Analysis 325

8.2.1 Measuring Dissimilarity between Observations on Binary Responses

To group together similar observations, clustering methods calculate a measure of **dissimilarity** between each pair of observations. Pairs within a cluster tend to have lower dissimilarity than pairs in different clusters. A clustering method is characterized by its dissimilarity measure and the algorithm for implementing the clustering.

When the variables are quantitative, a popular dissimilarity measure is *Euclidean distance*, which is the straight-line distance between the observations in multidimensional Euclidean space. For two observations $(x_1, \ldots, x_p)$ and $(y_1, \ldots, y_p)$ on p variables, this is $\sqrt{(x_1 - y_1)^2 + \cdots + (x_p - y_p)^2}$. With binary variables, the data file is a $n \times p$ table in which row i shows the p binary responses for observation i, with each response being an indicator that takes value 0 or 1. Table 8.1 summarizes the similarity and dissimilarity for a particular pair of observations. Of the p variables, a of them take the value 1 for both observations, and d of them take the value 0 for both. The proportion of the p variables that have a match is $(a + d)/(a + b + c + d)$. A simple dissimilarity measure is the proportion for which the outcome differs, which is $(b + c)/(a + b + c + d)$. In some applications, a common response of 1 is much more relevant than a common response of 0. With market basket data, for example, each person's observation consists of a very high proportion of 0 entries (i.e., items *not* bought), so necessarily a high proportion of variables has a common outcome. Then, an *asymmetric* similarity measure may be more relevant, such as $a/(a + b + c)$. The corresponding dissimilarity measure is $(b + c)/(a + b + c)$.

TABLE 8.1 Cross classification of two observations on p binary response variables, where $p = (a + b + c + d)$.

	Observation 2	
Observation 1	1	0
1	a	b
0	c	d

With high-dimensional data, such as market basket data, the challenges to clustering are many. Many irrelevant variables may have the impact of masking clusters, as clusters might exist for only a tiny subset of the variables. Dissimilarity measures then are less meaningful, as observations may be close for the most relevant variables but the curse of dimensionality may put them far apart in high-dimensional space. The clusters found need not reflect a true categorical classification.

8.2.2 Hierarchical Clustering Algorithm and Its Dendrogram

Agglomerative clustering is a popular algorithm that forms clusters by creating a *hierarchical* merging of the observations. The clusters at a particular level of the hierarchy result from merging clusters at the previous level. At one extreme, each observation forms its own cluster; at the other extreme, a single cluster contains all the observations. A step of the algorithm combines into a single cluster the pair of clusters having the smallest mean dissimilarity. The algorithm keeps combining clusters as long as the mean dissimilarity between a pair of clusters that could be combined is less than some chosen value.

The entire hierarchy for this clustering portrays an ordered sequence of clusters, starting with each observation as its own cluster and successively merging them. A graphical tree called a **dendrogram** portrays the hierarchical merging of the clusters, as a function of the mean dissimilarity between clusters being merged. An informal way to stop the agglomerative clustering looks for a natural break point in the dendrogram at which the mean dissimilarity changes substantially.

8.2.3 Example: Clustering States on Presidential Election Outcomes

Table 8.2 shows, for some U.S. states, the political party that won the electoral votes for that state for each Presidential election between 1980 and 2020. The `Elections` data file at the book's website shows results for all states and for the District of Columbia, with an indicator variable for the winner (0 = Republican, 1 = Democratic). For a pair of states, we measure dissimilarity by the number of election outcomes on which the states differ. For example, Arizona and California agree in 5 of the 11 elections, so have dissimilarity of 6.

TABLE 8.2 Statewide data on political party (D = Democratic, R = Republican) winning electoral votes in eleven Presidential elections, from `Elections` data file at book's website.

State	1980	1984	1988	1992	1996	2000	2004	2008	2012	2016	2020
Arizona	R	R	R	R	D	R	R	R	R	R	D
California	R	R	R	D	D	D	D	D	D	D	D
Colorado	R	R	R	D	R	R	R	D	D	D	D
Florida	R	R	R	R	D	R	R	D	D	R	R
Illinois	R	R	R	D	D	D	D	D	D	D	D
Massachusetts	R	R	D	D	D	D	D	D	D	D	D
Minnesota	D	R	D	D	D	D	D	D	D	D	D
Missouri	R	R	R	D	D	R	R	R	R	R	R
New Mexico	R	R	R	D	D	D	R	D	D	D	D
New York	R	R	D	D	D	D	D	D	D	D	D
Ohio	R	R	R	D	D	R	R	D	D	R	R
Texas	R	R	R	R	R	R	R	R	R	R	R
Virginia	R	R	R	R	R	R	R	D	D	D	D
Wyoming	R	R	R	R	R	R	R	R	R	R	R

To more easily portray the cluster-forming process and its dendrogram, we use only the 14 states in Table 8.2. The agglomerative clustering algorithm begins with 14 clusters, one for each state. The first step combines states that have the minimum dissimilarity, which are states such as Massachusetts and New York that have identical sets of responses and a dissimilarity of 0. At the next step, clusters are combined with the next smallest dissimilarity, such as the cluster containing Massachusetts and New York with the cluster containing California and Illinois, for which the dissimilarity is 1. By the stage at which only two clusters remain, one cluster has states that tended to vote Democratic and the other cluster has states that tended to vote Republican. Figure 8.4 shows the dendrogram. The bottom nodes of the figure are the initial 14 clusters. The top of the dendrogram joins all states into a single cluster. The two-cluster solution, below it, shows the Republican-leaning cluster (Florida, Ohio, Texas, Wyoming, Arizona, Missouri) and the Democratic-leaning cluster (Colorado, Virginia, Minnesota, New Mexico, California, Illinois, Massachusetts, New York). At the step of merging Minnesota with five other states, the mean dissimilarity between Minnesota and those states is $(4+3+3+2+2)/5 = 2.8$. Here is R code for these results:

```
> Elections <- read.table("http://stat4ds.rwth-aachen.de/data/Elections2.dat", header=T)
> Elections # 0 = Republican, 1 = Democratic electoral college winner
          state e1 e2 e3 e4 e5 e6 e7 e8 e9 e10 e11 # 11 election results
1       Arizona  0  0  0  0  1  0  0  0  0   0  1
2    California  0  0  0  1  1  1  1  1  1   1  1
  ...
```

```
14          Wyoming  0  0  0  0  0  0  0  0  0  0 0
> distances <- dist(Elections[, 3:13], method = "manhattan")
   # manhattan dissimilarity = no. of election outcomes that differ
> democlust <- hclust(distances, "average")    # hierarchical clustering
> plot(democlust, labels=Elections$state)
> library(gplots)         # heatmap portrays observations with dendrogram
> clust.meth <- function(d) hclust(d, method = "average")
> dist.meth <- function(x) dist(x,method = "manhattan")
> heatmap.2(as.matrix(Elections[, 3:13]), distfun=dist.meth, hclustfun=clust.meth,
+           labRow = Elections$state, dendrogram="row", key=FALSE, Colv=FALSE)
```

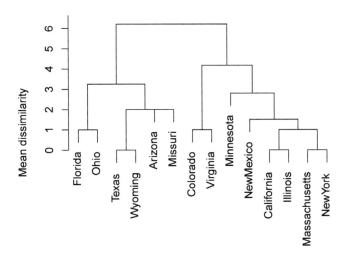

FIGURE 8.4 Dendrogram for cluster analysis of 14 states according to 11 presidential election results in Table 8.2: The vertical axis (height) measures mean dissimilarity, which is the mean number of election outcomes on which the states differed for the clusters being merged.

Figure 8.5 is a *heatmap*, which portrays all the observations together with the dendrogram. For instance, the first two rows of the heatmap show that New York and Massachusetts voted Republican in the first two elections but in none of the others.

For further details about clustering methods, see Everitt et al. (2011) and James et al. (2021, Section 12.4).

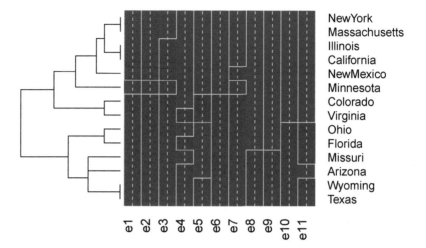

FIGURE 8.5 Heatmap showing 11 election results (e1 through e11, with red = Republican victory, blue = Democratic victory) and dendrogram for cluster analysis of states in Table 8.2.

8.3 Chapter Summary

Chapter 7 introduced *logistic regression* for modeling a binary response variable. This chapter presents alternative methods for **classification** of observations into categories of a binary response variable based on their explanatory variable values.

- **Linear discriminant analysis** yields a linear predictor formula that is more efficient than logistic regression when the explanatory variables have a normal distribution.

- Other methods have algorithms that do not provide prediction formulas but do provide classification predictions. A graphical **classification tree** portrays how a simple partitioning of explanatory variable values into rectangular regions can provide classifications. **k-nearest neighbors** uses response values for nearby observations to determine the predictions, and **neural networks** provide a multi-layered process consisting of hidden units that receives a weighted sum of its inputs and propagates an output to other hidden units and then eventually to an output prediction function. For quantitative response variables, analogous methods (e.g., *regression trees*) can also provide predicted values.

Cluster analysis groups observations on multiple variables into clusters of similar observations when the response variable is unknown for which the clusters are its categories. It provides a *dendrogram* for displaying how clusters combine in a hierarchical manner when we use a method such as *agglomerative clustering* to join clusters.

Exercises

Data Analysis and Applications

8.1 Consider the example in Section 8.1.2 of predicting whether a female horseshoe crab has any satellites. Now use only weight and color as explanatory variables.

(a) Use linear discriminant analysis to classify on y. Report and interpret Fisher's linear discriminant function.

(b) With $\pi_0 = 0.50$, show the posterior probabilities for the first crab in the data file and give the predicted y for a crab at that weight and color.

(c) Using cross-validation, form the classification table with $\pi_0 = 0.50$. Report the predicted sensitivity and specificity. Give the overall proportion of correct predictions and compare with results in Section 8.1.3 using all four explanatory variables.

(d) Construct the ROC curve and find the area under it for the linear discriminant analysis and for the corresponding logistic regression model. Compare to results in Section 8.1.3 using all four explanatory variables.

(e) Find the least squares fit of the linear probability model with weight and color explanatory variables, and interpret. Explain a disadvantage of this model compared to logistic regression.

8.2 Adult heights (in *cm*) in the U.S. have approximately a $N(161.7, 7^2)$ distribution for women and $N(175.4, 7^2)$ distribution for men. Let X = height and Y = gender (0 = woman, 1 = man). As in Exercise 7.34, for each value of y, randomly generate 100,000 observations on X.

(a) Use linear discriminant analysis for classifying on y for given values of x. With $\pi_0 = 0.50$, explain how the posterior probabilities and subsequent predictions relate to the overall $\bar{x}$.

(b) Using cross-validation, form the classification table with $\pi_0 = 0.50$. What proportion is correctly classified?

(c) Find the area under the ROC curve. Interpret.

8.3 In 1936, R. A. Fisher used linear discriminant analysis for Iris flower data.[12] Conduct a linear discriminant analysis using the `Iris` data file at the book's website for the *virginica* and *versicolor* species, with sepal length and petal length (in centimeters) as explanatory variables.

(a) Report the linear discriminant function. Interpret.

(b) Show the leave-one-out cross-validated classification table, with $\pi_0 = 0.50$. Report the sensitivity, specificity, and overall proportion of correct predictions.

(c) Construct the ROC curve. Report and interpret the area under it and compare to the area under the ROC curve for the logistic regression model.

(d) Construct and interpret a classification tree. How did you select λ? Report the sensitivity, specificity, and overall proportion of observations correctly predicted with the tree.

8.4 Refer to Exercise 8.1. Construct a classification tree, and prune strongly until the tree uses a single explanatory variable. Which crabs were predicted to have satellites? How does the proportion of correct predictions compare with the more complex tree in Figure 8.2?

---

[12]This is discussed in the *Iris flower data set* article at Wikipedia.

8.5 Refer to the horseshoe crab classification trees in Figure 8.2.

   (a) For each tree, sketch a plot of color against the carapace width regions for the tree. Based on the information at the terminal nodes, highlight the rectangular regions for which $\hat{y} = 1$.

   (b) Compare the appearance of the region with $\hat{y} = 1$ for classification trees, such as those in (a), with the region for which $\hat{y} = 1$ using linear discriminant analysis or logistic regression.

   (c) Using all four explanatory variables, construct classification trees with various λ pruning values. Summarize how the tree depends on λ. Select a tree that seems sensible. Explain how results agree or disagree with the results from logistic regression model-building.

8.6 The Kyphosis data file[13] at the book's website contains data on x = age (in months) and y = whether a subject has kyphosis (1 = yes, 0 = no), which is severe forward flexion of the spine following corrective spinal surgery. Construct a classification tree without any pruning, and summarize results. Why might an ordinary logistic regression model or linear discriminant analysis not detect the nature of this effect?

8.7 Figure 8.6 shows a classification tree for survival of the Titanic sinking, where *sibsp* is the number of spouses or siblings aboard and the figures in the terminal nodes show the proportion that survived and the percentage of observations at that node.

   (a) Specify the groups predicted to survive.

   (b) Find the percentage of correct predictions for this tree. What would this percentage be if you merely predicted that *everyone* died?

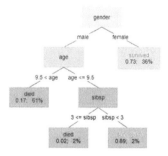

FIGURE 8.6 Classification tree for the Titanic sinking.
Source: https://commons.wikimedia.org/w/index.php?curid=90405437

8.8 A classification tree predicted whether, over a one-year period, elderly subjects participating in an assisted-living program disenroll from the program to enter a nursing home.[14] The sample consisted of 4654 individuals who had been enrolled in the program for at least a year and who did not die during that one-year period. If available online at your library, read the article cited in the footnote.

   (a) Specify the four questions asked in the classification tree.

   (b) In the classification tree, the authors treated the two types of misclassifications as having different costs: 13 times as high to predicting that someone would remain in the program who actually left it than to predicting that someone would leave the program who actually stayed. At a terminal node, the prediction taken is the response category that has the lowest misclassification cost. For the node of 931 subjects of age > 83, of whom 112

---

[13]From Section 10.2 of *Generalized Additive Models* by T. J. Hastie and R. J. Tishirani, Chapman & Hall (1990).
[14]D. Noe et al., *Chance*, **22**, no. 4: 58–62 (2009).

disenrolled and 819 stayed, show that the misclassification cost is lower if we predict that they all disenroll; so, this is the prediction for this terminal node.

8.9 Refer to Section 8.1.6. Use the k-nearest neighbor method for predicting horseshoe crab satellites with 3/4 of the sample in the training sample. Try various values for k and show their classification tables.

8.10 Refer to Section 8.1.6. Use the neural network method for predicting horseshoe crab satellites with 3/4 of the sample in the training sample. Report the classification tables using 0.50 and the sample proportion of cases with satellites as the cutoff point.

8.11 Refer to the Presidential elections data in Table 8.2 for 14 states. The observations were the same for New Jersey and Pennsylvania as llinois, and the same for Alabama as Wyoming. Conduct a cluster analysis, showing the dendrogram, using these three states together with the 14 states in Table 8.2. Interpret.

8.12 Conduct a cluster analysis for the complete **Elections** data file at the book's website, but without the elections of 1980 and 1984, in which nearly all states favored the Republican candidate (Ronald Reagan). Show the dendrogram, and compare results for the two-cluster solution to the analysis that also used those elections.

8.13 For 63 alligators caught in Lake George, Florida, the **Gators** data file[15] gives the alligator length (in meters) and whether the primary food type, in volume, found in the alligator's stomach was fish (1 = yes, 0 = no). Use a method from Chapter 7 or 8 to predict the lengths for which alligators' primary food choice is fish.

8.14 For the **spam** data[16] at **web.stanford.edu/~hastie/ElemStatLearn**, use a method presented in this chapter to select explanatory variables to classify whether a given email is spam. Summarize results in a short report, with edited software output in an appendix.

8.15 Go to a site with large data files, such as the UCI Machine Learning Repository (**archive.ics.uci.edu/ml**), Yahoo! Webscope (**webscope.sandbox.yahoo.com**), or the R package **ISLR** for the book by James et al. (2001). Select a data set and analyze, using a method presented in this chapter. Summarize your analysis in a short report.

Methods and Concepts

8.16 What does an ROC curve look like for the logistic regression null model? What is the area under the curve?

8.17 For classification on a binary response variable, summarize advantages and disadvantages of logistic regression, linear discriminant analysis, and classification trees.

8.18 Summarize advantages and disadvantages of k-nearest neighbors and neural networks compared with logistic regression.

8.19 For probabilities $\{\pi_j\}$ in c classes, *Simpson's diversity index* $D = \sum_j \pi_j^2$ is used to summarize diversity in ecological applications. In the context of classification trees, $1 - D$ is the *Gini impurity index*, and with $c = 2$, minimizing $1 - D$ is a possible way to determine how to split a variable in constructing a classification tree. Explain how to interpret D. As D increases, is the diversity greater, or less?

8.20 For a sample of olive oils, suppose you have data on several chemical properties and whether the olive oil is from Italy. For predicting the origin of a particular olive oil based on its chemical properties, discuss issues that would affect your decision of whether to use logistic regression, linear discriminant analysis, or classification trees. (An Internet search reveals many articles that have performed various analyses to model olive oil origin.)

---

[15]Thanks to Clint T. Moore and M. F. Delany for these data.
[16]Analyzed in the book by Hastie et al. (2009).

8.21 For predicting a quantitative response variable, conduct an Internet search or read part of a relevant book (such as Chapter 8 of James et al. (2021)) to learn about the *regression tree* method. Illustrate the method with an example, pointing out the advantages and disadvantages compared to regression analysis.

8.22 Suppose the variables for a cluster analysis are all quantitative. Read Section A.8.4 of the R Appendix and then conduct an Internet search or read part of a relevant book (such as Section 12.4 of James et al. (2021)) to learn about possible clustering methods. Explain what is meant by *Euclidean distance* for a measure of dissimilarity. Describe a hierarchical clustering algorithm that uses mean intercluster dissimilarity to link clusters. Discuss issues that can affect results, such as whether one uses the original variables or standardized versions and whether one fixes ahead of time the number of clusters.

8.23 With a huge number of binary variables, with p much larger than n, explain how one could form clusters of variables instead of clusters of observations.

8.24 As the basis for a statistical analysis, explain the difference between a *statistical model* and an *algorithm*. For each, explain the extent to which it can deal with summarizing effects, inferential statistics, and prediction.

9

Statistical Science: A Historical Overview

This final chapter provides a brief historical overview of how statistical science evolved to its present state. It is a relatively young mathematical science, with many of the key ideas developed only within the past century. The evolution of statistical science continues at a rapid pace, energized by the continual increase in computing power and by the diversity and size of available data sets. Section 9.1 summarizes this evolution. Section 9.2 then highlights pillars of the foundations of statistical science and pillars of wisdom for practicing data science.

9.1 The Evolution of Statistical Science *

For many years, the statistician Stephen Stigler, a distinguished professor at the University of Chicago, has been the foremost historian of statistical science. He has written extensively about how the theory and methods presented in this book evolved. Stigler's 1986 landmark book *The History of Statistics* is a fascinating in-depth overview of the history before 1900. Also noteworthy is his collection of essays on a variety of historical topics (Stigler 2002) and a book described in the next section that highlights the main pillars of the subject and the people mainly responsible for them. A book by David Salsburg (2002) provides an entertaining, non-technical presentation covering the 20th century. Julian Champkin has developed a compact graphical *Timeline of Statistics* overview of many of the key developments between the years 450 and 2012 at `www.statslife.org.uk/images/pdf/timeline-of-statistics.pdf`.

9.1.1 Evolution of Probability

Another relevant history, also surveyed in Stigler's 1986 book, is that of probability. Much of its development dates back to questions that arose in gambling settings in the 16th through 18th century. For example, in 1560 the Italian polymath Gerolamo Cardano calculated probabilities of different dice throws for gamblers, in 1654 the Frenchmen Blaise Pascal and Pierre de Fermat corresponded about ways to fairly divide stakes in gambling games, and books about probability for gambling situations included *On Reasoning in Games of Chance* in 1657 by the Dutch mathematician Christiaan Huygens and *The Doctrine of Chances* in 1718 by Abraham De Moivre, a French mathematician living in London to escape the persecution of Huguenots.

The development of probability led naturally to probability distributions that are the basis of statistical models and inference. The Swiss mathematician Jakob Bernoulli noted the law of large numbers for sample proportions, essentially by analyzing the binomial distribution for large n. His landmark book *Ars Conjectandi* was produced by his cousin in 1713, eight years after Bernoulli's death. The German mathematician Carl Friedrich Gauss is commonly credited with the discovery of the normal distribution in 1808, in motivating the

---

*Sections with an asterisk are optional.

DOI: 10.1201/9781003159834-9

least squares method. However, De Moivre had in 1733 noted how the binomial distribution is approximated by a probability density function of normal form when n is large.

The French scholar and polymath Pierre-Simon Laplace presented the Central Limit Theorem in a lecture in 1810, but may not have been aware of Gauss's work on the normal distribution until shortly thereafter. Regarded as one of the greatest scientists of all time, Laplace's publications began in the 1770s when merely in his mid 20's in age. His 1812 book *Théorie Analytique des Probabilités* can be regarded as the basis of modern probability theory and is influential also for the development of basic statistical methods. In that book, he stated,

> It is remarkable that a science which began with the consideration of games of chance should have become the most important object of human knowledge.... The most important questions of life are, for the most part, really only problems of probability.

However, an axiomatic development of probability did not occur until a 1933 article by a Russian mathematician, Andrey Kolmogorov.

Siméon Denis Poisson, often regarded as Laplace's successor in his interests and position, derived the Poisson distribution in 1837 as a limit of the binomial with an increasingly large number of binary observations and successively smaller probability of the outcome of interest in each one. This was merely one page of a book that dealt with other topics, such as generalizing the law of large numbers for proportions. His book first used the term *law of large numbers*. A more general version of the law of large numbers in terms of moments of arbitrary discrete or continuous random variables is due to the French mathematician I. J. Bienaymé in 1853. He showed it by proving what is now referred to as Chebyshev's inequality or the Bienaymé–Chebyshev inequality, with the argument presented in Section 3.2.5.

In 1761 the British ordained Nonconformist minister Thomas Bayes proved what is now called Bayes' theorem, although his notes on this were not edited and published until after his death, in 1764 by his literary executor Richard Price. This theorem was stated independently by Laplace in 1774. He extended it to a Bayesian theory of probability and basic statistical inference, referring to it as *inverse probability* because of applying probability to parameters, given observations, instead of the reverse. Laplace promoted the use of uniform prior distributions for unknown parameters such as the binomial probability, as a reasonable way of representing ignorance. These days we would probably be referring to *Laplace's Theorem* and *Laplacian statistics* were it not for Price's discovery of Bayes's work.

9.1.2   Evolution of Descriptive and Inferential Statistics

Early uses of the mean included Danish astronomer Tycho Brahe applying it in 1570 to reduce errors in estimating locations of planets and Oxford professor Henry Gellibrand introducing the term in 1635 in summarizing readings on a magnetic compass. The method of least squares (which generates the mean as the estimate of the intercept in the null model) was presented by the French mathematician Adrien-Marie Legendre in 1805. In 1809, however, Gauss claimed priority in stating that he had been using it since 1795. Gauss developed it further than Legendre, including linking it to probability and providing algorithms for computation.

The Belgian Adolphe Quetelet was influential in introducing statistical methods to the social sciences by formulating the concept of the "average man" and fitting distributions to social data, as summarized in his 1835 book *A Treatise on Man and the Development of His Faculties*. In the mid 19th century, descriptive statistics and graphics were first used in a way to have a substantial impact on public health by Florence Nightingale. Influenced by

Quetelet, Nightingale showed how to better record and summarize information from medical records and strongly advocated sanitary precautions that dramatically reduced mortality in the military and in the general public. Graphical illustrations had received little use before she showed how effective simple graphics such as pie charts were for conveying information about the large percentage of deaths in the Crimean War that were due to preventable causes rather than due to being on the battlefield. She became the first female member of the Royal Statistical Society and the first overseas member of the American Statistical Association.

The modern methods of statistical science as presented in Chapters 4–7 of this book started emerging only late in the 19th century and in the first half of the 20th century. In the late 1880s Francis Galton introduced bivariate regression and correlation and explained the concept of regression toward the mean. His other statistical work included introducing and showing the use of percentiles and investigating properties of the bivariate normal distribution. Galton was a highly creative polymath who did fundamental research in many disciplines, including genetics and statistics. His many notable contributions included devising weather maps and other types of graphical displays, pioneering fingerprint identification, studying inheritance of intelligence, and exploring Africa.[1] Galton's work was highly influential to Karl Pearson, who devised the product-moment estimate of the correlation. Pearson proposed a family of skewed distributions that includes the gamma and chi-squared and used the chi-squared to test hypotheses about multinomial probability values. Among his many other contributions, he promoted the use of the standard deviation (to which he gave the name) for measuring variability, devised the method of moments for estimating parameters, and originated principal component analysis.

Karl Pearson (1857–1936) should perhaps receive the most credit for founding an actual discipline of statistical science. He was its most influential contributor at the beginning of the twentieth century and he founded the first academic Statistics department at University College, London in 1911. However, the person who eventually became most responsible for modern statistical theory and methods was the British statistician and geneticist Ronald A. Fisher (1890–1962). His influential theoretical article in 1922 introduced maximum likelihood and key concepts such as sufficiency, information, and efficiency, following his specification in 1921 of the likelihood function.[2] Fisher pioneered principles of randomization and the design of experiments and developed the analysis of variance for comparing means, promoting the use of multiple-factor analyses rather than treating factors one-by-one in separate analyses. In its 14 editions, his book *Statistical Methods for Research Workers* (1st edition 1925) was highly influential in familiarizing scientists with new statistical methods.

For example, while working as a brewer in Guinness Breweries in Dublin, in 1908 William Sealy Gosset introduced the t distribution to evaluate random variability in a sample mean while accounting for estimating its standard error, but it was Fisher's book that explained its importance to statistical inference and presented a table of some percentiles for small df values. Like Francis Galton and Karl Pearson, Fisher had some interest in eugenics, but his focus evolved into creating the discipline of human genetics.[3]

Systematic development of tests of hypotheses, including the concepts of Type I and Type II errors and power, occurred in landmark articles in 1928 and 1933 by Egon Sharpe

---

[1] He is less fondly remembered for promoting the field of eugenics, devoted to improving the human race by selective breeding and encouraging sterilization of the unfit. Karl Pearson followed Galton in being a proponent of eugenics.

[2] An interesting article by A. W. F. Edwards surveys the history of likelihood; see *Int. Stat. Rev.* **42**: 9–15 (1974), available at www.jstor.org/stable/1402681.

[3] The book *In the Name of Eugenics* by D. J. Kevles (Knopf, 1985) examined the roles of Galton, Pearson, and others, and suggested that Fisher was concerned mainly with matters involving inheritance rather than political advocacy of eugenics.

Pearson (Karl Pearson's son) and the Polish statistician Jerzy Neyman, who strongly influenced the development of academic statistical science in the U.S. through his chairing of a department at the University of California, Berkeley. Related work by R. A. Fisher resulted in eventual popularity of *P*-values in significance testing.[4] Neyman and E. S. Pearson developed a simple version of a likelihood-ratio test and showed its optimality in the *Neyman–Pearson lemma*. In 1938 the American statistician Samuel Wilks further developed the theory and showed the large-sample chi-squared distribution of the likelihood-ratio statistic in a general context. Confidence intervals were introduced by Neyman in 1937 in connection with his earlier work with E. S. Pearson. The primary nonparametric tests, such as the Wilcoxon test for comparing mean ranks of two groups, were developed mainly between 1940 and 1955.

Generalized linear models became popular following a highly influential article in 1972 by the British statisticians John Nelder and Robert Wedderburn. Particular models had previously been developed and used, such as logistic regression by the physician–biostatistician Joseph Berkson of Mayo Clinic in 1944. A related *probit model* for binary response variables, for which response curves have the shape of a normal *cdf*, was used in 1935 by Chester Bliss and contained an appendix written by R. A. Fisher that introduced Fisher scoring for solving the likelihood equations. Loglinear models were developed in the early 1960s, primarily for evaluating association structure in multiway contingency tables in a series of articles by Leo Goodman at the University of Chicago. In 1972 British statistician David Cox introduced a regression model with proportional hazards structure for modeling survival times with censored data.[5]

In the last fifty years, key advances include the development of exploratory data analysis methods such as the box plot by John Tukey in the 1970s, the introduction of the bootstrap method in 1979 by Bradley Efron at Stanford University, the development since the 1980s of Markov chain Monte Carlo methods for approximating Bayesian posterior distributions that make Bayesian inference more easily available, and methods of functional data analysis for the nonparametric estimation of curves defined over time or space. Most recently, increasing availability of "big data" of various types has motivated the development of regularization methods, such as the lasso, and algorithm-driven non-model-based methods of *statistical learning* such as neural networks and classification and regression trees. These developments have also led to the increasing awareness of two cultures for data analysis—statistical modeling and algorithmic models.[6]

9.2 Pillars of Statistical Wisdom and Practice

9.2.1 Stigler's Seven Pillars of Statistical Wisdom

At the 175th anniversary of the founding of the American Statistical Association in Boston in 2014, the statistical science historian Stephen Stigler presented a stimulating talk, sharing his views about the pillars on which statistical science is based. He extended this lecture

---

[4] Informal significance testing dates back to an analysis by John Arbuthnot in 1710, who observed more males than females born in each of 82 years of data and noted that the probability of this extreme result is only $(0.50)^{82}$ if each year had a 50% chance of more births by either sex.

[5] For this and other contributions he was knighted in 1985 by Queen Elizabeth.

[6] Highlighted in the article by Leo Breiman, *Statistical Science*, **16**: 199–231. (2001), available by search at `https://projecteuclid.org`.

into a book (Stigler 2016). Here is a summary of his choices of seven pillars, with brief descriptions of their history:

1. **Aggregation** (*the targeted reduction/compression of data using sums, means*)
    Simple combination of observations was not as obvious an idea as one might think. Stigler noted that although the graphical depiction of summary totals goes back at least to Sumerian tablets of 3000 BC that showed total crops of various types by year, the use of the *mean* increased only slowly after its first documented use in 1635 by Henry Gellibrand of Oxford University. In the development of theory for statistical science, a key later concept relating to the aggregation of data was R. A. Fisher's definition of *sufficient statistics* (Section 4.2.3): For a particular assumed probability distribution for the data, the sufficient statistics summarize the data without any loss of information. This was one of many new ideas on statistical theory in Fisher's landmark 1922 article.

2. **Information** (*the "$\sqrt{n}$ rule" shows the diminishing value of more data*)
    How can we measure the accumulation of *information*? Are 20 observations twice as informative as 10 observations? In 1730 Abraham De Moivre noted that the spread of a binomial distribution is proportional to $\sqrt{n}$. Equivalently, the sample proportion estimator of the binomial parameter has standard error proportional to $1/\sqrt{n}$ (Sections 2.4.5 and 3.2.4). For example, we need 40 observations to have twice the information as 10 observations, where "twice the information" is characterized by half as large a standard error. This *square root law* is quite general. Estimators of nearly all parameters of common interest, including means and proportions and effect parameters in linear and generalized linear models, have standard errors that equal a measure of variability of the population sampled divided by $\sqrt{n}$. The formulas for these standard errors determine the sample size needed in an experiment or sample survey to obtain a desired level of precision.

3. **Likelihood** (*ML estimation, probability measures for statistical inferences*)
    The calibration of evidence on a probability scale can be based on the *likelihood function* (Section 4.2), for an assumed probability distribution for the data. In 1921 and 1922, R. A. Fisher introduced the likelihood function and characteristics of it, such as sufficiency, efficiency, and information. Calibration of evidence is accomplished through likelihood-based inference such as maximum likelihood (ML) point estimation and confidence intervals or through P-values of significance tests that are based on sampling distributions induced by the likelihood function.

4. **Intercomparison** (*comparing groups using internal data variation, such as by percentiles and t tests for means*)
    How can we compare two groups, in terms of their respective distributions for a quantitative variable? In his 1889 book *Natural Inheritance*, Francis Galton suggested comparing *percentiles* such as the median and quartiles obtained from the cumulative distributions for the groups. The percentile, simple as it is, was apparently not in common use until Galton highlighted its usefulness. R. A. Fisher showed how to use the t and F distributions through the *analysis of variance* (Section 6.5.3) to conduct formal statistical inference for comparing group means. Nonparametric methods (Section 5.8) enable us to make inferential comparisons without assuming a particular family of probability distributions for the groups. The *bootstrap* (Section 4.6) is a more modern advance that enables parametric or nonparametric comparisons in cases not easily handled by derivations with standard statistical theory.

5. **Regression** (*multivariate inference and Bayes Theorem*)
    In 1885 Francis Galton introduced the term *regression toward the mean* (Section 6.1.6),

with his observation that tall parents on the average produce somewhat shorter children than themselves, and likewise that short parents on average have somewhat taller children than themselves. For correlated variables, extreme observations on one of them tend to correspond to less-extreme observations on the other, so likewise children who are very tall or very short tend to have parents less-extreme in height. Galton developed the mechanism for studying conditional expectations in bivariate distributions. This led in the 1900s to extensions for multivariate analyses, such as multiple regression and generalized linear modeling. The formulation of conditional distributions also led indirectly to Bayesian methods (Section 4.7) for making posterior inference about a parameter θ conditional on data y, based on assumptions about the probability distribution of Y conditional on θ and a prior probability distribution for θ.

6. **Design** (*essential role of planning, using design-based inference*)

Modern ideas about *experimental design* are largely due to R. A. Fisher, who in the 1920s introduced the radical idea that designs could be based on varying multiple factors simultaneously through multifactor analysis of variance, rather than the prevalent approach of one-at-a-time investigations keeping everything else fixed. In the late 1900s, special designs were developed for designing and analyzing randomized clinical trials for the evaluation of new drugs, including sequential analyses that can be conducted over time as the data become available.

7. **Residual** (*exploring using models and model comparison*)

In 1831, the English mathematician John Herschel argued that to explain complicated phenomena, one could remove the effects of known causes, leaving a *residual* phenomenon to be explained (e.g., Section 6.3.2). In statistical science, this idea is manifested by tools that incorporate the structure of *statistical models* and use probabilistic-based inference. These include testing the significance of regression parameters and the more general comparison of nested models to analyze whether a more complex one explains significantly more variability than a simpler one. Such methods utilize the residual variability remaining after fitting a statistical model. Fundamental in the process of evaluating the needed complexity of a statistical model is the *bias/variance tradeoff* (Section 7.1.6), such as dealt with by the AIC measure to guard against overfitting.

These pillars represent statistical ideas that were revolutionary at their time of introduction. Each one pushed aside or overturned conventional scientific beliefs, such as pillar (2) showing that all data might be equally good but that adding data becomes successively less valuable. These seven pillars that constitute core ideas underlying statistical science are quite distinct from pillars of mathematics and computer science. They are also pillars of the overall knowledge about statistical science that you need to be an effective data scientist.

9.2.2   Seven Pillars of Wisdom for Practicing Data Science

To finish this book, we suggest seven pillars that should guide your own uses of the methods of statistical science. In your future analyses as a data scientist, we believe that you should keep these in your mind, realizing also that conducting proper analyses is an art and science, not something that can be done merely using a recipe.[7]

1. **Plan the study well**: Be transparent about the purpose of your study. An informative

---

[7] An interesting article with the theme of this section is "Ten simple rules for effective statistical practice," by R. Kass, B. Caffo, M. Davidian, X. L. Meng, B. Yu, and N. Reid in *PLOS Computational Biology* in 2016; see https://doi.org/10.1371/journal.pcbi.1004961.

and insightful study requires some understanding of the field to which the data refer and the context, including using existing theory to formulate appropriate questions to address with the analysis. Carefully consider which variables you need to observe to make useful conclusions. Try also to identify and observe lurking variables that could have an impact on any observed association. Determine how much data you need to obtain enough precision to make inferences useful.

2. **Data quality is paramount**: Whether an experiment or a survey or collecting observational data from the Internet, you need good data to conduct meaningful statistical analyses. In a survey, carefully word the questions so they are clear and appropriate for subsequent statistical analyses. Once data are available, make sure data cleaning is sufficient so that bias will not arise because of serious flaws in some observations. Note missing data, and if extensive, adjust analyses and conclusions to take the missingness into account.

3. **Be aware of potential sources of bias**: As you conduct analyses, keep in mind potential sources of bias, such as using samples that may not be representative of a population, searching only for significant results in software output or failing to report non-significant research results, not adjusting error rates for a large number of inferences conducted, paying attention only to results agreeing with your personal beliefs, treating observations as independent that are actually correlated, and neglecting to pay attention to lurking variables that affect conclusions about associations. Remember that association is not the same as causation, and that estimated effects of an explanatory variable on a response variable depend on whatever other variables are in the model.

4. **Expect variability and deal with it properly**: Handling variability is central to the practice of statistical science. Statistical analyses aim to assess the *signal* provided by the data, which is the interesting variability, in the presence of *noise*, which is variability that may be irrelevant or of secondary importance. Proper modeling deals with both types of variability. Usually we model the signal by describing the way the mean response depends on values of explanatory variables, and we model the noise by an appropriate choice of probability distribution for the random variability. This then leads to appropriate assessments of uncertainty, through standard errors of point estimates.

5. **Check assumptions and use appropriate statistical methods**: As you've seen, all methods of statistical inference methods have assumptions, such as requiring randomization and an appropriate choice of a parametric distribution. Be careful in using methods not robust to extreme outliers or other unusual patterns in the data, such as reporting means with highly skewed data. In using linear models, investigate plots and diagnostic measures to check whether the model is justified and whether certain observations are overly influential in the results. You should not try to use methods that the data do not justify. For example, with data gathered from a survey in which relatively few of the people contacted actually responded, methods of statistical inference are inappropriate. At best, perhaps the results suggest questions to address in studies with higher-quality data in the future. Keep in mind that statistical significance does not imply practical significance and should not substitute for estimating effect size. Confidence intervals for relevant measures are more informative than P-values from significance tests. (Recall the discussion in Section 5.6.)

6. **Aim for parsimony in methods, presentation, and interpretation**: Begin an analysis with simple graphical descriptions such as histograms, box plots, and scatterplots, to get a feel for the data. Related to the previous aim of only using methods justified by the data, don't try to use methods that are more complicated than needed.

When you do need to use a complex model but also need to report your results to an audience that is not especially statistically literate, report simple summaries that are easy to understand. For example, if you use logistic regression to model a binary response variable, you can report estimates of $P(Y = 1)$ (perhaps as a percentage rather than a proportion) at relevant settings of the explanatory variables. Rather than merely reporting a P-value, report the range of plausible values for a parameter or a probability, such as by providing a confidence interval or a margin of error together with any point estimate.

7. **Make analyses reproducible and encourage replication**: Make the data available together with complete details about the analyses and software coding you performed to obtain your results, so anyone else would be able to take the data and obtain exactly the same results. When results seem surprising or unusual in some way, replicate the study, or encourage others to do so, addressing questions and hypotheses raised by your study using another high-quality sample from the population of interest.

As you become more familiar with the main areas of statistical science and their methods, you may well identify other pillars of wisdom besides those described in this section that are fundamental in justifying your own decisions about how to conduct appropriate and informative statistical analyses. We hope that such pillars of wisdom become natural to you, and we wish you success and fulfillment in your own accomplishments as a data scientist!

A

Using R in Statistical Science

A.0 Basics of R

R is a free software for statistical computing and graphics that enjoys increasing popularity among data scientists. It is continuously enriched and updated by researchers who develop new statistical methods and supplement their published results with the associated R code. The website www.r-project.org has information about downloading and installing R. The *Comprehensive R Archive Network* (CRAN) at https://cran.r-project.org has a variety of add-on packages for data analysis and visualization. Many R users prefer to work in RStudio (https://rstudio.com/products/rstudio), which includes a console, syntax-highlighting editor supporting direct code execution, as well as tools for plotting, history, debugging, and workspace management.

This Appendix supplements the examples of R shown in this book, and the book's website has an R Appendix with more detail. Other helpful resources include the *Introduction to R* manual at https://cran.r-project.org/doc/manuals/R-intro.pdf, the Swirl tutoring system at https://swirlstats.com, and books by Hothorn and Everitt (2014), Wickham and Grolemund (2017), and Baumer et al. (2017).

A.0.1 Starting a Session, Entering Commands, and Quitting

Activation of R opens a console awaiting input at the prompt ($>$). To terminate an R session, type

```
> q()
```

or select 'Exit' in the 'File' Menu. Values are assigned to variables by the operator '$< -$' or '$=$'. To see the value of an object x, type x at the command prompt or put the assignment in parentheses, such as $(x < - \text{mean}(y))$. You can provide multiple commands on a line by separating them with ';' and enter comments following the # hashmark symbol. A command can expand to more than one line, in which case a $+$ appears at the beginning of the additional line(s). R is case-sensitive.

```
> y <- 7; Y <- 10; x <- sum(y + Y)
> y; Y; x        # equivalent to: (y <- 7); (Y <- 10); (x <- sum(y + Y))
[1] 7
[1] 10
[1] 17
> q()            # quits the session
```

Output starts with [1], indicating that this line initiates the results.

A.0.2 Installing and Loading R Packages

In addition to the base package, you can install from CRAN and then load user-contributed R packages. For example, to install the package binom and then load it in the workspace:

```
> install.packages("binom") # user asked to select a CRAN mirror to install the package
> library(binom)            # request to use installed package
```

The website `http://cran.r-project.org/web/packages` has an overview of all contributed packages at CRAN. The R (`software`) entry in the Subject Index of this book lists the R packages and functions used in this book.

A.0.3   R Functions and Data Structures

Tasks are performed in R through functions. To get help for an R function, use the command `help` or type ? before its name, such as `help(plot)` or `?plot` for a function for plotting data. Users can create their own functions but cannot use a name already used by R. For example, you cannot use `mean` for a mean of some values, because an R function exists with that name.

Data values can be synthesized in a variety of data structure types, including *vectors, matrices, arrays,* and *data frames.*[1] The data structures are known as *objects.* You can list the names of all objects in your workspace by typing `objects()` or `ls()`. The type of an object having name q is identified by typing `class(q)`. You can remove an object from the memory by typing its name inside the parentheses of `rm()`.

Vectors

A *vector* combines values in a one-dimensional vector. A vector can be created with the *combine* function c. Here are examples of vectors and their components, which can be numeric or characters:

```
> y <- c(4, 5, 6, 7); y           # equivalent to: y <- 4:7
[1] 4 5 6 7                        # and y <- seq(4, 7, 1)
> y1 <- c(1, 2.3, -3.5, exp(2)); y1 # numeric vector
[1] 1.000000  2.300000  -3.500000  7.389056
> y1[2]; y1[2:4]; y1[c(1:2, 4)]   # extract specific components
[1] 2.3
[1] 2.300000 -3.500000  7.389056
[1] 1.000000 2.300000 7.389056
> which(y1 > 2)                   # identify components with y1 > 2
[1] 2 4
> x <- c("A","B","C"); x          # character vector has components
[1] "A"  "B"  "C"                 # in quotes "..."
```

Helpful functions for creating vectors are the `seq` (*sequence*) function and the `rep` (*repeat*) function:

```
> seq(0, 10, 2)                   # from 0 to 10 in steps of size 2
[1]  0  2  4  6  8 10
> s2 <- rep(1:4, 3); s2           # repeat 3 times the integers 1 to 4
 [1] 1 2 3 4 1 2 3 4 1 2 3 4
> s3 <- rep(1:4, each=3); s3      # repeat 3 times each integer in 1 to 4
 [1] 1 1 1 2 2 2 3 3 3 4 4 4
```

You can assign labels to the values of a vector during its construction or later with the `names` function. Functions characterizing vectors include `length`, `min`, `max`, and `sum`.

```
> v1 <- c(a=1, 2:5, f=6); v1
a             f
1 2 3 4 5 6
> v2 <- 1:6; names(v2) = c("a","b","c","d","e","f"); v2
```

---

[1]Another data structure, *lists*, is described in in the R Appendix at the book's website.

```
  a b c d e f
  1 2 3 4 5 6
  > length(v2); sum(v2) # number of elements in vector, sum of elements
  [1] 6
  [1] 21
```

Use **sort** to sort the elements in increasing order (or decreasing, with the argument decreasing = TRUE) and **rank** to rank the elements.

Factors

A *factor* is a vector that represents a categorical variable and is required for some plots and statistical functions. Its values, numeric or character, are known as the factor *levels*. Levels that are numeric are treated merely as labels and not as quantitative characteristics.

```
  > q <- c("A","B","B","A","C","A","B","E","C","A","A","B"); q
   [1] "A" "B" "B" "A" "C" "A" "B" "E" "C" "A" "A" "B"
  > q_f <- factor(q); q_f
   [1] A B B A C A B E C A A B
  Levels: A B C E
  > table(q_f)        # frequency table for q_f
  q_f
  A B C E
  5 4 2 1
```

Matrix and array

A vector is one-dimensional. A two-dimensional array can be defined by the **matrix** function:

```
  > z <- 1:8
  > M1 <- matrix(z, nrow=2, ncol=4); M1 # 2 rows and 4 columns
        [,1] [,2] [,3] [,4]           # expand within columns
  [1,]    1    3    5    7
  [2,]    2    4    6    8
  > M2 <- matrix(z, nrow=2, ncol=4, byrow=TRUE); M2 # expand within rows
        [,1] [,2] [,3] [,4]
  [1,]    1    2    3    4
  [2,]    5    6    7    8
```

You can also construct a matrix by binding two or more vectors of the same length row-wise using **rbind** or column-wise using **cbind**. Useful functions for working with matrices include dim, nrow, ncol and t for providing the dimension, number of rows, number of columns, and the transpose. The functions **rowSums** and **colSums** find row and column sums.

```
  > r1 <- 1:5; r2 <- 6:10; r12 <- rbind(r1,r2); r12 # binds as rows
        [,1] [,2] [,3] [,4] [,5]                # cbind(r1,r2) binds as columns
  r1     1    2    3    4    5
  r2     6    7    8    9   10
  > rowSums(r12)
  r1 r2
  15 40
```

Functions and operators for numerical variables apply component-wise to numerical vectors and matrices, and %*% applies standard matrix multiplication:

```
  > M1*M2        # component-wise multiplication with above matrices
        [,1] [,2] [,3] [,4]
  [1,]    1    6   15   28
  [2,]   10   24   42   64
  > M1 %*% t(M2) # matrix multiplication of M1 by transpose of M2
```

```
        [,1] [,2]
[1,]    50  114
[2,]    60  140
```

The `array` function can construct a multidimensional array. For example, to re-organize a vector of length 12 in an array of dimension $2 \times 3 \times 2$:

```
> z1 <- 1:12
> z2 <- array(z1, c(2, 3, 2)) # array of dimension 2 by 3 by 2
```

Data frames

The most common way to store data in R is as a `data.frame` object. A data frame has the standard format of a data file, with columns corresponding to variables and rows to subjects, such as in Figure 1.1 in Chapter 1. This type of data structure is required by many R functions, such as the `plot` and `hist` functions. Variables in a data frame are specified by appending the $ operator:

```
> v1 <- 1:3
> v2 <- v1^2                    # squares the elements in v1
> D <- data.frame(v1, v2); D # binds v1 and v2 as columns in data frame
  v1 v2
1  1  1
2  2  4
3  3  9
> z <- D$v2; z                  # extracts v2 from D
[1]  1  4  9
> D[2,]                         # elements in row 2 of D
  v1 v2
2  2  4
> D[3,2]                        # element in row 3 and column 2, equivalent to D$v2[3]
[1] 9
```

A.0.4   Data Input in R

Simple data can be entered manually using the `c` or `scan` functions:

```
> y <- scan()
1: 2    # start typing the data
2: 5    # type one vector element on each line
3: 3
4:      # enter a blank line to signal the end of data reading
Read 3 items
```

R provides functions for importing data, supporting many formats including plain-text files and data files from software packages such as Excel. For plain-text data files, the basic function is `read.table`, as illustrated throughout this text (beginning in Section 1.4.1) to obtain data files from the text website. It reads a data file and creates a data frame from it. The argument is the file name, including the path to its directory. Useful functions for viewing the data are `names`, `dim`, `str`, and `print`.

```
> Carb <- read.table("http://stat4ds.rwth-aachen.de/data/Carbon.dat",
+          header=TRUE) # header=TRUE if variable names at top of file
> names(Carb)           # names of variables in data file
[1] "Nation" "CO2"
> dim(Carb)   # dimension of data frame (or matrix or array)
[1] 31  2     # 31 rows, 2 columns for 31 observations on 2 variables
```

```
> str(Carb)    # data structure of object
'data.frame': 31 obs. of  2 variables:
 $ Nation: chr  "Albania" "Austria" "Belgium" ...   # chr = character
 $ CO2   : num  2 6.9 8.3 6.2 5.9 4 5.3 9.2 5.9  ...# num = numerical
```

Data files are read using `read.csv` when they have comma separated values and `read.csv2` for semicolon separated data. For details, type `help(read.table)`. The R Appendix at the book's website describes other options for reading data, including procedures based on the `tidyverse` collection of R packages.

Data that are not created or reported as a `data.frame` must be put in this format before calling statistical functions. To query whether an object, say `Carb`, is a data frame, type `class(Carb)`.

A.0.5 R Control Flows

For programming, R control flow structures include the `if` and `if--else` statements and the `for`, `while`, and `repeat` loops, such as follows:

```
> x <- 2
> if (x>0) {y <- 2*x ; z <- 1} else {y <- -3*x+1 ; z <- 0};  y;  z
[1] 4
[1] 1
> f <- numeric(10)      # creates vector of length 10 containing 0 entries
> f[1] <- 1; f[2] <- 2 # assigns values to first two elements
> for (i in 3:10) {f[i] <- f[i-1] + 2*f[i-2]}; f
[1]   1   2   4   8  16  32  64 128 256 512
> y <- f[f <= 10]; y    # y consists of elements of f no greater than 10
[1] 1 2 4 8
> z <- y[-3]; z         # z same as y but without 3rd element
[1] 1 2 8
```

For expressing conditions, logical operators include < (less), <= (less or equal), > (greater), >= (greater or equal), == (equal), != (not equal) and the Boolean operators | (or) and & (and).

A.1   Chapter 1: R for Descriptive Statistics

A.1.1   Data Handling and Wrangling

Data sets can be messy, and data from many sources do not have the desired form for a data frame. In data science terminology, data in the axiomatic format of a data frame, in which each column corresponds to a characteristic (variable) and each row to a case (subject), are called **tidy data**. Organizing the data in a tidy form and cleaning and manipulating them is called **data wrangling**.[2] The `tidyverse` collection of R packages is designed for data wrangling. We illustrate a few features of `tidyverse` in this Appendix, such as the `ggplot2` package for creating graphics, with more information available at the R Appendix at the book's website. The `tidyr` package, with its functions `spread` and `gather`, is designed for reshaping data to a tidy form. Other `tidyverse` packages include `readr` for reading data, `forcats` for defining and treating factors, and `tidymodels` for classical and Bayesian modeling including GLMs.

---

[2]For an overview of data wrangling options, see `https://rstudio.com/wp-content/uploads/2015/02/data-wrangling-cheatsheet.pdf` and see Part IV of Irizarry (2019).

The `dplyr` package has many capabilities for viewing, manipulating, and analyzing a data frame. Section A.1.3 shows the `summarize` function for descriptive statistics, `slice` to exhibit cases by the position of the rows, `filter` to exhibit cases satisfying one or more conditions, and `select` to create a new data frame with a subset of the columns. Others described in the R Appendix at the book's website include `arrange` to arrange the observations in increasing order according to a variable and `mutate` to create a new variable and add it as a column to the data frame, and functions for joining data frames in different ways.

A.1.2 Histograms and Other Graphics

For data visualization, R provides powerful graphical tools. The `plot` function can produce scatterplots, box plots, and other types of plots. The `ggplot2` package in `tidyverse` offers options for elegant graphics that can be tailored to visualize complex data sets.[3] This section focuses on creating a histogram for a frequency distribution. With equal length classes (bins) for the values, various rules can determine the number of classes and their width. To graph variable y with k bins and bin width h, the rules specify k or h in $k = [\max(y) - \min(y)]/h$ and let k increase and h decrease as n increases. The default rule, called *Sturges*, takes $k = \log_2(n) + 1$. Its derivation assumes a bell-shaped distribution, and outliers can be problematic. The *Scott* rule takes $h = 3.49s/n^{1/3}$, for sample standard deviation s. For large n, Sturges' rule yields wider bins than Scott's and may oversmooth the histogram.

We illustrate R facilities for histograms using the `UN` data file from the book's website, consisting of nine variables measured for 42 nations, described in Exercise 1.24. We illustrate with the human development index (HDI), a summary measure with components referring to life expectancy at birth, educational attainment, and income per capita:

```
> UN <- read.table("http://stat4ds.rwth-aachen.de/data/UN.dat", header=TRUE)
> names(UN)          # names of the variables in the data file
[1] "Nation"  "GDP"    "HDI"    "GII"   "Fertility"   "CO2"
[7] "Homicide"  "Prison"   "Internet"
> hist(UN[,3], xlab="HDI", xlim=c(0.5, 1)) # default breaks="Sturges"
> hist(UN[,3], xlab="HDI", ylim=c(0, 20), breaks="Scott")
```

Figure A.1 shows histograms using the Sturges and Scott rules.

Usually histograms have bins of equal width. When the classes are prespecified, however, they need not be of equal length and caution is needed in forming histograms. We illustrate with data on `AGE` for the `GSS2018` data file, containing data on 14 variables for the 2018 General Social Survey. The histogram on the left in Figure A.2 results from prespecified age classes, as produced with the following code using a function from the `ggplot2` package:

```
> GSS <- read.table("http://stat4ds.rwth-aachen.de/data/GSS2018.dat", header=TRUE)
> age.cat <- cut(GSS$AGE, c(18, 25, 35, 50, 65, 75, 90),
+        include.lowest=TRUE, right=TRUE) # can create AGE categories
> table(age.cat)                          # used in histogram
[18,25] (25,35] (35,50] (50,65] (65,75] (75,90]
   240     432     578     591     315     185
> library(ggplot2)
> ggplot(GSS,aes(x=AGE))+geom_histogram(breaks=c(18,25,35,50,65,75,90),
+             color="dodgerblue4", fill="lightsteelblue")
```

The default values for the y-axis are the counts of the classes. However, when the classes are of unequal width, the bin areas are not then proportional to the relative frequencies. The correct scale for the y-axis is the *density*:

---

[3]`https://rstudio.com/wp-content/uploads/2015/03/ggplot2-cheatsheet.pdf` has a helpful overview of its logic, options, and features.

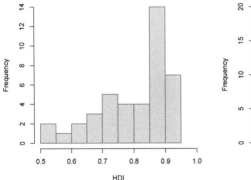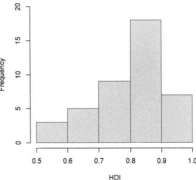

FIGURE A.1 Histograms for HDI in UN data file with number of bins and bin width specified by Sturges' rule (left) and Scott's rule (right).

```
> ggplot(GSS,aes(x=AGE))+geom_histogram(breaks=c(18,25,35,50,65,75,90),
+          aes(y =..density..), color="dodgerblue4", fill="lightsteelblue")
```

The proper histogram, for which the bin areas are relative frequencies, is on the right in Figure A.2.

A.1.3 Descriptive Statistics

We next present R facilities for descriptive statistics. For the UN data file, we form some summary statistics and box plots:

```
> summary(UN[,2:5]) # 5-number summary and mean for variables 2 through 5
      GDP               HDI              GII            Fertility
 Min.   : 4.40    Min.   :0.5000   Min.   :0.0300   Min.   :1.200
 1st Qu.:13.18    1st Qu.:0.7400   1st Qu.:0.0850   1st Qu.:1.700
 Median :27.45    Median :0.8600   Median :0.1850   Median :1.900
 Mean   :26.83    Mean   :0.8045   Mean   :0.2414   Mean   :2.038
 3rd Qu.:40.33    3rd Qu.:0.8975   3rd Qu.:0.3875   3rd Qu.:2.200
 Max.   :62.90    Max.   :0.9400   Max.   :0.5600   Max.   :6.000
> boxplot(UN[,2], xlab="GDP", horizontal=TRUE) # 2nd variable is GDP
> points(mean(UN[,2]), 1, col="blue", pch=18) # adds mean to box plot
> arrows(mean(UN[,2]) - sd(UN[,2]), 1, mean(UN[,2]) + sd(UN[,2]), 1,
      code=3, col="blue", angle=75, length=.1) # shows mean +- std dev
```

The R Appendix at the book's website shows the box plots, which also mark the sample mean and the interval within a standard deviation of the mean.

In finding descriptive summaries, we identify a categorical variable as a *factor*, so that the summary function provides its frequency distribution rather than statistics for quantitative variables, which are inappropriate. We illustrate with the **Income** data file, which lists annual income (in thousands of dollars) of 80 subjects classified by three categories of racial–ethnic status (Black, Hispanic, White).[4]

```
> Inc <- read.table("http://stat4ds.rwth-aachen.de/data/Income.dat", header=TRUE)
> head(Inc, 3)            # shows first 3 lines of data file
```

---

[4]The data are based on a much larger sample taken by the U.S. Bureau of the Census and are analyzed in Sections 6.5.2 and 6.5.5.

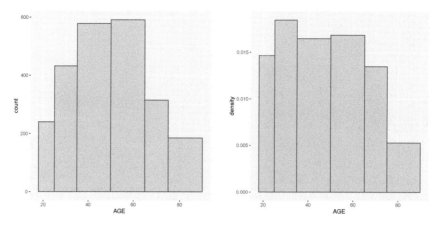

FIGURE A.2 Histograms for the ages of GSS participants, with bins of unequal width (left: incorrect, right: correct).

```
    income education race
1      16          10    B
2      18           7    B
3      26           9    B
> print(Inc[3:5,]) # prints observations 3-5 of the data file
    income education race
3      26           9    B
4      16          11    B
5      34          14    B
> Inc$race <- factor(Inc$race)
> summary(Inc) # shows frequency distribution for factors
       income            education        race
  Min.   : 16.00   Min.   : 7.00   B:16
  1st Qu.: 22.00   1st Qu.:10.00   H:14
  Median : 30.00   Median :12.00   W:50
  Mean   : 37.52   Mean   :12.69
  3rd Qu.: 46.50   3rd Qu.:15.00
  Max.   :120.00   Max.   :20.00
```

To generate descriptive statistics on a quantitative variable for each group in a categorical variable, we can use the `tapply` function as shown in Section 1.4.5 or the `aggregate` function as shown next:

```
> aggregate(Inc$income, by=list(Inc$race), summary) # describe income by race
  Group.1 x.Min. x.1st Qu. x.Median x.Mean x.3rd Qu. x.Max.
1       B  16.00     19.50    24.00  27.75     31.00  66.00
2       H  16.00     20.50    30.00  31.00     32.00  58.00
3       W  18.00     24.00    37.00  42.48     50.00 120.00
> aggregate(income ~ race, data=Inc, sd) # alternative form for aggregate, here
  race    income                        # standard deviation of income by race
1    B 13.28408
2    H 12.81225
3    W 22.86985
```

Identifying a nominal-scale categorical variable as a factor is crucial when the data file lists its values as numeric instead of character. For instance, if the data file listed race values as 1, 2, and 3 instead of B, H, and W, the `summary` function produces statistics that treat racial-ethnic status as quantitative unless we create a factor for race:

```
> Race <- as.numeric(Inc$race); summary(Race)
   Min. 1st Qu.  Median    Mean 3rd Qu.    Max. # inappropriate for
  1.000   2.000   3.000   2.425   3.000   3.000 # nominal variable
> summary(as.factor(Race))      # compare to summary(Race)
  1  2  3
 16 14 50
```

A categorical variable is summarized by a frequency table and can be visualized through a **bar graph**, with bar heights representing frequencies or proportions. We illustrate for racial-ethnic status in the `Income` data file, using the `ggplot` function in the `ggplot2` package:

```
> library(ggplot2)
# Bar graph of counts (not shown):
> ggplot(data=Inc, aes(x=race)) + geom_bar(width=0.5, fill="steelblue")
# Bar graph of percentages:
> library(scales)
> ggplot(data=Inc, aes(race)) +
+    geom_bar(aes(y=..prop.., group = 1), width=0.5, fill="steelblue") +
+    scale_y_continuous(labels=percent_format()) +
+    ylab("Percentage") + xlab("Racial-Ethnic Status")
# In ggplot command, "+" symbol must be at end of each line
#    rather than at beginning of next one.
```

Figure A.3 shows the bar graph.

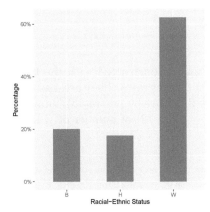

FIGURE A.3 Bar graph for racial-ethnic status of subjects in `Income` data file.

The `dplyr` package has many useful capabilities for manipulating data files and finding descriptive statistics. The `slice` command shows cases in a data frame by the position of the rows, `filter` shows cases that fulfill one or more conditions, and `select` can create a new data frame from a subset of the columns. The package employs the "pipe" operator %>%, which passes the object on the left-hand side as an argument of the function on the right-hand side.

```
> library(dplyr)
> slice(Inc, 2:4)                        # Or, in base R, Inc[2:4,]
   income education race                 # Base functions show actual
 1     18         7    B                 # row numbers of the data file
 2     26         9    B
 3     16        11    B
> Inc%>%filter(income >= 100)            # Or, in base R, Inc[Inc$income >= 100,]
   income education race
```

```
1    120         18    W
2    104         14    W
> Inc2 <- select(Inc, income, education) # Or, in base R, Inc2 <- Inc[,1:2]
> head(Inc2, 2)
  income education
1    16         10
2    18          7
```

The `dplyr` package can construct frequency distributions using the `count` function. The `summarize` command in `dplyr` can produce many descriptive statistics. The following illustrates, finding the mean and standard deviation of the income values in the `Inc` data frame. Grouping can be applied with the `group_by` function in combination with `summarize` to show descriptive statistics by group:

```
> Inc %>% count(race)
  race  n
1   B 16
2   H 14
3   W 50
> Inc %>% summarize(mean_inc = mean(income), sd_inc = sd(income))
  mean_inc sd_inc
1   37.525 20.673
> Inc %>% group_by(race) %>% summarize(n=n(), # n=n() is sample size
+                                      mean=mean(income), sd=sd(income))
# A tibble: 3 x 3           # can use tapply or aggregate in base R
  race      n  mean    sd  # to find statistics within groups
1 B        16  27.8  13.3
2 H        14  31    12.8
3 W        50  42.5  22.9
> library(purrr) # also provides descriptive statistics (not shown here)
> Inc %>% split(.$race) %>% map(summary)
```

Side-by-side box plots can be constructed with the `boxplot` function, as Section 1.4.5 shows for U.S. and Canadian murder rates. They are also available with the `ggplot` function in the `ggplot2` package. We illustrate by portraying simultaneously the effects on income of race and a binary splitting (≤ 12, > 12) of number of years of education, the other variable in the `Income` data file:

```
> library(ggplot2)
> educ.cat <- factor(Inc$education > 12, labels=c("up to 12","> 12"))
> ggplot(Inc, aes(x=educ.cat, y=income, fill=race)) + geom_boxplot() +
+        stat_summary(fun=mean, geom="point", shape=23, size=3) +
+        labs(x="Education (years)",y="Income (thousands of dollars)")
```

Figure A.4 shows the result. A *stacked histogram* is another graphical method for comparing distributions for two groups. See the R Appendix at the book's website.

R functions, beyond their standard usage, provide options controlled with the arguments. For example, the `mean` function can also provide the ***trimmed mean***. The mean is influenced strongly by *outliers*, and the $p\%$ *trimmed mean* eliminates their influence by excluding the $p\%$ lowest and $p\%$ highest data points before computing the mean. Let $y_{(1)} \leq y_{(2)} \leq \cdots \leq y_{(n)}$ denoted the ordered observations. For the data vector $(y_1, \ldots, y_{10}) = (11, 6, 12, 9, 68, 15, 5, 12, 23, 14)$ with sample mean $\bar{y} = 17.5$, $(y_{(1)}, \ldots, y_{(10)}) = (5, 6, 9, 11, 12, 12, 14, 15, 23, 68)$, and the 10% trimmed mean is $\frac{1}{8}\sum_{i=2}^{9} y_{(i)} = \frac{1}{8}(6+9+\cdots+23) = 12.75$, as shown next:

```
> y <- c(11, 6, 12, 9, 68, 15, 5, 12, 23, 14)
> mean(y); mean(y, 0.10); median(y) # mean, 10% trimmed mean, median
[1] 17.5
[1] 12.75 # 10% trimmed mean is mean of 80% central observations
[1] 12    # with skewed data, highly-trimmed mean moves toward median
```

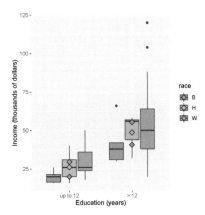

FIGURE A.4 Side-by-side box plots for income by racial-ethnic status and education, from `Income` data file.

A.1.4   Missing Values in Data Files

Many data files have missing observations on some or all variables. We illustrate with the GSS2018 data file:

```
> nrow(GSS) # sample size (no. of rows) for the GSS data frame
[1] 2348
> names(GSS)
 [1] "subject"  "AGE"  "SEX"  "RACE"  "EDUC" "WRKSTAT"  "MARITAL"
 [8] "EARNRS" "INCOME"  "RINCOME"  "PARTYID"  "GUNLAW"  "PRES16"
[14] "SMALLGAP" "TRCOURTS"
> summary(GSS$AGE)
  Min. 1st Qu  Median   Meanc 3rd Qu    Max. NA's # NA = not available
 18.00  34.00   48.00   48.97   63.00   89.00    7
```

Besides basic descriptive statistics, the output indicates the number of *not available* (NA) values per variable.

We could restrict the analysis to the subsample of cases that are complete for all variables, but this subsample can be small, losing much information. In the GSS data file, only 225 of the 2348 cases are complete:

```
> ind <- complete.cases(GSS) # indicator (logical: FALSE for NA)
> sum(ind)               # number of complete cases
[1] 225
```

It is better to remove cases with NA values selectively, separately for each variable. For example, only 7 age values are missing, and we can analyze all the other observations:

```
> sum(is.na(GSS$AGE))       # number of NA cases for variable age
 [1] 7
> mean(GSS$AGE, na.rm=TRUE) # na.rm=TRUE removes NA observations
[1] 48.97138
> head(GSS, 1)
  subject AGE SEX RACE EDUC WRKSTAT MARITAL EARNRS INCOME RINCOME ...
1       1  43   1    1   14       3       5      1     NA      NA ...
> ind.age <- complete.cases(GSS[,2]) # TRUE when AGE (var 2) reported
> GSSsub <- GSS[ind.age,]  # subsample without missing age values
> mean(GSSsub$AGE)         # equivalent to: mean(GSS$AGE, na.rm=TRUE)
[1] 48.97138
```

A graphical visualization of the extent and distribution of missing values, called a *heatmap*, is provided in the `visdat` package by the `vis_miss` function. An additional option clusters the NA values and the variables by the subjects to identify missingness patterns. For the GSS data file, the heatmap shown in Figure A.5 blacks out missing observations and is produced by:

```
> GSS2 <- data.frame(GSS$AGE, GSS$INCOME, GSS$RINCOME, GSS$PARTYID, GSS$GUNLAW)
> library(visdat)
> vis_miss(GSS2)
> vis_dat(GSS2)   # produces a variant of vis_miss(GSS2) with columns colored by
                  # the type of the corresponding variable (not shown)
> vis_miss(GSS2, cluster=TRUE)
```

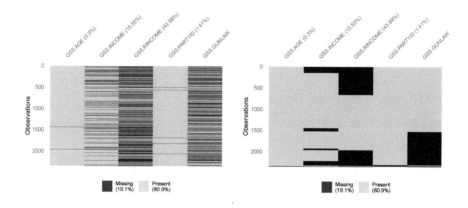

FIGURE A.5 Missing data heatmaps for the GSS2018 data file, without and with clustering according to missingness.

The heatmap shows that AGE and PARTYID have little missing data whereas the other variables (e.g. RINCOME, the respondent's income) are missing a lot. Overall 19.1% of the observations are missing for these five variables.

Identifying missing data is important in the *data wrangling* phase of a data analysis. Advanced methods of statistics, such as *data imputation*, analyze the data by estimating the missing observations.

A.1.5 Summarizing Bivariate Quantitative Data

Bivariate quantitative data can be visualized by scatterplots while the strength of their linear correlation is measured by the correlation, implemented in R by `plot` and `cor` functions, as illustrated in Section 1.5.1. Scatterplots can also portray the data and regression line for groups that are categories of a categorical variable in the data file. We illustrate for the Income data file:

```
> plot(Inc$income ~ Inc$educ, pch=as.character(Inc$race), cex=0.75,
+       ylab="Income (thousands of dollars)", xlab="Education (years)")
> abline(lm(Inc$income ~ Inc$educ))
 # regression lines fitted on subsamples defined by race:
> abline(lm(Inc$income~Inc$educ,subset=Inc$race=="B"), lty=4, col="red")
> abline(lm(Inc$income~Inc$educ,subset=Inc$race=="H"), lty=2, col=51)
> abline(lm(Inc$income~Inc$educ,subset=Inc$race=="W"), lty=5, col="blue")
> legend("topleft", legend=c("B","H","W"), lty=c(4,2,5),
+        col=c("red", 51, "blue"), cex=1.1, box.lty=0)
```

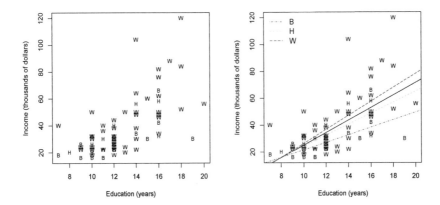

FIGURE A.6 Scatterplots of income by education with the fitted regression line: The second scatterplot shows the regression lines fitted to the subsamples of racial-ethnic status.

Figure A.6 shows the scatterplot between income and education and the fitted linear regression line, with data points marked by racial-ethnic status. The right plot in the figure shows the regression lines between income and education fitted separately to the racial-ethnic subsamples.

A.1.6 Summarizing Bivariate Categorical Data

The `dplyr` package can combine the `count` and `group_by` functions to construct frequency distributions of a categorical variable within values of another variable. For example, for the variable representing the response to the statement, 'For a society to be fair, differences in people's standard of living should be small.' in the GSS2018 data file, the following code creates the frequency distribution of SMALLGAP for males and females:

```
> library(dplyr)
> GSS$SEX <- factor(GSS$SEX, levels=c(1:2), labels = c("male", "female"))
> GSS$SMALLGAP <- factor(GSS$SMALLGAP, levels=c(1:5), labels =
+            c("strongly agree","agree","neutral","disagree","strongly disagree"))
> GSS %>% group_by(SEX) %>% count(SMALLGAP) # result not shown
```

A.2   Chapter 2: R for Probability Distributions

A.2.1   R Functions for Probability Distributions

Table A.1 lists probability distributions introduced in this text and their base names in R. For each distribution,[5] specified by its parameter values, R provides four functions:

- p for 'probability': the *cdf*
- q for 'quantile': inverse of the *cdf* (Section 2.5.6)

---

[5] For the multinomial distribution, only the `dmultinom` and `rmultinom` functions are available.

- d for 'density': the *pdf* or *pmf*
- r for 'random': random sample generation

TABLE A.1 Functions in R for common probability distributions.

Probability Distribution	Base name	Parameters	pdf or pmf
Beta	beta	α, β	Equation (2.20)
Binomial	binom	n, π	Equation (2.6)
Cauchy	cauchy	location, scale	Section 4.4.5
Chi-squared	chisq	*df*	Section 4.4.5
Exponential	exp	rate λ	Equation (2.12)
F	f	df_1, df_2	Section 6.4.1
Gamma	gamma	shape, scale	Equation (2.10)
Geometric	geom	π	Example 2.2.2
Hypergeometric	hyper	F, M, n	Equation (2.18)
Logistic	logis	location, scale	Section 7.2.1
Multinomial	multinom	n, $(\pi_1, \ldots, \pi_c)$	Equation (2.14)
Negative binomial	nbinom	k, π	Equation (2.19)
Normal	norm	μ, σ	Equation (2.8)
Poisson	pois	μ	Equation (2.7)
t	t	*df*	Section 4.4.1
Uniform	unif	min, max	Example 2.2.4

For example, for the normal distribution these are pnorm, qnorm, dnorm, and rnorm. In Sections 2.5.2 and 2.5.3 we found cumulative probabilities and quantiles for normal distributions using pnorm and qnorm. We used rnorm for simulations in Section 1.5.3.

Some probability distributions have alternative parameterizations. For example, the standard *pdf* parameterization in R of a gamma distribution is

$$ f(y; \theta, k) = \frac{1}{\theta^k \Gamma(k)} e^{-y/\theta} y^{k-1}, \quad y \geq 0; \quad f(y; \theta, k) = 0, \quad y < 0, $$

for *shape parameter* k and *scale parameter* θ. It has $\mu = k\theta$ and $\sigma = \sqrt{k}\theta$. The scale parameter relates to the λ *rate parameter* in equation (2.10) and the exponential special case (2.12) by $\theta = 1/\lambda$. The R functions for the gamma distribution provide the ability to choose parameterization in terms of scale or rate. For instance, rgamma(1000, shape=10, scale=2) is equivalent to rgamma(1000, shape=10, rate=1/2).

Probability functions (*pdf* and *pmf*) can be plotted using the d versions of the base functions. For example, the following code produces the graph of the *pmf* of a binomial distribution with $n = 3$ and $\pi = 0.5$, shown in Figure 2.5.

```
> y <- 0:3
> plot(y, dbinom(y, 3, 0.5), type="h", xaxt="n", lwd=8, lend=2,
+        col="dodgerblue4", ylim=c(0, 0.4), xlab="y", ylab="P(y)")
> axis(1, at = seq(0, 3, by = 1))
```

The code for producing the second plot in Figure 2.12 of gamma *pdf*s with different shape parameter values but all having $\mu = 10$ follows:

```
> y = seq(0, 40, 0.01)
> plot(y, dgamma(y,shape=10,scale=1), ylab="f(y)",type ="l") # mean=10
> lines(y, dgamma(y, shape=2, scale=5), col="green")          # scale = 1/lambda
```

```
> lines(y, dgamma(y, shape=1, scale=10), col="red")        # = mean/shape
> legend("topright", c("k=10","k=2","k=1"), lwd=2,
+          col=c("black","green","red"), box.lty=0)
```

For the curves to have $\mu = 10$, we set scale = 10/shape, because $\mu = k\theta = $ shape $\times$ scale. Replacing dgamma by pgamma yields the graphs of the *cdf*s.

A.2.2 Quantiles, *Q-Q* Plots, and the Normal Quantile Plot

For a continuous random variable, Section 2.5.6 defined the *p*th quantile (100*p* percentile) as the point *q* at which the *cdf* satisfies $F(q) = p$. For a discrete random variable, the *cdf* is a step function, and the *p*th quantile is defined as the minimum *q* such that $F(q) \geq p$. For instance, for the binomial distribution in Table 2.3 with $n = 12$ and $\pi = 0.50$, the *cdf* has $F(5) = 0.3872$ and $F(6) = 0.6128$, so the *p*th quantile is 6 for any $0.3872 < p \leq 0.6128$, such as $p = 0.40$ and 0.60 as shown in the following R code:

```
> cbind(5:6, pbinom(5:6, 12, 0.50))
       [,1]    [,2]
[1,]    5     0.3872
[2,]    6     0.6128
> qbinom(0.40, 12, 0.50); qbinom(0.60, 12, 0.50)
[1] 6
[1] 6
```

Figure A.7 illustrates. It shows, for instance, that 0.60 on the vertical *cdf* probability scale maps to the 0.60 quantile of 6 on the horizontal scale of binomial random variable values.

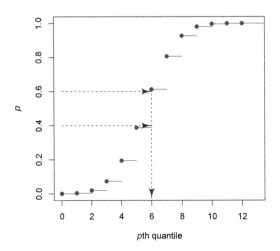

FIGURE A.7 The *cdf* of a binomial distribution with $n = 12$ and $\pi = 0.50$ with the 0.40th and 0.60th quantiles, both equal to 6.

Some inferential statistical methods assume that the data come from a particular distribution, often the normal. The *Q-Q* plot (*quantile-quantile plot*) is a graphical comparison of the observed sample data distribution with a theoretical distribution. As explained in Exercise 2.67, it plots the *order statistics* $y_{(1)} \leq y_{(2)} \leq \ldots \leq y_{(n)}$ of the data against the ordered quantiles $q_{\frac{1}{n+1}} \leq q_{\frac{2}{n+1}} \leq \ldots \leq q_{\frac{n}{n+1}}$ of the reference distribution. If $\{q_{\frac{i}{n+1}}\}$ and $\{y_i\}$ come from the same distribution, the points $\{(q_{\frac{1}{n+1}}, y_{(1)}), (q_{\frac{2}{n+1}}, y_{(2)}), \ldots, (q_{\frac{n}{n+1}}, y_{(n)})\}$ should approximately follow a straight line, more closely so when *n* is large. With the standard normal distribution for $\{q_{\frac{i}{n+1}}\}$ and a normal distribution assumed for $\{y_i\}$, the Q-Q plot is called a *normal quantile plot*. With a standard normal distribution assumed for $\{y_i\}$, the points should approximately follow the straight line $y = x$ having intercept 0 and slope 1, which R plots with the command abline(0,1). When the points deviate greatly from a straight line, this gives a visual indication of how the sample data distribution differs from the reference distribution.

We illustrate by generating random samples from a standard normal distribution, a t distribution (introduced in Section 4.4.1, symmetric around 0 like the standard normal but with thicker tails), an exponential distribution (2.12) with $\lambda = 1$, and a uniform distribution over $(0, 1)$. The qqnorm function creates normal quantile plots:

```
> Y1 <- rnorm(1000); Y2 <- rt(1000, df=3) # generating random samples
> Y3 <- rexp(1000); Y4 <- runif(1000)     # from four distributions
> par(mfrow=c(2, 2))                       # plots 4 graphs in a 2x2 matrix format
> qqnorm(Y1, col='blue', main='Y1 ~ N(0,1)'); abline(0,1)
> qqnorm(Y2, col='blue', main='Y2 ~ t(3)'); abline(0,1)
> qqnorm(Y3, col='blue', main='Y3 ~ exp(1)')
> qqnorm(Y4, col='blue', main='Y4 ~ uniform(0,1)')
```

Figure A.8 shows the normal quantile plots. The first plot shows excellent agreement, as expected, between the normal sample and the normal quantiles, with the points falling close to the straight line $y = x$. The plot for the sample from the t distribution indicates that more observations occur well out in the tails (i.e., larger $|t|$ values) than expected with a standard normal distribution. The plot for the uniform distribution indicates the opposite, fewer observations in the tails than expected with the normal distribution. The plot for the sample from the exponential distribution reflects the right skew of that distribution, with some quite large observations but no very small observations, reflecting its lower boundary of 0 for possible values.

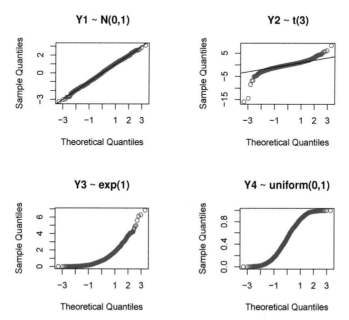

FIGURE A.8 Normal quantile plots, plotting quantiles of the standard normal distribution against quantiles of random samples from a $N(0,1)$ distribution, a t distribution with $df = 3$, an exponential distribution with $\lambda = 1$, and a uniform distribution over $[0, 1]$.

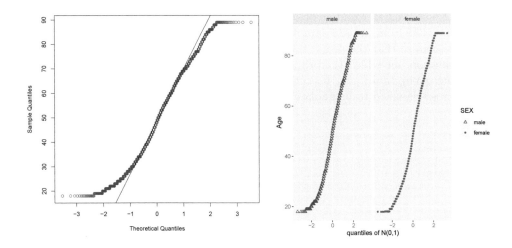

FIGURE A.9 Normal quantile (Q-Q) plots for the ages of respondents in the GSS2018 data file, overall and grouped by gender.

To illustrate the normal quantile plot for actual data, we construct it for the ages in the GRSS data frame created in Section A.1.2:

```
> ind.age <- complete.cases(GSS[,2]) # subsample without missing ages (variable 2)
> GSSsub <- GSS[ind.age,]            # new data frame without missing ages
> qqnorm(GSSsub$AGE, col="dodgerblue4"); qqline(GSSsub$AGE)
```

Figure A.9 (left) shows the plot. The `qqline` function adds the straight line corresponding to the trend in points if the sample distribution were normal. It suggests that the distribution has fewer observations in the tails than expected with the normal, reflecting subjects under 18 not being sampled in the GSS and very old subjects being in a smaller cohort and also dropping out because of deaths. (A histogram also shows evidence of non-normality.) The `ggplot2` package provides options for controlling the format of the plot according to groups defined by levels of a factor. The following shows the code for the Q-Q plots for the ages of females and of males, which is shown on the right in Figure A.9:

```
> library(ggplot2)
> GSS$SEX <- factor(GSS$SEX, labels = c("male","female"))
> p <- qplot(sample=AGE, data=GSS, color=SEX, shape=SEX);  # no output
# one qq-plot for males and females:
> p + scale_color_manual(values=c("blue", "red")) + scale_shape_manual(values=c(2,20)) +
  labs(x="quantiles of N(0,1)", y = "Age")
# separate qq-plot for males and females (facet_wrap):
> p + scale_color_manual(values=c("blue", "red")) + scale_shape_manual(values= c(2,20)) +
  labs(x="quantiles of N(0,1)", y="Age") + facet_wrap(~ SEX)
```

The `qqPlot` function in the `EnvStats` library can construct Q-Q plots for reference distributions other than the normal.

A.2.3   Joint and Conditional Probability Distributions

Section A.1.6 showed an example of sample conditional distributions, for discrete variables SEX and SMALLGAP from the GSS data file. Since we treated *smallgap* as the response variable, we formed them so that the proportions sum to 1 for each gender. We could also form the *joint* distribution, for which the proportions sum to 1 over all 10 cells of the contingency table. Contingency tables can be constructed by the `table` function, which requires the variables cross-classified to be `factors`.

```
> gender <-GSS$SEX; smallgap <- GSS$SMALLGAP
> fairsociety <- table(gender, smallgap)
> fairsociety               # contingency table with counts in cells (not shown)
> prop.table(fairsociety)   # joint cell proportions (total = 1)
        smallgap
gender    strongly agree  agree neutral disagree strongly disagree
   Male           0.0409 0.1220  0.1298   0.1594            0.0331
   Female         0.0505 0.1359  0.1672   0.1385            0.0226
```

For the multivariate normal distribution, probabilities, the *pdf*, quantiles, and random numbers can be computed using the `mvtnorm` package. The bivariate normal *pdf* plots as a bell-shaped surface in 3-dimensional space, as shown in Figure 2.15. The R Appendix at the book's website contains code for plotting the bivariate normal density in Figure 2.15, using the `plot3D` package.

A.3   Chapter 3: R for Sampling Distributions

Simulation to mimic simple random sampling is used to approximate sampling distributions and study their characteristics. Section 1.3.1 applied the `sample` function to randomly sample 5 integers from a discrete uniform distribution on $\{1, 2, \ldots, 60\}$. This sampling was done *without replacement*, meaning that a value cannot be sampled more than once. Sampling *with replacement* is also possible:

```
> sample(1:60, 5, replace = TRUE)
[1] 56 27 54 24 27                    # value 27 is observed twice
```

Sampling with replacement is appropriate with most statistical methods based on simulation, such as simulating sampling distributions and using the bootstrap (Section 4.6). The r versions of the random sampling functions for distributions shown in Table A.1, such as `rnorm` and `rpois`, use it.

A.3.1   Simulating the Sampling Distribution of a Statistic

Suppose we'd like to simulate the sampling distribution of some statistic, assuming a simple random sample from a particular probability distribution. We could write an R function to simulate a very large number of random samples from that distribution and then construct a histogram of the values of the statistic.

We illustrate for approximating the sampling distribution of $\bar{Y}$ for a random sample of size n from a Poisson distribution with μ. In the R function created in the following code, B is the number of random samples of size n simulated from the Poisson. We next discuss the steps in the function for $n = 10$, using the value $B = 100{,}000$ selected at the end of the code. Letting Y be a numeric vector of length $nB = 10(100{,}000) = 1{,}000{,}000$, we randomly

generate 1,000,000 Poisson random variables with mean denoted by *mu*. We then organize
these in a matrix with 10 columns and 100,000 rows. Each row of the matrix contains
a simulated random sample of size 10 from the Poisson distribution. The `apply` function
then finds the mean within each row. (In the second argument of the `apply` function, 1
indicates rows, 2 indicates columns, and `c(1, 2)` indicates rows and columns.) At this stage,
the vector *Ymean* is a vector of 100,000 means. The remaining code creates plots, showing
the sample data distribution for the first sample and the empirical sampling distribution
of the 100,000 simulated values of $\bar{y}$:

```
> pois_CLT <- function(n, mu, B) {
  # n:   vector of 2 sample sizes [e.g. n <- c(10, 100)]
  # mu: mean parameter of Poisson distribution
  # B:   number of simulated random samples from the Poisson
  par(mfrow = c(2, 2))
  for (i in 1:2){
    Y <- numeric(length=n[i]*B)
    Y <- matrix(rpois(n[i]*B, mu), ncol=n[i])
    Ymean <- apply(Y, 1, mean) # or, can do this with rowMeans(Y)
    barplot(table(Y[1,]), main=paste("n=", n[i]), xlab="y",
      col="lightsteelblue") # sample data dist. for first sample
    hist(Ymean, main=paste("n=",n[i]), xlab=expression(bar(y)),
      col="lightsteelblue") # histogram of B sample mean values
  } }
# implement:with 100000 random sample sizes of 10 and 100, mean = 0.7
> n <- c(10, 100)
> pois_CLT(n, 0.7, 100000)
```

Figure A.10 shows the results with $\mu = 0.7$, which we used to find the sampling distribution of the sample median in Section 3.4.3. We use both $n = 10$ and $n = 100$ to show the
impact of the Central Limit Theorem as n increases. The figures on the left are bar graphs of
the sample data distribution for the first of the 100,000 simulated random samples of size n.
With $\mu = 0.7$, a typical sample has a mode of 0, few if any observations above 3, and severe
skew to the right. The sampling distributions are shown on the right. With random samples
of size $n = 10$, the sampling distribution has somewhat of a bell shape but is still skewed to
the right. (It is a re-scaling of a Poisson with mean 7, since adding 10 independent Poissons
with mean 0.7 gives a Poisson with mean 7.) With $n = 100$, the sampling distribution is
bell-shaped, has a more symmetric appearance, and is narrower because the standard error
decreases as n increases.

By changing the function from the mean in the `apply` command, you can simulate
sampling distributions of other statistics, such as we did for the sample median in Section
3.4.3. By changing the `rpois` argument, you can simulate sampling distributions for other
probability distributions as well as other statistics.

A.3.2   Monte Carlo Simulation

The *Monte Carlo (MC) method* is a way to use simulation to investigate characteristics of
random variables, such as means and variances of their probability distributions.

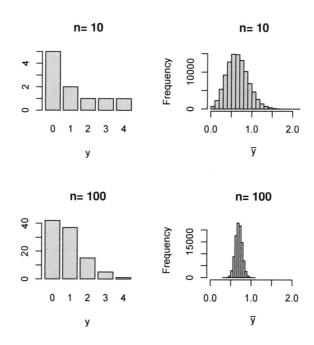

FIGURE A.10 Bar plot of sample data distribution (left) and histogram of empirical sampling distribution of sample mean (right), for random samples of size $n = 10$ (upper figures) and $n = 100$ (lower figures) from a Poisson distribution with $\mu = 0.7$.

Monte Carlo (MC) method

For a function g and a random variable Y with probability function f, consider

$$E[g(Y)] = \begin{cases} \sum_y g(y)f(y), & Y \text{ discrete} \\ \int_y g(y)f(y)dy, & Y \text{ continuous.} \end{cases}$$

If $Y_1, Y_2, \ldots, Y_B$ are independent random variables sampled from f, then $\frac{1}{B}\sum_{i=1}^{B} g(Y_i)$ is the **Monte Carlo (MC) estimator** of $E[g(Y)]$.

For a parameter θ, estimated by $\hat{\theta}$, we can use the Monte Carlo method to estimate the variance of the sampling distribution of $\hat{\theta}$ for a random sample $(Y_1, \ldots, Y_n)$. Here are the steps for a basic MC algorithm:

(1) For $j = 1, \ldots, B$, draw $\mathbf{y}^{(j)} = (y_{j1}, \ldots, y_{jn})$ independently from the distribution of interest.

(2) Use $\mathbf{y}^{(j)}$ to find $\hat{\theta}_j$ for sample j of size n, $j = 1, \ldots, B$.

(3) The Monte Carlo estimate of $E(\hat{\theta})$ is $\bar{\theta} = \frac{1}{B}\sum_{j=1}^{B} \hat{\theta}_j$.

(4) The Monte Carlo estimate of $\text{var}(\hat{\theta})$ is $\frac{1}{B}\sum_{j=1}^{B} \left(\hat{\theta}_j - \bar{\theta}\right)^2$.

For example, although we have a standard error formula for a sample mean, most probability distributions do not have a simple standard error formula for a sample median, so

Monte Carlo approximation is useful to approximate it. Let's investigate how the standard error of a sample median compares to that of a sample mean in sampling from a normal distribution. We create a function to take a large number B of simple random samples of size n from a $N(\mu, \sigma^2)$ distribution, calculate the median for each sample, and then find the standard deviation of those sample medians:

```
> sdmed <- function(B, n, mu, sigma){
          medians <- rep(0, B)
          for(i in 1:B){
          y <- rnorm(n, mu, sigma)
          medians[i] <- median(y)  }
          sd(medians)
          }
```

If IQ scores have a $N(100, 16^2)$ distribution, then for a simple random sample of size $n = 100$, $\bar{Y}$ has a standard error of $\sigma/\sqrt{n} = 16/\sqrt{100} = 1.60$. Let's approximate the standard error of the sample median by simulating $B = 1,000,000$ random samples of size $n = 100$ each, finding the 1,000,000 sample medians, and then finding the standard deviation of their values:

```
> sdmed(1000000, 100, 100, 16) # B=1000000, n=100, mu=100, sigma=16
[1] 1.990409
```

We approximate that the standard error is 1.99. In fact, for sampling from a normal population, the standard error of the sample median is 25% larger than the standard error of a sample mean. The sample mean tends to be closer than the sample median to the joint population mean and median of a normal distribution. Apparently the sample mean is a better estimator than the sample median of the center of a normal distribution. Constructing good estimators is the subject of Chapter 4.

A.4   Chapter 4: R for Estimation

The `maxLik` package has a function for ML estimation when you supply the log-likelihood function to be maximized. Output includes the standard errors of the ML estimates.

A.4.1   Confidence Intervals for Proportions

As shown in Section 4.3.4, several confidence intervals (CIs) for a proportion are available in R with the function `ciAllx` in the `proportion` package. The `binom` package and the `BinomCI` function in the `DescTools` package also offer several CIs, as shown in the R Appendix at the book's website, and the `BinomDiffCI` function in the `DescTools` package can construct CIs for the difference of proportions.

The `binom` package also contains a function to simulate the *actual coverage probability* that a CI contains the parameter. It generates a huge number of binomial samples with the chosen values of n and π and finds the proportion that truly contain π. This is useful for investigating small n cases in which a method based on the approximate normality of the sampling distribution of $\hat{\pi}$ may perform poorly. We illustrate with $n = 30$ when $\pi = 0.10$:

```
> library(binom)
> binom.coverage(0.10, 30, conf.level=0.95, c("asymptotic", "wilson"))
       method   p  n  coverage
1 asymptotic 0.1 30 0.80852 # Wald CI has true prob. = 0.81 of containing pi = 0.10
2     wilson 0.1 30 0.97417 # score CI
```

When we form a Wald 95% CI with $n = 30$ when $\pi = 0.10$, the actual probability that the CI contains π is only 0.81. With small n, we should not use this method when π may be close to 0 or 1.

A.4.2   Confidence Intervals for Means of Subgroups and Paired Differences

To show how to construct CIs for subgroups, for the UN data file we construct 95% CIs for the mean homicide rate for nations with low GDP (≤ 30) and high GDP (> 30). The `group_by` function of the `tidyverse` package can do this, as shown in the R Appendix at the book's website. Here, we use the `t.test` function in base R by forming subgroups:

```
> t.test(UN$Homicide[UN$GDP <= 30], conf.level=0.95)$conf.int
[1]  3.3074 10.6835
> t.test(UN$Homicide[UN$GDP > 30], conf.level=0.95)$conf.int
[1]  0.80322 1.68678
```

Section 4.4.3 found a CI for the mean weight change of anorexic young girls after receiving a cognitive behavioral (*cb*) therapy. For the changes of weight (*after–before*), we constructed the t CI for the mean. The original samples of the *before* weights and the *after* weights are *dependent*, having the same subjects for each measurement, so the method of Section 4.5.2 for comparing means for *independent* samples is not appropriate. A study that compares means using paired observations is called a ***paired design*** study. For the *before* and *after* weights, the *paired=TRUE* option with the `t.test` function finds the appropriate CI:

```
> Anor <- read.table("http://stat4ds.rwth-aachen.de/data/Anorexia.dat", header=TRUE)
> t.test(Anor$after[Anor$therapy=="cb"], Anor$before[Anor$therapy=="cb"],
+        paired=TRUE)$conf.int # default 95% CI
[1]  0.22689 5.78690
```

To find a confidence interval for the difference between two means, with independent or paired dependent samples. you can also use the `MeanDiffCI` function in the `DescTools` package, as shown in the R Appendix at the book's website. It provides the t interval that does not assume equal population variances and also has bootstrap options.

A.4.3   The t and Other Probability Distributions for Statistical Inference

The distributions commonly used in parametric statistical inference, other than the normal, are the t, χ^2 and F distributions. To understand the shape and properties of a family of distributions, it is helpful to plot their *pdf*s, as shown in Section A.2.1 for the gamma distribution. The R Appendix at the book's website has the code for Figure 4.5 showing the *pdf*s of t distributions for a selection of *df* values together with the standard normal *pdf* and the code for Figure 4.7 showing chi-squared *pdf*s for various *df* values.

To illustrate the convergence of the t distribution to the standard normal as *df* increases, we compare some quantiles of a t distribution with 3, 30, and 1000 degrees of freedom to the corresponding normal quantiles. For *df* values of about 30 and higher the quantiles are quite close, having the largest differences in the tails.

```
> quantiles <- c(0.50, 0.75, 0.90, 0.95, 0.99)
> qt(quantiles, 3) - qnorm(quantiles)      # e.g. 0.99 quantile for t
[1] 0.0000  0.0904  0.3562  0.7085  2.2144 #     is 2.2144 above N(0,1)
> qt(quantiles, 30) - qnorm(quantiles)
[1] 0.0000  0.0083  0.0289  0.0524  0.1309
> qt(quantiles, 1000) - qnorm(quantiles)   # difference decreases
[1] 0.0000  0.0002  0.0008  0.0015  0.0037 # as df increases
```

A.4.4 Empirical Cumulative Distribution Function

Some inferential methods assume that the data come from a family of distributions, such as the normal assumption when we form t confidence intervals. Other inferential methods, such as the *bootstrap* method (Section 4.6) and *nonparametric* methods (Section 5.8), do not make such an assumption. When the *cdf* is completely unknown, the natural estimator is its **empirical cumulative distribution function.**

Empirical cumulative distribution function

For independent random variables $Y_1, \ldots, Y_n$ from a particular distribution, the **empirical cumulative distribution function** is

$$F_n(y) = \frac{1}{n} \sum_{i=1}^{n} I(Y_i \le y),$$

where $I(\cdot)$ is the indicator function, $I(Y_i \le y) = \begin{cases} 1, & \text{if } Y_i \le y \\ 0, & \text{otherwise} \end{cases}$.

That is, $F_n(y)$ is the sample proportion of the n observations that fall at or below y.

We illustrate by generating a random sample of size $n = 10$ from the $N(100, 16^2)$ distribution of IQ values and constructing the empirical *cdf*:

```
> y <- rnorm(10, 100, 16)
> plot(ecdf(y), xlab="y", ylab="Empirical CDF", col="dodgerblue4") # ecdf = empirical cdf
> lines(seq(50, 150, by=.1), pnorm(seq(50,150,by=.1), 100, 16), col="red4", lwd=2)
```

Figure A.11 shows the empirical *cdf* and the *cdf* of the normal distribution from which the data were simulated. The empirical *cdf* is the *cdf* of the discrete distribution having probability $1/n$ at each observation, so it is a step function. The figure also shows an empirical *cdf* for a random sample of size $n = 50$. As n increases, the empirical *cdf* converges uniformly over y to the true underlying *cdf*.[6]

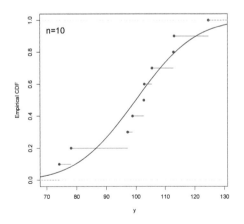
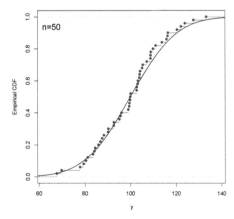

FIGURE A.11 Empirical cumulative distribution functions for random samples of sizes $n = 10$ and $n = 50$ from the $N(100, 16^2)$ distribution, showing also the $N(100, 16^2)$ *cdf*.

---

[6]This result is called the *Glivenko–Cantelli Theorem*, named after the probabilists who proved it in 1933.

In medical applications that focus on the survival time of patients following some procedure of diagnosis, it is common to focus on the empirical ***survival function***, $S_n(y) = 1 - F_n(y)$. At a particular value y, it shows the proportion of the sample that had survival time greater than y. It can be informative to compare two treatments by plotting their survival functions next to each other. See Section 5.8.4.[7]

A.4.5 Nonparametric and Parametric Bootstraps

The bootstrap uses Monte Carlo simulation to resample with replacement from the sample data distribution, for which the *cdf* is the empirical *cdf*. For a parameter θ, Section 4.6 showed how the bootstrap distribution produced by the large number of simulated values of $\hat{\theta}$ yields CIs for θ and a standard error for $\hat{\theta}$. The endpoints of the 95% percentile-based CI are the 0.025 and 0.975 quantiles of the bootstrap distribution. The R Appendix at the book's website shows other possibilities, such as one based on an approximate normal sampling distribution for $\hat{\theta}$ and a bootstrap approximation for its standard error.

The `boot` function in R implements the bootstrap method. It is also straightforward to program the required simulations and construct a percentile-based CI, applying the `sample` function to the sample data distribution. We illustrate for the median and standard deviation of the book shelf life (Section 4.6.2), taking 100,000 re-samples:

```
> Books <- read.table("http://stat4ds.rwth-aachen.de/data/Library.dat", header=TRUE)
> n <- 54; nboot <- 100000
> Psample <- matrix(0, nboot, n) # matrix of nboot rows and n columns
> for (i in 1:nboot) Psample[i,] <- sample(Books$P, n, replace=TRUE)
> MedianBoot <- apply(Psample, 1, median) # finds median in each row
> quantile(MedianBoot, c(0.025, 0.975))
 2.5%   97.5%                       # 95% percentile CI for median
  11    18.5
> SDBoot <- apply(Psample, 1, sd)
> quantile(SDBoot, c(0.025, 0.975)) # 95% percentile CI for standard deviation
    2.5%    97.5%
  13.398  35.807
```

The bootstrap method that simulates using the empirical *cdf* is sometimes referred to as the *nonparametric bootstrap*. The *parametric bootstrap* instead samples from a parametric distribution, with estimates substituted for unknown parameters. If the true distribution is close to that sampled distribution, this has the potential of improved performance.

To illustrate the two types of bootstrap, we contruct bootstrap CIs for the median selling prices of homes from the `Houses` data file analyzed in Section 7.1.3. The selling prices, in thousands of dollars, have distribution highly skewed to the right. We first use the nonparametric bootstrap:

```
> Houses <- read.table("http://stat4ds.rwth-aachen.de/data/Houses.dat", header=TRUE)
> mean(Houses$price); median(Houses$price); sd(Houses$price)
[1] 232.996 # sample mean selling price, in thousands of dollars
[1] 198.9   # sample median
[1] 151.893 # sample standard deviation
> library(boot)
> b.med <- boot(Houses$price, function(x,i){median(x[i])}, 100000)
> b.med
ORDINARY NONPARAMETRIC BOOTSTRAP
Bootstrap Statistics :b.med
      original   bias   std. error
t1*     198.9   0.843     8.287
> mean(b.med$t)
```

---

[7]For example, see https://en.wikipedia.org/wiki/Kaplan-Meier_estimator.

```
[1] 199.743
> boot.ci(b.med)
Intervals : # nonparametric 95% bootstrap CIs for population median
Level      Percentile            BCa
95%   (185.9, 217.3 )    (185.6, 215.6 )
```

For the parametric bootstrap, since the distribution is skewed to the right, we could try the gamma distribution. The **boot** package implements the parametric bootstrap by setting **sim="parametric"**, using the **ran.gen** function to specify the parametric distribution. We also specify functions to find the median and to randomly generate 100,000 random samples from a gamma distribution. The sample medians of the simulated bootstrap samples are saved under the vector *MedianBoot$t*. We can estimate the gamma parameters in the **EnvStats** package using the **egamma** function:

```
> library(EnvStats)
> p <- egamma(Houses$price, ci = FALSE)$parameters; p # estimate parameters
    shape      scale
 3.288145 70.859553
> library(boot)
> y.median <- function(y, i){return(median(y[i]))}
> gamma.rg <- function(y, p){rgamma(length(y), shape=3.29, scale=70.86)}
> MedianBoot = boot(Houses$price, y.median, 100000, sim="parametric",
+                   ran.gen=gamma.rg)
> quantile(MedianBoot$t, c(0.025, 0.975)) # 95% percentile CI
    2.5%    97.5%
  181.95   240.87
```

The 95% percentile CI for the population median is (181.9, 240.9), quite a bit wider than the nonparametric bootstrap percentile interval of (185.9, 217.3). A *Q-Q* plot suggests that the data have right-tail much longer than for the gamma distribution used in the bootstrap. A boxplot identifies the 7 observations above 500 as being outliers:

```
> library(EnvStats)
> qqPlot(Houses$price, distribution="gamma", estimate.params=TRUE)
> abline(0,1)
> boxplot(Houses$price) # plots not shown here
```

The empirical *cdf* may be quite different from the fitted gamma *cdf* used to perform the parametric bootstrap. The parametric bootstrap can be more effective than the nonparametric bootstrap when n is small, because the empirical distribution to which the nonparametric bootstrap applies is highly discrete. Otherwise, it is safer to use the nonparametric bootstrap unless you have considerable faith in the adequacy of the parametric model. Without further study of a sensible distribution to assume for selling price (e.g., considering possibilities such as the log-normal), it is safer to use the nonparametric bootstrap.

The bootstrap can also estimate the bias of an estimator. With estimate $\hat{\theta}_{obs}$ for the observed sample and B simulations in the bootstrap, the bias estimate is

$$\hat{b}(\hat{\theta}) = \left(\frac{1}{B} \sum_{j=1}^{B} \hat{\theta}_j \right) - \hat{\theta}_{obs}.$$

In the nonparametric bootstrap for the median selling price shown above, the bootstrap estimate of the median was 199.74, the sample median was 198.90, and the bias of the sample median is estimated to be 199.74 − 198.90 = 0.84.

A.4.6   Bayesian HPD Intervals Comparing Proportions

Section 4.7.6 introduced the highest posterior density (HPD) interval as an alternative to using posterior quantiles with equal tail (EQT) areas. One situation in which we recommend using the HPD interval instead of the EQT interval is when the posterior *pdf* is monotone increasing or decreasing from the boundary of the parameter space.

For example, in estimating a proportion π, suppose that all n trials are successes or all n trials are failures. When $y = n$ and we use a Jeffreys or a uniform prior for π, $f(\pi \mid y)$ is monotone increasing from 0 to 1. It is not then sensible to exclude 1.0 and nearby values from the posterior interval. Rather than forming an interval from the 2.5 to 97.5 percentiles of the posterior distribution, we use the interval from the 5.0 percentile to 1.0. When $y = 0$, $f(\pi \mid y)$ is monotone decreasing from 0, and a sensible posterior interval goes from 0.0 to the 95.0 percentile. For estimating a difference $\pi_1 - \pi_2$ with Jeffreys or more diffuse priors, the posterior density is monotone when one of the samples has all successes and the other sample has all failures.

A caution: Unlike EQT intervals, HPD intervals are not invariant under nonlinear transformations. We illustrate with π_1/π_2, sometimes called the *risk ratio* or *relative risk*. If a 95% HPD CI for π_1/π_2 is (L, U), the 95% HPD CI for π_2/π_1 is not (1/U, 1/L).

Consider the clinical trial example in Section 4.7.5 in which the 11 patients allocated to the experimental treatment were all successes and the only patient allocated to the control treatment was a failure. With uniform prior distributions, the posterior distributions were beta(12.0, 1.0) for π_1 and beta(12.0, 1.0) for π_2. For inference about the risk ratio, we obtain with simulation:

```
> library(PropCIs) # EQT intervals
> rrci.bayes(11, 11, 0, 1, 1.0, 1.0, 1.0, 1.0, 0.95, nsim = 1000000)
[1]  1.078 73.379  # EQT interval for pi1/pi2
> rrci.bayes(0, 1, 11, 11, 1.0, 1.0, 1.0, 1.0, 0.95, nsim = 1000000)
[1] 0.01363 0.92771 # EQT for pi2/pi1; endpoints (1/73.379, 1/1.078)
> library(HDInterval) # HPD interval for ratio of probabilities
> pi1 <- rbeta(1000000, 12.0, 1.0) # random sample from beta posterior
> pi2 <- rbeta(1000000, 1.0, 2.0)
> hdi(pi1/pi2, credMass=0.95)
  lower   upper
 0.6729 36.6303
> hdi(pi2/pi1, credMass=0.95)
    lower    upper
 7.820e-07 8.506e-01 # quite different from (1/36.63, 1/0.67)
```

The HPD 95% interval for π_1/π_2 is (0.673, 36.630). Taking reciprocals, this would suggest (0.027, 1.486) as plausible values for π_2/π_1, but the HPD 95% interval is (0.000, 0.851). The inference then depends on which group we identify as Group 1 and which we identify as Group 2! Because of this, we prefer EQT intervals for nonlinear functions of parameters.

When you can specify the posterior distribution, the HPD interval is also available in R with the **hpd** function of the **TeachingDemos** package. The **LearnBayes** package is a collection of functions helpful in learning the Bayesian approach to statistical inference. Albert (2009) is a related excellent introduction to applied Bayesian analysis and computations.

A.5 Chapter 5: R for Significance Testing

A.5.1 Bayes Factors and a Bayesian t Test

In a Bayesian framework, the *Bayes factor* (BF) expresses the change in our relative belief about two hypotheses after we have observed the data. Let $P(H)$ and $P(H \mid y)$ denote the prior and posterior probabilities for a hypothesis H. The BF in favor of the alternative hypothesis is

$$BF_{10}(y) = \frac{P(H_a \mid y)/P(H_0 \mid y)}{P(H_a)/P(H_0)} .$$

The following scale summarizes the BF strength of evidence against H_0:

$BF_{10}(y)$	Evidence against H_0
1–3	negligible
3–20	positive
20–150	strong
> 150	very strong

For comparing two means for a normal model with common variance, an alternative to the Bayesian analysis presented in Section 5.3.4 uses Bayes factors. We reparameterize by expressing the means as deviations from a common mean μ under H_0. Letting $\delta = (\mu_1 - \mu_2)/\sigma$ denote the standardized effect size, we set $\mu_1 = \mu + (\sigma\delta)/2$ and $\mu_2 = \mu - (\sigma\delta)/2$ and test $H_0: \delta = 0$ against $H_a: \delta \neq 0$. We express the prior distribution as $\pi_0(\mu, \sigma)$ under H_0 and $\pi_0(\mu, \sigma)\pi(\delta)$ under H_a. A relatively uninformative version takes $\pi_0(\mu, \sigma) = \pi_0(\mu)\pi_0(\sigma)$ with improper priors $\pi_0(\mu) = 1$ and $\pi_0(\sigma) \propto \sigma^{-1}$ for $\sigma > 0$ and $\pi(\delta)$ either normal or a version of the Cauchy that permits nonzero median.

The BayesFactor package can perform such a Bayesian t test. We illustrate for the example of Sections 5.3.2 and 5.3.5, comparing cognitive behavioral and control therapies for anorexia, using the default Cauchy prior for δ:

```
> y1 <- Anor$after[Anor$therapy=="cb"] - Anor$before[Anor$therapy=="cb"]
> y2 <- Anor$after[Anor$therapy=="c"] - Anor$before[Anor$therapy=="c"]
> t.anor <- t.test(y1, y2, var.equal=TRUE)
> t.anor
t = 1.676, df = 53, p-value = 0.09963 # classical t test
> library(BayesFactor)
> ttest.tstat(t = t.anor$statistic, n1 = length(y1), n2 = length(y2), simple = TRUE)
       B10 # Bayes factor
 0.8630774
> ttestBF(x = y1, y = y2) # output not shown
   # Sample from corresponding posterior distribution:
> samples = ttestBF(x = y1, y = y2, paired=FALSE,
+                    posterior = TRUE, iterations = 100000)
> quantile(samples[,"delta"], c(0.025, 0.975))
     2.5%    97.5% # posterior interval for standardized effect size
  -0.1086   0.8945
> mean(samples[,"delta"] < 0) # mean of indicator of negative values
[1] 0.0644                      # yields posterior P(delta < 0)
> densplot(samples[,"delta"]) # produces figure shown next
```

The estimated Bayes factor of $BF_{10}(y) = 0.86$ shows only weak evidence against H_0. The 95% posterior interval for the standardized effect difference δ is $(-0.11, 0.89)$. Although some plausible values for δ are negative, the posterior probability of a negative value is only 0.064. (The classical one-sided P-value is $0.0996/2 = 0.05$.) Figure A.12 plots the posterior density of δ.

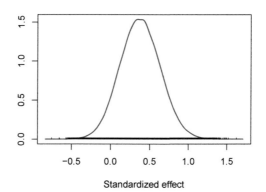

FIGURE A.12 Simulated posterior *pdf* for standardized effect size δ for comparing the *cb* and *control* groups of anorexia patients.

The BEST package provides another Bayesian alternative to the t test, not based on the Bayes Factor. The R Appendix at the book's website shows details.

A.5.2   Simulating the Exact Distribution of the Likelihood-Ratio Statistic

Section 5.7 introduced likelihood-ratio tests, for which the test statistic $2\log(\ell_1/\ell_0) = 2(L_1 - L_0)$ has an approximate chi-squared distribution with $df = 1$, for large n. Under H_0, it is often possible to simulate the true sampling distribution of the test statistic, so the chi-squared approximation is not needed.

We illustrate for the likelihood-ratio test of H_0: $\mu = \mu_0$ for the Poisson distribution. You can verify that the test statistic equals $2n[(\mu_0 - \hat{\mu}) - \hat{\mu}\log(\mu_0/\hat{\mu})]$, where $\hat{\mu} = \bar{y}$ is the ML estimate of μ under H_a. The following code simulates the exact distribution and compares it to the χ_1^2 distribution. We use a relatively small sample size of $n = 25$, when $\mu_0 = 5$, with $B = 100{,}000$ Monte Carlo simulations:

```
> LRT <- function(n, mu0, mu.hat){ # Poisson likelihood-ratio (LR) test statistic
            2*n*((mu0 - mu.hat) - mu.hat*log(mu0/mu.hat))}
  # Function returning vector of B values of LR test statistic
  #    for the B simulated Poisson(mu0) samples of size n:
> simstat <- function(B, n, mu0){ y <- rep(-1,B) # simulating Poisson
            for (i in 1:B){x <- rpois(n, mu0) # samples and applying
                    ML <- mean(x)       # LRT function to each
                    y[i] <- LRT(n, mu0, ML)}
            return(y) }
> n <- 25; mu0 <- 5; B <- 100000 # B = number of Monte Carlo samples
> stat <- simstat(B, n, mu0)
> hist(stat, prob=TRUE, border="blue", breaks="Scott")
> fchi2 <- function(x) {dchisq(x, 1)}
> curve(fchi2, from=0, to=max(stat), add=TRUE, col="red4",lwd=2)
> quantile(stat,probs=c(0.8,0.9,0.95,0.99)) # simulated exact quantiles
      80%    90%    95%    99%
   1.6301 2.7262 3.7440 6.6845
> qchisq(c(0.8, 0.9, 0.95, 0.99), 1) # chi-squared quantiles for df=1
[1] 1.6424 2.7055 3.8415 6.6349
```

The simulated quantiles of the exact sampling distribution are close to the χ_1^2 quantiles. Figure A.13 is a histogram of the 100,000 values of the likelihood-ratio test statistic and the χ_1^2 pdf. The approximation seems fairly good, even though n is relatively small.

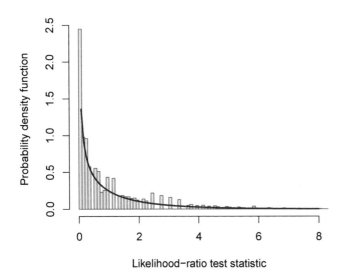

FIGURE A.13 Histogram of 100,000 values of likelihood-ratio test statistic and the χ_1^2 pdf, for random sampling from a Poisson distribution with $\mu_0 = 5$ and $n = 25$.

A.5.3 Nonparametric Statistics: Permutation Test and Wilcoxon Test

You can conduct the permutation test comparing means or medians of two groups in R using a function in the EnvStats package, as shown in Section 5.8.2. However, it uses the exact distribution only when $n_1 + n_2 \le 10$, and otherwise uses simulation. Here is an R package and function that can test the hypothesis of identical distributions against an alternative in which the means differ or one is larger than the other, using the exact permutation distribution:

```
> library(coin) # "coin = conditional inference" uses survival package
> time <- c(114, 203, 217, 254, 256, 284, 296, 4, 7, 24, 25, 48, 71, 294)
> group <- factor(rep(c(1,2), each=7))
> oneway_test(time ~ group, alt="greater", distribution="exact")
        Exact Two-Sample Fisher-PitmanPermutation Test
            p-value = 0.003788
```

An issue in nonparametric statistical inference based on ranks is the treatment of observations of equal rank (*ties*). The wilcox.test function used in Section 5.8.3 does not provide options for this. The coin package handles ties for a variety of measures for comparing groups and offers asymptotic, exact, and Monte Carlo approximations for exact approaches. The groups are defined as a factor. The R Appendix at the book's website shows how to use it for the Wilcoxon test.

A.6   Chapter 6: R for Linear Models

A.6.1   Linear Models with the lm Function

Symbols that can be used in the lm formula argument for linear models include

- x1:x2, for an interaction between x1 and x2

- x1*x2, which expands to x1 + x2 + x1:x2

- lm(y ~ 1) to fit the null model

- lm(y ~ -1 + x) to fit the model with explanatory variable x but no y-intercept

Functions available for displaying components of an lm object, following a command such as fit <- lm(y ~ x1 + x2 + x3), include

- summary(fit): displays a summary of results

- coef(fit): vector of model parameter estimates (coefficients)

- confint(fit): t confidence intervals for model parameters (default 95%)

- fitted.values(fit): fitted mean response values

- residuals(fit): residuals (observed – fitted)

- predict(fit, newdata=): predicted responses for new data

- plot(fit): diagnostic plots (discussed next)

A.6.2   Diagnostic Plots for Linear Models

Section 6.4.2 modeled Y = mental impairment, which has $\bar{y} = 27.30$ and $s_y = 5.46$, with explanatory variables life events and SES. For a linear model fit, the plot function can display several diagnostics:

```
> Mental <- read.table("http://stat4ds.rwth-aachen.de/data/Mental.dat", header=TRUE)
> fit <- lm(impair ~ life + ses, data=Mental)
> summary(fit)
              Estimate  Std. Error  t value  Pr(>|t|)
(Intercept)    28.2298     2.1742    12.984  2.38e-15
life            0.1033     0.0325     3.177   0.00300
ses            -0.0975     0.0291    -3.351   0.00186
-
> layout(matrix(1:4, 2, 2))   # multiple plots in 2x2 matrix layout
> plot(fit, which=c(1,2,4,5)) # diagnostic plots shown in figure
```

Figure A.14 shows four of the available diagnostic plots. These help us check the model assumptions that $E(Y)$ follows the linear model form and that Y has a normal distribution about $E(Y)$ with constant variance σ^2. The first display plots the residuals $\{y_i - \hat{\mu}_i\}$ against the fitted values $\{\hat{\mu}_i\}$. If the linear trend holds for $E(Y)$ and the conditional variance of Y is truly constant, these should fluctuate in a random manner, with similar variability throughout. With only 40 observations, the danger is over-interpreting, but this plot does not show any obvious abnormality. Observation 40 stands out as a relatively large residual, with observed y more than 10 higher than the fitted value. The residuals can also be plotted

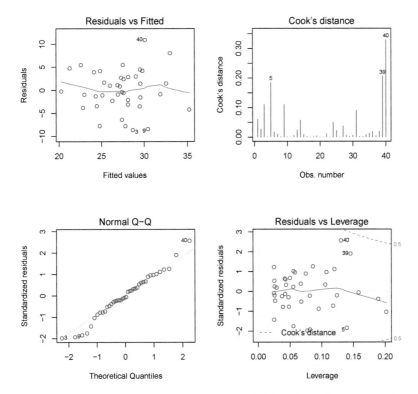

FIGURE A.14 Diagnostic plots for the linear model fitted to the `Mental` data file.

against each explanatory variable. Such a plot can reveal possible nonlinearity in an effect, such as when the residuals exhibit a U-shaped pattern. They can also highlight nonconstant variance, such as a fan-shaped pattern in which the residuals are markedly more spread out as the values of an explanatory variable increase.

Figure A.14 also shows Cook's distance values. From Section 6.2.8, a large Cook's distance highlights an observation that may be influential, because of having a relatively large residual and leverage. In this display, cases 5, 39 and 40 stand out. The plot of the residuals versus the leverage highlight these observations. In this plot, observations fall outside red dashed lines if their Cook's distance exceeds 0.5, which identifies them as potentially influential. Here, no observation has that large a Cook's distance, but when observation 40 is removed from the data file, the estimated life events effect weakens somewhat.

The figure also shows the normal quantile (Q-Q) plot. Introduced in Section A.2.2, this enables us to check the normal assumption for the conditional distribution of mental impairment that is the basis for using the t distribution in statistical inference, including prediction intervals. The assumption seems reasonable, as the trend in this Q-Q plot is not far from the straight line expected with normality.

A.6.3 Plots for Regression Bands and Posterior Distributions

In plots such as Figure 6.8 that show the confidence interval (6.8) for $E(Y)$ through lower and upper curves, the confidence levels are *pointwise*, applying at each point x_0 for x rather than for the entire set. With a single explanatory variable, confidence bands that apply simultaneously over the entire interval of x_0 values of interest are

$$(\hat{\beta}_0 + \hat{\beta}_1 x_0) \pm s\sqrt{2F_{1-\alpha;2,n-2}}\sqrt{\frac{1}{n} + \frac{(x_0 - \bar{x})^2}{\sum_{i=1}^{n}(x_i - \bar{x})^2}}$$

where $F_{1-\alpha;2,n-2}$ is the $(1 - \alpha)$ quantile of an $F_{2,n-2}$ distribution. The R Appendix at the book's website shows how to plot the bands using the `ggplot` function in the `tidyverse` package.

A key issue in Bayesian fitting of linear models with MCMC methods is the convergence of the Markov chain to the posterior distribution. With the `MCMCregress` function in the `MCMCpack` package, the reported time-series SE summarizes the simulation error by accounting for the positive correlation between successive values in the chain. Other diagnostics, beyond our scope, are available in the `coda` package. With `MCMCpack`, we can plot a posterior *pdf* using the `densplot` command. We show this next for the life events effect β_1 (the 2nd model parameter) in the Bayesian fitting of the linear model for mental impairment that used improper prior distributions for $\{\beta_j\}$ (Section 6.6.2):

```
> library(MCMCpack)
> fit.bayes <- MCMCregress(impair ~ life + ses, mcmc=5000000,
+              b0=0, B0=10^(-10), c0=10^(-10), d0=10^(-10), data=Mental)
> densplot(fit.bayes[,2], xlab="Life events effect", ylab="Posterior pdf")
```

Figure A.15 shows the plot. For this effect, the posterior mean was 0.103, with a standard error of 0.033.

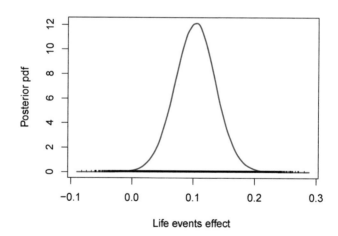

FIGURE A.15 Posterior *pdf* for the life events effect β_1 on mental impairment, in the linear model fitted to the `Mental` data file.

Bayesian fitting of linear models can also use the improper prior $f(\sigma^2) \propto 1/\sigma^2$ for $\sigma^2 > 0$ that, together with improper uniform priors over the real line for the regression parameters, yields posterior results that accord with classical inference. The R Appendix at the book's website shows details.

A.7 Chapter 7: R for Generalized Linear Models

A.7.1 The `glm` Function

The `glm` function in R for fitting generalized linear models has many optional arguments and saved components, such as those mentioned in Section A.6.1 for the `lm` function. For a saved object from fitting a model, say called `fit`, typing `names(fit)` yields an overview of what is saved for the object, including characteristics such as the deviance, AIC, coefficients, fitted values, converged, and residuals. For instance, the command `fit$converged` asks whether the Fisher scoring fitting algorithm converged. Useful follow-up functions include `confint` for profile likelihood confidence intervals.

Included in the output is the number of iterations needed for the Fisher scoring algorithm to converge, with a default maximum of 25. Normally this is small, but it may be large (e.g., 17 for the endometrial cancer example in Section 7.3.2) or not even converge when some ML estimates are infinite or do not exist. You can increase the maximum number of iterations, such as with the argument `maxit = 50` in the `glm` function, but convergence may still fail. In that case, you should not trust estimates shown in the output.

A.7.2 Plotting a Logistic Regression Model Fit

The following code[8] shows how to plot the fit of a logistic regression model with a single quantitative explanatory variable, illustrating with the Section 7.2.3 example of a dose-response study for flour beetles:

```
> Beetles <- read.table("http://stat4ds.rwth-aachen.de/data/Beetles_ungrouped.dat",
+   header=TRUE)
> fit <- glm(y ~ x, family = binomial(link=logit), data=Beetles)
> prob.fit <- function(z){
+           exp(fit$coef[1]+ fit$coef[2]*z)/(1+exp(fit$coef[1]+ fit$coef[2]*z))
+           }
> plot(prob.fit, from=min(Beetles$x), to=max(Beetles$x),
+       xlab="x", ylab="Estimated P(death)", col="dodgerblue4", lwd=2)
> x0 <- mean(Beetles$x); y0 <- prob.fit(mean(Beetles$x))
> points(x0, y0, pch=15, col='red') # marks estimated P(Y=1) at mean of x
```

Figure A.16 shows the plot, with a point added to show $\hat{P}(Y = 1 \mid X = \bar{x})$.

A.7.3 Model Selection for GLMs

For a particular data set, how do we select a model? For inference, we can compare two nested GLMs using their deviance difference (Section 7.1.5). To approximate well the relation in the population, we can use a model having relatively small value of AIC or BIC (Section 7.1.6). With many explanatory variables, it is not feasible to fit all possible models. It is standard to consider only *hierarchical models*, which means that if a model includes an interaction term, it should also contain the main effect terms that go into that interaction. One approach finds the best model with a certain number of explanatory variables according to a criterion such as adjusted R-squared. In R, the `regsubsets` function in the `leaps` package can do this.

---

[8]The `prob.fit` function is needed to find probability estimates for x-values other than those in the data set, such as the mean of x.

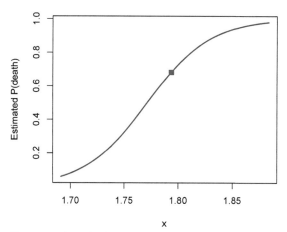

FIGURE A.16 Estimated probability of death for flour beetles as a function of dosage x of gaseous carbon disulfide, for `Beetles` data file.

Alternatively, algorithms exist that select explanatory variables, or delete them, in a stepwise manner. *Backward elimination* begins with a complex model and sequentially removes terms. One version uses AIC, at a particular stage removing the term for which AIC decreases the most, and stopping the process when it no longer decreases. An alternative, *forward selection*, starts with the null model and adds terms sequentially until further additions do not improve the fit. Some statisticians prefer backward elimination, feeling it safer to delete terms from an overly complex model than to add terms to an overly simple one. In exploratory studies, such a process can be informative when used cautiously, but it need not yield a meaningful model and has no theoretical basis. You should regard its results with skepticism. For the final model suggested by a particular selection procedure, any inferences conducted with it are highly approximate. In particular, P-values are likely to appear smaller than they should be and confidence intervals are likely to be too narrow, because the model was chosen that most closely reflects the data, in some sense. The inferences are more believable if performed for that model with a new set of data or using cross-validation. Also, with large n, the process may yield an overly complex model, such as containing interaction terms that are statistically significant but not practically significant. In R, the `step` function provides stepwise model selection procedures that apply on `lm` and `glm` objects. By default it compares AIC values in working forwards and backwards.

We illustrate for the data on house selling prices introduced in Exercise 6.15 and analyzed with a linear model and a gamma GLM in Section 7.1.3. In Section 7.1.3 we observed that the variability in selling prices increases noticeably as the mean selling price increases, so we'll use gamma GLMs. To predict selling prices (in thousands of dollars), we begin with all five explanatory variables (size of house in square feet, annual property tax bill in dollars, number of bedrooms, number of bathrooms, and whether the house is new) and their ten two-way interaction terms as potential explanatory variables. The initial model has AIC = 1087.85. After several backward steps this reduces to 1077.31:

```
> Houses <- read.table("http://stat4ds.rwth-aachen.de/data/Houses.dat", header=TRUE)
> step(glm(price ~ (size+taxes+new+bedrooms+baths)^2, family=Gamma(link=identity),
+          data=Houses))
Start:  AIC=1087.85
... # several steps not shown here
Step:  AIC=1077.31 # final model chosen with backward elimination
```

```
price ~ size+taxes+new+bedrooms+baths+size:new+size:baths+taxes:new+bedrooms:baths
> fit <- glm(formula = price ~ size+taxes+new+bedrooms+bath + size:new+size:baths
+                    + taxes:new+bedrooms:baths, family=Gamma(link=identity), data=Houses)
> summary(fit)
                  Estimate  Std. Error  t value  Pr(>|t|)
(Intercept)      8.486e+01   5.202e+01    1.631  0.106311
size             1.422e-01   4.153e-02    3.424  0.000932
taxes            6.030e-02   7.369e-03    8.183  1.71e-12
new             -1.397e+02   7.491e+01   -1.865  0.065465
bedrooms        -7.381e+01   2.737e+01   -2.697  0.008358
baths           -1.673e+01   3.178e+01   -0.526  0.600004
size:new         2.520e-01   8.321e-02    3.028  0.003209
size:baths      -3.601e-02   1.863e-02   -1.933  0.056394
taxes:new       -1.130e-01   5.332e-02   -2.118  0.036902
bedrooms:baths   2.800e+01   1.478e+01    1.894  0.061392
---
(Dispersion parameter for Gamma family taken to be 0.0618078)
    Null deviance: 31.9401  on 99  degrees of freedom
Residual deviance:  5.6313  on 90  degrees of freedom
AIC: 1077.3
```

The model chosen by backward elimination is still quite complex, having four interaction terms. Only a slightly higher AIC value (1080.7) results from taking out all interactions except the one between size and whether the house is new, which is by far the most significant among the interaction terms. Removing also the baths term gives the model selected based on the BIC criterion, implemented in the **step** function by the additional argument `k=log(n)`:

```
> n <- nrow(Houses)       # sample size
> step(glm(price ~ (size+taxes+new+bedrooms+baths)^2, family=Gamma(link=identity),
+           data=Houses), k=log(n))    # output not shown
```

The interpretation is much simpler, as the effects of taxes and bedrooms are main effects solely. Here is the R code:

```
> fit2 <- glm(price ~ size + taxes + new + bedrooms + size:new,
+              family = Gamma(link=identity), data=Houses)
> summary(fit2)
                  Estimate  Std. Error  t value  Pr(>|t|)
(Intercept)      3.923e+01   2.024e+01    1.938    0.0556
size             8.588e-02   1.837e-02    4.675  9.80e-06  # effect 0.086 for old homes
taxes            5.776e-02   7.563e-03    7.638  1.82e-11
new             -1.273e+02   7.557e+01   -1.685    0.0954
bedrooms        -2.135e+01   9.432e+00   -2.263    0.0259
size:new         8.956e-02   4.310e-02    2.078    0.0404  # size effect 0.086 + 0.090 for
---                                                         # new homes
(Dispersion parameter for Gamma family taken to be 0.06509439)
    Null deviance: 31.9401  on 99  degrees of freedom
Residual deviance:  6.3478  on 94  degrees of freedom
AIC: 1081.4
```

The estimated effect on selling price of a square-foot increase in size, adjusting for the other predictors, is 0.086 (i.e., $86) for older homes and (0.086 + 0.090) = 0.176 (i.e., $176) for newer homes.

Apart from the AIC not being much higher, how do we know that the fit of the simpler model is essentially as good in practical terms? A measure of how well the model predicts is given by the *correlation* between the observed response variable and the fitted values for the model. For a linear model, this is the *multiple correlation* (Section 6.3.3). For these data, the multiple correlation is 0.918 for the more complex model and 0.904 for the simpler one, very nearly as high, and this is without adjusting for the more complex model having many more terms:

```
> cor(Houses$price, fitted(fit)); cor(Houses$price, fitted(fit2))
[1] 0.9179869 # multiple correlation analog for model chosen by backward elimination
[1] 0.9037955 # multiple correlation analog for model with only size:new interaction
```

You can check that further simplification is also possible without much change in AIC or the multiple correlation. For instance, the simpler model yet that removes the bedrooms predictor has a multiple correlation of 0.903.

A.7.4 Correlated Responses: Marginal, Random Effects, and Transitional Models

Fitting of generalized linear models, like other methods presented in this book, assumes *independent* observations from the population of interest. Many studies observe the response variable for each subject repeatedly, at several times or under various conditions. Then, the repeated observations on a subject are typically positively correlated. A study that repeatedly observes the same variables for the same subjects over time is called a ***longitudinal study***. Such studies are common in health-related applications, such as when a physician evaluates patients at regular time intervals regarding whether a drug treatment is successful. In longitudinal studies, statistical analyses should take correlation of repeated observations into account. Analyses that ignore the correlation can have badly biased standard error estimators. GLMs can be generalized so that, while maintaining the capability to assume various probability distributions for the response variable and employ various link functions, model-fitting permits observations to be correlated. We next briefly describe the three basic types of models for doing this.

For subject i, let y_{it} be the observation at time $t = 1, \ldots, T$, which is a realization of a random variable Y_{it} with $\mu_{it} = E(Y_{it})$. Then, $\boldsymbol{Y}_i = (Y_{i1}, Y_{i2}, \ldots, Y_{iT})$ is a multivariate random variable. The first type of model specifies a GLM for each marginal distribution,

$$g(\mu_{it}) = \beta_{0t} + \beta_{1t}x_{i1t} + \cdots + \beta_{pt}x_{ipt}, \quad i = 1, 2, \ldots, n.$$

In special cases, values of explanatory variables and some effects may be the same for each t. For continuous responses, it is common to assume a multivariate normal distribution for $\boldsymbol{Y}_i$ to obtain a likelihood function that also has correlation parameters to account for within-subject responses being correlated. The model is fitted simultaneously for all t. For discrete responses, simple multivariate parametric families containing correlation parameters do not exist. A popular approach fits the model by solving *generalized estimating equations* (GEE) that resemble likelihood equations but without constructing a likelihood function. The equations utilize the analyst's naive guess about the form of the actual correlation structure for the repeated responses, such as the *exchangeable* structure by which responses for each pair of times have the same correlation, while using the empirical covariances for the sample data to help generate standard errors that are robust to violations of that naive guess. In this so-called ***marginal modeling*** approach, some software refers to the standard errors of the model parameter estimates as *sandwich* standard errors, because the covariance matrix on which they are based uses a formula that sandwiches the empirical information between two matrices that relate to the native guess about the correlation structure.

The second type of model uses ***random effects*** as a mechanism for generating positive correlations for the pairs of repeated responses. In one simple case, the model for Y_{it} has form

$$g(\mu_{it}) = u_i + \beta_{0t} + \beta_{1t}x_{i1t} + \cdots + \beta_{pt}x_{ipt}$$

The random effect u_i, called a *random intercept*, is an unobserved random variable that is typically assumed to have a $N(0, \sigma^2)$ distribution for unknown σ. A subject i with large positive (negative) u_i tends to have relatively high (low) values for each of $(y_{i1}, y_{i2}, \ldots, y_{iT})$, relative to other subjects with the same values of the explanatory variables. This tendency accentuates as σ increases, generating stronger correlations. The model is called a ***generalized linear mixed model*** because it has a mixture of random effects (the $\{u_i\}$ terms) and fixed effects (the β parameter coefficients of the explanatory variables). Such models can contain more than one random effect, such as ***multilevel models*** that have a hierarchical structure of random effects. For instance, a study of factors that affect student performance might measure each student's exam scores $(y_{i1}, y_{i2}, \ldots, y_{iT})$ on a battery of T exams. Students are nested within schools, and the model could incorporate a random effect for variability among students and another random effect for variability among schools.

In some applications, it can be informative to use previously observed responses as explanatory variables in modeling response t. The model can focus on the dependence of Y_{it} on $\{y_{i1}, y_{i2}, \ldots, y_{i,t-1}\}$ as well as the ordinary explanatory variables. Models that include past observations as explanatory variables are called ***transitional models***.

The book by Fitzmaurice et al. (2011) presents a good overview of these three main methods for modeling longitudinal data. An example showing how to use R to fit a marginal model and a generalized linear mixed model with random effects is in the website R Appendix for this book.

A.7.5 Modeling Time Series

When observations occur for a single entity over time, such as recording daily sales of a business over some period of time weekly, the observed data form a sequence $\{y_t\}$ that is a realization of a random process $\{Y_t\}$ called a *time series*. In such applications, prediction of future observations is sometimes more important than estimating and interpreting effects of explanatory variables. A ***time series model*** is a transitional model that often has as its primary goal predicting future responses based on responses observed so far, such as in economic projections.

Here, we briefly discuss a simple time series model for a quantitative response, to show a mechanism that yields observations that are correlated but in which those farther apart in time are less strongly correlated. The model assumes that $\{Y_1, Y_2, \ldots\}$ are *stationary*, which means that $E(Y_t)$, $\text{var}(Y_t)$, and $\rho_s = \text{corr}(Y_t, Y_{t+s})$ for $s = 1, 2, \ldots$ do not vary over time (t). The correlation ρ_s between observations s units apart in time is called the s-order *autocorrelation*, and the values $(\rho_1, \rho_2, \rho_3, \ldots)$ are called the *autocorrelation function*. The sequence of observations

$$Y_t - \mu = \phi(y_{t-1} - \mu) + \epsilon_t, \quad t = 1, 2, 3, \ldots,$$

where $|\phi| < 1$ and $\epsilon_t \sim N(0, \sigma^2)$ is independent of $\{Y_1, \ldots, Y_{t-1}\}$, is called an ***autoregressive process***. The expected deviation from the mean at time t is proportional to the previous deviation. This model satisfies $\rho_s = \phi^s$, with autocorrelation exponentially decreasing as the distance s between times increases. The process is a *Markov chain* (Section 2.6.7), because the distribution of $(Y_t \mid y_1, \ldots, y_{t-1})$ is the same as the distribution of $(Y_t \mid y_{t-1})$. In particular, $\text{corr}(Y_t, Y_{t+1}) = \phi$ but $\text{corr}(Y_t, Y_{t+2} \mid Y_{t+1}) = 0$.

To illustrate the use of R to generate an autoregressive process and to fit an autoregressive model and predict future observations, we start at $y_1 = 100$ and generate 200 observations with $\mu = 100$, $\phi = 0.90$, and $\sigma = 10$:

```
> y <- rep(0, 200)
> y[1] <- 100
```

```
> for (t in 2:200){
+                y[t] <- 100 + 0.90*(y[t-1] - 100) + rnorm(1,0,10)
+                }
> plot(y, xlim=c(0,210))              # plots the time index t against y[t]
> acf(y, lag.max=10, plot=FALSE)      # autocorrelation function
Autocorrelations of series 'y', by lag
   0     1     2     3     4     5     6     7     8     9    10
1.000 0.917 0.856 0.779 0.706 0.644 0.574 0.517 0.437 0.355 0.290
> fit <- ar(y, order.max = 1, method = c("mle")) # fit autoregressive model by ML
> fit$ar
[1] 0.9180788 # ML estimate of phi parameter in model
> pred10 <- predict(fit, n.ahead=10)                # predict next 10 observations on y
> pred10$pred # predicted y for next 10 observations
Start = 201   End = 210
[1] 66.146 68.350 70.374 72.231 73.937 75.503 76.940  78.260 79.472 80.58 4
> pred10$se   # standard errors of predicted values
[1] 10.275 13.949 16.419 18.243 19.649 20.761 21.653  22.378 22.971 23.459
points(201:210, pred10$pred, col="red") # add on plot next 10 predicted y values
```

Figure A.17 shows the time series. Observations that are close together in time tend to be quite close in value. The plot looks greatly different than if the observations were generated independently, which results for the special case of the model with $\phi = 0$. After generating the data, we use the `acf` function in R to find the sample autocorrelation function, relating to times t and $t + s$ with lag s between 1 and 10. The first-order sample autocorrelation ($s = 1$) is 0.921, and the values are weaker as the lag s increases. We then fit the autoregressive model with the `ar` function in R. The ML estimate of $\phi = 0.90$ is $\hat{\phi} = 0.918$. One can use the fit of the model to generate predictions of future observations as well as standard errors to reflect the precision of those predictions. Predicting ahead the next 10 observations, the R output shows that the predictions tend toward $\mu = 100$ but with standard error that increases as we look farther into the future. Figure A.17 also shows, in red, the predictions for the next 10 observations.

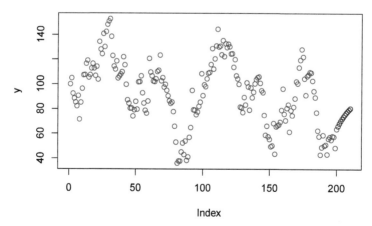

FIGURE A.17 Observations from autoregressive time series process, with predicted values of next 10 observations shown in red.

A more general autoregressive model, having order p instead of 1, is

$$Y_t - \mu = \sum_{j=1}^{p} \phi_j (y_{t-j} - \mu) + \epsilon_t, \quad t = 1, 2. \ldots$$

It uses the p observations before time t in the linear predictor. This process is a higher-order Markov chain, in which Y_t and $Y_{t-(p+1)}$ are conditionally independent, given the observations in between those two times. An alternative time series model, called a ***moving average*** model of order p, has form

$$Y_t - \mu = \sum_{j=1}^{p} \lambda_j \epsilon_{t-j} + \epsilon_t, \quad t = 1, 2, \ldots.$$

It has $\rho_s = 0$ for $s > p$, so it is appropriate if the sample autocorrelations drop off sharply after lag p. A more general *ARMA* model, more difficult for interpretation but potentially useful for prediction, can include both autoregressive and moving average terms. The models generalize also to include explanatory variables other than past observations of the response variable and to allow observations at irregular time intervals. See Brockwell and Davis (2016) and Cryer and Chan (2008) for introductions to time series modeling.

A.8 Chapter 8: R for Classification and Clustering

A.8.1 Visualization of Linear Discriminant Analysis Results

For linear discriminant analysis, the `ggplot2` package offers options to visualize the data and results. The following code illustrates, for the example using the `Crabs` data file to predict whether a female horseshoe crab has satellites (Section 8.1.2). That section notes that it is sufficient to use weight or carapace width together with color as explanatory variables. Here, we use width and color:

```
Crabs <- read.table("http://stat4ds.rwth-aachen.de/data/Crabs.dat", header=TRUE)
> library(MASS)
> fit.lda <- lda(y ~ width + color,data=Crabs) # linear discriminant analysis
> prob1 <- predict(fit.lda)$posterior[,2]        # estimated P(Y=1)
> predY <- predict(fit.lda)$class                # predicted class of Y
> library(ggplot2)
> Crabs$y <- factor(Crabs$y) # need factor response variable for ggplot2
> qplot(width, color, data=Crabs, col=y)         # first figure below
> qplot(width, color, data=Crabs, col=predY)     # second figure
> Crabs$pred.right = predY == Crabs$y
> round(mean(Crabs$pred.right),3)                # prediction accuracy
[1] 0.728                                         # without cross validation
> qplot(width, color, data=Crabs, col=pred.right) # third figure
```

Figure A.18 shows the plots. The first one shows the observed y values, at the various width and color values. The second plot shows the predicted responses. At each color, the crabs with greater widths were predicted to have $y = 1$, with the boundary for the predictions moving to higher width values as color darkness increases. The third plot identifies the crabs that were misclassified. Another possible plot, shown in the R Appendix at the book's website, shades the points according to their estimated probabilities.

A.8.2 Cross-Validation and Model Training

For classification methods, leave-one-out cross-validation (*loocv*) provides more realistic values for the probability of a correct classification. For penalized likelihood methods, Section 7.7.2 mentioned that the choice of tuning parameter λ can be based on k-fold cross-validation

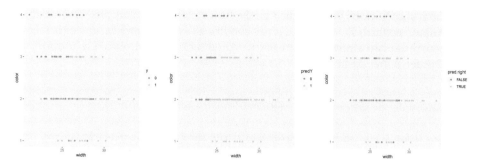

FIGURE A.18 Scatterplots of width and color values for linear discriminant analysis to predict y = whether a female horseshoe crabs has male satellites, showing (i) observed value of y, (ii) predicted value of y, (iii) misclassified observations

(k-fold *cv*). The *loocv* is the extreme case of k-fold *cv* for $k = n$. Increasing k, especially for large n, may be computationally difficult. In practice, the choice $k = 10$ is predominant, since it usually performs similarly to *loocv*.

Model training refers to randomly partitioning the data frame into a training sample (typically 70%–80% of the observations) and a test sample, fitting the model on the training sample, and checking the fit's accuracy when applied to the testing sample. Cross-validation is used for fitting the model, with 10-fold *cv* by default. The `caret` package for classification and regression training applies on models fitted in basic R packages such as `stats`, `MASS`, and `rpart`. One specifies the desired modeling function (`glm`, `lda`,...) in the `method=` argument of the `train` function. The `createDataPartition` function randomly partitions the data frame. We illustrate in the linear discriminant analysis context, for the horseshoe crabs example in Section 8.1.2, using 70% of the observations in the training sample:

```
> library(caret); library(ggplot2); library(MASS)
> Crabs$y <- factor(Crabs$y) # need factor response variable for ggplot2
> index = createDataPartition(y=Crabs$y, p=0.7, list=FALSE)
> train = Crabs[index,]  # training sample, 70% of observations
> test = Crabs[-index,]  # testing sample
> dim(train)
[1] 122   7 # 122 observations of 7 variables in training sample
> dim(test) # (8 variables if include pred.right in Crabs, as in above code)
[1] 51  7   # 51 observations of 7 variables in testing sample
> lda.fit = train(y ~ width + color, data=train, method="lda",
               trControl = trainControl(method = "cv", number=10))
> names(lda.fit) # lists what is saved under "lda.fit"; not shown
> predY.new = predict(lda.fit,test) # prediction for testing subsample
> table(predY.new, test$y)
predY.new  0  1 # output varies depending on training sample used
        0  5  2
        1 13 31
> round(mean(predY.new == test$y)*100, 2) # prediction accuracy
[1] 0.706
> qplot(width, color, data=test, col=y)          # first plot in Figure A.20
> test$pred.right = predY.new == test$y
> qplot(width,color, data=test, col=pred.right) # second plot in Figure A.20
```

Figure A.19 provides plots that are analogous to the first and third in Figure A.18, but now only for the 51 cases in the testing subsample. The first plot shows the actual y values and the second shows the misclassified observations.

Model training is an essential step with neural networks. The `keras` package (see Chollet and Allaire 2018) is useful for this method.

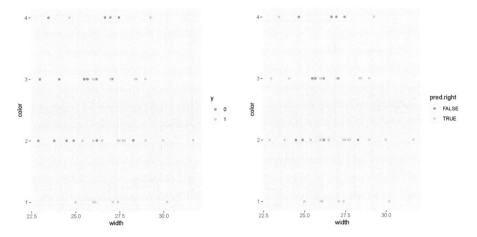

FIGURE A.19 Scatterplots of width and color values for horseshoe crabs in testing subsample, showing (i) observed value of y, (ii) misclassified observations.

A.8.3 Classification and Regression Trees

Section 8.1.4 discussed classification trees for binary response variable. The `rpart` and `tree` packages can also handle categorical response variables with multiple categories. For an example, see the R Appendix at the book's website.

The `rpart` and `tree` packages can also form trees when the response is quantitative, in which case the display is called a *regression tree*. The predicted value at a terminal node is the mean response for the subjects in the region of predictor values for that node. The site `https://cran.r-project.org/web/packages/rpart/vignettes/longintro.pdf` has useful examples of `rpart` for binary, multiple category, and quantitative responses.

A.8.4 Cluster Analysis with Quantitative Variables

Section 8.2 showed a hierarchical cluster analysis for binary variables, using the agglomerative clustering algorithm. An alternative clustering method, called *divisive hierarchical clustering*, applies in the opposite direction, starting with one cluster and splitting them until reaching a prespecified bound for the average dissimilarity. Methods for measuring the dissimilarity between clusters are called *linkage* methods. Section 8.2.3 used the average linkage.

For clustering when the variables are quantitative, the default dissimilarity measure for most software is *Euclidean distance*, which is a distance measure for multidimensional Euclidean space. For two observations $(x_1, \ldots, x_p)$ and $(y_1, \ldots, y_p)$ on p variables, this is $\sqrt{(x_1 - y_1)^2 + \cdots + (x_p - y_p)^2}$. We illustrate for the UN data file, using Euclidean distance and agglomerative clustering. Using the `agnes` function in the `cluster` package, we chose the linkage method (Ward distance) having the highest *agglomerative coefficient*, which is a measure of the strength of the clustering structure, values closer to 1 suggesting stronger structure. The R Appendix at the book's website shows code to produce the dendrogram in Figure A.20 and also shows a heatmap. The two-cluster solution seems to differentiate between economically-advanced Western nations and the other nations.

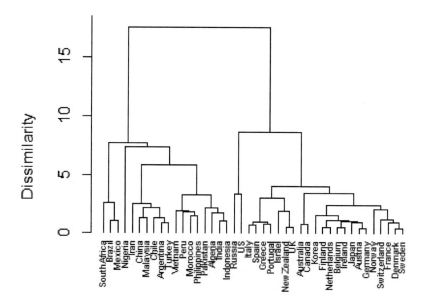

FIGURE A.20 Dendrogram for hierarchical clustering with the observations and variables in the UN data file.

Hierarchical clustering is not feasible for large data sets. For such cases, K-means clustering can estimate the optimal clustering for a prespecified number K of clusters. The `kmeans` function in the `cluster` package can do this. Clustering methods are also available in a modeling context. For example, *Gaussian mixture models* assume that k multivariate normal distributions generate the observations. Model-based clustering is available with the `mclust` package.

B

Using *Python* in *Statistical Science*

B.0 Basics of Python

This Appendix shows how to use the open source language **Python** for the examples for which this book's chapters show R code. The longer **Python** Appendix at the book's website shows additional code and many figures. We assume that the reader already has some familiarity with **Python**. For beginners, a variety of introductions are available on the Internet.[1] The code shown in this appendix uses version **Python 3.7**.

B.0.1 Python Preliminaries

Among *Python distributions*, especially handy is the open-source *Anaconda Individual Edition*.[2] We recommend running **Python** in an IDE (integrated development environment) such as *Spyder*, which is distributed with *Anaconda* and used in this Appendix. For the **Spyder** console, the screenshot in Figure B.1 illustrates some simple value assignments, computing, and the use of the **type** function. Code typed in the editor console can be run line-wise, or with a selection of lines, or as a whole script. The upper-right console lists the active variables, help, plots and list of files.

A wide variety of statistical functions and graphics are available in **Python** libraries. The following libraries are especially relevant for this book:

Library	Description
ipython	Interactive computing
mathplotlib	Tools for graphics and data visualization
NumPy	Numeric Python: operations for multidimensional arrays and linear algebra
pandas	Python data analysis library: creation of data frames and data manipulation
rp2	Python interface to R language: runs embedded R, providing access from Python
scipy	Scientific computing: algorithms, including statistical functions (scipy.stats) (http://scipy-lectures.org/intro)
seaborn	Statistical data visualization (based on matplotlib)
statistics	In base Python for simple descriptive statistics (https://docs.python.org/3/library/statistics.html)
statsmodels	Functions for statistical modeling and inference (https://www.statsmodels.org/stable/index.html)

This appendix shows the code as it appears in the IPython console, with the input/output (In [ ]:/Out [ ]:) indication, but merely showing ... : in place of repeated input

---

[1] Such as the documentation and tutorials at https://www.python.org and https://docs.python.org/3.7/tutorial/index.html

[2] See https://www.anaconda.com/products/individual and https://docs.anaconda.com/anaconda/user-guide.

DOI: 10.1201/9781003159834-B

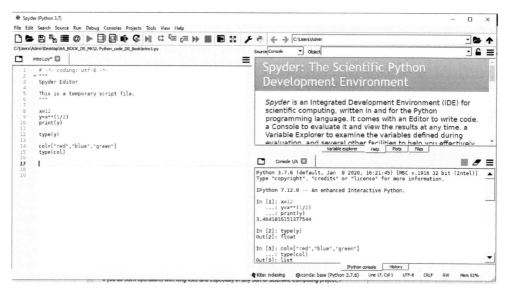

FIGURE B.1 Spyder console screenshot for **Python**.

indicators and with highly edited output. In **Python**, as in R, comments follow the # symbol. You should load needed libraries at the beginning of a session. For example, for dividing the entries of a vector a = [1,2,3,4] by a scalar (here 2), we use the **numpy** library, as shown in the following code:

```
In [1]: import numpy # use numpy library to compute with vectors
   ...: a = numpy.array([1,2,3,4]) # define a as an array
   ...: b = a/2
   ...: print(b)
[0.5 1.  1.5 2. ]
```

B.0.2   Data Structures and Data Input

Like R, **python** offers a variety of data structures, including the following:

- *Lists*: A list groups objects of the same type.

- *Tuples*: A tuple groups objects of different type.

- *Sets*: A set is an unordered collection of elements with no duplicate elements.

- *Dictionaries*: Dictionaries list unordered elements that are accessed by their position in the list, via indexing.

- *Arrays*: An array can consist of basic values—characters, integers, and floating point numbers.

- *Data frames*: A data frame is the convenient way to display a data file for statistical data analysis.

The first five are data structures of base **Python** while data frames apply in the **pandas** library. For a detailed description of options and examples, see Internet sites listed in the **Python** Appendix at the book's website.

Data files of various formats are easily read in **pandas** and commonly saved in CSV (comma-separated values) files. If the data separator is ',', a data file is read by `pd.read_csv('...')` with the name and location of the file within the quotes. Otherwise, the separator must be specified. For example, with data separated by spaces, such as those at the data website for this book, data files are read[3] by `pd.read_csv('...', sep='\s+')`.

B.1 Chapter 1: PYTHON for Descriptive Statistics

B.1.1 Random Number Generation

Here is how to implement the random number generation shown for R in Section 1.3.1:

```
In [1]: import random
   ...: randomlist = random.sample(range(1,60), 5) # randomly sample 5
   ...: print(randomlist)                          # integers from 1 to 60
[37, 31, 34, 3, 17]                                # without replacement
In [2]: import numpy as np
   ...: y = list(range(1, 60))
   ...: randomlist2 = np.random.choice(y, 5)       # sample with replacement
   ...: print(randomlist2)
[ 5 35  1 35 18]
```

Python can also randomly generate values from various distributions, such as shown in Sections B.1.5, B.2.1, and B.2.3.

B.1.2 Summary Statistics and Graphs for Quantitative Variables

This section shows how to use **Python** to find descriptive statistics for data analyzed in Chapter 1.

Descriptive statistics for carbon dioxide emissions

The following code reads the data file on per-capita carbon dioxide emissions for 31 European nations analyzed in Chapter 1 (starting in Section 1.4.1) and finds some descriptive statistics:

```
In [1]: import pandas as pd   # used to read data file
   ...: Carbon = pd.read_csv('http://stat4ds.rwth-aachen.de/data/
             Carbon.dat', sep='\s+') # values separator is a space
In [2]: Carbon            # prints the data file (not shown here)
In [3]: Carbon.shape      # dimensions of the array
Out[3]: (31, 2)           # (31 rows with 2 columns)
In [4]: Carbon.columns    # variables (columns) in the file
Out[4]: Index(['Nation', 'CO2'], dtype='object')
In [5]: Carbon.head()     # first 5 observations (starts numbering with 0)
Out[5]:
      Nation  CO2
0    Albania  2.0
1    Austria  6.9
2    Belgium  8.3
3     Bosnia  6.2
4   Bulgaria  5.9
In [6]: Carbon.tail ()    # last 5 observations (not shown here)
```

---

[3]To illustrate, see the example in Section B.1.2.

```
In [7]: Carbon.describe()    # n, mean, standard deviation, and five-number
Out[7]:                      # summary for numerical variables
            CO2
count   31.000000 # sample size n
mean     5.819355 # mean of observations in the data file
std      1.964929 # standard deviation
min      2.000000 # minimum value
25%      4.350000 # lower quartile (25th percentile)
50%      5.400000 # median (50th percentile)
75%      6.700000 # upper quartile (75th percentile)
max      9.900000 # maximum value
In [8]: Carbon['CO2'].mean()     # mean
Out[8]: 5.819354838709677
In [9]: Carbon['CO2'].std()      # standard deviation
Out[9]: 1.9649290665464592
In [10]: Carbon['CO2'].median() # median
Out[10]: 5.4
```

Next we construct[4] a histogram of CO2 with 8 bins of equal length. Select and run the four histogram commands together to produce the desired plot:

```
In [11]: import matplotlib.pyplot as plt
    ...: plt.hist(Carbon['CO2'], density=True, bins=8) # density=False
    ...: plt.ylabel('Proportion')                      # uses counts instead of
    ...: plt.xlabel('CO2')                              # proportions on y-axis
    ...: plt.title('Histogram of Carbon[CO2]')
```

A boxplot of CO2 (shown at the **Python** Appendix at the book's website) is derived by the following command:

```
In [12]: plt.boxplot(Carbon['CO2'], vert=False)        # at book's website Appendix
```

Side-by-side box plots for U.S. and Canadian murder rates

Section 1.4.5 showed side-by-side box plots to compare murder rates in the U.S. and Canada. Here is **Python** code for this figure, shown in Figure B.2, and for using the **groupby** command to report summary statistics by nation:

```
In [1]: import pandas as pd
   ...: import seaborn as sns
   ...: Crime = pd.read_csv('http://stat4ds.rwth-aachen.de/data/Murder2.dat', sep='\s+')
   ...: sns.boxplot(x='murder', y='nation', data=Crime, orient='h')
In [2]: Crime.groupby('nation')['murder'].describe()
Out[2]:
        count      mean       std  min   25%    50%    75%    max
nation
Canada   10.0  1.673000  1.184437  0.0  1.03  1.735  1.875   4.07
US       51.0  5.252941  3.725391  1.0  2.65  5.000  6.450  24.20
```

B.1.3   Descriptive Statistics for Bivariate Quantitative Data

For the example in Section 1.5.1 relating statewide suicide rates in the U.S. to the percentage of people who own guns, we show code to construct the scatter plot with the fitted regression line (shown at the **Python** Appendix at the book's website) and find the correlation and the linear regression parameter estimates:

---

[4]**Spyder** has the option of selecting whether graphs appear in a separate window (**%matplotlib qt**) or in the IPython console (**%matplotlib inline**). These commands have to be given directly in the IPython console.

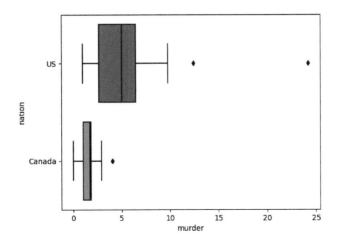

FIGURE B.2 Side-by-side box plots for U.S. and Canadian murder rates.

```
In [1]: import pandas as pd
   ...: import seaborn as sns
   ...: import matplotlib.pyplot as plt        # use for scatter plot
   ...: GS = pd.read_csv('http://stat4ds.rwth-aachen.de/data/Guns_Suicide.dat',
                         sep='\s+')
In [2]: GS.info()            # number of non-missing values per variable
 #   Column    Non-Null Count  Dtype
---  ------    --------------  -----
 0   state     51 non-null     object
 1   guns      51 non-null     float64
 2   suicide   51 non-null     float64

In [3]: GS.plot(kind='scatter', x='guns', y='suicide', color='blue', figsize=(10,7))
   ...: plt.xlabel('guns', size=14)
   ...: plt.ylabel('suicide', size=14)
In [4]: GS.corr()              # correlation matrix for pairs of
Out[4]:                        # variables in GS data file
           guns    suicide
guns     1.000000  0.738667 # corr. = 0.739 between guns and suicide
suicide  0.738667  1.000000

In [5]: import numpy as np  # scatter plot with linear regression line
   ...: coef = np.polyfit(GS['guns'], GS['suicide'], 1)
   ...: LR_fn = np.poly1d(coef)                 # LR_fn: returns fitted y values
   ...: fig = plt.figure(figsize=(10,7))        # submit next 4 lines together
   ...: plt.plot(GS['guns'],GS['suicide'],'o',GS['guns'],LR_fn(GS['guns']))
   ...: plt.xlabel('guns', size=14)
   ...: plt.ylabel('suicide', size=14)

In [6]: import statsmodels.formula.api as sm  # fit linear regression
   ...: mod = sm.ols(formula='suicide ~ guns', data=GS).fit()
   ...: print(mod.params)  # model parameter estimates
Intercept    7.390080
guns         0.193565       # slope estimate for effect of guns on suicide
```

The book's website shows further summary results of the model fitting.

B.1.4   Descriptive Statistics for Bivariate Categorical Data

We next show code for forming a contingency table and mosaic plot (shown at the Python Appendix at the book's website) for the Section 1.5.2 example of cross-classifying race and political party identification for data from a General Subject Survey:

```
In [1]: import numpy as np
   ...: import pandas as pd
   ...: import matplotlib as plt
   ...: PID = pd.read_csv('http://stat4ds.rwth-aachen.de/data/
                           PartyID.dat', sep='\s+')
   ...: PID_table = pd.crosstab(PID['race'], PID['id'], margins=False)
   ...: PID_table
Out[1]:
id       Democrat  Independent  Republican
race
black         281           65          30
other         124           77          52
white         633          272         704


In [2]: from scipy.stats.contingency import margins # find marginal
   ...: mr, mc = margins(PID_table)                  # distribution counts
   ...: print(mr)    # row marginal counts (output not shown)
   ...: print(mc)    # column marginal counts (output not shown)


In [3]: asarray = np.array(PID_table)/sum(np.array(PID_table))
   ...: probtable = pd.DataFrame(asarray, columns=['Democrat',
                                 'Independent','Republican'])
   ...: probtable.index=['black', 'white', 'other']
   ...: probtable   # joint probability table:
Out[3]:
       Democrat  Independent  Republican
black  0.270713     0.157005    0.038168
white  0.119461     0.185990    0.066158
other  0.609827     0.657005    0.895674


In [4]: asarray1 = np.array(PID_table)/mr
   ...: probtable1 = pd.DataFrame(asarray1, columns=['Democrat',
                                  'Independent','Republican'])
   ...: probtable1.index = ['black', 'white', 'other']
   ...: probtable1   # table with conditional probabilities within rows
Out[4]:
       Democrat  Independent  Republican
black  0.747340     0.172872    0.079787
white  0.490119     0.304348    0.205534
other  0.393412     0.169049    0.437539


In [5]: from statsmodels.graphics.mosaicplot import mosaic
   ...: fig, _ = mosaic(PID, index=['race', 'id'])    # mosaic plot
```

B.1.5   Simulating Samples from a Bell-Shaped Population

The simulation example in Section 1.5.3 took two random samples of size $n = 30$ each from a bell-shaped population[5] with a mean of 100 and a standard deviation of 16. The following code performs the simulation, finds sample means and standard deviations, and constructs histograms (shown at the Python Appendix at the book's website):

```
In [1]: import numpy as np
   ...: import matplotlib.pyplot as plt
```

---

[5]Specifically, the normal distribution introduced in Section 2.5.1

```
In [2]: mu, sigma = 100, 16        # specify popul. mean and standard dev.
In [3]: y1 = np.random.normal(mu, sigma, 30)      # random sample of n=30
   ...: y1.mean(), y1.std()
Out[3]: (101.46071134287304, 16.14904095192038)  # mean, standard dev.
In [4]: plt.hist(y1, bins='auto') # histogram (not shown)

In [5]: y2 = np.random.normal(mu, sigma, 30)      # 2nd random sample, n=30
   ...: y2.mean(), y2.std()
Out[5]: (100.29079228919267, 16.792865510807726)
In [6]: plt.hist(y2, bins='auto')
```

This example illustrates that descriptive statistics such as the sample mean can themselves be regarded as variables, their values varying from sample to sample. Chapter 3 provides results about the nature of that variation.

B.2   Chapter 2: PYTHON for Probability Distributions

B.2.1   Simulating a Probability as a Long-Run Relative Frequency

Section 2.1.1 used random number generation to illustrate the relative frequency definition of probability. To represent several observations having two possible outcomes on each, such as flips of a coin, we used the binomial distribution. Here is how to implement the examples in Python:

```
In [1]: import numpy as np
In [2]: y = list(range(0, 10))             # list integers from 0 to 9
   ...: randomlist = np.random.choice(y,7) # sample n=7 observations
   ...: print(randomlist)                  # with replacement
[1 4 6 8 3 2 2] # 0 and 1 represent rain, so rain occurs only on day 1
In [3]: np.random.binomial(7, 0.2, size=1) # 1 simulation of 7 flips
Out[3]: array([2])                         # obtain 2 heads in 7 flips
In [4]: n, p = 1, 0.2 # no. of flips (trials), prob(success) in each
   ...: s = np.random.binomial(n, p, 7)    # 7 simulations of n flips
   ...: print(s)
[0 0 0 1 1 0 0] # heads on flips 4 and 5 simulate rain on days 4 and 5
```

Next we illustrate the definition of the probability of an outcome as the long-run relative frequency of that outcome in n observations, with n taking values 100, 1000, 10000, 100000, 1000000, and with probability 0.20 for each observation:

```
In [1]: import numpy as np
In [2]: x1 = np.random.binomial(100, 0.20, 1); print(x1/100)
[0.18]      # proportion = 0.18 (e.g., 18 heads in 100 coin flips)
In [3]: x2 = np.random.binomial(1000, 0.20, 1); print(x2/1000)
[0.206]     # proportion of heads is 0.206 in n=1000 coin flips
In [4]: x3 = np.random.binomial(10000, 0.20, 1); print(x3/10000)
[0.2023]    # proportion of heads is 0.2023 in n=10000 coin flips
In [5]: x4 = np.random.binomial(100000, 0.20, 1); print(x4/100000)
[0.20037]   # proportion of heads is 0.20037 in n=100000 coin flips
In [6]: x5 = np.random.binomial(1000000, 0.20, 1); print(x5/1000000)
[0.199933] # proportion of heads is 0.199933 in n=1000000 coin flips
```

The Python Appendix at the book's website shows code to construct a figure, similar to Figure 2.1 in Chapter 2, to show how the sample proportion converges to the probability value as n increases.

B.2.2   Python Functions for Discrete Probability Distributions

Many discrete probability distributions have objects available in the `scipy.stats` module of the `scipy` library, including the binomial (`binom`), geometric (`geom`), multinomial (`multinomial`), Poisson (`poisson`), and negative binomial (`nbinom`). Each has arguments for the parameter values and for options such as displaying the *pmf*.

Binomial distribution

The `binom` object has several options for binomial distributions, including calculation of *pmf* or *cdf* values and random number generation. The following shows code for computing binomial probabilities and plotting a binomial *pmf* for the example in Section 2.4.2 about the Hispanic composition of a jury list, which has $n = 12$ and $\pi = 0.20$:

```
In [1]: import numpy as np
   ...: import matplotlib.pyplot as plt
   ...: from scipy.stats import binom
In [2]: binom.pmf(1, 12, 0.20)              # binomial P(Y=1) when n=12, pi=0.20
Out[2]: 0.2061584302079996
In [3]: fig, ax = plt.subplots(1, 1)
   ...: n, pi = 12, 0.20 # following creates plot of bin(12, 0.2) pmf
   ...: y = list(range(0, 13))                # y values between 0 and 12
   ...: ax.vlines(y, 0, binom.pmf(y, n, pi), colors='b', lw=5, alpha=0.5)
   ...: plt.xlabel('y'); plt.ylabel('P(y)')
   ...: plt.xticks(np.arange(min(y), max(y) + 1, 1.0))
In [4]: print(list(binom.pmf(y, n, pi))) # displays binomial probabilities
[0.06871947673599997, 0.2061584302079996, 0.28346784153599947,
0.23622320128000002, 0.1328755507199998, 0.05315022028799997,
0.01550214758399999, 0.003321888767999998, 0.0005190451199999995,
5.767168000000002e-05, 4.3253759999999935e-06, 1.9660799999999964e-07,
4.096000000000008e-09]
In [5]: mean, variance, skewness = binom.stats(n, pi, moments='mvs')
   ...: mean, variance, skewness  # compare to: print(mean, variance, skewness)
Out[5]: (array(2.4), array(1.92), array(0.4330127))
```

The following shows code to construct a figure similar to Figure 2.5, for a survey about legalized marijuana, with $n = 3$ and $\pi = 0.50$:

```
In [1]: from scipy.stats import binom
   ...: import matplotlib.pyplot as plt
   ...: fig, ax = plt.subplots(1, 1)
   ...: n, p = 3, 0.5
   ...: x = [0, 1, 2, 3]       # or: x = list(range(0, 4))
   ...: ax.vlines(x, 0, binom.pmf(x, n, p), colors='b', lw=5, alpha=0.5)
   ...: plt.xlabel('y')
   ...: plt.ylabel('P(y)')
   ...: plt.xticks(np.arange(min(x), max(x)+1, 1.0))
```

Poisson distribution

For a Poisson distribution, here is how to find probabilities of individual values using the *pmf* or of a range of values using the *cdf*, such as in the example in Section 2.4.7:

```
In [1]: from scipy.stats import poisson
In [2]: poisson.pmf(0, 2.3) # P(Y=0) if Poisson mean = 2.3
Out[2]: 0.10025884372280375
   # Difference of cdf values at 130 and 69 for Poisson with mean = 100:
In [3]: poisson.cdf(130, 100) - poisson.cdf(69, 100)
Out[3]: 0.9976322764993413
   # Probability within 2 standard deviations of mean (from 80 to 120):
In [4]: poisson.cdf(120, 100) - poisson.cdf(79, 100)
Out[4]: 0.9598793484053718
```

The `Python` Appendix at the book's website shows code for plotting the *pmf* of a Poisson distribution.

B.2.3   Python Functions for Continuous Probability Distributions

Many continuous probability distributions are available in the `scipy.stats` module of the `scipy` library, including the beta (`beta`), chi-squared (`chi2`), exponential (`expon`), F (`f`), gamma (`gamma`), logistic (`logistic`), log-normal (`lognorm`), normal (`norm`) and multivariate normal (`multivariate_normal`), t (`t`), and uniform (`uniform`). Each has arguments for the parameter values and for options such as displaying the *pdf*. For example, the `Python` Appendix at the book's website shows how to plot a uniform *pdf* and *cdf*.

Exponential and gamma distributions

The *pdf* of an exponential distribution can be plotted using the `expon` object of the `scipy.stats` module. Next we show how to plot an exponential *pdf* with $\lambda = 1$ (shown at the `Python` Appendix at the book's website), analogous to Figure 2.8 In Section 2.2.6. The following code also shows how to find the 0.05 and 0.95 quantiles of an exponential distribution, such as done with `R` in Section 2.5.6:

```
In [1]: import numpy as np
   ...: import scipy.stats as ss
   ...: from scipy.stats import expon
   ...: import matplotlib.pyplot as plt
   ...: x = np.linspace(0, 10, 5000)
   ...: lam = 1 # lambda parameter for the exponential pdf
   ...: y = ss.expon.pdf(x, 0, lam)
   ...: plt.plot(x, y, lw = 2, color = 'blue') # plot shown at book's
   ...: plt.xlabel('y'); plt.ylabel('f(y)')    # website appendix
In [2]: expon.ppf(0.05, scale=1), expon.ppf(0.95, scale=1) # scale is lambda parameter
Out[2]: (0.05129329438755, 2.9957322736)                   # of exponential distribution
```

Section 2.5.7 explained how the probability integral transformation can generate random observations from a continuous distribution, by randomly generating observations from a uniform distribution over [0, 1] and then taking the inverse *cdf* transformation. Here we randomly generate a million observations from that uniform distribution and then transform them to observations from an exponential distribution with $\lambda = 0.50$, also plotting a histogram of the randomly generated values, shown in Figure B.3:

```
In [1]: import numpy as np
   ...: import statistics
   ...: import matplotlib.pyplot as plt
   ...: X = np.random.uniform(0, 1, 1000000)
   ...: Y = -np.log(1 - X)/(0.50) # Y has exponential distribution, lambda = 0.50
   ...: statistics.mean(Y), statistics.stdev(Y)
Out[1]: (1.99864667507566, 1.99991458003761)  # E(Y) = std dev = 2.0
In [2]: plt.hist(Y, bins=50) # histogram is at book's website appendix
   ...: plt.xlabel('y'); plt.ylabel('Frequency')
   ...: plt.xlim(0, 15)
```

Figure 2.12 portrays gamma distributions with $\mu = 10$ and shape parameters $k = 1, 2$, and 10. The `Python` Appendix at the book's website shows code to construct such a plot.

Normal distribution

We use the *cdf* of a normal distribution to find tail probabilities or central probabilities. Next, using the *cdf* of the standard normal, we find the probabilities falling within 1, 2, and 3 standard deviations of the mean, as in the `R` code in Section 2.5.2:

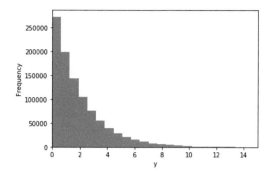

FIGURE B.3 Histogram of randomly generated values from an exponential distribution with $\lambda = 0.5$.

```
In [1]: from scipy.stats import norm
In [2]: norm.cdf(1) - norm.cdf(-1) # probability within 1 standard deviation of mean
Out[2]: 0.6826894921370859
In [3]: norm.cdf(2) - norm.cdf(-2) # probability within 2 standard deviation of mean
Out[3]: 0.9544997361036416
In [4]: norm.cdf(3) - norm.cdf(-3) # probability within 3 standard deviation of mean
Out[4]: 0.9973002039367398
```

Next we use **Python** for the Section 2.5.3 examples of finding probabilities and quantiles, such as finding the proportion of the self-employed who work between 50 and 70 hours a week, when the times have a $N(45, 15^2)$ distribution. We can apply normal distributions other than the standard normal by specifying μ and σ:

```
In [1]: from scipy.stats import norm
In [2]: norm.cdf(70,45,15) - norm.cdf(50,45,15) # mean = 45, standard dev. = 15
Out[2]: 0.32165098790894897        # probability between 50 and 70
In [3]: norm.ppf(0.99)             # 0.99 quantile of standard normal
Out[3]: 2.3263478740408408
In [4]: norm.ppf(0.99, 100, 16) # 0.99 normal quantile for IQ's
Out[4]: 137.22156598465347         # when mean = 100, standard deviation = 16
In [5]: norm.cdf(550, 500, 100) # SAT = 550 is 69th percentile
Out[5]: 0.6914624612740131         # when SAT mean = 500, standard deviation = 100
In [6]: norm.cdf(30, 18, 6)     # ACT =  30 is 97.7 percentile
Out[6]: 0.9772498680518208         # when ACT mean = 18, standard deviation = 6
```

The **Python** Appendix at the book's website shows code for plotting the *pdf* of a normal distribution over the *pmf* of a Poisson distribution, when both have $\mu = 100$ and $\sigma = 10$.

Q-Q Plots and the Normal Quantile Plot

Exercise 2.67 in Chapter 2 and Section A.2.2 in the R Appendix introduced the *Q-Q plot* (*quantile-quantile plot*) as a graphical comparison of an observed sample data distribution with a theoretical distribution. With the standard normal distribution for the theoretical quantiles, the Q-Q plot is called a *normal quantile plot*. If the observed data also come from a normal distribution, the points on the normal quantile plot should follow approximately a straight line, the deviations from a straight line reflecting random sampling variability. To illustrate how **Python** can construct this plot, we construct one for the carbon dioxide emissions values for the 31 European nations in the **Carbon** data file:

```
In [1]: import pandas as pd
   ...: from scipy.stats import probplot
```

```
    ...: from matplotlib import pyplot
In [2]: Carbon = pd.read_csv('http://stat4ds.rwth-aachen.de/data/
                Carbon.dat', sep='\s+')
In [3]: probplot(Carbon['CO2'], dist = 'norm', plot = pyplot)
In [4]: Carbon2 = pd.read_csv('http://stat4ds.rwth-aachen.de/data/
                Carbon_West.dat', sep='\s+')
In [5]: probplot(Carbon2['CO2'], dist = 'norm', plot = pyplot)
```

Figure B.4 shows the plot, on the left. It does not show any clear departure from normality, as with such a small n, the deviations from the straight line could merely be due to ordinary sampling variability. Figure B.4 (right) also shows the normal quantile plot for the `Carbon_West` data file at the book's website that adds four Western nations to the data file for Europe. The values are quite large for three nations (Australia, Canada, U.S.), and these appear on the upper-right part of the plot as values that are larger than expected for observations in the right-tail of a normal distribution. A couple of points on the lower-left part of the plot are not as small as expected for observations in the left tail of a normal distribution. This is a typical normal quantile plot display when the sample-data distribution is skewed to the right.

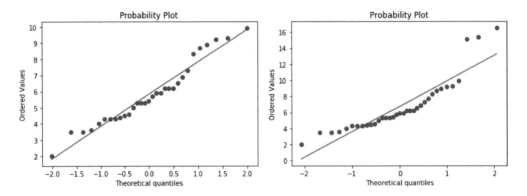

FIGURE B.4 Normal quantile plots for carbon dioxide emissions, for 31 European nations (left) and also including four other Western nations (right).

B.2.4 Expectations of Random Variables

Binomial distribution

For a sufficiently large number of simulations, the sample mean of a random sample from a binomial distribution is close to its expected value. Section 2.3.1 illustrated this for the example shown next with **Python**:

```
In [1]: import numpy as np # randomly generate 10000000 bin(3,0.5) rv's
In [2]: y = np.random.binomial(3, 0.5, 10000000)
In [3]: list(y[0: 10])        # first 10 of 10 million generated
Out[3]: [1, 2, 2, 3, 1, 2, 1, 1, 2, 1]
In [4]: sum(y)/10000000      # sample mean of 10000000 binomial outcomes
Out[4]: 1.4999395           # binomial expected value n(pi) = 3(0.5) = 1.5
```

For the example in Section 2.4.4 of gauging the popularity of a prime minister, using a sample survey with $n = 1500$ when $\pi = 0.60$, we use **Python** to find the mean and standard deviation of the relevant binomial distribution and find the probability within 2 and within 3 standard deviations of the mean:

```
In [1]: from scipy.stats import binom
   ...: n, p = 1500, 0.60
   ...: mu = binom.mean(n, p)      # mean of binomial(1500, 0.60)
   ...: sigma = binom.std(n, p)    # standard deviation of binomial(1500, 0.60)
   ...: mu, sigma
Out[1]: (900.0, 18.973665961010276)
In [2]: binom.cdf(mu + 2*sigma, n, p) - binom.cdf(mu - 2*sigma, n, p)
Out[2]: 0.9519324392528513        # probability within 2 standard dev's of mean
In [3]: binom.cdf(mu + 3*sigma, n,p) - binom.cdf(mu - 3*sigma, n,p)
Out[3]: 0.9971083299488276        # probability within 3 standard dev's of mean
```

Since this binomial distribution is approximately normal, the probabilities are close to the normal probabilities of 0.9545 and 0.9973.

Uniform distribution

Section 2.3.3 showed that a uniform random variable over the interval $[0, U]$ has $\mu = U/2$ and $\sigma = U/\sqrt{12}$. Here we use **Python** to find the mean and standard deviation of a simulated sample of 10 million random outcomes from a uniform $[0, 100]$ distribution, for which $\mu = 50.0$ and $\sigma = 28.8675$:

```
In [1]: import numpy as np
In [2]: n = 10000000
In [3]: y = np.random.uniform(0, 100, n)
In [4]: list(y[0 : 3])                          # first 3 simulated values
Out[4]:
[27.34765205743761,
 20.216650993789067,
 10.371009047647906]
In [5]: ymean = sum(y)/n                         # mean of 10000000 y values
In [6]: ysd = np.sqrt(sum((y-ymean)**2)/(n-1))   # standard deviation of y values
In [7]: ymean, ysd
Out[7]: (49.999411632715706, 28.86646306368665)
```

Finding the correlation for a joint probability distribution

For a particular joint probability distribution, we can find the correlation using equation (2.16). We illustrate for the correlation between income and happiness for the joint distribution in Table 2.5, using the fact that the covariance between a random variable and itself is the variance:

```
In [1]: import numpy as np
   ...: prob = [0.2, 0.1, 0.0, 0.1, 0.2, 0.1, 0.0, 0.1, 0.2]
   ...: x = [1,1,1,2,2,2,3,3,3]
   ...: y = [1,2,3,1,2,3,1,2,3]
   ...: covxy = np.cov(x, y, rowvar=False, aweights=prob)
   ...: varx = np.cov(x, x, rowvar=False, aweights=prob)
   ...: vary = np.cov(y, y, rowvar=False, aweights=prob)
   ...: r = covxy/(np.sqrt(varx*vary)) # 2x2 correlation matrix
   ...: print(round(r[0,1], 5))          # x-y correlation: element r[0,1]=r[1,0]
0.66667
```

B.3   Chapter 3: PYTHON for Sampling Distributions

B.3.1   Simulation to Illustrate a Sampling Distribution

To explain the concept of a sampling distribution, Section 3.1.1 used simulation to illustrate results of an exit poll in a U.S. Presidential election, when the probability is $\pi = 0.50$ of voting for Joe Biden. Here we use **Python** to do this for a random sample of 2271 voters:

```
In [1]: import numpy as np
   ...: n, p = 2271, 0.50               # values for binomial n, pi
   ...: x = np.random.binomial(n, p, 1) # 1 binomial experiment
   ...: print(x); print(x/n)
[1128]          # binomial random variable = 1128 Biden votes
[0.49669749]    # simulated proportion of Biden votes = 0.497
```

Next, we repeat this process of randomly sampling 2271 voters a million times, to investigate the variability in the results of the simulated proportion voting for Biden, when half of the population voted for him. Also shown is the code for deriving the histogram of the million simulated proportions. The **Python** Appendix at the book's website shows the histogram, which is similar to Figure 3.1.

```
In [2]: import matplotlib.pyplot as plt
   ...: import statistics     # use for mean and standard deviation functions
In [3]: results = np.random.binomial(n, p, 1000000)/n
   ...: statistics.mean(results)
Out[3]: 0.4999967811536768    # mean of million sample proportion values
In [4]: statistics.stdev(results)
Out[4]: 0.010503525956680382  # standard deviation of million sample proportions
In [5]: plt.hist(results, bins=14, edgecolor='k') # histogram
   ...: plt.xlabel('Sample proportion'); plt.ylabel('Frequency')
```

B.3.2   Law of Large Numbers

We next use **Python** to perform the simulation discussed in Section 3.2.5 to illustrate the law of large numbers result that the sample mean converges in probability to the population mean. We do this for simple random sampling with $n = 10$, 1000, and 10,000,000 from a uniform distribution over $[0, 100]$, for which $\mu = 50.0$:

```
In [1]: import numpy as np
   ...: n1, n2, n3 = 10, 1000, 10000000
   ...: y1 = np.random.uniform(0, 100, n1); mean1 = sum(y1)/n1
   ...: print(mean1)        # sample mean for  random sample of
27.12067089376516           # n = 10 from uniform [0, 100]
In [2]: y2 = np.random.uniform(0, 100, n2); mean2 = sum(y2)/n2
   ...: print(mean2)
49.955368338199484          # sample mean for n = 1000
In [3]: y3 = np.random.uniform(0, 100, n3); mean3 = sum(y3)/n3
   ...: print(mean3)
49.99943168403832           # sample mean for n = 10000000
```

B.4 Chapter 4: `PYTHON` for Estimation

B.4.1 Confidence Intervals for Proportions

We show confidence intervals (CIs) for a binomial proportion for the survey example of Section 4.3.4. Of the 1497 respondents in The Netherlands, 778 reported being atheists or agnostics:

```
In [1]: from statsmodels.stats.proportion import proportion_confint
In [2]: proportion_confint(778, 1497, method='normal') # default
Out[2]: (0.4943973906940667, 0.545014766954564)        # 95% Wald CI
In [3]: proportion_confint(778, 1497, method='wilson')
Out[3]: (0.4943793119474541, 0.5449319688365669)       # 95% Score CI
```

Python does not seem to currently have a function for finding a likelihood-ratio test-based CI for a proportion.

B.4.2 The t Distribution

We use the t distribution in the construction of a CI for the mean of a normal population. Section 4.4.1 shows R code for t cumulative probabilities and the t-quantiles used in CIs. The following shows **Python** code for the same calculations:

```
In [1]: import numpy as np
In [2]: df = np.array([1, 10, 30, 100, 1000, 10000])
   ...: from scipy.stats import t
   ...: t.ppf(0.975, df) # 0.975-quantiles for specified df values
Out[2]:
array([12.70620474,  2.22813885,  2.04227246,  1.98397152,  1.96233908,
        1.96020124])
In [3]: t.cdf(1.96020124, 10000)
Out[3]: 0.97500000000     # cumulative probability at t=1.96020124 when df=10000
```

The **Python** Appendix at the book's website shows code for plotting *pdf*s for t distributions of various degrees of freedom.

B.4.3 Confidence Intervals for Means

We next find descriptive statistics and CIs for the Section 4.4.3 example of analyzing weight changes of anorexic girls who are undergoing a cognitive behavioral therapy:

```
In [1]: import pandas as pd
   ...: import numpy as np
   ...: import matplotlib.pyplot as plt
In [2]: Anor = pd.read_csv('http://stat4ds.rwth-aachen.de/data/Anorexia.dat', sep='\s+')
In [3]: Anor.head(3)
Out[3]:
   subject therapy  before  after
0        1      cb    80.5   82.2
1        2      cb    84.9   85.6
2        3      cb    81.5   81.4
In [4]: change = Anor['after'] - Anor['before']
   ...: Anor['change'] = change    # add new variable to the data frame
   ...: Anor.loc[Anor['therapy'] == 'cb']['change'].describe()
Out[4]:         # showing only n and mean and standard deviation of change
count    29.000000
mean      3.006897
```

```
std          7.308504
In [5]: bins=list(range(-10,30,5))    # histogram with pre-specified bins:
   ...: plt.hist(Anor.loc[Anor['therapy']=='cb']['change'],
                 bins, edgecolor='k')
   ...: plt.xlabel('Weight change'); plt.ylabel('Frequency')
In [6]: changeCB = Anor.loc[Anor['therapy'] == 'cb']['change']
In [7]: import statsmodels.stats.api as sms
   ...: sms.DescrStatsW(changeCB).tconfint_mean() # default alpha=0.05
Out[7]: (0.2268901583588, 5.78690294509)        # 95% CI for mean change
In [8]: sms.DescrStatsW(changeCB).tconfint_mean(alpha=0.01)
Out[8]: (-0.743279444048, 6.75707254750)        # 99% CI for mean change
```

B.4.4   Confidence Intervals Comparing Means and Comparing Proportions

In R, the function for t tests for comparing means also provides the corresponding CI for the difference of means (Section 4.5.3). However, the functions in the statsmodels and scipy libraries for t tests do not also provide CIs. To construct these CIs, assuming equal or unequal population variances for the two groups, we provide the following[6] function:

```
In [1]: import numpy as np
   ...: from scipy.stats import t
In [2]: def t2ind_confint(y1, y2, equal_var = True, alpha = 0.05):
   ...:     # y1, y2: vectors or data frames of values for groups A and B
   ...:     n1 = len(y1); n2 = len(y2)
   ...:     v1 = np.var(y1)*n1/(n1-1); v2 = np.var(y2)*n2/(n2-1)
   ...:     if equal_var:
   ...:         df = n1 + n2 - 2
   ...:         vardiff = ((n1-1)*v1+(n2-1)*v2)/(n1+n2-2)*(1/n1 + 1/n2)
   ...:     else:
   ...:         df = (v1/n1 + v2/n2)**2/(v1**2/(n1**2*(n1-1)) + v2**2/(n2**2*(n2-1)))
   ...:         vardiff = v1/n1 + v2/n2
   ...:     se = np.sqrt(vardiff)
   ...:     qt = t.ppf(1 - alpha/2, df)       # t quantile for 100(1-alpha)% CI
   ...:     mean_diff = np.mean(y1) - np.mean(y2)
   ...:     confint = mean_diff + np.array([-1, 1]) * qt * se
   ...:     conf = 1 - alpha
   ...:     return mean_diff, confint, conf, df
   ...:
  # returns: mean(A) - mean(B), CI for mu_A - mu_B, confidence level, df
```

Next, we implement this function to find a 95% CI for the difference between the weight changes for the cognitive behavioral therapy and the control groups in the anorexia study:

```
# continue analysis from Section B.4.3 with Anor data file
In [3]: cogbehav = Anor.loc[Anor['therapy']=='cb']['change']
   ...: control = Anor.loc[Anor['therapy']=='c']['change']
In [4]: mean_diff, confint, conf, df = t2ind_confint(cogbehav,control)
   ...: print('mean1 - mean2 =', mean_diff)       # assume equal variances
   ...: print(conf, 'confidence interval:', confint)
   ...: print('df =', df)
mean1 - mean2 = 3.456896551724137
0.95 confidence interval: [-0.68013704  7.59393014]
df = 53
In [5]: mean_diff, confint, conf, df = t2ind_confint(cogbehav,control, equal_var=False)
                                        # permit unequal variances
   ...: print('mean1 - mean2 =', mean_diff)
   ...: print(conf, 'confidence interval:', confint)
```

---

[6]We introduce *v1* and *v2* because np.var() uses n instead of $n-1$ in the denominator.

```
    ...: print('df =', df)
mean1 - mean2 = 3.456896551724137
0.95 confidence interval: [-0.70446319  7.61825629]
df = 50.97065330426786
```

CIs for the difference of proportions for two independent samples are not provided directly in the standard **Python** libraries. Next, we provide a function that computes the Wald CI and implements it for the example in Section 4.5.5 about whether prayer helps coronary surgery patients:

```
In [1]: import numpy as np
   ...: from scipy.stats import norm
In [2]: def prop2_confint(y1, n1, y2, n2, alpha = 0.05):
   ...:     # y1, y2 : numbers of successes in groups A and B
   ...:     # n1, n2 : sample sizes in groups A and B
   ...:     prop1 = y1/n1; prop2 = y2/n2
   ...:     var = prop1*(1 - prop1)/n1 + prop2*(1 - prop2)/n2
   ...:     se = np.sqrt(var)
   ...:     qz = norm.ppf(1 - alpha/2)       # standard normal quantile
   ...:     prop_diff = prop1 - prop2
   ...:     confint = prop_diff + np.array([-1, 1]) * qz * se
   ...:     conf = 1 - alpha
   ...:     return prop_diff, confint, conf   # returns diff, CI, level
   ...:
# call the function for data on prayers and coronary surgery
In [3]: prop_diff, confint, conf = prop2_confint(315, 604, 304, 597)
   ...: print('prop1 - prop2 =', prop_diff)
   ...: print(conf, 'confidence interval:', confint)
prop1 - prop2 = 0.012310488489689096
0.95 CI: [-0.04421536  0.06883625]
```

B.4.5   Bootstrap Confidence Intervals

Section 4.6.2 constructed bootstrap CIs for the median and standard deviation. The following code uses the **bootstrapped** package to construct a percentile-based CI, for the variable in the **Library** data file giving the number of years since publication of the book. It also provides two options for constructing a box plot, with and without outliers:

```
In [1]: import pandas as pd
   ...: import numpy as np
   ...: import matplotlib.pyplot as plt
In [2]: Books = pd.read_csv('http://stat4ds.rwth-aachen.de/data/Library.dat', sep='\s+')
   ...: Books.head(3)
Out[2]:
   C  P # P = number of years since publication of book
0  1  3
1  9  9
2  4  4
In [3]: np.median(Books['P'])
Out[3]: 17.0
In [4]: plt.boxplot(Books['P'], vert=False)        # Box plot of 'P' with outliers
   ...: plt.xlabel('Years since publication')
In [5]: plt.boxplot(Books['P'], vert=False, showfliers=False)  # without outliers
   ...: plt.xlabel('Years since publication')

In [6]: pip install bootstrapped       # needs to be done once
In [7]: import bootstrapped.bootstrap as bs
   ...: import bootstrapped.stats_functions as bs_stats
In [8]: population = Books['P']
   ...: samples = np.array(population[:100000])
```

```
In [9]: print(bs.bootstrap(samples, stat_func = bs_stats.median))
17.0    (15.0, 23.0)                    # bootstrap 95% CI for median of P
In [10]: print(bs.bootstrap(samples, stat_func = bs_stats.std))
25.548688676  (15.567148, 37.952999)   # bootstrap 95% CI for standard deviation
```

B.4.6 Bayesian Posterior Intervals for Proportions and Means

We next show a **Python** implementation of the posterior interval for a proportion using the Jeffreys prior, which is the beta(0.5, 0.5) distribution, for the example in Section 4.7.3 about the proportion believing in hell. HPD regions can be found in **pymc3**, which has to be installed before being imported:

```
In [1]: from statsmodels.stats.proportion import proportion_confint
   ...: proportion_confint(814, 1142, method='jeffreys')
Out[1]: (0.686028505, 0.738463665)  # 95% Jeffreys posterior interval
In [2]: import pymc3
   ...: from scipy.stats import beta
In [3]: beta_dist = beta.rvs(size = 5000000, a = 814.5, b = 328.5)
   ...: print(pymc3.stats.hpd(beta_dist, alpha=0.05))
[0.68727542 0.73758295]                 # 95% HPD interval when use Jeffreys prior
In [4]: import numpy as np
   ...: print('[',np.quantile(beta_dist, 0.025),',', np.quantile(beta_dist, 0.975),']')
[ 0.6860454783123715 , 0.7384521768118637 ]    # ordinary 95% posterior interval
```

With normal priors and likelihood, the HPD posterior interval is the same as the percentile-based interval with equal tail probabilities. We next find a posterior interval for the mean weight change of anorexic girls, with the same approach as in Section 4.8.2 using **R**:

```
# continue analysis from Section B.4.3 with Anor data file
# (required is the variable: changeCB )
In [1]: import numpy as np
In [2]: from pymc3 import  *
   ...: data = dict(y = changeCB)
   ...: B0=10**(-7)                      # using priors: inverse gamma,
   ...: with Model() as model:
   ...:    # define highly disperse priors for variance and mean
   ...:    sigma = InverseGamma('sigma', B0, B0, testval=1.)
   ...:    intercept = Normal('Intercept', 0, sigma=1/B0)
   ...:    # define likelihood function for normal responses
   ...:    likelihood = Normal('y',mu=intercept,sigma=sigma,observed=changeCB)
   ...:    trace = sample(50000, cores=2)  # 100000 posterior samples
In [3]: np.mean(trace['Intercept'])
Out[4]: 3.007279525692707                # mean of posterior distribution
In [4]: np.std(trace['Intercept'])
Out[4]: 1.413687215567763                # standard deviation of posterior dist.
In [5]: pymc3.stats.hpd(trace['Intercept'], alpha=0.05)
Out[5]: array([0.31450337, 5.61027393])  # 95% posterior interval
```

For comparison, the classical 95% CI of (0.227, 5.787) for the population mean weight change gives similar substantive conclusions.

B.5   Chapter 5: `PYTHON` for Significance Testing

B.5.1   Significance Tests for Proportions

The significance test for a binomial proportion based on the large-sample normal distribution of the test statistic under H_0 can be implemented as shown next for the Section 5.2.2 example about climate change:

```
In [1]: import numpy as np
   ...: from statsmodels.stats.proportion import proportions_ztest
In [2]: stat, pval = proportions_ztest(524, 1008, 0.50)
   ...: print('{0:0.4f},'.format(stat),'{0:0.4f}'.format(pval))
1.2609, 0.2074
In [3]: from statsmodels.stats.proportion import proportion_confint
   ...: proportion_confint(524, 1008, method='wilson')
Out[3]: (0.48898223316199607, 0.5505496516518761)  # score 95% CI
```

The same **Python** function can test equality of two population proportions. Here is the code for the example of Section 5.4.2 comparing proportions suffering complications after heart surgery for prayer and non-prayer groups:

```
In [1]: import numpy as np
   ...: from statsmodels.stats.proportion import proportions_ztest
In [2]: count = np.array([315, 304])        # group 'success' counts
   ...: nobs = np.array([604, 597])         # group sample sizes
   ...: stat, pval = proportions_ztest(count, nobs)
   ...: print('{0:0.4f},'.format(stat),'{0:0.4f}'.format(pval))
0.4268, 0.6695            # z test statistic and two-sided P-value
```

B.5.2   Chi-Squared Tests Comparing Multiple Proportions in Contingency Tables

The analysis of two-way contingency tables presented in Section 5.4.4 and illustrated on the Happiness example of Section 5.4.5 can be implemented in Python as follows:

```
In [1]: import numpy as np
   ...: import pandas as pd
   ...: import matplotlib.pyplot as plt
   ...: Happy = pd.read_csv('http://stat4ds.rwth-aachen.de/data/Happy.dat', sep='\s+')
   ...: rowlabel=['Married', 'Divorced/Separated', 'Never married']
   ...: collabel=['Very happy', 'Pretty happy', 'Not too happy']
   ...: table = pd.crosstab(Happy['marital'], Happy['happiness'], margins = False)
   ...: table.index=rowlabel
   ...: table.columns=collabel
   ...: table                   # output not shown
# conditional distributions on happiness (proportions within rows):
In [2]: proptable = pd.crosstab(Happy['marital'], Happy['happiness'], normalize='index')
   ...: proptable.index=rowlabel
   ...: proptable.columns=collabel
   ...: proptable              # output not shown

In [3]: import statsmodels.api as sm    # expected frequencies under H0: independence
   ...: table = sm.stats.Table(table)
   ...: print(table.fittedvalues)              # output not shown
In [4]: X2 = table.test_nominal_association()  # chi-squared test of independence
   ...: print(X2)
df         4
pvalue     0.0
```

```
        statistic    197.407019249992
In [5]: table.standardized_resids                    # standardized residuals (not shown)
```

For the derivation of the mosaic plot, we first transform our data from numeric to string, since Python has no way to directly assign labels to the categories of the classification variables within the mosaic command. Coloring the cells according to the values of the standardized residuals is possible by setting the argument `statistic=True` (the default value is `False`), as done below. The mosaic plot is shown in the Python Appendix at the book's website.

```
In [5]: Happy.loc[Happy['happiness'] == 1, 'happiness'] = 'Very'
   ...: Happy.loc[Happy['happiness'] == 2, 'happiness'] = 'Pretty'
   ...: Happy.loc[Happy['happiness'] == 3, 'happiness'] = 'Not too'
   ...: Happy.loc[Happy['marital'] == 1, 'marital'] = 'Married'
   ...: Happy.loc[Happy['marital'] == 2, 'marital'] = 'Div/Sep'
   ...: Happy.loc[Happy['marital'] == 3, 'marital'] = 'Never'
   ...:
   ...: from statsmodels.graphics.mosaicplot import mosaic
   ...: fig, _ = mosaic(Happy, ['marital','happiness'], statistic=True)
```

B.5.3 Significance Tests for Means

To illustrate the t test for a mean, Section 5.2.5 tests whether the Hispanics in a GSS sample have population mean political ideology differing from the moderate value of 4.0, on an ordinal scale from 1 to 7. Here is this test in `Python`:

```
In [1]: import pandas as pd
   ...: Polid = pd.read_csv('http://stat4ds.rwth-aachen.de/data/Polid.dat', sep='\s+')
In [2]: Polid.head(2)
Out[2]:
        race  ideology
1  hispanic         1
2  hispanic         1
In [3]: from scipy import stats
   ...: stats.ttest_1samp(Polid.loc[Polid['race']=='hispanic']['ideology'], 4.0)
                                            # H_0 mean value is 4.0
Out[3]: Ttest_1sampResult(statistic=1.2827341281592484, pvalue=0.20039257254280335)
In [4]: import statsmodels.stats.api as sms
   ...: sms.DescrStatsW(Polid.loc[Polid['race']=='hispanic']['ideology']).tconfint_mean()
Out[4]: (3.9523333438892, 4.2265284447287)  # 95% CI for population mean
```

In discussing the impact of sample size on significance tests, namely that large n can result in statistical significance without practical significance, Section 5.6.2 conducted the test of H_0: $\mu = 4.0$ against H_a: $\mu \neq 4.0$ for political ideology of the entire sample. Here are the results and a corresponding CI:

```
In [5]: from scipy import stats
   ...: stats.ttest_1samp(Polid['ideology'], 4.0)
Out[5]: Ttest_1sampResult(statistic=3.8455584366605935, pvalue=0.00012319510560068636)
In [6]: Iimport statsmodels.stats.api as sms
   ...: sms.DescrStatsW(Polid['ideology']).tconfint_mean()
Out[6]: (4.05291076215289, 4.163011567944197)  # 95% CI for mu
```

B.5.4 Significance Tests Comparing Means

To illustrate the t test for comparing means for two independent random samples, for the anorexia study we test whether the population mean weight change differs between the cognitive behavioral therapy group and the control group. We can apply the test assuming that the two groups have equal variances or without that assumption (Section 5.3.2):

```
# continue analysis from Section B.4.4 with Anor data file
# (required are the variables: cogbehav, control )
In [7]: from scipy import stats
   ...: stats.ttest_ind(cogbehav, control, equal_var = True)
Out[7]: Ttest_indResult(statistic=1.6759971256, pvalue=0.09962901351)
In [8]: stats.ttest_ind(cogbehav, control, equal_var = False)
Out[8]: Ttest_indResult(statistic=1.667749692, pvalue=0.1014985957)
```

The CI for the difference between the means is not part of the output. For it, we constructed the **t2ind_confint** function in Section B.4.4.

To compare two means with independent samples, Section 5.3.5 showed how to use the modeling approach of Chapter 6, in which an indicator variable represents the two groups being compared. As in that section, we first show the classical analysis and then the Bayesian analysis, for the anorexia study comparing the mean weight change between the cognitive behavioral therapy and control groups:

```
In [9]: import statsmodels.formula.api as sm
   ...: Anor2 = Anor.loc[Anor['therapy'] != 'f']
   ...: change = Anor2['after'] - Anor2['before']; Anor2['change']=change
   ...: mod = sm.ols(formula='change ~ C(therapy)', data=Anor2).fit()
   ...: print(mod.summary())
=================================================================
                     coef   std err       t    P>|t|    [0.025  0.975]
-----------------------------------------------------------------
Intercept         -0.4500     1.498    -0.300   0.765    -3.454   2.554
C(therapy)[T.cb]   3.4569     2.063     1.676   0.100    -0.680   7.594
```

The analysis is equivalent to the one shown in the previous output that assumed equal variances for the groups. The estimated difference between the means of 3.457 has a standard error of 2.063 and a P-value of 0.10 for testing $H_0: \mu_1 = \mu_2$ against $H_a: \mu_1 \neq \mu_2$.

For the Bayesian analysis, we transform the **therapy** factor to a binary indicator variable x:

```
In [10]: from sklearn.preprocessing import LabelEncoder
    ...: LE = LabelEncoder()
    ...: Anor2['x'] = LE.fit_transform(Anor2['therapy'])
    ...: x = np.array(Anor2['x']) # x=0 controls (c), x=1 therapy (cb)
In [11]: from pymc3 import *
    ...: data = dict(x = x, y = change)
    ...: B0=10**(-8)
    ...: with Model() as model:
    ...:     # define very disperse prior distributions
    ...:     sigma = InverseGamma ('sigma', B0, B0, testval=1.)
    ...:     intercept = Normal('Intercept', 0, sigma = 1/B0)
    ...:     x_coeff = Normal('x', 0, sigma = 1/B0)
    ...:     # define likelihood function for normal response variable
    ...:     likelihood = Normal('y', mu = intercept + x_coeff * x,
                               sigma = sigma, observed = change)
    ...:     fit = sample(50000, cores=2) # posterior samples
In [12]: summary(fit)
Out[12]:
              mean     sd   hdi_3%  hdi_97% # actually 2.5% and 97.5%
Intercept   -0.444  1.543  -3.438    2.366
x            3.452  2.124  -0.517    7.449
sigma        7.749  0.781   6.333    9.220
In [13]: np.mean(fit['x'] < 0)
Out[13]: 0.05217
```

The posterior mean estimated difference of 3.45 has a posterior standard deviation of 2.12. The 95% posterior interval infers that the population mean difference falls between −0.52 and 7.45. This interval includes the value of 0, indicating it is plausible that $\mu_1 = \mu_2$. As an analog of a one-sided P-value, the Bayesian analysis reports that the posterior probability is 0.052 that the population mean weight change is smaller for the cognitive behavioral group than for the control group.

B.5.5 The Power of a Significance Test

The `statsmodels` library provides functions for the calculation of powers for basic significance tests. For the Section 5.5.6 example about the proportion of correct predictions in an astrology study, with $H_0 : \pi = 1/3$ and $H_a : \pi > 1/3$, we find the power at $\pi_1 = 0.50$. The `normal_power` function requires as input not the difference in probabilities but an effect size, defined for proportions as $2\arcsin(\sqrt{\pi_1}) - 2\arcsin(\sqrt{\pi_0})$:

```
In [1]: import numpy as np
   ...: from statsmodels.stats.power import normal_power
   ...: normal_power(2*(np.arcsin(np.sqrt(0.5))-np.arcsin(np.sqrt(1/3))), 116, 0.05,
                 alternative = 'larger', sigma = 1.)
Out[1]: 0.9780634871667955
```

The power at 0.50, which is $1 - P(\text{Type II error})$, equals 0.978.

B.5.6 Nonparametric Statistics: Permutation Test and Wilcoxon Test

Limited permutation tests are available of the hypothesis that two populations have identical distributions. We next show one that uses the difference of means as the test statistic to order all the possible samples, for the example of Section 5.8.2 about petting versus praise of dogs:

```
In [1]: pip install mlxtend
In [2]: from mlxtend.evaluate import permutation_test
   ...: data1 = [114, 203, 217, 254, 256, 284, 296]   # petting observations
   ...: data2 = [4, 7, 24, 25, 48, 71, 294]           # praise observations
   ...: p_value = permutation_test(data1, data2)
   ...: print(p_value)
0.006993006993006993            # P-value for default two-sided alternative
In [3]: p_value = permutation_test(data1, data2, func='x_mean > y_mean')
print(p_value)                  # one-sided test of greater mean for petting
0.0034965034965034965           # classical t one-sided P-value is 0.0017
```

Simulations can approximate the P-value (e.g., `'method = approximate'`, `num_rounds = 10000`) when it is infeasible to generate all permutations. This permutation test does not have the option of the test statistic being the difference between the sample medians, which the example in Section 5.8.2 used because of the potentially highly skewed distributions.

The **Python** Appendix at the book's website shows how to conduct permutation tests with the **permute** package, using simulation with the difference of means or the t test statistic to order the samples. Again, the difference of medians is not an option to order the samples.

The Wilcoxon test of the hypothesis that two populations have identical distributions, based on comparing the mean ranks of the two samples, is equivalent to the *Mann–Whitney test*. That test is performed by the `mannwhitneyu` function of `scipy.stats`. However, that function uses only the large-sample normal approximation for the distribution of the test statistic rather than an exact permutation analysis. The example of comparing petting with praise for dogs has very small samples ($n_1 = n_2 = 7$), so we show this analysis only for illustration:

```
In [4]: from scipy.stats import mannwhitneyu
   ...: stat, p = mannwhitneyu(data1, data2, use_continuity = False,
                                alternative = 'greater')
In [5]: print(stat,p)            # approximate, based on large-sample distribution
43.0 0.009043230657843692   # exact one-sided P-value is 0.0087
```

B.5.7 Kaplan-Meier Estimation of Survival Functions

The analysis of the survival times of the example in Section 5.8.4 can be implemented in Python using the `KaplanMeierFitter` function of `lifelines`. The plot of Kaplan-Meier estimators of survival functions for the drug and control groups as a function of time (see Figure 5.10) can be derived as shown below. The produced figure is shown in the Python Appendix at the book's website:

```
In [1]: import pandas as pd
   ...: Survival=pd.read_csv('http://stat4ds.rwth-aachen.de/data/Survival.dat',sep='\s+')
In [2]: import numpy as np
   ...: import pandas as pd
   ...: from lifelines import KaplanMeierFitter
   ...: kmf1 = KaplanMeierFitter()  # creates class to create an object
   ...: kmf2 = KaplanMeierFitter()
   ...: groups = Survival['group']
   ...: i1 = (groups == 1)          # group i1: drug
   ...: i2 = (groups == 0)          # group i2: control
   ...: T = Survival['time']
   ...: E = Survival['status']      # Event occured (=1)
   ...: kmf1.fit(T[i1], E[i1], label='drug')     # fits model for 1st group
   ...: a1 = kmf1.plot(ci_show=False)
   ...: a1.set_ylabel('Estimated P(survival)')
   ...: kmf2.fit(T[i2], E[i2], label='control')  # fits model for 2nd group
   ...: a2 = kmf2.plot(ax=a1,ci_show=False)
       ...: a2.set_xlabel('Time')
```

The chi-squared test for comparing the survival distributions with censored times is in Python referred as the *log-rank test* and conducted as shown next:

```
In [3]: from lifelines.statistics import logrank_test
   ...: results = logrank_test(T[i1],T[i2],event_observed_A=E[i1],event_observed_B=E[i2])
   ...: results.print_summary()
<lifelines.StatisticalResult: logrank_test>
                t_0 = -1
 null_distribution = chi squared
degrees_of_freedom = 1
         test_name = logrank_test
---
 test_statistic     p   -log2(p)
           6.25  0.01       6.33
```

B.6 Chapter 6: PYTHON for Linear Models

B.6.1 Fitting Linear Models

We illustrate Python fitting of linear models with the Scottish hill races data introduced in Section 6.1.4. The following code produces a scatterplot matrix for the record time for women, race distance, and race climb:

```
In [1]: import pandas as pd
   ...: Races =pd.read_csv('http://stat4ds.rwth-aachen.de/data/ScotsRaces.dat',sep='\s+')
In [2]: Races.head(3)
Out[2]:
             race  distance  climb   timeM   timeW
0       AnTeallach      10.6  1.062   74.68   89.72
1      ArrocharAlps      25.0  2.400  187.32  222.03
2  BaddinsgillRound    16.4  0.650   87.18  102.48
# create data frame containing variables for scatterplot matrix:
In [3]: Races2 = Races.drop(['timeM'], axis=1)
In [4]: import seaborn as sns
   ...: sns.set(style='ticks')
   ...: sns.pairplot(Races2)
```

Figure B.5 shows the scatterplot matrix. It portrays a histogram for each variable on the main diagonal.

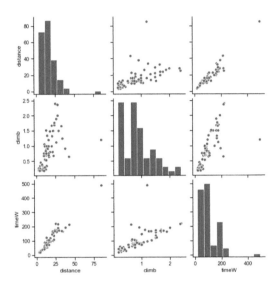

FIGURE B.5 Scatterplot matrix for women's record time, distance, and climb, for Scottish hill races data (Section 6.1.4), with histograms for variables on main diagonal.

We next fit a linear regression model for predicting the women's record time with distance as the sole explanatory variable, and then with both distance and climb as explanatory variables:

```
In [5]: import numpy as np
   ...: import statsmodels.formula.api as smf
   ...: fitd = smf.ols(formula='timeW ~ distance', data=Races).fit()
   ...: print(fitd.summary()) # edited output
             coef  std err       t  P>|t|      [0.025    0.975]
-----------------------------------------------------------------
Intercept   3.1076   4.537   0.685  0.496      -5.950   12.165
distance    5.8684   0.223  26.330  0.000       5.423    6.313
=================================================================
In [6]: fitdc = smf.ols(formula='timeW ~ distance + climb', data=Races).fit()
   ...: print(fitdc.summary())                  # edited output
             coef  std err       t  P>|t|      [0.025    0.975]
-----------------------------------------------------------------
Intercept  -14.5997   3.468  -4.210  0.000     -21.526   -7.674
distance     5.0362   0.168  29.919  0.000       4.700    5.372
climb       35.5610   3.700   9.610  0.000      28.171   42.951
```

To permit interaction, we place a colon between an interacting pair, as in R:

```
In [7]: fitdc_int = smf.ols(formula='timeW ~ distance + climb + distance:climb',
                            data=Races).fit()
    ...: print(fitdc_int.summary())
                      coef   std err        t    P>|t|     [0.025    0.975]
-----------------------------------------------------------------------------
Intercept          -5.0162     6.683   -0.751    0.456    -18.367    8.335
distance            4.3682     0.433   10.083    0.000      3.503    5.234
climb              23.9446     7.858    3.047    0.003      8.247   39.643
distance:climb      0.6582     0.394    1.669    0.100     -0.129    1.446
```

B.6.2   The Correlation and R-Squared

We next show the correlation matrix (**pandas** is required) containing correlations for pairs of variables in the reduced data frame. We also do this by excluding the outlying case 41 for the extremely long race, repeating the analysis of Section 6.1.5:

```
In [8]: Races2.corr() # Races2 is data frame without timeM
Out[8]:                   # correlation matrix for variables in Races2
            distance      climb     timeW
distance    1.000000   0.514471   0.955549
climb       0.514471   1.000000   0.685292
timeW       0.955549   0.685292   1.000000

In [9]: Races3 = Races2.loc[Races2.index != 40] # row 41 has index=40
    ...: Races3.corr()                          # (indices start at 0)
Out[9]:
            distance      climb     timeW
distance    1.000000   0.661714   0.920539
climb       0.661714   1.000000   0.851599
timeW       0.920539   0.851599   1.000000
```

We next find R^2, the multiple correlation, and the residual standard error and variance and marginal variance of the *timeW* response variable, using the model applied to the data file without the outlying observation:

```
# Race3 excludes case 41:
In [10]: fitdc2 = smf.ols(formula = 'timeW ~ distance + climb', data=Races3).fit()
     ...: print(fitdc2.summary()) # not shown here
     ...: print (fitdc2.params)    # parameter estimates without case 41
----------------------------------------------------------------------
Intercept    -8.931466
distance      4.172074            # 5.036 when include case 41
climb        43.852096            # 35.561 when include case 41
----------------------------------------------------------------------
In [11]: print ('R-Squared:', fitdc2.rsquared)
     ...: print ('adjusted R-Squared:', fitdc2.rsquared_adj)
R-Squared: 0.9519750513925197
adjusted R-Squared: 0.9504742717485359
In [12]: fitted = fitdc2.predict()              # model fitted values for timeW
In [13]: np.corrcoef(Races3.timeW, fitted)[0,1]  # multiple correlation
Out[13]: 0.9756920884134088
In [14]: residuals = fitdc2.resid
     ...: n=len(Races3.index); p=2                # p = number of explanatory var's
     ...: res_se = np.std(residuals)*np.sqrt(n/(n-(p+1)))
     ...: print ('residual standard error:', res_se)
residual standard error: 12.225327029914554
In [15]: res_se**2    # estimated error variance = squared residual standard error
Out[15]: 149.45862098835943
In [16]: np.var(Races3.timeW)*n/(n-1)           # estimated marginal variance
Out[16]: 3017.7975421076458                     # of women's record times
```

B.6.3 Diagnostics: Residuals and Cook's Distances for Linear Models

We next show how `Python` can use diagnostics to check model assumptions and detect influential observations. Section A.6.2 in the R appendix discussed how plots of the residuals can detect violations of model assumptions. We next show some residual plots that are available in `Python`. We first produce a histogram and a normal quantile plot[7] of the residuals, for the linear model for the complete Scottish hill races data with explanatory variables distance and climb:

```
In [17]: import matplotlib.pyplot as plt
    ...: import statsmodels.api as sm
    ...: import statsmodels.formula.api as smf
In [18]: fitdc = smf.ols(formula = 'timeW ~ distance + climb', data = Races).fit()
    ...: fitted = fitdc.predict()            # fitted values that predict timeW
    ...: residuals = fitdc.resid             # observed timeW - fitted value
In [19]: plt.hist(residuals, density=False)  # histogram (not shown)
    ...: plt.xlabel('residuals'); plt.ylabel('frequencies')
In [20]: import scipy.stats as stats
# qqplot of residuals:   (not shown)
In [21]: fig = sm.graphics.qqplot(residuals, dist=stats.norm, line='45', fit=True)
```

These two plots check whether the conditional distribution of the response variable is approximately normal, which is an assumption for making statistical inference with a linear model. Here, you can check that the histogram of the residuals is approximately bell-shaped and that the normal quantile plot shows a few outliers at the low and high ends, suggesting that the conditional distribution of *timeW* is approximately normal for this model. We do not show these two plots (which are shown in the `Python` appendix at the book's website), because these data are not a sample from a real or conceptual population and statistical inference is not relevant.

The other plots we consider *are* relevant, relating to the adequacy of the linear model itself. The following code constructs plots of the residuals against the observation index number and against the fitted values:

```
In [22]: index =  list(range(1, len(residuals) + 1))
In [23]: plt.scatter(index, residuals)     # residuals vs. observation index
    ...: plt.title(' ')
    ...: plt.xlabel('Index'); plt.ylabel('Residuals')
In [24]: plt.scatter(fitted, residuals)    # residuals vs. fitted values
    ...: plt.title(' ')
    ...: plt.xlabel('Fitted values'); plt.ylabel('Residuals')
```

Figure B.6 shows these two residual plots. The plot of the residuals against the index does not show any extreme values. The plot of the residuals against the fitted values shows the large residual for the observation that has much larger fitted value than the others, which is the outlying observation 41 that is a very long race.

Residuals plotted against each explanatory variable can highlight possible nonlinearity in an effect or severely nonconstant variance. A *partial regression plot* displays the relationship between a response variable and an explanatory variable after removing the effects of the other explanatory variables that are in the model. It does this by plotting the residuals from models using these two variables as responses and the other explanatory variable(s) as predictors. The least squares slope for the points in this plot is necessarily the same as the estimated partial slope for the multiple regression model. The following code plots residuals against each explanatory variable and constructs partial regression plots for each explanatory variable:

---

[7]Sections A.2.2 and B.2.3 introduced Q-Q plots and the normal quantile plot that uses the standard normal distribution for the theoretical quantiles.

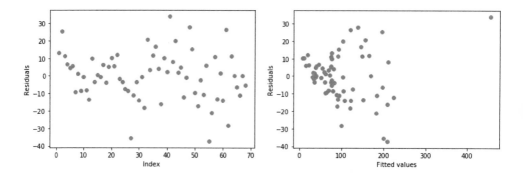

FIGURE B.6 Plots of residuals against observation index number and against fitted values for linear model for record times with distance and climb explanatory variables, in Scottish hill races.

```
# plots of residuals against each explanatory variable: (not shown)
In [25]: sm.graphics.plot_regress_exog(fitdc, 'distance', fig=plt.figure(figsize=(15, 8)))
In [26]: fig= sm.graphics.plot_regress_exog(fitdc,'climb',fig=plt.figure(figsize=(15, 8)))
# partial regression plot for each explanatory variable, adjusting for other:
In [27]: fig_dis = sm.graphics.plot_partregress('timeW','distance', ['climb'],
                   data = Races, obs_labels = False)
In [28]:fig_climb = sm.graphics.plot_partregress('timeW','climb', ['distance'],
                   data = Races, obs_labels = False)
```

You can check that the plots of residuals against each explanatory variable (shown in the **Python** Appendix at the book's website) reveal that the residuals tend to be small in absolute values at low values of distance and climb, suggesting (not surprisingly) that *timeW* tends to vary less at those low values. Figure B.7 shows the partial regression plots, which suggest that the partial effects of distance and climb are approximately linear and positive.

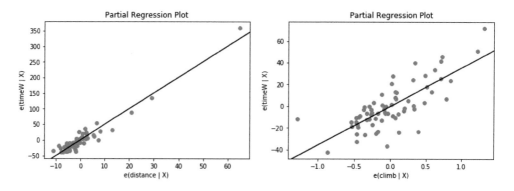

FIGURE B.7 Partial regression plots for effects of distance and climb on record times in Scottish hill races.

We next repeat with **Python** the analysis performed with **R** in Section 6.2.8 to use Cook's distances to detect potentially influential observations. Cook's distance is large when an observation has a large residual and a large leverage. The following code requests a plot of squared normalized residuals against the leverage:

```
In [29]: sm.graphics.plot_leverage_resid2(fitdc)
```

Figure B.8 shows the plot. We've seen in Figure B.6 that observation 41 (index 40 in Python) has a large residual, and Figure B.8 shows it also has a large leverage, highlighting it as potentially problematic.

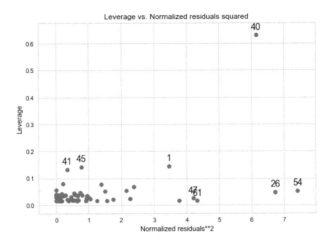

FIGURE B.8 Plot of leverage against squared normalized residuals for linear model for Scottish hill races.

Diagnostics for influential results can be saved in `fitdc.get_influence`, as shown in the following code.[8] To plot Cook's distances, we install the `yellowbrick` library. To create the plot, you need to define two new data frames, one containing the explanatory variables in the model and the other containing the response variable. This plot (shown in the Python Appendix at the book's website) and the following code detect the extremely large Cook's distance for observation 41:

```
In [30]: pip install yellowbrick
In [31]: influence = fitdc.get_influence()
    ...: leverage = influence.hat_matrix_diag    # hat values
    ...: cooks_d = influence.cooks_distance    # Cook's distances
In [32]: cooks_df = pd.DataFrame(cooks_d,index=['CooksDist','p-value'])
    ...: cooks_df = pd.DataFrame.transpose(cooks_df)
    ...: cooks_df.head(3)
Out[32]:
   CooksDist   p-value
0   0.007997   0.999008
1   0.216293   0.884759
2   0.004241   0.999615
In [33]: max(cooks_df. CooksDist)
Out[33]: 9.068276652414221
In [34]: cooks_df.CooksDist.idxmax(axis = 0)
Out[34]: 40 # case 41 has maximum Cook's Distance (index starts at 0)
In [35]: from yellowbrick.regressor import CooksDistance
    ...: X = Races.drop(['race', 'timeM', 'timeW'], axis=1)
    ...: y = Races['timeW']                    # y only has response variable
    ...: visualizer = CooksDistance()          # plot Cook's distances
    ...: visualizer.fit(X, y)                  # (not shown here)
In [36]: X1 = X.loc[X.index != 40]            # 41st case has index=40
    ...: y1 = y.loc[y.index != 40]
```

---

[8]The function `OLSInfluence` of `statsmodels.stats.outliers_influence`, which has to be imported, also provides them.

```
       ...: visualizer = CooksDistance()          # plot Cook's distances without
       ...: visualizer.fit(X1, y1)                # influential case (not shown)
```

B.6.4   Statistical Inference and Prediction for Linear Models

To illustrate statistical inference for linear models, Section 6.4.2 used a study of mental impairment, with life events and SES as explanatory variables. Here are inferential analyses for those data using **Python**, showing the global F test and individual t tests and CIs:

```
In [1]: import pandas as pd
   ...: Mental = pd.read_csv('http://stat4ds.rwth-aachen.de/data/Mental.dat', sep='\s+')
In [2]: Mental.corr() # correlation matrix
Out[2]:
           impair      life       ses
impair   1.000000  0.372221 -0.398568
life     0.372221  1.000000  0.123337
ses     -0.398568  0.123337  1.000000
In [3]: import statsmodels.formula.api as smf
   ...: fit = smf.ols(formula='impair ~ life + ses', data=Mental).fit()
   ...: print(fit.summary())                    # showing some of the output
============================================================================
DF Residuals: 37    F-statistic:              9.495 # F statistic tests
Df Model:      2    Prob (F-statistic): 0.000470 # H_0: beta1=beta2=0
============================================================================
              coef  std err        t   P>|t|     [0.025    0.975]
----------------------------------------------------------------------------
Intercept  28.2298    2.174   12.984   0.000     23.824    32.635
life        0.1033    0.032    3.177   0.003      0.037     0.169
ses        -0.0975    0.029   -3.351   0.002     -0.156    -0.039
```

We next find a CI for the regression line value $E(Y_0)$ and a prediction interval for a new observation Y_0, at fixed values of the explanatory variables. At their mean values, we find the 95% CI of (25.84, 28.76) for the mean mental impairment and 95% prediction interval of (17.95, 36.65) for a new observation Y_0. The following code is analogous to the R code in Section 6.4.5:

```
In [4]: newdata = pd.DataFrame({'life':[44.42], 'ses':[56.60]})
In [5]: predictions = fit.get_prediction(newdata)
   ...: pd.options.display.width = 0     # detection and adjustment of the display size
   ...: predictions.summary_frame(alpha = 0.05)
Out[5]: # shows predicted value, CI for E(Y_0), pred. interval for Y_0
    mean mean_se  mean_ci_lower mean_ci_upper obs_ci_lower obs_ci_upper
 27.2995 0.72044       25.839742     28.759226    17.952574    36.646394
```

If one asks for the predictions summary above without the `pd.options.display.width` command, then not all columns of the output are visible (the inner columns are omitted). Alternatively, one can control the number of columns to be printed, e.g., set equal to 10, by the command `pd.set_option('display.max_columns', 10)`.

The following code constructs these intervals simultaneously for all explanatory variable values in the sample used to fit the model:

```
In [6]: from statsmodels.stats.outliers_influence import summary_table
   ...: # summary_table returns: st: simple table,
   ...: # data: raw data of table, ss2: labels of table columns
   ...: st, data, ss2 = summary_table(fit, alpha = 0.05)
   ...: fittedvalues = data[:, 2]
   ...: predict_mean_se  = data[:, 3]
   ...: predict_mean_ci_low, predict_mean_ci_up = data[:, 4:6].T  # CI
   ...: predict_ci_low, predict_ci_up = data[:, 6:8].T            # PI
```

The `data` output of this function contains the fitted values (column 2), the lower and upper limits of the confidence interval for the mean (columns 4 and 5), and the lower and upper limits of the prediction interval (columns 6 and 7). The **Python** Appendix at the book's website shows code for constructing a scatterplot of the data for a particular explanatory variable together with the confidence interval and prediction interval at each data point.

B.6.5 Categorical Explanatory Variables in Linear Models

In `statsmodels`, a categorical explanatory variable is transformed to a factor by `C()`. Here we use it for the analysis of variance(ANOVA) in Section 6.5.2 for comparing mean incomes among three racial-ethnic groups:

```
In [1]: import pandas as pd
   ...: import statsmodels.formula.api as smf
   ...: Income = pd.read_csv('http://stat4ds.rwth-aachen.de/data/Income.dat', sep='\s+')
In [2]: Income.head(1)
Out[2]:
   income  education race       # race is categorical explanatory variable
0      16         10   B
In [3]: fit = smf.ols(formula = 'income ~ C(race)', data=Income).fit()
   ...: print(fit.summary())       # showing some output; F stat. tests
 F-statistic: 4.244   Prob (F-statistic): 0.0178   # H_0: equal means
===============================================================
                 coef   std err       t    P>|t|      [0.025  0.975]
---------------------------------------------------------------
Intercept      27.7500   4.968    5.586    0.000     17.857  37.643
C(race)[T.H]    3.2500   7.273    0.447    0.656    -11.232  17.732
C(race)[T.W]   14.7300   5.708    2.581    0.012      3.364  26.096
```

Next we show the ANOVA table and the Tukey multiple comparisons of the mean incomes for the three racial-ethnic groups, presented in Section 6.5.4:

```
In [4]: import statsmodels.api as sm
   ...: sm.stats.anova_lm(fit)             # ANOVA table
Out[4]:
            df    sum_sq      mean_sq        F    PR(>F)
C(race)    2.0   3352.47  1676.235000  4.244403  0.01784
Residual  77.0  30409.48   394.928312      NaN      NaN

In [5]: import statsmodels.stats.multicomp as mc
   ...: comp = mc.MultiComparison(Income['income'], Income['race'])
   ...: post_hoc_res = comp.tukeyhsd()
   ...: print(post_hoc_res.summary())
 Multiple Comparison of Means - Tukey HSD, FWER=0.05
=======================================================
group1 group2 meandiff p-adj   lower    upper   reject
-------------------------------------------------------
   B      H     3.25  0.8882 -14.1311 20.6311  False
   B      W    14.73  0.0312   1.0884 28.3716   True
   H      W    11.48  0.1426  -2.8809 25.8409  False
-------------------------------------------------------

# plot Tukey intervals:
In [6]: post_hoc_res.plot_simultaneous(ylabel='race', xlabel='mean income difference')
```

The *reject* column of the multiple comparisons table indicates whether one would reject the pair of groups having identical means, so we can conclude only that Black and White racial-ethnic groups have differing population mean annual incomes. The graphical display of the Tukey HSD comparisons is shown in the **Python** Appendix at the books's website.

We expand the model now, showing a quantitative explanatory variable (*education*) as well as a factor (*race*) and the corresponding ANOVA table, following the analysis of Section 6.5.5:

```
In [7]: fit2 = smf.ols(formula = 'income ~ C(race) + education', data=Income).fit()
   ...: print(fit2.summary())                    # part of the output
F-statistic:  21.75                    Prob (F-statistic): 2.85e-10
=================================================================
                   coef   std err        t     P>|t|    [0.025    0.975]
-----------------------------------------------------------------
Intercept      -26.5379     8.512    -3.118     0.003   -43.492    -9.584
C(race)[T.H]     5.9407     5.670     1.048     0.298    -5.352    17.234
C(race)[T.W]    10.8744     4.473     2.431     0.017     1.966    19.783
education        4.4317     0.619     7.158     0.000     3.199     5.665
=================================================================
In [8]: sm.stats.anova_lm(fit2, typ=2)                # Type II sums of squares
Out[8]:
                sum_sq    df         F        PR(>F)
C(race)      1460.583947   2.0   3.055573  5.292198e-02   # F test for each variable,
education   12245.231928   1.0  51.234580  4.422192e-10   # adjusted for other variable
Residual    18164.248072  76.0       NaN           NaN
```

The bottom of the output shows tests for the effect of each variable, adjusted for the other one. For example, the test that racial-ethnic status has no effect on mean annual income, adjusting for years of experience, has a test statistic of $F = 3.06$ and a P-value of 0.053. The **Python** Appendix at the book's website also shows **Python** results of fitting the model allowing interaction between race and education in their effects, similar to the R output in Section 6.5.7.

B.6.6   Bayesian Fitting of Linear Models

We next show **Python** for implementing the Bayesian fitting of a linear model to the mental impairment data, described in Section 6.6.2. This is conducted with the **pymc3** package, which needs to be imported first. The code shown next uses two MCMC chains of length 100,000 each, for which the MCMC approximation to the true fit seems to be reasonably good:

```
In [1]: import matplotlib.pyplot as plt
   ...: from pymc3 import *
   ...: import pymc3
   ...: import statsmodels.api as sm
   ...: from pandas.plotting import scatter_matrix
In [2]: Mental = pd.read_csv('http://stat4ds.rwth-aachen.de/data/Mental.dat', sep='\s+')
   : y = Mental.impair; life = Mental.life; ses = Mental.ses
In [3]: B0 = 10**(-20); C0 = 10**(-10)
# model specifications in PyMC3 are wrapped in a with-statement:
   ...: with Model() as model:                       # define prior distributions
   ...:     sigma = InverseGamma ('sigma', C0, C0, testval=1.)
   ...:     Intercept = Normal('Intercept', 0, sigma=1/B0)
   ...:     beta1 = Normal('beta1', 0, sigma=1/B0)   # very flat priors
   ...:     beta2 = Normal('beta2', 0, sigma=1/B0)
   ...:     # define likelihood function
   ...:     likelihood = Normal('y', mu=Intercept+beta1*life+beta2*ses,
                              sigma=sigma, observed = Mental.impair)
   ...:     trace = sample(100000, cores=2)          # 2x100000 posterior samples
In [4]: summary(trace)
Out[4]:
              mean     sd  hdi_2.5%  hdi_97.5%
Intercept   28.222  2.250    24.025     32.509
beta1        0.103  0.034     0.040      0.167
beta2       -0.097  0.030    -0.154     -0.040
```

```
sigma         4.653  0.561      3.659       5.715
In [5]: sum(trace['beta1'] < 0)/200000          # analog of one-sided P-value
Out[5]: 0.001405                                # for H_a: life events beta > 0
In [6]: sum(trace['beta2'] > 0)/200000          # analog of one-sided P-value
Out[6]: 0.000995                                # for H_a: SES beta < 0
```

Results are similar to the Bayesian results obtained with R and similar to the classical results in Section 6.4.2. The Python Appendix at the book's website also shows a figure portraying the posterior distributions of the model parameters.

B.7 Chapter 7: PYTHON for Generalized Linear Models

Linear models are special cases of GLMs, so models fitted to the Scottish hill races data in Section B.6.1 by least squares using `smf.ols` can equivalently be fitted as GLMs:

```
In [1]: import pandas as pd
   ...: Races=pd.read_csv('http://stat4ds.rwth-aachen.de/data/ScotsRaces.dat',sep='\s+')
In [2]: import statsmodels.formula.api as smf
In [3]: fitdc=smf.ols(formula='timeW ~ distance + climb', data=Races).fit()
   ...: print(fitdc.summary())        # edited output of least squares fit
==================================================================
             coef   std err      t    P>|t|     [0.025    0.975]
------------------------------------------------------------------
Intercept  -14.5997  3.468   -4.210   0.000   -21.526    -7.674
distance     5.0362  0.168   29.919   0.000     4.700     5.372
climb       35.5610  3.700    9.610   0.000    28.171    42.951
------------------------------------------------------------------

In [4]: fitdc.glm = smf.glm(formula='timeW ~ distance + climb',
                            data=Races).fit()
   ...: print(fitdc.glm.summary())    # edited output of GLM fit
==================================================================
             coef   std err      z    P>|z|     [0.025    0.975]
------------------------------------------------------------------
Intercept  -14.5997  3.468   -4.210   0.000   -21.397    -7.802
distance     5.0362  0.168   29.919   0.000     4.706     5.366
climb       35.5610  3.700    9.610   0.000    28.309    42.813
```

The default for `smf.glm` is the Gaussian (normal) distribution family with identity link function. The parameter estimates are identical to the least squares fit, but inference about individual coefficients differs slightly because the `glm` function uses normal distributions for the sampling distributions (regardless of the assumed distribution for Y), whereas the *ols* function uses the t distribution, which applies only with normal responses.

B.7.1 GLMs with Identity Link

Section 7.1.3 used GLMs with identity link function to model house selling prices. The scatterplot of the selling prices by size of home and whether it is new, such as shown in Figure 7.1, can be obtained in Python as follows:

```
In [1]: import pandas as pd
   ...: import matplotlib.pyplot as plt
In [2]: Houses = pd.read_csv('http://stat4ds.rwth-aachen.de/data/Houses.dat', sep='\s+')
In [3]: import seaborn as sns
   ...: Houses['house'] = Houses['new'].apply(lambda x: 'old' if x==0 else 'new')
   ...: sns.pairplot(x_vars=['size'], y_vars=['price'], data=Houses, hue='house', size=5)
```

We next fit the GLMs with identity link function discussed in Section 7.1.3, assuming normal (for which the identity link is the default) or gamma distributions for house selling price:

```
In [4]: import statsmodels.formula.api as smf
   ...: import statsmodels.api as sm
# GLM assuming normal response, identity link, permitting interaction
In [5]: fit1 = smf.glm(formula = 'price ~ size + new + size:new', data = Houses,
                       family = sm.families.Gaussian()).fit()
   ...: print(fit1.summary())                        # edited output
                  Generalized Linear Model Regression Results
=================================================================
               coef   std err        z     P>|z|     [0.025    0.975]
-----------------------------------------------------------------
Intercept   -33.3417   23.282    -1.432    0.152    -78.973    12.290
size          0.1567    0.014    11.082    0.000      0.129     0.184
new        -117.7913   76.511    -1.540    0.124   -267.751    32.168
size:new      0.0929    0.033     2.855    0.004      0.029     0.157
=================================================================
# GLM assuming gamma response, identity link, permitting interaction:
In [6]: gamma_mod = smf.glm(formula = 'price ~ size + new + size:new', data = Houses,
                       family = sm.families.Gamma(link = sm.families.links.identity))
   ...: fit2 = gamma_mod.fit()
   ...: print(fit2.summary())                        # edited output
                  Generalized Linear Model Regression Results
=================================================================
               coef   std err        z     P>|z|     [0.025    0.975]
-----------------------------------------------------------------
Intercept   -11.1764   19.461    -0.574    0.566    -49.320    26.967
size          0.1417    0.015     9.396    0.000      0.112     0.171
new        -116.8569   96.873    -1.206    0.228   -306.725    73.011
size:new      0.0974    0.055     1.769    0.077     -0.011     0.205
=================================================================
```

The interaction term is not needed for the gamma GLM, reflecting the greater variability in the response as the mean increases for that GLM.

We next conduct the analyses of the Covid-19 data set in Section 7.1.8 using normal and gamma GLMs. We fit a (1) normal linear model for the log counts (i.e., assuming a log-normal distribution for the response),(2) GLM using the log link for a normal response, (3) GLM using the log link for a gamma response:

```
In [1]: import pandas as pd
   ...: import numpy as np
   ...: import statsmodels.api as sm
   ...: import statsmodels.formula.api as smf
In [2]: Covid = pd.read_csv('http://stat4ds.rwth-aachen.de/data/Covid19.dat', sep='\s+')
In [3]: fit1 = smf.ols(formula='np.log(cases) ~ day', data=Covid).fit()
   ...: print(fit1.summary())           # normal linear model for log-counts
=================================================================
               coef   std err        t     P>|t|     [0.025    0.975]
-----------------------------------------------------------------
Intercept     2.8439    0.084    33.850    0.000      2.672     3.016
day           0.3088    0.005    67.377    0.000      0.299     0.318
=================================================================
In [4]: fit2 = smf.glm(formula = 'cases ~ day', family = sm.families.Gaussian
                       (link = sm.families.links.log), data = Covid).fit()
   ...: print(fit2.summary())           # normal GLM with log link
=================================================================
               coef   std err        z     P>|z|     [0.025    0.975]
-----------------------------------------------------------------
Intercept     5.3159    0.168    31.703    0.000      4.987     5.645
day           0.2129    0.006    37.090    0.000      0.202     0.224
=================================================================
In [5]: fit2.aic
```

```
Out[5]: 594.1435463614453
In [6]: fit3 = smf.glm(formula='cases ~ day', family = sm.families.Gamma
                    (link = sm.families.links.log), data = Covid).fit()
   ...: print(fit3.summary())          # gamma GLM with log link
================================================================
               coef   std err         z     P>|z|      [0.025     0.975]
----------------------------------------------------------------
Intercept    2.8572     0.077    36.972     0.000       2.706      3.009
day          0.3094     0.004    73.388     0.000       0.301      0.318
================================================================

In [7]: fit3.aic
Out[7]: 479.3853756004412          # better fit that normal GLM with log link
```

All three models assume an exponential relationship for the response over time, but results are similar with models (1) and (3) because they both permit the variability of the response to grow with its mean.

B.7.2   Logistic Regression: Logit Link with Binary Data

To illustrate logistic regression, Section 7.2.3 models the probability of death for flour beetles after five hours of exposure to various log-dosages of gaseous carbon disulfide. The response variable is binary with $y = 1$ for death and $y = 0$ for survival. We can fit the model with *grouped* data (Section 7.2.3) or with *ungrouped* data (i.e., using a data file having a separate row for each beetle in the sample; see Section 7.2.4). We first present the ungrouped-data analysis:

```
In [1]: import pandas as pd
   ...: import numpy as np
   ...: import statsmodels.api as sm
   ...: import statsmodels.formula.api as smf
   ...: import matplotlib.pyplot as plt
In [2]: Beetles = pd.read_csv('http://stat4ds.rwth-aachen.de/data/Beetles_ungrouped.dat',
                    sep='\s+')
In [3]: Beetles.head(2)
Out[3]:
       x   y
0  1.691   1
1  1.691   1
In [4]: Beetles.tail(1)
Out[4]:
480  1.884   1          # 481 observations in ungrouped data file
                        # logit link is binomial default with smf.glm
In [5]: fit = smf.glm('y ~ x', family = sm.families.Binomial(), data=Beetles).fit()
   ...: print(fit.summary())                    # edited output
               Generalized Linear Model Regression Results
Deviance:    372.35       Df Residuals:    479
================================================================
               coef   std err         z     P>|z|      [0.025     0.975]
----------------------------------------------------------------
Intercept  -60.7401     5.182   -11.722     0.000     -70.896    -50.584
x           34.2859     2.913    11.769     0.000      28.576     39.996
```

The following code shows how to plot the proportion of dead beetles versus the log dosage of gaseous carbon disulfide, showing also the fit of the logistic regression model:

```
In [6]: logdose = Beetles.x.unique()      # vector of unique values of x
   ...: yx=pd.crosstab(Beetles['y'],Beetles['x'], normalize='columns')
   ...: y_prop=yx.iloc[1]                  # vector of sample proportions of y=1
   ...: def f(t):
   ...:     return np.exp(fit.params[0] + fit.params[1]*t)/
```

```
                              (1 + np.exp(fit.params[0] + fit.params[1]*t))
        ...: t1 = np.arange(1.65, 1.95, 0.0001)
        ...: fig, ax = plt.subplots()
        ...: ax.plot(t1, f(t1),'blue')
        ...: ax.scatter(logdose, y_prop, s=5, color='red')
        ...: ax.set(xlabel='x', ylabel='P(Y=1)')
```

The figure itself is shown in the **Python** Appendix at the book's website.

Next we fit the logistic regression model to the grouped-data file for the beetles:

```
In [1]: import pandas as pd
   ...: from statsmodels.formula.api import glm
   ...: import statsmodels.api as sm
In [2]: Beetles2=pd.read_csv('http://stat4ds.rwth-aachen.de/data/Beetles.dat',sep='\s+')
In [3]: Beetles2
Out[3]:
   logdose  live  dead   n
0    1.691    53     6  59
1    1.724    47    13  60
2    1.755    44    18  62
3    1.784    28    28  56
4    1.811    11    52  63
5    1.837     6    53  59
6    1.861     1    61  62
7    1.884     0    60  60       # 8 observations in grouped data file
In [4]: fit = glm('dead + live ~ logdose', data = Beetles2,
                    family = sm.families.Binomial()).fit()
In [5]: print(fit.summary())     # same results as with ungrouped data
                    Generalized Linear Model Regression Results
Deviance:    11.116       Df Residuals:    6
=================================================================
               coef   std err        z   P>|z|     [0.025   0.975]
-----------------------------------------------------------------
Intercept  -60.7401    5.182   -11.722   0.000    -70.896  -50.584
logdose     34.2859    2.913    11.769   0.000     28.576   39.996
```

The deviance differs, since now the data file has 8 observations instead of 481, but the ML estimates and standard errors are identical.

Sections B.7.3 and B.8.1 show other examples of fitting logistic regression models using **Python**.

B.7.3 Separation and Bayesian Fitting in Logistic Regression

When the explanatory variable values satisfy *complete separation*, the glm function of statsmodels reports a separation error and does not provide results. We illustrate for the toy example of Section 7.2.6:

```
In [1]: import pandas as pd
   ...: import statsmodels.api as sm
   ...: import statsmodels.formula.api as smf
In [2]: toy = pd.DataFrame({'x': [1,2,3,4,5,6], 'y': [0,0,0,1,1,1]})
   ...: fit = smf.glm('y ~ x', family = sm.families.Binomial(), data=toy).fit()
PerfectSeparationError: Perfect separation, results not available
```

With *quasi-complete separation*, results are reported, but truly infinite estimates have enormous standard errors. We illustrate with the endometrial cancer example from Section 7.3.2, for which the ML estimate of the NV effect is truly infinite. Before fitting the logistic regression model, we standardize the quantitative explanatory variables (PI and EH), so we can compare the magnitudes of their estimated effects (which are truly finite):

```
In [1]: import pandas as pd
In [2]: Endo =pd.read_csv('http://stat4ds.rwth-aachen.de/data/Endometrial.dat',sep='\s+')
In [3]: pd.crosstab(Endo.NV, Endo.HG)
Out[3]:
HG   0   1
NV
0    49  17           # quasi-complete separation: no 'HG=0 and NV=1' cases
1    0   13
In [4]: from sklearn import preprocessing       # standardize PI and EH:
   ...: Endo['PI2'] = preprocessing.scale(Endo.PI)
   ...: Endo['EH2'] = preprocessing.scale(Endo.EH)
In [5]: Endo['NV2'] = Endo['NV'] - 0.5          # centers NV around 0
In [6]: import statsmodels.api as sm
   ...: import statsmodels.formula.api as smf
   ...: fit = smf.glm('HG ~ NV2 + PI2 + EH2',
          family = sm.families.Binomial(), data = Endo).fit()
   ...: print(fit.summary())        # true ML estimate for NV is infinite
============================================================================
              coef     std err        z     P>|z|      [0.025    0.975]
----------------------------------------------------------------------------
Intercept    9.8411   6338.889     0.002    0.999    -1.24e+04   1.24e+04
NV2         22.1856   1.27e+04     0.002    0.999    -2.48e+04   2.49e+04
PI2         -0.4191      0.440    -0.952    0.341       -1.282      0.444
EH2         -1.9097      0.556    -3.433    0.001       -3.000     -0.819
```

Python does not yet seem to have capability of Firth's penalized likelihood method (Section 7.7.1) or profile-likelihood CIs for the logistic regression model. However, Bayesian analysis is possible, which is especially useful when some ML estimates are infinite. For this, we use the function for GLMs of pymc3, which is simpler to apply and has code similar to standard GLM code. We illustrate for the endometrial cancer example,[9] using highly disperse normal prior distributions for the model parameters with $\mu = 0$ and $\sigma = 10$:

```
In [7]: import pymc3 as pm
   ...: from pymc3 import *
   ...: import numpy as np
In [7]: priors = {'Intercept': pm.Normal.dist(mu = 0, sd = 10),
   ...:            'Regressor': pm.Normal.dist(mu = 0, sd = 10)
   ...:           }
   ...: with pm.Model() as fit:
   ...:     pm.glm.GLM.from_formula('HG ~ NV2 + PI2 + EH2',
                  Endo, family = pm.glm.families.Binomial(), priors = priors)
   ...:     trace_fit = pm.sample(10000)
In [8]: summary(trace_fit)
Out[8]:
               mean      sd  hdi_2.5%  hdi_97.5%
Intercept     3.219   2.529    -0.649      8.149
NV2           9.123   5.036     1.270     18.618    # compare to infinite ML estimate
PI2          -0.475   0.453    -1.349      0.335
EH2          -2.131   0.594    -3.267     -1.054

In [9]: sum(trace_fit['NV2'] < 0)/20000
Out[9]: 0.0002                    # posterior probability of negative NV effect
```

Results are similar to those using R in Section 7.3.2. The Python Appendix at the book's website shows how to plot the posterior distributions of the model parameters.

B.7.4   Poisson Loglinear Model for Counts

To illustrate the modeling of count data, Section 7.4.2 used Poisson loglinear models for data on female horseshoe crabs, in which the response variable is the number of male satellites

---

[9]Warning: This is very slow compared with R.

during a mating season. Here is **Python** code for the model with explanatory variables weight and color, treating color as a factor:

```
In [1]: import pandas as pd
   ...: import statsmodels.api as sm
   ...: import statsmodels.formula.api as smf
In [2]: Crabs = pd.read_csv('http://stat4ds.rwth-aachen.de/data/Crabs.dat', sep='\s+')
In [3]: fit = smf.glm('sat ~ weight + C(color)',          # default log link
                      family=sm.families.Poisson(), data=Crabs).fit()
   ...: print(fit.summary())                              # edited output
                 Generalized Linear Model Regression Results
Deviance:   551.80      Df Residuals: 168
=================================================================
                  coef   std err        z    P>|z|     [0.025    0.975]
-----------------------------------------------------------------
Intercept       -0.0498    0.233   -0.214   0.831    -0.507     0.407
C(color)[T.2]   -0.2051    0.154   -1.334   0.182    -0.506     0.096
C(color)[T.3]   -0.4498    0.176   -2.560   0.010    -0.794    -0.105
C(color)[T.4]   -0.4520    0.208   -2.169   0.030    -0.861    -0.044
weight           0.5462    0.068    8.019   0.000     0.413     0.680
=================================================================

In [4]: fit.aic               # AIC indicates the fit is poorer than
Out[4]: 917.1026114781453     # negative binomial model in Section B.7.4
```

The output includes the residual deviance and its *df*. You can obtain the null deviance and its *df* by fitting the null model:

```
In [5]: fit0 = smf.glm('sat ~ 1', family = sm.families.Poisson(), data=Crabs).fit()
In [6]: fit0.deviance, fit0.df_resid
Out[6]: (632.791659200811, 172)
```

Python produces an analysis of variance (ANOVA) table only for linear models. For a GLM, we can construct an analogous analysis of deviance table, as shown next for summarizing likelihood-ratio tests for the explanatory variables in the loglinear model for horseshoe crab satellite counts:

```
In [7]: fitW = smf.glm('sat ~ weight', family = sm.families.Poisson(),
                       data=Crabs).fit()                # weight the sole predictor
   ...: fitC = smf.glm('sat ~ C(color)', family=sm.families.Poisson(),
                       data=Crabs).fit()                # color the sole predictor
   ...: D = fit.deviance; D1 = fitW.deviance; D2 = fitC.deviance
In [8]: df = fit.df_resid                  # residual degrees of freedom of the models
   ...: dfW = fitW.df_resid
   ...: dfC = fitC.df_resid
In [9]: from scipy import stats            # P-values for likelihood-ratio tests
   ...: P_weight = 1 - stats.chi2.cdf(D2 - D, dfC - df)
   ...: P_color = 1 - stats.chi2.cdf(D1 - D, dfW - df)
In [10]: pd.DataFrame({'Variable': ['weight','C(color)'],
                      'LR Chisq': [round(D2 - D, 3), round(D1 - D, 3)],
                      'df': [dfC - df, dfW - df],
                      'Pr(>Chisq)': [P_weight, P_color]})
    Variable  LR Chisq  df  Pr(>Chisq)
0     weight    57.334   1  3.6748e-14
1   C(color)     9.061   3  2.8485e-02  # color effect P-value = 0.028
```

To model a rate with a Poisson loglinear model, we use an offset. Here is code for an expanded version of the analysis in Section 7.4.3 of lung cancer survival, including histology as an additional prognostic factor:

```
In [1]: import pandas as pd
   ...: import numpy as np
   ...: import statsmodels.api as sm
```

```
        ...: import statsmodels.formula.api as smf
In [2]: Cancer = pd.read_csv('http://stat4ds.rwth-aachen.de/data/Cancer2.dat', sep='\s+')
In [3]: Cancer.head(2)
Out[3]:
   time  histology  stage  count  risktime
0     1          1      1      9       157
1     1          2      1      5        77
In [4]: logrisktime = np.log(Cancer.risktime)
   ...: fit = smf.glm('count ~ C(histology) + C(stage) + C(time)',
           family = sm.families.Poisson(), offset = logrisktime, data = Cancer).fit()
   ...: print(fit.summary())                              # edited output
=======================================================================
                     coef  std err       z  P>|z|   [0.025  0.975]
-----------------------------------------------------------------------
Intercept          -3.0093   0.167  -18.073  0.000   -3.336  -2.683
C(histology)[T.2]   0.1624   0.122    1.332  0.183   -0.077   0.401
C(histology)[T.3]   0.1075   0.147    0.729  0.466   -0.181   0.397
C(stage)[T.2]       0.4700   0.174    2.694  0.007    0.128   0.812
C(stage)[T.3]       1.3243   0.152    8.709  0.000    1.026   1.622
C(time)[T.2]       -0.1275   0.149   -0.855  0.393   -0.420   0.165
# to save space, not showing other time effects
```

After fitting the model, we can construct an analysis of deviance analog of an ANOVA table showing results of likelihood-ratio tests for the effects of individual explanatory variables, and construct CIs for effects (here, comparing stages 2 and 3 to stage 1):

```
In [5]: fit1 = smf.glm('count ~ C(stage) + C(time)',
            family = sm.families.Poisson(), offset = logrisktime,
            data = Cancer).fit()
   ...: fit2 = smf.glm('count ~ C(histology) + C(time)',
            family = sm.families.Poisson(), offset = logrisktime,
            data = Cancer).fit()
   ...: fit3 = smf.glm('count ~ C(histology) + C(stage)',
            family = sm.families.Poisson(), offset = logrisktime,
            data = Cancer).fit()
In [6]: D = fit.deviance; D1 = fit1.deviance
   ...: D2 = fit2.deviance; D3 = fit3.deviance
   ...: df = fit.df_resid; df1 = fit1.df_resid          # residual df values
   ...: df2 = fit2.df_resid; df3 = fit3.df_resid
   ...: from scipy import stats
   ...: P_hist = 1 - stats.chi2.cdf(D1 - D, df1 - df)   # like.-ratio
   ...: P_stage = 1 - stats.chi2.cdf(D2 - D, df2 - df)  # test P-values
   ...: P_time = 1 - stats.chi2.cdf(D3 - D, df3 - df)
In [7]: pd.DataFrame({'Variable':['C(histology)', 'C(stage)', 'C(time)'],
            'LR Chisq':[round(D1-D,3), round(D2-D,3), round(D3-D,3)],
            'df': [df1 - df, df2 - df, df3 - df],
            'Pr(>Chisq)': [P_hist, P_stage, P_time]})
       Variable  LR Chisq  df  Pr(>Chisq)
0  C(histology)     1.876   2    0.391317
1      C(stage)    99.155   2    0.000000
2       C(time)    11.383   6    0.077237

In [8]: CI = np.exp(fit.conf_int(alpha = 0.05))
   ...: CI.iloc[[3]]                    # 95% CI for multiplicative effect of
Out[8]:                                 # stage 2, compared to stage 1
                      0         1
C(stage)[T.2]  1.136683  2.252211
In [9]: CI.iloc[[4]]                    # 95% CI for multiplicative effect of
Out[9]:                                 # stage 3, compared to stage 1
                      0        1
C(stage)[T.3]  2.790695  5.06488
```

B.7.5   Negative Binomial Modeling of Count Data

Negative binomial modeling of count data has more flexibility than Poisson modeling, because the response variance can exceed the mean, permitting overdispersion. As in Section 7.5.3, we first show that the marginal distribution of the number of satellites for the female horseshoe crabs exhibits more variability than the Poisson permits and then plot a histogram of the satellite counts (not shown here):

```
In [1]: import pandas as pd
   ...: import numpy as np
   ...: import statsmodels.api as sm
   ...: import statsmodels.formula.api as smf
   ...: import matplotlib.pyplot as plt
In [2]: Crabs = pd.read_csv('http://stat4ds.rwth-aachen.de/data/Crabs.dat', sep='\s+')
In [3]: round(np.mean(Crabs.sat), 4)        # mean number of satellites
Out[3]: 2.9191
In [4]: round(np.var(Crabs.sat), 4)         # variance of number of satellites
Out[4]: 9.8547 # overdispersion: for Poisson, true variance = mean
In [5]: plt.hist(Crabs['sat'], density=True, bins=16, edgecolor='k')
   ...: plt.ylabel('Proportion'); plt.xlabel('Satellites');
```

To fit a negative binomial GLM, first we fit the model to estimate the dispersion parameter ($1/k$ in formula (7.7), called *alpha* in the **Python** output). This stage yields correct estimates for the model parameters but not for their standard errors. In a second step, we re-fit the negative binomial GLM, setting the dispersion parameter equal to the estimate derived in the first step:

```
In [6]: from statsmodels.discrete.discrete_model import NegativeBinomial
In [7]: model = NegativeBinomial.from_formula('sat ~ weight + C(color)',
              data = Crabs, loglike_method='nb2')
In [8]: fit_dispersion = model.fit()
   ...: print(fit_dispersion.summary())
Out[8]: # correct estimates but wrong std. errors; alpha = dispersion est.
==================================================================
                 coef   std err      z    P>|z|   [0.025    0.975]
------------------------------------------------------------------
Intercept      -0.4263   0.559   -0.762   0.446   -1.522    0.670
C(color)[T.2]  -0.2528   0.351   -0.721   0.471   -0.940    0.435
C(color)[T.3]  -0.5219   0.379   -1.376   0.169   -1.265    0.222
C(color)[T.4]  -0.4804   0.428   -1.124   0.261   -1.319    0.358
weight          0.7121   0.178    4.005   0.000    0.364    1.061
alpha           1.0420   0.190    5.489   0.000    0.670    1.414
==================================================================

In [9]: a = fit_dispersion.params[5]                  # a set equal to alpha
   ...: fit = smf.glm('sat ~ weight + C(color)', family =
                  sm.families.NegativeBinomial(alpha = a), data = Crabs).fit()
In [10]: print(fit.summary())                          # edited output
              Generalized Linear Model Regression Results
          Deviance:    196.56              Df Residuals: 168
==================================================================
                 coef   std err      z    P>|z|   [0.025    0.975]
------------------------------------------------------------------
Intercept      -0.4263   0.538   -0.792   0.428   -1.481    0.629
C(color)[T.2]  -0.2527   0.349   -0.725   0.468   -0.936    0.430
C(color)[T.3]  -0.5218   0.380   -1.373   0.170   -1.266    0.223
C(color)[T.4]  -0.4804   0.428   -1.122   0.262   -1.320    0.359
weight          0.7121   0.161    4.410   0.000    0.396    1.029
==================================================================

In [9]: print('AIC:', round(fit.aic, 3))
AIC: 755.935       # better fit than Poisson loglinear model in Section B.7.3
```

An analysis of deviance table can be constructed for this model, analogous to the tables constructed for the Poisson loglinear models in Section B.7.4.

B.7.6 Regularization: Penalized Logistic Regression Using the Lasso

The lasso regularization method is available with `glmnet`, which first has to be installed.[10] We illustrate it for the logistic regression model fitted on the student survey data, with response variable the opinion about whether abortion should be legal in the first three months of a pregnancy (1 = yes, 0 = no) and with 14 explanatory variables. The response and the explanatory variables in `glmnet` must be in separate arrays of type 'float64', using only the variables to be employed in the model. In our case, we therefore drop the variables `subject`, `abor` and `life` from the `Students` data frame. Using cross validation, the smoothing parameter that minimizes the mean prediction error is saved as *lambda_max_*, and the value from the one-standard-error rule is saved as *lambda_best_*. The latter is used for estimates and predictions unless the user selects an alternative value. The results shown next utilize it:

```
In [1]: conda install -c conda-forge glmnet
In [2]: import pandas as pd
   ...: import numpy as np
   ...: import matplotlib.pyplot as plt
   ...: from glmnet import LogitNet
In [3]: Students=pd.read_csv('http://stat4ds.rwth-aachen.de/data/Students.dat',sep='\s+')
   ...: y = Students.abor
   ...: x = Students.drop(['subject', 'abor', 'life'], axis = 1).astype('float64')
In [4]: fit = LogitNet()                  # ElasticNet() for regularized linear model
   ...: fit = fit.fit(x, y)
In [5]: print(fit.intercept_)
2.3671347098687052
In [6]: print(fit.coef_) # default: one std. error rule for smoothing.
[[ 0.          0.          0.          0.          0.          0.
   0.          0.          0.          0.          0.          0.
  -0.25995012 -0.18310286  0.          ]]    # only ideol and relig have
                                             # non-zero estimates
In [7]: print(fit.lambda_best_)              # smoothing parameter for one se rule
[0.12677869]
In [8]: print(fit.lambda_max_)               # smoothing to minimize prediction error
0.037826288644684083                         # less smoothing
In [9]: p = fit.predict(x)                    # predict abortion response category
   ...: prob = fit.predict_proba(x)           # probability estimates
```

The `Python` Appendix at the book's website shows code to plot the lasso model parameter estimates as a function of the smoothing parameter, similar to Figure 7.9. By default, `LogitNet` applies 3-fold cross-validation. The `Python` Appendix at the book's website shows how to change this to 10-fold.

B.8   Chapter 8: PYTHON for Classification and Clustering

B.8.1   Linear Discriminant Analysis

We illustrate a linear discriminant analysis (LDA) for the example in Section 8.1.2 of whether female horseshoe crabs have male satellites ($y = 1$, yes; $y = 0$, no). That section notes that it is sufficient to use weight or carapace width together with color as explanatory variables, and here we use width and color. In `Python`, `sklearn` requires the response variable and the explanatory variables (y and X) to be `numpy arrays`. We find the linear

---

[10]See `https://pypi.org/project/glmnet`

discriminant function,[11] the prediction for Y and the posterior probabilities for the two categories of Y at a particular setting of the explanatory variables, and then show how to find these for the horseshoe crabs in the sample:

```
In [1]: import pandas as pd
   ...: import numpy as np
   ...: import matplotlib.pyplot as plt
In [2]: Crabs = pd.read_csv('http://stat4ds.rwth-aachen.de/data/Crabs.dat', sep='\s+')
In [3]: y = np.asarray(Crabs['y'])          # we form X so it has only width and color
   ...: X = np.asarray(Crabs.drop(['crab','sat','y','weight','spine'], axis=1))
   ...: from sklearn.discriminant_analysis  import LinearDiscriminantAnalysis
   ...: lda = LinearDiscriminantAnalysis(priors=None)
   ...: lda.fit(X, y)
In [4]: lda.coef_
Out[4]: array([[ 0.429729, -0.552606]])  # coefficients of linear discriminant function
In [5]: print(lda.predict([[30, 3]]))     # predict y at x1 = 30, x2 = 3
[1]       # predicted y = 1 (yes for satellites) at width = 30, color = 3
In [6]: print(lda.predict_proba([[30, 3]]))
[[0.11866592 0.88133408]]                 # posterior probabilities for y=0 and y=1
# category predictions and associated probabilities for the sample:
In [7]: y_pred = lda.predict(X)
   ...: y_pred_prob = lda.predict_proba(X)
In [8]: print(y_pred)                      # only first line shown, for crabs 1 - 35
[1 0 1 0 1 0 1 0 0 1 0 1 1 0 1 1 1 1 0 1 0 1 0 1 0 0 1 1 1 1 1 1 1 1 1]
In [9]: print(y_pred_prob)  # estimates of post. [P(Y=0),P(Y=1)] shown only for two crabs
[0.1385732  0.8614268 ]                    # crab 1 had width x1 = 28.3, color x2 = 2
[0.77168388 0.22831612]                    # crab 2 had width x1 = 22.5, color x2 = 3
```

The reported predictions and posterior probabilities take the prior probability π_0 for $P(Y = 1)$ to be the default value, which is the sample proportion with $y = 1$. You can set an alternative, such as by replacing *priors=None* with *priors = (0.5, 0.5)*.

A scatterplot of the explanatory variable values can show the actual y values and use a background color to show the predicted value. The **Python** Appendix at the book's website shows code for doing this. Figure B.9 shows the plot.

We can evaluate the quality of prediction achieved by a LDA or a logistic regression model with a classification table and ROC curve (Section 8.1.3). The **Python** Appendix at the book's website shows how to obtain a classification table. Using the observed category membership for our data (y) and the LDA predicted probabilities for $Y = 1$, here is code for constructing the ROC curve and finding the area under the curve to summarize the predictive power:

```
In [10]: def plot_roc(fpr, tpr):
   ...:     splot= plt.subplot()
   ...:     roc_auc = auc(fpr, tpr)
   ...:     plt.figure(1, figsize=(12, 6))
   ...:     plt.plot(fpr, tpr, lw=2, alpha=0.7, color='red', label='AUC=%0.4f'%(roc_auc))
   ...:     plt.plot([0, 1], [0, 1], linestyle='--', lw = 0.7, color = 'k',alpha = .4)
   ...:     plt.xlim([-0.05, 1.05]); plt.ylim([-0.05, 1.05])
   ...:     plt.xlabel('1 - Specificity'); plt.ylabel('Sensitivity')
   ...:     plt.legend(loc = 'lower right')
   ...:     return splot

In [11]: from sklearn.metrics import roc_curve
   ...: from sklearn.metrics import auc
In [12]: fpr, tpr, thresholds = roc_curve(y, y_pred_prob[:,1])
   ...: roc_auc = auc(fpr, tpr); roc_auc        # area under ROC curve
Out[12]: 0.7640947399011915
In [13]: plot_roc(fpr, tpr)                      # plots the ROC curve
```

---

[11]The linear discriminant coefficients provided by the default singular value decomposition solver (*solver='svd'*) differ slightly from those found by R, but the estimated probabilities are the same.

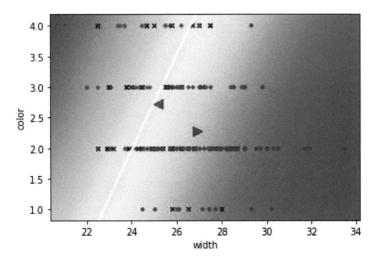

FIGURE B.9 Scatterplot for width and color of horseshoe crabs. The region of values that have $\hat{y} = 0$ (relatively low width and dark color) is shaded in red and the region of values that have $\hat{y} = 1$ (relatively high width and light color) is shaded in blue. The points use those same colors to show the actual y values, with x indicating an incorrect prediction.

The ROC curve is also relevant for predictions made using logistic regression. Next we fit that model to these data and find the ROC curve and the area under it:

```
In [14]: import statsmodels.api as sm
    ...: import statsmodels.formula.api as smf
In [15]: fit = smf.glm('y ~ width + color', family = sm.families.Binomial(),
                       data=Crabs).fit()
In [16]: print(fit.summary())
              Generalized Linear Model Regression Results
              coef    std err        z     P>|z|    [0.025    0.975]
-----------------------------------------------------------------------
Intercept  -10.0708    2.807    -3.588    0.000   -15.572    -4.569
width        0.4583    0.104     4.406    0.000     0.254     0.662
color       -0.5090    0.224    -2.276    0.023    -0.947    -0.071
=======================================================================
In [17]: predictions = fit.predict()
In [18]: fpr, tpr, thresholds = roc_curve(y, predictions)
In [19]: auc(fpr, tpr)                   # area under ROC curve
Out[19]: 0.762205754141238
In [20]: plot_roc(fpr, tpr)              # plots the ROC curve
```

Figure B.10 shows the ROC curves for LDA and logistic regression.

B.8.2   Classification Trees and Neural Networks for Prediction

To illustrate **Python** construction of a classification tree, we use the example in Section 8.1.4 of classification of horseshoe crabs on whether male satellites are present, continuing the analysis of the previous section using carapace width and color as predictors. The impurity criterion for splitting can be the default Gini impurity or an entropy measure corresponding to maximizing the binomial log-likelihood function. Options to control the pruning of a classification tree include setting the maximal number of leaf (terminal) nodes or setting a

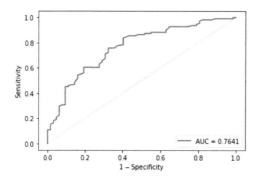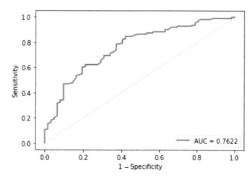

FIGURE B.10 ROC curves for the prediction about horseshoe crab satellites (yes or no), using width and color explanatory variables, for LDA (left) and logistic regression (right).

complexity parameter (*ccp_alpha*). Here we show code for the tree that sets the number of terminal nodes equal to 3, which is the size of the second tree shown in Figure 8.1.4:

```
# continuing with Crabs file and X and y arrays previously formed
In [21]: from sklearn import tree
   ...: clf = tree.DecisionTreeClassifier(criterion = 'gini', max_leaf_nodes=3).fit(X, y)
In [22]: X_names=['width', 'color']
   ...: y_names=['no', 'yes']
   ...: fig, axes = plt.subplots(nrows = 1, ncols = 1, figsize = (4,4), dpi=300)
   ...: # classification tree shown in figure:
   ...: tree.plot_tree(clf, feature_names = X_names, class_names = y_names, filled=True)
In [23]: from sklearn import metrics
   ...: y_pred = clf.predict(X)
   ...: print('Accuracy:', metrics.accuracy_score(y, y_pred))
Accuracy: 0.716763006              # proportion correct = (44 + 75 + 5)/173 = 0.717
```

Figure B.11 shows the classification tree obtained, which surprisingly differs somewhat from the one in Section 8.1.4 using **R** with the same (*gini*) criterion. It predicts that the crabs that have satellites are the ones of width greater than 25.85 *cm* that are in color classes 1, 2, and 3, of which the terminal node tells us that 13 did not have satellites and 75 did. For these data, the overall proportion of correct predictions with this tree is $(44 + 75 + 5)/173$ = 0.717. The tree constructed with three terminal nodes by **R**, shown in Figure 8.2, also predicted satellites for horseshoe crabs of color 4 with width above 25.85 *cm* and those of colors 1 and 2 with width less than 25.85 *cm*.

To illustrate **Python** for a neural network analysis, we continue the analysis for the horseshoe crabs with width and color explanatory variables, using as the threshold for probability predictions the standard (0.50):

```
In [24]: from sklearn.neural_network import MLPClassifier
   ...: clf = MLPClassifier(solver = 'lbfgs')
In [25]: from sklearn.model_selection import train_test_split
   ...: # use 2/3 to train, 1/3 to test
   ...: X_train, X_test, y_train, y_test = train_test_split(X, y, test_size=0.33)
In [26]: clf.fit(X_train, y_train)
   ...: y_pred = clf.predict(X_test)     # y predictions for test data
   ...: y_pred_prob = clf.predict_proba(X_test)
In [27]: from sklearn.metrics import confusion_matrix
In [28]: confusion_matrix = confusion_matrix(y_test, y_pred)
   ...: print(confusion_matrix)   # classification table
classification table:
[[10  7]                # accuracy proportion (10 + 38)/58 = 0.828
 [ 3 38]]               # this is random, depending on which 2/3 chosen for training
```

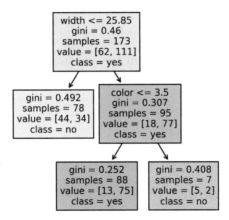

FIGURE B.11 Classification tree for whether a female crab satellite class is *yes* ($\hat{y} = 1$, in blue) or *no* ($\hat{y} = 0$, in orange).

The default solver used in `MLPClassifier` is a stochastic gradient-based optimizer called 'adam'. Here we instead used the quasi-Newton type optimizer 'lbfgs', which is preferable for small data sets in terms of convergence and performance. This classifier does not have an option for controlling the threshold probability for predictions, so the `Python` Appendix at the book's website provides a function for this and shows the analysis using the sample proportion with $y = 1$ (0.64) as the threshold.

B.8.3   Cluster Analysis

Hierarchical clustering can be performed with various linkage methods and norms for computing the linkage. For quantitative variables with the 'ward' linkage (Section A.8.4), which is the default, only the 'euclidean' norm is available. For the criterion to stop the clustering, one can specify the number of desired clusters or specity a linkage distance threshold. We illustrate hierarchical clustering with 'average' linkage and 'manhattan' distance for the example of Section 8.2.3 of clustering U.S. states by results of ten Presidential elections:

```
In [1]: import pandas as pd
   ...: from sklearn.cluster import AgglomerativeClustering
   ...: Elections = pd.read_csv('http://stat4ds.rwth-aachen.de/data/Elections2.dat',
                                  sep='\s+')
   ...: Elections.head(2)
Out[1]:
   number       state  e1  e2  e3  e4  e5  e6  e7  e8  e9  e10
0       1     Arizona   0   0   0   0   1   0   0   0   0    0
1       2  California   0   0   0   1   1   1   1   1   1    1
In [2]: y = np.array(Elections['state'])
   ...: state = ['Arizona','California','Colorado','Florida','Illinois','Massachusetts',
            'Minnesota','Missouri','NewMexico','NewYork','Ohio','Texas','Virginia','Wyoming']
   ...: X = np.array(Elections.drop(['number','state'], axis=1))
   ...: clustering = AgglomerativeClustering(n_clusters = None, affinity = 'manhattan',
                     linkage = 'average', distance_threshold = 0.01).fit(X)
In [3]: cluster = clustering.labels_
In [4]: import matplotlib.pyplot as plt
   ...: import scipy.cluster.hierarchy as sch
   ...: # Calculate the distance matrix:
In [5]: Z = sch.linkage(X, method = 'average', metric = 'cityblock')
   ...: plt.figure(figsize = (10, 7))
```

```
...: # form dendrogram (not shown):
...: sch.dendrogram(Z, orientation = 'top', labels = state, leaf_rotation = 80,
                    distance_sort = 'descending', show_leaf_counts = False)
```

We next construct the heatmap with the dendrogram. Rather than apply it to the
np.array X, it is better to apply it to a data frame (X1 below) so that the plot can have
labels (here, the states):

```
In [6]: import seaborn as sns
   ...: sns.set(color_codes = True)
In [7]: X1 = Elections.drop(['number', 'state'], axis=1)
   ...: X1.index = state
In [8]: g = sns.clustermap(X1, metric = 'cityblock',
           method = 'average', figsize=(7, 5), col_cluster = False,
           dendrogram_ratio = (.1, .2), cbar_pos=(0, .2, .03, .4),
           xticklabels = True,    # adds variables as labels
           yticklabels = True,    # adds states as labels
           cmap = 'coolwarm')     # heatmap with dendrogram
```

Figure B.12 shows the dendrogram and heatmap produced with this code.

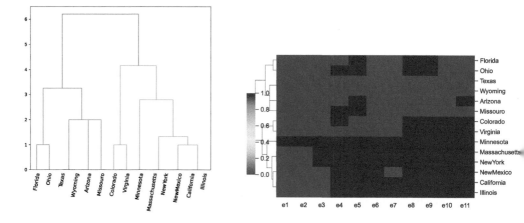

FIGURE B.12 Dendrogram and heatmap with dendrogram for the cluster analysis of the
election data.

C

Brief Solutions to Exercises

This appendix provides brief solutions or hints to odd numbered exercises of all chapters.

C.1 Chapter 1: Solutions to Exercises

1.1 (a) (i) an individual voter, (ii) the 1882 voters of exit poll, (iii) the 11.1 million voters
   (b) Statistic: Sample percentage of 52.5% who voted for Feinstein
      Parameter: Population percentage of 54.2% who voted for Feinstein

1.3 (a) Quantitative; (b) categorical; (c) categorical; (d) quantitative

1.5 Ordinal, because categories have natural ordering.

1.7 In R, for students numbered 00001 to 52000,

```
> sample(1:52000, 10)              # (output not shown)
```

1.9 Median = 4, mode = 2, expect mean larger than median (distribution is skewed right).

1.11 Skewed to the right, because the mean is much larger than the median.

1.13 (a) 63,000 to 75,000; (b) 57,000 to 81,000; (c) 51,000 to 87,000. 100,000 would be unusual.

1.15 Skewed right (distances of median from LQ and min. are less than from UQ and max.).

1.17
```
> Murder <- read.table("http://stat4ds.rwth-aachen.de/data/Murder.dat", header=TRUE)
> Murder1 <- Murder[Murder$state!="DC",]    # data frame without D.C.
```

(a)
```
> mean(Murder1$murder); sd(Murder1$murder)  # mean = 4.87, st. dev. = 2.59
```

(b) Min.=1.0, LQ=2.6, median=4.85, U = 6.2, max.=12.4, somewhat skewed right
```
> summary(Murder1$murder); boxplot(Murder1$murder)
```

(c) Repeat the analysis above for `Murder1$murder`. The DC is a large outlier, causing the mean to increase and the range to increase dramatically.

1.19 (a) Highly skewed right
```
> Houses <- read.table("http://stat4ds.rwth-aachen.de/data/Houses.dat",
+                       header=TRUE);  attach(Houses)
> PriceH <- hist(price); hist(price)        # save histogram to use its breaks
> breaks <- PriceH$breaks                   # breaks used in histogram
> freq <- table(cut(Houses$price,breaks, right=FALSE))
> cbind(freq,freq/nrow(Houses))             # frequency table (not shown)
```

(b) $\bar{y}$ = 233.0, s = 151.9; 85%, not close to 68% because highly skewed

DOI: 10.1201/9781003159834-C

```
                   > length(case[mean(price)-sd(price)<price & price<mean(price+sd(price)]) /
                   +     nrow(Houses)
```

(c)   ```
        > boxplot(price) # shows many large observations that are outliers
        ```

(d)     ```
        > tapply(Houses$price, Houses$new, summary)   # (output not shown)
        ```

New homes tend to have higher selling prices.

1.21 Correlation = 0.278 (positive but weak), predicted college GPA is 2.75 + 0.22 (high school GPA), which is 3.6 for high school GPA of 4.0.

1.23
```
> attach(Students)
> table(relig, abor)   # (output not shown)
```

The very religious are less likely to support legal abortion (only 2 of the 9 supporters).

1.25
```
> Races <- read.table("http://stat4ds.rwth-aachen.de/data/ScotsRaces.dat", header=TRUE
> attach(Races)
> par(mfrow=c(2,2))              # a matrix of 2x2 plots in one graph
> boxplot(timeM); boxplot(timeW)
> hist(timeM); hist(timeW)
> summary(timeM)                 # (output not shown)
> summary(timeW)                 # (output not shown)
> dev.off()                      # reset the graphical parameter mfrow
> plot(timeM, timeW)
> cor(timeM, timeW)              # output: [1] 0.9958732
> summary(lm(timeW ~ timeM))     # (output not shown)
```

Both distributions are skewed right with an extreme outlier. Men's and women's record times are very strongly correlated (predict one based on the other with a linear equation).

1.27
```
> Sheep <- read.table("http://stat4ds.rwth-aachen.de/data/Sheep.dat",header=TRUE)
> attach(Sheep)
> tapply(weight, survival, summary)    # (output not shown)
> tapply(weight, survival, sd)         # (output not shown)
> boxplot(weight ~ survival, xlab="weight", horizontal=TRUE)
```

1.29 Every possible sample is not equally likely; e.g. two people listed next to each other on the list cannot both be in sample.

1.31 (b) is the correct response.

1.33 Observational. No, correlation does not imply causation.

1.35 When n is only 20, the shape is highly irregular, varying a lot from sample to sample.

1.37 Estimate (ii) because those having more friends are more likely to be sampled.

1.39 (a) Range summarizes only two most extreme observations whereas s uses all the data.
     (b) IQR is not affected by outliers; the range is greatly affected by a single outlier.

1.41 The standard deviation of the $\bar{y}$ values generated should be about 2.9 when $n = 30$ for each sample and 0.5 when $n = 1000$ for each sample.

1.43 $[\sum_i (y_i + c)]/n = \bar{y} + c$; $\sum_i [(y_i + c) - (\bar{y} + c)]^2 = \sum_i (y_i - \bar{y})^2 = s^2$ and s do not change. $[\sum_i (cy_i)]/n = c\bar{y}$; $\sum_i (cy_i - c\bar{y})^2/(n-1) = c^2 s^2$ and thus s multiplies by $|c|$.

1.45 (a) 1, (b) 1/4, (c) 1/9, much larger than the values 32%, 5%, close to 0% for a bell-shape; Chebyshev applies to *any* distribution, not only bell-shaped ones.

1.47 Setting the derivative of f with respect to c equal to zero gives $c = (\sum_i y_i)/n = \bar{y}$ (critical point). Since f is a convex function of c, the critical point $\bar{y}$ corresponds to a global minimum.

1.49 (a) is the correct response.

C.2   Chapter 2: Solutions to Exercises

2.1 Repeat the steps of the example in Section 2.1.1, for a rain probability of 0.30 (let say that generating a random digit from $0, 1, \ldots, 9$, the outcomes 0, 1 and 2 denote rain).

2.3 (a) X given Y

(b) Need also $P(Y = white)$. Using 0.60 for it, $P(Y = w \mid X = w) = 0.903$.

2.5 (a) $(365)^3$ sample points for the 3 birthdays, $(365)(364)(363)$ of which are all different.

(b) Probability that at least 2 out of 23 have the same birthday is $1 - 0.493 = 0.507$.

(c)
```
> ind <- 0; iter <- 100000
> for(i in 1:iter){
+ s <- sample(1:365,50,replace=TRUE); d <- unique(s)
+ ind <- ind + as.numeric(length(d)!=length(s)) }
> ind/iter
```

2.7
```
> rbinom(1, 30000000, 0.50)/10000000  # theoretical expected value = 1.5000
```

2.9 (a) (i) $P(Y = 10) = 0.000$, (ii) $P(Y = 0) = 0.107$ (e.g., in R with $\texttt{dbinom(0, 10, 0.20)}$).

(b) $\mu = n\pi = 10(0.20) = 2$ and $\sigma = \sqrt{n\pi(1 - \pi)} = \sqrt{10(0.20)(0.80)} = 1.265$.

2.11 Solving $|1 - 2\pi|/\sqrt{n\pi(1 - \pi)} \le c$ for n, and for $\pi = 0.20$, $c = 0.3$, this is 25.

2.13 (a) $(5/6)^6 = 0.335$ (b) Geometric distribution $f(y) = (5/6)^{y-1}(1/6)$, $y = 1, 2, 3, \ldots$

2.15 If the company insures a very large number of homes n and the event that a home burns down on any particular week is independent from home to home and has the same tiny probability π for all insured homes. For very large n and very small π, the binomial distribution is approximated by the Poisson with $\mu = n\pi$.

2.17 The standard normal probability between $z = 1.40$ and $z = -0.60$ is 0.645.

2.19 (a) A: 0.159, B: 0.309 (b) 0.660 (c) 0.746

2.21 Mean and standard deviation both increase (their values are proportional to $1/\lambda$).

2.23
```
> Afterlife <- read.table("http://stat4ds.rwth-aachen.de/data/Afterlife.dat",
+                    header=TRUE);   attach(Afterlife)
> proportions(table(religion, postlife))          # sample joint distribution
> proportions(table(postlife)); proportions(table(religion)) # sample marginal dist.
> proportions(table(religion, postlife), 1)        # sample conditional dist.
```

2.25 $E(Y) = E[E(Y \mid X)] = E[70 + 0.60(X - 70)] = 70 + 0.60[E(X) - 70] = 70$.

2.27
```
> x <- rnorm(1000, 162, 7);   y <- rnorm(1000, 3.0 + 0.40*x, 8)
> plot(x, y);   cor(x, y)           # weak positive association
> mean(x); sd(x); mean(y); sd(y)
```

2.29 De Morgan's law extends to $(A_1 \cup A_2 \cup \cdots \cup A_p)^c = A_1^c A_2^c \cdots A_p^c$.

2.31 $f(x \mid y) = \frac{f(y|x)f_1(x)}{\int_a f(y|a)f_1(a)\,da}$.

2.33 $P(X = x \mid Y = y) = \frac{P(X=x \text{ and } Y=y)}{P(Y=y)} = \frac{P(Y=y|X=x)P(X=x)}{P(Y=y)} = \frac{P(Y=y)P(X=x)}{P(Y=y)} = P(X = x)$

2.35 The probability of an event for a continuous random variable is the area under the *pdf* for that event. For the event consisting of a single point, this area is 0.

2.37 $f(y) = (1 - \pi)^y \pi$, $\quad y = 0, 1, 2, \ldots$.

2.39 Prove that $E[Y(Y - 1)] = \sum_{y=0}^{\infty} y(y - 1) f(y; \mu) = \mu^2$. Thus, $E(Y^2) = E(Y) + \mu^2 = \mu + \mu^2$.

2.41 For any real number x, the *pdf* at value $y = \mu - x$ is the same as at value $y = \mu + x$.

2.43 (a) Solving $F(y; \lambda) = 1 - e^{-\lambda y} = 0.50$ for y yields median $= -\log(0.5)/\lambda = 0.693/\lambda$.

   (b) From Section 2.5.6 and for $p = 0.25$ and $p = 0.75$, these are $0.288/\lambda$ and $1.386/\lambda$.

   (c) $E(Y) = \int_0^\infty y \lambda e^{-\lambda y} dy = \frac{1}{\lambda} \int_0^\infty \frac{\lambda^2}{\Gamma(2)} e^{-\lambda y} y^{2-1} dy = \frac{1}{\lambda}$, because the argument of the integral is a gamma *pdf* with parameters λ and $k = 2$, which integrates to 1. This is greater than the median because the distribution is skewed right.

   (d) Analogously to (c), prove that $E(Y^2) = \frac{2}{\lambda^2}$, so $\sigma^2 = E(Y^2) - \mu^2 = \frac{1}{\lambda^2}$.

2.45 Substituting $\lambda = k/\mu$ in (2.10) and (2.11) yields the result.

2.47 Every y value with $(y - \mu) = c$ and thus $(y - \mu)^3 = c^3$ has a corresponding y value with $(y - \mu) = -c$ and thus $(y - \mu)^3 = -c^3$ having the same value of $f(y)$, so integrating or summing over all y values gives $E(Y - \mu)^3 = 0$.

2.49 Consider that the standard deviation $\sqrt{\pi(1 - \pi)/n}$ converges toward 0 as $n \to \infty$. Also, the binomial disribution is increasingly bell-shaped around its mean $n\pi$ as n increases.

2.51 If g is concave, then $-g$ is convex, so $E[-g(Y)] \geq -g[E(Y)]$, so $E[g(Y)] \leq g[E(Y)]$. Prove that $g(y) = \log(y)$ is concave and $g(y) = 1/y$ is convex for $y > 0$.

2.53 X has a uniform distribution (see Section 2.5.7).

2.55 $E(Y) = E[E(Y \mid \lambda)] = E(\lambda) = \mu$.

2.57 (a) This is the product of the separate probability mass functions, by independence.

   (b) E.g., if we know $Y_1 = c$, then Y_2 cannot be larger than $n - c$. It cannot be Poisson distributed (Poisson has positive probabilities for every nonnegative integer value).

   (c) The conditional probability is $P[(Y_1 = y_1, \ldots, Y_c = y_c) \mid \sum_j Y_j = n] = \frac{n!}{\prod_i y_i!} \prod_i \pi_i^{y_i}$ where $\{\pi_i = \mu_i/(\sum_j \mu_j)\}$. This is the multinomial $(n, \{\pi_i\})$ distribution.

2.59 Your next move depends only on where you are now, not where you were in the past.

2.61 It is an application of the previous exercise.

2.63 (a) $E(X + Y) = E(X) + E(Y) = \mu_x + \mu_y$, so
   $\text{var}(X + Y) = E[(X - \mu_x) + (Y - \mu_y)]^2 = \text{var}(X) + \text{var}(Y) + 2\text{cov}(X, Y)$.

   (b) Analogous to (a).

2.65 (a) For simplicity of notation, take all means $= 0$, since they don't affect covariation. Then prove that $\text{cov}(X, Y) = \text{cov}(U + V, U + W) = \text{var}(U)$. Thus,
   $\text{corr}(X, Y) = \frac{\text{cov}(X,Y)}{\sqrt{[\text{var}(U+V)][\text{var}(U+W)]}} = \frac{\text{var}(U)}{\sqrt{[\text{var}(U)+\text{var}(V)][\text{var}(U)+\text{var}(W)]}}$.

   (b) As $\text{var}(U)$ increases, for fixed $\text{var}(V)$ and $\text{var}(W)$, $\text{corr}(X, Y)$ increases.

2.67 (a)
```
> Y <- rnorm(10) # similarly for n=100 and n=1000
> qqnorm(Y, col='blue', main='Y ~ N(0,1)'); abline(0,1)
```

(b) | `> Y <- rnorm(1000, 0, 16); qqnorm(Y) # slope of points is about 16`

(c) Analogous to (b) using `rexp(1000)` and `runif(1000)`. For interpretation, see the discussion in the R appendix.

(d) For the uniform$(0, 1)$, $q_i = i/(n + 1)$.

2.69 $Y = y$ if y successes occur in the first $y + k - 1$ trials and then a failure occurs on trial $y + k$. $\binom{y+k-1}{y}$ is the number of ways y successes can occur in $y + k - 1$ trials. The probability of each sequence with k failures and y successes is $\pi^y(1 - \pi)^k$, so the total $P(Y = y) = \binom{y+k-1}{y}\pi^y(1 - \pi)^k$.

2.71 (a) $G(y) = P(Y \leq y) = P[\log(Y) \leq \log(y)] = P[X \leq \log(y)] = F[\log(y)]$, so $g(y) = (1/y)f[\log(y)] = [1/y(\sqrt{2\pi}\sigma)]\exp\{-[\log(y) - \mu]^2/2\sigma^2\}$.

(b) Since $Y = e^X$ and $E(Y) = E(e^X)$, use the *mgf* of X for $t = 1, 2$, to get $E(Y) = E(e^X) = m(1)$ and $E(Y^2) = m(2)$.

(c) $P(Y \leq e^\mu) = P[\log(Y) \leq \mu] = 0.50$ (μ: mean of the normal distribution for $\log(Y)$).

(d) $\exp(\overline{x}) = \exp[(\Sigma_i \log(y_i))/n] = \exp[\log(\prod y_i)^{1/n}] = (\prod_i y_i)^{1/n}$.

2.73 (a) The *pdf* is nonnegative with $\int f(y)dy = \int_1^\infty \alpha/y^{\alpha+1}dy = -(1/y)^\alpha\Big|_{y=1}^{y=\infty} = 1$.

(b) $E(Y) = \alpha/(\alpha - 1)$ (c) With $\alpha = 0$, $\Sigma_{y=1}^\infty(c/y) = \infty$ for all c.

C.3   Chapter 3: Solutions to Exercises

3.1 | `> results <- rbinom(1000000, 2123, 0.50)/2123; summary(results); hist(results)`

If $\pi = 0.50$, we expect sample proportions between about 0.44 and 0.56 (min and max of the simulated values); 0.61 is unusually large, so we can predict that Klobuchar won.

3.3 The simulation (can be conducted analogous to Exercise 3.1) shows that $\hat{\pi} = 0.59$ is not highly unusual if $\pi = 0.5$. Notice that $\hat{\pi} = 0.59$ is within 3 standard errors from 0.5:

| `> 0.5 + c(-1,1)*3*sqrt(0.5*0.5/49)`   `# [1] 0.2857143 0.7142857`

3.5 (a) The theoretical standard errors $\sigma/\sqrt{n}$ are 1.00 when $\sigma = 5$ and 1.60 when $\sigma = 8$. The simulations had standard deviations very close to the theoretical values.

(b) | `> pgamma(25, shape=16, scale=1.25) - pgamma(15, ,shape=16, scale=1.25)`
`[1] 0.6879025  # close to 2/3 and similar to value for normal distributions`

3.7 (i) since as n increases, the standard deviation of the *number* of heads increases.

3.9 (a) (1,1), (1,2), ..., (1,6), (2,1), (2,2), ..., (2,6) , ...(6,1), (6,2), ..., (6,6)

$\overline{y}$	1	1.5	2	2.5	3	3.5	4	4.5	5	5.5	6
Probability	$\frac{1}{36}$	$\frac{2}{36}$	$\frac{3}{36}$	$\frac{4}{36}$	$\frac{5}{36}$	$\frac{6}{36}$	$\frac{5}{36}$	$\frac{4}{36}$	$\frac{3}{36}$	$\frac{2}{36}$	$\frac{1}{36}$

(b) With more rolls, $\overline{Y}$ converges to a normal distribution (Central Limit Theorem).

(c) | `> y <- NULL; for(i in 1:10000){y[i,] <- mean(sample(1:6, 10, replace=TRUE))}`
`> hist(y)    # the empirical sampling distribution is bell-shaped`

3.11
```
> mean(rpois(10,5));mean(rpois(1000,5));mean(rpois(100000,5));mean(rpois(10000000,5))
```

3.13 Code for simulating the sampling distribution of $\bar{y}$ for $n = 2$:

```
> y <- NULL;  n <- 2
> for(i in 1:100000){y[i] <- mean(runif(n, 0, 1))}       # sample mean for case i
> hist(y) # empirical sampling distribution of sample mean for samples of size n
```

This sampling distribution has a triangular shape. Run this with successively larger sample sizes to see the CLT convergence to a normal distribution.

3.15 (a) No, probably skewed right.

    (b) Normal by CLT, mean = 5.5, standard error = $3.9/\sqrt{1000} = 0.123$.

    (c) Almost certainly population mean is within 3 standard errors of sample mean.

3.17 (a) For $y = 1$ for females and $y = 0$ for males, $P(1) = 0.60$ and $P(0) = 0.40$.

    (b) $y = 1$ has proportion $18/50 = 0.36$ and $y = 0$ has proportion 0.64.

    (c) Bell-shaped (CLT), mean 0.60, standard error 0.069; 18 females very unusual.

3.19
```
> y <- rpois(1000000, 100000); mean(sqrt(y)); var(sqrt(y))
[1] 316.2278
[1] 0.2498776 # by delta method, variance close to 1/4 when Poisson mean is large
```

3.21
```
> y <- rnorm(25, 3.0, 0.4) # random sample of n=25 from population
> summary(y); hist(y)      # describes sample data distribution
> ybar <- rnorm(100000, 3.0, 0.4/sqrt(25)); hist(ybar)  # sample distribution of Ybar
```

3.23 (a) Unlike the population distribution, the empirical sampling distribution is bell-shaped, by the CLT. (b) The CLT holds for large n, not for $n = 2$.

3.25 The theoretical values are 0.50 for the mean and 0.05 for the standard deviation.

```
> y <-NULL; for(i in 1:10000){y[i] <- mean(rbinom(100, 1, 0.5)) }; mean(y); sd(y)
```

3.27 (a) For $\pi = 0$ or 1, $\sqrt{\pi(1-\pi)/n} = 0$. If $\pi = 1$, necessarily every trial is a success and $\hat{\pi} = 1.0$. There cannot be any variability.

    (b) The corresponding standard error formula is maximized at $\pi = 0.50$. It is easier to make a precise inference about π when it is near 0 or 1 than when it is near 0.50.

3.29
```
> expo_median <- function(n, lambda, B=10000){
+     par(mfrow=c(1,2), pin=c(2.2, 2.2))
+     for(i in 1:2){Y <- numeric(length=n[i]*B);
+       Y <- matrix(rexp(n[i]*B, lambda), ncol=n[i])
+       Ymed <- apply(Y, 1, median); hist(Ymed)}}
> n <- c(10, 100); expo_median(n, 1, 100000)   # call function for lambda=1
```

The sampling distribution of the sample median is skewed right for $n = 10$ but is approximately normal for $n = 100$.

3.31 The population distribution (see the exit poll example in the chapter).

3.33 (c) is the correct response.

3.35 (a): sample data tends to look like the population distribution (need not be bell-shaped). (b): population distributions can have any shape regardless of population size. (d): the sampling distribution gets narrower and bell-shaped as n increases and may be very different from the population distribution.

3.37 The finite population correction equals: (a) 0.995. (b) 0 when $N = n$, so the standard error is 0. (c) 1, so the standard error simplifies to σ.

3.39 Convergence in probability is stronger and implies convergence in distribution. The opposite is true only if that distribution has all its probability at a single point.

3.41 Use that for $g(\pi) = \arcsin(\sqrt{\pi})$, $g'(\pi) = 1/2\sqrt{\pi(1-\pi)}$ and multiply the square of this by the variance of $\hat{\pi}$.

3.43 Use that for the given function $g(t)$ it holds $[g(T) - g(0)] \approx (T-0)g'(0) = 0$ and $[g(T) - g(0)] \approx [(T-0)g'(0) + \frac{1}{2}(T-0)^2 g''(0)] = T^2$, being exact since g is quadratic.

3.45 (a) $E(e^{tT}) = E(\prod_i e^{tY_i}) = \prod_i m_i(t)$. (b) $m_T(t) = \prod_i m_i(t) = e^{n\mu t + n\sigma^2 t^2/2}$, i.e. the *mgf* of a $N(n\mu, n\sigma^2)$. (c) Poisson with mean $\sum_i \mu_i$. (d) $E(e^{tY_i}) = \pi(e^t) + (1-\pi)(e^0)$. The product of n of these gives the *mgf* for binom(n, π). (e) If $\pi_1 = \cdots = \pi_n$. (f) The exponential distribution is the gamma with $k = 1$. The product of n exponential *mgf*'s gives a gamma *mgf*. As n increases, this is approximately normal (by CLT).

C.4 Chapter 4: Solutions to Exercises

4.1
```
> y <- NULL; for(i in 1:100000){x <- rnorm(100, 0, 1)
+            y[i] <- (quantile(x, 0.75) + quantile(x, 0.25))/2 }; sd(y) # = 0.1108
```

The standard error of the sample mean is $\sigma/\sqrt{n} = 1/\sqrt{100} = 0.10$, so the sample mean seems to be a slightly better estimator.

4.3 $\hat{\pi} = 0.60$. The log function is monotone increasing and does not affect the value at which the function is maximized.

4.5 (a) Sample percentage for legalization increased from 19.6% (1973) to 66.4% (2018).

(b)
```
> library(proportion);  ciAllx(938, 1447, 0.05)
       method    x LowerLimit UpperLimit
1        Wald  938  0.6236337  0.6728417   # in 2018 a majority
4       Score  938  0.6232707  0.6724198   # favored legalization
```

4.7 Setting $0.05 = 1.96\sqrt{0.5(0.5)/n}$ yields $n = (1.96)^2(0.5)(0.5)/(0.05)^2 = 384$.

4.9 (a) Histogram shows skew to right. Sample point estimates are $\bar{y} = 20.33, s = 3.68$.
(b) $20.33 \pm 2.045(3.68)/\sqrt{30}$, which is $(18.96, 21.71)$.

```
> Chicago <- read.table("http://stat4ds.rwth-aachen.de/data/Chicago.dat",header=T)
> hist(Chicago$income); mean(Chicago$income); sd(Chicago$income); qt(0.025, 29)
> t.test(Chicago$income)$conf.int
```

4.11 (a) The 95% CI $\bar{y} \pm t_{\alpha/2, n-1}(s/\sqrt{n})$ is $(0.74, 2.66)$. (b) Now the CI is $(-1.46, 8.86)$, dramatically affected by the outlier.

4.13 (a) $\bar{y} = 7.29$, $s = 7.18$ (b) $se = 1.74$, $df = 16$, CI is $(3.6, 11.0)$. (c)

```
> family <- Anor$after[Anor$therapy=="f"] - Anor$before[Anor$therapy=="f"]
> t.test(family, control, var.equal=TRUE, conf.level=0.95)
95 percent confidence interval:   2.880164 12.549248
```

4.15 The 95% Wald CIs are (0.844, 0.883) for females, (0.716, 0.772) for males, and (0.085, 0.153) for the difference between the population proportions for females and males.

4.17 The plot suggests thicker or longer tails than the standard normal has:

```
> y <- rt(10000, 3); qqnorm(y, col='blue', main='y ~ t(3)'); abline(0,1)
```

4.19 (a) We can be 95% confident that the population median falls between 2 and 7 years:

```
> Books <- read.table("http://stat4ds.rwth-aachen.de/data/Library.dat",header=TRUE)
> boxplot(Books$C, xlab="Years since checked out", horizontal=TRUE)
> library(boot); boot.results <- boot(Books$C, function(x,i){median(x[i])}, 10000)
> boot.results; boot.ci(boot.results)
```

(b)

```
> boot.results2 <- boot(Books$C, function(x,i){sd(x[i])}, 100000)
> boot.results2; boot.ci(boot.results2)
Level      Percentile            BCa
95%      ( 8.03, 20.69 )    ( 9.92, 22.36 )
```

4.21 (a) A bootstrap CI for the trimmed mean is much narrower than the ordinary t CI:

```
> y <- rt(1000, 1) # 1000  observations from Cauchy (t distribution with df=1)
> boot.results <- boot(y, function(x,i){mean(x[i], 0.05)}, 10000)
> boot.ci(boot.results);  t.test(y)
```

(b) For heavy-tailed distributions, the sample median estimator seems more precise:

```
> boot.results2 <- boot(y,function(x,i){median(x[i])}, 10000); boot.ci(boot.results2)
Level      Percentile            BCa
95%      (-0.1264, 0.0756 )    (-0.1214, 0.0772 )
```

4.23 (a) ML estimate: $y/n = 1.0$ (b) Bayesian estimate: $(y+1)/(n+2) = 0.917$.

4.25 (a)
```
> library(proportion)
> ciBAx(0, 25, 0.05, 1.0, 1.0)
  x       LBAQx        UBAQx        LBAHx       UBAHx    # First: percentile CI
1 0 0.0009732879 0.1322746 2.440083e-10 0.1088304    # Second: HPD interval
```

(b) The equal-tail percentile interval cannot include exactly 0, because its lower bound is the 0.025 quantile of the beta posterior, which is > 0.

4.27 (a) Posterior mean estimate: 7.27, 95% eq.-tail percentile post. interval: (3.59, 10.95).

(b) 95% CI (3.58, 10.94). Similar results but different interpretations (Section 4.8.2).

4.29 For $\pi_1 = P(HG = 1 \mid NV = 1)$ and $\pi_2 = P(HG = 1 \mid NV = 0)$, the 95% Wald CI for $\pi_1 = \pi_2$ is (0.637, 0.848) which is unreliable, because $\hat{\pi}_1 = 1$. The score CI is (0.501, 0.833) and the Bayesian posterior interval is (0.479, 0.801).

4.31 The sample standard deviations are quite different, so it is safer to use the confidence interval that does not assume $\sigma_1 = \sigma_2$:

```
> Houses <- read.table("http://stat4ds.rwth-aachen.de/data/Houses.dat", header=TRUE)
> sd(Houses$price[Houses$new=="1"]); sd(Houses$price[Houses$new=="0"])
> t.test(Houses$price[Houses$new==1], Houses$price[Houses$new==0], var.equal=FALSE)
```

4.33
```
> n <- 100; y <- z <- NULL
> for(i in 1:100000){x <- rnorm(n, 0, 1); y[i] <- mean(x); z[i] <- median(x)}
par(mfrow=c(1,2), pin=c(2.3, 2.5)) # control the plots layout (two in a row) and size
plot(density(y)); plot(density(z))
> sum(y^2)/100000 # MSE for sample mean    # = 0.01000186 (better)
> sum(z^2)/100000 # MSE for sample median  # = 0.01552494
```

4.35 False for nonlinear functions. For instance, when $\sigma > 0$, even though $E(Y) = \mu$, with the function $g(y) = y^2$, $E(Y^2) > [E(Y)]^2 = (\mu)^2$.

4.37 (a) For a normal distribution $f(M) = f(\mu) = 1/\sqrt{2\pi}\sigma$ so the variance is approximately $1/4[f(M)]^2 n = \pi\sigma^2/2n$. (b) $\text{var}(\overline{Y})/\text{var}(\widehat{M}) = (\sigma^2/n)/[\pi\sigma^2/2n] = 2/\pi$. (c) The uniform has $f(M) = 1/\theta$ and $\widehat{M}$ has approximate variance $\theta^2/4n$. The sample mean is a much better estimator (its variance is a third that of the sample median).

4.39 (a) $L(\lambda) = n\log(\lambda) - \lambda\sum_i y_i$ for $\lambda > 0$. (b) The ML estimator is $\hat{\lambda} = 1/\overline{Y}$. (c) As n increases, $L(\lambda)$ becomes narrower, more parabolic, and a narrower range of λ values are plausible. (d) $I(\lambda) = n/\lambda^2$; the asymptotic distribution of $\hat{\lambda}$ is $N(\lambda, \lambda^2/n)$.

4.41 (a) $\ell(\lambda) = \left(\frac{\lambda^k}{\Gamma(k)}\right)^n e^{-\lambda\sum_i y_i} \prod_i(y_i^{k-1})$; use $\partial L(\lambda)/\partial\lambda = kn/\lambda - \sum_i y_i = 0$ to yield $\hat{\lambda} = k/\overline{Y}$. (b) The ML estimator of $E(Y)$ is $k/\hat{\lambda} = \overline{Y}$. (c) Using (2.11) and (4.3), $I(\lambda) = nk/\lambda^2$, so the large sample variance is $1/I(\lambda) = \lambda^2/kn$.

4.43 (a) $\hat{\mu} = \sum_i[\log(y_i)]/n$ and $\hat{\sigma}^2 = (1/n)\sum_i[\log(y_i)-\hat{\mu}]^2$. (b) The estimated standard error of $\hat{\mu} = \sum_i[\log(Y_i)]/n$ is $\hat{\sigma}/\sqrt{n}$. (c) $\hat{\mu}_y = e^{\hat{\mu}+\hat{\sigma}^2/2}$ and $\hat{\sigma}_y^2 = [e^{\hat{\sigma}^2} - 1][\hat{\mu}_y]^2$.

4.45 (a) $L(\pi) = 2y_1\log(\pi) + y_2\log(2) + y_2\log(\pi) + y_2\log(1-\pi) + 2y_3\log(1-\pi) + c$, where c is a constant, and $\hat{\pi} = (2y_1 + y_2)/2n$. (b) $I(\pi) = -E[\partial^2 L(\pi)/\partial\pi^2] = 2n/\pi(1-\pi)$ and the large-sample standard error of $\hat{\pi}$ is $\sqrt{\pi(1-\pi)/2n}$. (c) Use $\hat{\pi} \pm 1.96\sqrt{\hat{\pi}(1-\hat{\pi})/2n}$.

4.47 (a) Normal or t quantiles used in the margin of error decreases as the confidence level decreases. (b) Standard errors have $\sqrt{n}$ in the denominator, so diminish as n increases.

4.49 The standard error for estimating a mean is $\sigma/\sqrt{n}$, so to obtain a certain margin of error M, you need a larger n when σ is larger.

4.51 (a) is the correct response.

4.53 (a) incorrect: we make inference about μ, $\overline{y}$ is known. (b) correct. (c) incorrect: the CI is not summarizing the sample data distribution. (d) correct. (e) incorrect: the percentage of times $\overline{y}$ values would fall between 6.8 and 8.0 could be anything.

4.55 Express $X_1^2 + X_2^2$ as a sum of $d_1 + d_2$ squared indep. standard normal random variables.

4.57 (a) From the definition of a t random variable with $df = 1$, $Y = \frac{Z}{\sqrt{X^2/1}}$ where X^2 is a squared standard normal. So, Y is a ratio of standard normal random variables. (b) Sample mean is not converging (the mean does not exist for a Cauchy distribution); quantiles are converging to the true values.

```
> y <- rcauchy(10000000); mean(y); median(y); quantile(y,0.25); boxplot(y)
> summary(y)
     Min.   1st Qu.   Median    Mean  3rd Qu.      Max.    # extreme outliers
 -2159764        -1        0       5        1  33344648    # affect mean
```

4.59 From the Bayesian interval, the probability is 0.95 that μ is between 23.5 and 25.0. For the classical interval, with repeated samples, in the long run the CI would contain μ 95% of the time.

4.61 The posterior distribution is gamma with shape parameter $k^* = k + \sum_i y_i$ and rate parameter $\lambda^* = \lambda + n$. The mean is k^*/λ^* which is approximately $\overline{y}$ for large n.

4.63 (a) From Section 4.2.5, $U(\mathbf{y};\mu) = \frac{n(\bar{y}-\mu)}{\mu}$ and $I(\mu) = \frac{n}{\mu}$. (b) $\frac{U(\mathbf{y},\mu)}{\sqrt{I(\mu)}} = \frac{\sqrt{n}(\bar{y}-\mu)}{\sqrt{\mu}}$ and the score CI is the endpoints of the solution of the quadratic equation resulting from $\sqrt{n}(\bar{y}-\mu)/\sqrt{\mu} = \pm z_{\alpha/2}$.

4.65 (a) $\tilde{\pi} = \left(\frac{n}{n+2c}\right)\frac{Y}{n} + \left(\frac{2c}{n+2c}\right)\frac{1}{2}$ gives weight to $\hat{\pi}$ that decreases in c. (b) $|\text{bias}| = |1-2\pi|/(2+n/c)$ increases in c and $\text{var}(\tilde{\pi}) = n\pi(1-\pi)/(n+2c)^2$ decreases in c. (c) From Section 4.7.2, $\tilde{\pi}$ results using a beta prior for π with $\alpha = \beta = c$, say uniform ($c = 1$). As n increases, the weight given $(1/2)$ decreases and $\tilde{\pi}$ is more similar to $\hat{\pi}$.

4.67 (a) $\hat{\pi} = y/n$ and the midpoint of the 95% CI is $[\hat{\pi}+(1.96)^2/2n]/[1+(1.96)^2/n]$. Replacing 1.96 by 2.0, this is approximately $(y+2)/(n+4)$. (b) Follows replacing 1.96 by 2.

4.69 (a) $P(H,H) = P(H)P(H) = 0.25$ and $P(H,T) = P(H)P(T) = 0.25$ for two independent flips. $P(T,H) = \pi/2$ and $P(T,T) = (1-\pi)/2$. (b) $P(\text{head on second flip}) = 0.25 + \pi/2$. Equating this to $\tilde{\pi}$ yields $\hat{\pi} = 2(\tilde{\pi}-0.25)$. (c) (i) 0, (ii) 0.50

4.71 (a) $P(|\hat{\theta}-\theta| \geq \epsilon) = P[(\hat{\theta}-\theta)^2 \geq \epsilon^2) \leq E[(\hat{\theta}-\theta)]^2/\epsilon^2$. Since $E(\hat{\theta}-\theta)^2 \to 0$, the right-hand side goes to 0 as $n \to \infty$, so $\hat{\theta} \overset{p}{\to} \theta$. (b) If $E(\hat{\theta}) \to \theta$, then bias $\to 0$ and together with $\text{var}(\hat{\theta}) \to 0$, we have $\text{MSE}(\hat{\theta}) \to 0$ and then part (a) implies that $\hat{\theta} \overset{p}{\to} \theta$.

4.73 (a) $E(Z_i^2) = \text{var}(Z_i) = 1$, so $E(\chi_d^2) = E(Z_1^2 + \cdots + Z_d^2) = d$. (b) $X^2/d = (Z_1^2 + \cdots + Z_d^2)/d$, which by the law of large numbers converges to $E(Z^2) = 1$, so $\sqrt{X^2/d} \overset{p}{\to} 1$ Then, $T = Z/\sqrt{X^2/d}$ converges in distribution to that of Z.

4.75 (a) From equation (2.6), $f(y;\pi,n) = (1-\pi)^n\binom{n}{y}\exp\left[y\left(\log\frac{\pi}{1-\pi}\right)\right]$ (b) $\ell(\theta) = [B(\theta)]^n[\prod_i h(y_i)]\exp(\theta\sum_i y_i)$. The term involving the data and the parameter uses the data only through $\sum_i y_i$.

4.77 The distribution of the number of observations below the median follows by the definition of the median. For this example, $n = 54$ so $a = 20$ and $b = 34$, giving values 11 and 19.

4.79 $\frac{T(\mathbf{Y})-\theta}{\sigma_T} \leq 1.645$ is equivalent to $\theta \geq T(\mathbf{Y}) - 1.645\sigma_T = T_L(\mathbf{Y})$. For the proportion in Exercise 4.5, using the estimated standard error, $T_L(\mathbf{y}) = \hat{\pi} - 1.645\sqrt{\hat{\pi}(1-\hat{\pi})/n} = 0.628$.

4.81 The posterior expected loss $r_p^*(\hat{\theta} \mid \mathbf{y}) = E[(\theta-\hat{\theta})^2 \mid \mathbf{Y} = \mathbf{y}] = E[(\theta - E(\theta \mid \mathbf{y})^2 \mid \mathbf{Y} = \mathbf{y}] + [E(\theta \mid \mathbf{y}) - \hat{\theta}]^2$ is minimized when $[E(\theta \mid \mathbf{y}) - \hat{\theta}]^2 = 0$, that is, when $\hat{\theta} = E(\theta \mid \mathbf{y})$.

C.5   Chapter 5: Solutions to Exercises

5.1 (a) $H_0: \pi = 0.50$; (b) H_a: Population correlation > 0; (c) $H_0: \mu_1 = \mu_2$

5.3 $H_0: \pi = 0.50$, $H_a: \pi \neq 0.50$, $z = 26.8$, P-value < 0.0001 (extremely strong evidence against H_0). Since $\hat{\pi} > 0.5$, conclude that legalization is supported by a majority of Canadians.

5.5 $z = -0.26$ has P-value $= 0.60$ and we cannot reject H_0 (it is plausible that $\pi = 1/3$).

5.7 (a) $H_0: \mu = 2.0$, $H_a: \mu \neq 2.0$ (b) $t = 20.8$ and the P-value gives very strong evidence against H_0 (can conclude that $\mu > 2.0$).

5.9 The calculation of the *P*-value assumes a normal population distribution (to get the *t* sampling distribution) but in practice the population distribution is not exactly normal.

5.11 Insufficient evidence to conclude that the population mean ideology differs for Hispanics and Whites; strong evidence that it is lower for Blacks than for Whites/Hispanics.

5.13 The significance tests give strong evidence of a difference (*P*-values essentially 0) but do not tell us how much of a difference. The 95% CIs comparing strong Democrats to strong Republicans are (0.71, 1.33) for 1974 and (2.67, 3.07) for 2018.

5.15 Effect size for height is 1.96 and for marathon time 0.675. Effect is greater for height.

5.17
```
> Anor <- read.table("http://stat4ds.rwth-aachen.de/data/Anorexia.dat", header=TRUE)
> cogbehav <- Anor$after[Anor$therapy=="cb"] - Anor$before[Anor$therapy=="cb"]
> control  <- Anor$after[Anor$therapy=="c"] - Anor$before[Anor$therapy=="c"]
> cogbehav[15] <- 2.9; mean(control); mean(cogbehav); sd(control); sd(cogbehav)
> t.test(cogbehav, control, var.equal=TRUE)
```

Compare output to results in Section 5.3.2. A single outlier can have a substantial effect when the sample size is not very large.

5.19 Test statistic $z = 3.04$ and for $H_a: \pi_1 \neq \pi_2$, *P*-value = 0.002 gives strong evidence that the population proportion believing in life after death is higher for women.

5.21
```
> prop.test(c(133, 429), c(429, 487), correct=FALSE) # extremely strong evidence
X-squared = 313.5, df = 1, p-value < 2.2e-16        # of association
```

5.23 It is possible that happiness and gender are independent:
```
> Happy <- read.table("http://stat4ds.rwth-aachen.de/data/Happy.dat", header=TRUE)
> Gender <- Happy$gender; Happiness <- factor(Happy$happiness)
> levels(Happiness) <- c("Very", "Pretty", "Not too")
> GH.tab <- table(Gender, Happiness); chisq.test(GH.tab)   # (a)
> chisq.test(GH.tab)$expected                              # (b)
> stdres <- chisq.test(GH.tab)$stdres; stdres #
> library(vcd); mosaic(GH.tab, gp=shading_Friendly, residuals=stdres)
```

5.25 Continuing the code of Exercise 5.23, we conclude that it is plausible the divorced/separated and never married subjects to have the same conditional distribution on happiness, but those two combined differ from the married subjects:
```
> Marital <- factor(Happy$marital); levels(Marital) <-c("Married","Div/Sep","Never")
> MH.tab <- table(Marital, Happiness); MH.tab[2:3,];  chisq.test(MH.tab[2:3,])
> rbind(MH.tab[1,], MH.tab[2,]+MH.tab[3,])
> chisq.test(rbind(MH.tab[1,], MH.tab[2,]+MH.tab[3,]))
```

5.27 Relative to what's expected under independence of party ID and race, there are more Black Democrats and White Republicans and other-category Independents. Do also pairwise comparisons of groups for a particular response category.

5.29 For π = probability of greater relief with new analgesic than standard, testing H_0: $\pi = 0.50$ has *P*-value = 0046, giving considerable but not overwhelming evidence in favor of the new analgesic.

5.31 Assuming the two populations of interest (1: Fahal, 2: Daymaniyat) to be independent, compare the means of their clutch sizes ($H_0 : \mu_1 = \mu_2$ vs. $H_a : \mu_1 \neq \mu_2$) and the population proportions of failed nests ($H_0 : \pi_1 = \pi_2$ vs. $H_a : \pi_1 \neq \pi_2$). The Z-test is not suitable for the proportions comparison, since $y_1 = 1$ (very low for asymptotic inference). Using uniform priors, the 95% equal tailed posterior interval for $\pi_2 - \pi_1$ is (0.154 0.316).

5.33 (a) Jones has $z = 2.0$ and Smith has $z = 1.90$. The result is statistically significant only for Jones, even though in practical terms the results are very similar. (b) The 95% CIs for π [Jones: $(0.501, 0.599)$, Smith: $(0.499, 0.596)$] are almost identical, but the first does not contain 0.50, in agreement with its statistical significance.

5.35 Since $P(\text{fail to rej. } H_0 \mid \text{effect}) = 0.5$ and $P(\text{effect}) = 0.10$, $P(\text{No effect} \mid \text{rej. } H_0) = 0.47$.

5.37 The P-values are about 0.10 for all three methods.

5.39 (a) Test $H_0: \mu_1 = \mu_2$ vs. $H_a: \mu_1 \neq \mu_2$, without assuming equal population variances (the standard deviation of the prices for new and older homes are quite different): P-value=0.006. The 95% CI for $\mu_1 - \mu_2$ is $(79.6\ 377.6)$.

(b)
```
> median(PriceNew); median(PriceOld); library(EnvStats)
> test <- twoSamplePermutationTestLocation(PriceNew, PriceOld, fcn="median",
+    alternative="two.sided", exact=FALSE, n.permutations=100000); test$p.value
[1] 1e-05 # very strong evidence of a higher median selling price for new homes
```

5.41 Extremely strong evidence of a difference between the survival distributions (P-value = 0.00004, see Section 5.8.4). Estimated medians: 23 (drug group) and 8 (control group).

5.43 There are many plausible values for the parameter, not just the H_0 value, as a confidence interval for the parameter shows.

5.45 Prior and posterior $P(\mu_1 = \mu_2) = 0$, since the joint prior and posterior density of (μ_1, μ_2) are continuous and the volume over the diagonal line $\mu_1 = \mu_2$ under these pdf's is 0.

5.47 Reject H_0 at $\alpha = 0.01$ level is equivalent to the 99% confidence interval not containing the H_0 value of the parameter.

5.49 (b) and (d) are correct.

5.51 (a) We reject H_0 if α is any value ≥ 0.057. Of the set of values ≥ 0.057, 0.057 is the minimum and thus the smallest α-level at which H_0 can be rejected. (b) For any $\alpha \leq 0.057$, H_0 is not rejected and 100 falls in the corresponding $(1 - \alpha)$ CI (ranges between 94.3% CI and 99.9999...% CI). The narrowest is the 94.3% CI.

5.53 It is so difficult to convict anyone that many guilty people are found to be not guilty, thus making many Type II errors at the cost of a tiny chance of Type I error.

5.55 (a) $P(\text{Type II error})$ decreases as H_0 is more badly false. (b) Because at $\pi = 0.50$, the probability of rejecting H_0 is 0.05 (i.e., $P(\text{Type I error})$), so the probability of not rejecting H_0 is 0.95. (c) As n increases, $P(\text{Type II error})$ decreases.

5.57 With $H_a: \mu_1 > \mu_2$, the critical value for the rejection region will be smaller than with $H_a: \mu_1 \neq \mu_2$. So, it is easier to reject H_0 and thus less likely to make a Type II error.

5.59 Even if H_0 is true in all 40 cases, we expect to reject H_0 about $40(0.05) = 2$ times. Those two results could well be Type I errors.

5.61 See Section 5.6.4.

5.63 (a) From Section 4.2.5 with $\hat{\mu} = \bar{y}$, $2[L(\hat{\mu}) - L(\mu_0)] = 2n\{\bar{y}[\log(\bar{y}) - \log(\mu_0)] - (\bar{y} - \mu_0)\}$. (b) Use the R functions LRT and simstat (Section A.5.2 of the R Appendix) and verify the good approximation by the limiting chi-squared distribution:

```
> n <- 25; mu0 <- 3; B <- 100000;   stat <- simstat(B, n, mu0)
> hist(stat, prob=TRUE, border="blue", breaks="Scott")
> fchi2 <- function(x) {dchisq(x, 1)}; curve(fchi2, from=0, to=max(stat), add=T)
```

(c) 95% LR based CI: (3.27, 4.84); 95% Wald CI: (3.22, 4.78). (d) The maximized log-likelihood is $L(\hat{\mu}) = (n_1 + n_2)\{\bar{y}[\log(\bar{y})] - \bar{y}\}$ under H_0, and $L(\hat{\mu}_1, \hat{\mu}_2) = n_1[\bar{y}_1 \log(\bar{y}_1) - \bar{y}_1] + n_2[\bar{y}_2 \log(\bar{y}_2) - \bar{y}_2]$ under H_a. The LR test statistic is $2[L(\hat{\mu}_1, \hat{\mu}_2) - L(\hat{\mu})]$.

5.65 (a) Using $\hat{\pi}_j = y_j/n$, $2[L(\hat{\pi}_1, \cdots, \hat{\pi}_c) - L(\pi_{10}, \cdots, \pi_{c0})] = 2[\sum_j y_j \log(y_j/n) - \sum_j y_j \log(\pi_{j0})]$. There are $c - 1$ unknown parameters under H_a and none under H_0. Thus, $df = c - 1$.
(b) The test statistic is $2 \sum_j y_j \log(6y_j/100) = 3.17$ and H_0 is plausible (P-value=0.67).
(c)

```
> y <- rmultinom(1000000, 100, prob=rep(1/6,6)); T = colSums(2*(y*log(6*y/100)))
> 1 - ecdf(T)(3.17)   # [1] 0.683381
```

5.67 (a) $U(\mathbf{y}; \mu) = (1/\mu) \sum_i y_i - n$, $I(\mu) = n/\mu$ and the value of the score test statistic at $\mathbf{y}$ is $z = U(\mathbf{y}, \mu_0)/\sqrt{I(\mu_0)} = [(1/\mu_0)(\sum_i y_i) - n]/\sqrt{n/\mu_0}$. (b) Use that $I(\mu) = n/\mu$ and that $\sqrt{\bar{y}/n}$ is the estimated standard error. (c) With $\hat{\mu} = \bar{y}$, $2[L(\hat{\mu}) - L(\mu_0)] = 2n\{\bar{y}[\log(\bar{y}) - \log(\mu_0)] - (\bar{y} - \mu_0)\}$. (d) The Wald CI is $\bar{y} \pm z_{\alpha/2}\sqrt{\bar{y}/n}$. The score CI is the set of μ_0 for which $|z| = |\bar{y} - \mu_0|/\sqrt{\mu_0/n} \le z_{\alpha/2}$ (obtained by solving a quadratic equation).

5.69 For H_0: identical population distributions, the t test assumes that this common distribution in H_0 is normal while the permutation test makes no distributional assumption. Interpret the P-value of the permutation test.

5.71 An equal tailed 95% CI for $\mu_1 - \mu_2$ based on the inversion of a permutation test is derived by allocating a lower and an upper value for $\mu_1 - \mu_2$ at which the test has P-value=0.05. Trying various values for $\mu_1 - \mu_2$, we get the CI (67, 248).

5.73 (a) $F(T)$ and $1 - F(T)$ are left- and right-tail probabilities, which are one-sided P-values. The cdf of $U = 1 - F(T)$ is $G(u) = 1 - P[F(T) \le 1 - u] = u$, for $0 \le u \le 1$, i.e. uniform.
(b)

```
> y <- rbinom(1000000, 1500, 0.50); z <- (y/1500 - 0.50)/sqrt(0.5*0.5/1500)
> p <- 1 - pnorm(z); hist(p)   # approximately uniform
```

5.75 (a) $\ell(\theta)/\ell(\theta') = [B(\theta)/B(\theta')]^n \exp\{[Q(\theta) - Q(\theta')] \sum_i R(y_i)\}$: Since Q is monotone increasing, this is an increasing function of $\sum_i R(y_i)$. (b) The binomial is in the exponential distribution with $Q(\pi) = \log[\pi/(1-\pi)]$, which is monotone increasing in π, and $R(y) = y$, so $T = \sum_i R(y_i) = \sum_i y_i$.

C.6   Chapter 6: Solutions to Exercises

6.1 (a) The prediction equation for men's record time is $\hat{\mu} = -2.83 + 0.87x$, for a given women's record time x. The predicted men's record time for $x = 490.05$ min. is 423.94 min. (b) The correlation is positive and very strong (0.996). (c) The fit is quite similar but goes through the origin. For an increase in women's record time of t, men's record time is predicted to increase by $0.85t$.

6.3 Hawaii (observation 11) is an outlier, Delaware (observation 8) less so; their Cook's distance values of 0.28 and 0.17 are much larger than all the others. Removing Hawaii, the correlation changes from 0.698 to 0.782.

6.5 (a)

```
> Covid <-read.table("http://stat4ds.rwth-aachen.de/data/Covid19.dat",header=T)
> plot(Covid$day, Covid$cases); plot(Covid$day, log(Covid$cases))
```

(b) Very strong linear relation when the response variable is the log of number of cases:

```
> cor(Covid$cases, Covid$day); cor(log(Covid$cases), Covid$day)
[1] 0.7937368
[1] 0.9968212
```

(c) The prediction for $\log(Y)$ is $2.844 + 0.309x$ for $x =$ day, so the prediction for Y is $\exp(2.844 + 0.309x) = 17.18(1.362)^x$.

6.7 Observation 41 is highly influential, with a Cook's distance of 7.88, and no other observation has a Cook's distance above 1. Deleting observation 41, the estimate of the interaction parameter changes from the substantively important effect of 0.658 (P-value=0.100) to the unimportant effect of -0.033 (highly non-significant with P-value=0.933).

6.9 We obtain a 72.4% reduction in error in predicting y using x compared to predicting it using $\bar{y}$. A scatterplot shows a positive trend, so the correlation is $r = +\sqrt{r^2} = 0.85$.

6.11 (a) Test statistic $F = 2.18$ (P-value $= 0.10$): only weak evidence that at least one of the explanatory variables has a true effect in the corresponding population. (b) For H_0: $\beta_1 = 0$, test statistic $t = 2.06$ ($df = 56$, P-value $= 0.044$): Reject H_0 (*hsgpa* has a positive effect on *cogpa*, adjusting for *tv* and *sport*). (c) Using the Bonferroni approach we need P-value ≤ 0.0167 to reject H_0. So the *hsgpa* effect is not significant with this correction. (d)Testing the significance of *tv*, adjusting for *hsgpa* and *sport*, and then the significance of *sport*, adjusting for *hsgpa*, we conclude that, among these variables, only *hsgpa* has a significant effect on the mean college GPA. Fit this model and present it.

6.13 The test of equal population means has test statistic $F = 9.62$ (P-value < 0.0001), giving strong evidence of at least one difference. The Tukey multiple comparison method indicates that Hispanics and Whites tend to be more conservative than Blacks, on the average, but there is no significant difference between Whites and Hispanics.

6.15 (a)

```
> Houses <- read.table("http://stat4ds.rwth-aachen.de/data/Houses.dat",header=T)
> attach(Houses); pch.list <- NULL; col.list <- NULL
> pch.list[new=="0"] <- 20; pch.list[new=="1"] <- 4        # pick symbols
> col.list[new=="0"] <- "blue"; col.list[new=="1"] <- "red" # pick colors
> plot(size, price, pch=pch.list, col=col.list)  # control symbols/colors
> legend("topleft",  title="age of house", inset=0.02, legend= c("old","new"),
       pch=c(20,4), col=c("dodgerblue4","red4"), cex=0.9,box.lty=0)
```

(b) The mean price is estimated to increase by \$17,420 for a 100 square foot increase in size and is \$86,604 higher for new than for older homes, adjusting for the other explanatory variable. (c) $R^2 = 0.72$. Interpret as in the example of Section 6.3.4. (d) Test statistic $t = 3.095$ ($df = 97$, $P = 0.003$) is highly significant, indicating that the population mean selling price is higher for new homes. (e) If the model truly holds, 95% CI for the population mean selling price is (258.721, 323.207) and 95% prediction interval for another new house of that size is (179.270, 402.658), in thousand dollars. (f) Observation 64 has the maximum Cook's distance of 1.28. Without it, R^2 increases from 0.723 to 0.772. The effect of a home being new decreases from 86.60 to 61.96!

6.17 (a) $H_0: \mu_1 = \mu_2 = \mu_3$ is rejected, giving strong evidence that at least two of the population means differ. (b) The Tukey multiple comparisons suggest that the f group has greater population mean weight change than the c, but it is plausible that the population means are the same for the other two pairs. (c) The mean weight after was estimated to be 4.1 pounds higher for the cb group than c and 8.66 pounds higher for the f group than c, adjusting for the weight before. $H_0: \beta_1 = \beta_2 = 0$ is rejected, interpret.

6.19 For very flat prior distributions, we have similar results as least squares:

```
> fit.bayes <- MCMCregress(timeW ~ distance + climb, mcmc=5000000, b0=0, B0=10^{-10},
+                          c0=10^(-10), d0=10^(-10), data = Races[-41,])
> summary(fit.bayes)
> fit <- lm(timeW ~ distance + climb, , data = Races[-41,])
> summary(fit) # classical least squares approach
```

6.21 For the main effects model, the Highland Fling observation for women has Cook's distance = 2.78 (next largest is 0.32, for the Highland Fling observation for men). The fit of the main effects model without that race is:

```
> RacesMW <- read.table("http://stat4ds.rwth-aachen.de/data/ScotsRacesMW.dat",
  header=T)
> Cd <- cooks.distance(fit); tail(sort(Cd), 3)
        70        41        109
0.1435206 0.3204229 2.7814732
> RacesMW[c(41,109),]
            race distance climb   time gender
41  HighlandFling      85   1.2 439.15      1
109 HighlandFling      85   1.2 490.05      0
# without Highland Fling:
> fit2 <- lm(time ~ distance + climb + gender, data=RacesMW[-c(41,109),])
> summary(fit2)
```

For a particular race, we predict that the record time is 15.3 min. lower for men than women. The fit is slightly improved by permitting interactions between pairs of variables.

6.23 For the model permitting interaction, the prediction equation between y = weight and x = foot length is $\hat{\mu} = -1955.27 + 24.55x$ for female and $\hat{\mu} = -1397.21 + 20.03x$ for male hares. It has $R^2 = 0.549$, and the model without interaction has $R^2 = 0.544$, so the fit is as good for most practical purposes even though the test of H_0: no interaction has a P-value of 0.012. No values of Cook's distance are exceptionally large for either model.

6.25 Solutions will vary by the actual values and the guesses made.

6.27 To minimize $f(\beta_0) = \Sigma_i (y_i - \beta_0)^2$, we take its derivative with respect to β_0 and set it equal to zero, giving $\hat{\beta}_0 = (\Sigma_i y_i)/n$. The second derivative at $\hat{\beta}_0$ is positive, so we have found the minimum.

6.29 (a) For this model, β_0 is $E(Y)$ when $x = \mu_x$, so it is much more relevant that the ordinary intercept when x does not take values near 0. (b) β_0 is $E(Y)$ when $x = \min(\{x_i\})$.

6.31 When x and y are standardized, $\bar{x} = \bar{y} = 0$ so $\hat{\beta}_0 = \bar{y} - \hat{\beta}_1\bar{x} = 0$. Also, $s_x = s_y$ so that $r = \hat{\beta}_1(s_x/s_y) = \hat{\beta}_1$ and the prediction equation is $\hat{\mu}_i = rx_i$.

6.33 Suppose that the systolic blood pressure readings vary around a mean of 120 and the correlation between readings for a person at two times separated by a month is 0.67. Then, for people with systolic blood pressure 150 originally, on the average we would expect the reading a month later to be 2/3 as far from 120, with a mean of 140.

6.35 (a) $E(X \mid Y = y) = \mu_X + \rho(\sigma_X/\sigma_Y)(y - \mu_Y)$

(b) $\beta_1/(1/\beta_1^*) = \beta_1\beta_1^* = [\rho(\sigma_Y/\sigma_X)][\rho(\sigma_X/\sigma_Y)] = \rho^2$.

6.37 Prediction equation: $\hat{\mu} = -28.34 + 6.21x$. As n grows, it would get closer to $-25.0 + 6.0x$.

6.39 The Spearman correlation changes only from 0.850 to 0.851 when we remove the outlying observation. It is more robust than the ordinary correlation to outliers.

6.41 (a) $\hat{\beta}_1$ has a normal sampling distribution. For the calculation of $E(\hat{\beta}_1)$ prove first that $E(\overline{Y}) = \beta_0 + \beta_1\overline{x}$ and $E(Y_i - \overline{Y}) = \beta_1(x_i - \overline{x})$. For the calculation of $\text{var}(\hat{\beta}_1)$, prove that $\hat{\beta}_1 = \frac{1}{\sum_{i=1}^{n}(x_i-\overline{x})^2} \sum_{i=1}^{n}[(x_i-\overline{x})Y_i]$. (b) With more variation in x or with more observations, $[\sum_i(x_i - \overline{x})^2]$ increases and $\text{var}(\hat{\beta}_1)$ decreases (i, iii). With less variation in y given x, σ^2 decreases and $\text{var}(\hat{\beta}_1)$ decreases (ii).

6.43 Healthier people are more likely to play at least a round of golf a week and more likely to be alive a decade later.

6.45 A possible lurking variable is family's income. You could check for this by observing the association between X and Y separately for different groups of people stratified on family income.

6.47 (a) Conditioning on $U = u$, $\text{corr}(X, Y) = \text{corr}(V, W) = 0$. (b) If U is a common partial cause of X and Y, then both X and Y tend to increase in U. So a positive correlation between them will be observed even though they are uncorrelated for fixed U.

6.49 $r^2 = (TSS-SSE)/TSS$ is estimating the population ratio $[\text{var}(Y) - \text{var}(Y \mid X)]/\text{var}(Y)$. For larger range of sampled x-values, we expect $\text{var}(Y)$ to be larger, whereas the standard model treats $\text{var}(Y \mid X)$ as being the same for any sampled x values.

6.51 Expand $\sum_i(y_i - \overline{y})^2 = \sum_i[y_i - \hat{\mu}_i) + (\hat{\mu}_i - \overline{y})]^2$ and use $\sum_i(y_i - \hat{\mu}_i)\overline{y} = \overline{y}\sum_i e_i = 0$ by the first likelihood equation in Section 6.2.6. Also, $\sum_i(y_i - \hat{\mu}_i)\hat{\mu}_i = \sum_i(y_i - \hat{\mu}_i)(\sum_j \beta_j x_{ij})$ and $\sum_i(y_i - \hat{\mu}_i)x_{ij} = 0$ by the second likelihood equation.

6.53 Use the form of a t random variable T in Section 4.4.5, the definition of an F random variable in Section 6.4.1, to find the distribution of $T^2 = \frac{Z^2/1}{X^2/d}$.

6.55 (a) At $x_0 = \overline{x}$, $\hat{\beta}_0 + \hat{\beta}_1 x_0 = \overline{y}$ by the least squares formula for $\hat{\beta}_0$, so the CI is $\overline{y} \pm t_{\alpha/2,n-(p+1)}(s/\sqrt{n})$ (for the marginal distribution set $p = 0$). (b) $\sum_{i=1}^{n}(x_i - \overline{x})^2$ increases and the standard error used in the margin of error decreases.

6.57 (a) Highly skewed to the left, since r cannot take a value much larger than ρ. (b) A $100(1-\alpha)\%$ CI for $T(\rho)$ is $T(r) \pm z_{\alpha/2}\sqrt{1/(n-3)}$. Substitute each endpoint for T in the inverse transformation $\rho = (e^{2T} - 1)/(e^{2T} + 1)$ to get the endpoints of the CI for ρ.

6.59 Note that $\cup_j B_j = \cup_j E_j$ and $B_j \subseteq E_j$, but the $\{B_j\}$ are disjoint, and so $P(\cup_j E_j) = P(\cup_j B_j) = \sum_j P(B_j) \le \sum_{j=1}^{t} P(E_j)$, since $P(B_j) \le P(E_j)$ for all j.

6.61 Using the expression of the ML function of Section 6.4.6 and with $\hat{\sigma}_0^2 = SSE_0/n$ and $\hat{\sigma}_1^2 = SSE_1/n$ the ML variance estimates for the simpler and the more complex model, the likelihood ratio becomes $(1 + (p_1 - p_0)/(n - (p_1 + 1))F)^{n/2}$ for the F statistic (6.9).

6.63 The effect β_2 is the difference between $E(Y)$ for the group with $z = 1$ and that with $z = 0$ at $x = \mu_x$. Without centering, β_2 is the difference between $E(Y)$ for the same groups but at $x = 0$, which may not be a relevant place to make a comparison.

6.65 As n increases, the model matrix X has more rows, each term on the main diagonal of $X^T X$ has a greater number of terms in its sum of squares and is therefore larger, and the main diagonal elements of $(X^T X)^{-1}$ tend to be smaller.

C.7 Chapter 7: Solutions to Exercises

7.1 (a) Prices may vary more at higher values for taxes, suggesting that a GLM assuming a gamma distribution may be more appropriate. (b) Adjusting for taxes, the estimated mean price for new homes is 86.2 (80.5) thousand dollars higher than for older homes with the normal (gamma) model. (c) The estimated variability is $\hat{\sigma} = 78.82$ at each value for the estimated mean for the normal model and $\hat{\sigma} = 0.2955\hat{\mu}$ for the gamma model, which varies between 29.55 (for $\hat{\mu} = 100$) and 147.75 (for $\hat{\mu} = 500$) thousand dollars. (d) The gamma model has considerably smaller AIC and is preferred by that criterion.

7.3 The more complex model gives a perfect fit, having as many parameters as observations. The SSE values are decreasing in the model's complexity while the actual sum of squares around the true mean not. The later can be lower for the simpler straight-line model.

7.5 (a) The logistic regression model fit suggests that the heavier sheep were more likely to survive ($\hat{\beta}_1 > 0$, stat. significant). (b) $\hat{\pi} > 0.50$ when weight $x > -\hat{\beta}_0/\hat{\beta}_1 = 11.57$ kg.

7.7
```
> Afterlife <-read.table("http://stat4ds.rwth-aachen.de/data/Afterlife.dat",header=T)
> y <- ifelse(Afterlife$postlife == 1, 1, 0)
> fit <- glm(y ~ factor(religion)+factor(gender), family=binomial, data=Afterlife)
> summary(fit)
```

The probability of believing in the afterlife seems to be somewhat greater for females than males, adjusting for religion, and quite a bit lower for the Jewish religious category than the Protestant and Catholic categories, adjusting for gender.

7.9 (a) The model fit is $\text{logit}(\hat{\pi}) = -1.417 + 0.069D - 1.659T$. The estimated odds of a sore throat for those using a tracheal tube are $e^{-1.659} = 0.19$ times the estimated odds for those using a laryngeal mask airway, for a given duration of surgery. Interpret effect D analogously. (b) The prediction equation is $\text{logit}(\hat{\pi}) = -4.42 + 0.103D$ when $T = 1$ and $\text{logit}(\hat{\pi}) = 0.0498 + 0.0285D$ when $T = 0$ but the interaction is not statistically significant.

7.11 The model with main effects d and v seems to fit well (residual deviance is small). Interpret the main effects analogously to the example in Section 7.2.3.

7.13 The gender effect is -0.273 for non-citizens and $-0.273 - 1.083 = -1.356$ for citizens. The estimated odds of employment for women are $\exp(-0.263) = 0.76$ times those for men for non-citizens and $\exp(-1.356) = 0.26$ for citizens.

7.15 (a) The odds of death due to suicide by firearm was 374.49 times higher in the U.S. than in the UK. The risk ratio was 374.46. When the proportions are close to 0, odds ratio and risk ratio are very close. (b) Risk ratio = 3.71, odds ratio = 13.34 much larger and more similar to square of risk ratio, which is 13.80. (c) $\text{logit}[P(Y = 1)] = \beta_0 + \beta_1 x$, where y = climate change should be a top priority (1 = yes, 0 = no) and x = political party (1 = Democrat, 0 = Republican), for which $\hat{\beta}_1 = 2.59$.

7.17 (a) True ML estimate $\hat{\beta}_1 = \infty$, reported $\hat{\beta}_1 = 2.363$ with $se = 5805.9$ very large. For explanation see Section 7.2.6. (b) The estimate of β_1 is 0.089 instead of ∞, and the 95% CI is (0.015, 0.324) instead of over the entire real line given by the ordinary Wald CI.

7.19 Federer beats Murray all 5 times that they met, for a sample proportion of 1.00. Fitting the model provides smoothing of the sample proportions and gives estimated odds 5.50 and estimated probability of a Federer win of $\exp(1.704)/[1 + \exp(1.704)] = 0.85$.

7.21 (a) An exceptionally heavy crab (observation 141) weighing 5.2 *kg* that had 7 satellites is an outlier. Without it, the weight effect changes from 0.546 to 0.663. (b) With color treated in a quantitative manner, we estimate that the expected number of satellites multiplies by $e^{-0.173} = 0.84$ for each increase of a category in color darkness. AIC is less for this model (914.1 compared with 917.1), suggesting that this model may better reflect the true relationship. (c) This model is better according to both statistical significance (P-value = 0.006 for the test of no interaction) and AIC (lower value). (d) With the negative binomial assumption, the interaction is not significant. The simple main effects model is adequate and is much better according to AIC than the Poisson models.

7.23 No, because the sample mean and variance should not be dramatically different (are equal for the Poisson distribution). Also for the Poisson, the mode is the integer part of the mean, so the modal response would be 5, not 0.

7.25 Factors that cause heterogeneity, such as changing weather from day to day, whether the day is on a holiday or weekend, time of year.

7.27 The NV effect is estimated to be ∞ with the classical approach, 18.33 with the uninformative Bayesian approach using prior standard deviations $\sigma = 100$, 2.93 with the penalized likelihood approach, 2.51 with the lasso using lowest sample mean prediction error, and 1.57 using the one-standard-error rule.

7.29 In summary, no significant difference between females and males, but each tend to be happier when married than in the other two categories.

7.31 $E[g(Y)] \neq g[E(Y)]$ when g is nonlinear. With the GLM, one can recover information about $E(Y)$ by applying g^{-1} to the linear predictor.

7.33 A difference of probabilities equal to d between the treatments for each lab does not imply that the difference of logits between the treatments is the same for each lab. For instance, consider the probabilities of success 0.9 for treatment A and 0.8 for treatment B in one lab and probabilities 0.6 and 0.5 in the other lab.

7.35 Compute $\partial \hat{\pi}_i / \partial x_{ij}$ applying the quotient rule. Since $\hat{\pi}_i(1 - \hat{\pi}_i) \leq 0.25$ for every i, $\hat{\beta}_j/4$ is an upper bound for the size of the effect.

7.37 (a) See Section 5.6.2. (b) The interaction term is highly statistically significant (the difference of deviances between the main effects model and interaction model is 27.4 with $df = 1$), but n is huge ($n = 72,200$). The dissimilarity values of 0.0060 and 0.0056 show that for either model less than 1% of the data would need to be moved to achieve a perfect fit. This suggests that both models fit most of the data very well and the more complex model does not fit much better in a practical sense.

7.39 Consider sampling married couples and observing Y = number with a college education, with possible values 0, 1, and 2. Perhaps π follows a beta distribution with $\alpha < 1$ and $\beta < 1$, which has modes at 0 and 1, and then we observe mainly $Y = 0$ or $Y = 2$, since there are relatively fewer cases for which just one of the partners has college education. This is not possible with an ordinary binomial distribution, which is unimodal.

7.41 When λ has the gamma distribution (7.6), $E(Y) = E[E(Y \mid \lambda)] = E(\lambda) = \mu$ and $\text{var}(Y) = E[\text{var}(Y \mid \lambda)] + \text{var}[E(Y \mid \lambda)] = \mu + \mu^k/k$, which are the mean and variance of a negative binomial distribution (Section 7.5.2).

7.43 The model has a parameter π attached to the distribution with $P(Y = 0) = 1$ and parameter $(1 - \pi)$ attached to a discrete distribution on the nonnegative integers such as the Poisson or negative binomial. Example: The number of times you went to a theatre to see a movie in the past year.

7.45 Because the variability is not constant, residuals would not tend to have similar magnitudes over all values of explanatory variables.

7.47 Since the ML estimate $\hat{\beta}$ satisfies $L'(\hat{\beta}) = 0$, dropping higher-order terms in the expansion yields $0 \approx L'(\beta^{(0)}) + (\hat{\beta} - \beta^{(0)})L''(\beta^{(0)})$. Solving for $\hat{\beta}$ yields $\hat{\beta}^{(1)} = \beta^{(0)} - L'(\beta^{(0)})/L''(\beta^{(0)})$, which we use as the next approximation for $\hat{\beta}$. Using the same argument, replacing $\beta^{(0)}$ by $\beta^{(t)}$, we get the general expression.

7.49 (a) The log-likelihood function involves the data together with the parameters only through these terms. (b) For the derivation of the likelihood equation consult Section 7.6.2. Based on the likelihood equations we have that for each j, $E(\sum_{i=1}^{n} Y_i x_{ij}) = \sum_{i=1}^{n} \pi_i x_{ij}$, so the equations equate the sufficient statistics to their expected values. (c) The likelihood equation with $x_{i0} = 1$ for all i simplifies to $\sum_{i=1}^{n} y_i = n\pi$, so $\hat{\pi} = \bar{y}$.

7.51 (a) $L(\hat{\mu}; y) = \log\left[\prod_{i=1}^{n} \frac{e^{-\hat{\mu}_i} (\hat{\mu}_i)^{y_i}}{y_i!} \right]$ (b) The deviance equals $D(y; \hat{\mu}) = 2[L(y; y) - L(\hat{\mu}; y)]$. (c) When a model with log link contains an intercept term, the likelihood equation implied by that parameter is $\sum_i y_i = \sum_i \hat{\mu}_i$ and the deviance simplifies to the provided expression.

7.53 $\partial\hat{\mu}_i/\partial x_{ij} = \hat{\beta}_j \hat{\mu}_i$ which sum over i to $\hat{\beta}_j(\sum_i \hat{\mu}_i)$. The likelihood equation for $j = 0$ in terms of the ML estimates is $\sum_i y_i = \sum_i \hat{\mu}_i$, so $\frac{1}{n} \sum_i (\partial\hat{\mu}_i/\partial x_{ij}) = \frac{1}{n}\hat{\beta}_j(\sum_i y_i)$.

7.55 (a) As n increases, $\boldsymbol{X}$ has more rows and you sum more positive terms to get the diagonal elements of $\boldsymbol{X}^T\hat{\boldsymbol{D}}\boldsymbol{X}$, so the values tend to be smaller in the inverse matrix that gives the variances of the estimates. (b) As $\{\hat{\pi}_i\}$ tend to fall close to 0 or close to 1, the main diagonal elements of $\boldsymbol{X}^T\hat{\boldsymbol{D}}\boldsymbol{X}$ tend to be smaller, and thus larger in the inverse matrix.

7.57 (a) The three S-shaped curves have the same shape and do not cross anywhere, reflecting that necessarily $0 \le P(Y_i \le 1) \le P(Y_i \le 2) \le P(Y_i \le 3) \le 1$. With different effects, the curves would cross and some cumulative probabilities would be out of their proper order. (b) Model happiness (not too happy, pretty happy, very happy) or quality of life (poor, fair, good, excellent) using explanatory variables age, annual income, gender, race, attained education, whether married.

7.59 (a) Let A, C, and M be indicator variables taking values 1 = yes, 0 = no. For $i, j, k = 0, 1$, let $\mu_{ijk} = nP(A = i, C = j, M = k)$ be the expected frequencies for the cells. The model is $\mu_{ijk} = \beta_0 + \beta_1 A + \beta_2 C + \beta_3 M + \beta_4 AC + \beta_5 AM + \beta_6 CM$. (b) The AC conditional log odds ratio at level k of M is $\log[(\mu_{11k}\mu_{22k})(\mu_{12k}\mu_{21k})]$ which, substituting the loglinear model formula, simplifies to β_4. (c) The residual deviance is 0.374 ($df = 1$). The estimated conditional log odds ratios are 2.986 between M and A and 2.848 between M and C, identical to the estimates for the coefficient of the AM and CM terms in the loglinear model.

C.8   Chapter 8: Solutions to Exercises

8.1 (a) 1.533(weight)-0.588(color). (b) Would be predicted to have satellites (posterior probability 0.786). (c) Sensitivity: 0.676, specificity: 0.710, overall proportion of correct predictions: 0.688 (as good as in Section 8.1.3 using all four explanatory variables). (d) The areas under the curve of 0.761 for linear discriminant analysis and 0.7605 for logistic regression are as good as 0.770 for linear discriminant analysis using all four explanatory variables. (e) The estimated probability of a satellite increases by 0.285 for a 1 *kg* increase in weight, adjusting for color, and decreases by 0.109 by an increase of 1 in color darkness, adjusting for weight. Disadvantage: for sufficiently small values of color and large values of weight, $\hat{P}(Y = 1) > 1$ (happens for 6 crabs in this sample).

8.3 (a) 1.638(sepal length)-3.152(petal length), suggests that the posterior $P(Y = 1)$ increases (decreases) as sepal (petal) length increases. (b) Sensitivity, specificity and overall proportion of correct predictions are all 0.94. (c) Area under the ROC curve close to 1 with both methods, indicating excellent performance. (d) Simple tree for $\lambda = 0$ predicts $y = 1$ if petal length ≥ 4.75 *cm*. It correctly predicts 49 of 55 predicted to have $y = 1$ and 44 of 45 predicted to have $y = 0$, with an overall proportion correct of 0.93.

8.5 (a) For the more highly-pruned tree, the only region predicted not to have satellites is the rectangular region with colors 3 and 4 and carapace width < 25.85 *cm*. (b) Linear discriminant analysis or logistic regression results in a single line passing through this space with $\hat{y} = 1$ on one side of the line and $\hat{y} = 0$ on the other. (c) Simple classification trees using solely weight or solely width or weight with color or width with color seem adequate. Results agree with corresponding logistic regression model fits (satellites are more likely for lighter-colored crabs with greater weight or greater carapace width).

8.7 (a) All males of age ≤ 9.5 years who had fewer then 3 siblings, and all females. (b) 80.65%, compared to 71.94% correct if predicted that everyone died.

8.9 We get perfect prediction using only a single neighbor! Other solutions may differ slightly, because of the random selection for the training and test samples.

8.11 New Jersey (NJ) and Pennsylvania (P) join the initial cluster with Illinois, and Alabama (A) that with Wyoming. In two-cluster summary: NJ and P are Democratic-leaning and A is Republican-leaning.

8.13 By logistic regression, alligators of length greater than 1.99 meters have greater than a 50% chance of having fish as primary food choice.

8.15 Answers will vary according to data chosen.

8.17 See Section 8.1.5.

8.19 We can interpret D as the probability that two randomly selected subjects fall in the same class, so larger D reflects less diversity.

8.21 Regression trees have the advantage of being simple to explain and to portray values that lead to various predicted values; can portray a complex non-linear relationship (might not be discovered by regression methods). Disadvantages include not providing a framework for inference and simple numerical summaries of effects.

8.23 Interchange variables and cases in the data file used for the clustering, so each row is a different variable and each column is a different observation.

Bibliography

Agresti, A. (2015). *Foundations of Linear and Generalized Linear Models*. Hoboken, NJ:Wiley.

Agresti, A. (2019). *An Introduction to Categorical Data Analysis*, 3rd ed. Hoboken, NJ:Wiley.

Agresti, A., Franklin, C., and Klingenberg, B. (2021). *Statistics: The Art and Science of Learning from Data*, 5th ed. Hoboken, NJ:Pearson.

Albert, J. (2009). *Bayesian Computation with R*, 2nd ed. New York:Springer.

Allison, P.D. (2014). *Event History and Survival Analysis*, 2nd ed. Los Angeles:Sage.

Baumer B. S., Kaplan D. T., and Horton N. J. (2017). *Modern Data Science with R*, Boca Raton, FL: CRC Press.

Burnham, K. P., and Anderson, D. R. (2002). *Model Selection and Multi-Model Inference* 2nd ed. New York: Springer-Verlag.

Carlin, B., and Louis, T. (2008). *Bayesian Methods for Data Analysis*, 3rd ed. Boca Raton, FL: CRC Press.

Casella, G., and Berger, R. (2002) *Statistical Inference*, 2nd edition. Belmont, CA: Wadsworth and Brooks/Cole.

Chollet, F., and Allaire, J. J. (2018). *Deep Learning with R*. Shelter Island, NY:Manning Publications.

Cryer, J. D., and Chan, K.-S. (2008). *Time Series Analysis, with Applications in R*. New York:Springer Publishing.

Davison, A. C. (2003). *Statistical Models*. Cambridge, UK:Cambridge University Press.

Ellenberg, J. (2014). *How Not to Be Wrong: The Power of Mathematical Thinking*. London, UK:Penguin Books.

Everitt, B. S., Landau, S., Leese, M., and Stahl, D. (2011). *Cluster Analysis*, 5th edition. Hoboken, NJ:Wiley.

Fitzmaurice, G., Laird, N., and Ware, J. 2011. *Applied Longitudinal Analysis*, 2nd edition. Hoboken, NJ:Wiley.

Gelman, A., and Hill, J. (2006). *Data Analysis Using Regression and Multilevel/Hierarchical Models*. Cambridge, UK:Cambridge Univ. Press.

Hastie, T., Tibshirani, R., and Friedman, J. (2009). *The Elements of Statistical Learning*, 2nd ed. New York:Springer.

Hoff, P. D. (2009). *A First Course in Bayesian Statistical Methods*. New York:Springer.

Hollander, M., Wolfe, D., and Chicken, E. (2013). *Nonparametric Statistical Methods*, 3rd ed. Hoboken, NJ:Wiley.

Hothorn, T., and Everitt, B. S. (2014). *A Handbook of Statistical Analyses Using R*, 3rd ed. CRC Press, Boca Raton FL.

Irizarry, R. A. *Introduction to Data Science*. (2019). Boca Raton, FL:Chapman and Hall/CRC.

James, G., D. Witten, T. Hastie, and R. Tibshirani. (2021) *An Introduction to Statistical Learning*, 2nd edition. New York:Springer.

Kateri, M. (2014). *Contingency Table Analysis: Methods and Implementation Using R*. New York: Birkhäuser.

Rashid, T. (2016). *Make Your Own Neural Network*. Amazon.

Salsburg, D. (2002). *The Lady Tasting Tea: How Statistics Revolutionized Science in the Twentieth Century*. New York:W. H. Freeman.

Shumway, R. H., and Stoffer, D. S. (2017). *Time Series Analysis and Its Applications, with R Examples*, 4th ed. New York:Springer.

Stigler, S. M. (1986). *The History of Statistics: The Measurement of Uncertainty before 1900*. Cambridge, MA:Harvard University Press.

Stigler, S. M. (2002). *Statistics on the Table*. Cambridge, MA:Harvard University Press.

Stigler, S. M. (2016). *The Seven Pillars of Statistical Wisdom*. Cambridge, MA:Harvard University Press.

Tukey, J. W. (1977). *Exploratory Data Analysis*. Boston, MA:Addison–Wesley.

Tutz, G. 2011. *Structured Regression for Categorical Data*. Cambridge, UK:Cambridge Univ. Press.

Wickham, H., and Grolemund, G. (2017) *R for Data Science: Import, Tidy, Transform, Visualize, and Model Data*. O'Reilly Media Inc., Sebastopol, CA.

Example Index

Subject Index

T - #0133 - 230425 - C486 - 254/178/21 [23] - CB - 9780367748456 - Gloss Lamination